W9-BBB-846

McGraw-Hill Series in Political Science

JOSEPH P. HARRIS, *Consulting Editor*

DYNAMICS OF INTERNATIONAL RELATIONS

McGRAW-HILL SERIES IN POLITICAL SCIENCE

JOSEPH P. HARRIS, *Consulting Editor*

✔ ✔ ✔

327
H

Dynamics of
International Relations

ERNST B. HAAS

University of California (Berkeley)

ALLEN S. WHITING

The Rand Corporation

McGRAW-HILL BOOK COMPANY, INC.

New York   Toronto   London

1956

Wingate College Library

DYNAMICS OF INTERNATIONAL RELATIONS

Copyright © 1956 by the McGraw-Hill Book Company, Inc. Printed in the United States of America. All rights reserved. This book, or parts thereof, may not be reproduced in any form without permission of the publishers.

Library of Congress Catalog Card Number 55–8897

II

To Alice and Hil

PREFACE

As a separate field of study, international relations is a relative newcomer to the college curriculum. Yet in three or four decades of growth it has mushroomed from a review of diplomatic history to an all-embracive approach, often including elements of history, geography, economics, sociology, politics, and in some cases anthropology. Out of this compendium of social sciences have emerged two distinct theses underlying studies of international relations. One posits world affairs in terms of man's search for morality, stability, and community. The other stresses the Hobbesian power drive. Woodrow Wilson and Machiavelli provide the rival foci around which the study of international relations tends to coalesce.

For the authors, neither thesis is wholly satisfactory as a frame of reference for analyzing the dynamics of international relations. Power of and by itself does not appear as a meaningful concept under which all major data of international relations can be subsumed. Nor does the alleged struggle between "realism" and "idealism" provide an unambiguous framework for political analysis. We consider power to be merely a conditioner of means chosen to implement given ends of policy. Furthermore, we believe that the modes of thought associated with the value-structures implicit in idealism as well as in realism are useful tools of analysis only in so far as they shed light on the ends men seek to gain in politics.

This book, therefore, represents an effort to work out a different methodology for the study of international relations, as well as to provide the student with a basic text. As a major premise, we assume that the ends of foreign policy are qualitatively similar to ends implicit in any other field of politics. Whatever "laws" of political behavior, group conduct, and elite leadership can be isolated and identified in the domestic field are therefore considered applicable to the international field as well. In both cases the agent of action is man acting within a group. We doubt that this group is necessarily identical with that called the nation. Hence we have attempted to synthesize the study of political behavior and social action with an analysis of international relations as one manifestation of group aspirations.

The resulting interpretation of political processes among national communities centers on Max Weber's "actors." Groups, elites, and, to a lesser extent, nations are the primary actors studied. The scheme of international affairs which emerges is thus a compendium of the ways in which shapers

11451

and conditioners of policy view their mutual interrelations, in terms of their native ideological and institutional frameworks. While the dynamic nature of ideology and institutions must, of course, be granted, the emphasis of this interpretation nevertheless tends to be placed upon the contemporary distribution and impact of given social forces. Although attention is given to possible changes in the now dominant pattern of international relations, such forecasting is in each case made dependent upon logically necessary changes in ideology and institutional patterns. To this extent, then, our interpretation is deterministic.

The methodological challenge of this approach has been severe. Empirical material is frequently unavailable or inaccessible, especially in the case of underdeveloped countries and totalitarian regimes. Some of the generalizations in Part I, therefore, are closer to the abstract "model" type of treatment than to detailed empirical formulation. Chapter 4 is especially open to the charge of being an overly abstract statement of processes for which there is no unambiguous empirical support. If our formulation errs, therefore, we hope that the effort will act as a stimulus to further and more precise investigation.

We make no claim to any unique value or to finality in offering this type of analysis. Rather, we feel that it will throw light upon certain important aspects of social relations across national boundaries which tend to be neglected in contemporary discussions. Certainly, this frame of reference for the study of international relations is not the only possible one, nor is it necessarily the best. We feel that it is helpful for an understanding of behavior and therefore as a guide to what is possible in terms of changes in patterns of national conduct.

In political science, as in all the social sciences, all methodology is partial and incomplete. As a major caveat to the reader, we must point out that this approach is not designed to yield a normative appreciation of international relations. We have tried to examine how things are, not how they should be. We have excluded value judgments as rigorously as the limited validity of the concept of "ethical neutrality" permits.

In its mechanics, this book differs from other texts in the field in the minimization of historical material. Such materials have been selected largely from the period since 1914, with particular emphasis upon events since 1945. The decision to utilize more recent illustrative examples rather than earlier ones stems from our conviction that the contemporary undergraduate is far better informed on recent history. Therefore our examples will carry more meaning in terms of his memory and experiences and obviate the necessity for a complete statement of the historical setting. No attempt is made to present a systematic historical review of international relations.

On occasion, however, it has been considered useful to include detailed case studies of specific situations in order to illustrate fairly complex points.

Naturally, we selected such case-study material on the basis of available data and in the belief that the situation reviewed is typical of the problem under analysis. The bibliographies listed at the end of each chapter aim at making available further case-study material for the use of the instructor. They are *not* intended as comprehensive general listings of works in the field.

Our method of footnoting also requires a word of explanation. We feel that at the undergraduate level of instruction footnote material is of less significance to the student than to the instructor eager to trace the origin of ideas and materials included. Hence we refrained from footnoting such factual data as enjoy general acceptance and from including listings of works making points similar or identical with ours. Instead, we restricted notes to facts and statistics not generally known or accepted and to sources of specific quotations. Similarly, we sought to exclude quotations from secondary works and concentrated instead on primary contributions.

The approach and methodology used in this text have been elaborated jointly by us both, as a result of many discussions extending over a period of years and much experimentation in our teaching of the subject. Parts I, V, and VI in their entirety, as well as Chapters 12, 13, and 16 in Part IV were written by Ernst B. Haas. Parts II and III in their entirety and Chapters 14 and 15 of Part IV are the work of Allen S. Whiting. Yet each chapter bears the imprint of both authors, in form as well as in content.

Our debt to other writers and teachers is obviously immense. To list all who have stimulated our thinking would burden the reader and tax the memory. We must, however, single out our dependence on the work of Max Weber, Karl Mannheim, Harold Lasswell, and Robert M. MacIver and on the many social scientists who have profited from their insights. We owe a great debt of gratitude to many of our colleagues for patiently listening to our ideas, reading portions of the manuscript, and supplying us with suggestions and material. Our thanks are due especially to Paul Seabury, Norman Jacobson, Richard Scott, George Lenczowski, all at the University of California (Berkeley); to Rupert Emerson at Harvard; and to George Blanksten at Northwestern University. Margaret Fisher of the *India Press Digest* and Hildegarde Millar and her staff of the Bureau of International Relations at Berkeley generously furnished materials. Fred von der Mehden contributed his patient and understanding services as a research assistant at Berkeley, while Charles Gilbert likewise provided valuable services while an assistant to Allen S. Whiting at Northwestern University. Both of us owe a great deal to our graduate seminars for discussing, testing, and elaborating ideas, in addition to making available data not previously examined within our framework. Naturally, we alone bear responsibility for mistakes of fact or errors of interpretation. Our wives, Hildegarde Haas and Alice C. Whiting, not only made the work possible through their patience, constructive criticism, and full cooperation but also helped in typing and in the preparation of maps and illustrations.

Finally, appreciation is acknowledged for permission to quote from works published by the Macmillan Company; McGraw-Hill Book Company, Inc.; Cambridge University Press; Carnegie Endowment for International Peace; John Wiley & Sons, Inc.; Harper & Brothers; Harcourt, Brace and Company, Inc.; Oxford University Press; Alfred A. Knopf, Inc.; George W. Stewart, Publisher, Inc.; The Beacon Press; Stanford University Press; The Viking Press, Inc.; Simon and Schuster, Inc.; Rinehart & Company, Inc.; Princeton University Press; University of Illinois Press; University of California Press; University of Pennsylvania Press; Rutgers University Press; Appleton-Century-Crofts, Inc.; International Missionary Council; and International Publishers Co., Inc. Acknowledgment is also made to the following periodicals for the same courtesy: *Foreign Affairs, Public Opinion Quarterly, Far Eastern Survey, The New York Times, World Politics, Middle East Affairs, Harvard Business Review, New York Herald-Tribune,* and *Fortune Magazine.*

ERNST B. HAAS
ALLEN S. WHITING

CONTENTS

INTRODUCTION

Students in American colleges and universities have a new set of textbooks written for their guidance after every major foreign war. At the turn of the century hostilities with Spain produced treatises and texts on world politics and colonial government and gave new impetus to the history of diplomacy and international law. World War I brought in its wake a number of textbooks devoted to international relations, organization, and law. Today the student has at his disposal a choice of new guidebooks to the field of international politics. The quantity of these manuals is impressive. More important is the redistribution of emphasis, such as appears in the present volume.

Although it is too early to describe these variations with complete confidence, some tentative characterizations may be made. The texts reflect in part the emergence of a generation of specialists more numerous and often more experienced at the policy level than their predecessors. The gigantic scope of war and continuing crisis brought into existence a new army of experts on various geographical areas and provided exceptional opportunities for the experts—young and old—to play advisory or deciding roles.

There was a time when courses in international politics were largely devoted to contemporary history. It was possible to rewrite the *New York Times* or the London *Times* and to put between book covers a running account of "The Foreign Policy of Altruria, 1870–1914; During World War I; Since." The manual of current events has been losing ground since the 1930s at least; and the trend appears to be continuing if not accelerating. It would, I suggest, be a mistake to abandon this emphasis entirely, since an elementary task of an introduction to world politics is to provide a concise view of world developments and to familiarize the student with names, dates, and places. To an increasing extent this chore is being taken over by historians who overcome parochial dispositions to confound the history of the United States and Western Europe with world history. The specialists in both political history and the political process share responsibility for making clear to the student the principal trends in the structures and ideologies of the world arena. The authors of the present text characterize these trends; and an important exercise for a serious student is to evaluate the nature and balance maintained among these trends.

Among text writers one tradition has been to indoctrinate the reader with a strong set of policy preferences. The scholars who prepared the earlier manuals knew they were pioneers. A typical incentive for pioneering was a desire to influence the ship of state by influencing the state of mind of the educated elite of America (the minority of the nation exposed to the perils and opportunities of a college course). The earlier writers were a small band relatively poor in academic tradition and comparatively undisciplined by the reciprocal criticisms of a large and competent corps of fellow specialists. Working under such handicaps, it might be supposed that an author would take special precautions to put the student on notice of his biases. But a review of the texts confirms, in my opinion, the judgment of Quincy Wright: [1]

. . . that there has been a degree of indoctrination in American undergraduate education in international relations hardly compatible with the theory of what education should be in a liberal democracy. During a half century college education has successively and, in a measure, successfully guided opinion in the United States toward isolationism, toward international organization, and toward power politics as the central theme of American foreign policy. It may be suggested that if education had actually gone to the roots of the subject, perhaps in the realm of social psychology, such rapid shifts would not have occurred.

The dominant aim of the present authors, I believe, is "to go to the roots of the subject" and to provide the student with self-correcting tools of thought and observation. Hence they present a theoretical model of the political process and provide an opportunity to obtain experience in applying—and revising—the model. At the same time the policy emphasis does not disappear. The authors make it clear that their long-range-value goals are the realization of human dignity, and that they understand these goals. It is also evident that their primary audience are the participants in American politics, and that they can specify the long- and middle-range objectives of United States policy in relatively definite terms. The tone in presenting preferences is candid and clarifying. The style is an invitation to inquire and discuss—and to choose responsibly.

While there is no strict agreement among scholars concerning the most valid model of international politics, an approximate consensus exists. It is recognized, for instance, that great prominence must be given to such variables as power "expectations" and "demands" on the part of decision makers who are identified in varying degree with nations, parties, and other participating units. Since the conception of power occupies a crucial position, it must be handled with clarity and caution. It is obvious that power refers to a relationship among people, but so does the giving or obtaining of claims to wealth, respect, and other values. The problem is to select the distinctive marks of a power relation, drawing the line for analytic purposes between a

[1] *The Study of International Relations,* Appleton-Century-Crofts, New York, 1955, p. 72.

relationship that "involves extreme coercion" (like war or threat of war) and situations in which coercion is less "extreme" or less obviously "involved." As usual in scholarly work, it is less important that *A* agree with *B* than that *A* and *B* make their meaning so explicit that their statements are mutually translatable. The student will improve his skill if he watches the complex interplay of definition and exemplification in the present text, searching for seeming ambiguities and inconsistencies.

Some popular—and scholarly—disagreements about the topic of power come from failure to draw a clear distinction in a given context between the evaluation of power as a primary goal (a "scope value") and as a "base value" employed for the purpose of achieving other values at a later date. Even such a sentimentalized term as "power politics" can be usefully defined if such distinctions are made, so that "power as a base for power" is analytically separable from "wealth as a base for power" or "power as a base for wealth." The present text uses a number of pertinent tools of analysis, and the student will find his skill improving as he examines the connection between "cases" and "concepts."

The present textbook continues the trend to rely upon a balance between "cases" and "analytic formulations" as a teaching device. Beginning in the law schools the case method has quietly permeated the American academic community. However, the method has never been as important in political science as it has been in legal education. Lawyers use cases as precedents to be referred to in estimating and influencing the future response of courts. Political scientists use cases to gain familiarity with the frames of reference of decision makers. Serious intellectual work begins when the scholar has become acquainted with enough cases to formulate hypotheses and methods capable of explaining under what conditions one set of policy outcomes is more probable than another. This calls for the use of a comprehensive system of categories and propositions, and makes it important to balance "case studies" and "process analysis." It seems to me that the case studies in this volume are exceptionally pertinent and precise, and that students will discover that these studies usually reflect independent research on original sources.

One merit of "indoctrination" texts was that they gave the student a rather comprehensive set of expectations about the future course of world affairs. At one time the dominant outlook was sanguine, and the League of Nations and other organs appeared to have a favorable future. Beginning in the thirties the future suddenly darkened—in textbooks as well as in headlines. The brief return of sanguine expectations at the end of World War II was quickly dashed by the bipolar tension between the Soviet Union and the United States. Today the thoughtful student (and participant in world affairs) will not fail to think through the major lines of future development, and to assign some "exponent of probability" to each of these "developmental constructs." The brief hints in the last chapter of the present book need to be amplified, and a student will perform an important task if he writes out his detailed "estimates of the future" grounded on various postulates about the rate and nature of scientific and technical growth (in weapons, production, population) and the changes in the prevailing expectations of the elites of the world concerning the policies (domestic and foreign) that maximize values and minimize losses. The practice of making such conceptions explicit will to some extent immunize the individual from the "psychic infection" of headlines, "inside dopesters," and "psychological warriors," as well as from fluctuations of mood generated by the ups and downs of private life. This introduction to international politics is an invitation to begin a lifelong program of inquiry and participation in a process in which one is irretrievably involved regardless of intention.

HAROLD D. LASSWELL
Professor of Law and Political Science
Yale University

PART ONE

NATIONAL COMMUNITIES AND INTERNATIONAL SOCIETY

Chapter 1

THE FACTS OF INTERDEPENDENCE AND THEIR DENIAL

"If men define situations as real, they are real in their consequences." [1] So wrote W. I. Thomas, a sociologist, in an effort to give a succinct formulation of the prime conditioner of human behavior, man's dependence on his own beliefs. Unlike the controlled conditions of the scientist's laboratory, the world of human behavior, whether from the sociological, economic, or political viewpoint, finds man responding differently according to the way he views a given set of conditions. Politics is the result not only of man's varying aspirations, but also of man's varying evaluation of the situation which confronts him. The wellsprings of political action are twofold: the manner in which the political actors—the individuals participating in the making of political decisions—view their aims, and the manner in which the political actors view the environment in which they seek to achieve these aims.

1. Nations, Values, and Global Interdependence. Men are organized into nations. When an individual is labeled as an "Egyptian," "German," "Russian," or "American" he is identified with the social group to which he owes allegiance and loyalty and which is most important in shaping his life. This, of course, is not to say that he may not belong to other groups as well: his family, his labor union or professional association, his social class or religious sect. Whether these groups or the nation are of more crucial importance in explaining his role and conduct depends upon the amount of loyalty he shows toward each of these affiliations.

In our era, however, it seems to be true that it is the nation which outweighs these other centers of loyalty in terms of its conditioning impact.

---

[1] W. I. Thomas, as quoted by R. Merton, *Social Theory and Social Structure,* Free Press, Glencoe, Ill., 1949.

1

The doctrines, beliefs, and values associated with the nation are usually the shapers of the individual's demands and evaluations in his relations with the individuals of other nations. National belief systems tend to be made up of values which are exclusive: they reject, or at least they consider as suspect, the values and motives of other nations.

Yet there is ample evidence every day that, despite this tendency toward exclusiveness in the values of nations, the contemporary world is marked by a high degree of interdependence. The very fact that war always seems to be with us indicates our dependence on the intentions, values, and aims of our allies and enemies. The further fact that some values are actively shared with individuals of other nations—through religious, professional, and humanitarian bonds—highlights another facet of interdependence. The existence of international business and personal relations and the conduct of a network of international trade and investment clearly demonstrate areas of great dependence on others.

International life, therefore, is characterized by a pervasive paradox: nations and their values are exclusive, yet they depend on one another in many key aspects of life. Which is more important, exclusiveness or the recognition of interdependence? Which is more crucial in explaining motives, conduct, policy, and the pattern of international life? An examination of the recognition of and the reaction to war, global values, personal relations, and international trade may suggest an answer.

2. War and Global Interdependence. While there is only scant evidence of any loyalty to globally accepted values, it can easily be shown that in terms of individual and group suffering, frustration, and untimely death an excellent case for common international values could be made. The cold facts of modern warfare might be thought adequate proof that emphasis on national rather than international values can lead only to more suffering and more death.

Statistics of War. Thus in World War I, the total number of dead, wounded, missing, and prisoners reached 37,500,000. In World War II, which lasted six years, a total of 22 million persons lost their lives. The additional millions maimed, blinded, exposed for years to malnutrition, starvation, and exposure and suffering from radiation burns have never been accurately counted. The soldiers killed in battle numbered 15,300,000, distributed as follows: [2]

Soviet Union	7,500,000	United Kingdom	300,000
Germany	3,000,000	United States	300,000
China	2,200,000	Italy	300,000
Japan	1,500,000	France	200,000

This, of course, takes no account of the casualties suffered by Belgium, Hol-

[2] F. L. Schuman, *International Politics*, 4th ed., McGraw-Hill, New York, p. 388.

land, Norway, Finland, Poland, Yugoslavia, Romania, Greece, Brazil, and the Philippines.

These casualty statistics support the argument that the world's interdependence is patent because the individual citizen has a stake in peace. Much the same conclusion might be drawn from financial statistics. The American taxpayer contributed no less than $80,142,000,000 between 1940 and 1950 to the waging of war by his allies and toward the cost of reconstructing the damage wrought by the war. The Allies received $48,701,000,000 worth of military supplies from the United States until 1945 and $31,441,000,000 worth of relief and reconstruction assistance since then to undo the destruction brought about by the original investment.

It should be stressed that all these statistics apply to a setting in which only two atom bombs and no hydrogen bombs were used. The effect of weapons to which the world has grown accustomed since 1945 can only be surmised. Astronomical as the cost of human and material resources has been since 1914, nuclear warfare threatens to offer more staggering statistics should World War III engulf us.

Reactions to War. The plain fact that war has occurred in the past and that it may easily recur in the future, bringing with it the destruction of modern civilization, is the chief argument that interdependence among nations does exist. The equally plain fact that national values are not easily abandoned, however, stands out in modern international relations. That the possibility of war and unprecedented suffering implies interdependence is evident if there is a desire to avoid this type of carnage. Yet a recognition of this interdependence in the national values of each sovereign state has not led to identical patterns of thought on the subject and therefore did not result in identical policies toward war and peace. Interdependence was accepted as given, to be sure, but the acceptance led to two opposite reactions: the attempt to banish war through alliances, international law, and international organization on the one hand, and neutrality, withdrawal, or isolationism on the other. Both imply recognition of interdependence, and both are rational in terms of the values of their proponents.

Alliances, international law, and international organization imply the hope that a potential warmaker will be deterred from violence if he is confronted with the certainty of immediate armed opposition. Whether this certainty takes the form of bilateral or multilateral pacts or of universally applicable codes of law and conduct in case of violence makes little difference. Thus it was expected that the alliance between France and Soviet Russia, in the mid-thirties, would deter Nazi Germany; it was also hoped that the guarantee expressed in the League of Nations Covenant, that every member would come to the assistance of every other member who was illegally attacked, would be adequate to deter Japan from invading China. In either case, the recognition of interdependence implied the willingness of the key states of the world to jump into the fray and defend the victim of war. Recognition was to take the form of waging war to preserve peace, thereby demonstrating the futility of wars to potential new attackers.

This reaction to modern war, however, is no more common than its direct opposite: the desire to stay out of war altogether by remaining neutral and seeking isolation from world affairs. Thus Great Britain and France did nothing for eight years while Japan seized Manchuria (1931), Italy conquered Ethiopia (1935), Germany rearmed openly (1936), Japan attacked and conquered large parts of China (1937), and Germany annexed Austria (1938) and marched into Czechoslovakia (1939). The cost of resistance to German, Italian, and Japanese policy was considered too high. Interdependence in terms of the horrors of war was a more potent restraint on British and French policy than interdependence seen as the protecting of China, Ethiopia, Austria, and Czechoslovakia against the marching dictators.

Similarly, the United States sought to avoid entanglement in all wars—and all wars outside the Western Hemisphere were considered of no relevance to American interests—through rigid neutrality acts. Thus it was hoped to keep the Chinese as well as the European imbroglio away from American shores.

A reversal in the neutralist reaction to interdependence came only when the warlike policies of Germany and Japan were thought to threaten the interests of Britain, France, and the United States directly. When Germany, in September of 1939, attacked her next victim—Poland—France and Britain realized that life in Europe under established national values was no longer safe, so long as the Nazis prevailed. However, while the Allies came to assist Poland, the smaller European nations continued to seek protection in neutrality and isolation from the conflict, only to be invaded later by Germany. In the case of the United States, only the realization that the demise of the Allies and the victory of Germany and Japan would sooner or later threaten American national values and aspirations persuaded the government to extend aid to Britain and China. However, it was the Japanese attack on Pearl Harbor which catapulted America into active participation in the war. Thus the isolationist reaction to interdependence gave way to the building of alliances and new international organizations only *after* global conflict had become a reality.

While contemporary American policy recognizes the interdependence imposed by modern war through participation in the United Nations, the North Atlantic Pact, and the Organization of American States, other nations continue to adopt the opposite course. India, Egypt, Indonesia, Burma, and Switzerland seek aloofness from conflict through neutrality. Britain and France search for protection against war by joining alliances *and* by neutralizing potential sources of armed violence in Germany and the Far East.

Thus the facts of war and peace alone can tell little about the anatomy of interdependence. The same statistics and the same suffering can and do lead to active participation in world affairs and to the search for isolation from them. Hence it is necessary to investigate other aspirations which may lead to the creation and assertion of interdependence: commercial, religious, financial, cultural, and welfare factors.

3. International Sharing of Values in Commerce, Religion, and Labor. John Stuart Mill thought that "it is commerce which is rapidly rendering war obsolete, by strengthening and multiplying the personal interests which are in natural opposition to it."[3] No doubt Mill was overoptimistic in attributing so much importance to commerce. He stressed the fundamental truth, however, that increasing interdependence among nations may come to be recognized as a result of all sorts of personal and group interests which overlap national boundaries.

The international sharing of values is one such interest. Frequently groups in several national communities have identical or similar ideologies and claims. They may then band together in an effort to realize their aspirations through common national and international policy, by forming themselves into an international interest group. Such developments are most pronounced in the fields of commerce, religion, education, labor, and the professions.

Business and Agriculture. The extent to which businessmen and industrialists of all developed nations recognize common aspirations is indicated by the fact that they established a private international organization to advance their interests, the International Chamber of Commerce. Membership includes all important national chambers of commerce, shipping firms, banks, and industrial corporations. The organization claims that "its recommendations represent the consensus of world business opinion, arrived at after expert investigation and after full consultation of all its national groups."[4] Furthermore, it claims credit for having facilitated if not arranged a number of important international financial agreements. The Chamber demonstrates interdependence of its affiliated interest groups even more cogently by arguing today for protection against nationalization of property and a universal code of rights for foreign business investments. Thus its interests enjoy the support of a distinct international business ideology common to Western-type business organization the world over.

Agricultural cooperative societies in many countries recognize a parallel interdependence. Through the International Co-operative Alliance they exchange information on production and marketing techniques, prices and supplies. They argue for national legislation favoring their cause and even engage in common purchases and sales of their products, thus forming in effect an international "chain store."[5]

---

[3] *Principles of Political Economy,* 7th ed., London, 1929, p. 582.
[4] L. C. White, *International Non-governmental Organizations,* Rutgers University Press, New Brunswick, N.J., 1951, pp. 19–32.
[5] *Ibid.,* pp. 32–35.

Churches and Professional Groups. An international ideology is the keystone of the shared values represented by religious groups in many countries. Organizationally these groups have banded together through the World Conference on Faith and Order, the International Missionary Council, the World Student Christian Federation, the World Alliance of YMCA's, and most recently through the World Council of Churches, which was created to "provide for some symbolic act by which from time to time the unity of the Christian movement can be brought visibly before the imagination of the Church and of the world." [6]

Members of the free professions—lawyers, teachers, engineers—recognize a similar interdependence. International social-science associations provide for the interchange of information and research techniques expected to raise the levels of scientific investigation everywhere. Astronomers, geologists, chemists, physicists, and medical men all have their international associations and their International Council of Scientific Unions in order to profit from each other's work and experience and to enhance the values of their calling. Teachers' groups, such as the New Education Fellowship depending on thirty-one national sections and twenty-one magazines in fifteen languages, seek to establish an international outlook and better teaching methods.

Labor. It is in the field of international labor associations, however, that a most direct link with the ideological struggles of our era is in evidence. Communist labor unions from China, Czechoslovakia, France, Italy, Latin America, and the Soviet Union are united in the World Federation of Trade Unions. This organization is dedicated to supporting the foreign policy of the Soviet Union and therefore uses its strength among workingmen to attack and weaken non-Communist trade unions everywhere. These non-Communist unions, however, have banded together in the International Confederation of Free Trade Unions—with tens of millions of members from Western Europe, the United States, Scandinavia, and the British Commonwealth—to protect the freedom of the worker against domination by Communist and Fascist parties and governments. Thus each association is dedicated to defending its ideology by international means, thereby giving living proof to a recognition of a measure of interdependence by labor. This is indicated, for instance, by the international support given by the Free Confederation to the workers of East Germany when they revolted against their government in 1953, and by the attacks leveled against American aid to Western Europe by the Communist Federation in 1948.

Clearly, national interest groups which profess purposes and values shared by their counterparts elsewhere do indeed recognize a certain amount of interdependence through the common interests which they seek to defend. To the extent that their national values are thereby transcended by wider

6 *Ibid.*, p. 153.

loyalties, the exclusive nature of the national community tends to be weakened.

4. Interdependence Based on Personal and Corporate Relations. The positive interdependence of shared values is not the only link uniting groups and individuals across international frontiers. The activities of large-scale business enterprise and giant corporations, as well as the dealings of small exporters and importers, provide a direct and immediate demonstration of the dependence of groups in one country on events and attitudes in other lands. Such interdependence, however, need not imply any sharing of values at all. Business dealings may be anonymous; personal relations are usually entirely subordinate to the aspirations of managerial groups, who may deal with their opposite numbers across the ocean without caring about their values and ideologies. Dependence on events and attitudes elsewhere, then, does not imply an active sharing of values.

Corporate Relations. Specific corporations, domiciled and incorporated in one country but with interests, establishments, and sources of income in many countries, provide the first example of this interdependence. The International Telephone and Telegraph Corporation of New York is such a firm. It owns and operates municipal and national telephone systems in seven Latin-American states in addition to pre–World War II operations of systems in Italy, Spain, Turkey, Romania, and Shanghai. I.T.&T. owns subsidiaries which manufacture telephone and telegraph equipment in the United States, France, Belgium, Britain, and Germany; it maintains factories in South America, Western Europe, the Balkan countries, and Scandinavia; in addition it has sales offices in all these countries as well as in China, Japan, and Singapore. I.T.&T.'s underwater telegraph cable lines connect the United States with the Far East and Western Europe, Panama with Mexico, Buenos Aires with Rio de Janeiro. The company operates overland telegraph lines between most of the major South American cities and between Washington and San Francisco, and its radiotelegraph and radiotelephone circuits connect major cities across the seven seas.[7]

To the directors and investors of I.T.&T., concentrated in New York, any political or economic development in South America, Europe, and the Far East is a direct demonstration of interdependence, a demonstration which may mean millions of dollars earned or lost. It is apparent that American corporations—or any foreign corporation—with business interests abroad, such as General Motors, Ford, Anaconda Copper, or Alcoa, are by nature deeply involved in the dynamics of international relations. It must be borne in mind that American business-owned property abroad was worth 13.5 billion dollars in 1952.

An even more direct example of international business interdependence is

[7] This record of I.T.&T.'s operations applies to the year 1939. Some details are no longer applicable. See *Fortune Magazine,* September, 1945, pp. 145 ff.

furnished by the corporate form called the "cartel." Here several corporations, or varying nationalities, combine and cooperate for specific purposes rather than having one company active in several fields of endeavor abroad.[8] Cartels may involve joint control over the production or mining of specific commodities or minerals, the fixing of selling prices for these products, and the sharing of patents. Frequently, markets may be split among the participating companies so as to avoid competition between them. A case study of a simple cartel is furnished us by the Iraq Petroleum Company (I.P.C.), which has a monopoly over the production and marketing of all oil in Iraq, Syria, Israel, Jordan, Oman, Hadhramaut, and Aden. Four oil companies own 23.75 per cent each of I.P.C.'s stock, namely, Anglo-Iranian Oil Co. (British), Royal Dutch Shell (Dutch-British), Compagnie Française des Pétroles (French), and Near East Development Corp., owned in equal shares by Standard Oil of New Jersey (American) and Socony-Vacuum (also American).

Personal Relations. Less striking though equally important are the intimate relations which exist among thousands of small business firms in various countries. Exporters in Bombay, Singapore, Beirut, Genoa, Bordeaux, and Lima depend on importers in New York, Hamburg, London, and San Francisco for continuous business activity. Exporting firms in the United States and Britain, similarly, depend on thousands of small importing firms elsewhere in the world for the successful purchase and marketing of their products. These individuals carry on trade in the less spectacular products—leather belts, fine fabrics, cuckoo clocks, briar pipes, and caviar. Interdependence, then, is no less in the case of the small business operated by one individual or a partnership.

Similarly, close personal relations between individuals of different countries are brought about by immigration and emigration. American culture and life is a living example of this factor. Since 1945, furthermore, millions of people have left their native countries in Eastern and Central Europe, either as a result of forced population exchanges or to flee from political persecution and economic hardships. While immigration into the United States has shrunk, large-scale international population movements elsewhere still take place. Since the emigrant usually retains close personal ties with his relatives and friends in his native country—political conditions permitting—his loyalty tends to be divided between his adopted and his native land; he continues to associate his values and aspirations with those prevalent in the "old country." So long as this remains true a further element of value sharing, though probably temporary, across national boundaries occurs.

5. The Stake of the Individual in International Trade and Investment. *Trade and Employment.* International corporations and associations and ties of emigrants with their country of origin provide examples of interdependence

---

[8] The term "cartel" is subject to various definitions. It is used in the broadest possible sense here. The term "consortium" is sometimes applied to the I.P.C.

which are directly experienced in their daily pursuits by those concerned. Interdependence, however, is equally evident—though not directly experienced in terms of personal relations—in the role one country may play in the economy of another. If the United States were to cease buying coffee in Brazil and hemp in the Philippines tomorrow, thousands upon thousands of Brazilians and Filipinos would be thrown out of work. The Great Depression of 1929 to 1933 demonstrated once and for all that all countries active in international trade suffer if unemployment rises in any major trading country. Unemployment decreases income and purchasing power and hence makes it difficult for the former consumers of foreign products to maintain their consumption. As a result, exports to the depression-ridden country decrease, and unemployment is bound to rise in the exporting country, thus reducing its income and purchasing power.

The dependence of high living standards in the American economy—relatively self-sufficient though it is—on a high level of foreign trade is proved readily enough. In 1947 no less than 2,364,000 jobs depended on foreign trade, and today the figure is much higher. Of United States raw cotton production, 15 per cent is exported, while the corresponding figures for other products are as follows: wheat, 35 per cent; tobacco, 20 per cent; rice, 40 per cent; and agricultural machinery, 20 per cent.[9] Before the depression in 1929, American exports in agricultural commodities alone totaled 5 billion dollars. By 1932 the figure had shrunk to 1.6 billion dollars, while the United States shipped 48 per cent less cotton, 64 per cent less machinery, and 90 per cent less wheat and flour abroad. The State Department estimated that 40 million acres of farmland would have had to find some alternative use if this depression trade picture had continued for any length of time.[10] The foreclosing of mortgages and the impoverished farmer of the thirties bore eloquent testimony to this aspect of international interdependence.

Trade and Investment. But the international flow of goods does not tell the whole story. Living standards and employment in any one country are also very much dependent upon the flow of capital for investments from one country to another. Take Great Britain as an example. In 1939 she maintained one of the highest standards of living in Europe even though she imported perhaps 70 per cent of her food needs. These imports were paid for by drawing on income that British individuals had previously invested abroad. In order to pay for the strategic imports necessary in the production of armaments after 1939, however, Britain was forced to accumulate a foreign debt of 14 billion dollars and to liquidate 4.5 billion dollars of her foreign investments. Once the war ended, of course, the income from

---

[9] U.S. Department of State, *World Trade and the United States,* Publication 3492, Commercial Policy Series 119, 1949.

[10] Francis B. Sayre, *The Dependence of Domestic Markets upon Foreign Trade,* U.S. Department of State Publication 1340, Commercial Policy Series 61, 1939, p. 5.

these former investments was no longer available to pay for the renewed food needs of the British people. Hence in 1945 Britain imported 67 per cent less than in 1939. Since in 1939 Britain had purchased one-sixth of all American exports, employment in the United States might have been permanently affected unless Britain had been enabled to resume large-scale purchases from abroad. Because she lacked the capital to do this, the United States decided to lend her 3.75 billion dollars. As one American official explained,[11]

> The British could have existed [without the loan] by cutting their imports and the living standards. They would have cut their purchases from the United States, and other countries, to the very bone. This they would have had to do indefinitely and it would have meant very bad business for us. . . . We sold the British much more than we bought from them. We want to revive and increase that trade.

The interdependence of high living standards in the United States and Britain, then, demanded that capital be made available in order to make possible the purchase and sale of goods.

Economic Development. Interdependence may even be more dramatically illustrated by examining the capital needs of underdeveloped countries who wish to maximize production and living standards. The countries of Southeast Asia—India, Pakistan, Ceylon, Malaya, and British Borneo—have undertaken a cooperative six-year development plan which calls for the speedy investment of no less than 5.2 billion dollars. Of this sum these countries can raise only 2.2 billion dollars through taxes and domestic savings. Investments contributed by other countries must amount to 2.3 billion dollars in order to carry out the plan, in order to raise the standard of living of the Indian peasant above the starvation level. The failure to recognize economic aspirations will result in unemployment, depression, and unrest in industrialized countries and hunger, primitiveness, and xenophobia in underdeveloped areas.[12]

Strategic Materials. Access to strategic raw materials is one of the most potent factors making for world interdependence. Since minerals essential in modern technology are distributed over the world in uneven quantities and since no one country possesses a sufficient amount of certain key materials, trade and investment are essential even in time of peace. Once the possibility of war with its implied disruption of normal trade channels is faced, however, the strategic materials problem is directly linked to national survival. Nickel, for instance, is largely concentrated in Canada. Mercury can be obtained in large quantities only from Italy, Spain, Mexico, the United States, and the

[11] Fred M. Vinson and Dean Acheson, *The British Loan—What It Means to Us,* U.S. Department of State Publication 2454, Commercial Policy Series 81, 1946.

[12] John R. E. Carr-Gregg, "The Colombo Plan," *International Conciliation,* no. 467, January, 1951, pp. 38, 51. The remaining 700 million dollars is to be raised from funds presently owed by Britain to India, Pakistan, and Ceylon.

Soviet Union, while asbestos seems to be concentrated in Canada, South Africa, and the Soviet Union.

The dependence of the United States on certain strategic materials is plainly shown in these figures:

Material	Production		Consumption		Import demand	
	1950	1975	1950	1975	1950	1975
Copper, thousand short tons...........	900	800	1,300	1,800	230	1,000
Iron ore, million short tons.............	110	130	130	200	20	70
Zinc, thousand short tons..............	620	750	1,100	1,500	130	750
Lead, thousand short tons.............	450	300	750	1,200	300	900
Tin, thousand long tons...............	0	0	75	85	75	85

SOURCE: The President's Materials Policy Commission, *Resources for Freedom*, Washington, 1952, vol. I, p. 58. (Figures are approximate and rounded.)

Hence the American government is now following a policy of encouraging the importation and advance building of stockpiles of these minerals for emergency use, as well as the long-range investment of American capital in suitable mines abroad.

All these demonstrations of physical, ideological, and institutional inter-dependence merely beg the basic question: "Does recognition of dependence on other nations imply recognition of a body of value higher than that of each nation?" The answer seems to be "No." Hence it is necessary to examine the needs and ideologies of groups and nations which have kept—and continue to keep—the recognition of interdependence from unifying sovereign nations into a larger community.

6. Aloofness as a Reaction to Interdependence. One response to the challenge of recognized interdependence, as has been seen, is the growth of beliefs and values transcending loyalty to the national state. The other response possible, however, is the desire to minimize contacts with other nations and to withdraw from them. Mere facts do not shape political conduct. The interpretation of these facts in terms of the national values which determine concrete policy decisions is the keystone of political analysis. Hence both responses to the challenge of interdependence deserve careful study.

Groups which espouse isolationism, neutralism, or withdrawal do not deny the facts of dependence on others. On the contrary, they recognize involvement but prize their own values so highly that they prefer to maintain them intact without having to compromise with the values of others. Active co-operation in international relations, like peaceful political life within the national community, calls for constant compromising between values and interests. A group devoted to the defense of its own aspirations, however, may well be unwilling to pay the price of compromise. It will then advocate national policies of meeting deficiencies and needs through the unilateral assertion of national strength rather than through cooperative measures. Dependence on others frequently has resulted in a reinforced desire to maintain exclusive national values, instead of sharing them.

British Neutralism. Thus the wing of the British Labor party led by Aneurin Bevan espouses a foreign policy for the United Kingdom in which the principles of socialism are given first priority. The Labor Left, as it is called, opposes war on principle. It opposes capitalism and believes that the interests of a capitalist nation must inevitably drive it toward war. It holds that governments dominated by business cannot want peace and therefore are unable to negotiate in good faith. Such regimes always are held to favor a high level of armaments production, thereby reducing the standard of living of the working classes. The British Labor Left therefore opposes rearmament, since the physical welfare of the masses is its first and most important policy aim. Its leaders also oppose a British foreign policy of implacable hostility to the Soviet Union and caution against close British identification with American policy. A Republican American administration stands for everything the Labor Left abhors: armaments, impatience with the welfare state, warlike hostility to communism, and "power politics." Bevan has no wish to compromise his interpretation of British values by being "tied to a capitalist policy" or to establish "close liaison with a private monopoly capitalism." Hence the Labor Left also opposes being "dragged at the heels of American big business and their representatives" and has no wish for "tying of the economy of Britain with that of Capitalist America." [13]

Withdrawal of Britain from certain aspects of world affairs is clearly implied in this attitude. British values of mass welfare are considered incompatible with an American policy of long-range armed opposition to Russia. Bevan would have Britain follow an independent and peaceful international policy, free from involvement with American aims in Western Europe and the Far East.

Indian Neutralism. The unwillingness of the bulk of Indian opinion to compromise its national and group values finds expression in a different form. India's policy of "nonalignment" with any of the dominant blocs and alliances nevertheless is an attempt to withdraw from an unpalatable aspect of world affairs. Proudly asserting the uniqueness of Indian values, one newspaper noted, "There is nothing to be unnerved at if India is at times misunderstood by any of the armed camps. National interest and national self-respect alike demand that India should not align herself with any of the

---

[13] For these and other citations see Leon D. Epstein, "The British Labor Left and U.S. Foreign Policy," *American Political Science Review,* December, 1951, pp. 983 ff.

armed blocs sacrificing her brain and judgment." [14] For Prime Minister Nehru and his segment of the ruling Congress party, both American and Soviet policies and their concomitant alliance systems are unacceptable. Both imply war over competing national myths which India cannot wholly share. Indian policy stands for the peaceful coexistence of capitalism and communism. If the two antagonistic myths have to fight, Indian leaders wish to stay out of the war and therefore have steadfastly refused to ally themselves with either camp. Noninvolvement, neutrality, and mediation between the two giant blocs are India's recipe of withdrawal.

The Atlantic Pact [settles] almost irrevocably the future course of events. The Powers are not drifting towards war; on the contrary, they are inviting it and preparing for it as being inevitable. . . . There is just the faintest hope that war might still be averted by the pressure of neutral opinion in Europe as well as in Asia. That is not much but still the only hope against the triumph of the jungle principle on a scale too dreadful even to contemplate.[15]

In this fashion, the doctrine of nonviolence in politics, accepted by many Indians, is kept from being compromised out of existence. India's role as a noncapitalist and non-Communist neutral mediator is being preserved, while New Delhi eschews being definitely allied with Washington or Moscow. Consequently, India is thrown back upon her own resources in case of conflict with either camp. Her isolation compels her to "go it alone," since no outside power is pledged to come to her assistance.

American Unilateralism. A marked unwillingness to meet interdependence by compromising national values with those of other states is equally characteristic of the American form of aloofness—isolationism. Thus participation in the United Nations and in the North Atlantic Treaty Organization (NATO) has not infrequently imposed the necessity on American policy makers to revise policy aims so as to make them acceptable to the other member states of these organizations. Postponing the creation of the Southeast Asian alliance and the rearmament of Germany are cogent examples.

Hence some Americans, like General MacArthur, demanded an American course of "going it alone," even outside the UN and NATO. These groups minimize the dependence of America on its allies and prefer unilateral action to the yielding of values to the pressure of interdependence. They attacked the UN and NATO precisely because these bodies make interallied compromises inevitable. Said one American senator,[16]

The cold, clever, calculating, power-seeking U.N. still is there, just where it was at San Francisco, hidden behind the idealism. This network of international agencies

---

[14] *Allahabad Amrita Bazar Patrika*, Dec. 26, 1950. Quoted in F. S. C. Northrop, *The Taming of the Nations*, Macmillan, New York, 1952, p. 39.

[15] *Hindustan Standard*, Dec. 21, 1950. Quoted in Northrop, *op. cit.*, p. 38.

[16] Hon. William E. Jenner, *Congressional Record*, Aug. 18, 1952, pp. A5246, A5250.

Wingate College Library

has now selected and trained a huge aggressive bureaucracy which is working inside every country, building world government while we sleep. This collectivist bureaucracy has set up UNESCO to penetrate into every private agency in every country . . . to spin its web of propaganda in every town and village in this country.

The symbol of American patriotism is invoked in order to demonstrate the "treason" implied in giving up any portion of national beliefs. Threats to withdraw from the UN are commonly heard when policies in that organization are advocated which run counter to key American ideological tenets. Opposition to compromising any portion of American values is voiced whenever powerful veterans' organizations gather at their yearly meetings. School boards take action against teachers who use textbooks based on international rather than exclusively American precepts. Demands are heard that economic aid be cut off to countries which violate the ideology of free enterprise in their domestic legislation. Compromises with any nation espousing atheism are held equally repugnant to the purity of American nationalism. The desire to remain aloof if international relations cannot be conducted wholly in accord with these doctrines follows naturally from the realization that interdependence imposes ideological compromise.

Some desire to withdraw is marked in the attitudes of most nations. Participation in the actions of international organizations, for instance, is restricted and qualified by almost all states in accord with their unique values. Groups and individuals tending toward a measure of withdrawal exist everywhere. Their role in policy making is at least as significant as that of their rivals who may be ready to make the compromise.

7. The Limitations of Internationally Shared Values. Apart from these general attitudes favoring involvement or withdrawal in international relations, it has been noted that certain groups share specific aspirations with similar groups in other countries. The International Confederation of Free Trade Unions and the International Chamber of Commerce are the result of active value sharing across national frontiers. Yet it appears that the leaders of the participating trade unions no less than the business elite remain attached to their national loyalties while actively seeking international ties. In case of a conflict between international and national loyalties it is almost always the latter which emerges victorious. How is the paradox to be explained? How important is the international sharing of values in redirecting the ideologies of individuals and groups after a degree of interdependence has been recognized?

There is no guarantee that even in a mass membership organization like the American Federation of Labor, which does belong to an international labor group with shared values, the leadership really represents the views of its rank-and-file supporters on each and every issue. No matter how firmly the facts of interdependence may be ingrained in the minds of the leaders, on issues which appear remote to immediate interests and needs, no mass support for the leadership can be anticipated. Once an international emergency has catapulted key states into war, universal value systems have a tendency to be submerged in the dominant national myths. Interest groups with internationally shared values flourish in time of peace and harmony and lapse into inaction and indifference in time of crisis. Clearly, even in such groups, then, divisive forces are likely to supplant shared values—at least temporarily.

Nor can shared values survive indefinitely as a result of immigrant loyalties. For one or two generations, to be sure, such loyalties continue to be divided. But as the process of assimilation takes root, loyalty to the adopted community invariably supplants the earlier attachments. If it fails to do so, the new national community tends to treat the immigrant as "subversive" and takes measures to exclude him from participation in the social and political life of the nation in time of crisis. Immigrant loyalties have rarely been a force for world integration. Frequently they have acted instead as a catalyst of hostilities if their attachment to the original home country continued to outweigh developing loyalties to the adopted state.

Finally, can international personal relationships which come about as a result of close ties between business firms be considered as making for increased recognition of interdependence? The answer once more seems to be in the negative. Mutual interdependence in terms of dollars and cents is no substitute for loyalty to a common myth. To be sure, international trade may be disrupted by war; but then new business relationships may be formed, just as casual as the original ties and just as liable to interruption if war should develop. In short, close business relations do not imply personal friendship.

8. International Trade or National Self-sufficiency? The limitations of shared values in international life result in the victory of national values during times of crisis. Those who share aspirations with others abroad are rendered incapable of acting in accordance with their convictions because the aspirations involved appear unimportant—if not treasonable—to the bulk of the nation. A brisk trade among nations, by contrast, does not even imply the existence of shared values or the desire to bridge ideological gaps. It reflects only the interests of groups who stand to profit from this activity, regardless of their private endorsement of internationalism or their support of virulent chauvinism. Further, international trade may be used merely as a vehicle for realizing a policy of national exclusion from the rest of the world.

Self-sufficiency. Thus in Nazi Germany, foreign trade was conducted on the principle of political advantage only. Goods of no use to the German war machine were exported at low prices, and only goods which would either enhance the war potential of Germany or make other countries permanently dependent upon Germany were imported, at high prices if politically desirable. The policy of the Soviet Union has been much the same. Exported goods are the ones which the ruling elite does not need for purposes of cementing its internal strength. Imported goods exclude only the type required for increasing the industrial strength or the political contentment of the community. Not interdependence but self-sufficiency and national strength are the criteria of policy making in any authoritarian state.

But the authoritarians are by no means alone in not using international trade. During the Great Depression, it was the consistent policy of most democratic countries to minimize interdependence and to achieve as much self-sufficiency as possible. Foreign goods were uniformly discriminated against in order to make unnecessary their importation. It was hoped that domestic industries supplanting the formerly imported manufactures and commodities would develop, and through proper domestic policies such aims were frequently achieved. The net result sometimes was increased employment at home, but all too frequently at the expense of increased unemployment abroad. Even democracies tend to practice policies of self-sufficiency and deny interdependence when this appears as an easier way of achieving domestic prosperity, regardless of the disastrous results such policies may have for countries which cannot make the necessary internal adjustments.

Furthermore, in times of international political crisis, the search for strategic and military self-sufficiency is just as characteristic of democracies as it is of authoritarian communities. The disruption of American rubber imports from Indonesia in 1941 called into existence the domestic synthetic-rubber industry, which in the future is likely to ruin the American market for Indonesian natural rubber. If political disharmony makes the exportation of "strategic" commodities to the potential adversary unwise, even a democracy will place embargoes on specific exports and limit thereby the flow of international trade, as the United States has done in recent years.

Group Aims and Economic Exclusiveness. Policies of economic exclusiveness and discrimination, like any other policy, are the result of the aims of specific groups. When depression strikes and unemployment figures skyrocket, labor organizations in all industrial countries are the first to demand policies of discrimination against foreign goods. Similarly, manufacturers' trade associations will clamor for policies of discrimination and exclusion, and for much the same reason: to be able to acquire the market formerly held by foreign producers. Associations of shippers will back them with slogans of "ship and travel American," and farmers' groups will clamor for policies of excluding foreign agricultural commodities. At the same time, however, they will also demand that their own surplus crops be shipped abroad in order to keep them from suffering losses.

This pattern is a typical one in a democratic community in which the recognition of international interdependence is just as likely to result in a response of withdrawal as in policies of encouraging further trading contacts. To the dairyman, for example, interdependence is a tragedy which he seeks to soften by appropriate policy demands. His claims in a setting of competing national loyalties are more easily accepted by the community than those of the free traders and business interests with a stake in free trade.

9. International Investment or National Planning? Arguments extolling the need for capital, similarly, must be matched with the counterarguments emphasizing a strictly national viewpoint in the allocation of foreign investment. No one disputes the objective need for foreign funds if the standard of living of the Asian countries, for instance, is to be raised. But the conditions governing the furnishing of such funds is quite another matter. Thus some American investors insist that capital-importing countries permit a maximum of freedom of action to the foreign lender and restrict him in no way with "socialistic" legislation. One spokesman for American investors declared: "The first thing that all governments must be made to understand is that . . . investments must be principally based upon the profit motive. . . . It must not be expected that corporations managed in the interest of public shareholders should have to consider investment . . . on humanitarian, political, social or military grounds." [17]

Further, it must be remembered that when governments make loans to other governments they may have still other factors in view which bear no necessary relation to the aspirations of the capital-importing nation. America encourages the investment of huge funds in mines abroad in order to stimulate the importation and stockpiling of strategic materials, i.e., "strategic" from the American point of view. Such a judgment, however, need not be shared by the country on whose territory the strategic mines may be located, and once more one national investment policy comes into conflict with another. American investment policy in the Middle East oil fields may bear a distinct relation to the economic demands of oil companies and the strategic needs of the United States Navy. But it cannot be taken for granted that these policies also meet the needs of the Arab peoples, who may have quite different plans for their resources. They may insist that oil exploitation be geared to their own economic, social, and educational advancement, aims to which Standard Oil of New Jersey may not be sympathetic.

Thus the new countries of Asia have not been slow in indicating that their own capital needs cannot necessarily be squared with the demands of the capital-exporting countries. When a marked dichotomy in aims between a capital-importing and a capital-exporting country has come to the fore, nationals of underdeveloped countries have been heard to mutter that a new imperialism is "advancing behind dollar loans." No wonder that, in the deliberations of the United Nations, delegates from Latin America and Asia demand that economic development take place only under specific safeguards devised by the governments of the capital-hungry states.

Capital exporters and capital importers, private firms, and government

[17] National Foreign Trade Council, *Point Four Program—Forum,* 1949, p. 4.

lending agencies all have differing aims and claims. No general pattern of international investment recognizing each nation's dependence on every other nation can take shape so long as the plans for utilizing the funds differ basically. Recognized interdependence, therefore, has failed to produce a world-wide consensus on proper policies for enhancing the welfare of all. National aims continue to carry the day.

10. The Toleration of War. Within the state, differences over cultural values, economic policy, the rate of investment, and the stockpiling of strategic materials are settled by peaceful means. It is the essence of a community that violence between groups is banished; that "heads are counted rather than broken" in democratic political controversy. Clearly, much less repugnance to use violence characterizes international relations. The very fact that the recognition of interdependence among nations in all possible areas of human activity has not given rise to a larger loyalty indicates that a different method of settling competing claims prevails. That method is war. The continued toleration of war is both the result of the absence of a larger loyalty and the prime symptom of incomplete global integration.

Even the advent of atomic and hydrogen bombs has failed to deter man's acceptance of "inevitable war," despite the probable consequences of that war. On the contrary, as Harold Lasswell has said,[18]

The absence of moral revulsion is one of the dominant characteristics of our day. This callousness does not come primarily from the love of cruelty but rather from terror arising from the expectation of unlimited violence. . . . The American government killed more civilians with more dispatch at Hiroshima and Nagasaki than have ever been exterminated at one time in history. And there was no moral revulsion that threw out of office, and out of contact with decent human beings, every official who had any direct responsibility for the act.

Precisely because national communities expect further international violence, they seem to have resigned themselves to the recurrence of war. Instead of mustering overwhelming public pressure in favor of such international control measures as might be adopted to make harmless large-scale atomic warfare, the American community seems to feel that the security of its national way of life is best assured by maximizing the national advantage in these weapons. Instead of stressing the interdependence of the world in terms of the unprecedented destructiveness of modern weapons, one American general has said: [19]

Retaliation is the only way of gaining the decision over our opponent. . . . The result [of the first enemy attack] may be a casualty list of 25,000,000 men, women

[18] Harold D. Lasswell and Daniel Lerner (eds.), *The Policy Sciences*, Stanford University Press, Stanford, Calif., 1951, pp. 110–111.

[19] Gen. George C. Kenney, in address to 21st Women's Patriotic Conference on National Defense, Washington, Jan. 26, 1947. Cited in F. L. Schuman, *International Politics*, 4th ed., McGraw-Hill, New York, 1948, p. 919.

and children in the first 24 hours. . . . To stop our enemy from continuing his assault, we must be prepared to carry the war to him. . . .

Intensive strategic bombing is held out as the proper way to meet this threat. One opinion survey showed that when asked, "What do you think we in this country should do to try to cut down the possibility of war with Russia?" 29 per cent of those polled answered in terms of hostile measures, 28 per cent in terms of conciliatory attempts, 13 per cent had miscellaneous suggestions, and 35 per cent had no opinion whatever.[20]

Other opinion surveys support the contention that resignation to war rather than enthusiasm for it is the dominant attitude. Thus in Iowa 55 per cent of the respondents expected war, in Texas 61 per cent and in Minnesota 74 per cent, at least at the time the survey was taken.[21] No adequate surveys of this kind are available for all other countries, but in France 78 per cent of the respondents expected their country to be pulled into a conflict between the United States and the Soviet Union.[22]

Thus the expectation of future violence is part and parcel of political consciousness. As long as this fatalistic mode of thought continues, no demonstration of interdependence can be expected to change national loyalties to devotion to a global system of values. Anticipation of violence seems to breed continued acceptance of national values and interests and not a desire to transcend them. So long as this holds true the recognition of interdependence among nations alone will not contribute to the integration of the earth into one community. The dynamics of international relations, then, remains centered on the conflict of interests rather than on the community of interests.

ADDITIONAL CASE-STUDY MATERIAL

Atomic Energy Study Group of the Royal Institute of International Affairs: *Atomic Energy; Its International Implications,* London, 1948.
Barbask, J.: "International Labor Confederations: CIT and CTAL," *Monthly Labor Review,* May, 1948.
Carr, E. H.: "Two Currents in World Labor," *Foreign Affairs,* vol. 25, October, 1946.
Carr-Gregg, John R. E.: "The Colombo Plan," *International Conciliation,* no. 467, January, 1951.
Condliffe, J. B.: "International Trade and Economic Nationalism," *International Conciliation,* no. 476, December, 1951.
Diebold, W.: *Trade and Payments in Western Europe, 1947–51,* Harper, New York, 1952.
Epstein, L. D.: "The British Labor Left and U.S. Foreign Policy," *American Political Science Review,* vol. 45, December, 1951.
Glover, E.: *War, Sadism and Pacifism,* G. Allen, London, 1947.
Goormaghtigh, J.: "European Integration," *International Conciliation,* no. 469, February, 1953.

[20] Minnesota Poll, Dec. 25, 1949, *International Journal of Opinion and Attitude Research,* vol. 4, no. 1, spring, 1950, p. 143. Percentages add to more than 100 because some respondents gave more than one answer.
[21] Texas Poll, Dec. 25, 1949, *International Journal of Opinion and Attitude Research,* vol. 4, no. 1, spring, 1950, p. 144. Iowa Poll, July 2, 1950, *ibid.,* no. 3, fall, 1950, p. 457. Minnesota Poll, Aug. 20, 1950, *ibid.,* p. 457.
[22] G. Rotvand, "NATO—A French View," *International Journal,* spring, 1952, p. 108.

Haas, Ernst B.: "Imperialism and Economic Development in Asia," *Journal of International Affairs,* vol. 4, no. 2, spring, 1950.

Kohn, H.: *Pan-Slavism: Its History and Ideology,* Notre Dame University, South Bend, Ind., 1953.

Lasswell, H. D., and D. Lerner (eds.): *The Policy Sciences,* Stanford University Press, Stanford, Calif., 1951.

Loftus, J. A.: "Middle East Oil: The Pattern of Control," *Middle East Journal,* vol. 2, January, 1948.

Mill, J. S.: *Principles of Political Economy,* 7th ed., London, 1929.

Mott, J. R.: *Cooperation and the World Mission,* International Missionary Council, New York, 1935.

National Foreign Trade Council: *Point Four Program—Forum,* 1949.

Northrop, F. S. C.: *The Taming of the Nations,* Macmillan, New York, 1952.

President's Materials Policy Commission: *Resources for Freedom,* 1952.

Queener, L.: "The Development of Internationalist Attitudes," *Journal of Social Psychology,* vol. 29, May, 1949.

Reeves, W. H., and P. D. Dickens: "Private Foreign Investments; A Means of World Economic Development," *Political Science Quarterly,* vol. 64, June, 1949.

Roper, E.: "American Attitudes on World Organization," *Public Opinion Quarterly,* vol. 17, no. 4, winter, 1953–1954.

Rotvand, G.: "NATO—A French View," *International Journal,* spring, 1952.

Royal Institute of International Affairs: *Nationalism,* Oxford, New York, 1939.

Sayre, F. B.: *The Dependence of Domestic Markets upon Foreign Trade,* U.S. Department of State Publication 1340, Commercial Policy Series 61, 1939.

U.S. Department of State: *World Trade and the United States,* Publication 3492, Commercial Policy Series 119, 1949.

Vinson, F. M., and D. Acheson: *The British Loan—What It Means to Us,* U.S. Department of State Publication 2454, Commercial Policy Series 81, 1946.

White, L. C.: *International Non-governmental Organization,* Rutgers University Press, New Brunswick, N. J., 1951.

Whittlesey, C. R.: *National Interest and International Cartels,* Macmillan, New York, 1946.

Williams, B. H.: "The Spread of Technology and the Relative Strength of States," *Social Science,* October, 1949.

Chapter 2

INDIVIDUALS, GROUPS, AND THE NATION

Chapter 1 has shown how, despite widespread recognition of international interdependence, national loyalties and values remain dominant. Conversely, internationally shared values fail to enjoy a support similar to that of their national competitors. Implicit in this finding is the conclusion that, while nations form cohesive communities, the complex of interdependent nations is merely a pattern of voluntary associations of limited scope and duration.

This fails to answer the basic question of how nations become cohesive communities while the society of states remains unintegrated. For a fuller understanding of the dominance of society over community, it is necessary to analyze more closely the terms and concepts used in discussions of interdependence. What are *values, interests,* and *ideologies?* What part do they play in political action? What is the relationship between individual opinions and group ideologies, between group interests and national policy?

This approach to international relations regards individuals and groups as basic constituent elements. It denies that the actors upon the world stage are nations or states, conceived as monolithic units with fixed policies dictated by immutable injunctions of geography, principle, and power. It focuses on the *dynamic* aspects of international relations, the ever-shifting aims and demands which flourish *within* nations and which cause recurring conflict and compromise *between* them. It tries to discover what men seek through political action, which men direct the political actors, and finally how that action determines the pattern of international relations. Only an examination of the motives of men and groups of men can make clear the tangled pattern of international relations.

1. The Role of the Individual. Philosophy and psychology have long grappled with the question: "What makes men believe and behave as they do?" One clue may be furnished by an examination of the interaction between the individual and his environment, leading in turn to an appreciation of the relation between belief and behavior.

Attitudes and Opinions. Specific judgments the individual makes about his environment and his role in that environment can be traced to more or less clearly defined attitudes that he holds about himself and the world in which he lives. These attitudes spring from his many associations and experiences in life. The family in which he is raised, the nursery in which he plays, the street gang with which he spends his afternoons, and the schools in which he is educated imbue him with a set of assumptions and generalizations about his social environment which in due time become his standards of judgment for evaluating the world and his relation to it. If he is exposed to strongly religious strands of thought during this formative period, he may develop spiritual-ethical preferences and standards toward the world. A background of upper-class wealth and superiority of status may give him a set of standards in which he regards himself as superior to others and give him the desire to retain that superiority of status. A middle-class individual imbued with the idea that all are equal and should have equal access to the honors of life, in turn may grow up with a set of standards which will enable him to aspire toward advancement in status. Frames of reference and standards by which to judge behavior in society develop into opinions about society, opinions shaped by basic attitudes.

Thus when the individual polled by the local inquiring reporter indicates that he prefers social security to individual bargaining with his employer he is reflecting an attitude. When the important manufacturer expresses his preference for a minimum of government regulation of business it is his attitude on the place of business enterprise in the community which determines his position. To arrive at an opinion the individual may, to be sure, analyze the relevant issues dispassionately and come to a conclusion accordingly. It is much more likely, however, that the opinion adopted corresponds to the social position in which the individual happens to find himself or to which he aspires. He thinks as he is expected to think by his associates. He conforms to the general attitudes which tend to characterize the larger groups with which he is associated.

Multiple Attitudes and Affiliations. But to what does the individual choose to conform? Which attitudes is he likely to reject and which will he adopt as his own? Clearly, persons hold a multiplicity of separate attitudes on diverse aspects of public affairs and these attitudes produce a large cluster of demands and claims, not necessarily consistent with each other. Thus the manufacturer anxious to minimize government regulation over his business —implying few laws and low taxes—may also favor a high degree of national preparedness against Soviet attack, an attitude calling for detailed legislation and possible emergency control over business and certainly implying a high rate of taxation. Which of these attitudes will determine his conduct? Will our manufacturer associate his demands with the American Legion's preparedness program or the National Association of Manufacturers' call for lower taxes?

No definite answer is possible. In situations of conflicting attitudes and demands group affiliations by the individual will be determined by the importance he attaches to these separate aspirations and by the ease with which they may be satisfied without compromising one or the other out of existence. Hence attitudes may be said to suffer blunting as they must be brought into conformity with competing attitudes held by the same person, even though this may take place only when the individual is compelled to *act* on his convictions.

Further, the multiplicity of attitudes which can be entertained simultaneously brings with it identification of the individual with many groups, each of which is expected to satisfy certain of his demands. Identification proceeds on the basis of personal decisions as to what kind of group affiliation will be able to do justice to the maximum of aspirations. Devotion to low taxes brings with it one kind of affiliation; desire for military preparedness another; the search for a foreign market may produce a third, even though sales may be sought in the territory of the very state which is feared as an enemy of the manufacturer's nation. The limits of identification are determined by the degree to which these attitudes conflict with one another. A choice as to which affiliation should enjoy primacy may then be necessary, though no conclusion can be hazarded on how a given individual will choose. In the absence of this dilemma, however, the multiplicity of competing attitudes on the part of each single individual explains the tendency for an individual to identify with several groups and for groups to identify with one another or to share attitudes.

In a democratic community a maximum of emphasis is placed upon the individual's attitudes and opinions. Democracy highlights interplay of individual opinions, which determines the policies of the government. Through elections, debates, voting, and discussion in lodges, labor unions, and clubs, no less than through informal exchange of views, the individual is expected to form an opinion about current issues and to try to influence policy making accordingly.

In fact, however, the individual tends to act far otherwise. Thus it is reported that in the United States "about 3 out of 10 voters are unaware of almost every event in American foreign affairs," that "about 65 out of every 100 voters admit that they rarely discuss foreign affairs," and that "only about 25 out of every 100 voters can be considered reasonably well-informed." [1] The less an issue can be identified with the local community or the more complex it becomes, the greater the probability of individual indifference toward the issue. Vetoes in the Security Council or cabinet crises in Western Europe mean little to the stenographer in Des Moines or the fruit grower in Sacramento, each with his own immediate problems which demand his full attention. Furthermore, where awareness of "foreign affairs" exists, the very complexity and incomprehensibility of the issues often induce a feeling of helplessness and withdrawal on the part of the individual, evidenced

---

[1] L. Markel, *Public Opinion and Foreign Policy*, Harper, New York, 1949, p. 9.

by the "no opinion" responses found in public opinion polls. Ignorance of issues is thus frequently linked to individual indifference.

Opinion Leaders. This combination of ignorance and indifference leads often to a desperate mass demand that "something be done" about whatever international situation proves so frustrating. Reasoned judgments about complex relationships cannot be made if the locally fashioned attitudes toward the world prove too simple for a solution or if they are too rigid to permit adaptation to changing external phenomena. Under these conditions, the individual who cannot cope with issues the democratic system expects him to analyze rationally will frequently turn to the "expert" for guidance. Thus, the task of forming opinions is partly shifted by the individual to a set of other individuals who are considered better prepared and fitted.

The crucial question is: "Who are the 'experts'?" Broadly speaking, the population of a democratic and pluralistic community can be divided into persons who are closely identified with an organized group, such as fraternal and veterans' organizations, churches, labor unions, ethnic groups, and the like, and persons who are not members of such bodies. Members of organized groups which take a position on political issues generally pay heed to the opinions of their own presidents, program chairmen, and policy committees. The leaders of the group become the experts on political issues and thereby exert a tremendous influence in the formation of opinion. Of course, not all members of such groups think as the leadership counsels. The union member does not necessarily vote the Democratic ticket merely because his officers support the Democratic party. Yet the nonconforming member as well as the relatively unattached individual in a community also tend to be influenced by experts. For them it may be the favorite radio or television commentator who attains a position of respect and thereby is able to shape opinions among his followers. Whether identified with a well-organized group or independent, the individual is incessantly influenced by others better informed than he in the formation of his opinions.

The individual, of course, does not thereby become merely a pawn of the real opinion shapers. Leaders tend to be severely restricted in the way in which they guide their followers. Generally both the leaders and the followers share basic attitudes and agree on essentials. Leaders therefore guide in the sense of giving specific direction to an already existing preference. The basic preferences, however, are determined for the leaders by the attitudes of the individuals who are ready to follow and respect them. Policy making in a democracy, therefore, rests less on the allegedly independent and autonomous individual than on numbers of opinion-forming persons conversant with the issues, sharing the attitudes of the individuals who support them, and able to translate these general attitudes into more precise policy aims.

In an authoritarian community, by contrast, the individual is expected to behave quite differently. He is spared the task of forming opinions, and if he does form them independently he runs the fatal risk of violating the officially sanctioned opinions. Proper attitudes are defined for the individual by his leaders, who are thought to be endowed with superhuman powers of insight and understanding, infallible and omniscient. Instead of the individual being confronted by a series of groups with differing attitudes, in an authoritarian community there is usually only one group with one set of "right" attitudes, to which opposing notions constitute heresy, deviation, or treason.

The problem of attitudes in an authoritarian community, therefore, is not the enabling of individuals to make independent decisions. Rather it is the problem of fostering the attitudes favored by the ruling elite among the mass of individuals constituting the community. Constant propaganda, to which every form of expression in the society must be subordinated, is the method used to achieve such acquiescence. The problem of attitude formation and expression is reduced to the problem of manipulation.

2. The Role of Groups in a Community. When Aristotle declared that man is a social animal he was merely uttering a truism. Yet the truism is fundamental to an understanding of political decision making. Because the isolated individual, as an independent and autonomous thinking organism, does not in and by himself make decisions for a whole community, emphasis is necessarily thrown on groupings of individuals acting together to achieve a common aim. Individual attitudes, in becoming group-shared attitudes, thereby acquire the momentum necessary for translating them into actual fact, or to retain them in fact if they already are established. Every labor union, every chamber of commerce, church, veterans' organization, or fraternal lodge is a group of individuals exhibiting shared attitudes—in terms of better living conditions, higher prices, veterans' medical benefits, or mere good fellowship—and anxious to have other groups accept these shared attitudes. Groups are of political significance only if they exhibit this desire to generalize their own shared attitudes, to make the whole community in some measure subject to them.

Ideologies. When attitudes become shared they seem to undergo an intensification. Instead of being merely predispositions with respect to the social environment they frequently become a series of beliefs, assumptions, and even dogma. They acquire an inner consistency, a body of interconnected tenets. By acquiring greater rigidity and precision than individual attitudes, group-shared attitudes become ideologies, bodies of belief and opinion so detailed and emphatic as to provide over-all interpretations of society and history. A group which possesses an ideology is thus enabled to "understand" and interpret the world in which it lives and functions, the physical and human reality which surrounds it, in terms of these beliefs. Thus capitalist ideology bases its concrete policy demands upon a theory of society and economics in which the role of the free individual business unit is extolled.

Communist ideology bases its demands on the notion that only the collective and planned utilization of industry can produce maximum social benefits.

Each ideology has its own interpretation of "reality." Quakers see reality as a gradual approach by the individual to God in terms of personal contact and therefore interpret political life as an approximation to God's will. Marxists see reality as the displacement of one economically dominant group by another and therefore proceed to interpret political activity in terms of the inevitable overthrow of the feudal system or the capitalist system.

Rival ideologies exist side by side within the nonauthoritarian community and try to assert their own superiority; the groups identified with each ideology in fact struggle for supremacy or at least toleration. However, the intensity of this struggle may differ radically. Thus in a democratic community, even though ideologies do compete and their adherents try to displace each other, it is taken for granted that most, if not all, ideologies shall be given their time and place for expression. No one group asserts the right to displace others forcibly. Toleration of differing ideologies and groups tends to exist. In an authoritarian community this does not hold true. The very process through which the authoritarian leaders gain power implies the forcible exclusion of rival ideologies. The advent to power by one group with one ideology spells the end of other ideologies. The winning set of beliefs is now supreme and it alone may be advocated and taught. Thus in democratic communities and in the initial phases of authoritarian settings the struggle between groups and their ideologies is the key to the understanding of politics.

Values and Interests. Ideologies are the bodies of doctrine through which group aims are defined. But how do they find application in the political actions of individuals and groups? Each political judgment contains a decision of what is "good" or "bad" in terms of the decision maker's attitudes, opinions, and finally "values." The industrialist who advocates free private enterprise comes to his conclusion after deciding that he values his freedom to make independent business decisions and that the enjoyment of this freedom conduces to the progress of industry generally. The prosperous sheep raiser who argues for a high tariff on imports of wool values his independent role and seeks to protect it by protecting his income. The member of the American Medical Association opposes socialized medicine because he values the autonomy of his relations with his patients and his freedom to charge unregulated fees. Opinions which have been made rigid and buttressed through ideological doctrine have become group-shared values; and values determine each of these positions.

Values, then, are the constituent elements of which ideologies are made up. They determine what ideas, situations, and institutions the group would like to see established or cemented, and what conditions it would like to abolish or prevent from being established. In analyzing international relations in terms of ideologies, therefore, the examination of group demands and aims must be related to the specific values which make up the group's ideology.

When values are defended or advocated in the competitive arena of democratic politics or in the revolutionary debut of an authoritarian movement, they are referred to as "interests." Interests are values expressed in action. The values of the National Association of Manufacturers or the British Trade Union Council become the interests of these groups when they encounter the aims and demands of their opponents. Thus one may speak of the interest of the NAM in the preservation of free private enterprise at home and abroad and of the interest of labor in full employment and high wages. In each case, this expression of group interest merely gives formal content to the body of values believed in by the group. *Thus values and interests are the internal and external aspects of a given group ideology.*

Interest Groups and Elites. Turning from the individual citizen with his attitudes to the organized group with its ideology, therefore, political action can be defined as a contest between interest-determined preferences. Each politically active group makes demands upon other groups, demands based on the values and interests accepted, advocated, and defended by that group. Hence the label "interest group" is usually used in this situation. It is the leadership of such organizations which is continually active in shaping political aims and demands on the basis of its ideology.

Once more, it is the nature of this leadership which is of crucial importance for the study of political behavior. Neither the unattached individual nor the member of an interest group participates directly in policy making. The values and attitudes of the membership, to be sure, act as the general guidelines limiting the freedom of action of the leadership and insistent demands by the members must be heeded by the leaders if they wish to remain in control of their groups. Within these bounds, however, the political demands of interest groups are defined not by the members so much as by their leaders.

But who are these leaders? Generally, each interest group is ruled by its set of elected officers. These persons frequently tend to perpetuate their sway over long periods; or, more commonly still, new officers are chosen from a relatively small group of individuals considered especially fit for the position. Trade-union policy is made by a small body of professional labor leaders, just as big-business interests are formulated by an inner sanctum of top corporation executives. Church ideology and interests are the business of congresses and committees of outstanding clergymen, and the leadership of veterans' organizations is selected from those who have attained positions of importance in their fields.

If several interest groups with similar claims are ruled for long periods by the same individuals, or by the same type of individuals, an "elite" comes into being. An elite is a body of like-minded persons habitually in charge of politically significant groups and attempting to have the entire community respect the values and beliefs peculiar to it. Thus, in the United States there are a labor-union elite, a big-business elite, a Protestant and a Catholic church elite, an elite speaking for small businessmen, one or several farmers' elites, and the like. The opinions, values, ideologies, and political aspirations

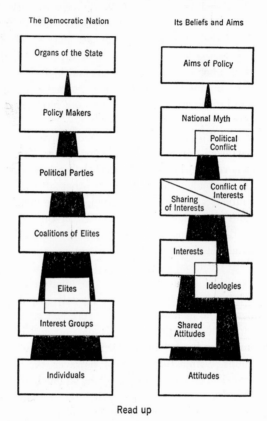

Read up

Individuals, groups, and the state in a democratic community

of key elites, therefore, are the crucial elements in the making of public policy.

In a democracy elites enter into conflict with one another. Thus the process of policy making in a democracy is more specifically a struggle among the elites of key interest groups. The hallmark of a democratic community is the coexistence of large numbers of such elites, demanding, adjusting, and compromising with each other. If the population of a democracy be presented as a pyramid, millions of puzzling, wondering, thinking, and voting individuals make up the bottom layer. These in turn become politically significant when they band together—in the middle layers of the pyramid—into thousands of competing interest groups. The political demands of interest groups are given concrete shape by some hundreds of elites leading the groups, while final policy emerges at the apex of the pyramid at the hands of a score of political leaders over whom rival elites struggle for control. The direct influence of the individual on the making of policy therefore diminishes in direct ratio to his distance from the apex.

In an authoritarian setting, by contrast, no such competition of elites prevails. The right to participate in the definition of policy demands is vested only in the single political party permitted or in the limited number of in-

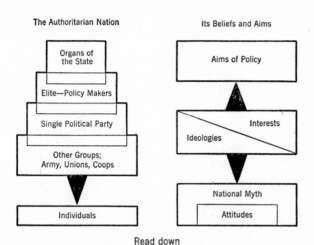

The Authoritarian Nation   Its Beliefs and Aims

Organs of the State

Elite—Policy Makers

Single Political Party

Other Groups; Army, Unions, Coops

Individuals

Aims of Policy

Interests

Ideologies

National Myth

Attitudes

Read down

Individuals, elites, and the state in an authoritarian community

terest groups which control the community. Hence there is no question of linking the individual or the lower ranks of group membership with values and interests. Individuals are not expected to take the initiative, and interest groups—apart from the ruling ones—may exist in name but not in substance. In such a setting, who constitutes the elite? Modern authoritarian systems fall into two categories: those dominated by a single group—the Communist Party—and the fascist systems which characteristically rest on a compromise between several elites. In a communist dictatorship, therefore, the ruling and the only real interest group is the Communist Party, with its carefully selected membership, special status, and special mission. The party is superior to all other formal associations in the community and controls them. The elite in such a system, then, consists of the individuals who habitually occupy key positions of influence within the party: the party secretaries and the members of central committees and presidiums. State, party, government, and community are ruled by the same individuals. In a fascist dictatorship, however, the elite is usually a mixture of all interest groups sharing power. The ruling elite of Spain, for instance, consists of army leaders, Church dignitaries, members of the landed aristocracy (who also tend to occupy key positions in the army and Church), and the leaders of the only political party, the Falange.

3. The Community and Its Myth: Nationalism. The discussion of interest groups and their conflicts has stressed the divisive influence of this process on the community within which the conflict takes place. However, it has yet to define what a "community" is in international relations. Of all the communities, that which today is called the "nation" is probably the most cohesive and certainly the most important. As Reinhold Niebuhr described it: [2]

> The modern nation is the human group of strongest social cohesion, of most undisputed central authority and of most clearly defined membership. The church may have challenged its pre-eminence in the Middle Ages, and the economic class may compete with it for the loyalty of men in our own day; yet it remains, as it has been since the seventeenth century, the most absolute of all human associations.

Life in a community in our days means life in a national community. Life in the American community commands—and receives—more loyalty than life in Minnesota, New York City, the Middle West, or Harlem. The Frenchman will identify himself with France first and his native province second, and the educated Indian will proclaim loyalty to India before stating his attachment to Bengal. Gone are the days when a famous intellectual could proclaim that "if we find a place in the world where we can rest with our property, a field to feed us, a house to shelter us: have we not there the Fatherland?" [3] The fatherland today is the nation, and the individual's attachment to the nation, for better or for worse, is not defined by whatever material advantages membership in the given national community may afford him.

For the study of international relations, then, the nation is the community. Still, how do national communities differ from other forms of association among individuals and groups? Since national communities obviously are not the only collective bodies of significance, what distinguishes their characteristic features from those of the family, the interest group, the village, town, or province?

Objective Criteria of Nationhood. Many writers have conceived of the political community as a series of groups within a more or less compact geographical area in a state of mutual dependence upon one another. Physical interdependence between groups—farmers relying on markets in towns, industrial establishments relying for their consumers among the farmers, etc. —has been considered the chief feature responsible for the existence of a larger community of interests, beyond the more limited association of specific interest groups.

---

[2] R. Niebuhr, *Moral Man and Immoral Society,* Scribner, New York, 1932, p. 83.

[3] Goethe in *Frankfurter Gelehrte Anzeigen* (1772), as quoted in H. Kohn, *The Idea of Nationalism,* Macmillan, New York, 1944, p. 377.

Physical interdependence, of course, is a phenomenon of great importance. Without it, relations between individuals and groups would be confined to social and family affairs. It is doubtful, however, whether such interdependence alone can be credited with being the chief feature of a political community. There are communities whose members are, in fact, not particularly interdependent. Units with complete social and economic autonomy, independent of each other in terms of needs, can still make up a community in the full sense of the word.

But if the nation and our membership in it cannot be defined in terms of physical interdependence, how can we set the nation apart from other associations of people? Some have argued that distinctive race marks the members of one nation from those of another. Yet persons of Oriental, Negro, and Caucasian racial origin comprise the nation known as the United States of America. This as well as other multiracial national communities refute this definition. Others suggest that a common language, literature, and literary tradition serve as the identifying mark of the nation. In Switzerland, however, there are four national languages, in Belgium two, and in India at least five, each with its own literature and tradition. A common religion is held out by still others, and a common historical experience by a further group. Obviously, a common religion will explain few if any contemporary nations, and a common historical experience, important though it is, will not explain the emergence of national sentiment in places such as the Gold Coast which lacked all common experience until a few decades ago. It is plain that none of these objective factors serves to set the national community apart from other associations of men.

Shared Values and Nationalism. Still, even if the nation is not definable on the basis of objective criteria, it obviously flourishes as a dominant non-voluntary association. How is this possible? More specifically, how can a national community, built on unity and solidarity, emerge from the strife and division implicit in the struggle among competing elites and ideologies? In most communities—whether democratic and pluralistic or authoritarian and monolithic—a measure of unity can be attained because of the agreement on essentials. The process of attaining unity in an authoritarian community will be discussed in a later section. In a democracy, interest groups, despite their different ideologies, can attain a measure of agreement because compromise is generally an integral portion of all beliefs.

Furthermore, since individuals do not belong to merely one group but usually participate in several at the same time, there tends to be a degree of attitude sharing not only within a given group but between interest groups as well. This attitude sharing coexists with conflicting aims among groups. The National Association of Manufacturers and the American Federation of Labor have consistently opposing interests in the field of wages. They have nevertheless common interests in regard to the preservation of individual liberty, national defense, and the essentials of the democratic process. Therefore it is possible to formulate policy aims—or interests—which are common to the whole community. Yet this rarely happens. Most items of policy are adopted as a result of compromises of interests among several elites and the acquiescence of the opposing elites. The continuing belief that their long-range interests will still be served by the community keeps the defeated elites within the fold.

Such objective factors as physical interdependence, religion, and race having failed in distinguishing the nation from other associations, there remains the subjective factor of belief in a common system of values. A national community, therefore, is a complex of individuals, groups, and elites united by a body of beliefs transcending their own restricted ideologies and distinguishing them from the rest of mankind, so that their national values make up the highest doctrine to which they profess political loyalty.

The national community, it must be concluded, is nothing more than "a portion of mankind . . . if they are united among themselves by common sympathies, which do not exist between them and any others—which make them cooperate with each other more willingly than with other people, desire to be under the same government and desire that it should be government by themselves or a portion of themselves exclusively." [4] It does not matter whether they are of one religion or of many, of short historical association or of long, united in language and literature or divided in separate language groups, of a homogeneous race or a heterogeneous mixture. So long as Frenchmen, subjectively, consider themselves united by closer bonds than the bonds which tie them to Englishmen, Belgians, or Germans, there will be a French national community. A will to live together, regardless of the objective bond of association, in a society larger than the town, province, interest group, or family, constitutes the only identifiable element in the consciousness of national life.

The National Myth. The elements common to all group ideologies in a given community will be referred to as the community's national "myth," or as nationalism. It differs from ideology in that it stands above the beliefs of the community's constituent groups and thereby unites them. The national myth is a compound of the common elements found in the differing and competing ideologies within the nation. The myth cannot be proved "right" or "wrong," "good" or "bad," "true" or "false." What matters is that it exists because it is professed and believed in by the groups and individuals who identify themselves with it. The national myth of the United States is the assertion, preservation, and defense of the democratic process, assuring a maximum of individual freedom and a minimum of group dictation. The national myth of the Soviet Union is the creation and defense of a classless society in which no one is exploited and all share fairly in the economic

---

[4] J. S. Mill, *Representative Government*, London, 1876, p. 120.

production of the community. Neither myth can be demonstrated as "true" in actual life, but both are held by a sufficient number of individuals and groups to give cohesion to the respective communities.

Myths do not develop spontaneously. In a democratic community they originate as part of the ideology of one or several founding groups and are diffused throughout the collectivity by a gradual process of evolution, education, and propaganda. A democracy may originate through the expressed will and consent of all the major elites within it. But it may also develop as a result of war, conquest, or internal revolution, in which case consent by all elites to the myth cannot be expected at the outset. Thus it is clear that even in a democratic community constant efforts are made to maintain the myth and to propagate it. The "American way of life," for instance, is imbued in children by means of daily salutes to the flag and daily recitations of the pledge of allegiance. The British "way" is supported in Britain by the playing of "God Save the Queen" at theater performances and daily over the air. In countless other ways the elements of the myth are incorporated into the elementary and high school curriculum, into the rites of public and civic functions, and even into the ceremonials surrounding the activities of most private associations and interest groups. In fact, such groups themselves insist on maintaining and protesting their loyalty to the national myth. It remains true nevertheless that a democracy must tolerate varying interpretations of the common belief system by all groups and elites and that none is considered endowed with omniscient insight into its dictates. It is this feature which distinguishes a democratic from an authoritarian nationalism.

Unlike the common beliefs of a democratic community, the myth in an authoritarian community does not grow as the result of the free sharing of values among interest groups. Authoritarian elites gain power by excluding their rivals from positions of prominence. Interest groups professing aims repugnant to the leadership are suppressed or eliminated. Opposition elites disappear from the political scene after the revolutionary success of the authoritarian group. The content of the national doctrine, therefore, is determined not by compromise and value sharing but by imposition. The ideology of the authoritarian elite becomes the community's myth. During the process of establishing this ideology, the tools of the ruling group are manipulation and coercion. Symbols of loyalty which are expected to find a receptive audience among the masses are exploited and used to unify the aspirations of the community. Coercion—as through periodic purges of the elite and the surveillance of the masses by the secret police—is always in the background to support manipulative measures, should these be unsuccessful.

After this process has gone on for some decades, it is quite likely that the entire community accepts the elite's ideology as its national myth without doubt or reservation. Thus even an authoritarian community may rest on a consensus because no scheme of values other than the officially sanctioned one is permitted expression. If there is no desire to challenge the elite's version of the national myth, the absence of dispute may indicate unity and solidarity surpassing that of the democratic community.

The content of the myth—democratic or authoritarian—is emotional rather than rational. It appeals to the individual's desire to be identified with others who share his attitudes and to find self-gratification in such identification. It defies proof or refutation by means of formal logic. In a democracy, the continuing viability of such identification is demonstrated by the willingness of the minority to abide by the decision of the majority even if its aims are completely disregarded. So long as the primary requisite of the community's myth—the observation of the democratic process—is faithfully observed, the minority will obey the majority's decisions. Democratic decision making has been observed, and therefore the decision is "legitimate" even from the defeated minority's point of view. Only continued and flagrant violation of a minority's aspirations will cause its disaffection, resulting in the shattering of community consciousness and in the outbreak of civil war.

This, however, is not the process whereby the myth of an authoritarian community remains viable. No problem of majority and minority interpretation arises. The elite, or, more commonly, the leader at the head of the elite, is exclusively capable of interpreting the myth. Authoritarian leadership is almost always "charismatic." The leader possessed of the charisma is believed to possess superhuman powers of insight into history and the fate of the community. His judgment is almost omniscient and therefore beyond challenge by others. A Hitler or a Stalin alone decreed what Germany or the Soviet Union expected and demanded in a given situation. Their views *were* the Nazi and Soviet myths, not merely important interpretations of them. As long as charismatic leadership, therefore, remains the accepted mode of decision making for a community, a unanimous consensus on the content of the national myth can be expected.

Exclusiveness and Nationalism. With all its emphasis on individual identification and individual consent to its processes, even the democratic community is not really a voluntary organization. Membership in a community is considered so obvious and natural by most individuals that they never stop to question their own "belonging." While membership in interest groups is certainly a voluntary act which can easily be undone by resignation or withdrawal from such a group, it is possible to "resign" from the community only through emigration. For the overwhelming number of individuals, however, there is no wish to resign. Their preeminent loyalty is to their community; indeed, the main condition of a successful and viable community is that loyalty to it be stronger than loyalty to the interest groups of which it is composed. As long as individuals are "born into" a community rather than "joining" it, the community will continue to attract individual loyalty more than can be true of most interest groups.

Without nationalism the pursuit of a foreign policy by any one national community in our era would be inconceivable. If the population remained indifferent to its own values, if it failed to support the myth, no government could count on the cooperation of its citizens in the prosecution of policy. In the event of conflict with other nations, the failure of the population to identify itself with the claims and demands of its leaders would condemn any policy to failure. Hence the myth enters into the conduct of foreign relations.

It is of the essence of each national body of beliefs that the community espousing it will, in some degree, consider its own institutions, its way of life, and its values superior to that of all other national myths, i.e., the beliefs of other countries. Its whole sense of identity is intimately tied up with such feelings. Thus the "American way of life" or the "classless society," significant elements in the American and Soviet myths, are by definition considered superior by their supporters to other ways of life. The Frenchman will point to the superiority of French civilization and the Indian to the spiritual quali-ties in his native value system in the effort to prove to himself—and to others —the superiority of his national beliefs. So long as these myths do not com-pete with each other, the feelings of superiority do not enter the realm of international relations. Since national communities, like interest groups within each community, however, have mutually incompatible claims upon each other, these beliefs leave their national compartments and enter the arena of competition and conflict. American policy will then be justified—to Ameri-cans as well as to members of other national communities—as necessary to the preservation of the "American way of life," while Soviet policy, similarly, will draw its justification from the desire to maintain or to expand the "class-less society." Whether these justifications represent the true aims under-lying the respective policies is here beside the point. It is of importance to note that national loyalty to a given policy is maintained by having the policy accord with the national myth. If national beliefs are of an extremely bellicose nature, implying the marked inferiority of other national doctrines, the conditions for active conflict are given. Nazi insistence that the German myth of racial superiority justified the conquest of other national commu-nities was at least one factor making for an active German policy of con-quering the rest of Europe. Thus the content of each national myth and the degree of energy with which the content is advanced outside the national community is in itself a vital factor in the dynamics of international relations.

4. The State and Its Government. National communities are the units of international relations. But even though individuals consider themselves part of a national community and identify themselves with its institutions, when some concrete measures are to be taken by the community they speak of it as the "state" and refer to the agency which formulated and executes these specific measures as the "government." The state, in short, is the formal incorporation of the community into an entity which can formulate policy and make decisions, the government, and carry out its decisions by means of compulsory measures, the law. The state differs from all other associations in that membership in it is mandatory. It follows that the rules formulated by the government for the community are binding on all persons, whether they consented to these rules or not. The consequence of disobeying the by-laws of an interest group is expulsion or resignation. The consequence of disobeying the state's law may be fines and jail sentences, or death. The difference is fundamental: the interest group aims only at the realization of group aims and is limited in membership; the state claims to preserve order for *all* the interest groups making up the community and is therefore coterminal with the community in membership.

While the community functions as a state in regulating its internal problems and in maintaining contact with other national communities, decisions to make rules and enforce them on the community are still made by specific groups and individuals who are also members of the community. If relationships in the community and between national communities are relationships between elites, as we saw earlier, decision making on the part of the state is equally a process of adjusting or settling competing aims between elites.

Government and Authoritarian Elites. One of the differences between the authoritarian and democratic forms of government lies in the question of whether policy is made directly by elites, or by policy makers—politicians and statesmen—influenced by the elites of various interest groups. Whenever policy for a whole community is made by a single interest group acting directly as the government the result is an authoritarian regime. The same is true whenever the government consists of a coalition of specific interest groups which have succeeded in permanently excluding others from positions of influence. The Soviet Union is an example of the first case. The only group in a position of control is the Communist Party. Its members direct the Russian government, the economy, the army, and the arts and sciences, as well as the daily life of the community. Rival centers of influence do not exist. In such a system, elite, government, and state are identical so long as the ruling group retains its unity of purpose.

In Nazi Germany the picture was more complex. A state as authoritarian as the Soviet Union, it nevertheless did not originate as the rule of one elite but as the coalition of several elites seeking to eliminate competing groups permanently from the government. These elites—the Nazi party, the army, the bureaucracy, and big industry—agreed to share in the government so as to exclude from lawmaking the elites representing labor, the churches, the peasants, and the small businessman. As in the case of the Soviet Union, these ruling elites governed the German state directly rather than merely seeking to influence a special elite of politicians. Since state power and governmental authority were in the hands of a few groups, only their aims were to be realized.

Government and Democratic Elites. In the democratic state the picture is otherwise. Government consists not primarily of representatives of a given elite or interest group, but of professional politicians, who in turn are influenced by the rival elites leading the interest groups. At election time each interest group will endorse or condemn the party or politician which supports or opposes its aims. During the lawmaking process, it will lobby at the legislature, send letters and telegrams to the lawmakers, and promise gratitude or revenge depending on whether the politician meets or opposes the group's aims. The politician, in turn, in order to secure their support to be reelected, will try to please as many interest groups as he can without appearing as a hypocrite. Thus the democratic state at any one time is ruled by a particular set of politicians—the party which won the election—associated with and influenced by a given set of elites of certain interest groups. Generally, the ruling party will legislate in order to translate the aims of the supporting elites into reality. The opposing party, or parties, associated with a rival set of elites representing rival interest groups will seek to prevent passage of such legislation in order to meet the interests of its supporters.

While it is generally true that political decisions result from the power which one coalition of elites can muster over the power of the opposing coalition, certain facets of the decision-making process remain to be explained. Shifts in opinion and in power are usually reflected with considerable accuracy in the composition of the legislature. The professional politicians who sit in the parliaments and congresses of democratic nations tend to be responsive to the ever-changing pattern of elite pressure and thereby introduce a dynamic force into the process of making policy.

Yet shifts in opinion and the alternation of elites represented in the legislature are not necessarily accompanied by proportional changes in the nature of the executive branch of a democratic government. Members of the cabinet may be selected from identical social and economic groups regardless of reversals of party strength. This is particularly true in the American system, under which no sharp ideological cleavages divide the two major parties. Civil servants, though varying in importance as policy makers from country to country, often remain in key positions despite shifts in elite power. Military and naval officers retain crucial decision-making roles regardless of whether Republicans or Democrats control the national legislature. In short, a static element of continuity is introduced into democratic government by the continued presence of decision makers recruited from identical elites despite reversals of party strength at election time. Hence the values of persons within the executive branch, whether military or civilian, Democratic or Republican, may be of supreme significance in specific decisions, although the elites concerned may not be directly represented in the legislative branch of government.

The essence of democracy, thus, does not lie in the absence of elites but in the fact that the rule of any one coalition of elites can be terminated or altered by shifts in opinion in the community. The participation of all interest groups and their ruling elites is thereby assured. So long as the basic beliefs of most democratic communities—the observation of human and political rights and free participation in the making of decisions—is observed, the ruling coalition will never be able to perpetuate its own sway in the face of a numerically stronger and united opposition.

5. The State and the Use of Power. In the definition of the state, it was noted that the state formally rules by means of law. Law comes into existence as the result of the capacity of an elite or a coalition of elites to impose its interests and values on the community. The ability to make generally binding rules, therefore, is a reflection of political "power." The concept of power is crucial in any discussion of domestic or international politics.

"Power," wrote one official of the Department of State, "is the capacity to achieve intended results." [5] Power is here conceived as the objective ability of an elite to carry out its will through possession of armies, military equipment, or propaganda instruments or by the acquiescence of those who are expected to comply with that will. More meaningfully, perhaps, power has been defined in subjective terms as "the probability that one actor within a social relationship will be in a position to carry out his own will despite resistance, regardless of the basis on which probability rests." [6] Here, it is the *opinion* of those who make rules and decisions that compliance with these rules will come about which is of significance, regardless of whether actual quantitative superiority of force exists. It is this latter meaning which is of primary significance in the dynamics of international relations, since decisions are made on the basis of the amount of power *thought* to be available to each state.

While a completely objective definition of power is impossible as long as we are focusing on the political actor—who remains subject to his own and his group's ideology in making his assessments—certain types of power relationships can be differentiated from others, despite this difficulty. The United States is obviously "more powerful" than Haiti, irrespective of the values of Haitian or American leaders, in terms of the physical endowment of each to inflict deprivation upon the other. In such situations, power can be roughly measured. Yet it remains true that the ideology-determined unwillingness to make use of measurably superior power—and such unwillingness cannot be quantitatively assessed in a given situation—operates effectively to reduce the ability to impose deprivation. While the observer can specify the amount of physical power available, the statesman remains sub-

---

[5] Charles B. Marshall, "The Nature of Foreign Policy," *Department of State Bulletin,* Mar. 17, 1952, p. 418.

[6] M. Weber, *Theory of Social and Economic Organization,* Oxford, New York, 1947, p. 152.

ject to the intangible strictures imposed by his own thought and behavior pattern, including the social pressures amidst which he makes decisions.

Ends and Means in Policy. Ends are defined by group interests, and the ends of state policy are, as has been seen, determined by the interests of ruling elites. Means are determined by ideologies, too, but the amount of power thought to be available to the policy makers is crucial as well. Power, then, relates only to the means chosen by the elite to translate its underlying aims into reality.

It is frequently argued, however, that power refers to ends as well as to means. This contention rests on the assumption that all political behavior stems from a "power drive"—that individuals, groups, organizations, and states are interested primarily in acquiring greater power for its own sake. Even if it were granted that *individuals* enjoy the exercise of power and like to gather more and more of the elements of force in their own hands, it would not follow that groups and organizations are similarly motivated. Groups represent the shared values and demands of their members. Leaders are constrained to remain faithful to the aspirations of their supporters even if, incidentally, they gratify a personal desire for power in the exercise of their leadership.

In terms of their political relevance, therefore, group aims remain tied to values and interests. Commonly, a group seeks to strengthen its position and to increase its resources so as to be able to achieve its basic aims more effectively at a later time. Superficially, then, all groups and all states seek power: in armaments, trade, strategic position, and ideological appeal abroad. Yet this power is merely accumulated so as to achieve the basic ends dictated by ideology. For these reasons, then, power relates only to means and is not an end in itself, and it will be so treated in this discussion of the dynamics of international relations.

Domination over the state is one of the positions which elites and political parties seek in order to achieve their aims. Once such a position is achieved, the mechanism of law makes it possible for the victorious group to impose its ends upon the entire population. Hence control over the state and lawmaking machinery is the supreme prize of political conflict.

This crucial capacity of the state, the power to regulate all other associations within it, is generally referred to as "sovereignty." The origins of the sovereignty concept are intimately tied up with monarchical past of the European states. Prior to the emergence of democratic governments in Europe, during the seventeenth and eighteenth centuries, the power of the ruling monarch, in theory, was absolute. He made, abrogated, and amended the law. His personal will was the law. He possessed what Bodin called "supreme power *over* law." He acknowledged no authority above him to make law for him either within his realm or in his relations with other rulers. He possessed complete sovereignty and hence he was called the sovereign. Binding law for several sovereigns could be made only by common agreement between them, not by a higher authority.

The internal aspect of sovereignty underwent a series of marked changes at the end of the eighteenth century. With the rise of parliamentary democracy in Europe and the United States, some sovereigns were abolished, and the powers of others were reduced and made subject to the will of the legislature. Hence, the internal meaning of the whole sovereignty concept took a different form. The basic law of the land—of the national community—was no longer the will of the monarch but the constitution of the state. Sovereign powers could be exercised by the government only within the areas permitted by that constitution; they were *subject to* the law instead of standing above it.

But since the constitution of the state is really the reflection of the bonds of unity which tie together the interest groups of the national community, we may conclude that the sovereign power of the constitution is nothing else but the formal incorporation of the central myth, the "way of life" of the community. Hence internal sovereignty in modern national states is always subject to the myth of the community, to majority opinion among the groups and individuals making up the community. Sovereign powers, then, are no longer "sovereign" in the original sense of the term.

The case is otherwise with the external aspects of sovereignty. There the modern democratic community is the direct heir of the monarchical tradition. The sovereign power of each monarch to be bound only by his own consent in his relations with other monarchs was taken over by the parliamentary democracies almost without change. The very interest groups which acknowledge the existence of a common myth within the community deny a common myth uniting all national communities. States remain "sovereign," i.e., no higher authority may make law for them. Consent and agreement, as in the case of the monarchs, remain the only method for making states subject to a law higher than that of the national legislature, or the national constitution. In the absence of a central myth for all national states, there can be no supranational authority. As one famous British statesman put it: [7]

If a situation were to be forced upon us [Great Britain] in which peace could only be preserved by the surrender of the great and beneficent position Britain has won by centuries of heroism and achievement, by allowing Britain to be treated, when her interests were vitally affected, as if she were of no account in the cabinet of nations, then I say emphatically that peace at that price would be a humiliation intolerable for a great country like ours to endure.

Given the absence of a central myth, of which sovereignty is merely the external symptom, willingness to use violence more readily than within a community follows automatically. The impact of these beliefs and forces on

[7] Lloyd George's Mansion House speech, 1911. Quoted in Niebuhr, *op. cit.*, p. 92

the interplay of conflict and compromise in international relations now remains to be analyzed.

ADDITIONAL CASE-STUDY MATERIAL

Arendt, H.: "Imperialism, Nationalism and Chauvinism," *Review of Politics,* vol. 7, October, 1945.
————: *Origins of Totalitarianism,* Harcourt, Brace, New York, 1951.
Cantril, H.: *The Psychology of Social Movements,* Wiley, New York, 1941.
Carr, E. H.: *Nationalism and After,* Macmillan, New York, 1945.
Chandler, R.: *Rosenberg's National Myth,* Cornell University Press, Ithaca, N.Y., 1945.
Coleman, J. S.: "Nationalism in Tropical Africa," *American Political Science Review,* vol. 48, 1954.
Deutsch, K.: *Nationalism and Social Communication,* Wiley, New York, 1953.
————: *Political Community at the International Level: Problems of Definition and Measurement,* Publication 2, Foreign Policy Analysis Series, Princeton, N.J., 1953.
Frenkel-Brunswik, E.: "Interaction of Psychological and Sociological Factors in Political Behavior," *American Political Science Review,* vol. 46, 1952.
Hayes, C. J.: *Essays on Nationalism,* Macmillan, New York, 1928.
Hoffer, E.: *The True Believer,* Harper, New York, 1951.
Knickerbocker, I.: "Leadership: A Conception and Some Implications," *Journal of Social Issues,* vol. 4, 1948.
Kohn, H.: *The Idea of Nationalism,* Macmillan, New York, 1944.
Lasswell, H. D.: *World Politics and Personal Insecurity,* McGraw-Hill, New York, 1935.
Leiserson, A.: "Notes on the Theory of Political Opinion Formation," *American Political Science Review,* vol. 47, 1953.
Lindsay, A. D.: *The Modern Democratic State,* Oxford, New York, 1947.
Mabbot, J. D.: "Conflict of Ideologies," *Philosophy,* July, 1948.
MacIver, R. M.: *Web of Government,* Macmillan, New York, 1951.
Mannheim, K.: *Ideology and Utopia,* Harcourt, Brace, New York, 1936.
Markel, L.: *Public Opinion and Foreign Policy,* Harper, New York, 1949.
Marshall, C. B.: "The Nature of Foreign Policy," *Department of State Bulletin,* Mar. 17, 1952.
May, M.: *A Social Psychology of War and Peace,* Yale University Press, New Haven, Conn., 1943.
Merton, R.: *Social Theory and Social Structure,* Free Press, Glencoe, Ill., 1949.
Mill, J. S.: *Representative Government,* Oxford, New York, 1948.
Murphy, G. (ed.): *Human Nature and Enduring Peace,* Reynal & Hitchcock, New York, 1945.
Niebuhr, R.: *Moral Man and Immoral Society,* Scribner, New York, 1932.
Renan, E.: *What Is a Nation?* London, 1896.
Royal Institute of International Affairs: *Nationalism,* Oxford, New York, 1939.
Seligman, L.: "The Study of Political Leadership," *American Political Science Review,* vol. 44, 1950.
Sulzbach, W.: *National Consciousness,* American Council on Public Affairs, Washington, 1943.
Truman, D. B.: *The Governmental Process,* Knopf, New York, 1951.
Weber, M.: *Theory of Social and Economic Organization,* Oxford, New York, 1947.
Wright, Q. (ed.): *The World Community,* University of Chicago Press, Chicago, 1948.
————: *A Study of War,* 2 vols., University of Chicago Press, Chicago, 1942.
————: *Problems of Stability and Progress in International Relations,* University of California Press, Berkeley, Calif., 1954.

Chapter 3

CONFLICTS OF INTEREST

1. Interest Groups and International Relations. The preceding chapter analyzed the role of organized groups in the making of policy; this chapter will examine the relationship between the interests and values of groups and the processes of international politics. Not all groups possess an equal amount of direct and continuing interest in the foreign policy of their state. Hence it is necessary to distinguish among the various degrees of intensity exhibited by specific organizations in their efforts to shape foreign policy.

Degrees of Interest in Foreign Policy. Organized groups may be classified in these categories, depending upon the degree of intensity of their concern in foreign policy:

1. Groups which have a continuing, direct, and permanent stake in foreign policy, such as foreign traders, shippers, and groups stressing the spiritual interdependence of peoples.

2. Groups whose major function is the realization of demands related to the ordering of the national community but which must, on numerous occasions, take a direct interest in foreign affairs because the nature of their ideologies makes them realize the dependence of domestic victory on external achievement. Such groups will participate in policy decisions of a general kind as well as voicing their demands on very specific issues. Labor unions and trade associations are typical examples of this kind of interest.

3. Groups interested only in the general problems of foreign policy making, but not necessarily concerned about specific issues which arise, among which are patriotic societies, veterans' groups, and civic and educational organizations.

4. Groups which are usually preoccupied by purely internal questions, but which on occasion will see a direct and immediate stake in a specific item of foreign policy, without entering into an over-all debate.

5. Groups generally not interested at all in foreign relations and policy, but deeply aroused in times of crisis and emergency. It is this last category which usually includes the overwhelming majority of individuals in a given nation.

Shippers and traders with a continuing stake in international relations are not slow to make their wishes known to the government of their state. When

Congress debates foreign-aid bills, the National Federation of American Shipping invariably demands that 50 per cent of all aid be transported in American bottoms. When a seemingly humanitarian proposal is debated, such as the sending of wheat to India to avert famine, an organization like the Textile Bag Manufacturers Association might demand that the wheat be shipped only if it does not interfere with a regular supply of jute—which comes from India's rival, Pakistan—a commodity from which sacking and bags are made.[1] This type of group claim is clear.

Organizations representing all of labor or all of industry—as distinguished from specific business interests like shippers—are persuaded to concern themselves with broad policy issues as well as with specific problems. The United States National Association of Manufacturers or the Federation of British Industries will do their best to influence policy making on such broad issues as the initiation of foreign-aid programs or the pace of rearmament. The same is true of the American Federation of Labor or the British Trades Unions Congress. These issues affect the material and ideological interests of these groups. Moreover, they will also be active on behalf of policy decisions implying support for or opposition to a foreign nation dominated by a hostile—or friendly—ideology, such as socialism. Specific issues such as trade treaties or the tariff on cheese and watches, however, also engage the attention of these groups, so that they are compelled to interest themselves in foreign relations almost continuously, but on a broader base than is true of the first category.

By contrast, groups with only a general interest in the broad principles of foreign policy will not usually exert pressure on the government on specific items of policy. The American Legion, the French War Veterans, or the American League of Women Voters will be more likely to attempt to influence their nations' entry or nonentry into an international organization like the United Nations. They will argue for or against policies of military as opposed to economic assistance to allies abroad, but they will rarely take a stand on specific trade treaties or monetary agreements. Their influence, in short, is to be found in situations demanding an over-all policy decision.

The opposite is true of scientific societies or special religious groups. They are preoccupied by internal questions and will take an interest in international affairs only when a specific issue arises. Thus physicists may suddenly take an interest in foreign affairs when they wish to advance nuclear research by facilitating a freer exchange of scientific information. Christian Scientists, though not usually concerned with foreign relations, may nevertheless begin an active pressure campaign to prevent their country's entry into the World Health Organization—an institution likely to violate some

---

[1] Examples of such demands can be found in *India Emergency Assistance Act of 1951*, Hearings on H.R. 2692, U.S. House of Representatives, 82d Cong., 1st Sess., 1951, pp. 163, 217.

of their religious principles. Once their aim is achieved, however, such groups are likely to lose interest in international policy making.

The Individual and Foreign Policy. The overwhelming majority of individuals everywhere quite obviously fit none of the categories mentioned above. The farmer preoccupied with his harvest, the laborer with his daily wage, and the professional man with his own routine generally do not partake in thinking or worrying about foreign policy beyond reading the evening paper. Whether an individual is affiliated with an interest group or not, unless he is directly concerned with the immediate impact of a given foreign policy decision he is not likely to know or care much about an issue or even consider it important in his own life until "interdependence" is dramatically driven home to him. Because he lacks a continuing tie with foreign affairs, the individual tends to be passive and to rely upon the elites with whom he is identified for his information and attitudes on international issues.

If, in a well-integrated national community with a minimum of bitter intergroup conflicts, such information or pressure comes from highly respected leaders, the response of the mass of individuals is likely to be a strong one. Further, if an appeal to support a particular foreign policy takes the form of invoking the protection of the community's body of beliefs, individuals of all strata tend to react with considerable unity and determination regardless of interest-group affiliation. However, in communities marked by bitter group antagonisms, such as modern France or Italy, no such unified response can be expected simply because the national myth enjoys less support and no single respected leadership exists. Americans of all types respond when the "American way of life" seems threatened by a new myth—communism or Nazism—and Indians, Egyptians, and Britons respond in the same fashion when their "ways of life" seem exposed to danger because of the activities of a foreign state. We may conclude, therefore, that even though the overwhelming mass of individuals does not usually see any direct relationship between foreign affairs issues and their own lives, once the issue takes on the form of a national crisis in which the survival of their common aspirations seems endangered, a strong and unified response can be expected, a response which may by no means subside into indifference when the external danger is averted.

"National Interest." Some writers and many statesmen have labeled the apparently permanently fixed features of the foreign policy of any nation as its "national interest." However, policy aims undergo change as the interests of elites alter and as new groups attain positions of influence. Given the domestic conflict for the realization of rival interests, can one actually point to a national interest? Is it possible to define some overriding set of aspirations not only common to the whole nation but also capable of guiding the statesman in making policy?

An official of the U.S. Department of State answers affirmatively. He sees the national interest in those broad policy aims which are beyond political controversy, such as maintenance of peace, preservation of security, maximization of prosperity, and the protection of one's own citizens abroad.[2] More specific values, even though they may be shared by many groups in the community, seem to have nothing to do with the national interest. Preservation of democratic institutions abroad, for instance, finds no expression in this definition. In one sense this is a conception with which it is impossible to disagree. Obviously, these generalities are aims to which everyone is devoted, regardless of his group or political affiliation. At the same time, however, this definition of the national interest is much too vague to permit the policy maker to reach specific decisions on key issues. The mere "desire for peace," for instance, is an inadequate criterion for a reasoned judgment on whether an Iranian oil nationalization scheme should be supported or opposed, whether Western Europe should be given more food instead of tanks, or whether democracy in Japan should be encouraged. This view of the national interest must lead to the conclusion that "national interest is a useful term when you are engaged in pressing upon public attention your own view about foreign affairs. It may be doubted, however, whether except in very general terms, such things as prosperity and peace can be shown to mold policy." [3]

Others argue that the national interest is the sum of all those geographic, economic, political, and ideological elements which have historically been associated with the preservation of each state. Again, the attempt to apply this concept to a specific issue leaves some doubt as to what these elements might be. Different groups will emphasize different elements. Individual values and ideologies will argue for the primacy of one or another constituent of the "national" interest, and no agreement on the sum will emerge. Competing group values continually assert themselves in the community defining them as "historical" and "permanent" elements. No national myth is comprehensive enough, except in a highly authoritarian setting, to preclude this kind of controversy over basic aims.

It must be concluded, therefore, that the concept of the national interest means little more than the claims on other states which correspond to the specific aims of ruling groups. The "little more" is dependent upon the extent to which the opposition's views intrude on policy making. To the extent that policy corresponds in its broad outline to the values of the whole community in general and to the specific ideologies of opposition groups in particular, a true national interest is being defended. The charge of "un-American" or "un-British" or "un-Indian" is a charge which no government can tolerate for long and expect to remain in power. No government can afford

---

[2] C. B. Marshall, "The National Interest and Current World Problems," *Department of State Bulletin,* May 5, 1952, pp. 696–702.

[3] Carl J. Friedrich, *Foreign Policy in the Making,* Norton, New York, 1938, p. 95.

to depart for long in its specific policy aims from what the national myth dictates. It is this need which gives to national foreign policies whatever relative consistency they may possess from government to government, from election to election.

In the large number of issues, however, in which there is no direct relation to these broad consensual forces, the view of the ruling groups alone defines the national interest, which therefore is not necessarily permanent, consistent, or national.

2. Conflict and the International Society. Within each national community, agreement exists on a *procedure* for the making of policy. Each national myth specifies how decisions among clashing groups shall be reached, whether through elections, lobbying, or charismatic leadership. Each myth is rooted in the conviction that a common life is both inescapable and desirable.

In the international society the picture is different. Interdependence is only partially and intermittently accepted. There is no agreement on ends, or even on the procedure whereby binding and enforceable decisions can be reached. The inescapable conviction of a common life does not yet exist everywhere. The ends sought by one set of groups, for instance, in the Soviet Union, are by no means reconcilable with the ends professed by groups in India, Australia, or the United States.

Irreconcilable Group Aims. Rival claims of struggling elites within the community, then, tend to be less severe in proportion to the acceptance of common values. A landed aristocracy will not resist violently the demands of its tenant farmers for the redistribution of land if that aristocracy and its opponents both accept the doctrine of peaceful adjustment and common long-range aims. The central feature of international relations, however, is the fact that the international rivalry among various elites is far more intense than is true within the nation. The professed and tacit ends frequently are mutually exclusive in international politics. The coexistence of two sets of struggling elites may be held by each to be impossible; one must be decisively defeated by physical force. The Communist elite aspires to world revolution and the overthrow of the democratic-capitalist elites. The democratic-capitalist elite of the United States aspires to contain communism within a given area. The Indian nationalist elite counted itself strong when its opposition before 1947—the colonial-conservative elite of Britain—was weak. Conversely, the British elite counted itself strong when its Indian opponents—Nehru, Gandhi, and others—were safely behind bars. Ends, in short, may be so defined as to be mutually exclusive. The more intensely the end is held, the more irreconcilable it becomes with respect to rival ends of others. The intensity of feeling clearly makes difficult even the agreement on procedure which, as has been seen, is the most important point of agreement between clashing elites of the same nationality.

International Political Movements. However, the spectacular existence of at least one international political movement today—the Communist Party—calls for reconsideration of this conclusion. This movement is an example of active value sharing regardless of diverse national myths. Adherence to one set of rules and to one set of leaders characterizes Communists in France, Greece, Peru, Egypt, Indonesia, and China, as well as the United States and the Soviet Union. Is the dominance of the national myth breaking down for significant sections of the world's population? This may well be the case, though the process is still in its beginnings and has not advanced far enough to challenge definitely the earlier conclusion.

The emergence of the Communist creed as an internationally shared value system is not the only possible development away from nationalism. The phenomenon now called "regionalism" gives proof of that fact. The integration of Eastern Europe under the pressure of the supranational Communist movement finds its counterpart in the growing institutions common to the states of Western Europe. Once more shared values are in evidence. Both Catholicism and socialism are active ideologies working for the union of Europe west of the Elbe River, and in so doing they are challenging the supremacy of the old national myths. The North Atlantic Treaty Organization, which includes Canada and the United States in addition to Western Europe, is a similar example of the emergence of supranational institutions as the result of shared values: defense of Western democracy against the threat of communism. Thus shared values—political, religious, economic, or moral—can operate internationally in bringing about larger loyalties and more comprehensive myth systems, a process to be explored in a later section. It remains true in the meantime, however, that in the remainder of the world and especially between the main centers of world conflict no such development is discernible.

International Society. With the exception of world communism and growing regional loyalties, the most important feature of international relations is the mass belief that ties between groups across international frontiers are qualitatively different from relations between groups within nations. International ties still tend to be regarded as short-term in nature, easily terminable, and confined to specific definable needs. Withdrawal from international agreements and organizations is simple. Pressure for such withdrawal—not infrequently acted upon—is always present in any national community. A trade treaty which hurts specific domestic interest groups, e.g., the dairy farmer, may easily be terminated by increasing the tariff on Danish blue cheese. A radio convention which hinders the free broadcasting of propaganda falls quietly into disuse.

In short, global international relations lack the symptoms of a community. The ease of withdrawal, of "resignation," provides the key. The basic feature of a community is the permanent identification of groups and individuals with a larger unit. An association, by contrast, is voluntary; joining it implies merely the expectation that individual needs can be met by membership. If the expectation fails to be gratified, membership can be terminated. So it tends to be with international relations. They are "societal" in nature in that the loyalties created are temporary and peripheral. Withdrawal, however difficult in terms of physical interdependence and welfare, is nevertheless considered possible and often is desirable both emotionally and ideologically. There is no "community of states." There is only a "society of states." Ours is an international society, not a world community.

Sovereignty and Society. It is often argued that the existence of absolute external sovereignty is the main cause of international anarchy. Sovereignty is held to be the sole obstacle to genuine international community in which the constituent members can no longer act in defiance of the will of the majority. This argument misses the essential point that sovereignty as such is a symptom rather than a cause of anarchy. Apart from the problem of *how* sovereignty can be restricted except by voluntary consent or forcible conquest, sovereignty is nothing more than a legal fiction based on the essential sociological fact that groups within states enjoy a cohesion not found among states themselves. Were devotion to a common myth evident in international relations, there would be no need for asserting sovereign independence for each nation. The key to international anarchy, therefore, lies not in the concept of sovereignty but in the identification of elites with rival ends, rooted in group ideologies and differing national myths.

The Implication of Violence. This intensity of identification increases the probability that violent means for the gratification of aims will be an instrument of international relations. Mutually contradictory claims of ruling groups in the international arena harbor the seeds of violent conflict if these claims enjoy the support of the national myth, if competing interest groups are strongly supported by "public opinion" in their home countries. The Nazi elite, as long as it was able to represent its claims upon the democratic world as the expression of the whole community for independence and peace and survival, was able to rally the unswerving support of the German people to its personal cause. The same is true of the Soviet Union's Communist elite. The picture in democratic communities is no different provided the ruling groups succeed in identifying the indifferent segment of the nation with their cause.

In substance, then, the integrity of national beliefs and institutions is the supreme end for which nations will struggle, however that integrity may be defined. To the Nazis it was the "hegemony of the Aryan people over Europe"; to the Indians, the "expulsion of the British imperialists"; to the Americans, "making the world safe for democracy." As long as national myths receiving the wide support of groups and individuals continue to have rival and irreconcilable claims upon each other, the seeds of violence remain firmly embedded in the dynamics of international relations.

3. Restraints on International Violence. International politics is often called a "struggle for power" or "power politics," but in this regard it does not differ from domestic politics; all politics involves conflict. The essential difference is that domestic political conflicts are subject to restraints which are lacking in the world scene. In short, all politics is power politics, only international politics is "more so."

Relative Intensity of Conflicts. The relatively unrestrained application of power in international politics does not mean that all international conflicts necessarily lead to war. In domestic politics, conflicts of interests which are of a relatively nonviolent nature and which can be settled with a minimum of strife may be distinguished from other conflicts which require decades of propaganda, elections, court fights, and government crises before they are settled. The question of whether the local coroner should be elected or appointed does involve rival interests, and a referendum may be necessary to decide it. But no one would deny that the "conflict" implicit in this situation is of a different order as compared to the general issue of whether labor or industry should be supreme in the making of economic policy. So it is in international politics. Conflicts over fishing rights, airport facilities, double taxation, trade restrictions, and immigration ordinarily do not lead to armed action or war, although they certainly are conflicts involving rival claims of interest groups.

If, however, any of these conflicting issues were to be strongly identified with the national values of the states involved and thereby become a political issue affecting the whole nation, then the conflict might well become acute. Thus the American immigration policy aimed at the exclusion of Japanese on racial grounds poisoned United States–Japanese relations for decades and furnished the cause for a marked anti-American sentiment in Japan precisely because discrimination implied mass national inferiority to the Japanese. But it may also be concluded that the likelihood that international conflicts will lead to war decreases as the destructive potential of warfare becomes greater. Atomic destruction on the scale of Hiroshima is not likely to be risked merely over immigration disputes.

Material Restraints on Violence. What are the restraints on the use of this latent violence in international affairs? If there is no common myth, no international government, and no law in the domestic sense of the term among nations, how can there be formal restraints upon the free application of force by rival elites? These restraints, to be sure, are not really of an institutional character at all. It is most doubtful, for instance, that either international law or international organizations *as institutions* act as a restraining hand upon the use of force. Instead, the actual restraints upon the use of force are implicit in the ideological and material setting of the participating elites themselves. The restraints are self-imposed and self-administered; they do not originate from some outside power.

The single most important restraint is the unwillingness of many interest groups to have recourse to force in a given issue because of anticipated adverse consequences in terms of material disadvantages. A fear of monetary losses abroad or a fear of severe and shattering damage at home are frequently sufficient deterrents from the ready appeal to violence. Further, the ability of the potential enemy to inflict losses and damage is, of course, the primary feature which induces a given interest group to assume the attitude of restraint. On the basis of this tendency, then, it may be concluded that a rough equality of power may act as a restraining force simply because neither side can be confident of an easy victory.

Ideological Restraints on Violence. Ideological opposition to the use of violence can be an equally powerful deterrent to war. Pacifism provides one extreme of ideological conviction against any appeal to power. By itself, pacifism as an ideology of small groups has never sufficed to keep any state neutral or disarmed or unwilling to resist attack. However, if a national pacifist orientation were to emerge it might become a deterring force of considerable moment. Thus the marriage of pacifism and socialism was of great importance in bringing about the mutinies and revolutions which marked the end of World War I in 1918. That same combination induced the British Labor party to tolerate German expansion after 1935 without so much as a pretense at resistance. Nor is pacifism, alone or in combination, the only possible ideology opposing violence. The ideology of isolationism, of avoiding involvement in the affairs and conflicts of other countries, has operated as a powerful deterrent to American, Swiss, and on occasion British participation in wars. Even if some groups did advocate the use of force, a dominant mass feeling of indifference or even hostility to the foreign issue may make impossible the commitment to war. Thus, in the United States it took a Pearl Harbor to make the indifferent portion of the population ready to resort to force, even though certain groups had been advocating American participation in World War II for some time previously. The ideology of isolation had acted as a most effective deterrent to American entry into the conflict for over two years.

Ideological and material opposition to violence is the chief restraint on the ready use of force. For some, force in a given situation just "doesn't pay," and for others it is morally and spiritually repulsive. No government will be able to assert its claims against other governments in a conflict situation of some intensity if either of these attitudes prevails in the claimant country. These restraints are self-contained within the ideologies and myths of given communities. They are not institutionalized or incorporated into specific organs or principles of government. There are two further restraints, however, which do qualify as distinct institutions of international politics and which are often credited with acting as deterrents to war: international law and international organizations.

Institutional Restraints on Violence. If the multitude of international treaties, conventions, charters, and covenants were taken at their face value, it would have to be concluded that any use of force other than in self-defense is illegal now and has been illegal at least since 1928, if not since 1919. Not only do they outlaw the use of force, except for self-defense, but they make available specifically defined procedures—arbitration, mediation, conciliation—by which governments can settle disputes without having to call upon their armies. Law, as within the national community, does provide remedies for infractions of rights. However, all international law is subject to the voluntary consent of each state, and no item of law can be enforced without the consent of the alleged violator. Hence these principles lose most of their effectiveness as deterrents to war. A law which is superimposed upon some eighty sovereign peoples acknowledging no common myth and no permanent common purpose, professing mutually hostile rather than complementary ends, is not law in the same sense as that made by Congress in Washington. While international law makes possible the peaceful solution of thousands of disputes and tensions every year, most of these disputes are of the "coroner" variety, i.e., they are of so subordinate a nature that they would not give rise to violence anyway.

Much the same is true of international organization as an institution. The United Nations, for instance, is empowered to define the limits within which war may take place—limits which will be discussed in detail elsewhere. But if any one of its members chooses to disobey these limitations, the only method by which it can be brought to compliance is United Nations "enforcement action," i.e., violence rechristened but otherwise unchanged. Far from eliminating the use of violence or necessarily reducing its incidence, international organization implies the utilization of force by the society of states rather than by single states. It remains to be demonstrated that the institution of international organization is able to act as a restraining force against the ready appeal to arms in crises in which the unilateral action of single states would not have deterred the use of violence equally well.

All four restraining forces, then, are subject to limitation. The institutional restraints upon the use of force are weak in proportion to the heterogeneity and division of the world into mutually hostile groups. Law and organization in themselves are powerless to persuade given elites that their survival is not at stake in specific situations of conflict. Nor can the self-imposed restraints of material or moral opposition to violence be relied upon as ever valid deterrents to war. As national survival comes to be accepted as the highest end of the community, the moral restraint to war tends to be sloughed off more and more until the power position of the community comes to be accepted as the only true criterion of action. In such a crisis situation only the rational fear that war may destroy more than it is expected to save may prevent the outbreak of hostilities. This check, of course, is dependent at any one time on the existence of a sufficiently powerful body of opinion. Such opinion cannot be expected to be present in all crisis situations. Indeed, despite these restraints on the free application of force, the likelihood that rival group claims will be settled by appeal to force, in degrees varying from threats and demonstrations to full war, is as great now as it has been at all times in international relations.

4. The State of Nature and the Search for Security. It is the absence of effective restraints on violence which has persuaded many theorists and observers to conclude that international politics is power politics in the fullest possible sense of the term and that the relations between sovereign states are not unlike life in the jungle. Political theorists have called this condition the "state of nature," in which, according to Hobbes, human life is "nasty, mean, brutish, and short." Life in the state of nature is based on the war of all against all. Each unit is the enemy of each other unit. The security of one must of necessity be the insecurity of the others. When moralists inveigh against "power politics" they have in mind the condition of absolute rivalry and absolute distrust which dictates policies of absolute superiority of power. In the state of nature—assuming this characterization to be an accurate one —the search for security by each state is the single dominating factor, and since the search for security by one implies the future insecurity of the others, the search for security by one state must be countered by the power policies of others. Hence conflict is held to be inevitable on every level of activity and policy in the state of nature.

Changing Nature of Policy Aims. This characterization of international relations need not be accepted even though the expectation of violence does indeed obtain in world politics. Continued enmity assumes constant aims of unbroken opposition at all times. No such constancy in aims can be demonstrated to exist in actuality. As elites and interest groups change, values, ideologies, and ends change with them. Enmity may be converted into friendship and vice versa by these inevitable shifts in motive. Furthermore, not all disagreements imply war to the bitter end, as has been seen. Conflicts may range in intensity from polite disagreements over tax rates, which are easily solved by negotiation or arbitration, through squabbles over immigration quotas, all the way to questions of the possible coexistence of basically hostile belief systems. It is only on the level of basic and intensely held ends that conflicts tend to develop into violence. Short of this extreme, conflict does not imply permanent warfare, permanent distrust, and the permanent search for more national power. Therefore, in a discussion of the dynamics of international relations it is not necessary to assume that every relationship is a pairing or comparison of power, with war lurking around the corner. It remains true, nevertheless, that in times of profound distrust—and we live in such an era now—the expectation of violence is such that the security of one antagonist does indeed imply the insecurity of the other in the relations between the superpowers.

Security, then, emerges as the key term in the foreign policies of states. It is a far more accurate description than "struggle for power" or "power politics," because it reduces power once more to its proper role as a conditioner of means and not an end. The over-all end of state policy is the security of the ruling group, internally, externally, and in combination. Security is an end which enjoys universal validity: every elite attempts to protect its own position, to perpetuate itself—in short, to make itself secure. But the pursuit of power in this process is no more than the instrument through which security is to be achieved. Security, once attained in relation to a specific foreign state, need no longer be implemented with a continuing search for more and more power. But conversely, situations arise in which complete security is never attained because the potential antagonist matches every increase in power with an additional increment of his own.

The Relativity of Security. When it is argued that security is the shibboleth of policy, the universally recognized end toward which elites direct their policies, is it possible to specify more precisely whose security is to be protected against whom? In the abstract, of course, one speaks of the security of nations or states which have to be protected against the aggressive designs of other nations. This identification of security with a need of the whole national community can be true in actuality only if one assumes the general acceptance of common ends, adhered to not only by isolated groups but by the whole people. It would then involve the nation's myth, and security would mean the defense of the nation's way of life against some rival, irreconcilable, and hostile way of life. Only in this situation is it justifiable to equate the nation with an individual person fighting for his own survival or welfare.

In many cases, however, the security concept cannot be equated with the will or the interest of the whole nation. The principle does not always imply unanimous agreement on the immutable needs of the nation. On the contrary, it is subject to the varying interpretations and understandings of the particular groups concerned. Security may mean, therefore, the particular conception of interest *for given groups* in the nation at a given time, but not necessarily for the whole nation for all time. Specific group aims, based on ideologies but not necessarily on national myths, define the security needs of given groups. There is no permanent, all-inclusive, and universally valid definition of security for any one state.

However, it remains true that state policy against other states does indeed reflect definable notions of security: the security of elites, of coalitions of elites, and in some cases of the whole nation. The vital process of defining the policy aims of nations in accordance with the security principle, therefore, must now be examined in detail.

ADDITIONAL CASE-STUDY MATERIAL

Beard, Charles A.: *The Idea of National Interest,* Macmillan, New York, 1934.

Briggs, H.: "New Dimensions in International Law," *American Political Science Review,* vol. 46, 1952.

Cook, T. I., and Malcolm Moos: "Foreign Policy: The Realism of Idealism," *American Political Science Review,* vol. 46, 1952.

———— and ————: "The American Idea of International Interest," *American Political Science Review,* vol. 47, 1953.

Corbett, P. E.: *Law and Society in the Relations of States,* Harcourt, Brace, New York, 1951.

Friedrich, Carl J.: *Foreign Policy in the Making,* Norton, New York, 1938.

Haas, E. B.: "The Balance of Power as a Guide to Policy-making," *Journal of Politics,* vol. 15, 1953.

————: "The United States of Europe: Four Approaches to the Purpose and Form of a European Federation," *Political Science Quarterly,* vol. 63, 1948.

Hall, H. Duncan: "The British Commonwealth of Nations," *American Political Science Review,* vol. 47, 1953.

Levi, Werner: *Fundamentals of World Organization,* University of Minnesota Press, Minneapolis, 1950.

Marshall, C. B.: "The National Interest and Current World Problems," *Department of State Bulletin,* May 5, 1952.

Morgenthau, Hans J.: *Politics among Nations,* 2d ed., Knopf, New York, 1954.

————: *In Defense of the National Interest,* Knopf, New York, 1951.

Wright, Q.: "The Nature of Political Conflict," *Western Political Quarterly,* July, 1951.

Documentary case-study material on the demands and roles of interest groups on foreign policy issues may be found in any set of congressional hearings, especially in those dealing with foreign-aid programs.

Chapter 4

THE DEFINITION OF POLICY AIMS

Despite the absence of a meaningful concept of national interest, policy aims *are* defined and decisions on relations with other states *are* made. In order to trace the process through which this is achieved and to arrive at a broad scheme of what the typical aims of national foreign policy are in practice it is necessary to look once more at the forces which shape politics within each nation.

1. Ideology, Myth, and the Definition of Policy Aims. This discussion of individuals, groups, communities, societies, and intergroup contact across national boundaries has been concerned with the ideas and aspirations of men as they impinge upon one another. It requires another type of discussion —the analysis of the constituents of national power—to put these human aims and intentions in the framework of the possible: the objective factors allowing or prohibiting the satisfaction of aims. The two discussions are opposite sides of the same coin. Policy consists of the underlying aim, the definition of the goal to be attained, and therefore refers to individual and group motives. Policy, however, also consists of an appraisal of the physical means, techniques, and manipulations possible within the limitations of national power to translate policy aims into reality at some future time. National foreign policies must be treated as an amalgam of interests and of the group appraisal of the objective factual environment in which policy operates. This, in turn, calls for a second look at our concept of ideology, to determine the extent to which group aspirations include an appreciation of the means available for carrying out basic aims.

Ends, Means, and Ideology. Interest groups and communities may demand a foreign policy on any ideological grounds. Some may call for global social-security benefits, unlimited foreign trade, or universal peace. Others may advocate the maintenance of the domestic as well as the international *status quo* and the maximization of national security. Humanitarians may demand measures for the prevention of cruelty to animals and thus give outward expression to their values. Or the establishment of Christian, Moslem, or Hinayana Buddhist beliefs everywhere can be made the end of policy. Such interests can be as wide as the range of human experience and hope.

The striking fact remains, however, that not all ideological demands—even if held by powerful groups—find expression in international relations. Conviction is not enough to translate hope into policy. Means must be found to attain these ends, and the adoption of means calls for the marshaling of the factors of national power. Consciousness of power and means is least developed at the level of the individual. In his formation and articulation of policy, the individual gives little effort to devising ways for translating opinion and hope into action. Nor can the unexpert citizen be expected to master the complexities of production statistics and population pressures in hope of implementing his ideas on policy. The large interest group is also unlikely to give much thought to the problem of means. Ideology still tends to assert itself without paying much attention to ways of realizing its demands.

Thus a local union may vote to bar further immigration of competing workingmen on the basis of its values, or the American Polish Congress may call for a policy of liberating oppressed peoples. Neither may give much thought as to how these aims can be made to dovetail with other, perhaps antagonistic, group demands. Ends receive all attention; means tend to be neglected on this level of political action.

Ends, Means, and Elites. The picture changes once the values of the group are in the hands of the leadership—the elite. In a democratic setting elites rarely are so strong that they can hope to attain their aims without allying themselves with other elites. Alliances—often mere marriages of convenience—are the common result, and alliances bring with them the need for compromising group values. Thus a process of diluting the demands of specific ideologies sets in. A given coalition of elites will have to share the ideologies of the constituent groups in order to present a common front. In the American setting, the compromises among the groups identified with the Democratic party provides a cogent example. Northern labor organizations, Southern business groups, and Western farmers have all cooperated and compromised in fashioning the program of the Democrats since 1932. Each of the participating elites had to give up a portion of its demands, at least temporarily, in order to make a common front with the others. The level of ideology, further, was partially pushed back in this process, and the groups tended to combine on the level of the national myth. They sought to fashion their aims in such a manner as to conform with the common values and beliefs of other American groups to whom they appealed for support, thus tending toward a common denominator of generally accepted values and interests.

In so doing a more consistent appreciation of the ways of realizing policy aims emerges. Elites seek to achieve their program, and hence they must bear in mind continually how to go about implementing their aims. The process of compromising among elites includes the process of finding means as well as reconciling ends. Policy which is attractive but which cannot be realized for lack of power tends to be sloughed off; only the attainable remains in the program.

The ability of an elite to ally itself with other groups, however, can be severely limited. If there is no fundamental ideological cleavage between groups, elites encounter no serious obstacle in their search for friends. They combine freely and in the process identify themselves with a political party which meets their interests most closely. Yet an elite which refuses to compromise its demands must go into politics alone. The Italian and French Communist parties define their programs, values, and interests in such a fashion as to preclude any real cooperation with other groups and parties. They stand outside the national myth on a number of issues. Hence the ends of these groups do not lose their exclusive and clear character since no compromising is ever indulged in for prolonged periods.

Ends, Means, and Policy Makers. The appreciation of means becomes an even more significant factor in the definition of specific policy aims once we reach the level of the policy maker, the government. Policy makers, to be sure, frequently are members of elites, and they always seek to translate their beliefs into reality. However, because they represent a political party which is itself dependent upon the support of many groups, they must compromise almost incessantly. They can never follow a policy repugnant to the myth of the community, because they cannot risk being left without the support of the overwhelming majority of groups and individuals in the event of international conflict. Hence many a politician and statesman must think twice before embarking on a foreign policy of speedily translating the values of his group into demands upon foreign nations. Only a secure autocrat can afford to ignore the wishes of his domestic supporters and opponents and to follow his personal values and preferences. The Secretary of State of the United States, the Foreign Minister of India, no less than the head of the Soviet Union's Foreign Office, must weigh alternative policy ends in terms of the demands and aims of their supporters, of the entire national community, and in terms of the physical means available for carrying out the policy. Reducing the international strength of communism may have been an ideological tenet of almost all American interest groups, elites, and parties since 1947. But President Truman's policy of "containing the Soviet Union" through economic aid to Europe could take shape only after disagreements between farmers and labor, small business and big business, among dozens of interested bodies, had been adjusted. Only then did Congress pass the appropriations bills providing the money whereby the actual military, diplomatic, and economic means of containment were made available.

Thus it is on the level of the policy maker that compromises between elites are finally translated into compromises with all groups, producing the necessary power for carrying out a policy. The process of defining policy ends, then, includes within it the appreciation of means, even if this occurs only on the highest level of community action, the level of the state.

Ends, Means, and the Civil Service. Little has so far been said about the "professionals" in government, the civil servant whose task it is to administer and implement a policy, once aims have been defined. Does the administrator merely follow and carry out policy directives which have been worked out for him by policy makers and their supporting elites? Or does he take the initiative in proposing aims of policy and the means for realizing them? Does he have an ideology like members of other groups, and if so, does his ideology impinge upon ends and means? Were his values to oppose those of the policy maker, the administrator might attempt to sabotage a policy with which he disagrees and whose implementation has been entrusted to him. The relationship of a nation's civil service to the definition of interests, therefore, remains to be clarified.

In principle, a member of a civil service of any kind is expected to be "neutral" with respect to ideology. It is his sole task to carry out policies whose ends have been defined by others; it is not for him to question those ends. Yet the statement of the principle tells us little. A policy of aiding Western Europe through American financial support may have been decided by policy makers in Washington. The civil servant may then be called upon to spell out in detail how this aid is to be tendered, since he is the economic expert most conversant with the complexities of financial relationships. Though his advice is apparently limited to the means through which this policy is to be pursued, ideology may well find its way into the picture at this stage. Sir Horace Wilson, a British civil servant of some renown, put forward this rather ambiguous interpretation of an administrator's responsibility with respect to advice on means: [1]

Broadly speaking, the main quality that is required seems to me to be a capacity to take the facts about a particular subject, to put them into shape, to suggest the deductions that might be drawn from them, to propose the lines of policy that might be adopted in relation to them, and generally to apply a constructive analytical mind to what I would call the policy of the Ministry.

Which facts will the civil servant select? Which deductions will he stress and which will be slurred over? What values will be in his mind when "lines of policy" are to be suggested? A highly placed civil servant may influence policy making directly through the expert advice he gives to the politician. Moreover, top-level civil servants have been known to take the initiative in suggesting and defining the very ends of policy. Their adoption, of course, depends on the extent to which they meet the values and political judgments of superiors in the government. It is plain, nevertheless, that in the social

---

[1] Testimony to the Tomlin Commission, as cited in R. G. Neumann, *European and Comparative Government,* McGraw-Hill, New York, 1951, p. 59.

hierarchy the ideologies of civil servants are a factor to be taken into account. In some nations, to be sure, severe institutional and traditional limitations exist to cut down this possibility. Thus the British civil service enjoys a high reputation for political neutrality. The same civil servants worked loyally for Conservative as well as socialist policy makers, despite the difference in ends professed by the two parties. The civil service may possess such a tight code of professional ethics as to preclude the intrusion of the bureaucrat's ideology, as in Britain. In the civil servant's scheme of values, the code of neutral service takes precedence over the desire to express ideological preferences in policy. Yet the same has not always been true of the United States. Administrators are dropped or transferred frequently when a new party takes over the government or when a new set of policy aims is to be achieved. Administrative appointments with the advent of the New Deal in 1933 and its demise in 1953 illustrate this tendency. Thus policy makers frequently have to assure success for their political aims by controlling civil servants whose ideologies make them poor instruments for implementation.

The ends of a nation's foreign policy are defined on each level of the social hierarchy: individuals, interest groups, elites, political parties, and the government itself. Ideology enters at each level, though the clarity and uniqueness of group values tend to be sloughed off and compromised away as the process of definition reaches the higher levels. At the highest stage the overall policy emerges. Its final ends may be described in three basic types: self-preservation, self-extension, and self-abnegation. The next three sections examine these ends for which nations strive in their relations.

2. Ends of Self-preservation. Self-preservation implies the desire to maintain social, economic, institutional, ideological, and therefore political systems as they are at a given point in time. The wish to maintain a given set of institutions is a *minimum* aim which almost all groups, elites, and national communities profess almost all the time. Sometimes this minimum wish gives way to a more ambitious set of demands; in that case, ends of self-extension take the place of the more limited desire to maintain the *status quo*. Finally, particular ideological or physical conditions may persuade elites and nations to abnegate, more or less voluntarily, aims of preserving what they possess and to cut down their political commitments and programs. For the most part self-preservation, however, is the group aim of overwhelming importance.[2]

No party likes to lose an election, and no social group wishes to be ousted through a revolution. Corporation executives like to be and to remain in prominent political positions, and so do union leaders. Collective suicide and the voluntary changing of institutions by those who profit from them are rare in history. The existing advantages of deference, respect, and status

[2] This breakdown is an adaptation of the "goals" of policy discussed by Arnold Wolfers, "The Pole of Power and the Pole of Indifference," *World Politics*, October, 1951, pp. 39–63.

enjoyed by an elite constitute its major asset. These advantages are not lightly relinquished and tend to be bitterly defended.

Group Status and Self-preservation. If self-preservation in this sense is practiced by groups within the state, nations in their relations with each other certainly betray no intention of seeing their institutions threatened, the "way of life" endangered, by the policies of some other nation. A threat to the institutions, beliefs, and myths of a nation implies a threat to the status and position of the elites which benefit from these features. A world-wide blow to the prestige of Communist dogma not only implies a weakening of the status of Communist leaders in France, India, and Brazil, but may also imply a shock to the position occupied by leaders of the Soviet elite. The failure of Leon Trotsky to achieve world revolution contributed to his loss of position at home. A blow to free private enterprise struck by the Labor party in Britain is considered a defeat for the ideology of free private enterprise in the United States. Hence business groups will seek to protect their interest in America by opposing socialism in Britain, though this desire may not necessarily find its way into the foreign policy of the United States. Elites acting in self-defense, then, must protect their interpretation of the national myth if they wish to protect their own status.

Self-preservation as an aim in international relations refers to the position and status *already achieved* by nations and groups within nations. Those who would create a new set of institutions nationally and internationally in conformance with their beliefs and aspirations aim at self-extension and not at self-preservation. Ends of self-preservation imply a minimum of demands upon groups and nations outside the national community. They imply satisfaction with the way things are at any one time. While minor adjustments and changes in relations with groups elsewhere are not precluded in the ends of self-preservation, drastic changes and revisions of the *status quo* are foreign to this orientation.

Self-preservation and Peace. Hence ends of self-preservation, if professed by all elites in all important nations at the same time, are conducive to peaceful international relations. Demands for adjustments can be met with negotiations instead of bitter propaganda campaigns or war. Conflicts of interests arise even if self-preservation is the universal end of policy followed everywhere, since even self-preservation may call for rival claims in the same area. But a negotiated peaceful settlement is almost always possible in situations of this type. Protection of one's own established interests rarely implies the necessity of defeating or eliminating a rival completely.

A point may be reached in the relations between two nations, however, at which even ends of self-preservation from each other come into such violent conflict that the stage of open hostilities or the near-violent state of political warfare is attained. The distrust dividing two nations may be so great as to invest such ends of self-preservation with all the destruction-laden implications of nuclear war. Hostility between American and Soviet ruling groups, even though each may aim only at its own salvation, seems to approach this extreme.

Activities Aiming at Self-preservation. Such an extreme state of affairs definitely does not characterize the bulk of contacts among the eighty-three sovereign states of our time.[3] While diplomatic protests, airplane incidents, blockades, and cold and hot wars made the headlines, the overwhelming majority of circumstances in international relations reflect national and group aims of self-preservation. Because these are free from the stigma of violent conflict, they receive little publicity.

Thus the area of protecting the interests of nationals abroad is of major importance among the unspectacular aims of self-preservation. Businessmen engaged in transactions with businessmen in other countries frequently seek the protection of their home governments. Travelers call upon the services of their consuls to advise them about their rights and duties in foreign territory. Trade agreements pave the way for the exchange of goods and services, and treaties regulating fisheries on the high seas or in territorial waters make it possible for the fishermen of several nations to earn a living under orderly conditions. Agreements on immigration, dual nationality, and double taxation attempt to ease the lot of those who seek to better their lives by settling in foreign countries. In each of these instances the interests of some group are protected by arrangements with other governments. While the services of consuls are particularly important for the businessman active abroad, every citizen profits from them when he travels. Corporations with interests in other nations benefit from treaties on double taxation; land-hungry peasants migrating to the New World profit from treaties on immigration. Reciprocal trade and tariff pacts benefit exporters and consumers.

Self-preservation and Neutrality. Ordinarily, the standard foreign policy pursued by a nation with no foreseeable claims upon any other nation is one of neutrality. Whether self-imposed or guaranteed by others, neutrality reflects the fundamental national desire not to participate in any conflict leading to a state of hostilities. A neutral nation thereby publicly declares its lack of concern with the rivalries dividing others, though it may maintain a large armed force to demonstrate its intention to defend itself against an unprovoked attack. This, indeed, had been the policy of the Scandinavian countries, Holland, and Belgium in 1940, who had thereby made an alliance with France and Britain a diplomatic impossibility. Neutrality continues to be the rigorous policy of Switzerland today. It signifies an intent to practice exclusively a policy of self-preservation to the point of not wishing to give

---

[3] Our criterion for sovereign statehood is the *pro forma* capacity to enter into diplomatic relations with other states through the existence of a foreign ministry, regardless of whether the ministry is *in fact* able to make independent policy. Thus Outer Mongolia and North Korea are included, while Byelorussia and the Ukraine are not.

a state determined upon self-extension an excuse for unleashing an attack. Still, the defense of a policy of neutrality has frequently involved countries in war despite the fact that they had no wish to enter it. In such situations the cause for involvement was the desire for self-extension on the part of elites in the attacking country, as demonstrated by Germany's attacks on Scandinavia and the Low Countries in 1940.

Self-preservation and Domestic Strife. Even groups seeking self-preservation and no more may be driven to a foreign policy of conflict—if not open war—in order to defend themselves against the onslaught of domestic rather than foreign enemies. In times of extreme domestic tension among elites, a policy of uniting a badly divided nation against some real or alleged outside threat frequently seems useful to a ruling group. Elites, fearful of losing their position in the nation as a result of sharp ideological and group conflict, as in periods of rapid industrialization and large-scale social change, attempt to displace the attention of the disaffected portion of the nation away from its grievances and toward some outside target. International bankers, capitalist imperialists, communist conspirators, or any other appropriate symbol may serve this purpose. Yet the aim of the group initiating such a policy remains one of self-preservation against the claims of its domestic enemies.

This form of the search for self-preservation rarely results in war, though the "Hate America" or "Hate the Jews" campaigns may give rise to such propaganda barrages as to make war appear imminent. Relations between states may then become embittered, but if an authoritarian elite makes use of these means they can generally be stopped as speedily as they are begun. Thus both Nazi Germany and the Soviet Union have been frequent practitioners of the art of displacement through propaganda, for purposes of self-preservation rather than self-extension. A policy of hostility and propaganda toward the capitalist world on the part of Russia has been correlated with periods of domestic tension. Hitler's and Mussolini's propaganda attacks against Britain, Russia, or the United States could be similarly explained when they were not conducted in preparation for a diplomatic or military attack. As soon as an authoritarian elite feels more secure domestically, it usually stops this type of foreign policy and ends its propaganda campaign.

Ends of self-preservation may even persuade ruling groups to adopt policies alien to their ideologies, particularly in democratic communities. The opposition party may come forward with a series of demands which the governing party can ill afford to rebuff for fear of losing control of the government. Self-preservation within the domestic sociopolitical context may then dictate a partial acceptance of the opposition's demands, bringing with it immediate consequences in the foreign relations of the nation.

Thus the German Socialists, Catholics, and Democrats during the 1920s believed in a policy of peace and disarmament. Yet they felt insecure of their position in the ideologically torn Germany of that time; in the hope of conciliating their Nationalist opponents, they consented to building battleships and tanks. The vacillating and ambiguous China policy of the Truman Administration, from 1948 until 1952, can partly be explained on similar grounds. With the complete military victory of the Chinese Communist elite, in 1948 and 1949, the Democratic administration was prepared to recognize the new regime and enter into regular diplomatic relations with it. The fact that it failed to do so and instead followed a policy of frank disapproval and open hostility to Peiping—long before Chinese participation in the Korean War—is largely due to the violent criticism with which the Republican opposition greeted the intention to recognize. Ideological conflict over the issue threatened to damage the prestige of the Democratic party and its allied elites. The Truman Administration met its critics by not recognizing Red China and by attempting to isolate it, while stopping short of the warlike measures that extreme critics were advocating for the United States. Self-preservation thus forced a ruling group into a foreign policy it did not entirely welcome but also kept it from following this policy to its logical conclusion.

Subsumed under these broad aims of self-preservation, whether practiced by specific elites or entire nations, may be any number of subsidiary aims and aspirations. The desire for economic gain or financial security ranks high among these. The wish to remain true to one's cultural traditions and maintain intact the values of group or nation enter constantly as aims of self-preservation, as does the omnipresent need for physical security. Some or all of these enter into the definition of any foreign policy at all times, since self-preservation operates under different labels for different groups.

Ends and Means in Self-preservation. A sharp distinction between *ends* of self-preservation and possible *means* of self-extension is crucial in this analysis. A foreign policy characterized by the extension of national power on a global scale should not be mistaken for a policy inspired by aims of self-extension. Witness the trend of American policy since 1947. Washington maintains air and naval bases in Italy, Libya, Morocco, Japan, and Okinawa. It gives extensive military and economic assistance to almost every country not in the Soviet sphere. Its military, economic, and technical-assistance experts function almost everywhere, while its armed forces dot Central Europe and the Far East. Yet a perusal of American opinion and ideology will indicate an insignificant number of groups who glory in this expansion of American influence. On the contrary, a significant number of elites oppose this trend and argue for a retrenchment of operations. In short, there are no important ends of self-extension operative in American ideologies. Means of self-extension, however, jump to the eye. Thus, here is a classic example of means of self-extension being used to attain ends of self-preservation, and no more.

The possibility that means of self-extension may be adopted in order to secure ends of self-preservation raises the key problem of how opposing nations evaluate and identify each other's policy aims. Granted that American policy is one of self-preservation, must not its use of expansive means be interpreted as *bona fide* expansion by the Soviet Union? For the Soviet policy maker it may make very little difference whether the construction of American airfields in Libya is attributable to a desire to protect American interests in Europe or to a plan to bomb Russia and to subdue her. Similarly, for the American statesman the Soviet acquisition of Port Arthur may constitute evidence of Soviet expansive desires since the base may be used to attack Japan. Yet the Soviet aim may merely have been one of self-preservation, the desire to protect Siberian industrial centers. Thus the opposing nation is not always willing or able to benefit from the distinction between means of self-extension and ends of self-preservation. Conflict may well be the result of the failure to make the distinction. Means are mistaken for ends; imperialistic desires are assumed to propel the antagonist while he may merely be trying to protect what he already holds. It is therefore of the highest importance for the preservation of peace and the survival of states that policy makers properly identify policies of others, assess correctly the aims of their opponents, and not mistake means for ends.

3. Ends of Self-extension. If ends of self-preservation can be generally identified with peace, or conflict short of war, ends of self-extension by definition suggest violence and battle. Self-extension implies the imposition by groups or nations of their values and institutions upon members of other social or political systems. It includes the desire to foist unwanted goods and undesired economic and social institutions upon other nations. It allows for the desire to conquer lands and peoples or to dominate them without actually attacking their government. Self-extension refers to the will of an elite to make others subservient to its ideology and to convert them against their preferences. To mold other nations in the image of the molder is an act of self-extension, as is the desire to "liberate" other peoples when the process of liberation implies the exportation and imposition of the liberator's values and institutions. Ends of self-extension, therefore, are identical with what is generally called "imperialism."

Since the search for imperial expansion usually results in the resistance of those at whose expense the process takes place, war is implicit in such relationships. In fact, some writers hold that policies of expansion are inevitable because war is considered desirable and pleasurable by man. Thus Frederick L. Schuman argues that [4]

War is a habit that men enjoy, as they enjoy drunkenness, gluttony, fornication, gambling and crime. Its vast superiority over all other forms of sin is that it embraces all the vices and casts over them the thrilling shadow of danger and the glittering cloak of honor, thereby making them "heroic" or at least permissible.

[4] F. L. Schuman, *The Commonwealth of Man,* Knopf, New York, 1952, p. 45.

Since the roots of this psychological drive are held to be deeply embedded in men's minds, policies of self-extension are seen to be as natural as life itself. Yet if this analysis is true, what accounts for the fact that most nations do not follow policies of self-extension? How does it fit the fact that the American people signally failed to rejoice about the Korean War or the fact that India and neutralists in Europe desperately wish to avoid being involved in war? Clearly, policies of self-extension are not inevitable. If they were and if their causes were to be found in the psychology of brutality, all nations would always be bent on imperialism.

Economic Self-extension. Among the many factors which may prompt an elite or a nation to seek expansion is the desire for economic and financial gain. Industrial raw materials can sometimes be obtained more readily and more cheaply if they are seized rather than purchased in international trade. Industries desiring markets for sales and outlets for investable funds have been known to prefer going into another country in which they could be active without fear of competition from other states. Hence they would argue for the annexation of the desired country, or at least press for some kind of indirect control short of annexation which would still give them the desired advantage. Because of such factors, protectorates have been established over weaker nations.

The process of expansion is easily summarized. Individual traders penetrated an area, or settlers began taking and tilling land. Then, to protect themselves from the reprisals of the peoples already domiciled in the area, the home government was called upon to extend its jurisdiction over the region. Oil and mining concessions were sought by investors, and subsequently their government might be asked to protect their interests if the investment happened to be in a weak country with unstable political institutions, leading to the establishment of a protectorate or veiled control over the native regime by the foreign corporation and its government. Economic extension, however, need not lead to outside control. United States railroads and Argentine meat plants were established largely through European capital without a resulting pattern of European control over American or Argentine institutions. Hence economic factors lead to imperial control only under the special circumstances of the expanding country's ideology permitting control and manipulation and the victimized community's inability to resist.

Cultural Self-extension. A more pervasive factor than economic ends of self-extension has been the desire to expand culturally and socially. When economic considerations are the aim of the expanding group, no attempt is necessarily made to convert the victimized nation to the values and myths of the expanding one. Culturally and socially conditioned imperialism, however, rests on the fundamental aim of making other peoples subject to a new myth or ideology and of imposing the institutions associated with these beliefs.

Yet cultural imperialism is not identical with international propaganda.

Americans consider that democracy is the best form of government, applicable everywhere. They spend a portion of their budget on teaching other nations efficient production methods, agricultural techniques, and the virtues of modern plumbing. Indian diplomats abroad like to lecture others on the superiority of the Gandhian doctrine of nonviolence, and European elites pride themselves on their possession of culture in contrast to the alleged American preoccupation with movies, comic books, and dishwashing machines. Each of these claims and beliefs reflects a desire for cultural and social affirmation; but since no attempt is made to *impose* these values and institutions upon others, they do not imply active ends of self-extension.

Cultural imperialism is an active end of national policy whenever elites claim a "civilizing mission" or a "white man's burden" for themselves. The French groups who found hospitals, schools, armies, and systems of law according to their precepts in Madagascar, Morocco, and Tahiti claim to be carrying civilization—i.e., their own values—to the subject groups. The Britons who penetrated and ruled Nigeria, Sarawak, and Aden, in imposing values and institutions of their own upon the peoples of these regions, claimed to bear the white man's civilizing burden. Both nations were following ends of self-extension at the same time. Cultural self-extension is equally implicit in policies of racial superiority, which seek to give special rights and positions to "master races" while subjugating "inferior races" in the process. Nazi Germany sought to realize policy aims of cultural self-extension by subjugating "inferior races" (i.e., Poles, Russians, Greeks) as well as assimilating with kindred ethnic groups (i.e., Scandinavians). Thus German racial doctrines were imposed in both cases. Nor was cultural imperialism absent from the American policy aim, professed in the years immediately following World War II, of "democratizing" Germany and Japan. Since neither the defeated German nor Japanese elites expressed any particular wish to be "democratized" and since the occupation authorities did not seek the approval of their former enemies, the creation of democratic institutions and the dissemination of democratic values were, in effect, acts of imposition. Americans exported their own beliefs because they—like most other nations—consider their national myth superior and worthy of imitation elsewhere.

Social Status and Self-extension. Finally, ends of self-extension are commonly professed by interest groups and elites who wish to live up to their group code, their ideology. If this set of beliefs happens to be based on notions of military honor and personal glory, ends of self-extension are implicit within it. If the domestic political and social setting restricts the freedom of such elites to realize their aims for ideological self-assertion, they may well turn to foreign areas as fields of operation. In so doing they seek to maximize and strengthen their social and political status and gain deference from the subjugated population. Imperial expansion may mean profit and economic security to the mining concessionaire and the opportunity to impose his religious values to the missionary. But it means status, deference, and a secure social position for the military and civil administrator who leaves his native country to rule the "backward" people over whom his government has asserted control. For the French and British aristocracies, increasingly challenged at home at the end of the nineteenth century, the acquisition of colonial empire implied a new claim to position and social status, since it was the members of these elite groups who monopolized the important empire administrative and military posts. In such a setting, ends of self-extension then serve to buttress the claims and roles of specific groups fearful of their future at home and bent on finding a scope for action abroad.

Self-extension Drives and Colonialism. The growth and preservation of large colonial empires is the result of the interaction of all these facets of self-extension. Britain annexed most of South and Central Africa and all of India and Burma because of the combination of economic, ideological, and group-status drives in the last quarter of the nineteenth century. She established her control over the Middle East through protectorates and mandates a little later for the same reasons. France's colonial drive in North and West Africa, in the Pacific and in Southeast Asia is attributable to the same interaction of factors. Industrialists, exporters, civil servants, military and naval officers, intellectuals, and religious groups all profited from the expansion, as did the millions of Frenchmen and Britishers who settled in the colonies as permanent residents. The entire population, in so far as it accepted the ideology of civilizing non-Western nations, benefited from the ends of self-extension in finding emotional satisfaction from the exportation of national values. The same is true of the Continental empire which certain German groups wished to found for Germany before 1918 and which the Nazis actually realized. It is also true of the Japanese elites who wished to build a "Greater East Asia Co-prosperity Sphere" for Japan after 1931. Whether empire building proceeds in Africa or the Pacific, or whether it is undertaken in regions neighboring the expanding community, in Eastern Europe or the Chinese mainland, the ends of self-extension professed by the expanding groups are always an interaction of economic, ideological, and status aims.

But cannot self-extension be considered self-preservation after a colonial empire has been stabilized? Do aims of expansion not give way to ends of retaining what has been acquired, after the original imperial impulse has run its course? It can be argued that the desire of France and Britain to retain their overseas territories is an aim of self-preservation, since no demands for further expansion exist. It can be argued, further, that the countries of Eastern Europe which are now so closely tied to the Soviet Union as to approximate colonial status will no longer be the victims of imperialism once they accept their position and come to consider themselves parts of a greater Communist realm.

It is true that today the old colonial empires are shrinking. It is also true that the Soviet manipulators of Eastern Europe have a great many supporters among the Czech, Polish, Hungarian, and Romanian populations who are tied to Moscow. However, so long as elites in the imperial nations continue to pursue ends of self-extension, imperialism continues to prevail even though it be static. Elites still wish to impose their values and institutions upon alien peoples and races, regardless of the indifference or opposition of the subject groups to these aims, as in Indochina or Kenya. Hence imperialism continues to be a factor in the dynamics of international relations so long as these ends survive and so long as the subject groups cling to their own institutions and values.

4. Ends of Self-abnegation. While history is full of examples of groups seeking to preserve or to expand their positions, few examples of *voluntary* abnegation of values and interests are apparent. Voluntary withdrawal from the whirlpool of politics, such as the self-imposed neutrality of Switzerland, or of Holland and Belgium after 1936, usually stems from self-preservation and not self-abnegation. Self-abnegation as a group aim implies the willingness to relinquish control, to retrench and withdraw—and not to resist if attacked. The ideology of Mohandas K. Gandhi, leader of the Indian independence movement until 1947, is one of the few clear political doctrines espousing self-abnegation. Nonviolence is the supreme value of the ideology. Political aims are to be achieved exclusively by peaceful means. Thus when Japan attacked and invaded India in 1942 Gandhi favored a policy of noncooperation with the invader but opposed military countermeasures. The fact that he failed to convince other Indian leaders of the wisdom of this policy indicates, however, that its ability to appeal to groups is extremely limited. In short, complete and consistent self-abnegation is so rarely accepted as a group aim or national policy that it does not significantly enter into international relations in its pure form.

Yet the growth and decline of colonial empires show that in some form self-abnegation is being practiced. British policy since 1946 is a case in point. India, Burma, Pakistan, and Ceylon were given their freedom after centuries of direct and indirect imperial rule. The Gold Coast and Nigeria are now in the process of achieving the same status. It is the professed aim of British colonial policy to prepare gradually all subject areas for self-government or independence. How can such policy aims be explained except as examples of voluntary self-abnegation?

It is true that the military position of Great Britain after World War II was not such as to make possible the reconquest or forceful retention of rebellious colonies. Strong independence movements were active in each of the nations which are now free. Restraining these movements would have involved military and economic hardships which the majority of British interest groups were unwilling to undergo. Yet both the Dutch and French governments, faced with exactly the same challenges and burdens in Southeast Asia, decided to fight and not to abnegate voluntarily. What accounts for the difference in group aims?

Differences in ideology between the British on the one hand and the French on the other are here of crucial importance. While British investors were no more anxious than their French colleagues to lose their money and influence abroad, there had grown up in Britain a belief that imperialism was morally inconsistent with democracy. The Labor party, essentially socialist in its ideology, had come to power in 1945. It could accept imperial rule only on the condition that it be used as a means for enabling colonial peoples to attain self-government or independence. Its values called for economic progress through the restraining of free enterprise. Hence the party was more indifferent to the interests of established economic groups than had been true of its Conservative rival. Its beliefs did not sanction the use of force to beat down colonial independence movements and sought solutions instead through compromise with them and gradual emancipation. Furthermore, through the force of this ideology, many sections within the Conservative party became more or less convinced of the preferability of Labor's position. In short, the ideological climate in Britain had so changed by 1945 as to make a policy of partial self-abnegation a political reality. Certainly British elites hoped that the freed nations would leave British industry and plantations intact, and they tried to induce the new nations to remain associated with Britain through the Commonwealth. Yet the fact that tremendous concessions rather than force were used to achieve these aims indicates that under specific ideological conditions, policies approximating self-abnegation may be undertaken. The fact remains, however, that such policies are the exception rather than the rule in international relations.

5. Group Interests in Conflict: A Case Study—United States Policy toward the Soviet Union, 1917 to 1933. Self-preservation, self-extension, and self-abnegation are extremely broad categories. Ideologies which recognize economic, cultural, and status interests can be identified with each one. Therefore the definition of foreign policy on the basis of only one type of ends can take place only if the policy makers of the community profess one homogeneous set of beliefs. This is rarely the case. While our categories of policy aims provide a point of reference for the identification of group aims, they cannot be expected to occur in a pure and unmixed form in the actual conflict and compromise of interests which determine foreign policy. Commonly, groups professing self-extension and others dedicated to self-preservation compete for influence within the same political framework. Ideologies concerned with these ends may and do alternate in the relative vogue they enjoy in a community, but aims identified with each one also vie for recognition every time a policy decision is to be made. Analysis of groups and their demands in international relations requires identification of the mode of thought and the policy demands which they may put forward in any one situation. The making of American policy toward the Soviet Union from 1917 to 1933 serves as a case study to illustrate the complexity of the process.[5]

Recognition or Opposition as Choices. In September of 1917, World War I had been in progress for over three years. The front was stalemated in France: neither Germany nor the Allies seemed to be able to win. While the Allies were slowly crushing Turkey, Germany and Austria were defeating Italy. Russia, now under the "provisional" government of the democratic parties led by Alexander Kerensky, tried to stave off the Austro-German onslaught, but gave way as famine, discontent, and war-weariness spread among her armies and her population. The United States had become a belligerent on the Allied side in April, and was therefore engaged in a common military effort with Russia to defeat Germany and Austria-Hungary.

In November of 1917, however, the victory of the Bolshevik Revolution in Russia changed that picture considerably. The new regime proclaimed the necessity for ending Russia's part in the war and stood for the general destruction of capitalist and parliamentary institutions. More important, perhaps, it wished to foment world revolution and use its success in Russia merely as a point of departure for the universal overthrow of capitalism and democracy.

American groups had two alternatives: to ignore the revolution and continue cooperation with Russia, or to take the ideological content of Lenin's party at face value and oppose it. On the one hand, several already recognized ends in American policy could be served by a course of continued cooperation. Russia might remain in the war, fight Germany to the finish, and also help American efforts to restrain Japanese expansion in the Far East. Cooperation could serve the established policy of expanding American exports and investments to Russia. Finally, a policy of recognizing and dealing with the Soviet regime might facilitate its "conversion" to Western concepts and a sloughing off of its anticapitalist and antidemocratic precepts. On the other hand, a policy of opposition could be adopted in the hope of destroying the fledgling Soviets and thereby wiping out a potential center of attack against American institutions and values. A policy of opposition would deprive the Soviets of recognition, credits, economic aid, and foodstuffs and thus weaken the regime. Support of anti-Bolshevik groups in the civil war which erupted in Russia in 1918 might win a more stable Russian government, predisposed to favor American economic and political interests.

The policy of opposition was adopted and practiced until 1933, when the Soviet regime was legally recognized by the United States and normal diplomatic and economic relations established. What aims were responsible for the initial decision to oppose and the subsequent move to recognize Russia? The

---

[5] The following material has been selected from W. A. Williams, *American Russian Relations, 1781–1947*, Rinehart, New York, 1952.

demands and activities of key interest groups in the United States can be analyzed to obtain an impression of the dynamics of policy making. Ends can be separated from means, ends of self-preservation from those of self-extension, as well as the relationship between them and the economic, spiritual, and military aims of specific groups in America.

Forces and Beliefs Favoring Recognition. Military strategy provided a cogent set of considerations in favor of recognition. The American military and Red Cross personnel stationed in Russia wanted the United States to recognize *any* Russian government in order to keep Russia in the war and opposed to Germany.[6] Further, certain American leaders, including Colonel House, were willing to recognize Lenin and Trotsky and use their claims in the Far East to oppose the expansionist desires of Japan.[7] The aim at the root of these demands was self-preservation: the protection of a set of interests already defined.

The same was true later of economic groups and interests favoring recognition. Thus former Red Cross official Raymond Robins insisted that recognition would increase trade, and trade would help all segments of the American economy. Senator Borah agreed and even held that the depression of 1929 could be overcome by a more active trade with the Soviets. The president of General Motors Export Company commented that this position was "so sound from the standpoint . . . of economics that [it admits] of no controversy." [8] Still other economic and financial interests, during the twenties, took the lead in obtaining concessions in Russia for the development of automobile, machine-tool, agricultural-implement, and manganese industries. American engineering consultants, architects, and designers flocked to the Soviet Union and added their voices to the clamor for recognition.[9]

A final reason persuading certain groups and individuals to favor recognition lay in a general desire to strengthen American values and institutions. Thus Borah and Robins equated the safety of American beliefs with a stable world and the prevalence of peace, which in turn required the recognition of every nonaggressive government. They foresaw nothing but future tension if the ostracism of Russia were to continue. Self-preservation was the keynote again.

Yet a note of self-extension was equally prominent in another aspect of these demands. Robins, Borah, diplomat William Bullitt, and financier Alexander Gumberg also hoped that by recognizing, aiding, and influencing the fledgling Soviet regime they might be enabled to transform it into a less totalitarian and anticapitalist set of institutions. They counted on Soviet dearth of funds, on starvation and military weakness, to induce the Soviet leaders to make domestic and international concessions to the America which

[6] *Ibid.,* pp. 109, 115, 120, 135.
[7] *Ibid.,* pp. 127, 140, 151, 186.

[8] *Ibid.,* pp. 218, 236.
[9] *Ibid.,* pp. 142, 145–146, 160, 217, 223.

was to recognize and aid them.[10] Hence their ends were geared to the extension of American views on government and society, even though their arguments remained ineffective in persuading the bulk of American opinion.

What was the ideological framework of these proponents of recognition? The dilemma of many liberals on the issue is well illustrated by the vacillations of President Woodrow Wilson. The Democratic President believed in gradual reform—at home and abroad—but opposed revolution and therefore had little patience with the Bolsheviks. Thus he wavered between policies of moderation and attempts at negotiation with Moscow on the one hand, and a course of opposition and intervention on the other. Once the latter was decided, however, Wilson seemed to regret it and was instrumental in terminating the American share in the military effort to unseat the Bolsheviks. Other liberals, by contrast, believed in the possibility of transforming the Soviet regime into an image of the socially and economically "progressive" system which they favored at home and abroad. Peace through adaptation to new international forces and institutions was held out as desirable and dictated these modes of defining American interests, in sharp opposition to the viewpoint prevalent among conservatives.[11]

American Socialists and Communists welcomed the Soviet victory and of course favored recognition accordingly. Yet their values were symbols of opposition to the great mass of Americans; they were considered un-American, undesirable, and, in some cases, criminal. Socialist sympathies for the Soviets undoubtedly contributed to the reinforcement of antirecognition sentiment, especially since left-wing labor leaders were then being blamed for union violence and industrial unrest.

Forces and Beliefs Opposing Recognition. The military rationale of self-preservation loomed in the antirecognition camp as well. Thus President Hoover, when concerned over the future of the Far East in 1931, was disinclined to oppose Japan, in part at least because he hoped to create an antidote to Soviet power in that area.[12] Similar arguments were voiced as early as 1919.

Self-preservation, moreover, was the main consideration of a number of important economic groups in the United States. Lumber interests urged continued nonrecognition in order to exclude Russian competition. Manganese producers agreed. Important segments of American labor opposed the Soviet Union on the economic grounds that Soviet slave labor—reckoned at 1 million persons in 1930—would furnish unfair competition for American unions.[13] Conversely, the American decision to abandon the nonrecognition in 1933 was partly the result of the conversion of many of these groups to Borah's position, hoping to overcome the depression by greater foreign trade.

[10] *Ibid.*, pp. 142, 145–146, 160.
[11] *Ibid.*, pp. 107, 123, 115, 146, 124, 203.
[12] *Ibid.*, pp. 127, 226.
[13] *Ibid.*, pp. 203, 223, 224.

Opposition to recognition was also strong among economic groups bent on self-extension. The hope of using the temporary eclipse of Russia's external power to acquire American control over the Chinese Eastern Railway provides one example. While this aim was espoused only by a few railroad interests and the State Department,[14] a much more ambitious end was sought by the American-Russian Chamber of Commerce in its general demand that the demise of Russia be used as a wedge to permit American capital and enterprise to penetrate the Russian market to the exclusion of other foreign interests. In the words of one backer of this scheme, he was "trying to get a coterie of bankers organized . . . who would take hold of Russia in a large way." [15]

While this program was never consistently implemented by Washington, Herbert Hoover, on becoming Secretary of Commerce in 1921, used its rationale in his administration of the American famine relief program. "The relief measures," said Hoover, "will build a situation which, combined with the other factors, will enable the Americans to undertake the leadership in the reconstruction of Russia when the proper moment arrives." [16] Relief was to become a means for commercial expansion.

Opposition to recognition was most vocally and consistently developed, moreover, on the general level of ideology and values. This is shown in the positions of the American Federation of Labor and the Allied Patriotic Societies. Samuel Gompers, for the AFL, held that toleration of a communist workers' movement would endanger the nonpolitical character of American labor and give a bad name to unionism. And the patriots demanded that "we not only commend the policy of non-recognition . . . but condemn the attempts of certain financial interests to compromise such a policy." [17] Self-preservation was the keynote: the success of communism seemed to imperil the stability of these domestic institutions and groups.

To the extent that these sentiments called for a policy of intervention, however, they approached the end of self-extension. Democrat Robert Lansing as well as Republicans Hoover and Charles E. Hughes thus were anxious to suppress the revolution. An American consul in Russia insisted on aiding "all classes of Russians standing for law and order," while Lansing expressed his "disappointment and amazement" with respect to the "class despotism" in Russia and favored American backing for any Russian movement which would give the country a military dictatorship.[18] The National Civic Federation, which included Samuel Gompers as well as important industrial leaders, heartily concurred. In 1921, Hoover announced that negotiations with the Soviets were possible only after the "abandonment of their present economic

---

[14] *Ibid.*, pp. 106, 163, 183.
[15] *Ibid.*, pp. 148–149, 152.
[16] *Ibid.*, p. 193.

[17] *Ibid.*, p. 237.
[18] *Ibid.*, pp. 112, 116, 117.

system," a decision with which Secretary of State Hughes agreed.[19] Hughes took this stand in opposition to members of his own party who urged recognition in order to make investment in Russia easier. No economic arguments could shake his determination not to deal with Moscow, a stand based on his conviction that no aid of any kind be extended to a Communist government. His position was backed by groups of financiers who owned Soviet-canceled czarist bonds. These financiers sought to use nonrecognition as a weapon to force Moscow to pay.

The ideological framework of the opponents of recognition deserves attention. Conservatives generally rallied to the nonrecognition banner because they opposed the values associated with the Bolshevik cause. Lansing argued that the revolution was bound to "make the ignorant and incapable mass of humanity dominant in the earth" and he confided to his diary that "the correct policy for a government which believes in political institutions as they now exist and based on nationality and private property is to leave these dangerous idealists alone and have no direct dealings with them." [20] Hoover and Hughes, of course, concurred because of their parallel belief in the "naturalness" of private property as the key to a stable society.[21]

Since conservatism was the dominant ideological feature of America in the twenties, it is hardly surprising that key labor, fraternal, patriotic, and business leaders tended to agree. The same is true of the professional policy makers in the State Department. These men—Miles, Polk, Phillips, and Kelley—supported the aims of their chiefs. If the civil-service code dictates the identification of the civil servant with whatever ideology has gained political recognition in the elected portions of the government, no different approach could have been expected. Condemnations of Russia and the Russians as "not much superior to animals with brutal instincts" occurred in staff memoranda. As late as 1933, Robert Kelley still argued that "difficulties arising out of the profound differences between the economic and social structure of the two countries" would prevent normal relations; and he made it quite clear that he favored the use of this issue to prevent recognition altogether.[22] When the prorecognition forces carried the day, the pattern of conservative thinking among these civil servants by no means evaporated at the same time.

Ends and Means. Strikingly, a hierarchy of ends appeared in this array of aims, of varying importance to the policy maker and of varying significance to the many groups who participated in the definition of policy. Furthermore, what appeared as ends to some were no more than a useful set of means to others.

First, the relationship between ends and means was expressed in the

[19] *Ibid.*, pp. 137, 181–182, 190.
[20] *Ibid.*, pp. 106, 117, 123.
[21] *Ibid.*, pp. 181, 183.
[22] *Ibid.*, pp. 108, 117, 219, 239.

struggle between economic and political factors. Thus Senator Borah and Secretary Hughes, for entirely different reasons, were willing to use economic measures to achieve a more basic political purpose. Politics was the end; economics provided the means. On the one hand, Borah was committed to a policy of peace and therefore encouraged the recognition of Moscow to eliminate indefinite hostility. To this end, he encouraged the expansion of Soviet-American trade and investments. On the other hand, Secretary Hughes opposed the Soviet regime on political grounds and wished its early dissolution. Hence he refused to give Soviet traders credit facilities in the United States and turned a deaf ear to American exporters who demanded a relaxation of credit and export restrictions. He also used the economic means of boycott to serve his political convictions, at some financial disadvantage to his own political supporters in the ranks of business. Similarly to the State Department people who entertained the notion of linking economic with military and diplomatic intervention, the economic aspect once more was merely an instrument. Thus Lansing left no doubt that to him economic penetration was no more than a lever to unseat Lenin's group.[23]

The reverse, however, was true of the opposing groups in the United States who argued for and against recognition on economic grounds alone. Concessionaires and traders who wished to enter the promising Soviet market were interested only in facilitating their private ends. They argued for recognition, after 1921, in order to find access to Russia easier, regardless of the impact of Communist thought on the United States. Recognition was for them a political means to an economic end. Similarly, the affiliates of the American-Russian Chamber of Commerce and the societies of bondholders who exerted pressure on Washington to make the Soviets pay the debts of the czarist government put economic interests first. One wished intervention in Russia in 1917 in order to penetrate the Russian economy, and the other argued for nonrecognition in order to put pressure on Russia to pay. Whether the intervention resulted in the overthrow of the Communist regime was immaterial to them. Political measures again were merely instruments to an economic end.

Nor is the problem of means and ends clear-cut in as "humanitarian" an area as famine relief. To be sure, the major ends of American social workers and relief officials in Russia in 1921 were to avert starvation. To those who initiated and financed the policy, however, relief was a means to the dual end of gaining information about the Russian economy and trying to create conditions of well-being in Russia which would make the doctrinaire appeal of communism less inviting. Much the same reasoning also held true in the ranks of those who favored a generally pro-Soviet policy. They also backed relief and trade as a means of exerting pressure on Russia's rulers. They hoped for a gradual and voluntary transformation of Communist institutions

[23] *Ibid.*, p. 149.

and therefore supported every American move to expand Western concepts, especially in such "nonpolitical" arenas as famine relief. Thus what appeared as ultimate ends to some groups represented instruments toward a more basic end to others.

Essentially the same holds true in the realm of military thought. To the military attachés who wished to keep Russia in the war in 1917, the winning of the war was the major end. To the statesmen in Washington, postwar relations between Communist Russia and the world were of more significance than the problem of whether the war was won in 1918 or 1920. To the military, the war itself is the end to be kept in mind in the making of diplomatic decisions. To the diplomat, by contrast, the military effort is merely part of a larger picture of international relations. Policy aims and decisions must differ accordingly, as they did in the setting of 1917.

Nor can military ends always be differentiated easily from economic aims, and vice versa. Certainly in the decision to intervene militarily in Siberia, in the summer of 1918, both considerations were present. For those who, like Colonel House, saw in the intervention a measure to stop the Japanese, the military effort was the main end. Yet for those who wished to acquire control over the Chinese Eastern Railway, military intervention was an instrument to serve an economic aim. Finally, for the group which saw in Admiral Kolchak's Siberian government the proper antidote to Lenin's Communist regime in Moscow, military intervention was a means to effect the political displacement of the Bolsheviks. Three different conceptions of ends and means—and consequently three different appraisals of the success or failure of the whole policy—thus entered into a given policy in a specific situation.

Importance of Correct Identification. The complexity of the policy-making process in the instance of the alternatives of recognizing or opposing the Soviet Union is indeed formidable. The identification of ends of self-extension and their separation from aspirations limited to self-preservation was particularly difficult, since sometimes one was used as a means to realize the other. Essentially the same difficulty prevails if we try to analyze the definition of policy aims of any other complex pluralistic community. Did Japan expand into China and Manchuria because she wanted to preserve her vulnerable economy or because she wished to impose her institutions on the Chinese? Were the leaders of the Soviet Union interested in protecting their western frontier against new German invasions in 1945, and was that why they all but annexed Eastern Europe, or were they anxious to impose Communist institutions and values on the Poles and Hungarians? In short, how can ends of policy ever be identified with any degree of certainty?

Facile labeling of any policy as self-preservation or self-extension is not only inaccurate but highly dangerous. Misidentification may result in wrong decisions on the part of the statesman and in a misreading of history on the part of the social scientist. Yet identification is essential to understand the forces in one's own country and those of its antagonists. Only a careful study of interest groups and their aspirations, policy statements, ideological pronouncements, lobbying, propaganda symbols, legislative debates, and trends in public opinion can give any assurance that specific policies are directed at self-extension or self-preservation. The outward effects and manifestations of foreign policy are inadequate criteria of the intentions underlying them. Group aims explain the adoption of given policies; group aims contain the keys to what is self-preservation, self-extension, or self-abnegation.

6. Can Consistent Policy Be Made? In international politics, it can now be concluded, different groups profess different ends. Further, they base their definition of ends on varying ideologies. Finally, they do not always agree whether a given item in the foreign policy of their nation is an end in itself or whether it serves as a means toward an end. Hence, from the point of view of the participating interest groups in the community, a clear agreement on how the ends of policy differ from the means selected to achieve them cannot be expected. Consequently the evaluation of a given policy as a success or a failure will rarely be unanimous. From the point of view of some it will appear as a resounding victory over alien groups, while from the ideologically defined position of other groups it may fall far short of this achievement.

The Case of Korea. The inability of a complex pluralistic community to come to a clear agreement on what are ends and means in foreign policy raises the key problem of how a rational integration of policy can be brought about. The conduct of the Korean War by the United States is a clear case in point. From the point of view of many groups identified with the Democratic party, the end of the war was the containment of Communist power by pushing the North Korean and Chinese armies back over the 38th parallel. Military, propaganda, economic, and diplomatic measures were merely the means for achieving this basic aim. However, from the point of view of some groups identified with the Republican party the end of the war was to defeat communism in Asia by striking at the nerve-center of Red Chinese strength and unifying Korea under the pro-American Syngman Rhee government. Policy ends being defined differently, the truce at the 38th parallel was viewed as a symbol of success by the Democrats and became a stigma of defeat for some Republicans. From the viewpoint of the latter a gross disproportion between ends and means prevailed, since American military and diplomatic strength was not used to full advantage: Korea was not unified, Manchuria was not bombed, and Chinese Nationalist attacks on the mainland were given less support than might have been possible. Since United

States policy tended to vacillate between these two approaches, neither ends nor means were rigidly defined, and no agreement was possible on generally acceptable means for a clear policy aim of self-preservation in East Asia.

Consistent Policy in a Democracy. Since values are implicit in the definition of basic aims and since the more interest groups compete for influence the greater the number of rival values becomes, agreement on ends and means grows increasingly difficult in the more complex communities, especially democracies. Yet even democracies may produce a consensus which eliminates the difficulty. The mere fact that nationalism continues to be the single most cohesive bond may imply the possibility of near unanimity on what are ends and which means they subsume for implementation. Given this possibility, means will be adjusted rationally to the collective ends they are to serve. If, for example, there were unanimous American agreement on the need to extend democracy by defeating communism in Russia, such unanimity would make easy the adoption of the proper military, diplomatic, and propaganda means, calculated specifically for the attainment of this single overriding end.

However, as soon as this agreement is riddled by varying conceptions of *why* communism should be defeated and *what kind* of democracy is to take its place, consensus evaporates and the discussion over means to be adopted becomes an integral part of the controversy over ends. In short, means cannot be rationally adjusted to the ends they are to serve if there is no agreement on what the end is.

Consistent Policy under Totalitarianism. Nor is the problem of ends and means much simpler in the case of totalitarian systems. When the ruling elite is a coalition of various interests—as in Nazi Germany—much the same difficulties are encountered as in the case of democratic practices. Here the problem is that of reconciling various ideologies and views on ends into an integrated policy. But in the case of the Soviet Union the problem is just as real. Is the basic aim of the Soviet government self-preservation or self-extension? Does the question arise if the basic incompatibility of communism with capitalism and the need for conflict between them is accepted as dogma? Soviet policy offers no unambiguous clues in answer, and certainly Communist ideology has shown sufficient "flexibility" to make deduction from ideological principles a most hazardous procedure.

Thus in 1935 Soviet leaders spoke only of the need for peace, collective security, and steady internal economic growth. Yet at the time the Soviet Union was comparatively weak and on the defensive against Japan and a resurgent Germany. The policy contrasts strikingly with statements made since 1945, in which the theme of self-extension has been heard. Furthermore, Soviet policies have commonly borne the imprint of expansive intent. As ideology and objective conditions change, even the policy aims of relatively homogeneous elites undergo transformations in which the problem of what is an aim of policy and what is merely a tactical means is far from plain.

Standard Means of Policy. No doubt, it would be most helpful for the analysis of the dynamics of international relations if a simple symmetry could be established in which ends of policy are linked with values, interests, and ideology, while means remain neutral with respect to these features. If it were possible to proceed in this manner, concentration on ends alone would afford the majority of insights needed in our quest, since means would merely be the ideologically neutral techniques which any group anywhere would adopt in striving for the fulfillment of its aims. As has been seen, however, no such simple symmetry exists. Ends are defined not by generally accepted aims but by the preferences peculiar to the value system of each group and nation. Means, therefore, remain indissolubly mixed with group values and group aims. Far from being neutral, they are themselves part and parcel of the values which policy makers and elites profess.

Nevertheless, definite techniques in the conduct of international relations occur with such regularity in our era—regardless of the democratic or authoritarian character of the community using them—that it is justifiable to retain our distinction between ends and means. Among these techniques are diplomacy, the search for allies and the building of alliance systems, the large-scale application of external propaganda to make friends and weaken enemies, the use of economic and social methods for purposes of assuring domestic prosperity, and the increasingly significant use of identical methods for the political end of strengthening one's friends and hurting one's enemies. Finally, war—declared or undeclared, hot or cold, with the United Nations or without—remains a technique of international relations which continues ever present in the minds of policy makers and the expectations of nations. All these methods of conducting foreign relations are accepted as standard practices by all nations, whatever their ideologies and myths may be.

In introducing the discussion of means in international relations, however, it remains true that policy makers are *not* free to adopt any technique which may be expected to yield results. The application of specific means is possible only if the values of the community and the ideology of the elite or government permit it. Just as a democracy is prevented by its myth from undertaking a preventive war—even though this may be "rational" under certain conditions—so is a dictatorship usually bound to remain within the strictures of its own symbols. If the Soviet Union professes peace and uses the peace theme in its external and internal propaganda, it limits its ability to go to war under any and all circumstances. Thus means remain linked to values and ideology, thereby limiting the freedom of action of elites and policy makers.

Within this framework, then, it is necessary to move from the problem of ends to those of national power and of means. Without losing sight of the all-pervasive influence of ends, the factors of power which condition the definition of aims in the first place must be examined. Then can follow a discussion of the various means for carrying out policy aims, of the problems inherent in their use as well as their abuse.

ADDITIONAL CASE-STUDY MATERIAL

Bendix, R., and S. Lipset (eds.): *Class, Status and Power,* Free Press, Glencoe, Ill., 1953.

Furniss, E. S., Jr.: *The Office of the Premier in French Foreign Policy-making: An Application of Decision-making Analysis,* Foreign Policy Analysis Project 5, Princeton University, Organizational Behavior Section, Princeton, N.J., 1954.

Lundberg, I. C.: "World Revolution, American Plan," *Harper's,* December, 1948.

Macmahon, Arthur W.: *Administration in Foreign Affairs,* University of Alabama Press, University, Ala., 1953.

Marvel, William W.: "Foreign Aid and United States Security," unpublished Ph.D. dissertation, Princeton University, Princeton, N.J., 1951.

Merton, R. K.: "Role of the Intellectual in Public Bureaucracy," *Social Forces,* vol. 23, 1945.

———: "Social Structure and Anomie," *American Sociological Review,* vol. 3, 1938.

Michels, R.: *Political Parties,* Free Press, Glencoe, Ill., 1949.

Neumann, F.: *Behemoth,* Oxford, New York, 1944.

Neumann, R. G.: *European and Comparative Government,* McGraw-Hill, New York, 1951.

Osgood, R. E.: *Ideals and Self-interest in America's Foreign Relations,* University of Chicago Press, Chicago, 1953.

Parsons, T.: *Essays in Sociological Theory, Pure and Applied,* Free Press, Glencoe, Ill., 1949.

Rappaport, Armin: "The Navy League of the United States," *The South Atlantic Quarterly,* vol. 53, April, 1954.

Scalapino, R. A.: *Democracy and the Party Movement in Prewar Japan,* University of California Press, Berkeley, Calif., 1953.

Schuman, F. L.: *The Commonwealth of Man,* Knopf, New York, 1952.

Snyder, R., H. W. Bruck, and B. Sapin: *Decision-making as an Approach to the Study of International Politics,* Foreign Policy Analysis Project 3, Princeton University, Organizational Behavior Section, Princeton, N.J., 1954.

Stein, Harold (ed.): *Public Administration and Policy Development,* Harcourt, Brace, New York, 1952.

U.S. Department of State, *Postwar Foreign Policy Preparation,* 1949.

Williams, W. A.: *American Russian Relations, 1781–1947,* Rinehart, New York, 1952.

———: "The Legend of Isolationism in the 1920's," *Science and Society,* vol. 18, winter, 1954.

PART TWO

FACTORS OF POWER

Chapter 5

TANGIBLE FACTORS OF POWER

1. Power: Meaning and Significance. Epigrams and mottos insult reality; they force complex life into simple words. Perhaps few sayings have been more repeated with reference to the nature of power in international relations than the familiar "God is on the side of the biggest battalions." Measuring power solely in physical prowess, this concept is countered by an equally familiar aphorism, "Nothing is so powerful as an idea which has arrived." This second saying would define power in philosophical or ideological terms. Both approaches assume power is composed of a single factor, to the subordination of all other factors. Obviously this is not the case. Soviet Russia and the United States, the two most powerful countries in the world, enjoy supremacy because of their physical strength and because of the attraction of their ideology. Neither Soviet steel output nor American atomic bombs alone hold vast sections of Asia and Europe to a pro-Moscow or a pro-Washington orientation. Neither battalions nor ideas separately suffice to explain the power of these two countries in all areas of the globe.

For purposes of this discussion, then, power is a function of many factors, some of them tangible, such as raw materials and industrial production, some of them intangible, such as technology and morale. Power is synonymous with strength and might be defined as the amount of force available to a nation's elite toward the accomplishment of any given aid. Note that power is not synonymous with ends; nations do not vie *for* power but their struggle is *of* power, for ends rooted in values and interests. Furthermore, power is not synonymous with means, the way in which ends are achieved. It provides the force whereby means succeed, be they military, economic, political, or psychological. To put it another way, policy makers frame their problem in three questions: "What do we wish to accomplish?" "What ways may we employ to accomplish it?" and "What strength is at our disposal in support of these different ways?"

By approaching power through the eyes of the policy maker, it is possible to see its subjective role, suggested in Chapter 2. Gross disparities of power may be viewed differently according to the calculations of different elites, as dramatically evidenced by the Japanese military groups in World War II, who added a war with the United States to a four-year struggle to conquer China. True, only total war provides the final definitive test of power. But power is a constant referrent in nonmilitary international relations. Elites act and react according to their expectations of severe deprivations which they can inflict on others and/or which others can inflict on them. In this sense power is what men conceive it to be, a calculation of power factors related to nations or groups of nations.

In addition, power has objective reality, capable of measurement by the scientific observer. Such measurement is necessary if we are to judge the degree of fantasy or reality in the view of policy makers. While it is impossible to pinpoint the power factor which may determine victory or defeat in two closely balanced countries which have radically different points of strength and weakness, the majority of instances permit rational calculation of comparative power sufficient to determine the ability of one side to inflict severe deprivation upon the other.

Therefore the factors of power must be examined as regarded by those who determine international relations, to see what they consider sources of strength and weakness and what ways they adopt for maximizing strength. At the same time understanding the dynamics of power enables the observer independently to assess the validity of power calculations by elites. Tangible factors of location, topography, climate, size, population, raw materials, and productivity combine with intangible factors of technology, propaganda, and morale to produce the total power view of our study.

Power is the amount of force *available* to elites; and one of the three questions posed by policy makers is: "What means might be employed in search of ends?" This raises the first obstacle to absolute power, for national power is of importance only when it is capable of being used. Statistics showing human and industrial resources are meaningless unless they are related to the ends and means of policy. As has been shown, values and interests determine what ruling groups wish to accomplish and also how they may accomplish it. Apparent power may not be available to a nation's elite if its ideology precludes use of that power. Thus, for purposes of international relations, that power does not exist; it cannot be translated into action. Postwar America was the most "powerful" nation in terms of industrial output and atomic bombs, but prevailing ideology denied use of these bombs against a Communist bloc, nullifying much of this "power."

The example of postwar American policy, particularly in Korea, suggested a second limitation upon evaluation of power, namely, counterpower in the hands of other nations. Taken alone, American production figures tell nothing of America's world position. Juxtaposed with those of Soviet Russia, they present a crude picture of defensive, if not offensive, strength.

TABLE 1. WESTERN EUROPE–UNITED STATES–SOVIET UNION: STATISTICS OF RELATIVE POWER

	Population, estimated, 1953	Production, thousand metric tons, estimated, 1953		
		Coal and lignite	Crude steel	Crude petroleum
United States...................	159,629,000	439,031	101,250	318,929
Europe, west of Iron Curtain........	311,000,000	624,546	62,511	4,842
Soviet Union and Eastern Europe....	294,000,000	434,300	48,223	62,715

SOURCE: *U.N. Statistical Yearbook*, United Nations, Statistical Office, New York, 1954. Population, pp. 24–33; coal and lignite, pp. 113–116; crude steel, pp. 233–234; crude petroleum, pp. 118–119.

However, by adding the output of Western Europe to the Soviet bloc, its collective power significantly balances that of the United States. Thus power is a relative concept whose content changes according to differing combinations of opposing nations. Countries are powerful only in comparison with other countries in a given combination of alliance and counteralliance.

Just as the dynamics of international relations compel national power to be measured in terms of the possible combinations of power which might be arranged against it, so the dynamics of human development subject power to a third limitation, that of time and technological change. Changes in technology affect power no less than changes in alliances. England's world supremacy in the nineteenth century rested on her monopoly of capital, her primacy in the Industrial Revolution, and her consequent control of the seas. One hundred years later, the United States became the center of international capital control, with an ascendant place in the Atomic Revolution, and enjoying limited but widespread control of the skies. England's industrial preeminence of 1850 gave way to the more advanced American industrial giant of 1940, in turn closely challenged by the new Russian industrial nexus of 1955. In the mid-nineteenth century, control of coal established power. In the mid-twentieth century, control of oil became paramount. For the future, it appears to be control of uranium which will determine victor and vanquished. It is not inconceivable that technology may one day make sand a basic factor of power, turning North Africa and Outer Mongolia into pivotal areas of development.

Power, then, is never absolute but relative, to be measured in terms of its possessors, in terms of its competitors, and in terms of its future. No brief treatment such as this can hope to give a definitive power picture of the major states, nor is such a statistical analysis necessary for the present purpose. Rather it is necessary to grasp the basic means of analyzing power, appreciate its place in the larger picture of international relations, and finally obtain a working knowledge of the relative strength of major regions of the globe.

2. Physical Foundations. *Geopolitics.* Taking first the tangible factors of power, the most immediate and rudimentary are those connected with physical geography, namely, location, topography, climate, and size. Just as in analyzing the strength of a building, one begins not with the steel and concrete framework but with the foundation upon which it rests, so with the strength of a nation the analysis begins with the basic factor of land and the influences at work upon it. Because of the permanence of this factor as contrasted with man's relatively brief history, various efforts have been made to build a science of international relations in terms of geography and politics, known as *geopolitics*. Ranging from generalizations on national characteristics allegedly derived from climate or race, to systematic studies of land versus naval and air warfare, these efforts have won the attention of statesmen and strategists, anxious to find rules for success in self-preservation or self-extension.

Successive technological revolutions in military tactics have forced continued revisions in geopolitical theories, but basically they may be divided into those which focus on a central land mass as a base of operations, and those which seek to surround a land mass with peripheral control. The first concept considers the Eurasian continent, stretching roughly from central Germany to central Russia, as a strategic heartland which contains sufficient size for maneuver, resources for exploitation, and population for mobilization as to be virtually impregnable, if not able to dominate the world. According to this theory, control of this heartland by any single power would give it an unsurpassable advantage over the rest of the globe. A second geopolitical theory, directly contrary to the first, views the European and Asian coastline as a rimland, control of which assures domination over the vital sea lanes of the Pacific and Atlantic Oceans. In varied form, rimland theories also assume that any nation which wins the rimland also wins hegemony over the inner land masses as well as the outer sea lanes.

As in all single-factor analyses of national power, geopolitics fails to provide a comprehensive guide for the policy maker, but its influence is recurrent nevertheless. Because it uses the immediately perceived factors of location and size, it provides a convenient rationale for claim to territory on so-called strategic grounds. Reduced to its proper perspective, geopolitics provides fruitful insights into the weight that policy makers accord the physical foundations of location, topography, climate, and size in the scales of national power.

Location. Location defines a nation's spatial relationship with the rest of the world. It may be one of marine isolation, as with Australia, or of land communication, as with Korea. The people of Down Under may feel left out of the international spotlight, but at the same time their country's peaceful existence is in part a result of its distance from the centers of international conflict. Conversely, Korea has been termed a dagger, aimed both at the heart of Japan and the heart of Manchuria. Its ancient culture disintegrated under successive wars between foreign powers, occupation, and liberation which shook Korea from 1870 to the present. Astride the communication lines leading to China, Russia, and Japan, it seems destined to remain forever under the "protection" of whichever neighbor enjoys domination at the time. Location may bring mixed blessings, as in the case of Germany. Situated at the crossroads of European commerce, Germany enjoys a position of influence unparalleled by that of its neighbors. At the same time, lying between the Communist heartland and the NATO coalition, Germany cannot look forward to avoiding the ravages of war should East and West collide.

Location is one of the transitory factors of power, its importance varying according to technological as well as political developments. For almost a century, the Suez Canal has given Egypt an importance in international relations far above that of other Middle Eastern countries. Substitution of air for sea power, as well as the transshipment of Middle Eastern oil by pipeline instead of tanker through the Persian Gulf, radically lessens the strategic importance of Suez and with it Egypt.

Conversely, Arctic stretches, traditionally regarded as worthless wasteland, suddenly catapult into the headlines as scenes of military maneuvers and as bases for meteorological stations. Because the shortest routes between Russia and the United States pass over the polar region, possession of Arctic territory is held vital to the security of both countries. Ten years hence, rocket weapons may nullify importance of the Arctic, and it, too, will pass into the limbo of "has-been" locations.

Topography. Topography, the configuration of land, works less obviously on a nation's power than does location, though with a higher degree of permanence, at least in its internal aspects. Mountains endow Japan with an abundance of water power but ruthlessly limit the amount of arable soil. Great rivers provide China with avenues of cheap transportation and irrigation but periodically have swept over vast areas in destructive floods. Both America and Russia enjoy wide diversity of topography, permitting mining in mountains, extensive farming on great plains, and the harnessing of rivers for power. In the Soviet Union—as compared to West Europe—however, rivers prove less of an asset because their flow is mainly on a north-south axis, whereas Russian transport needs extend east and west. One need only compare the topography of desert-dominated North Africa with that of rolling West Europe to see the effect of topography upon food and communication, ingredients of power.

While it is true that the internal effects of topography can be altered somewhat by human effort, physical foundations are least amenable to human change of all factors of power. Vast irrigation projects in India, China, and Russia can raise the food output of Asia, but these in turn require tremendous investment of capital. Great dikes may hold back the seas from Holland's rich lowlands, but the danger of national catastrophe, man-made as in World War II or natural as in 1952, remains forever in the background.

In its external consequences, topography conditions the accessibility of a nation. In time of peace, easy access may be a desirable feature for the development of foreign trade. War, however, may make limited access an asset, as both mountain-ringed Tibet and ocean-bounded America have discovered. So-called natural barriers have steadily shrunk with the development of faster means of travel, until today the English Channel is like an ancient moat surrounding a castle, of questionable effectiveness in stemming a determined, well-equipped invader. Similarly, oil locked in the northern stretches of Labrador or uranium in the Belgian Congo prove readily accessible to the combined assault of air, sea, and land communication.

Climate. Climate, a function both of location and topography, remains a constant factor of power, as a determinant of both agricultural output and human activity. Drought can impoverish wealthy Texans or wipe out near-starvation Chinese. Winter can tie up Europe's transportation, exhaust England's coal supplies, or freeze most of Russia's ports. Balanced seasons can bulge American granaries to the point of overflow, or give Eastern Europe exportable surpluses with which to purchase industrial equipment. Perhaps no clearer cause-and-effect relationship of climate and power, at least in the short-run sense, is provided than by the dilemma of British coal. Short in supply since the end of World War II, largely because of technological problems connected with labor costs, market price, and mining methods, British coal has barely met British needs. So acute was this problem in the summer of 1953, the *Manchester Guardian Weekly* commented,[1]

> The difference between this year and last in mean national temperatures . . . has been only 0.4 of a degree Fahrenheit. Our industrial survival may hang by a thread, but it should surely hang by a slightly thicker thread than four-tenths of a degree of temperature. . . . These figures show what havoc a few weeks of snow or prolonged frost could bring to national life next winter. . . . By the beginning of winter the position may be even more precarious.

[1] *Manchester Guardian Weekly*, July 2, 1953, p. 9.

In a different sense, human activity appears conditioned by climate. A glance at the globe reveals that almost all of contemporary history has centered in the temperate zone of the Northern Hemisphere. That this coincides with mineral-laden land masses is undoubtedly part of the reason, but there seems little doubt that man does not seek out the extreme climates in which to build civilization. Air-conditioning and central heating notwithstanding, climate still restricts and channelizes human endeavor in one section of the globe.

Size. Finally, there is size, probably the most deceptive of the physical foundations of power. Size is deceptive enough in itself, given the primitive symbolism which equates bigness with strength and smallness with weakness. However, man has increased its deceptiveness by his abuse of maps. Entire generations, schooled by the Mercator projection, believed that Greenland, northern Canada, and Siberia were the dominant land masses of the Northern Hemisphere and that the shortest routes from Japan to America and from America to Europe spanned the Pacific and Atlantic Oceans. Although Columbus proved the world to be round, mapmakers continued to distort it into flatness, rendering true only that part near the equator. In moving from sea to air travel, man has simultaneously improved his map making, so that our picture of the world now more closely approximates reality.

Japan is the classic illustration of the disparity between size and power. Many scoffed at its chances of defeating the United States in 1941, yet spacewise, this was no more improbable than Japan's victory over czarist Russia in 1905. Indeed, plenitude of space proved detrimental to Russia because it required shipment of men and munitions across more than six thousand miles of single-track railroad. To be sure, size played a role in Japan's defeat by America, in that congested Japan had little room in which to disperse her factories and depopulate her cities. Consequently American air and naval bombardment took a heavy toll which might otherwise have been avoided. The fact remains that the significance of size was completely reversed in the two campaigns, and in neither instance was success a consequence merely of size.

Size may play a most perverse role in the balance sheet of a nation's power. In peacetime, Russia's 8.5 million square miles of territory poses serious transportation problems. While the principal concentration of industry and population fills a triangle running from Leningrad near the Baltic Sea, to Odessa on the Black Sea, to the Kuznetsk Basin in Siberia, its minerals are scattered throughout the distant northern and far eastern stretches of the U.S.S.R. The economics of peace demand proximity of resources and manufacture. However, the logistics of war make Russia's size a definite asset, provided it is a war of maneuver, unlike the Russo-Japanese War. Celebrated in military chronicles are the Russian retreats of 1812 and 1940, the first sucking Napoleon into defeat on the wintry plains of Moscow, the second luring

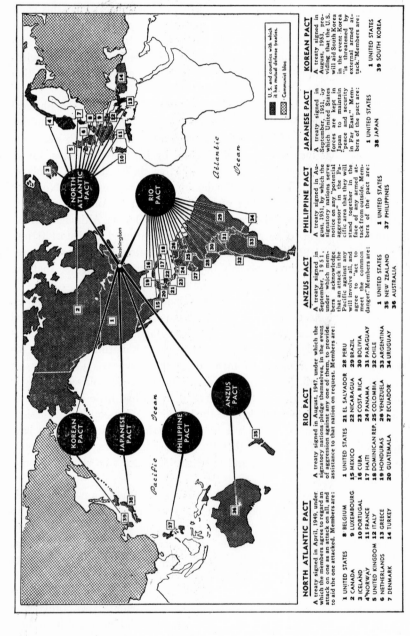

U. S. and countries with which it has mutual defense treaties.

Communist bloc

KOREAN PACT

A treaty signed in August, 1953, providing that the U.S. will aid South Korea in the event Korea "is threatened by external armed attack."Members are:

1 UNITED STATES
39 SOUTH KOREA

JAPANESE PACT

A treaty signed in September, 1951, by which United States forces are kept in Japan to maintain peace and security in Far East." Members of the pact are:

1 UNITED STATES
38 JAPAN

PHILIPINE PACT

A treaty signed in August, 1951, by which the signatory nations serve notice on any "potential aggressor" in the Pacific area that they will stand together in the face of any armed attack from outside. Members of the pact are:

1 UNITED STATES
37 PHILIPPINES

ANZUS PACT

A treaty signed in September, 1951, under which members acknowledge that an attack in the Pacific against any will involve all, and agree to "act to meet the common danger." Members are:

1 UNITED STATES
35 NEW ZEALAND
36 AUSTRALIA

RIO PACT

A treaty signed in August, 1947, under which the signatory nations pledge themselves, in the event of aggression against any one of them, to provide assistance to that nation on request. Members are:

1 UNITED STATES
15 MEXICO
16 CUBA
17 HAITI
18 DOMINICAN REP.
19 HONDURAS
20 GUATEMALA
21 EL SALVADOR
22 NICARAGUA
23 COSTA RICA
24 PANAMA
25 COLOMBIA
26 VENEZUELA
27 ECUADOR
28 PERU
29 BRAZIL
30 BOLIVIA
31 PARAGUAY
32 CHILE
33 ARGENTINA
34 URUGUAY

NORTH ATLANTIC PACT

A treaty signed in April, 1949, under which the members agree to regard an attack on one as an attack on all, and to aid the one attacked. Members are:

1 UNITED STATES
2 CANADA
3 ICELAND
4 NORWAY
5 UNITED KINGDOM
6 NETHERLANDS
7 DENMARK
8 BELGIUM
9 LUXEMBOURG
10 PORTUGAL
11 FRANCE
12 ITALY
13 GREECE
14 TURKEY

The world: Mercator's projection. SOURCE: *The New York Times*, Feb. 14, 1954.

Hitler's legions to decimation before both Moscow and Stalingrad. Russia's size permitted her to bargain away vast chunks of territory in exchange for time to regroup her civilian and military forces further inland, compelling the enemy to extend his lines of supply and to spread thinly his occupation

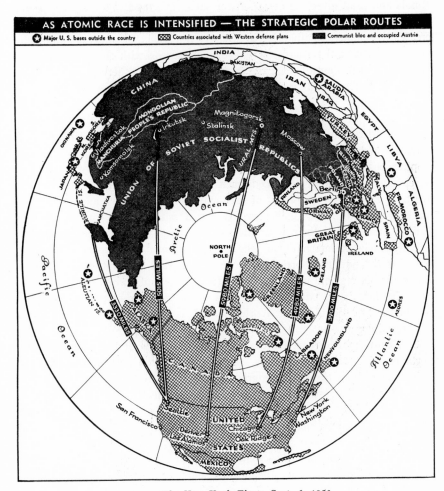

SOURCE: *The New York Times,* Sept. 6, 1953.

armies. Clearly size does not determine victor and vanquished, but it often plays a pivotal role in the strategy of warfare.

Size as a transitory factor of power is best illustrated by its changing importance under different means of transportation. Impressive as are the land masses of Eurasia and North America, they are spanned in hours by jet planes or rocket-propelled missiles. Arctic areas traditionally beyond the reach of Russian planners are now exploited for their mineral wealth as well as for their strategic potentialities. Barriers to peaceful economic development fall before the conquests of technology, as do barriers to military invasion.

If two of the largest nations at the mid-point of the twentieth century, Russia and the United States, are at the same time the two strongest powers, it is only in part because of their size. Extending over so large an area increases the chances of diversity in climate, abundance of minerals, and richness of agricultural resources. However, comparison with similar land areas of North Africa, Central Asia, and Australia proves that there is no guarantee that large territory will include these many factors of power.

While it may not be true that size creates greatness, it may very well limit it. Fragmentation of Western Europe into small national units impeded the flow of trade and the pooling of resources. Countries such as Holland and France which could increase their size, figuratively speaking, by colonial empires possessed a marked advantage over Germany and Italy which had fewer overseas holdings. Forced back increasingly on its own resources, Western Europe's patchwork of national economic plans and individual markets proved highly ineffective compared with Soviet Russia and the United States, with their vast internal markets and integrated economies. The dynamics of international relations transformed the impact of size, by reducing the national barriers and working toward integration of Western Europe into a regional unit. As a static factor, size had limited power in these countries for almost two centuries. The dynamic factor of political change, within the first decade after World War II, is reducing the role size plays in determining the power of the area.

3. Natural Resources: Fallacy and Fact. In view of the overriding importance of industrial resources, the average person remains surprisingly uninformed about the basic materials of energy and manufacture. He hears alarmist cries forecasting industrial collapse for the United States should it be denied Middle Eastern oil, or for Great Britain should it fail to increase coal output, or for Soviet Russia should it be forced to rely on its own steel production in an all-out mobilization race with the United States. Before World War II, professional as well as armchair strategists predicted American military impotence once the world's source of natural rubber in Southeast Asia fell into the hands of Japan. Although there were temporary hardships, no serious consequences resulted. Denial of natural rubber forced America into research and production of synthetic rubber. By 1953, it was producing 800 thousand tons a year of synthetic, compared with 450 thousand tons a year of imported rubber.[2] Although the economics of synthetic versus natural rubber remain debatable, from a national-power standpoint the gain of self-sufficiency offsets the loss in higher production costs.

[2] *The New York Times,* June 5, 1953.

Still, it remains true that all invention depends upon energy and raw materials of some kind. Synthetic rubber is the product of electricity generated by energy resources and of chemicals derived from petroleum materials and coal. Science can substitute one thing for another, but it has yet to create something out of nothing. Necessity may be the mother of invention in that it compels men to find substitutes for crucial items in short supply, but invention depends today upon an abundance of other items. Industry provides experience vital for advancing knowledge; money provides research facilities, necessary for experimentation. The meaning and nature of resources give clues to understanding the present power of Russia and the United States, the potential power of China and India, and the declining power of Germany and Japan.

Before discussing the specific energy resources and raw materials important as factors of power, a few general points should be established. First, resources do not create power; they must be exploited. Iron deposits, thought to be among the largest in the world, lay deep in Brazilian jungles and played no role in world politics until World War II. Suddenly emergence of a good-neighbor policy brought American loans and advice to Brazil, war created a market for Brazilian ore, and the miracles of modern technology worked feats of preventive medicine as well as industrialization, to turn long-standing iron deposits into a factor of power.[3] Significant is the fact that in the last analysis, the power of the United States increased as did the power of Brazil, perhaps to a greater degree. This illustrates the importance of changing what E. W. Zimmerman calls "neutral stuff," unexploited resources, into a factor of power, as well as of the difference between possession by one country and utilization by another.

Refining the concept of resources, it becomes clear that other resources, which may be termed "human," are necessary to work on those we term "natural." These human resources will be considered later, but suffice to say that capital, labor, and technology must be available to translate raw materials into industrial output. The equation works both ways, for without natural resources all the capital, labor, and technology will be of little use.

Another characteristic feature of natural resources is their changeability due to technological improvement. Contrary to popular belief, "resources *are* not, they *become;* they are not static but expand and contract in response to human wants and human actions." [4] Uranium became of world-wide significance only after expenditure of billions of dollars and man-hours unlocked the secrets of atomic fission. Rocks and earth suddenly became valuable resources, as their uranium content acquired meaning for national power. "Creation" of a new resource, in this case uranium, "destroys" another re-

[3] E. W. Zimmerman, *World Resources and Industries,* 2d ed., Harper, New York, 1951, p. 15.
[4] *Ibid.,* p. 15.

source, coal. As uranium becomes increasingly important as a source of energy, coal may prove less desirable and ultimately become as archaic as wood is today. Parallel with this development will be the transformation of coal-rich nations into secondary powers unless they can develop atomic energy or utilize their coal reserves in another manner. Similarly, technological development may increase the power of a given coal deposit tenfold in as many decades by increasing the energy produced by burning the same amount of coal. In this way, the physical measurement of coal remains the same but in a power sense the deposit is now ten times larger than it was under existing technological conditions a century earlier—or, allowing for the amount consumed in the interval, perhaps nine times as large. Thus resources have been "created" while being consumed.

Connected with this second item, the changeable nature of resources, lies the third and last observation, namely, that only a handful of countries know the limits of their resources and raw materials. Surveying the earth's crust is an extensive task. Initial surveys only establish the probable areas wherein resources may be found; they almost never indicate the depth of the area or the amount of the resources, much less the cost of exploitation and the quality of the resource. More will be said about this problem of estimating reserves in connection with the specific ingredients of energy resources, particularly coal and oil.

4. Distribution of Energy Resources. Vital in distinguishing energy resources is the concept of renewability. Fund resources are those which are exhaustible, such as coal, oil, and natural gas. Flow resources are those which renew themselves, such as water, sunshine, and, if properly utilized, wood. Fund resources face rapid depletion in many parts of the globe, forcing increased attention to flow resources as a source of energy. A second distinction in energy resources is between animate and inanimate, but only inanimate sources will be considered at this point.

Coal. King Coal still rules the world of energy production, despite the dramatic upsurge of oil, water, natural gas, and now uranium. It generates more electricity than all other fuels combined. More than two-thirds of Soviet electricity comes from "black gold." Coke, a refined state of coal, produces the tremendous heat vital to the blast furnace, the starting point of steel. As motive power, coal carried England's ships to control of world empire, it moved America's locomotives across a continent of conquest, and it built Russia's Five Year Plans into an industrial colossus in only twenty years. In addition to its energy uses, coal provides gases, oils, tar, and pitch on which the world of chemical industrialization is based, and carbon derived from coke is a necessary ingredient for the manufacture of steel. Small wonder that the economics of coal give it pivotal weight in the scales of power.

In viewing the force at the disposal of his country or that of his opponent, the policy maker must translate figures on coal reserves in terms of quality and location. With respect to quality, it need only be noted that good coking coal, essential for blast furnaces, is relatively rare. Its two major concentrations are the Connellsville region near Pittsburgh, in the United States, and the Ruhr region of Western Europe. British coking coal is less in quantity and quality, while both Soviet Russia and Japan face shortages, serious for the latter, in terms of their industrial needs. More generally found is lignite, a low-grade coal uneconomical in use compared with anthracite and bituminous, familiarly known as "hard" and "soft," coal.[5]

Location plays an important part because of coal's tremendous bulk and its corresponding high cost of transportation, especially across land. Soviet coal, for example, is less advantageously located than that of England or the United States, since the vast majority of Soviet coal deposits lie at the opposite end of the continent from its principal population and industrial concentrations. Moscow is more than 500 miles from the Donets coal field, the most productive high-grade coal area in Russia, while Leningrad lies 1,000 miles away. Kuznetsk, the second largest producing field, lies some 1,500 miles from Tashkent, its principal consumption point, thus requiring one-third of the coal mined to be used in transportation.[6] Most of the coal around Moscow and in the Urals is lignite, although if Russia wishes to increase her dependence on areas beyond her immediate borders, high-grade Polish coal is reasonably near Leningrad and the central manufacturing region.

Where is the world's coal located? To name the principal regions of industrial activity is to answer this question. The United States is blessed with virtually limitless reserves in terms of its anticipated needs. Western Europe has a rich supply in the Ruhr and Great Britain, although the latter is plagued with unfavorable working conditions and low productivity. Soviet Russia, with the qualifications already mentioned, has an inexhaustible series of coal deposits in its central, far eastern, and northern regions. Asia's known deposits are concentrated in India, already utilizing them in her iron and steel industries, and North China. China is only beginning to tap the Fushun coal bed near Mukden, Manchuria, thought to be the thickest bed of bituminous coal in the world.[7] From 1933 to 1945, Japan's annexation of Manchuria provided Nippon with an annual output of almost 20 million tons of coal. Denial of this valuable source of coke plays a major role in limiting Japan's present power in the Pacific.

Oil. Oil, like coal, meets a variety of needs in an industrial economy, chief of which is energy production. Whether it is low-grade diesel fuel moving trucks, busses, and locomotives, or high-octane gasoline propelling airplanes, oil provides the motive force for much of man's transportation and industry.

---

[5] *Ibid.*, p. 467.
[6] A. Bergson (ed.), *Soviet Economic Growth,* Row, Peterson, Evanston, Ill., 1953, "Industrial Resources" by Chauncey D. Harris, p. 171.
[7] Zimmerman, *op. cit.*, p. 469.

Virtually unknown to Western Europe's coal-dominated industry, oil plays a pivotal role in America's power, and promises to be of increasing importance in that of Soviet Russia. In addition, it moves the ships of many countries, including the vast armadas of Great Britain and the United States.

Oil, unlike coal, appears definitely limited in its distribution, being relatively distant from most centers of industry. For the industrialist as well as the militarist, oil deposits are the "beauty spots" on the face of the globe. The two largest of these beauty spots are the Middle East and the Caribbean. The cluster of wells in southern Russia, Iran, Iraq, Arabia, Romania, and Egypt tap one vast oil region, while those of South Central United States, Mexico, and Venezuela pump the second largest reserve concentration. Between them, the two beauty spots of oil combine almost two-thirds of the world's total proved reserves, with the greater amount in the Middle East.

Overlooking for a moment the combined Anglo-American domination over most of the oil lying outside the Soviet area, the resources immediately available to the major countries can be considered. Exhaustive geological surveys show that Japan and Western Europe have little or no oil, while according to partial surveys China and Eastern Europe have only nominal amounts. Quite different is the story of the United States, though here so much fact and fancy has surrounded the story of oil that the average person probably has a hazy, if correct, idea of how much is available to meet American needs.

In the first place, it is necessary to stress a point mentioned briefly earlier: that there is no knowledge as to total reserves in the Western Hemisphere, including the United States. The term "proved reserves" means merely the known inventories on which present oil production depends, obtainable under existing economic and operating conditions. This gives no indication of oil in untested areas. In addition, more efficient production methods have increased the yield so successfully that 5 billion barrels of "proved reserves" forty years ago might yield only half a billion or a billion barrels, whereas today the yield might hit 3 billion barrels.[8] Further increases in productivity from improved refining techniques call for upward revisions in proved-reserves estimates. Thus the picture is brightened by increased yields from known fields; it is further brightened by the discovery of new fields. Since 1950 more than 40,000 new wells a year have been drilled in the United States, keeping America's proved reserves of oil increasing at a rate of almost 1 billion barrels per year.[9] Despite an annual consumption of more than 2 billion barrels, America's proved oil reserves actually continue to increase. The clue to the paradox lies in the changeable nature and the ambiguous meaning of oil "reserves."

Taking into consideration the oil lying outside the continental United States but immediately available within the Western Hemisphere, America's

[8] *Ibid.*, p. 507.
[9] Standard Oil Company (New Jersey), *Facts about Oil Imports,* 1953, p. 41.

oil reserves become truly phenomenal. Not only do northern discoveries promise to make Canada a major supplier in the near future, but Venezuela's output in 1948 was more than double that for all of the U.S.S.R. and Eastern Europe, hitting almost 500 million barrels. With lesser deposits in Mexico, Colombia, and Alaska, America seems well situated with respect to oil. Nevertheless, private American oil interests as well as official governmental policy have invested considerable capital and diplomacy in Middle East oil. Although this provides a convenient supply base for Western Europe and the NATO navies, it does not appear to be as important in terms of American strength as in terms of Russian weakness. Loss of Middle East oil supplies might curtail American transportation but would hardly spell disaster in terms of power. On the other hand, Middle East oil would increase Soviet oil supplies more than tenfold, once problems of transportation into Russia were solved. Russia's problem lies not in reserves, of which she appears to have plenty, but in production, limited by her lack of capital and extensive refinery damage in World War II. Thus in terms of power, deprivation of Middle East oil would not cripple the United States, but should it simultaneously move into the Soviet Union, the present disparity in oil production would be eliminated with the new advantage resting with the communist bloc.

Iran's sudden move to nationalize its foreign-held oil in 1952 brought dramatic emphasis to the implications of oil control in international relations. As an official congressional report showed,[10]

The outstanding characteristic of the world's petroleum industry is the dominant position of seven international companies . . . five American . . . and two British-Dutch. . . . Apart from Mexico and Russian-controlled countries, these seven companies control directly or indirectly most of the world's petroleum business. . . . Control is held not only through direct corporate holdings, by parents, subsidiaries, and affiliates of the seven, but also through such indirect means as interlocking directorates, joint ownership of affiliates, inter-company crude purchase contracts, and marketing agreements.

Twentieth-century international relations in the Middle East is the complex story of British, French, and American competition for control of rich oil deposits, culminating in extensive international cartels. With the resurgence of nationalism in the area after World War II, bringing with it attacks on foreign control of national resources and national politics, the role of diplomacy as a function of both national power and private interests takes on added significance in the Middle East.

Outside these two major oil centers, the world has few areas for immediate exploitation. Indonesia's reserves provide potential energy resources for India and Japan, although transportation is a critical problem for the latter.

[10] *The International Petroleum Cartel,* Staff Report to the Federal Trade Commission Submitted to the Subcommittee on Monopoly of the Select Committee on Small Business, U.S. Senate, 1952, pp. 22–23.

Synthetic-oil production in Germany and Soviet Russia adds insignificant amounts, but the stubborn fact remains that to the best of present knowledge, oil resources are limited in location as well as in utilization. With only 6 per cent of the world's population, the United States consumes more than 80 per cent of the world's oil output. The significance of this has not escaped Soviet planners, whose target for 1955 was approximately 70 million tons, or more than six times Russia's 1946 production.[11] The comparative ease with which oil may be transported gives it marked economic advantage over coal in the Soviet Union.

Natural Gas and Water. Natural gas, a newcomer in the field of energy resources, promises to play an increasingly important role in the scales of power. Already it provides more than one-fifth of the heat energy produced in the United States, and its production there is expanding rapidly, based on tremendous reserves far exceeding present needs.[12] Coal-short France and Italy hope to bolster their economies with natural gas, while modest production efforts in the Soviet Union do not threaten the extensive reserves reported there.[13] As with uranium and atomic power, production costs and attendant problems preclude prediction as to the future of this new energy resource. However, it seems safe to conclude that neither natural gas nor atomic power will seriously alter the preponderance of American and Russian power, and they may well enhance it, particularly when compared with Asia.

Last, but certainly not least in the realm of energy, is hydroelectric power. Unlike coal, oil, and natural gas, water is self-renewing, a flow resource. Far from being "free" simply because it exists in abundance, it is the most costly fuel in terms of initial investment. Harnessing water power usually requires huge dams, reservoirs, turbines, and generators and an extensive transmission system. So costly is its development that it seems certain that, unlike other energy materials, the overwhelming amount of potential water reserves will never be tapped by man. Nevertheless, its role is crucial for some countries and is becoming more so for others. No policy maker's picture of power factors would be complete without an understanding of the economics of hydro development.

At the risk of being repetitious, it should be noted that the United States generates the largest amount of hydroelectric power in the world. To be sure, water plays a proportionately more important role in the economies of other countries such as Norway and Switzerland. In raw quantitative terms, however, the power potential of such engineering giants as Hoover, Grand Coulee, and Shasta dams staggers the imagination. As yet they operate far below capacity, but as American industry decentralizes, well-located hydro sources

---

[11] United Nations, Economic Commission for Europe, *Economic Survey of Europe since the War,* Geneva, 1953, p. 42.

[12] *The New York Times,* July 5, 1953.

[13] Bergson, *op. cit.,* p. 174.

will replace costly transportation of distant coal. Dramatic use of hydro-electric power came with production of atomic bombs at Hanford, Washington, drawing power from the Columbia River Valley projects; similar use of the Tennessee Valley Authority made Oak Ridge possible.

Some comparison of American and Russian hydro output may be grasped from the fact that Soviet planners hoped, in 1955, to produce a little more than one-third as much water power as did the United States in 1949.[14] Both countries have spurred vast multipurpose river projects within the past decade, simultaneously irrigating deserts, preventing floods, and generating electricity. Obstacles to further river exploitation in Russia lie in her poor distribution of water power and in her high proportion of rivers which freeze in the winter. Nevertheless, such projects as the Volga-Don Canal and the Turkmen Canal have tripled hydroelectric output between 1950 and 1955, with water furnishing a little more than one-fifth of all Russia's electricity today.

Turning to the lesser industrial areas, hydroelectricity is vital to Japan, whose rugged mountains provide ready energy in their swollen streams. Similarly, the Scandinavian countries as well as Switzerland, France, Germany, and Italy all depend upon water for much of their energy. Because of this, the absence of oil in West Europe is less important than might otherwise be thought. China's hydroelectric possibilities promise rapid expansion of power generation if she can secure the equipment necessary for harnessing her mighty rivers and for transmitting the power over her vast land area. Nothing could transform China's economy more rapidly than extensive hydro-electric projects.

Coal, oil, natural gas, and water—these furnish man with the bulk of his industrial energy. In addition, substitutes such as peat and fuel wood play a minor role in some areas, principally in Soviet Russia. With a virtually unlimited supply of peat in Siberia and excellent deposits around Moscow, Soviet peat consumption exceeded 53 million tons in 1955, a valuable substitute for low-grade heating needs.

Despite the tremendous attention given atomic energy, it remains principally a military weapon and as yet plays no role in general industrial use. Its development as a source of motive power for military vessels, such as submarines, indicates its future potentialities, particularly for the oil-poor merchant fleets of Britain and Norway. However, the large investment of technology and capital necessary to develop atomic energy to the point of being an economic source of energy precludes further consideration of it as a factor of power at this time. Another decade must pass before its impact can be fairly appraised.

These statistics can now be placed together to show their relationship in

[14] Zimmerman, *op. cit.*, p. 601; United Nations, Economic Commission for Europe, *op. cit.*, p. 44.

the scales of power. With Soviet output of electricity tripling since the end of World War II, India's industrialization reaching new heights, and China's economic progress moving ahead under forced draft, energy evaluations may be seriously revised by 1970. For the immediate future, however, the following figures will remain decisive:

TABLE 2. PRODUCTION OF COMMERCIAL SOURCES OF ENERGY

	United States	Western Europe and colonies	Soviet Union	China	India	Japan
Coal and lignite, thousand metric tons, 1953......	439,031	626,885	320,000	53,000 *	36,422	48,017
Crude petroleum, thousand metric tons, 1953..	318,929	48,347	52,500	389 *	—	284
Electric energy, thousand kilowatts, 1952........	463,055	1,112,912	116,400	1,420	6,120	51,647
Natural gas, million cubic meters, 1952..........	226,917	3,419	?	31	—	111

* W. W. Rostow, *The Prospects for Communist China*, Wiley, New York, 1954, p. 239. Statistics refer to 1952.

SOURCE: *U.N. Statistical Yearbook*, United Nations, Statistical Office, New York, 1954. Coal and lignite, pp. 113–116; crude petroleum, pp. 118–119; electric energy, pp. 256–262; natural gas, p. 117. A dash indicates that the country produces or possesses no quantity of the product in question. A question mark indicates no information is available on the amount of production of the product in question.

5. Natural Resources: Industrial Raw Materials. Like energy resources of the fund variety, metal resources are exhaustible supply; unlike energy resources, however, they are durable goods. This year's coal must be replaced next year, but this year's steel production will exist for decades, first in a finished product of considerable durability, and then in scrap which is reprocessed to create more steel. This facilitates the use of metals as a factor of power but does not make them more important, because without energy fuels, metals cannot be manufactured; once manufactured, the finished product cannot be utilized without energy.

Iron. If coal is the basic energy resource today, then iron ore is certainly the basic metal resource. To be sure, high-grade steel requires strengthening alloys, such as tungsten, molybdenum, manganese, and aluminum, but quantitatively iron ore plays the major role in its manufacture, and without iron and steel, no nation can aspire to international prominence. To name the concentrations of iron deposits is not to name the major world powers, since many rich iron centers such as Venezuela export their ore to other countries. Conversely, however, to name the major powers is to name the nations which enjoy ready access to iron ore supplies, namely, the United States, Great Britain, France, Germany, and Soviet Russia. Of these, the United States undoubtedly enjoys the ascendant position, possessing extensive deposits within its own borders, as well as access to extremely rich supplies in Labrador and Venezuela. Production in these last two areas is only beginning to hit its stride, but even preliminary studies there indicate that no shortage of iron ore faces the United States for at least a generation to come.

Western Europe's iron supplies center mainly in France, Sweden, the United Kingdom, and Spain, in that order. Taken as a unit, the area has more than ample iron reserves. Iron-ore production, however, threatens to be a bottleneck in Western Europe partly because of transportation problems involved in exploiting interior reserves. Another major obstacle is that each country has traditionally limited ore output to the amount consumable in its own blast furnaces.

Soviet Russia's iron-ore reserves more than suffice for her needs, although like Western Europe, technological problems of exploitation qualify her position somewhat. Although her total deposits comprise more than half the world's total estimated reserves, within the next fifteen years Soviet Russia may well have shortages of well-placed, high-grade ore.[15] Like coal, iron-ore statistics must be translated in terms of quality and location. Low-grade ores require special processing if they are to be used for smelting. Unless deposits lie within easy reach of coal supplies, and preferably near major points of consumption as well, extremely complex transportation problems result. These can be especially important in a country like Soviet Russia whose transportation facilities barely meet the heavy demands of serving a large population scattered over extensive territory.

Outside these areas, only China and India presently show promise of exploiting iron deposits for national power. In the case of China, poor location of iron with respect to coal limits development to Manchuria for the time being. India, however, enjoys the coal-iron supremacy of South Asia, and should remain the leading industrial power of the area for many years. Japan's dilemma underscores the fact that there is no substitute for possession of raw materials. Desperately in need of iron ore, Japan seized the rich deposits of Manchuria in 1931. Throughout the thirties, she imported huge amounts of scrap iron from the United States. Between natural ore and recovery from scrap, she was able to build her iron and steel output into a substantial industrial and military machine, capable of waging war against the United States for almost four years. Supplies of scrap ended shortly before hostilities began, however, and Manchurian production, never adequate

---

[15] Bergson, *op. cit.*, p. 163.

for Japan's needs, was further limited by American air and naval operations. Japan's deficiency in iron and steel doomed her to defeat.

Other Metals. As already suggested, steel varies widely in its qualities and uses. Gradations in strength come from introduction of alloys, metals, and ores other than iron into the production of steel. For high-speed cutting tools, cobalt and tungsten must be added to provide sharp cutting edges at high temperatures. Stainless steel requires chromium and nickel. Manganese exists in small amounts in all steels, but additional increments give great toughness and resistance to abrasion for steel used in dredging and drilling equipment. These so-called ferroalloys spell the difference between success and failure in the critical areas of machine and tool production, where durability and precision play so vital a role in modern industry.

With respect to ferroalloys, both the United States and Western Europe appear to stand at a disadvantage as compared with Soviet Russia. Not only are Russia's reserves good and her production adequate for her needs, but she enjoys an exportable surplus of manganese and chromium. In contrast, the United States relies heavily upon Africa and South America for manganese, chromium, cobalt, nickel, and tin. Almost half her bauxite, from which aluminum is produced, is imported, as are large amounts of tungsten, copper, and lead. Similarly, Western Europe draws heavily on Africa for many ferroalloys, and in case of further political upheaval there or of vulnerable supply lines in wartime, critical shortages will pose serious problems for policy makers.

Only two items of note remain to complete this survey of industrial raw materials. Copper exists primarily in North and South America and in Africa, yet it occupies a central role in the entire electrical industry as the only metal, other than silver, which will conduct electricity economically. Aluminum's lightness and strength make it essential for advanced aeronautics, particularly supersonic missiles. Aluminum is made from bauxite, and this ore, as well as copper, is found primarily in North and South America, and in Africa. These copper and bauxite deposits lie under the exclusive control of American, Belgian, and French corporations. Of the other nations, only Russia appears to have any appreciable amount of these critical items. However, Soviet production of both copper and aluminum appears to face technological problems and imports of copper ore and bauxite, the latter from nearby Hungary, have traditionally been necessary to fill an important metal shortage.

A glance at the table below quickly reveals the tremendous disparity among various areas in terms of raw-materials output, as well as the pivotal position of Western Europe in the international scales of power. Together with energy resources, raw materials predetermine, to a large extent, our next level of analysis, that of industrial output.

TABLE 3. RAW-MATERIAL RESOURCES (RESERVES)

	United States, Canada, and Latin America	Western Europe	Africa	Soviet Union and East Europe	China	India
Iron ore (proved reserves), 10^6 metric tons.........	19,248	16,893	250	1,009.3	400	400
Iron ore (actual reserves), 10^6 metric tons.........	12,570	11,370	1,240	4,720	500	3,600
Manganese, million tons...	At least 45	—	Several hundred	250–600	—	At least 150
Bauxite, million metric tons..................	560	230	300	320	200	250
Copper, thousand tons of contained metal (measured, indicated, and inferred)...............	107,000	—	108,000	16,000	—	—

SOURCE: Iron ore, manganese, and copper, United Nations, *Proceedings of the Scientific Conference on the Conservation and Utilization of Resources*, vol. II, *Mineral Resources*, New York, 1951, pp. 10–11, 145; bauxite, U.S. President's Materials Policy Commission, *Resources for Freedom*, vol. II, 1952, p. 138. A dash indicates that the country possesses no quantity of the resource in question.

6. Human Resources. The natural endowments of nations have been examined in terms of physical foundations, energy resources, and raw materials. The policy maker's analysis of national power has been traced through the various factors of location, topography, climate, and size, as well as factors of fuels and metals resources. The focus must now shift from what lies beneath a nation's territory to what it produces above that territory. In order that "neutral stuff" become immediate power, man-made ingredients must work upon it. These human resources, capital, technology, and labor, must combine with natural resources before industry for peace and war can develop. The human resources provide the link between statistics on natural resources and statistics on industrial production. Not always measurable, capital, technology, and labor nevertheless play central roles in national power. If a country has sufficient capital, it may purchase abroad what it lacks at home, as Great Britain has done for centuries. If it has sufficient technology, or know-how, it may invent substitutes for items of which it is in short supply, as Germany did down to 1945. If it has sufficient labor, it may use men instead of machines to build a modern industrial economy, as Soviet Russia did between 1930 and 1950, and as China hopes to do. If a country has all three in good supply, however, or even any two in particular abundance, it may expect to enjoy a dominant place in the hierarchy of national power.

Capital. England's history well illustrates the importance of capital as a factor of national power. Although her land was no better endowed than that of many other European nations, her ascendant position in the Industrial Revolution gave her a near monopoly in manufactured items. These proved to be valuable exports which, together with income from her vast merchant fleet, furnished England with capital for investment and for purchasing raw materials abroad. In the nineteenth century, British domination of world capital placed her in an advantageous position in international trade. However, more recent and advanced industrialization in the United States thrived on a vast storehouse of raw materials within her own borders as well as the world demand for America's wartime production from 1914 to 1918 and again from 1939 to 1945. These conditions catapulted the United States into the No. 1 creditor position, while World War II turned England from creditor into debtor. New York, rather than London, became banker of the world, with American capital providing the chief prop for European reconstruction and development after World War II, and American investments appearing together with those of Britain and France in underdeveloped areas. Simultaneously the United States stepped into the role of world leader held by Great Britain throughout the nineteenth and early twentieth centuries.

It may be helpful to take a specific industry, oil. Middle Eastern and South American nations without capital were forced to open their land to European and North American investors if they were to derive any advantage from their natural resources. Costly drilling apparatus must be expended in many futile efforts before oil is struck. Vast networks of pipelines, tankers, railroads, and trucks must transport the crude oil to gigantic catalytic cracking plants and refineries. There advanced scientific methods transform crude oil into its many derivatives, including gasoline, fuel oils, kerosene, and lubricants. Only a wealthy government treasury or a pooling of private earnings can finance exploitation of oil reserves.

Technology. Technology, the second human resource, is closely allied with capital. Without monetary wealth no means are available for training men through providing education and research facilities. Furthermore, accumulative experience advances technological research so fundamentally that technology may be considered directly a function of a nation's industrial development. In this sense, wealth begets wealth, for the more highly industrialized a country is, the more advanced may be its use of resources and raw materials and the larger will be its pool of trained engineers and scientists. The association of capital and technology in the realm of national power is well illustrated by atomic energy. To be sure, atomic development drew upon technological discoveries in many countries, including Japan, Germany, Italy,

Great Britain, and the United States. However, it was America's ability to invest 2 billion dollars, to draw upon the research facilities of six major universities, to devote the energies of several hundred scientists, and to build an entire city for atomic development—all while fighting a major war in the Pacific and Atlantic areas—that gave the United States the initial use of the atomic bomb. Not for four years thereafter was Soviet Russia able to produce her first atomic explosion. During this time the United States possessed a significant power advantage, which, while it was not used actively by America, may have been a passive deterrent to Soviet policy makers.

Technology as a human resource was dramatized in the race by both Russia and America for capture of German scientists in 1945. These men had worked successfully on the first guided missiles, and had valuable experience in rocket and jet propulsion. Their possession by the two nations contesting for hegemony in major areas of the globe tended to equate the strength of both contestants. However, it increased the bipolarity of power in giving Russia and America a joint monopoly of advanced means of war. Thus, both in peace and war, technology is essential to national strength.

Labor. Only in most recent times has man developed a systematic store of knowledge about one of the most basic of human resources, population. Qualitatively, of course, labor varies widely between the advanced industrial nations of Europe and the so-called backward agrarian nations of South America, Africa, the Middle East, and Asia. Qualitative differences, however, other than those directly connected with technology, play a subsidiary role in national strength. Although ignorance of machinery and the fundamentals of mechanics caused much waste and inefficiency in Russia's Five Year Plans, it did not prevent them from succeeding. The rapidity with which modern China has moved from the age of oxcarts to the age of jets shows that experience in running machines—if not in building them—is readily grasped by peoples throughout the world.

More important are quantitative differences between countries, because a labor shortage in Western Europe cannot be alleviated in the short run and places Western Europe at an initial disadvantage in comparison with Soviet Russia. Within Western Europe, the picture is different between the highly industrialized countries in the north and the more agricultural areas of the south. Great Britain, for instance, faces a constantly aging population, and her labor shortage is already acute. Italy, on the other hand, with an expanding population has an overt unemployment problem coupled with serious underemployment in her agricultural districts. Taken in the large, however, Western Europe's labor force of young men by 1970—i.e., those between fifteen and thirty-four years of age—will account for only 39 per cent of her total manpower. It is overwhelmingly outnumbered by the 51 per cent of total manpower in the corresponding age brackets available in Soviet Russia.[16]

[16] Political and Economic Planning, *Population Policy in Great Britain,* London, 1948, p. 30.

The less industrialized areas have been intentionally omitted from these comparative figures, since differentials in capital, technology, and resources strip such comparisons of all meaning. Admittedly Europe's greater output per worker, through better use of motive power, offsets much of the disparity between its labor population and that of Russia, but it by no means equates the two areas. In terms of military manpower, of course, the figures become even more significant, since firepower inequalities are much smaller than productivity differentials.

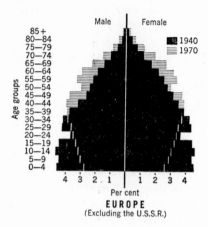

Population and age groups, Europe, 1940 and 1970. SOURCE: F. W. Notestein and Others, *The Future Population of Europe and the Soviet Union,* League of Nations, Geneva, 1944, p. 112.

Labor abundance can, to a certain degree, offset capital and technological shortages. Russia, for example, built huge canals, cut vast stretches of timber, and mined quantities of coal, salt, gold, and uranium with millions of persons under forced labor. Their energy was expendable in the true sense of the word, making up for lack of machinery during the heavy industrialization of the thirties and the forties. Similarly in China, millions of man-hours moved tons of earth for construction of the mighty dikes and dams controlling China's rivers, allowing the Communists to work miracles of conservation and irrigation without the gigantic apparatus employed in building Hoover Dam and Grand Coulee. This is not to compare economy or efficiency here; it is merely to state that certain jobs can be done without the use of advanced machinery, capital, or technology, provided there is enough manpower. Militarily, losses of 5 to 1 could be sustained by Soviet Russia against Western Europe, or by China against America, without destroying the relative manpower advantage of the Communist areas over the non-Communist regions.

7. Industrial Production. Capital, technology, and labor combine to work upon energy resources and industrial raw materials. The end product on which policy makers the world over fix their attention is industrial output, the nation's productivity. Here, expressed in millions of motor vehicles, appliances, construction tools, and related items, is the most accurate reflection of immediate, short-run strength. Translated into tanks, planes, guns, and munitions, it becomes the basis of military calculations and spells defeat or victory for contesting states. Industrial production does not necessarily give the policy maker a picture of the standard of living of different countries, since output must then be related to population, in order to see how much is produced per capita. Furthermore, it would have to be broken down into detailed consumption patterns, to find out how much steel went into automobiles and buildings as compared with tanks and guns, or whether a minor-

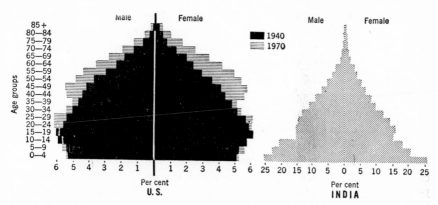

Population and age groups, United States and India, 1940 and 1970. SOURCE: *Fortune Magazine*, February, 1944, p. 162.

ity of the country consumed a majority of the national product. Stripped of these refinements, however, the figures provide a convenient index of industrial strength, readily translated into military strength, a vital factor of power.

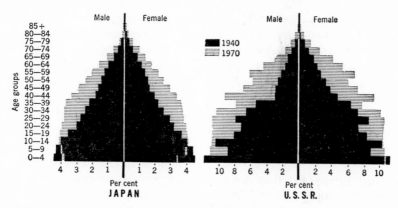

Population and age groups, Soviet Union and Japan, 1940 and 1970. SOURCE: *Fortune Magazine*, February, 1944, p. 163.

Living Standards. Naturally, the more items are included in the tabulation, the more comprehensive a picture it gives of a nation's power, industrially speaking. Basic are iron and steel figures, for they determine the scope of manufacture for most machines of construction and destruction. But light industry may tell how a nation adds to its industrial base by international trade, exchanging consumers' goods for producers' goods. Something can also be learned about the intangible factor of morale by examining output in key items such as clothing, housing, and household necessities.

A nation's standard of living is frequently considered as an important index of national morale; yet realistic appraisal of the divergent ways of living strips this approach of much of the significance commonly attributed to it. Propagandists of various nations claim that comparisons of consumption will win wars of words, if not of weapons. Shoe production figures prominently in United States' propaganda to the effect that the average American consumes four pairs of footgear a year. If we learn that the average Russian has only one pair of shoes a year and his Indian counterpart goes shoeless, can we develop hypotheses about the respective morale or loyalty of the Russian and Indian worker, compared with that of the American? Only by ignoring the lessons of sociology and anthropology can such cross-cultural conclusions be drawn, solely on the basis of production figures. In the Korean War—ignoring the larger strategical questions and focusing solely on the armies involved—the best-fed troops in the world, coming from one of the best-clothed, best-housed, and most-bathed nations in the world, met their match in troops subsisting on rice, coming from a nation of cotton padding and straw huts, knowing none of the vaunted joys of modern plumbing.

The comparison of one nation's consumption patterns for past and present is far more important than international comparisons at any one point in time. The Italian worker or the Hungarian peasant may know little and care less about the well-being of his British or American counterpart, but he is vitally concerned with whether his own life is improving, remaining the same, or deteriorating. In the summer of 1953, long-smoldering resentment over depressed living conditions, coupled with increased demands for productivity, resulted in workers' uprisings throughout the Communist-dominated East European countries. Strikes, demonstrations, and outright sabotage forced the governments to revise their industrial plans, increasing consumer output while cutting back targets in heavy industrial equipment. Similarly, concern over inflation and the slow deterioration in the standard of living prevented France and Italy from extensive rearmament despite continued pressure from their NATO partners, particularly the United States. Conversely, continued improvement in the general living conditions of the Soviet Union between 1945 and 1955 gave that country greater strength than revealed in a cursory comparison of Soviet and American consumption. Few Soviet citizens today can remember any period of greater material benefits, an important clue to the source of one type of support which Soviet rulers enjoy.

Industrial Production. With these points in mind, it is now possible to examine the end product of human and natural resources, industrial output.

It is neither proof of future potential nor conclusive as to military strength. However, the following figures indicate the basic power relationships of the major countries and areas. By shifting figures and combining areas, it is possible to see the strength of various alliances and their effect upon the respective power positions of the major countries.

TABLE 4. INDUSTRIAL PRODUCTION

	United States	Western Europe	Soviet Union *	China †	India	Japan
Crude steel, thousand metric tons, 1953....	101,250	62,511	38,000	1,215	1,531	7,662
Automobiles, noncommercial, 1952........	4,320,794	1,267,846	428,000	—	—	4,677
Automobiles, commercial, 1952..........	1,218,765	550,019	?	—	—	34,377
Cement, thousand metric tons, 1952.......	42,394	58,188	12,000	2,311	3,594	7,118
Cotton spindles, thousands, 1954........	22,960	52,667	8,380	2,784	11,721	7,766
Cotton looms, 1952....	398,501	290,193	233,000	56,580	198,473	290,193
Merchant vessels, thousand gross reg. tonnage, launched 1952..	528	3,868	?	?	—	557

* All statistics for the Soviet Union from United Nations, Economic Commission for Europe, *Economic Survey of Europe since the War*, Geneva, 1953, except for crude steel, which is in *Statistical Yearbook*, p. 233. Automobiles (1950), pp. 42–43; cement (1951), p. 49; cotton spindles (1951), p. 270; cotton looms (1951), p. 270.

† All statistics for China from W. W. Rostow, *The Prospects for Communist China*, Wiley, New York, 1954, p. 239. In the case of China the cotton-spindle figure represents cotton yarn produced, and the cotton-loom figure refers to cotton cloth produced. All figures for 1952.

SOURCE: *U.N. Statistical Yearbook*, United Nations, Statistical Office, New York, 1954. Crude steel, pp. 233–234; automobiles, p. 244; cement, pp. 224–226; cotton spindles, p. 186; cotton looms, p. 187; merchant vessels, p. 243. A dash indicates that the country produces no quantity of the product in question. A question mark indicates no information is available on the amount of production.

8. Military Strength. Military strength is the most decisive, most publicized, and most incalculable factor of power. Its role as arbiter of victor and vanquished is celebrated. As long as war remains the court of last resort for international conflict, military force is vital to survival. No less obvious is the central place accorded military power in contemporary society, from the most sensational magazine and newspaper columns to the most serious debates of national cabinets and legislatures. Devouring raw materials at an insatiable rate and turning national budgets topsy-turvy, military demands make a mockery of man's efforts to allocate resources in order to raise living standards constantly. Socialist and capitalist economies alike find themselves chained to ever-climbing military appropriations, forcing both to adopt measures at variance with their economic premises. Yet despite these familiar observations, military strength, of all the factors confronting policy makers, remains least susceptible to accurate measurement in the scales of power. Contrary to popular belief, it is not only the tight secrecy surrounding military data which precludes accurate estimate of comparative national strength. Even with all the statistics on the numbers of troops, aircraft, guided missiles, ships, tanks, munitions, and so-called secret weapons, no policy maker could make an accurate judgment concerning the preponderance of military power, except in the obvious cases where extreme disparity exists.

Two levels of analysis defy the layman's armchair strategy. First he must surmount the problem of comparing dissimilar ingredients. Iron and steel remain essentially the same the world over. Given so many tons of crude-steel production, a nation may produce only so many dozen ships or so many million automobiles. However, every weapon has both a counterdefense and a rival weapon. America possesses the largest atomic-bomb stockpile in the world. Undoubtedly the Soviet Union has prepared defensive measures against atomic attack and may also have a rival type of explosive. Only actual combat reveals which side has superior forces, yet the policy maker must decide on a course of action before he has such valuable knowledge. The United States possesses a fleet larger than that of all other navies combined; the Soviet Union has the biggest submarine navy in the world. Even given statistics on both sides, the superiority of one over the other cannot be deduced without testing American antisubmarine devices and Soviet countermeasures. To add one more dimension to our problem, American seapower faces Russian airpower. Traditional rivalries among exponents of land, sea, and air strength compel the civilian planner to cast a skeptical eye on the dogmatic claims of superiority enthusiastically pushed by army, navy, and air groups.

The second level of analysis hindering meaningful discussion in terms of comparative military forces is that of time and technology. Past wars are refought in memoirs; future wars are prefought on maps. Theories advanced in both cases run afoul of time and technology. The last war cannot show how to win the next one, because in the meantime new means of offense and defense have been discovered. Even less possible is it to win the next war without fighting it, because the full devotion of an opponent's inventive efforts to military strategy may well bring up an unforeseen development completely upsetting the most careful calculations of military planners. In World War I, trench warfare dominated battle strategy. In World War II, tank units unleashed a blitzkrieg war of mobility, completely by-passing France's vaunted Maginot Line, with its concrete fortifications and trenches. In World War II, the airplane moved at will over battlefield and city, relatively unharmed by the antiaircraft weapons of those below. In World War III, supersonic, electronically guided missiles may track the giant bomber to certain destruction.

Perhaps the only significant way in which military strength can be approached is through other factors of power, for in the last analysis, superiority in natural and human resources spells industrial superiority. This, in turn, indicates the probable outcome of conflict, though prediction may still be impossible, given the initial advantage of surprise attack and its attendant widespread destruction. World War II provides an excellent example of the industrial approach, rather than the military approach, to the question of national strength. In 1940, the United States Army, based solely on volunteers, trained with broomsticks instead of rifles and drove trucks painted with signs reading "tank." In 1941, Japan attacked the United States without warning, sinking the bulk of America's Pacific fleet in the Hawaiian Islands and destroying its bomber force in the Philippines. Within a few months, Japan cut off America's supply lines to the tin, rubber, oil, hemp, and jute of Southeast Asia. Only four years later, Japan lay in smoking ruins, its navy and merchant marine totally destroyed, its major cities completely devastated by fire and atomic explosion. In contrast, the United States, unharmed by war, had expanded its home industrial base while simultaneously fighting a war against Japan, Germany, and Italy and providing equipment for the Allies in Africa, Russia, and Asia. The story is told, not in symbolic charts of comparative military strength in 1940–1941, but in the tangible factors of power which determined America's relative superiority in terms of physical foundations, energy resources, raw materials, and industrial production.

ADDITIONAL CASE-STUDY MATERIAL

Bergson, A. (ed.): *Soviet Economic Growth,* Row, Peterson, Evanston, Ill., 1953.
Brady, R.: *Crisis in Britain,* University of California Press, Berkeley, Calif., 1950.
Cohen, J. B.: *Japan's Economy in War and Reconstruction,* University of Minnesota Press, Minneapolis, 1949.
Cressey, G. B.: *The Basis of Soviet Strength,* McGraw-Hill, New York, 1945.
Gordon, D. L., and R. J. Dangerfield: *The Hidden Weapon; The Story of Economic Warfare,* Harper, New York, 1947.
Guillaume, A.: *Soviet Arms and Soviet Power,* Combat, Washington, 1949.
James, W. M.: *The Influence of Sea Power on the History of the British People,* Cambridge, New York, 1948.
Lorimer, F.: *The Population of the Soviet Union; History and Prospects,* League of Nations, Geneva, 1946.
McDougall, F. L.: "Food and Population," *International Conciliation,* December, 1952.
Paleston, W. D.: *The Influence of Sea Power in World War II,* Yale University Press, New Haven, Conn., 1947.
Prasad, B.: *India's Hindu Moslem Questions,* G. Allen, London, 1946.
Russell, Sir E. J.: "Asia's Food Problems and Their Impact on Western Countries," *International Affairs,* vol. 26, July, 1950.
Schwartz, H.: *Russia's Soviet Economy,* Prentice-Hall, New York, 1950.
Sprout, H., and M. Sprout: *Foundations of National Power,* Princeton University Press, Princeton, N.J., 1951.

Standard Oil Company (New Jersey): *Facts about Oil Imports,* 1953.

Strausz-Hupé, R.: *The Balance of Tomorrow,* Putnam, New York, 1945.

Timasheff, N. S.: "The Strength and Weaknesses of the Soviet Union," *Review of Politics,* vol. 10, October, 1948.

U.N. Statistical Yearbook, United Nations, Statistical Office, New York, 1954.

Williams, B. H.: "The Spread of Technology and the Relative Strength of States," *Social Science,* October, 1949.

Woytinsky, W. S.: *World Population and Production,* Twentieth Century Fund, New York, 1953.

Zimmerman, E. W.: *World Resources and Industries,* 2d ed., Harper, New York, 1951.

Chapter 6

INTANGIBLE FACTORS OF POWER

1. Population: Meaning and Significance. Having analyzed the strength of his nation and its neighbors in terms of the physical foundations and related tangible factors of power, such as energy resources, raw materials, and industrial output, the policy maker must move to intangible factors of national power. Capital, technology, and labor already came under focus in examining the link between natural resources and industrial strength, but a comprehensive analysis of human resources must detail population changes, uncover differences between populations which affect unity or cohesiveness, and finally come to grips with that important ingredient of national strength, morale. In this way, gross population figures assume meaning in terms of prospective quantitative growth or decline of a nation's human resources, and a breakdown of census statistics in terms of racial, ethnic, socioeconomic, and religious groups provides insights into the qualitative nature of a given population. As with tangible factors of power, some areas of weakness resist human ingenuity, while others may be overcome by proper procedures. Although population changes as a whole appear less susceptible to man-made correctives, group tensions can be fashioned into unity or exploited into disunity by various means, chief of which is propaganda. Thus a brief study of propaganda, its assets and liabilities, will round out the discussion of the intangible factors of power, human resources.

Population figures, like size, prove highly deceptive indices of power, taken in gross form.

The Case of Germany and Russia. Thus Germany triumphed in battle over numerically superior czarist Russia. World War I saw outnumbered German legions defeat Russian armies, despite diversion of German manpower to the Western front against England and France. World War II found Germany unable to repeat her earlier victory, although Nazi armies fought to the gates of Moscow and Stalingrad, killing or capturing millions of Russian soldiers and civilians and laying waste Russia's key industrial and agricultural centers. One important difference between 1914 and 1941 lay in the qualitative transformation of Russia's human resources, changing mere quantitative superiority to actual power superiority.

Quantitatively, Germany has had far fewer persons between twenty and

111

forty-five years of age than has Russia. With a declining ratio of births over deaths, Germany's inferiority became more acute annually, especially when placed against Russia's increasing population. By 1941, less than 14 million Germans in the twenty to forty-five age bracket faced almost 35 million Russians. The precedent of World War I argued persuasively for discounting the Russian figure as composed of diverse racial, ethnic, and socioeconomic groups which would break away from the regime in open revolt, or at least would refuse to marshal their fullest energies behind the war. Hitler's hopes of victory, based partly on illusions of native Teutonic superiority over Slavs, received a critical upset when only an insignificant number of the Soviet population proved disloyal in World War II.[1] What explains this transformation between World Wars I and II? To be sure, Soviet Russia had built an industrial base of considerable magnitude, absent in the earlier conflict. Yet had the strains within the population remained constant, the combined impact of internal disunity and external pressure would have wrecked that industrial base, just as the czarist empire crumbled to defeat and revolution in 1917. Through persuasion as well as through coercion, Soviet leaders had built unity from the diverse groups within Russia, providing a common myth, an efficient government, and consciousness of a common cause. Bigger battalions became stronger battalions. Should a similar transformation occur in China, it will have parallel consequences in any future conflict between China and Japan.

   2. Demography and Power. In evaluating Russian strength, German strategists had to take into account both quantitative and qualitative developments. For the former problem, expressed in the rate of growth or decline in the populations of Germany and Russia, they depended upon demography, the study of population growth. It is not enough to know the comparative size of nations' populations. It is also essential to know how much of the population is of working age, whether this group is getting larger or smaller, and how that trend may be affected in the future. Basic to demography are comprehensive statistics, yet between one-fourth and one-third of the world's population is still uncovered by official census records.[2] China's first modern census came in 1953, and no breakdown of total figures was released to the outside world. Only in the past twenty years has interest in demography persuaded Europe's governments to make systematic studies in terms of age, sex, and employment. Consequently, population data are fragmentary in terms of the total world and brief in terms of man's life on earth. Nevertheless, demographers can furnish policy makers with illuminating hypotheses concerning population development and its role as a factor of power.

   [1] George Fischer, *Soviet Opposition to Stalin,* Harvard University Press, Cambridge, Mass., 1952.
   [2] E. W. Zimmerman, *World Resources and Industries,* Harper, New York, 2d ed., 1951, p. 99.

Stages of Population Growth. Demographers agree that populations remained relatively dormant prior to the Industrial Revolution, dipping somewhat with respect to catastrophes of famine and disease, but otherwise remaining in balance with the food supply available in simple, agrarian conditions. In the next two centuries, however, industrialization spread from the northwestern corner of Europe throughout much of the world, carrying with it patterns of population change so striking as to be described in stages of natural phenomena. There is debate as to the universality of these so-called "laws" of population growth, but omitting the effects of migration, three essential stages emerge. The first, or preindustrial, stage finds population stability maintained through high birth rates and high death rates. With the second, or early industrial, stage improved farming increases food output, permitting more people to live off the same amount of land. The attendant increase in birth rates is highlighted by an even more dramatic decline in death rates, following the introduction of sanitation and preventive medicine. Particularly sharp is the fall in infant mortality. So rapid is the nation's increase in numbers, it is said to be undergoing a population explosion. In the third, or advanced industrial, stage various social and cultural factors set in, causing a decline in the birth rate and hence a fall in net reproductivity. Death rates stabilize at a low figure with the tapering off of medical discoveries. Declining birth rates may eventually fail to keep up with losses through death, resulting in an absolute decline in the total population. Populations in this stage have a high proportion of older persons, since life span is increasing but births are decreasing. It is believed that a fourth stage may develop which would stabilize birth and death rates, leaving them in equal relationship as in the first stage, and thus leveling off the population at a constant but higher figure than in the preindustrial era. So far, however, no nation has reached this fourth, or "postindustrial," stage.

It is impossible to explain conclusively the reasons for the varied phenomena in this population cycle, nor are the causes as interesting as the effect. Suffice to say that so far as the third, or advanced industrial, stage is concerned, man's most exerted efforts have failed to effect any marked change in the trend of declining births. Experiments by Nazi Germany and Fascist Italy in this respect are inconclusive but discourage those who would stabilize or increase their populations in defiance of the population cycle. Minor deviations from the general pattern, such as France's increase in births after World War II despite a long-established declining birth rate, do not as yet call for revisions in the over-all analysis. It remains to be seen what will come of efforts to reverse trends in the second, or early industrial, stage. India, already plagued with periodic famines and starvation, hopes to industrialize and at the same time avoid population explosions. Experiments in birth control there are spotty and so far inconclusive, but symptoms of population explosions in India remain evident.

Populations, then, are a highly unstable factor of power, subject to dynamic changes according to certain external phenomena. Germany's demographic studies showed that if her position vis-à-vis Soviet Russia was one of inferiority in 1940, it would be far more so by 1950. Hitler's determination to conquer parts of Russia thus compelled him to act according to a timetable fixed, in part, by the dynamics of population change.

Comparative Population Strength. While there is considerable disagreement among demographers as to the absolute numbers within each country to be expected in 1970, projections from present trends agree as to the future relationship between nations. Northwestern Europe and the United States are not only in an inferior position, populationwise, with respect to the greater part of the Eurasian land mass, but their position promises to become increasingly worse. While the rate of population growth is declining in the United States, at least the total population will continue to expand. In Great Britain, France, and Germany, however, absolute decreases in population are expected by some demographers. Conversely, Spain, Italy, and all of Eastern Europe are experiencing rising rates of population increase. Serious wartime losses disrupted Soviet population trends, but conservative estimates predict the net reproductivity rate will hold its own for the next fifteen years, and some experts believe that Russia, like Eastern Europe, will continue to increase at an ever faster rate.[3]

Turning to Asia, the pattern follows the demographic picture perfectly, with Japan's population continuing its phenomenal growth of the past decades although showing signs of tapering off its reproductivity rate. China and India, already the first and second most populous countries in the world respectively, feel the first tremors of population explosions, and anticipate more as health facilities improve and industrialization increases.

If these figures are qualified further, it will be found that the declining populations of Great Britain and France are also aging. Thus an ever higher proportion of the population is simultaneously removed from productivity and becomes a burden on the active labor force. Put another way, more people are becoming dependent upon the production of less people. To maintain a standing army of a given size, Britain and France must lower the standards for recruitment annually, given the declining number of persons in younger age brackets. In the Soviet area, just the opposite is true, since the most rapidly expanding sector of the population is in the younger generation. Shown below in population pyramids, arranged according to age groups, are the key sectors of the globe. No words could express more eloquently the comparative quantitative population power of the communist bloc and India as compared with the West.

---

[3] W. Eason, "Population and Labor Force," in A. Bergson (ed.), *Soviet Economic Growth,* Row, Peterson, Evanston, Ill., 1953, pp. 100 ff.

APPROXIMATE POPULATION SIZES, 1955

China (estimated)..................... 571,000,000
India (estimated)..................... 357,000,000
Europe (without the Soviet Union)...... 340,000,000
Soviet Union.......................... 193,000,000
United States......................... 160,000,000
Japan................................. 83,000,000

Before going on to a qualitative analysis of populations in terms of unity and group tensions, one last historical observation should be made. Western man has long been aware of his numerical inferiority when compared with the colored populations of Asia and Africa. References to the "yellow peril" and "Asia's countless hordes" abound in Occidental polemics of the last century. Yet the fact remains that in contemporary history it has been the white man who has invaded and ravaged the red, yellow, brown, and black peoples of the world. His monopoly of mechanical power offset his numerical inferiority, permitting him to extend his rule over most of the world's land area. Perhaps the most significant development of our time is the smashing of that monopoly and with it the overthrow of the white man's rule. Only now are the world centers of population gaining political and economic maturity, introducing new significance into hitherto meaningless population figures.

3. Populations and Groups. Despite the everyday use of such terms as "the Germans," "the Chinese," and "the British," these terms simplify a highly complex picture. Within each nation there are groups, be they racial, ethnic, religious, or the omnipresent socioeconomic groups. The old saying "40 million Frenchmen can't be wrong" might well have been footnoted, "nor can they agree." Instead of "40 million Frenchmen," one might speak of 7.5 million peasants, 4.5 million manufacturing workers, 2.6 million service workers, 2.4 million tradesmen, etc.[4] Similarly, instead of "40 million Frenchmen," one might speak of 38.7 million Catholics, 1 million Protestants, and 0.2 million Jews.[5] Divergent groups spell divergent desires. To bring unity out of diversity is to maximize the power inherent in the total population. Therefore the policy maker must examine his population as well as that of his opponents to see what groups exist and how they may affect national unity, an important factor of national power. In addition to weighing groups in the scales of power, he must appraise their effect upon foreign policy. Conflicting group interests and demands must be resolved by the policy maker if his final policy is to win the support of important sectors of the populace. His policy may require a high level of military appropriations, but if this is strongly opposed by business and consumer interests, necessary

[4] *Annuaire Statistique,* Paris, 1952, p. 353; figures as of 1946.
[5] *Encyclopaedia Britannica Yearbook, 1953.*

revenue may not be forthcoming and the policy will fail. Foreign policy may be affected in a less direct manner, when group tensions within a nation mount to the point of challenging an elite's continued control of government. In this case, the ruling group may seek to alleviate internal tension by channeling it against another nation, "scapegoating" an external "devil." An otherwise conciliatory foreign policy thus becomes overtly hostile largely because of group tensions within the population.

Focusing on unity as a factor of power, we find that while populations may be numerically categorized in terms of age, productivity, and food supply, their cohesiveness or morale is not subject to statistical analysis. Group identification is a difficult task at best, depending not only on the raw data assembled from census reports but also upon the definition of groups utilized by the analyst. Racial groups may be identified according to color or genealogy; socioeconomic groups may be identified according to means of livelihood, earning ability, or consumption patterns. Once groups have been identified, some way must be found of measuring the degree of tension among them, and determining how susceptible it is to outside influences. Obviously there is a lack of precision and a high degree of subjectivity threatening any analysis of human resources, yet without such an analysis serious misjudgments of a nation's power can result. Canada's strength cannot be computed without an understanding of the schisms between French and English and the attendant economic obstacles preventing equal development of all the country's resources.

As was noted in Chapter 1, the individual plays his role in the political arena through participation with persons sharing similar attitudes and views, in other words, by joining with a group. His act of joining may be conscious or unconscious, voluntary or involuntary, but it is marked by his acceptance of a way of thinking, an ideology. Seen in this light, the existence of groups within a nation inevitably poses minimal problems of communication. In so far as these groups possess differing frames of reference, or a different sense of reality, the policy maker's appeal for support must use varying approaches. In so far as they possess differing values and interests, conflict and competition must be regulated, lest the nation be torn asunder by internecine warfare. Bearing these points in mind, it remains to examine the various types of informal groups which, by means of organized interest groups, affect national power and foreign policy, and then to study the types of tensions they may arouse and the means of alleviating those tensions.

Racial Groups. Race as a determinant of group affiliation continues to occupy first place in most population analyses, not because it generates the greatest tension, but because in many ways it is the most readily identifiable means of group affiliation. Inherited physical characteristics, whether of color, size, or facial features, establish an initial differentiation between members of different races. This initial differentiation is usually heightened by the tendency to attribute cultural differences to racial origin, thus assuming that members of different races also have different values and interests. By systematizing these cultural and racial differences into a pattern or stereotype, members of diverse races form group images of those outside their group. In this way, it is more than race which separates racial groups, since the group image, the way in which men view other men, assumes separation on the basis of race, value, and interest. Ideology of racial groups reinforces identification, although that identification basically is in inherited physical characteristics.

The concept of group image as a definer of reality is well illustrated by the relationship of white and yellow races in the United States. Chinese coolies, brought to the western United States in the mid-nineteenth century for construction on transcontinental railroads, were enthusiastically described by employers who imported them as thrifty, sober, and law-abiding.[6] In order to win their acceptance as cheap labor among the new settlers, a group image much more favorable than reality developed in the press and fiction of the time. However, after railroad construction was finished, no ready work lay at hand for these Chinese, and increased labor competition made their presence resented by white workers. Again with little regard for reality, a new group image typed the formerly "frugal" Chinese as possessing a "lowered plane of living." Once "worthy citizens," they were now "unassimilable," "opium-ridden," and "crime breeders." Such rapid changes in group images as shown in communication media may not be paralleled completely by the personal way in which individual members of groups view one another, but there is no denying the subtle and persistent influence of word and picture in shaping human relations.

Race groups are least assimilable of all groups within nations and the most easily identifiable; hence they often pose the most serious challenges to national unity and provide the easiest avenue of approach for an outside nation, determined to exploit disunity. Hostile group images intensify suspicion of the different, of the strange or unknown. The physical properties of racial groups as well as the attendant group images combine to make race the most durable factor of group affiliation within a nation. Since in many countries with more than one race, political control is monopolized by members of a dominant race, analysis of racial tensions provides significant insights into a nation's strengths and weaknesses.

Ethnic Groups. Ethnic groups are less easily identifiable, being based on acquired cultural characteristics derived from point of family origin, whether in the present or past generation. Language, folkways, and dress set off members of diverse ethnic groups. As with race groups, these differences often become stereotyped into group images, tending to intensify differences between ethnic groups. The problem of communication among ethnic groups is

[6] B. Shrieke, *Alien Americans*, Viking, New York, 1936.

particularly severe if, as in the Balkans, separate dialects or languages remain as hallmarks of ethnic origin. National unity and foreign policy become immediately intertwined when ethnic minorities border on a so-called "mother" country, sharing a common language and culture at variance with the ruling group of the state in which the ethnic minority is located.

Racial and ethnic groups share several characteristics which distinguish them from other groups in our analysis. First and foremost, membership in them is almost wholly involuntary. Only in marginal instances is an individual able to pass from one racial group to another; his physical characteristics remain with him for life. It is, of course, much simpler to change ethnic group affiliation than racial group, but problems of integration into new cultural patterns are formidable. Initially, persons are born into ethnic groups; they do not choose them of free will. Movement between racial or ethnic groups is often rigidly controlled by the dominant group in the population. Prohibited intermarriage, segregated living, and discriminatory employment all discourage individuals from shifting membership in these groups. Thus they play a fairly constant role in a nation's population picture, with few significant changes within one generation.

Another basic characteristic of racial and ethnic groups is the great degree to which they are rooted in the most elemental of all groups, the family. Here is the area of greatest attitude formation; here is the most dynamic center of ideological reinforcement. Bonds of belief forged in the home may withstand tremendous pressures from other groups, be they school, factory, or community. Thus the ideologies of racial and ethnic groups prove more comprehensive in development than of other groups, increasing their divisive powers considerably.

Socioeconomic Groups. Economic groups generally cut across racial and ethnic lines and are commonly distinguished by their means of earning a livelihood, although income categorizations are sometimes employed. Imprecision in so general a term as "economic group" permits extremes of classification, on the one hand the broad Marxist generalization of producing classes, on the other the highly detailed United States census breakdown of occupational skills. More concrete for analyzing groups and their role in policy formulation is the term "socioeconomic group." This associates job with role, with social prestige. It is not only means of livelihood that identifies socioeconomic groups, but the place they hold in the social and political hierarchy of a community.

Socioeconomic groups vary considerably in their fluidity of membership and mobility in the social hierarchy. At one extreme, China's scholar bureaucracy for centuries recruited its members exclusively through a comprehensive, complicated set of Confucian examinations. Becoming literate required years of training, a luxury often enjoyed only by sons of officials or landholders. Since government could be conducted only by the limited literate section of the populace, the ascendancy of the scholar-official was assured. Fluidity and mobility remained at a minimum. At the other extreme, Soviet Russia's managerial elite increased tenfold between 1930 and 1940 with the tremendous expansion of industry under the Five Year Plans, the provision of free technical training to all regardless of social origin, and the high casualty rate within the ranks of more experienced technicians because of purges which followed economic disorder. Status was won easily, in terms of productivity, but removed swiftly, by means of purge. Fluidity and mobility were at a maximum.

Differing racial and ethnic groups are extant in some populations but not in others. Socioeconomic groups, however, exist in all countries. Policy makers, by definition, are members of socioeconomic groups, sometimes a separate one in itself, the bureaucracy. The more industrialized a nation, the more diversified are its socioeconomic groupings. Often highly articulate and operating in small but highly important areas of a nation's economic or political structure, these groups can generate tensions capable of shattering national unity and of drastically reducing industrial power. Their conflicting demands pose constant problems to those confronted with maximizing industrial as well as human resources in time of international conflict.

Religious Groups. Religious groups occupy the last, and probably least important, position in this study of groups which affect national power. Identified basically in terms of organized spiritual affiliation, they encompass all-embracing world beliefs such as Buddhism, Mohammedanism, Catholicism, and Judaism, as well as smaller regional sects such as Wahabis, Uniates, Quakers, and Seventh-day Adventists. Grouping themselves around an identity of value, they are highly fluid in membership in most of the world, except where remnants of caste remain, as in part of India.

As with all attempts to systematize human beings and human behavior, marginal situations arise which defy simple classification. Reference to Judaism under religious groups may be justifiable so far as the orthodox Jew is concerned, but what of the millions who are identified as Jews but do not practice the orthodox faith? They are neither a racial, ethnic (except for those born of Israeli citizenship), socioeconomic, nor religious group. They are, in different communities and in different circumstances, identified according to one or more, possibly all, of these classifications. Tensions arising from anti-Semitism, then, provide a unique example of group pressures within a community, and can be explained only in terms of the surrounding circumstances in each separate instance.

4. Group Tensions and National Power. Group tensions manifest themselves in various ways, posing a series of challenges to those anxious to maximize national unity and strength. Some tensions subside readily; others require slow and arduous solution. Evaluation of groups as a qualifying factor of national power must be two-dimensional, in terms of both challenge and response. Only by examining the way in which group conflicts weaken nations, and then reviewing the possible means of alleviating those tensions, can we get a complete picture of the interaction of population and power, of cohesiveness and national morale.

Racial Tensions. Racial tensions, reflected in a continuum ranging from passive prejudice to explosive race riots, concern policy makers because they disrupt a nation internally and in some cases threaten the continued control of the dominant racial group. South Africa, ruled by whites but overwhelmingly populated by Negroes, has often seethed with racial tensions which repeatedly since World War II have verged on complete rebellion. Police brutality, extended curfew hours, ruthless denial of political, economic, and social privileges, all have failed to subdue the Negroes, who have answered with widespread passive resistance and intermittent rioting. Discrimination against Indians living in South Africa raised the internal problem to international proportions, with charges against the South African government being pressed by India in the United Nations. Internally and externally, racial tensions threaten to burst this country asunder.

Elsewhere in Africa, racial tensions threaten to oust European whites who, for more than two centuries, have found prestige and profit in colonial holdings. The peaceful evolution of the Gold Coast contrasts sharply with the bloody internecine warfare of Kenya. Greater familiarity with the mechanics of struggle, whether by ballot or by bullet, promises to move African leaders to new positions of strength in demanding independence, or at least equality.

Less serious in import but no less dramatic are racial tensions in the United States. American insecurities springing from racial unrest between white and yellow played an important role in the first half of the twentieth century. Agitation against persons of Oriental descent living along the West Coast resulted in restrictive educational and housing laws for California before World War I. Although the agitation stemmed largely from local white labor organizations seeking to restrict labor supply and opportunistic politicians seeking to ride an ultrapatriotic bandwagon, its consequences for American foreign policy were far-reaching. Japan's concern over the fate of its nationals living in California prompted President Theodore Roosevelt to conclude a "gentleman's agreement" restricting Japanese emigration to the United States. In 1923, reverberations of the California controversy reached the Supreme Court and Congress, with judicial decisions upholding restrictive racial covenants and legislation aimed at excluding Orientals from further entry into the United States. The Oriental Exclusion Act, as had been feared by the Department of State, inflamed anti-American passions in Japan and provided a convenient whipping boy for bellicose, nationalistic circles in Japan. Though obviously not the cause of the Japanese attack at Pearl Harbor in 1941, racial tensions nevertheless played a part in worsening

Japanese-American relations at a time when other sources of international friction between the two powers were on the increase.

Ethnic Tensions. Ethnic tensions abound in modern times, with much of Europe's interwar history the tale of entire areas becoming pawns of international politics. To take only one example, Czechoslovakia's creation in 1919 brought within the borders of the newly founded state 3 million Germans, centered in the northwestern region, called Sudetenland. Failing to win acceptance by Czechs and Slovaks and to integrate fully into the country, these Germans provided a recurrent source of friction. Their social, political, and educational grievances often went ignored, until Adolf Hitler expressed concern for the so-called "lost Germans" living outside the Third Reich. Manufacturing new grievances and playing upon old ones, his fifth-column agitators succeeded in widening the gulf of suspicion and distrust within Czechoslovakia. Finally in 1938, Hitler forced the Czech government to cede the area to Germany, gaining simultaneously control of Czechoslovakia's only good line of defense. Conquest of the rest of the country came easy to Germany the following year. It was a classic example of ethnic tensions being exploited successfully by a foreign nation, reducing Czechoslovakia's national strength to zero.

Socioeconomic Tensions. Socioeconomic tensions may paralyze a nation's economy by workers' strikes or peasant riots. They may cripple a nation's political power by blocking cabinet formations or by impeding administration of law and order. They may lower a nation's military power by reducing morale at the front because of unrest at home, or by arousing revolt between soldier and officer. All these manifestations of socioeconomic tension erupted in czarist Russia during World War I, bringing about the downfall both of the imperial Romanov dynasty and of the short-lived Provisional Government of March to November, 1917. Peasants in the hinterland released their pent-up demands by seizing land and burning manors, and defied government attempts to collect food for the starving cities. Strikes and industrial disorder slowed deliveries of munitions to the front, already suffering from defeat. Armies recruited largely from the peasant population became increasingly restive under the aristocratic officer corps; desertions from czarist forces exceeded proportionately those of all other combatants in World War I. Paralysis in the government, stagnation of the economy, and defeat at the front combined to topple czarist Russia. Its successor, the Provisional Government, failed to solve the dilemma and only a complete overturn of the old socioeconomic order by the Bolsheviks succeeded in reestablishing national unity and strength, albeit after civil war and extreme measures of repression.

According to Marxist analysis, socioeconomic tensions are inevitable in all nonsocialist countries and must result in the overthrow of the existing

systems everywhere. Without going so far, it is clear that they plague many
states in the world. Peasant-landlord tensions in particular lie at the root
of much governmental instability in the Middle East and Southeast Asia, as
well as at the heart of the two great revolutions of our century, in Russia
and in China. Similarly, tensions between management and labor limit productivity in many sectors of European industry, and are reflected in the
sizable Communist vote consistently returned in French and Italian elections
since World War II. Absenteeism, high labor turnover, and deteriorations in
quality all attend industrial unrest in Eastern Europe, while alternate policies
of pacifying and policing the peasants suggest deep-rooted problems between
Communist elites and rural populations. No more meaningful or persistent
source of weakness in the national power pattern can be found than that
arising from socioeconomic tensions.

Religious Tensions. Religious tensions generally have been decreasingly
important in the Western world, although they assumed new significance in
Eastern Europe after World War II. Newly organized Communist governments unleashed a systematic campaign against all churches, arousing stubborn resistance, particularly in Protestant East Germany and in Catholic
Poland. Despite occasional rumblings and reverberations from these areas,
this may well be Europe's last serious religious controversy. In Asia, however,
religious tensions exploded with dramatic violence between Hindus and
Moslems as India emerged from colonial rule. So bitter proved the animosity
that partition seemed the only solution, leaving the major land mass to India
but splitting in two the Moslem state of Pakistan. Subsequent migration of
Hindus and Moslems to their respective nations was accompanied by wholesale slaughter, in which thousands of persons died in frenzied religious riots.
Religious tensions continued to beset the Nehru government with problems.
Internally pockets of unrest remained subject to Communist exploitation,
while externally, a prolonged dispute with Pakistan concerning jurisdiction
over Kashmir threatened to embroil both countries in full-scale war.

Concern over religious tensions, although subsiding, remains operative
today. Soviet Russia has within its orbit millions of Moslems whose sympathies may lie with the Moslem nations of the Middle East, millions of
Jews whose allegiance may give Israel priority in time of conflict, and
millions of Catholics whose loyalty to Rome may make them unwilling subjects of Moscow. Less complex situations with greater or lesser significance
may be found in Germany, France, Canada, and the United States. Paradoxically, members of religious groups live in greater security, the weaker
is the cohesiveness of their faith, for as national values take precedence over
religious values, ruling groups can afford to become more tolerant of divergent
religious groups within the body politic. With the triumph of "my country,
right or wrong" over "thou shalt not kill," questions of religious differences
diminish in importance as a factor of power.

5. Alleviations of Tensions to Preserve Power. Faced with the challenge of group tensions, elites have a choice of responses, assuming that their aim is maximizing national power by unifying the population. Ranging from the ruthless use of force and repression to the skilled manipulation of hostilities and displacement, these responses vary in success according to the type of challenge. Because there is no sure cure for internal conflicts which weaken a nation in time of crisis, group tensions continue to confound policy makers.

Repression. Most obvious and immediate of all methods used to alleviate group tensions is repression or elimination of one of the conflicting groups. The alleviation may be permanent, if one of the groups is exterminated. Within the Soviet Union, socioeconomic tensions between the wealthier stratum of the peasant class and the Communist elite resulted in extermination of several millions of so-called "kulaks" in the collectivization period of Soviet agriculture. Such extreme measures are seldom acceptable in non-authoritarian nations, and they involve a potential weakening of national strength by the very loss of so large a segment of human resources. More practical means of eliminating entire groups came with population transfers, first attempted after World War I, but employed on a mass scale in Europe and Asia after World War II. So serious was the interwar problem of Europe's ethnic minorities that many statesmen believed repatriation was the best solution. Transferral of millions of Germans, Poles, and Russians in Europe, and millions more of Hindus and Moslems in India, uprooted entire communities from long-established homes. This response eliminated ethnic tensions, to be sure, but socioeconomic tensions sprang from the newcomers in strange lands, often destitute and with no immediate occupation. Such wholesale migrations furnish dramatic proof of the importance given population homogeneity by elites, but they also reveal the problems inherent in the use of force as a means of accomplishing it.

The most common use of repression in dealing with group tensions is non-violent political and economic domination by a ruling group. By using the authority of government and the control of wealth, it seeks to keep subservient groups so weak as to make dissent impossible. No better example of the internal and external consequences of such a policy can be found than in czarist Russia. Great Russians, fanning out from the ancient capital of Moscovy, conquered many races and many ethnic groups, including White Russians, Ukrainians, Kazakhs, Mongols, and all other peoples between the Baltic Sea and the Pacific Ocean, from northern Siberia down to inner Asia. Truly a "prison of nations," czarist officialdom systematically excluded non-Russians from political posts, attempted to Russify entire peoples by means of compulsory lingual unity, and in some instances instituted pogroms against special groups such as the Jews. Socioeconomic strains accumulated under the oppressive life of serfdom and the deplorable conditions which followed its abolition. Workers were denied political rights, and their organizations were permeated with police-spies and *agents provocateurs*. When reforms instituted shortly before World War I provided a quasi parliament an opportunity to vent grievances against the government, it was summarily dismissed.

The consequences are too well known to require more than brief summary. From without, German efforts to alienate Poles, Finns, Ukrainians, and others resulted in centrifugal forces which weakened the Russian empire along its vast periphery. In March, 1917, the czarist government fell; in July, the last Russian offensive failed to win a decisive victory on the Eastern front; in January, 1918, the Germans, through the treaty of Brest-Litovsk, removed Russia from the war and dismembered large chunks of the old Russian empire.

Repression may be applied against all group tensions, regardless of their origin. Its success depends upon the extent of its application. Partial repression may merely increase the latent strains of disunity and only delay the day of reckoning between groups. Total repression, or group liquidation, is not without other risks to national power, but is undoubtedly effective so far as alleviating the initial tension is concerned.

Assimilation and Integration. Assimilation of racial and ethnic groups parallels repression only in that it seeks to eliminate the source of tension by eliminating one of the groups. In the United States, great waves of immigration at the end of the nineteenth century brought millions of Europeans to American shores, to be dispersed over the vast continent and remolded under the impact of mass production and mass consumption. Public education provided second-generation immigrants with a common language. Films and other communication media established a common cultural pattern. While concentrations of Irish, Italians, Poles, Germans, and more recently Puerto Ricans aroused minor ethnic tensions in metropolitan areas and influenced foreign policy discussions in Congress, America presents an ethnically placid scene compared to Europe. It is not only distance which explains the weakness of ties between the "mother country" and American ethnic groups. Assimilation provides a more meaningful answer: the mass impact of American culture with its overriding desire to conform, to be like the heroes and heroines of Hollywood's films and New York's magazines.

Assimilation has proved less successful with racial than with ethnic groups in the United States, although the notable failure of repression against black and yellow groups is turning private and public efforts more and more to methods of assimilation. Crucial to success of this response is fluidity and mobility of movement within the socioeconomic hierarchy of the community. Access to elite status must remain open to all persons, regardless of race or ethnic origin, lest the national myth of egalitarian values become so distorted in reality that individuals find it of greater advantage to remain as hyphenated identities, as German-Americans or Polish-Americans. As the individual ascends the socioeconomic ladder, however, he identifies himself less and less with racial and ethnic groups, although sometimes relying on their support for election or for business. His assimilation is not only a function of mass consumption and mass communication, but also a function of the American socioeconomic framework.

Totally different responses to challenges of racial, ethnic, and socioeconomic group tensions typify the Soviet Union. Although both the American and the Russian approaches seek the same end, a cohesive community, they use diametrically opposite means. The United States seeks to assimilate all peoples into one larger culture; the Soviet Union seeks to emphasize cultural differences between groups while removing conflict by means of control from the center. Learning from czarist Russia lessons of repression and its consequences, Lenin and his followers attempted to achieve unity in diversity. Politically, a federal structure granted territorial recognition to various groups, with varying amounts of autonomy being accorded in proportion to the size of the ethnic group concerned. This not only symbolized self-rule, but placed representatives of the more than forty different ethnic and racial groups in the highest organs of government in the Soviet Union, a thing unknown under the old regime. Culturally, the slogan "National in form, socialist in content" sanctioned cultural differences in such external manifestations as language and arts, while maintaining cultural unity by the internal content of the message conveyed. Instead of stamping out minority languages, the Soviets have actually increased the number of written languages in Russia, compiling dictionaries for hitherto unwritten Asian dialects. Music, films, and paintings depict traditional Armenian, Mongolian, Estonian, and Azerbaijanian crafts. The meaning is always Marxism-Leninism-Stalinism, but the symbols vary according to group. Together with certain symbols propagated throughout the Soviet Union, such as the red star, Lenin's tomb, and the Kremlin towers, these ethnic symbols reduce tensions to a minimal degree, while political representation in the central government at Moscow permits identification of the various regions with the over-all entity, the Soviet Union.

To be sure, neither American assimilation nor Soviet integration enjoys full success. In the United States, no Catholic has succeeded in winning the Presidency, and only one Jew has reached the Senate in recent years. Soviet political appointments have shown a steadily decreasing proportion of Jews in top levels, until today only a few hold positions of importance in the Russian Communist Party and a handful are in key positions in the Soviet government. Such practices suggest a barely perceptible level of group tension, largely along religious lines. Similarly, repeated Soviet diatribes against "bourgeois chauvinism" indicate that divisive ethnic pride and prejudices continue to generate tension in many parts of the country. That neither nation suffered any obvious loss of national power in World War II from these points of friction, however, indicates their insignificance in the larger picture of international relations.

The Appeal to Nationalism. Persuasion and coercion, the twin tools of political manipulation, operate in both the American and Russian systems, although in different proportions. Soviet coercion against kulaks has already been cited; similar measures against the Volga Germans in World War II resulted in their complete disappearance in Siberian concentration camps. American coercion against those of Japanese ancestry led to the incarceration of 115,000 persons resident on the West Coast at the outbreak of World War II, with considerable property loss and problems of relocation after Japan was defeated. Both systems, however, employ a response to group tensions which has been mentioned but not examined closely, namely, the appeal to the national myth, to values and interests shared in common by all groups within the national community.

The individual is simultaneously member of a racial, ethnic, socioeconomic, and perhaps religious group. Racial ideology may stress hostility toward persons of different color; socioeconomic interests may demand accommodation with fellow associates. If racial and economic values conflict, which is to triumph? Obviously the answer varies with individual and incident, yet the fact remains that individuals belong to different groups with conflicting sets of interests and values. Just as we have described the pluralistic state, so Gordon Allport calls this the pluralistic personality, or *personae*. As another authority, Max Horkeimer, comments,[7]

Education, whether in the family, the school, or the outside world, seems to provide the individual with a set of masks rather than a coherent integrated personality. . . . The child learns almost instinctively that different situations demand different values. . . . The social roots of the personae phenomenon lie in the very existence of modern man in a constant dichotomy between public and private life.

If multiple-group membership complicates a simple scheme of group analysis, it also explains one means of alleviating group tensions. By appealing to a rival set of values held by an individual belonging to several groups, his overt hostility may be tempered and tension eased. Elites may hold up principles of proletarian solidarity or of religious brotherhood, in a successful effort to bring unity out of disunity. Thus World War II presented the anomaly of one generation of Americans with Japanese ancestry being interned in concentration camps while the next generation fought along with other American units overseas. Negro participation in America's military effort was unmarred by disloyalty or disaffection, despite segregation in the armed forces and continued tensions at home. Nisei and Negro were simultaneously Americans, sharing a system of values which explicitly promised equality for all, inferiority for none. Means to this end traditionally lie in peaceful political action. Given the frontal assault of fascism against all non-Teutonic races and against all democratic values, participation in the war was definitely in keeping with the interests and values of minority races in the United States.

[7] H. Cantril (ed.), *Tensions That Cause Wars*, University of Illinois Press, Urbana, Ill., 1950, p. 230.

Because multiple-group membership permits an appeal to national values for all groups, be they racial, ethnic, socioeconomic, or religious, it does not follow that the appeal will be successful. Nationalism as a cohesive factor in time of crisis is an indeterminate influence, seldom studied scientifically. General observation indicates, however, that it is fallacious to presume that an external attack automatically unites the groups within a target nation. To be sure, limited studies suggest that light attacks and remote misses in air bombardments may bring increased cohesiveness from the attending assurance of survival power, impetus to unite against the enemy, and tangible evidence of enemy aggression. As one post–World War II report concluded, "In contrast to the powerful reinforcement of fear reactions which occurs among those who are near-misses, the level of fear is *diminished* among the remote-misses, i.e., those who are exposed to an air raid in which they do not directly experience a narrow escape or direct personal loss. . . . [They] show increased capacity to withstand the emotional stress of subsequent air attacks." [8] The same report noted, however, that disruption of food supplies, destruction of housing, and breakdown of medical facilities after prolonged attack increased group tension and significantly lowered morale.

The twentieth century abounds in instances where nationalism failed to unify populations against external attack. During World War II, Chinese Communists and Nationalists waged pitched battles against one another, although Japanese troops continued to tighten their stranglehold on China's main centers of population and industry. Fifth-column operations helped to win quick victories for Nazi Germany in Denmark, Norway, Holland, Belgium, and, to a lesser extent, France. Appeal to national values and interests embodied in the myth which unites the divergent groups within a population is, then, only another type of response to group tensions. It is no certain cure.

Displacement. The final type of response important for study of international relations and the role that group tensions play internally as well as externally is that of displacement. Displacing, or transferring hostility between groups to a common enemy or "scapegoat," springs from the same phenomenon as an appeal to national values, namely, multiple-group membership. Just as groups within the national community share certain wants in common, so they share certain fears. Acting as a lightning rod, the scapegoat channels potential revolt away from the threatened group and grounds it safely in elite-directed hostility. As Harold Lasswell noted, "One of the principal functions of symbols of remote objects, like nations and classes, is to serve as targets for the relief of many of the tensions which might discharge disastrously in face-to-face relations." [9]

Displacement of tensions within a nation may alleviate one type of group

[8] I. L. Janis, *Air War and Emotional Stress*, McGraw-Hill, New York, 1951, p. 123.
[9] H. Lasswell, *World Politics and Personal Insecurity*, McGraw-Hill, New York, 1935, p. 73.

tension while heightening another. Adolf Hitler came to power amidst mass unemployment, mass dissatisfaction with Germany's inferior position in the society of nations, and growing fears of Communist disorder. Pitting group against group, he whipped up frenzied assemblages of supporters, channeling all their insecurities and frustrations into hatred of an internal scapegoat, the Jews. Typical of Hitler's anti-Semitic tirades is the following excerpt: [10]

> The Jew today is the great agitator for the complete destruction of Germany. Wherever in the world we read about attacks on Germany, Jews are their fabricators; indeed just as both before and during the War, the Jewish stock exchange and Marxist press deliberately added fuel to the hate for Germany, until State after State abandoned neutrality and entered the service of the World War coalition against their true national interests.

Hitler's external scapegoat, Bolshevism, came in for less consistent treatment, particularly during the period of the Nazi-Soviet pact. However, Judaism and Bolshevism, often merged into a single symbol, served the Nazi regime as a perpetual excuse for internal failure and prod for increased unity. Use of the Jews exacerbated Hitler's foreign relations, particularly with the United States, while his disparaging treatment of Slavs and the Russians led to war and ultimately defeat. Scapegoating, then, may serve to unify a population but, if directed externally, becomes an immediate problem of foreign policy.

Fundamental to scapegoating—indeed, to most methods of alleviating group tension—is proper use of propaganda. Before proceeding to analyze the role of the policy maker as a member of a group or groups in the national community, the relationship of propaganda and national power must first be reviewed, in order to understand the factors which condition its use.

6. Propaganda and Power. Internally, propaganda, as its name implies, propagates or spreads the basic myth of the community, necessary for engendering faith in and loyalty to prevailing principles. It may be a distortion of reality, deifying Lenin and Lincoln as symbols of national unity, or it may be a simple reproduction of flag or monument. Propaganda is not defined in terms of truth or falsehood, good or evil, but in terms of intent. If information is communicated in order to improve skills or to increase knowledge, it is called education. If its aim is to shape political attitudes or actions, it is called propaganda.

As has been shown, various responses are open to elites who wish to manipulate tensions so as to unify populations. Except for the extreme measure of complete group elimination, propaganda, the handmaiden of persuasion, plays a pivotal role in every response, whether it is repression, assimilation, integrated diversity, appeal to national values, or displacement. Externally, propaganda attempts to strengthen bonds among allies and weaken the power

[10] A. Hitler, *Mein Kampf*, Reynal & Hitchcock, New York, 1941, p. 906.

of opponents by dividing them and their peoples. This external use of propaganda as a tool of foreign policy necessitates counterpropaganda by the ruling group of the target nation, thus placing another emphasis upon persuasion as a means of achieving unity. As Hans Speier, renowned propaganda analyst, has noted, the propagandist "tries to strengthen the authority of the government among the governed, so that the governed will like to do what the government wants them to do, and dislike doing what the government wants to be left undone. Both as a public-relations man of the police and as a celebrator of governmental accomplishments, the propagandist eliminates dissent in the political community." [11]

Limitations of Propaganda. As with all factors of power, propaganda has both quantitative and qualitative aspects. Quantitatively, it holds statistical supremacy among all man's productive efforts. Should no catastrophe destroy the perishable items of contemporary civilization, future historians will be swamped with newspapers, magazines, books, pamphlets, wire and tape recordings, films, microfilms, and other means whereby rulers and ruled record their words of wisdom. These words command twentieth-century man to act or not-act, to hate or love, to believe or disbelieve.

Despite this staggering quantity of verbiage, dissent and doubt remain, even in the most authoritarian community. One clue to propaganda's limitations lies in the very fact that man encounters so much of it. In a democratic-pluralistic community, competing elites counter each other's appeals, often leaving target groups in a passive, confused condition. American foreign policy vacillated between isolation and intervention in the years before Pearl Harbor, partly because of a heated propaganda campaign between an America First group and a Committee to Defend America by Helping the Allies. Ethnic tensions mounted as pro-German and pro-British attitudes clashed, leaving much of the country uncommitted to any attitude and consequently unable to support any policy. Thus "neutralization" nullifies propaganda because in pluralistic communities every propaganda has its counterpart. In another example of "neutralization," trade-union members subject to propaganda pressures from both Catholic and Communist sources were found to have moderate or mixed views about the Soviet Union, and as the author of the study observed, "People are prone to avoid the conflict of contending propaganda by rejecting one of the contestants or by withdrawing their attention from the contest. . . . Although continued exposure to conflicting propaganda apparently makes for moderation of opinion, such moderation is more likely to be a manifestation of confusion and contradiction than the careful weighing of the different viewpoints." [12]

In the authoritarian, oligarchical community, such crosscurrents and inner

---

[11] E. Kris and H. Speier, *German Radio Propaganda*, Oxford, New York, 1944, p. 4.

[12] M. Krisberg, "Cross-pressures and Attitudes: A Study of the Influence of Conflicting Propaganda on Opinions Regarding American-Soviet Relations," *Public Opinion Quarterly*, vol. 13, 1949, p. 15.

contradictions are less frequent. Quantitative measurement of propaganda takes on more significance when it is primarily the decision of a single agency which decides the appeal or "line" to be taken throughout a country, as in Nazi Germany or Soviet Russia. However, even here mere tabulation of the volume of words addressed to target groups is hampered by the phenomenon of "saturation." Repetition engenders belief, particularly when unchallenged by counterstatement, but it also appears to reach a point of diminishing returns, ultimately engendering skepticism and disbelief. As with the boy who repeatedly called "Wolf!" until one day his pleas failed to bring response, so with totalitarian propagandists, the problem arises of how to affect attitudes and actions if message content remains the same. Joseph Goebbels, propagandist *extraordinaire* for Nazi Germany, sought to avoid repetition if the desired result had already been achieved, if the theme proved boring, or if the message seemed unimpressive. He worried lest abuse of propaganda encourage Germans to "read between the lines." [13] Like a sponge which can absorb only so much liquid, the mind accepts just so much message content, and further repetition brings negative results.

Techniques of Propaganda. Quantitatively, propaganda is impressive only superficially. The most basic challenge to this superficial evidence of its power potential lies in the fact that because groups must be appealed to within their own ideological framework, propaganda must be directed and shaped for a specific target. Thus the question is not merely, "How much was said to how many?" but rather, "What was said to whom?" This changes a quantitative to a qualitative analysis, a vital step in bringing propaganda into proper focus. Substituting depth of communication for extent of communication emphasizes a cardinal principle of successful propaganda: it must not only be heard or seen; it must be acted upon.

It is not necessary to recapitulate the many differences which distinguish racial, ethnic, socioeconomic, and religious groups. Suffice to say that both basic differences in values and interests and acquired differences in behavior limit the effectiveness of so-called mass communication. It is highly significant that the Soviet elite relies upon face-to-face agitators as a basic means of propaganda dissemination, despite that elite's monopoly control of radio, television, film, and all printed matter. These agitators, always members of the Communist Party and thus subject to control from above, are chosen from regular workers in the various factories, farms, and institutions throughout the country and remain in daily contact with their fellow workers.[14] Thus they combine knowledge of the policy of line to be propagated, received principally through a semimonthly handbook, with knowledge of the group toward which the message is directed. Unlike the radio broadcaster, they can

[13] L. W. Doob, "Goebbels' Principles of Propaganda," *Public Opinion Quarterly,* vol. 14, 1950, p. 435.

[14] A. Inkeles, *Public Opinion in Soviet Russia,* Harvard University Press, Cambridge, Mass., 1950, pp. 67 ff.

see and be seen, an asset in establishing confidence and in judging reaction. Unlike the newspaper, they decide the time and circumstance under which the message is received. Unlike the film, their audience is bound together by face-to-face verbal contact. In brief, use of the agitator follows the pattern of the most basic group, the family, and seeks to approximate the conditions which make it the primary molder of attitude and action.

The greater the anticipated crisis within Soviet Russia, the more extensive is the use of the agitator. In July, 1953, Lavrenti P. Beria, head of the Soviet secret police and member of the all-important Presidium of the Central Committee of the Communist Party, was suddenly removed from office amidst charges of being a "traitor and foreign hireling." Beria's removal was prompted by socioeconomic as well as by ethnic tensions. Even before the news of his dismissal was announced in the press, 2,000 members of the Central Committees of the Moscow environs assembled in the stately Hall of Columns to receive the news from a top Moscow Communist. Later that day, similar meetings were held in all the major cities, auto works, tractor factories, and collective farms. For almost two weeks afterward, mass meetings across the entire Soviet Union explained Beria's dismissal to all groups and individuals. Harrison Salisbury, *New York Times* correspondent in Moscow, cabled,[15]

The pattern of these meetings was the same in each instance. . . . The party speaker was followed in the case of the factory meetings by spokesmen from the ranks—steel workers, mechanics, and so on, all of whom pledged eternal loyalty to the party and the Government and praised the wisdom and vigilance . . . in unmasking in such timely fashion Beria's perfidy. . . . They [the party and government] want all the people in the shops and offices and factories and farms to have a chance to hear at first hand from informed party spokesmen exactly what Beria has been charged with and what the case is against him.

Communication, then, need not be mechanically perfect or psychologically oriented in order to be successful propaganda. Conversely, however, all the mechanical inventions and psychological studies come to naught if the propagandist is unable to bridge the differences which separate various groups within his community. Appeal to national values alone will not always suffice, as has already been demonstrated. Manipulation of symbols thought to represent basic needs rooted in man and associated with unconscious fears or desires undoubtedly is highly effective. However, in the only case where such manipulation was given priority over all other means of propaganda, in Nazi Germany, group tensions remained in peace and war, in victory and defeat. It is insight, not inventiveness, which enables elites to employ propaganda toward furthering national unity and relieving internal tensions.

In sum, then, propaganda cannot be measured in terms of volume. It must

[15] H. Salisbury, "On the Surface Moscow Is Calm," *The New York Times Magazine,* July 19, 1953, p. 31.

be defined by a policy, directed at a group, and evaluated in terms of responsive attitudes and actions. It demands of the propagandist and of the policy maker an ability to communicate within the frame of reference of specific groups, despite the fact that the policy maker and propagandists are themselves members of groups which may have divergent values and interests. This study of group tensions will therefore be completed with an examination of the position of the policy maker vis-à-vis groups within the national community.

7. Group Tensions and Ruling Groups. Because policy makers are members of groups, they are not always free to choose which of several responses they will use for a given situation. Their group ideology may rule out certain means of alleviating tension. They are thus unable to rise above the conflict, as it were, and apply the solution which might violate the interests of the group to which they belong.

The Example of China. Thus Kuomintang China, under the leadership of Chiang Kai-shek, suffered from policy makers whose separate group interests conflicted with the appeal to national ideology propagated by Chiang himself. Dr. Sun Yat-sen, founder of the Chinese Republic, laid the basis for a new national ideology in his famous Three People's Principles, often translated as People's Democracy, People's Livelihood, and People's Nationalism. Claiming the mantle of Sun, Chiang Kai-shek endeavored to unify China on the basis of this ideology. However his party, the Kuomintang, included various groups whose interests were antithetical to these principles, and in order to maintain his position as leader of the Kuomintang, Chiang risked national unity to preserve Kuomintang unity. People's Democracy, for example, proved unacceptable to autocratically minded military men, particularly the Whampoa group whose personal ties to Chiang Kai-shek stemmed from association in his earlier military life. Another faction known as the Organization, or "CC clique," maintained control of civilian organization by means of a secret police and steadfastly opposed implementation of People's Democracy. The principle of People's Livelihood became increasingly important after World War II when graft and inflation destroyed all semblance of economic stability in Nationalist China. Solutions of this problem were unacceptable to dominant business interests represented by the so-called Political Study group, men whose governmental and private positions combined to give them control over monetary policy for their own profit. Finally, the principle of People's Nationalism, as it had been expressed by Dr. Sun, involved an antiforeign and particularly anti-Western attitude that proved anathema to the Political Study group, which relied upon American capital loans for temporary palliatives to China's economic needs.[16]

---

[16] T. S. Chien, *The Government and Politics of China,* Harvard University Press, Cambridge, Mass., 1950, p. 129. See also R. C. North, *Kuomintang and Chinese Communist Elites,* Stanford University Press, Stanford, Calif., 1952, pp. 72 ff.

In sum, appeal to the Three People's Principles could not bring about national unity, as long as implementation of those principles jeopardized the interests of the three main groups conditioning national policy. The military, the party organizers, and the bureaucratic capitalists had conflicting ideologies which remained in harmony only by their common allegiance to Chiang Kai-shek as a leader. Their failure to support a national ideology foredoomed Chiang's efforts to failure.

Resort to various responses is determined not only by the types of tensions but also by the way in which the policy maker views those tensions—in other words, by the group affiliation of the policy maker. The closer his ties with groups involved in tensions, the less able he is to transcend partisanship and to adopt solutions prejudicial to the groups involved for the sake of national unity. The less flexible is the ideology of the policy maker existing in a group apart, the more will he turn to displacement or repression in order to safeguard any challenge to his ruling position, a characteristic response of authoritarian elites.

8. Morale and National Power. It is apparent that in the extreme instances of revolution and civil war, disintegration from group tensions nullifies national power. Apart from such gross manifestations of disunity, however, the degree of cohesiveness within populations must be inferred less directly than by observation of a community's outward behavior. Working from more measurable data already established in studying other factors of power, it is possible to evaluate the morale of a given population and its probable impact upon that nation's total power. For instance, production and revenue figures may disclose wide gaps between productive capacity and actual output, between production and distribution of wealth, or between former and present standards of living. Any or all of these dislocations suggest socioeconomic tensions within the nation. Further clues may be found in statistics on crime and suicide, the resort to political trials, or the intensification of disciplinary measures. Content analysis of communication media may disclose references to particular racial, ethnic, or religious groups, indicating tensions by the frequency and direction of those references.

Overt signs of disunity, short of revolution, include strikes, riots, and resistance to government appeals for recruitment or bond purchases. Migration, where it is given an opportunity to express itself, provides eloquent evidence of internal disunity, as shown by the millions who fled the Soviet bloc of countries in the decade after World War II. Finally, desertion from the armed forces provides rare but significant indications of internal tensions which threaten national power.

Group tensions, then, in terms of identification, manifestation, and alleviation, play a twofold role in the dynamics of international relations. They influence foreign policy directly through the explicit demands of conflicting ideologies, and indirectly through displacement of internal tensions. Human resources, combined with physical foundations and industrial production, determine the amount of power available to the policy maker in support of means. As such, they are central to the study of international relations.

ADDITIONAL CASE-STUDY MATERIAL

Arsenian, S.: "Wartime Propaganda in the Middle East," *Middle East Journal,* vol. 2, October, 1948.

Bergson, A. (ed.): *Soviet Economic Growth,* Row, Peterson, Evanston, Ill., 1953.

Bernstein, J. M.: "Myth of National Unity in Japan," *Amerasia,* Jan. 25, 1945.

Cantril, H.: *Tensions That Cause Wars,* University of Illinois Press, Urbana, Ill., 1950.

Chamberlin, W.: *The Ukraine: A Submerged Nation,* Macmillan, New York, 1944.

Chien, T. S.: *The Government and Politics of China,* Harvard University Press, Cambridge, Mass., 1950.

Curtiss, J. S.: "Soviet Patriotic Feeling during World War II," *South Atlantic Quarterly,* April, 1946.

Doob, F. W.: "Goebbels' Principles of Propaganda," *Public Opinion Quarterly,* vol. 14, 1950.

Embree, J. F.: *The Japanese Nation; A Social Survey,* Rinehart, New York, 1945.

Fischer, G.: *Soviet Opposition to Stalin,* Harvard University Press, Cambridge, Mass.

Grodzins, M.: *Americans Betrayed; Politics and the Japanese Evacuation,* University of Chicago Press, Chicago, 1949.

Gurian, W.: "Hitler—The Simplifier of German Nationalism," *Review of Politics,* vol. 7, October, 1945.

Hofstee, E. W.: "Population Pressure and the Future of Western Civilization in Europe," *American Journal of Sociology,* vol. 55, May, 1950.

Inkeles, A.: "Social Stratification and Mobility in the Soviet Union," *American Sociological Review,* vol. 15, August, 1950.

Janis, I. L.: *Air War and Emotional Stress,* McGraw-Hill, New York, 1951.

Janowsky, O. I.: *Nationalities and National Minorities,* Macmillan, New York, 1945.

Korsotovetz, V. de: "The Religious Factor in Eastern Europe," *Contemporary Review,* vol. 174, November, 1948.

Kris, E., and H. Speier: *German Radio Propaganda,* Oxford, New York, 1944.

Krisberg, M.: "Cross-pressures and Attitudes: A Study of the Influence of Conflicting Propaganda on Opinions Regarding American-Soviet Relations," *Public Opinion Quarterly,* vol. 13, 1949.

Lamont, C.: *The Peoples of the Soviet Union,* Harcourt, Brace, New York, 1946.

Lasswell, H.: *World Politics and Personal Insecurity,* McGraw-Hill, New York, 1935.

Lerner, D.: *Sykewar; Psychological Warfare against Germany, D Day to V-E Day,* Stewart, New York, 1949.

Salisbury, H.: "On the Surface Moscow Is Calm," *The New York Times Magazine,* July 19, 1953.

Shils, A., and M. Janowitz: "Cohesion and Disintegration in the Wehrmacht in World War II," *Public Opinion Quarterly,* vol. 2, summer, 1948.

Shrieke, B.: *Alien Americans,* Viking, New York, 1936.

Thompson, W. S.: *Population and Peace in the Pacific,* University of Chicago Press, Chicago, 1946.

———: "Population Growth and Control in Relation to World Peace," *Yale Law Journal,* August, 1946.

Wilcox, E.: *Acres and People, The Eternal Problem of China and India,* Orange Judd, New York, 1947.

Zimmerman, E. W.: *World Resources and Industries,* rev. ed., Harper, New York, 1951.

PART THREE

POLICY IMPLEMENTATION: THE MEANS OF INTERNATIONAL RELATIONS

Chapter 7

DIPLOMACY

1. Properties of Diplomacy. The basic choice confronting policy makers is a choice between means of violence and means of nonviolence. The interrelationship of these alternatives was aptly summarized in the classic aphorism of Karl von Clausewitz, "War is politics carried on by other means." Among those who deprecate the contemporary conduct of foreign policy, both spheres are viewed with undisguised hostility, war because of its slaughter, diplomacy because of its duplicity. Indeed, many would establish a causal relationship between diplomacy and war. In their view, negotiations represent little more than an assemblage of nattily dressed gentlemen, carefully concealed from the eyes of the world and particularly of their respective nations, concluding nefarious deals whereby populations are bartered, principles are abandoned, and nations are committed to war for private interests.

War and Diplomacy. Such critical judgments may have possessed limited validity in past centuries, but they do not reflect the essential properties of diplomacy today. By positing war and diplomacy as alternative means of policy, it is by no means implied that they are completely separate from one another. The inability of diplomacy to resolve conflicts of aims may lead to war. The inability of war to win total capitulation or total annihilation may require diplomacy to negotiate an armistice. The difference in role should be clear, however. In peace, diplomacy represents the accumulative political and economic pressures upon each side, formalized in the exchange of demands and concessions between negotiators. In terminating a war, diplomacy represents the accumulative political, economic, and military pressures, formalized in ratification of a peace treaty between victor and vanquished.

Diplomacy, in short, may be called the handmaiden to compromise in the dynamics of international relations.

To define the pivotal role of diplomacy as a means of foreign policy does not endow it with all-inclusive, infallible powers. Its role has become increasingly circumscribed with the rise of democratic-pluralistic systems and authoritarian regimes. Its record has led many to regard it with distrust, if not disgust. This chapter will examine the properties and problems of diplomacy and analyze the impact of the twentieth century upon its conduct.

Statesmen utilize the exchange of views and discussion, central constituents of diplomacy, for any of three basic aims. Negotiators may seek to embarrass the opposite party in the eyes of a particular group, perhaps an ally or neutral, by forcing that party into an ideologically unfavorable position. Alternatively, negotiators may enter into discussions for the sole purpose of "buying time," winning a suspension of activity in some area so that additional power may be amassed for the employment of other means. Neither of these instances presumes the third purpose of diplomacy, namely, the intention of settling whatever problem exists between the parties by means of discussion and compromise, so-called negotiations "in good faith."

Diplomacy Designed to Embarrass. While it is the third aim of diplomacy, the settlement of conflicting ends by means of negotiation, which will concern this discussion most, a few words about the first two aims are necessary. Perhaps no better example of diplomacy as a means of embarrassing an opponent exists than the repeated conferences on disarmament. Sometimes disarmament proposals represent a genuine desire to lessen military expenditures. More generally, however, they are advanced with the foreknowledge that they will never be accepted, but with the hope of forcing the other side to refuse disarmament and thereby impugn its motivations before the world. Soviet Russia has repeatedly advanced dramatic proposals for disarmament in the past thirty years, while its ideology decries "bourgeois pacifism" and its internal propaganda consistently emphasizes the impossibility of capitalism to exist without a large armaments program. The apparent paradox is explained by the fact that these proposals are aimed at embarrassing other states, not at lowering the level of armaments. As noted in a semiofficial Soviet analysis of diplomacy published in 1945,[1]

The idea of disarmament has been for centuries one of the favorite means whereby diplomacy conceals basic motives and plans. . . . Every proposal for disarmament can count inevitably on the widest popularity and support on the part of public opinion. But of course, the proponent of such a step will always have foreseen that his partners in the diplomatic game properly understand his intentions.

[1] V. Potemkin (ed.), *Istoriia Diplomatii* ("History of Diplomacy"), Moscow, 1945, vol. III, pp. 708–709.

Diplomacy Designed to Gain Time. Negotiations are frequently utilized as a means of delaying events when one side anticipates an imminent advantageous shift in the power relationship between the two parties. During the first year of negotiations in the Korean War, both sides launched large-scale offensives while obstructing talks over alleged truce-zone violations and lesser questions of prestige. As the talks continued into their second year, it became evident that a genuine military stalemate prevented either side from improving its position to any great extent. While there is no way of ascertaining to what degree negotiations were motivated by either of these first two aims, it seems apparent that both were operative to some extent. It is significant that attempts at embarrassment were a direct function of the publicity attending the truce talks. When both sides arrived at a final settlement, it was only after two months of secret session.

The greater the tension between conflicting elites in the international arena, the more frequently negotiations are designed to embarrass or to delay. Thus a decade of diplomacy between Soviet Russia and the United States, 1945 to 1955, shows little evidence of negotiations aimed at a compromise of conflicting ends, but considerable evidence of negotiations aimed at embarrassment or delay. However, in the last analysis settlement of a non-violent nature necessarily entails the third use of diplomacy, as a means of compromise between hostile as well as between nonhostile states.

Diplomacy and Clashing Interests. In analyzing the properties of diplomacy, it is vital to note its role in resolving conflicting interests by means of compromise. Because interests do conflict, diplomacy is not a hail-fellow-well-met session. Negotiations are undertaken by policy makers to accomplish certain ends, determined by the interests of the dominant elite or elites within their own countries. Refusal to recognize this fact leads to unfounded optimism over the possibilities of diplomacy. Characteristic of one outgrowth of Western humanistic liberalism was the portrayal of diplomacy as a general get-together of reasonable men, whose differences would soon melt away under the atmosphere of congeniality and "getting to know each other better." As summarized by President Franklin Roosevelt during World War II, "The idea of a conference is to confer, to get the other fellow's point of view. It is quite possible that you might get a good idea from somebody else outside of our own borders. It is quite possible that you might persuade the other fellow that some idea that you had was a pretty good idea." [2] While this approach is often applicable among acknowledged allies, its basic assumptions appear somewhat unrealistic. With respect to negotiations among elites with sharply conflicting interests, it is doomed to failure.

[2] President Franklin D. Roosevelt, speaking at an "off-the-record" press conference following the Moscow conference, Oct. 29, 1944, quoted in J. Rosenman, *Working with Roosevelt,* Harper, New York, 1952, p. 404.

If diplomacy is designed as a means of settlement, however, it would be erroneous to stress conflict to the exclusion of compromise. One reaction to the fallacies of the humanistic approach would substitute an attitude described by an Indian diplomat as "pistols for two, coffee for one," more suggestive of the dueling ground than the conference table.[3] This intransigent approach is well suited for purposes of embarrassment or delay, but bodes ill for the purpose of settlement through compromise. Much of post-1945 diplomacy finds statesmen appearing as staunch defenders of vital principles, demanding complete acceptance of specified programs. Secretary of State Dean Acheson's phrase "total diplomacy," with its implied parallel of "total war," exemplifies this postwar attitude of no compromise. While his phrase symbolized the intensity of conflict between the interests of the Soviet and American elites, it tended to limit the processes of negotiations to embarrassment and harassment of opponents, and to exclude settlement of existing tensions.

This discussion of diplomacy as a means of negotiating settlement, then, will assume neither a spirit of *bonhomie* nor its opposite, a refusal to compromise any interest, to prevail among the participants. Furthermore, the examination of diplomacy as a means of carrying out policy will exclude policy formulation as such. At the same time, by stressing negotiations, it will exclude the diplomat's roles as symbol of state, propagandist, and reporter-at-large. To be sure, diplomats do more than confer with their counterparts from other countries. They advise home offices on policy alternatives, they represent their government at public functions and assist nationals abroad, they make speeches and hold press conferences, and they analyze conditions in countries to which they are assigned. However, the focus at this point is determined not by the actor but by the purpose of his actions. This discussion is not concerned with the diplomat as such, but rather with his special job of negotiating.

Diplomacy and Power. Among the properties of diplomacy are three crucial factors: power, policy, and personnel. All must be effective if the means are to attain the end. The nature of power has already been examined. Its role in diplomacy is constant and conditioning. Seldom introduced into negotiations directly, it remains sufficiently concealed to permit discretion but sufficiently revealed to strengthen the hand of the nation whose alternative to negotiations is economic or military warfare. Thus negotiators must always consider the consequences if their efforts should fail, and the degree to which they are willing to compromise may be directly related with the way in which they view their own power relative to that of their opponent.

Diplomacy is often thought to be a substitute for power, enabling the small nation to maneuver dexterously among the bigger countries to its

[3] V. K. Krishna Menon, to the Political and Security Committee of the United Nations, quoted in *The New York Times*, Aug. 26, 1953, p. 3.

own advantage. Admittedly, the weaker a nation, the more it must rely on diplomacy as a means of accomplishing its ends of foreign policy. By associating themselves with strong partners, by threatening to shift their allegiance between closely matched opponents, or by carefully avoiding situations which might endanger their position, elites of small countries may preserve their interests for a considerably longer period than might be thought possible in terms of their industrial or military power. However, the history of Czechoslovakia during the interwar period reveals that, in the last analysis, diplomacy without power is indeed limited.

Czechoslovakia, carved out of the old Austro-Hungarian Empire at the end of World War I, found itself plagued with ethnic minorities, chiefly Germans, Poles, and Hungarians, which provided the respective neighboring countries with irredentist ambitions. Incapable of amassing sufficient power to guarantee Czech independence, Eduard Beneš, architect of Prague's foreign policy from 1919 to 1939, declared,[4]

Our state is the key to the whole postwar structure of Central Europe. If it is touched . . . the peace of Europe [is] seriously infringed. . . . It is for that reason that . . . our international position and our internal stability are a matter of great interest equally to France and the Soviet Union, equally to England and Italy, and to the Little Entente, as they ought to be to Germany, and to Poland.

Following this formula, Czech foreign policy between the wars attempted to build security through bilateral and regional pacts, and to stress collective security through the League of Nations. Two cardinal weaknesses in Czechoslovakia's position doomed her to failure, however. Germany, Hungary, and Poland remained hostile to Czech independence, refusing to underwrite her territorial inviolability in treaty form. Furthermore, what guarantees Beneš did receive, principally from France and Russia, failed to be met because of British-French unwillingness to risk war with Germany for the sake of Czechoslovakia. In 1938, the Munich conference, to which Czechoslovakia was not even invited, conceded the strategic Sudetenland to Hitler; in 1939, Nazi troups marched into Prague, unopposed. Not only was Czech diplomacy unable to still the demands of its hostile neighbors, but it was forced to rely on the promises of its vacillating allies. Annexation was the result.

Diplomacy proved no substitute for power in the case of Czechoslovakia. It could prolong its existence; it could attain limited ends of self-preservation. In the last analysis, however, Beneš's policy of collective security remained fatally dependent upon the power of other countries, countries whose policy makers inevitably placed their own interests above those of Beneš.

4 P. Zinner, "Czechoslovakia: The Diplomacy of Eduard Beneš," in G. Craig and F. Gilbert (eds.), *The Diplomats, 1919–1939,* Princeton University Press, Princeton, N.J., 1953, pp. 107–108.

Diplomacy and Policy. Policy, the second prerequisite for diplomacy, received a general analysis in previous chapters. Suffice to say that where there is no policy, diplomacy is doomed to failure; where policy is ill conceived, success is most improbable. Negotiators without directives may concede vital interests for the sake of agreement or refuse possible concessions for the sake of intransigence. Not only must the ends of policy be clear to the diplomat, but he must have a precise understanding of the limits within which he may bargain to achieve those ends. Assumption by the diplomat of the responsibility of formulating policy and negotiating for its attainment may lead to his repudiation in a democracy, to his extermination in an authoritarian country.

Diplomacy and Personnel. It is personnel, the third factor of diplomacy, which is of chief concern here. Diplomacy may be conducted by heads of state, foreign secretaries, overseas staffs of ambassadors and career experts, special representatives, or military leaders. Different consequences attend each of these negotiators, yet all of them are employed, often indiscriminately, in contemporary diplomacy. In the past decade, to take just one American example of each type, President Franklin D. Roosevelt, Secretary of State James Byrnes, Ambassador Charles Bohlen, special representative Paul Hoffman, and General George Marshall played pivotal roles in negotiations with Soviet Russia, the NATO countries, and China. Able personnel can seldom work miracles without power or policy, but the strongest accumulation of power or the most carefully formulated policy may be of little avail if the personnel conducting diplomacy is ill chosen.

2. Personnel in Diplomacy: Heads of State. Most dramatic among those who move across the pages of diplomatic history are, of course, the heads of state. At times of crisis, the familiar cry is heard for a meeting of the Big Two—or Three—or Four—in the hope that somehow these men can succeed where others have failed. The personages have certainly varied, including such figures as Woodrow Wilson, Franklin Roosevelt, and Harry Truman; Adolf Hitler, Benito Mussolini, and Joseph Stalin. The record, however, indicates that definite liabilities as well as definite advantages are inherent in the use of heads of state as negotiators of international issues.

Advantages of Diplomacy by Heads of State. Probably the chief advantage in negotiations among world leaders is their ability to commit their countries to a given agreement, to a greater extent than any other person. Thus in Soviet-American relations, the feeling on the Russian side that a President's word carried greatest weight was paralleled by the American supposition that only Stalin or his avowed successor could negotiate matters freely. The fallacy in the Russian position is patent. Congress may upset Presidential agreements by blocking funds for implementing the decision or by refusing to approve a treaty, while the life of a President's administration and hence the strength of his personal word cannot be assured for more than four years.

There is no proof that the American assumption about the freedom of Soviet leaders is false, but at the very least, catering to this assumption necessitates direct negotiations with the Soviet leader, reinforcing his fallacious interpretation of the President's power. At one point during the Teheran conference of 1943 between Stalin and Roosevelt, Russian attempts to win acquiescence to annexation of the Baltic countries and part of Poland were rebuffed by Roosevelt, partly on the grounds that ethnic groups in the United States of Lithuanian, Latvian, Estonian, and Polish origin would raise political obstacles against such a move. Stalin's prompt response, advocating some "propaganda work" by the President, showed little familiarity with the relationship between the White House and Congress.[5] Far more complex problems arose from the 1945 Yalta agreement, concluded by Stalin, Roosevelt, and Churchill personally but kept secret in part from the Department of State, as well as from the American Congress. Subsequent American administrations did not consider themselves bound completely by an agreement signed by Roosevelt, and various moves were made to repudiate its terms. Although the Soviet Union remained in possession of the territory occupied by it under the Yalta agreement, it was ultimately force, not diplomacy, which determined its position.

Disadvantages of Diplomacy by Heads of State. While heads of state can claim maximum responsibility for conducting negotiations, they suffer from minimum experience in such activity. Seldom does a figure arise, such as Sir Winston Churchill, who combines considerable experience in all areas of politics. More frequently it is a man like Neville Chamberlain or Harry Truman, unschooled in the legal niceties of drafting notes, unfamiliar with the complex economic and military problems attending political issues, and unversed in the nuances of international communication, who heads the executive branch of government. The rare opportunity for a President or Prime Minister to essay the field of diplomacy affords him little experience or background as a guide. Communication of aims and comprehension of those of an opponent pose twin problems to negotiators. The single meeting of the Big Two or Big Three leaders barely suffices to acquaint the participants with each other, much less with their conflicting interests. Familiarity among negotiators need not lead to friendship, but it facilitates communication in the basic sense of the word.

Further, the burden of executive duties, weighing heavily on all contemporary leaders, precludes careful preparation for negotiations and limits their duration. Impending legislation, party politics, and the complex task of managing an industrialized community seriously limit the effectiveness of heads of state as diplomats. While the statesman's attention is divided, negotiations may require complete concentration. Whether it is German unification, Far Eastern tensions, or disarmament, contemporary conflicts of

[5] R. Sherwood, *Roosevelt and Hopkins*, Harper, New York, 1948, p. 796.

interest combine political and economic problems of utmost complexity. The chief executive who tackles diplomacy while keeping in constant touch with his capital via cable, telephone, or teletype is incapable of devoting the careful, patient, and judicious care that negotiations demand. Perhaps nothing is more striking than the difficult task of simultaneously playing politics at home and abroad, as revealed in the memoirs of Sir Winston Churchill and the studies of Franklin Roosevelt.

Another consequence of diplomacy by national leaders is epitomized in the references to "Churchill's strategy" and "Roosevelt's policy." In so far as policy does represent the individual negotiating rather than the interests of the prevailing coalition of elites, diplomacy is likely to receive little support or implementation from others. The risk of personalization of policy increases in direct proportion to the status of the negotiator. The effect of such personalization is to imply continuity of policy or observance of negotiated agreement only so long as the individual concerned remains in office. Removal by election defeat or death immediately places in jeopardy understandings supposedly based on personal relations. For instance, it seemed to strengthen the wartime coalition of the United States and Soviet Russia for Roosevelt to declare that he "got along fine with Marshal Stalin." [6] However, Roosevelt's death in April, 1945, had serious repercussions on American-Soviet relations, largely because of the conviction held by many Americans and Russians alike that policy had been personalized. Those who agreed with the course of American-Russian relations believed "getting along" would be quite difficult in the future; those who disagreed with past actions demanded a change in approach with the change in president.

Finally, perhaps the most serious consequence of negotiations by heads of the state is the pressure upon them, politically speaking, to produce results. Paralleling this is the tendency toward an attitude of utter futility should negotiations by such exalted persons collapse. Within their respective countries, political opponents wait for any sign of concession, weakness, or "betrayals of the national interest," compelling the negotiators to issue verbose communiqués, implying everything while saying nothing. The necessity of coming home with "peace in our time" or "victory for our side" gives the heads of state, particularly in democratic communities, little leeway. Externally the failure of heads of state to effect a happy compromise may lead to intensification of tension and precipitate a genuine international crisis. In short, a fresh effort at diplomacy may be precluded and stalemate, perhaps sharper conflict, results.

3. Foreign Secretaries and Professionals. While some of the problems attending negotiation by heads of state continue when foreign secretaries take over diplomacy, there are marked advantages nevertheless. Secretaries of state and foreign ministers usually combine a high degree of responsibility,

[6] Rosenman, *op. cit.*, p. 413.

although not necessarily commanding party control in America, with intimate knowledge of the over-all foreign policy in its many aspects. This permits them to relate the given issues to other issues of concern, while their administrative position provides them ready access to extensive briefings on the details of specific problems. In addition, long experience in policy and diplomacy is more likely to be found in a foreign secretary than in the head of state, although the last decade of American appointments is erratic in this respect, ranging from neophytes, such as Edward Stettinius and James Byrnes, to highly experienced men, such as Dean Acheson and John Foster Dulles.

Foreign secretaries often enjoy the advantage of frequent contacts with their counterparts, particularly when, as in Great Britain and France, they occupy the office over many years. Communication comes more easily; misunderstandings are quickly clarified. As with the heads of state, however, personalization of policy is a parallel liability. Failure of negotiations to attain desired ends may be a political burden for an experienced and capable foreign secretary, regardless of the degree to which he was responsible for the policy determining such negotiations or the obstacles encountered during the conference.

By and large, these are minor shortcomings in foreign secretaries as diplomats. Far more serious is the tremendous load of responsibility which rests on their shoulders, as on those of the chief executive. Secretary of State James Byrnes, for example, traveled almost 70,000 miles and spent almost eight months at conferences abroad during the period July 6, 1945, to October 17, 1946. At the same time, he directed extensive changes in the Department of State, supervised American legations to the United Nations, and maintained constant liaison with a recalcitrant Republican Congress, determined to avoid what it felt were the failures of the preceding Democratic regime.[7] In a day of concurrent crises in Europe, Africa, the Middle East, and Southeast Asia, not to mention less dramatic but no less demanding problems in conferences of the United Nations and its related agencies, the foreign secretary can ill afford the time and attention consumed in the minutiae of negotiations. During absence from his Department, important decisions of policy must be left to seconds-in-command or thrashed out over long-distance telephone, a difficult procedure at best.

Professional Diplomats. Negotiations, then, rest most easily with the conventional channels of diplomatic activity, the professional overseas staff of ambassadors and career experts. Here is found the combination best suited for negotiations: experience, delegated responsibility, knowledge of local conditions, relative anonymity, and freedom from other duties. The ideally trained diplomat, perceptive in judgment and discreet in manner, patient in temperament and loyal in action, is indeed a valued instrument for the

[7] J. Byrnes, *Speaking Frankly,* Harper, New York, 1947.

implementation of any foreign policy. Were these qualities uniformly present in overseas officials, diplomacy would be of a highly different nature. However, the presence of politically appointed ambassadors, prominent in the service of the United States, brings inexperience and jealousy into the embassies abroad. The long-experienced professional diplomat may look with a jaundiced eye upon the advice of the foreign office and, trusting to his own judgment, strike off on an independent course of action. Finally, the most serious liability besetting the use of overseas staff in negotiations is the tendency of personal prejudices, rooted in lengthy contact with the local area, to becloud judgment and perhaps subvert policy. Generally it appears that the better acquainted a diplomat becomes with an area, the more sympathetic is his association with that area, although in some instances, notably in Soviet Russia, the longer he is in residence the more hostile he becomes to his environment. In neither case does the person on the spot enjoy as rational an approach to his negotiations as the envoy newly arrived on the scene.

Sir Nevile Henderson, British Ambassador to Nazi Germany from 1937 to 1939, included many if not all of these weaknesses and played no small role in the failure of British policy to accomplish its ends during this period.[8] Henderson's appointment was correctly understood by himself and others as being a slap at the British Foreign Office, and in his close association with Prime Minister Chamberlain he often by-passed the authorized center of policy formulation. Henderson's many years in Turkey, Egypt, France, Yugoslavia, and Argentina gave him confidence of judgment, considerably enhanced by his desire to effect a historic junction of British and German policy. Finally, his admitted desire to see the "good side" of Germany precluded the partiality which all diplomats must have for the policies of their own foreign office.

As a consequence, while Britain was supposedly attempting to restrain Germany from moving against Austria and Czechoslovakia, Henderson was assuring German leaders that the Austrian premier "had acted with precipitous folly" in resisting Nazi pressure, that "England fully understood the historical need for a solution of this question [annexation of Austria] in the Reich German sense," and that "he personally had no sympathy at all with the Czechs and moreover considered the placing of Sudeten Germans under Czech domination to be a grave mistake." [9] Partly because of this, Britain's repeated attempts to negotiate a settlement with Hitler which would safeguard the independence of the small countries came to naught.

4. Special and Military Representatives. Two other types of negotiators, special representatives and military staffs, need to be discussed. Both types

---

[8] F. Gilbert, "Two British Ambassadors: Perth and Henderson," in Craig and Gilbert, *op. cit.*, pp. 537–554.
   [9] *Ibid.*, pp. 538–541.

play an increasingly important role in negotiations since World War II, largely because of American reliance upon them in preference to professional diplomats. Each has certain assets and liabilities, but in brief neither can be said to combine the advantages of either foreign secretaries or overseas career officials.

Special representatives, whether politicians, businessmen, or professors, often lack experience and occasionally lack responsibility. Accustomed to the give-and-take of discussion among groups sharing common interests, even if they conflict in ideologies, the special representative may be perplexed by the inability of his counterpart to "understand" or "accept" his point of view. Alternatively, he may be elated to find "agreement" in principle, only to discover that implementation in practice is far removed from what he had expected. Perhaps less significant is the question of responsibility, but it should be noted that the expert, drafted temporarily from another occupation for service as a negotiator, may be considerably less affected by the outcome of the discussions than the head of state, the foreign secretary, or the career diplomat. This is not to imply that he necessarily enters his job irresponsibly, but rather to point up possible distinctions between the government servant and the negotiator drawn from another walk of life.

Offsetting shortcomings in experience and responsibility may be expert knowledge of the problem, gained through years of business or academic work in the field. In addition, the "fresh" approach of an outsider, unsaddled with bureaucratic traditions and petty prejudices, argues persuasively for using a special representative to tackle a particularly knotty problem. Philip E. Mosely, long a close scholar of Russian foreign policy and intimately acquainted with Balkan politics, played an important role in negotiating the postwar treaties for Hungary, Bulgaria, and Romania. Similarly, reliance of President Roosevelt upon Harry Hopkins in negotiations with the Russians was determined in part by the ideological opposition within official American circles concerning the Soviet Union which appeared to limit the readiness to negotiate of many persons. In part, it was also determined by Hopkins' willingness to work literally beyond the point of human endurance and the President's confidence in his ability to understand New Deal ends and means as could few other persons. These advantages are not to be minimized, and they explain why the United States has found so-called "amateur diplomats" —such as Elihu Root, Harriman, and Wallace—extremely helpful at times. However, in so far as the use of special representatives arouses suspicions and jealousies on the part of official channels thus by-passed by the chief executive, it places an added strain within the governmental system. As for the quality of such negotiations, it is obviously dependent upon the judgment of a single person who is responsible for choosing the special representative, rather than upon the time-tested performance of persons who have made a career of negotiating.

Military negotiators, aside from those concerned with ending hostilities, bring an entirely different orientation to diplomacy from any of the above groups. Their advantage lies in combining politics with strategy in the sense that they eliminate the artificial distinction observed by excluding military men from peacetime policy, and abandoning everything to them during war. Equally important are the shortcomings attending the use of military staffs as negotiators. By training, soldiers see states in terms of ally and enemy, in terms of defense and offense. They may ignore the possibility of negotiating so as both to win friends (allies) and influence people (neutrals). Thus uncommitted divisions pose a threat which can be eliminated by bringing them over to one side, or at least clearly defined by their transferal to the other side.

This mathematical determination of policy and its impact upon diplomacy is illustrated by American policy in Europe. Despite the deep misgivings among British and French circles concerning the political consequences of giving succor to Franco Spain, American military strategists proceeded to negotiate for bases on the Iberian peninsula, necessitating simultaneous bolstering of the Franco government as an ally against communism. More immediate and far-reaching was the impact of a similar military decision, namely, the invitation to Tito's Yugoslavia to enter into military discussion with the United States. By moving closer to Tito, America moved further from Italy and found herself enmeshed in the constant struggle of both Mediterranean countries for the key port of Trieste. In the summer of 1953, Alcide de Gasperi, prime minister of Italy, toppled from office largely because of his loss of Right Wing, nationalist support over the question of Tito and Trieste. De Gasperi's commitment to the United States, formalized through Italy's participation in NATO, became his downfall when American policy moved against the interests of a group crucial to De Gasperi's survival. The consequences of his fall for Italy's internal politics as well as for the over-all position of the NATO alliance provide dramatic illustration of how military negotiations may conflict with other aspects of foreign policy.

5. Types of Diplomacy. So far, diplomacy has been discussed in terms of its aims and participants. Diplomacy may also be analyzed in terms of its conduct. Negotiations fall into two major categories, bilateral and multilateral, but variations on these themes call for more detailed examination of different types of diplomacy and their effect upon problems common to this means of international relations.

Bilateral negotiations are the simplest and most customary type of diplomacy, encompassing a multitude of issues ranging from the routine establishment of diplomatic immunities to the conclusion of alliances for world conquest. Conducted in privacy, they are the diplomat's dream of the personal tête-à-tête, enabling an exchange of views in which the fewest external distractions intrude. Conducted publicly, they become the diplomat's nightmare, complete with poses for the photographers and notes for the historians. Bilateral negotiations best serve the purpose of splitting a possible coalition, and have been utilized quite successfully by both Nazi Germany and Soviet Russia in preventing East European countries from forming a common front against either of the two larger nations.

Bilateral diplomacy may serve as a steppingstone to multilateral diplomacy, when negotiations *à deux* among several pairs of countries culminate in an over-all merging of views toward a common objective. The initial negotiations remain bilateral; the final results are, however, multilateral. Particularly effective when the range of interests may be very diverse concerning a given issue, this combination of types characterized the negotiations leading up to the Japanese Peace Treaty. As early as January, 1951, John Foster Dulles entered into conversations with Japanese spokesmen. He then communicated separately with the various allies which had participated in the war with Japan, advancing the United States' proposals and sounding out their views. After months of these bilateral negotiations, the majority of Allied powers together with Japan convened in San Francisco where, in September, 1951, they signed the Japanese Peace Treaty. The brevity of the conference underscored the importance of the earlier bilateral talks in settling in advance the major terms of the treaty. This method bridges full-fledged bilateral and multilateral types of diplomacy, in that it discourages the formation of blocs while aiming at a coordination among several different countries. Perhaps more than any other type of diplomacy, it requires utmost skill on the part of the diplomat exercising the initiating, coordinating function.

Diplomacy by conference, as the name implies, brings under one roof all the negotiators for the purpose of discussing general problems of international tension. Secrecy is impeded by the increased number of participants in comparison with the previous types, particularly so when the conference is attended by staffs of interpreters, consultants, and reporters. Such meetings vary widely in scope, ranging from tightly organized conferences of foreign ministers which have grappled over the postwar problems of Trieste, Austria, and Germany, to the omnibus parleys of the interwar period, such as the 1921 Washington Conference which discussed general naval disarmament, evacuation of Japanese troops from the Russian Far East, China's grievances against the West, and the Anglo-Japanese alliance. Although the success of negotiations appears to vary in inverse proportion to the number of conflicting interests involved, the Washington Conference resolved a number of outstanding problems, while the post-1945 foreign ministers' meetings often achieved little but discouragement in diplomacy by conference.

Although no invention of the twentieth century, diplomacy by conference became a widely advocated means of resolving international tensions after World War I. Its obstacles to secrecy, its tendency toward informality, and the conviction that more heads meant more wisdom, combined to make this a popular type of diplomacy. These factors were all marked at the Washington Conference, opened dramatically by the United States Secretary of State who, with little regard for tradition, devoted his "welcoming address" to a precise blueprint for the voluntary destruction of the major navies then afloat or on the ways. After winning this gambit, the United States permitted representatives of a Soviet satellite, the Far Eastern Republic, to attend the conference as "observer" but not as "participant." In this way, anti-Japanese materials, distributed in the corridors by F.E.R. delegates, served the American interests by building up pressure against Nippon, while the exclusion of Soviet Russia remained compatible with Washington's refusal to recognize Moscow.

Another decade of conferences, however, saw informality lead to confusion and publicity lead to propaganda. More heads seemed to result in more conflicts of interest, rather than in more wisdom. Diplomacy by conference fell from its ascendant position and became simply another type of diplomacy, eminently suited for certain situations where many different interests desire expression on a particular problem, but less adaptable to major points of tension. Diplomacy by conference during the interwar period, with its high level of publicity and voluminous records, contrasts sharply with the many secret conferences in world capitals which have marked the post-1945 era.

International organization is a final step of multilateral diplomacy. Differing from diplomacy by conference chiefly in its institutionalization, with regular meetings, officers, rules, and even permanent representatives, it stands as the culmination of man's efforts to resolve conflict by negotiation. Although its results are recorded in formal debate and voting, international organization relies considerably upon bilateral and multilateral diplomacy, both secret and public, which serve to iron out differences of interest before and during consideration of issues in the open meetings. Here lies the closest approximation of international diplomacy to domestic methods of politics in the pluralistic community, epitomized in the bargaining for votes, logrolling, and similar techniques familiar in legislative assemblies. Nothing better illustrates the continuing, but transformed, role of diplomacy in contemporary international relations.

6. Problems of Diplomacy. *Agendas.* For the casual observer, little significance is attached to the fixing of an agenda; yet success or failure may rest upon this initial procedure of negotiation. In the truce talks at Panmunjom, for instance, Communist and United Nations delegates wrangled for almost two months over what they were to discuss, each side seeking to insert or to keep out issues in accordance with its own policy. One of the problems confronting the delegates was how to agree on the items to be discussed at a political conference designed to follow the completion of an armistice agreement. This raised even more complex matters than drawing up the initial agenda for the truce talks. After weeks of deadlock, both sides temporarily shelved their differences by resorting to the all-inclusive, ambiguous term "etc." with reference to the issues to be included on the political agenda.

It is clear that without agreement on the precise matters to be discussed, negotiators cannot get specific powers and directives from their governments. They must enter a conference room prepared for anything yet agreeing to nothing. Days may pass with new issues being raised simply to avoid discussion of old issues. Far from being trivial, the agenda narrows the attention of the delegates to a few carefully selected, well-defined conflicts of interest chosen from among the many points of friction which may exist between nations. Its importance increases in direct proportion to the number of countries participating, so that diplomacy by conference or in international organization is almost wholly dependent upon a well-worked-out agenda.

Secrecy. In sharp contrast to the scant attention accorded the agenda by the public at large, the problem of secrecy has been widely touted as the all-pervading, pernicious evil of diplomacy, if not the basic cause of war. Such varied figures as Woodrow Wilson and Leon Trotsky foreswore secret diplomacy after World War I, the first championing "open covenants openly arrived at," and the second declaring, "The abolition of secret diplomacy is the primary condition of an honourable, popular, really democratic foreign policy." [10] Yet both the United States and Soviet Russia resorted to secret diplomacy within a few years of these pronunciamentos. Despite klieg lights and television cameras, flash bulbs and imaginative reporters, microphones and intrepid commentators, secrecy remains an essential ingredient of diplomacy.

Enough has been said already about the conflict of interests and the necessity of compromise to indicate the basic manner in which negotiations must be conducted. Every proposal has its counterproposal; every concession requires its counterconcession. It is a skilled game of advance and retreat, and only the actual participants can separate bluff from sincerity, can distinguish between compromise and capitulation. As long as there is to be a tomorrow, today's negotiations are part of the game, the significance of which may not be evident until the last day has arrived and final agreement—or disagreement—is reached.

Any break in secrecy may upset the entire course of the game. Negotiators may be saddled with proposals or remarks which were intended solely for the conference hall but which, broadcast at large, become issues of prestige for the individual, the government, or the public at home. Compromises on points of importance may be blocked if groups sharply opposed

---

[10] E. H. Carr, *The Bolshevik Revolution, 1917–1923*, Macmillan, New York, vol. 3, p. 14.

to such compromise learn of what is to be given up before knowing what is to be gained in return. The tendency of the publicity-conscious diplomat to play to the gallery, winning applause at home for his intransigence abroad, is hardly conducive to fruitful negotiations. Heated exchanges in the privacy of the conference room may prove less serious after a good meal or a night's sleep, but once recorded in public print or transmitted over television screens, they become a matter of "national honor," increasing the tension not only between nations but also within nations, between those who would negotiate and those who oppose negotiations.

These are but a few reasons why secrecy and diplomacy continue to go hand in hand. The case against secrecy is too celebrated, particularly in democratic countries, to require repetition here. Suffice to say that coupled with distrust of a group operating in a foreign milieu amidst "alien" interests is hostility to anything which violates the democratic value of full, open discussion. It is no accident that with the ascendancy of the liberal humanistic approach to international relations, evidenced immediately after World War I in the speeches of President Wilson, diplomacy by conference and by international organization became prominent. Both types received support partly because of their supposed abjuration of secrecy. By abandoning secrecy, diplomats were to be compelled by the "pressure of world opinion" to act judiciously, to arrive at peaceful compromise, and thereby to avoid war. As has been shown by this analysis, "world" public opinion is a figment of the phrasemaker's imagination. Opinion is nationally conditioned, and within nations it is the vociferous voice of conflicting group interests. Thus abandoning secrecy produced not a monolithic world opinion but a cacophony of national aims and interests.

Secrecy continues, not only in bilateral but in multilateral negotiations as well. Obviously the more persons present, the more difficult it is to maintain. "Leaks" to the outside through clusters of delegates, translators, and advisors are far more probable in diplomacy by conference and by international organization than between spokesmen of two countries. Nevertheless, secret diplomacy is a continuing phenomenon, even in so highly publicized an operation as the United Nations. Consultations in corridors, exchange of views between foreign offices, and officially closed sessions of the Security Council all mark the deliberations of UN delegates. Indeed, Lester Pearson, president of the Seventh Session of the General Assembly, called for more "quiet and confidential" discussion, warning, "It is often harmful for the negotiation of policy always to be conducted in glass houses which are often too tempting a target for brickbats. It is all too easy to strike attitudes in public, only to find later that we are stuck with them. Open diplomacy now tends to become frozen diplomacy." [11]

In World War II, as in World War I, secret negotiations resolved conflict

[11] *New York Herald Tribune,* Sept. 27, 1953.

among the allies on both sides, and secret agreements parceled out spoils to the victor nations. The Korean War dragged on through two years of quasi-secret truce talks, ending only after two months of fully confidential discussions. During the postwar decade, top-level conferences, whether of World War II Allies, NATO, or Cominform countries, have invariably invoked secrecy at time of crucial decision. In short, it must be concluded that the democratic value of full, open discussion has proved inapplicable for many vital aspects of international relations.

Communication. Communication, fundamental to negotiations, poses a multitude of problems, ranging from the obvious one of language differences to the extremely complex one of culture differences. A significant setback came with the abandonment of a lingua franca as the universal medium of diplomacy. The challenge of communicating in six or seven languages has resulted in hordes of skilled linguists providing simultaneous translations sped to committees via mimeograph. Pitfalls remain, however, as illustrated in the postwar negotiations between American and Soviet representatives concerning the peace treaties for the defeated Axis nations. Translation of the Russian word *vlast,* as "authority," implied that certain prerogatives would be granted the Soviet *Kommandatura* in Berlin, whereas the Soviet use of the word *vlast* actually meant that complete and unlimited power would be vested in the Russian official.[12] Similarly, American advocacy of "an aggressive policy" meant a positive, forward-moving policy, whereas the Russian translation, with the word *aggressivnost,* implied a policy of attack against other countries.

Much more profound differences rooted in cultural development continue to play an important role in negotiations, despite the rapid improvement in interpretation and translation. It would be misleading to assert that international tensions spring from cultural barriers to communication exclusively, for as has already been shown, group interests and ideologies do clash in the international arena even if the antagonists "understand each other." However, settlement of conflicts of interest is often impeded by cultural differences which obstruct communication in the most fundamental way. During World War II, for example, exchange of information and aid between America and Russia constantly ran afoul of misunderstandings rooted in the difference between the democratic-pluralistic-capitalist community and the authoritarian-socialistic community. Many American official and nonofficial groups continued to express open doubt throughout the war over the wisdom of helping Stalin to fight Hitler. Soviet suspicions of duplicity in Washington ignored the basic character of the American governmental system which permitted expression of views at total variance with official policy. No less difficult was American reaction to the refusal of lower-echelon Rus-

---

[12] P. Mosely, "Some Soviet Techniques of Negotiation," in R. Dennett and J. Johnson (eds.): *Negotiating with the Russians,* World Peace Foundation, Boston, 1951, p. 295.

sian officials to give information on Soviet industrial and military problems, or to implement agreements unless specific orders came from the Kremlin elite. American accusations of obstructionism or bad faith based on such instances overlooked their inevitable connection with the rigid authoritarian regime.

In the actual process of negotiations, cultural differences continued to plague American-Russian relations. American negotiators, accustomed to the give-and-take of bargaining and placing a high value upon compromise in the national myth, frequently modified proposals in the attempt to reach a middle ground of agreement. Russian reaction was one of bewilderment and distrust, regarding the Americans as elusive and insincere because they did not stick by a position. Conversely, Soviet negotiators, accustomed to rigid directives and strict adherence to a disciplined line, put forth one proposal and kept repeating it for days, sometimes weeks, on end. American reaction found the Soviet diplomats boring and intransigent. Each side bargained according to its culture, to the detriment of diplomacy.[13]

As negotiations move from concrete matters such as regulation of currency exchange and the reduction of tariffs to less easily definable problems such as freely held elections and drawing of boundaries along ethnic lines, cross-cultural difficulty in communication increases accordingly. American reliance upon "agreements in principle" proved fatal with respect to the Yalta conference, wherein all parties agreed to the holding of "free, democratic elections" in East European countries. The Soviet interpretation of "democratic parties" as "antifascist parties" aimed at exclusion of all groups hostile to communism, whereas the American interpretation of the identical phrase aimed at the exclusion of only those groups actively engaged in support of Nazi Germany or Fascist Italy during World War II. A particularly ironic example of such ambiguity arising from resort to principles lacking universal definition is Article 4 of the United Nations Charter, wherein membership to the UN is declared open to "all other peace-loving states" which accept the Charter's obligations and which "are willing and able to carry out these obligations." By implication, the original United Nations members were peace-loving, yet membership was originally limited to countries which had declared war against the Axis.

Concluding Negotiations. Assuming barriers of agenda, secrecy, and communication to have been surmounted, diplomats must still meet the problem of concluding negotiations. Mechanical difficulties occasionally arise in the necessity that all parties agree to say the same thing at the same time about the negotiations. Far more important is the necessity of all parties meaning the same thing by what they agree to say. If negotiations have ended in compromise, each delegate must make his concession palatable because of domestic groups, yet be tactful about his gains because of relations with

---

[13] *Ibid.*, pp. 277 ff.

negotiators of other countries. With modern communication denying national leaders privacy of discussion with their community, the utmost care is required lest critics at home prevent settlement abroad.

The most serious problems arise, however, when no results come from negotiations. Recriminations, denials, and new accusations increase the tensions which negotiations were designed to relieve. Sometimes intricately worded formulas give the impression of success where only disagreement exists. Such deception, while dangerous, may be the only recourse for negotiators who wish to try again at a later date. In this sense, international organizations prove more amenable to deadlock than do conferences, for their very existence gives promise of renewed efforts at compromise and often no special attention is accorded to disagreement. The collapse of conferences, however, whether on reparations, disarmament, or tariffs, seems to symbolize imminent crisis and conflict, catching up the policy maker in the backwash of public reaction and limiting his freedom to negotiate further.

7. Twentieth-century Diplomacy. Having reviewed the properties of diplomacy as well as problems inherent in its operation, it is now necessary to survey the impact of contemporary events upon the role of diplomacy in international relations. It requires little elaboration to show that the twentieth century has transformed diplomacy radically from the previous centuries when aristocratic representatives of royal courts convened to discuss matters of boundaries, consular exchange, and colonies. Those who advocate "traditional diplomacy" tend to ignore the basic developments of the Industrial Era which make a return to diplomacy's so-called Golden Age an impossibility. History cannot be reversed, nor can the factors be denied which limit diplomacy's role in the modern world.

Diplomacy and Ideology. Perhaps the most fundamental transformation in domestic and international politics came with the shattering of the closed circle of pre-Industrial Europe, in which a traditional aristocracy ruling over various principalities shared common interests and ideologies. Conflicts over territory could be settled by brief if bloody wars between armed mercenaries. Court circles exchanged diplomats, and those who traveled among Europe's many capitals were affiliated by common socioeconomic, if not paternal, background. The ideological gap widened with the French Revolution, but some semblance of community remained during much of the early nineteenth century. With the ever-widening access of competing elites to positions of policy making, marked on the one hand by the rise of democracy and on the other by the rise of dictatorship, diplomats represented ever more diverging interests and ideologies, sharpening conflict and lessening compromise.

One need only compare the chronicles of pre-1914 diplomacy and witness the intimate exchange of mutual grief between representatives of belligerent powers on the eve of World War I, with the interwar record of diplomacy wherein issues of democracy, fascism, and communism plunged diplomats into ideological controversy which precluded negotiation and compromise. In 1914, war came after repeated tensions met by conferences, some of which had been successful, some of which had failed. Throughout the memoirs of the participants runs the plaintive lament of fear and regret when conflicts of interest proved incapable of solution and war resulted. In 1939, war came after repeated tensions met by conferences, none of which had succeeded. Ideological convictions of diplomats, no less rigid in those of democracies than in those of dictatorships, fill both private and public papers with references to the futility of negotiation, the inevitability of conflict, and the incompatibility of differing value systems.

The ideological rigidity of fascist and Communist negotiators is well known. Less familiar is the manner in which American diplomats, fixed with one or another frame of reference, reduced the role of diplomat from negotiator to crusader. William E. Dodd, American Ambassador to Germany from 1933 to 1938, went to Nazi Germany determined to instill it with his Jeffersonian liberalism and to reexperience his image of pre-1914 Germany as he had known it in university life at Liepzig.[14] Hitler's famous blood purge of 1934, in which prominent civilian and military figures were assassinated or disappeared, shocked Dodd so much that he left a calling card at the home of one of the purged reading, "I hope we may see you soon." [15] For the next four years, he never had a private interview with Hitler, and his emotional reaction to the values propounded by the Nazi regime precluded any use of negotiations with Dodd as diplomat.

Another instance of the ideological impact upon diplomacy is the case of American Ambassador William Bullitt, envoy to Moscow from 1933 to 1936. Bullitt's experience on a dramatic mission in 1919 which took him to the newly founded Soviet Republic and to conferences with Lenin and Chicherin predisposed him to the values of the Russian Revolution. As the new American Ambassador to the Soviet Union in 1933, Bullitt went full of hopes for the accomplishment of the revolution, only to be rudely surprised at the inhumanity of the dictatorship as well as the brusqueness with which Soviet officials reacted to American policy. Swinging from undisguised friendship to undisguised hostility, Bullitt became as bitterly anti-Soviet as he had been pro-Soviet, and even after his transferal from Moscow to Paris in 1936 he continued to work against negotiations with the Russians because of what he considered their ideological shortcomings.

The point need be labored no further. Diplomacy's concern with men's clashing ideologies makes a mockery of the terms customarily used to describe the traditional envoy to foreign lands: courteous, tactful, and endeavoring to better relations whenever possible. Beneath the similarities in

[14] F. Ford, "Three Observers in Berlin: Rumbold, Dodd, and François-Poncet," in Craig and Gilbert, *op. cit.*, p. 448.
[15] *Ibid.*, p. 451.

protocol and procedures lie deep differences between eighteenth-century and twentieth-century negotiations.

Diplomacy and Domestic Pressures. Another consequence of the rise of democracy and dictatorship is the growing restriction upon diplomats as negotiators. In the democratic-pluralistic community, competing elites vie in the shaping of policy and assure attainment of their separate interests by insisting on a close check of diplomats and their activities. Postwar American diplomacy in China provides dramatic evidence of the push and pull of conflicting group interests. They resulted in a purge of those connected with the China policy of 1945–1949, highlighting the risk of suggesting or executing policies antithetical to different groups. As phrased in an unfavorable report against John Carter Vincent, career minister and active in American-Chinese relations from 1924 to 1947, his "studied praise of Chinese Communists and equally studied criticism of the Chiang Kai-shek government throughout a period when it was the declared and established policy of the United States to support Chiang Kai-shek's government," contributed to his dismissal in 1953.[16] The implication that professional foreign service officers should shape their reports so as to avoid disagreement with potentially powerful groups at home was clear from the fate of Vincent and his associates.

Just as the political structure of democracies precludes the traditional freedom for diplomacy, so the foundations of the authoritarian state limit, if not eliminate, the autonomy of the diplomat. With the monopoly of decision making in the hands of a single elite, as in Soviet Russia, or a limited combination of elites as in Nazi Germany, there can be little leeway accorded negotiators in far-off conferences. Although a semblance of so-called professional diplomacy remains in the authoritarian community, with the conventional apparatus of a foreign office and career diplomats overseas, the record shows constant domination by the party and surveillance by the secret police.[17] Thus, the experience of an American negotiator with considerable experience in Soviet-American diplomacy leads him to conclude, "The present-day Soviet representative can hardly be called a 'negotiator' in the customary sense. He is rather treated as a mechanical mouthpiece for views and demands formulated centrally in Moscow."[18]

Diplomacy and Political Institutions. The rise of democracy and dictatorship altered the role of the diplomat in still another way. Under the *ancien régime* negotiations progressed within limited social circles; responses within those circles indicated possible success or failure of a policy, and the diplomat's suggestions back to his foreign office accordingly could recommend new

---

[16] United States Civil Service Loyalty Review Board report, expressing "reasonable doubt as to the loyalty" of John Carter Vincent, in *The New York Times,* Dec. 16, 1952, p. 37. Vincent's "resignation" as of Mar. 31, 1953, was accepted by Secretary of State John Foster Dulles after reviewing Vincent's case. See Chap. 13 for a detailed treatment.

[17] For a detailed treatment of Nazi diplomacy see Chap. 16.

[18] P. Mosely, *op. cit.*, p. 272.

approaches in accordance with the situation confronting him. In short, his role as a negotiator was considerably enhanced by his ability to appraise the actions and reactions of his partners in negotiation. With the emergence of democracies and pluralism, the variables confronting the envoy to a democratic state become incapable of analysis by one man. He now faces a variety of interest groups ranging from the so-called "kitchen cabinet" surrounding the chief executive to the innumerable, vociferous commentators of radio, newspaper, and television.

Although the situation is precisely the opposite in a dictatorship from that in a democracy, the diplomat's job is no simpler. With decision making resting in the hands of one man or a small group of men, carefully concealed from all outside view, "the prognostication of political developments degenerated into a kind of psychological guessing game." [19] Isolated from all contact with the citizenry, restricted to the daily outpourings of government-controlled press and radio, the envoy to an authoritarian regime bears little resemblance to his predecessor in the salons of Paris or the garden parties of London. His view of the situation is extremely limited, not to mention the progressive deterioration of his emotional balance.

Even if all other factors remained equal, which they did not, the post-1919 political developments by their very nature seriously revised the role of diplomacy. Democracy and dictatorship, the two vehicles whereby new elites aspired to replace the old order, changed the ideological focus of diplomacy, severely limited its autonomy, and paralyzed much of its sensory apparatus. These consequences came not from any misunderstanding of diplomacy's role or abuse of its prerogatives but rather from the inherent structure of the two systems of government.

Linked with the rise of democracy and dictatorship but not inherent in their system is the emergence of other groups in the realm of international relations, with the subsequent intensification of the interrelation of foreign and domestic tensions. Whereas once the diplomat enjoyed a near-monopoly of contact with foreign countries, shared only peripherally with the trader and the missionary, today he must watch propagandists, military strategists, economic interests, and instruments of subversion operate side by side with, if not above and beyond, the efforts of diplomacy. The continual confusion in Western Europe resulting from the conflicting policies emanating simultaneously from the Departments of State, Commerce, and Defense illustrates the dilemma of the diplomat charged with effecting closer cooperation among the non-Communist countries. Similarly, no details are necessary to highlight the perpetual quandary of Soviet foreign policy, seeking intermittently to ease tensions between Moscow and the West yet beholden to an international Communist movement, openly dedicated to subvert dissident groups in foreign countries and aiding revolutions throughout the colonial world.

[19] Gilbert, *op. cit.*, p. 547.

It is true that both democracy and dictatorship may suddenly cut through these contradictions and in time of crisis resolve conflicts of interest by direct negotiation at the highest level. Such instances are rare, however, and do not negate the limitations of the diplomats resulting from the complex machinations of international economic interests, subversive organizations, and military strategists.

In the face of these political developments, it seems unfair to assail science and technology as the undoers of diplomacy, yet such is the argument of many who believe that it is rapidity of communication which has transformed diplomats into messenger boys. Admittedly, telecommunications permit capitals to by-pass their diplomats or to bind them to daily directives. When heads of state can communicate by telephone, as Churchill and Roosevelt did so frequently during World War II, or when negotiators can communicate with their home capitals by means of teletype, as did American representatives at the Korean truce talks, there is little need for vesting the diplomat with discretionary powers in negotiation. However, reliance upon such means of communication is symptomatic of a deeper factor in contemporary developments, the impact of history.

The Discrediting of Diplomacy. It is not overstating the case to say that nothing has so discredited diplomacy as the way in which men have viewed diplomacy's past record. France, alone of the post-1919 nations, failed to hold diplomacy in disrepute for the very reason that World War I was not regarded as the nefarious product of secret diplomacy, that diplomacy brought France badly needed allies against militarily superior Germany, and that the armistice awarded France Alsace-Lorraine, a constant goal of French policy since 1870.[20] Wilson's hostile attitude to diplomacy has already been described. Lloyd George, Prime Minister of Great Britain during and after World War I, remarked, "Diplomats were invented to waste time. It is simply a waste of time to let [important matters] be discussed by men who are not authorized to speak for their countries."[21] Franklin Roosevelt thought of the foreign service as a profession of perfection, characterizing the formula for success in it as "(a) you are loyal to the service, (b) you do nothing to offend people, and (c) you are not intoxicated at public functions."[22] As for the dictators, their remarks were no more complimentary. Leon Trotsky, newly appointed People's Commissar for Foreign Affairs in November, 1917, declared, "I will issue a few revolutionary proclamations to the peoples of the world and then shut up shop."[23] Adolf Hitler allegedly declared that Ribbentrop was the only man who told him "the truth about foreign coun-

[20] R. Challener, "The French Foreign Office: The Era of Philippe Berthelot," in Craig and Gilbert, *op. cit.*, p. 50.
[21] A. Kennedy, *Old Diplomacy and New,* London, 1922, pp. 364-365.
[22] W. Kaufmann, "Two American Ambassadors: Bullitt and Kennedy," in Craig and Gilbert, *op. cit.*, p. 655.
[23] Carr, *op. cit.*, p. 16.

tries," and later complained that "the reports of the Foreign Office were miserable. They always had the same quintessence: that we ought to do nothing." [24]

British and American rejections of diplomacy stemmed from ideological aversion to war and the supposition that with less diplomacy there would be less war, as well as from ideological preference for egalitarian, market-place politics which seemed antithetical to the professional, close-mouthed diplomatic official. Nazi and Communist rejections of diplomacy stemmed from ideological predispositions for revolutionary action instead of compromise and from a hostility to any group, including professional diplomats, which seemed to carry on traditions of the *ancien régime*.

If these considerations aroused distrust of diplomacy in the eyes of key groups the world over, the events of the 1930s and 1940s aroused disgust for diplomacy, particularly in the Western world. No two areas were more celebrated by the abuse accorded them than Munich and Yalta. At Munich in 1938, Chamberlain, Daladier, and Mussolini agreed to Hitler's demand for Sudeten Czechoslovakia. At Yalta in 1945, Churchill and Roosevelt, among other things, acceded to Stalin's demand for concessions in Manchuria and independence for Outer Mongolia, both at the expense of China. The term "appeasement" came to mean dishonor and to connote bartering defenseless peoples and strategic areas with world conquerers in return for temporary peace. Applied to Yalta, it meant betraying American principles to the interest of world communism.

Men view the present not only in terms of what they hope of the future but also in terms of what they remember of the past. It is impossible to analyze international events since 1945 without spotlighting the symbolic importance of Munich and Yalta. Intensifying the distrust and disgust with which the diplomat is often viewed is the fatalism which has pervaded the attitude of many groups in the postwar world concerning the inevitability of war and the uselessness of negotiations. As noted in Secretary of State Acheson's phrase "total diplomacy," the association of diplomacy with war seems almost indelible at this point.

Thus, negotiations during much of the postwar decade have been restricted to activities *within* the spheres dominated by the Soviet Union and the United States, rather than between these spheres. In this sense, to be sure, diplomacy has been a constant preoccupation of Western nations as the complex alliance system, built through diplomacy, requires ever-widening areas of negotiation to maintain it. To emphasize diplomacy's role within the so-called "friendly" sphere, however, is not to deny the negative record of negotiations between so-called "unfriendly" spheres. While the records are not yet available for full examination where such negotiations have been attempted, there is much to suggest that neither side undertook them on

[24] Gilbert, *op. cit.*, pp. 423–425.

the premise with which this discussion has approached diplomacy, namely, that settlement of given issues was the desired end.

Diplomacy, then, as a means of conducting foreign policy has little or no resemblance to the classical concepts of negotiation. Its form as well as its content bears the marks of the twentieth-century world, in which the intensification of conflict conditions the role of diplomacy and not vice versa. It remains true that in areas of international contact not permeated by the cold war, diplomacy continues to function and frequently produce agreements. In the great areas touched by the ideological struggle of our era, however, diplomacy is operative continually only on the interallied level, the "friendly sphere." But as long as men strive to settle all differences by compromise, whether before or after battle, negotiations will be necessary and diplomacy will be called upon.

ADDITIONAL CASE-STUDY MATERIAL

Byrnes, J.: *Speaking Frankly,* Harper, New York, 1947.
Carr, E. H.: *The Bolshevik Revolution, 1917–1923,* Macmillan, New York, 1950.
Churchill, Sir Winston: *The Second World War: The Gathering Storm, Their Finest Hour, The Grand Alliance, The Hinge of Fate, Closing the Ring, Triumph and Tragedy,* Houghton Mifflin, Boston, 1948–1953.
Ciano, Count Galeazzo: *The Ciano Diaries, 1939–1943,* Doubleday, New York, 1945.
Craig, G.: "High Tide of Appeasement: The Road to Munich, 1937–1938," *Political Science Quarterly,* vol. 65, March, 1950.
——— and F. Gilbert: "The Professional Diplomat and His Problems, 1919–1939," *World Politics,* vol. 6, January, 1952.
——— and ——— (eds.): *The Diplomats, 1919–1939,* Princeton University Press, Princeton, N.J., 1953.
Dennett, R., and J. Johnson (eds.): *Negotiating with the Russians,* World Peace Foundation, Boston, 1951.
Feis, H.: *The Road to Pearl Harbor,* Princeton University Press, Princeton, N.J., 1950.
François-Poncet, A.: *The Fateful Years; Memoirs of a French Ambassador in Berlin, 1931–1938,* Harcourt, Brace, New York, 1949.
Franklin, W.: *Protection of Foreign Interests; A Study in Diplomatic and Consular Practice,* GPO, Washington, 1946.
Haas, E.: "The Impact of Modern Weapons on Diplomacy," *World Affairs Interpreter,* winter, 1953.
Hankey, Lord: *Diplomacy by Conference; Studies in Public Affairs, 1926–1946,* Putnam, New York, 1947.
Hull, C.: *The Memoirs of Cordell Hull,* Macmillan, New York, 1948.
Kennedy, A.: *Old Diplomacy and New,* Appleton, New York, 1923.
Marshall, J.: "Citizen Diplomacy," *American Political Science Review,* vol. 43, February, 1949.
Mosely, P. E.: "Peace Making," *International Organization,* vol. 2, February, 1947.
Mowat, R. B.: *Diplomacy and Peace,* McBride, New York, 1936.
Nicolson, H.: *Diplomacy,* Oxford, New York, 1950.
Petrie, Sir C.: "The Strategic Element in Modern Diplomacy," *Quarterly Review,* July, 1952.
Rosenman, J.: *Working with Roosevelt,* Harper, New York, 1952.
Sherwood, R. E.: *Roosevelt and Hopkins,* Harper, New York, 1948.
Vansittart, Lord: "The Decline of Diplomacy," *Foreign Affairs,* vol. 28, January, 1950.
Webster, C. K.: *The Congress of Vienna,* Oxford, New York, 1919.
Wheeler-Bennett, J. W.: "Twenty Years of Russo-German Relations, 1919–1939," *Foreign Affairs,* vol. 25, October, 1946.

Chapter 8

ALLIANCES

1. Why Ally? Diplomacy enjoys few moments of greater grandeur than those surrounding the signing of an alliance, a solemn exchange of vows to merge power and policy of two or more nations for the attainment of specified ends. The familiar pledges "to consult and to agree on all necessary measures and actions," signed by the dignitaries of states amidst the hum of cameras and the explosions of flash bulbs, would seem to deny the conflict of interests so emphasized in Chapter 3. If no communal consciousness exists beyond national boundaries, how does one account for the innumerable alliances which fill the pages of history from time immemorial?

Firmness of the Alliance. One answer lies in sheer necessity. Unable to achieve their ends unilaterally, policy makers seek to augment power by securing help from another nation. Beyond this aim, common to all alliances, lies a broad continuum of purpose, varying according to the degree to which the interests of the allies are compatible. At one extreme stands the alliance concluded between elites with totally different ends but sharing a similar view of means. One partner aims at extending his territory at the expense of a third party; the other partner seeks to protect himself from possible attack by that third party. Ends of self-extension and self-preservation demand the pooling of power by the partners. At the opposite end of the continuum stands the agreement concluded between elites with identical interests, agreeing both as to ends and means. Between these two extremes fall the majority of alliances, representing limited compatibility of interests, entailing a certain amount of collaboration, and varying with respect to extent and duration of operation.

Alliances, then, do not preclude the existence of conflicting interests, much less of differing ideologies. Many pacts of mutual assistance have foundered upon the rock of conflicting interests and failed to meet the situation for which they were designed. Few alliances have led to lasting collaboration, much less federation, among the signatories. As will be seen in the examination of the so-called Axis pacts—embracing Nazi Germany, Fascist Italy, and imperial Japan—and of the North Atlantic Treaty Organization (NATO), the degree of conflict of interests within an alliance may determine ultimate success or failure.

If conflicts of interest remain among allies, will any pledges undertaken with such ceremony ever be observed? This depends upon the way in which the partners view the alliance at the time when action is called for its clauses. It would be false to assume that statesmen undertake contractual obligations lightly with no moral compulsion whatsoever to observe these obligations. The extreme caution with which elites enter alliance systems testifies to the contrary. Nevertheless, because policy is determined primarily by interests within nations, and because these interests change under the dynamics of national as well as international relations, no absolute certainty accompanies the formation of any alliance that it can survive the vicissitudes of time and tension.

To deny certainty, however, is not to deny probability. Herein lies the clue to why alliances continue to be formed despite the absence of some higher sanction to enforce their observance. A signed commitment alters the situation as it is viewed not only by the signatories but by those outside the alliance. Whatever pomp and circumstance attend the final agreement serve to symbolize an element of stability and permanency which the allies would introduce into the uncertain world of human behavior. The calculated risk of defection by a partner is preferable to the certainty of failure by unilateral action. Any degree of probability that can be introduced into the actions of other countries is a decided asset for the policy maker. Alliances serve this purpose, reducing the freedom of action of allied elites by changing their status in the view of all outside as well as inside the system.

Alliances for Self-preservation. As for specific motivations behind alliances, the overwhelming majority of contractual obligations are undertaken for the purpose of self-preservation. It was popularly believed during the interwar period that all alliances represented aggressive plots against the peace. However, it is more commonly fear of a third party rather than design upon it which prompts countries to pool their power and to coordinate their policies. This fear manifests itself in three basic types of guarantee contract, varying according to the amount of responsibility assumed by the signatories. The first and most widely encountered is the simple mutual-defense treaty whereby all parties assume an equal responsibility toward the security of the signatories. Thus NATO members have pledged to regard "an armed attack against one or more" of the signatories as "an attack against them all."

A second type imposes an unequal burden because of the extreme disparity in power among the partners, excluding reciprocity of obligation. The security pact signed in September, 1951, between the United States and Japan provided for the stationing of American troops in Japan, the latter country lacking a strong military organization at the time. According to Article 1, American forces "may be utilized to maintain . . . the security of Japan against armed attack from without, including assistance given at the express request of the Japanese government to put down large-scale internal riots and disturbances in Japan caused through instigation or intervention by an outside Power or Powers." Japan assumed no similar commitment to the United States. Even if, unlike the United States–Japan agreement, reciprocal obligations are specified, unequal burden remains where there is patent disparity of power, as between the United States and South Korea, or between the Soviet Union and Bulgaria.

Although these are the most prevalent types of defensive alliances, a third type has been used in which two potential antagonists receive identical guarantees from a third party, without that third party receiving any guarantees in return. The Locarno Pact of 1925 bound Great Britain and Italy to assist either France and Belgium on the one hand, or Germany on the other, depending upon which side was invaded in violation of the Franco-Belgian-German frontier. The obligation was limited to Germany's western borders. Furthermore, it did not bind Germany, France, or Belgium to render any assistance to Great Britain or Italy if these two countries became involved in conflict with other countries. Unlike the second type of treaty, this does not presume an inequality of power between two signatories but rather an approximation of power between them which can be radically altered by the agreed intervention of a third party.

Alliances for Self-extension. Alliances of self-extension, unlike those of self-preservation, seldom express their intent so boldly. Indeed, the almost universal condemnation of aggression usually compels pacts of self-extension to be clothed in defensive terms. However, secret protocols often reveal their true purpose, as in the so-called "Treaty of Nonaggression" concluded between Nazi Germany and Soviet Russia in August, 1939. Confidential articles provided for Soviet domination of the Baltic lands north of Lithuania, division of Poland between Germany and Russia, and Soviet freedom of action in Bessarabia, then part of Romania.

Occasionally aims of self-extension, at least on the part of one of the signatories, can be seen in the phrasing of the *casus foederis,* the situation in which the commitments assumed under the pact become operative. In the so-called "Pact of Steel" concluded between Germany and Italy in May, 1940, Article 3 stipulated, "If it should happen, against the wishes and hopes of the contracting parties, that one of them becomes involved in warlike complications with another Power or Powers, the other contracting party will come to its aid as an ally and will support it with all its military forces on land, on sea, and in the air." The absence of any reference to "being attacked by another power" distinguished this from pacts of self-preservation such as those quoted earlier.

Although the majority of alliances are concluded for the purposes of self-preservation, the dynamics of international relations often transform them into pacts of self-extension, for at least one of the parties. Before World War I, Germany, Austria-Hungary, and Italy formed the Triple Alliance, designed by its architect, Bismarck, as a purely defensive system. After his death, however, influential groups in Austria-Hungary came to view it as a means of self-extension. The original intent was changed, but German policy considered the obligations to remain binding and so supported Austria-Hungary in exerting pressure upon Serbia, a situation which touched off World War I.

Proper identification of the purposes behind an alliance is often difficult but is always vital for those outside the alliance. The original defensive nature of the Triple Alliance remained in doubt among many French groups, partly because its existence was known but its terms were secret, partly because Italian actions suggested ends of self-extension. Alarmed at her apparent isolation, France concluded a defensive alliance with Russia, to remain in effect as long as did the Triple Alliance. Great Britain later affiliated herself with the Russian-French arrangement, though not in a fully formalized alliance. Consequently, Europe was divided into two alliance systems, both originally defensive in purpose, which, because of the gradual transformation of elites, tended to forgo their defensive nature and to heighten tension between the two groups. So marked was this dual phenomenon of suspicion stemming from misidentification of purpose and of transformation stemming from reinterpretation of interest that one noted historian concluded,[1]

> The greatest single underlying cause of the War was the system of secret alliances which . . . gradually divided Europe into two hostile groups of Powers who were increasingly suspicious of one another and who steadily built up greater and greater armies and navies. . . . Members of each group felt bound to support each other, even in matters where they had no direct interest, because failure to give support would have weakened the solidarity of the group.

2. Wartime Alliances. Contractual obligations assumed in war differ radically in certain respects from those assumed in peace. While the bulk of this chapter will center on those concluded in peace, attention must be given wartime alliances because of the particular conditions under which they are negotiated and because of their frequent evolution into alliances of self-extension, regardless of the original intent of the signatories.

Wartime alliances originate at the behest of a sorely pressed nation in need of additional power to win the conflict. This precludes the careful sounding of interests and the definition of ends other than that of defeating a common enemy. If help is sought from a party not otherwise faced with becoming involved in the conflict, it is generally purchased with the promise of spoils. Thus from the start, wartime alliances may contain serious divergences in ends, that of the wooer being self-preservation, that of the wooed being self-extension.

---

[1] S. B. Fay, *The Origins of the World War,* Macmillan, New York, 1928, vol. I, p. 34.

Strains in Wartime Alliances. Once concluded, the wartime alliance operates under continual tension. Military operations seldom pose burdens of
similar magnitude upon all allies, thereby fostering recriminations among
partners. If a separate peace offers tangible advantage to an ally, suspicion
prevails within the coalition. Blackmail may pose a serious threat, since rup-
turing of the alliance carries with it probable defeat for the partner left alone
against the enemy. Furthermore, the illusion of unity so necessary for deceiving the foe as well as for maintaining morale within the alliance distorts
reality by concealing all conflicts of interest. Avoidance of argument, often
accompanied by pledges to resolve disagreements when the war is won, increases the tension under which the alliance operates. The successful wartime
alliance inevitably results in means, if not ends, of self-extension on the
part of one or more of the members. Bribery to bring additional groups into
the war may take the form of territorial or economic rewards. Defeat offers
the opportunity to compensate at the expense of the vanquished for losses
suffered, as well as to lessen the power of the defeated to become a threat in
the future. Finally, differences among the allies over the nature of their
rewards are enhanced by the fact that their power relationship at the end of
the conflict often differs radically from that prevailing when the alliance
was concluded and promises were exchanged. Where armies have marched,
interests may already be consolidated, in violation of equity among partners
if not in violation of specified agreements.

Illustrative of these points is the coalition of Great Britain, Soviet Russia,
and the United States, which defeated the forces of Germany, Italy, and
Japan in World War II. Although British-American cooperation evolved
gradually as Britain's situation became increasingly critical between 1939
and 1941, affiliation with the Soviet Union was precipitated by the German
attack of June, 1941, followed by months of Nazi victory on the Russian
front. With the Japanese attack upon Pearl Harbor in December, 1941, the
coalition faced the prospect of a long, arduous war at best, defeat of one
or more of its members at worst.

Although most differences among the Allies appeared strategic in nature,
conduct of the war necessarily affected settlement of the peace, for it was
evident to the participants that political influence accompanied armies. No
better illustration of this problem can be found than the question of a second
front. From 1941 to 1944, the bulk of Continental fighting took place between
German and Russian troops, resulting in continual Russian insistence on a
cross-channel landing by British and American units to relieve the pressure
on the eastern front. Britain, arguing on grounds of manpower shortage as
well as of German airpower, held out for Mediterranean landings along what
Churchill termed "the soft underbelly of the Axis." Invasions of Italy and
the Balkans would guarantee access to Middle Eastern oil, keep open vital

supply routes to Soviet Russia through Iran, and provide additional bases for bombing German industry.

These differences in strategy, dictated by the essential differences in British and Russian factors of power, took on an added dimension from conflicts of political interest inherited from earlier times. Following Chamberlain's appeasement of Nazi Germany from 1937 to 1939, Soviet suspicions interpreted British strategy as aiming at embroiling Germany and Russia in prolonged conflict which would weaken both to the advantage of England. Delay in opening a second front bolstered this view of the situation. Furthermore, the proposed landing of British troops in the Balkans was thought by Soviet policy makers to be aimed at the exclusion of Russian influence in East Europe. On the other side, Churchill viewed Russian demands for a second front as designed to cripple Britain militarily while excluding England from the Middle East and the eastern Mediterranean.

American strategy was complicated by the war in the Pacific and the need to provide the bulk of material for a second front in Europe, regardless of where it might be. Ultimately, American, Russian, and British interests were satisfied in part—but by no means altogether—with invasions of North Africa, Sicily, and Italy, being followed by a cross-channel invasion of France and the Lowlands in June, 1944. In the Pacific, however, American and Russian interests collided. Soviet refusal to enter the war against Japan until Germany had been defeated precluded operations from the Siberian mainland and left America with virtually all of the major fighting that took place aside from that in China. Only at Yalta, in February of 1945, did Soviet Russia agree to attack Japan three months after the defeat of Germany, this agreement being won by territorial awards at the expense of Japan and China.

Strains over the Peace. No less serious were the conflicts of interest inherent in the postwar settlement. The Soviet elite, twice assaulted by Germany within thirty years, aimed at domination of Eastern Europe and permanent weakening of Germany. British policy makers, anxious for Middle Eastern oil and traditionally opposed to one-nation hegemony of Europe, be it German or Russian, aspired at influence in the Balkans and a restructured, if somewhat emasculated, Germany to check further Russian penetration. Churchill's fear of a separate Russian-German peace along lines compatible with Soviet interests combined with a desire to win Soviet acceptance of British interests before the military situation determined the final position of the armies. As a result, he and Foreign Minister Anthony Eden pressed for some sort of settlement in 1942 which would define spheres of influence after victory. However, American policy makers, lacking well-defined interests in Europe but facing sizable ethnic minorities at home whose concern over the postwar settlement was of political importance to

Congress as well as to the President, aimed at avoiding any commitments to either Britain or Russia, with the hope of settling all problems at postwar conferences. Basic to the position of Roosevelt and Secretary Hull was an aversion to territorial annexation by any of the victors and an insistence upon the establishment of democracy on the American pattern in all the liberated or conquered territories. This conflicted directly with Russian designs upon Eastern Europe, which sought the establishment of friendly, i.e., communist-controlled, regimes.

During the course of hostilities as well as in the effort to build a peace system, the Allies of World War II differed over ends and means. Sir Winston Churchill's term "the Grand Alliance" is as inaccurate a term for their co-operation as that of an American observer who called it "the Strange Alliance." [2] It can be argued in support of the adjective "grand" that the world-wide alliance succeeded in its basic objective, defeat of the Axis nations. Against use of this adjective, however, stands the complex record of conflict of interests which threatened to rend it asunder repeatedly during the war. It can be argued in support of the adjective "strange" that the coalition joined communism and capitalism, imperialism and anticolonialism. Against use of this adjective stands the history of limited consensus which binds alliances in general and wartime alliances in particular. Admittedly politics does make strange bedfellows; in this sense all alliances are "strange." The World War II coalition, with its widely diverging ideologies, had much in common with that of World War I, which embraced czarist Russia, imperial Japan, republican France, parliamentary-monarchical Britain, and finally presidential America. Viewed in perspective, the joining of Soviet Russia, Great Britain, and the United States seems neither "grand" nor "strange."

Self-preservation versus Self-extension in 1945. As with many other war-time alliances, that of World War II appears to have developed from one of self-preservation into one of self-extension, at least for some if not all of the partners. For Great Britain, this meant nothing more than the maintenance of colonial holdings wherever consonant with the force at hand. As put by Winston Churchill, "I did not become the King's First Minister in order to preside over the liquidation of the British Empire." [3]

Until archives are opened, it is impossible to assess accurately the degree to which the United States and Soviet Russia pursued ends of self-extension in 1945. Certainly means of self-extension are evident in contradiction of earlier pledges to refrain from such steps. In 1941, the grandiloquent phrases of the Atlantic Charter, signed by Great Britain and the United States and adhered to later by Soviet Russia, forswore "territorial changes that do not

---

[2] Sir Winston Churchill, *The Grand Alliance,* Houghton Mifflin, Boston, 1951; J. R. Deane, *The Strange Alliance,* Viking, New York, 1947.

[3] *The War Speeches of the Rt. Hon. Winston S. Churchill,* Cassell and Co., London, vol. II, p. 344.

accord with the freely expressed wishes of the peoples concerned" and promised all peoples choice of "the form of government under which they will live." Churchill made no secret of his intention to exclude the British Empire from these provisions. Soviet annexations and indirect expansion in Eastern Europe hardly meet these clauses. Russia's Far Eastern gains included southern Sakhalin and the Kurile Islands from Japan and rights in Manchuria won at the expense of China. A Russian-dominated government in North Korea completed the picture.

By comparison, American actions appear both temperate and limited, but there is no denying their incompatibility with the self-denying provisions of the Atlantic Charter. Territorial gains centered around such Pacific islands as Okinawa, taken from Japan to become key United States naval bases. Far more drastic was the attempt to remold Japan's entire political, economic, and social system in the image of American values, and the effort to democratize the German social system by mass denazification trials and complete political tutelage.

Such is the pattern of British, Russian, and American policy in 1945, far removed from the ends of self-preservation which joined the three nations in 1941. Again, it should be emphasized that this evolution is not peculiar to the World War II alliance; its pattern recurs throughout the conflicts of history. It is because of these differences in formation and evolution that wartime alliances remain in a category by themselves, sharing problems in common with peacetime alliances but also facing situations markedly different from those with which we are most concerned.

3. Choosing Allies. In the actual process of forming, maintaining, and utilizing an alliance, conditions of peace offer far more opportunity for alternatives in decision making than do conditions of war. Seldom is the actual survival of the community at stake, compelling haste in the winning of allies. Never are the tensions as great, threatening one partner with extinction should the other partner default in his obligation. At the same time, with the lessened pressures of peace come increased problems of maintaining unity among divergent interests lacking a common threat to keep them compatible. The Rome-Berlin-Tokyo system of the prewar period and the North Atlantic Treaty Organization of the postwar period illustrate the mechanics of alliances with respect to these factors. By analyzing a pact of self-extension and a pact of self-preservation, it will be possible to note the similarities as well as the differences inherent in the two types of alliance.

Ideology and Power. Assuming that the ends of the alliance have been determined, there remains the selection of allies. Two factors determine choice of partners: power and interest. Since the purpose of an alliance is to augment the power of an elite unable to attain its ends unilaterally, the ally must be strong. However, the interests of the ally must not preclude utilization of his power in behalf of the alliance. Similarity of interest without sufficient power can accomplish nothing; conversely, strong allies whose interests remain incompatible cannot remain in harmony. It is fallacious to debate alliances based on "common ideology" as opposed to alliances based on "power politics." It is not power *or* interest, but power *and* interest, which determine an effective alliance.

NATO illustrates this generalization. Thus the NATO members shared an initial aversion to communism, particularly as utilized by Soviet Russia as a means of self-extension. It by no means followed from this, however, that they were predisposed to representative democracy, capitalism, or the other values championed by the architect of NATO, the United States. Turkey, Portugal, and Great Britain illustrate the wide divergence in religious, political, and economic values held by the member states. Although NATO has not yet been put to the definitive test of external attack, there is no evidence that these ideological and institutional dissimilarities have worked an undue hardship upon its operations.

In the Rome-Berlin-Tokyo system, there were many shared values in terms of authoritarian elites, embracing a more or less systematic fascist philosophy of racial superiority, worship of force and violence, and determination to control or crush all lesser states. Despite the ideological affinity of the three partners, however, they seldom coordinated policy, frequently duped one another, and never acquired the minimal integration necessary for success of the alliance.

While ideology often plays a subsidiary role in alliances, incapable by itself of making or breaking the system, ideological affinity is a welcome factor among allies. It has undoubtedly proved an asset in relations between Soviet Russia and Communist China, whatever conflicts of interest may have arisen. Similarly, it has played a role in NATO by limiting the participation of Spain, because of the political instability in France and the deep hostility toward Franco entertained by important interest groups of France's Center and Left. States may be included or excluded, then, according to ideology *if* this proves essential to over-all consensus among the partners.

Common Interests in NATO. It is interest, determined by ideology but not identical with it, which conditions in part the choice of allies. In March, 1947, Great Britain and France concluded a fifty-year pact of mutual assistance. This concept of common defense for Western Europe expanded into the Brussels Treaty of March, 1948, linking Great Britain, France, Luxembourg, Belgium, and the Netherlands. The initial point of tangency for the partners was defense against any country which might threaten their security. While France saw Germany as the implicit target of the alliance in view of the threefold German attack on France in less than seventy years, Great Britain saw the pact equally motivated by possibility of Russian expansion beyond the Elbe. Such differences lessened with the swift increase in Soviet power, manifested in a succession of Communist governments in Eastern Europe and culminating in the *coup d'état* in Czechoslovakia of February, 1948. The recognized weakness of the Brussels partners impelled them to turn to the United States to underwrite the pact. Months of proposals and counterproposals resulted in the North Atlantic Treaty of April, 1949, linking the United Kingdom, Canada, Belgium, Denmark, France, Iceland, Italy, Luxembourg, Netherlands, Norway, Portugal, and the United States in a common defense system. By 1955, Greece, Turkey, and West Germany had entered the organization, bringing to fifteen the number of NATO members. In the evolution of NATO from the original British-French agreement, one common point of interest has determined the choice of ally: defense against a possible enemy, be it Russia or Germany.

Factors of power likewise determine an alliance, although here NATO is on less solid ground. Critics contend that the pact was weakened by ignoring the factor of location in bringing Turkey into an alliance with Norway. Both countries border on the Soviet Union yet are separated by several thousand miles of territory. Furthermore, NATO long remained of two minds concerning the wisdom of excluding Western Germany, with its military and industrial potential, from defense of Western Europe as a whole. Advocates of the Greek-Turkish move argued that by flanking the Soviet Union the pact had become stronger, particularly in view of well-equipped Turkish armies within striking distance of the oil-rich Caucasus. As for Western Germany, a series of measures attempted, with varying success, to plan strategy both with and without participation of German units. Meanwhile American officials endeavored to win over French groups which opposed German entrance into NATO. Obviously NATO's considerations of power cannot be proved correct until the test of battle, but so far it appears that most if not all of the members represent added increments of power.

Common Interests in the Axis. NATO and the Axis differ sharply with respect to their success in the choice of allies. A pact of self-preservation such as NATO is essentially a passive, reacting instrument operating in a readily defined sphere, the *status quo,* with a clearly defined method, military defense against a common enemy. A pact of self-extension, such as the Axis, however, is basically an active, initiating instrument. Its sphere of operation is contingent upon the appetites of its members. Its method of procedure runs the gamut of means from diplomacy to total war. Power and interest play a particularly critical role in determining the strength or weakness of such an alliance.

Adolf Hitler, founder of the Axis, failed to cope satisfactorily with either interest or power. Intensely committed ideologically, he felt that only Benito Mussolini was worthy of participating in the New Order.[4] Accordingly, the two dictators concluded the Pact of Steel in May, 1939. However, Hitler,

---

[4] For the best analysis of the Hitler-Mussolini relationship see E. Wiskemann, *The Rome-Berlin Axis,* Oxford, New York, 1949.

even after concluding this pact, continued to regard Italy with a mixture of contempt and suspicion, considering Mussolini the only person capable of keeping Italy in the alliance. Hitler never respected his partner's power. Italian economic and military weakness dictated a policy of peace, anathema to Hitler's intentions. From the start, the Axis was plagued by this dilemma, manifested in Mussolini's refusal to march with Germany against Poland in September, 1939, in Germany's providing Italy with her sole supply of coal after March, 1940, in the poor showing of Italian troops against France in June, 1940, and in the failure of the Italian navy to offset German weakness in the Mediterranean throughout the war.

Furthermore, Hitler's obsession with ideology overlooked conflicts of interest stemming from factors other than power. His antireligious tirades nettled Italian Catholics, while his division of Poland in alliance with Soviet Russia brought open dissent in Rome. Mussolini's designs upon the French navy, as well as upon French colonies, clashed with Hitler's decision to conclude a somewhat moderate peace with France in 1940, hoping thereby to interest England in peace on a compromise basis. Finally, Italian ambitions in Central and Eastern Europe, while less tenacious than those of Germany, placed an added strain upon the Rome-Berlin Axis. In short, Hitler's choice of an ally in Italy suffered both in terms of power and of interest.

It was in part these weaknesses which necessitated the Nazi-Soviet Nonaggression Treaty of August, 1939. Attempts to integrate Soviet Russia into the Axis system failed, however, conflicts of interest being too great between Russia and Germany, as well as between Russia and Japan. Hitler's choice of Japan as an ally exhibited far more acumen in terms of power and interest than that of Italy. Japan's Pacific force was indeed imposing, provided Great Britain remained tied down in Europe and the United States remained neutral. Japanese interests might be meshed with those of Germany without friction provided both countries assailed similar objectives simultaneously, whether Soviet Russia or the Western democracies. The principal clash of interests inherent in the German-Japanese relationship lay in the failure of Germany to defeat Great Britain before attacking Soviet Russia on the one hand, and on the other, the refusal of dominant groups in Japan to move against the Soviet Union before securing control of the raw materials, particularly oil, of Southeast Asia—control which was challenged not only by Great Britain but also by the United States.

Complicating Hitler's choice of allies was his refusal to compromise his interests with those of his allies. Nazi ideology was a scheme of European domination, Germanic superiority, and Hitlerian infallibility. By definition, then, Nazi interests precluded any genuine alliance. Hitler's short-lived compact with Soviet Russia foundered, in part, because of his refusal to share Eastern Europe with Bolshevism. The Tripartite Pact failed to reap rich rewards, in part, because of Hitler's insistence on keeping Japan in the dark concerning the planned attack against Russia, resulting in a Tokyo-Moscow pact of nonaggression only two months before the war began. His reluctance to compensate Italy in North Africa or to treat Rome as an equal partner in formulation of policy only widened the gulf already separating the two countries. Hitler's view of his allies proved fatal to the integration necessary in any alliance, particularly one of self-extension.

Expanding the Alliance. Alliances vary considerably according to their flexibility of membership. In so far as all alliances of self-extension are directed against target groups and most alliances of self-preservation have an implicit, if not an explicit, threat in view, it is obvious that few are completely open to all comers. One such exception was the Locarno Treaty, which permitted additional nations to subscribe to the initial conditions. Its sponsors at one time hoped to extend its guarantees to areas other than the French-Belgian-German frontier. More usual are the NATO and Axis systems which permit an unspecified number of additional allies after the original contract is completed but implicitly bar "the enemy," be it one country or a counter-alliance.

The addition of allies is determined by the same factors as the original alliance, but the problems increase in complexity because of the probability of reinterpretation or violation of the original purpose. NATO's defensive responsibilities were considerably altered, for instance, when commitments limited to Western Europe were extended into the Middle East by the addition of Greece and Turkey. Changes of a more profound nature complicated the question of adding Germany, which claims so-called "lost" territories annexed by Poland in 1945, while NATO is an avowedly defensive system. Similarly, the strategic design of the Rome-Berlin Axis, based on contiguous partners, was radically altered with the addition of Japan, separated from Germany and Italy by the continental expanse of Soviet Russia. Choice of allies becomes increasingly important as more members are brought into the system, thereby lowering the common denominator of interest without necessarily increasing the over-all power.

4. Drafting the Alliance. Assuming that the parties are agreed as to the ends of policy, negotiators then strive to define the *casus foederis,* the situation which is to bring obligatory action on the part of the allies, to establish machinery for implementing the terms of the treaty, and to specify the duration of the pact. Although words seldom prove as important as events in determining the operation of an alliance, comparison of key articles in recent treaties will reveal differences in attitude on the part of the allies which often result in differences of behavior.

No article receives more attention than that containing the *casus foederis.* Sometimes, as in the Brussels pact, a so-called "hair-trigger" clause specified automatic action in the case of crisis: "If any of the High Contracting Parties should be the object of an armed attack in Europe, the other High Contracting Parties will . . . afford the Party so attacked all the military and other aid and assistance in their power." [5] The corresponding clause in NATO, at the insistence of the United States Congress, was more qualified: "The Parties agree that an armed attack against one or more of them in Europe or North America shall be considered an attack against them all . . . each of them . . . will assist the Party or Parties so attacked by taking . . . *such actions as it deems necessary,* including the use of armed force." [6]

The extreme caution with which many groups within the United States view contractual obligations is best exemplified by the Australian–New Zealand–United States (ANZUS) treaty, which reads: "Each Party recognizes that an attack in the Pacific area on any of the Parties would be dangerous to its own peace and security and declares that it would act to meet the common danger in accord with its constitutional processes." [7] No reference is made to military action, nor is any implication of automatic response indicated. The same approach characterizes the South East Asian Treaty (SEATO) which, since 1954, links the United States, Britain, France, New Zealand, Australia, Pakistan, Thailand, and the Philippines in the defense of the territorial *status quo* of the South Asian lands of the members. Despite American, Philippine, and Australian demands for tighter obligations and a more intense union of the members, British, French, and Pakistani misgivings about the alliance compelled the minimal definition of the *casus foederis* finally adopted.

In sharp contrast, the Axis pacts included both military and "hair-trigger" provisions. Thus the Pact of Steel read, "If . . . one of them becomes involved in warlike complications with another Power or Powers, the other Contracting Party will come to its aid . . . with all its military forces on land, on sea, and in the air." [8] Similarly, the Tripartite Pact pledged Japan, Germany, and Italy "to assist one another with all political, economic and military means when one of the three Contracting Parties is attacked by a power at present not involved in the European War or in the Sino-Japanese conflict." [9]

The limitations of drafting cannot be overemphasized. Despite the greater rigidity of Axis terminology, Italy did not enter the war at the side of Germany until June, 1940. Conversely, despite the ambiguities in the obligations undertaken by the United States, there is little indication that American response will be any less prompt in case of attack on Western Europe than if a "hair-trigger" clause had been inserted. Drafting serves a twofold purpose: it attempts to represent the way in which the allies view their obliga-

[5] Art. 4 of Brussels Treaty, concluded Mar. 17, 1948.
[6] Art. 5 of the North Atlantic Treaty, concluded Apr. 4, 1949. Italics supplied.
[7] Art. 4 of ANZUS Mutual Security Treaty, concluded Sept. 5, 1951.
[8] Art. 3 of Pact of Steel, concluded in May, 1939.
[9] Art. 3 of Tripartite Pact, concluded Sept. 27, 1940.

tions at the time of signature, and it increases the probability of response at some future date. As such, it merits attention without adulation.

Consultation Machinery. A second problem confronting those negotiating an alliance is in providing ways of implementing the provisions of the pact. Often this is left to supplementary protocols, worked out between military rather than diplomatic staffs. This permits greater flexibility, particularly on the part of parliamentary systems which demand ratification of a treaty but which exclude parliamentary participation in executive agreements or military plans. Mutual defense pacts often pledge "to consult whenever necessary," an article which provides for machinery in the most general terms. Typical was the Tripartite Pact, calling for "a Joint Technical Commission, the members of which are to be appointed by . . . Japan, Germany and Italy [which] will meet without delay." [10] These provisions remained a dead letter.

The North Atlantic Treaty varies only slightly in this respect, although far more meaning has been given its provisions which establish "a council, on which each of them [the members] shall be represented, to consider matters concerning the implementation of this Treaty. The Council shall be so organized as to be able to meet promptly at any time. The Council shall set up such subsidiary bodies as may be necessary; in particular it shall establish immediately a defense committee." [11] The highly personalized nature of the Axis system contrasts with the institutionalized structure of NATO. Given the premium placed on coordination within an alliance, such machinery may determine the success or failure in maintaining and utilizing the alliance.

Finally, negotiators must provide for termination of the treaty, the least important of their various problems. Commitments may be undertaken according to time, in terms of years, or according to objective, in terms of winning a war. Seldom are alliances held to be in force "indefinitely," as is the ANZUS pact.[12] More frequently obligations are considered binding, as in the Pact of Steel, for ten years, whereupon the treaty may be reviewed. NATO members may review the treaty after ten years but are bound by its obligations for at least twenty years, after which release can be obtained only by filing notice of intent to renounce membership one year in advance. The Russian-French alliance of 1894 illustrates duration contingent upon event, the pact specifically to remain in force as long as the Triple Alliance continued. However, deeds rather than words determine the longevity of an alliance. Its duration is dependent upon how it is maintained more than upon how it is drafted.

5. Maintaining the Alliance. One certainty in international relations is the certainty of change. No matter what the conditions under which an

[10] Art. 4 of Tripartite Pact.
[11] Art. 9 of North Atlantic Treaty.
[12] Art. 10 of ANZUS Mutual Security Treaty.

alliance is drafted, it is inevitable that there will be significant changes, within as well as without the system, before the alliance is utilized. Interpretations of interest as well as relationships of power are transformed under the impact of political as well as technological developments. Difficult as are the problems of choosing allies and drafting agreements, maintenance of an alliance indeed seems to be the most thorny issue confronting policy makers.

Internal Strains and Shifts. Within the alliance system, an elite's interpretation of interest may change or the elite itself may change. NATO's origin coincided with growing alarm over Soviet moves in Central Europe; its implementation made promising progress after the outbreak of the Korean War. Failure of the Soviet Union to move beyond its sphere of influence in Europe, and stabilization of the Korean conflict combined to lessen the sense of emergency with which West European elites viewed the situation. Slackening of rearmament and increased reluctance to admit West Germany into NATO were the results.

Reinterpretation of interest may come when an elite assumes new obligations outside the alliance which necessarily impinge upon its relationship with the other partners. Illustrative of this is the United States, now connecting an interlocking system of alliances which spans more than half the globe. Before entering NATO, it was already a member of the Rio Treaty of 1947, binding twenty-one American republics to a pledge whereby "armed attack by any State against an American State shall be considered as an attack against all American States." By joining NATO in 1949, the United States bridged two defense systems extending from the northern tip of Norway to the southern tip of Argentina. In 1951, the United States assumed security commitments separately with Japan and the Philippines, and jointly with Australia and New Zealand. In 1953, it undertook to guarantee the independence of the Republic of South Korea in a mutual-security pact.

Although there is no legal obligation for Norway to come to the defense of Australia or Argentina under these pacts, the fact that they all interlock through the medium of the United States does link Norway indirectly to the security of Australia and Argentina. West European defense depends upon the strength of the United States. Every added American commitment spreads that strength more thinly, diverting it to areas other than Western Europe. In 1949, NATO represented America's primary responsibility. In 1951, Pacific pacts lessened that emphasis. Reinterpretation of American interest came without change in the Washington administration during the interval. It is facile to say that the world is round, that peace is indivisible, or that the struggle is global. Such phrases mean little to West Europeans whose reliance upon American men and munitions makes them loath to see such items committed to defense of South Korea. Similarly, Latin-American governments grumble when the Yankee colossus turns its assistance to other hemispheres while economic and military problems exist nearer home.

Reinterpretation of interest may accompany a change in elite, bringing new tensions within the alliance system. No such tension followed immediately upon the change of American administration in 1952, principally because President Eisenhower represented groups within the Republican party whose interests with respect to NATO paralleled those dominant in the Democratic party. However, a change of French government in 1953, which forced out Robert Schuman as Foreign Minister, indicated increasing hostility to integration of West Germany into NATO as demanded by the United States. Similarly the downfall of Prime Minister de Gasperi in Italy, several months later, weakened that country's participation in NATO. In both France and Italy continued pressure from neutralist groups on the Right and Left, coupled with large Communist movements, made NATO's future difficult at best. Further influence by neutralist and Communist elites might paralyze the alliance.

No less serious a challenge to maintenance of an alliance is that posed by changes of power relationships within the alliance. The objection of many French groups to bringing West Germany into NATO stemmed largely from the fear that in due course Germany would become the most powerful European member of NATO and as such might subvert the defensive nature of the pact in order to rewin territory held by Poland since 1945. Similarly, congressional cuts in military appropriations and threatening dips in Wall Street bring cries of alarm from America's partners who fear any decrease in the United States military or economic strength. Having committed themselves to NATO in the face of considerable internal as well as external opposition, West European policy makers can ill afford an adverse change in American power.

External Changes. In addition to these shifts in interest and power, policy makers must consider similar shifts which occur outside the alliance. Since the birth of NATO, debate has raged concerning possible changes in the interests of the Soviet elite, debate which intensified following personnel changes within that elite occasioned by the death of Stalin in March, 1953. Apparent changes in the target group raise two problems for maintenance of an alliance. On the one hand, they affect the way in which the members view their obligations under the alliance. Relaxation of NATO rearmament whenever Moscow's gestures have appeared less bellicose illustrates the impossibility of long-range planning when the way partners view the alliance changes with every move of the target group.

On the other hand, possible changes in the target group must be explored because they may permit different planning within the alliance. Rearmament is a continual burden in Western Europe. By dismissing a priori all Soviet moves as concealing a belligerent intent, NATO commits its members to an indefinite period of inflation and lower standards of living. However, by properly interpreting the situation within the Soviet bloc as less threatening in 1952–1953, a "stretch-out" of defense preparations meant an increase in NATO's effectiveness. Not only was a temporary respite given to strained economies, but materials and energies were harbored for use at a later time, producing more effective weapons in terms of the ultimate challenge. Failure

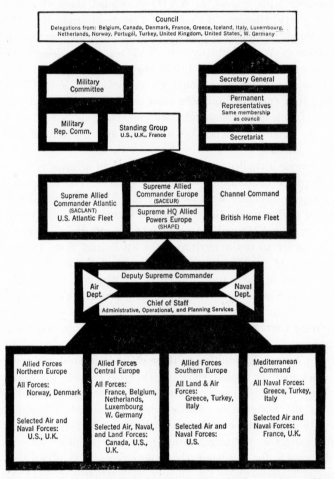

Structure of the North Atlantic Treaty Organization, spring, 1955

to adapt an alliance to such shifts of interest in other elites may lead to temporary and purposeless strength, expending energies unnecessarily which might be better used in a different way or at a different time.

Adapting to Change: NATO Planning. NATO's efforts to cope with this plenitude of change have indeed been unprecedented. The actual organs of common action which have been created to realize these aims are pictured on the accompanying chart. Broadly speaking, they may be divided into a civilian and a military branch. The civilian organs—the Council, Secretary

General, the Permanent Representatives, and the international Secretariat—jointly plan policy and make recommendations to the member governments. After these plans have been accepted, they are then carried out not only by the national governmental services individually but also through the joint military organs which comprise the remainder of the chart.

It is in the Council that plans prepared by the joint staffs are approved, rejected, or modified. Since all members are equally represented on the Council, it has developed into the organ of compromise and consultation wherein divergent policy aims are discussed and adjusted. Since unanimity is required, compromises must be acceptable to all members. Those who serve on the Council may be the heads of state or the foreign, defense, or finance ministers, depending on the nature of the topic which needs discussing and adjusting. The separate identities of the member nations are, of course, maintained at this level of discussion.

In addition, the body of Permanent Representatives plans policy continually, even when the Council is not in session. Although this organ also consists of instructed government delegates, they function under the guidance of a Secretary General, responsible to no single government, and receive help from an international body of civil servants loyal to NATO as a collective entity. Thus, NATO policy planning combines international civil servants with instructed representatives who naturally forgo much of their distinct national predilections through this amalgamation. The extraordinary nature of the combined Secretariat–Permanent Representatives organ is made plain by examining the nature of its work. Far from confining itself to collecting information and making legal studies, it constantly surveys the military requirements of the allies, examines their separate economic and financial conditions and resources, and attempts integrated and collective plans for reconciling economic capacity with military needs. It goes still further. The Secretariat actually reviews and criticizes the efforts made by member governments to meet their assigned tasks and sets up numerical targets to be met in national recruitment, organization, and industrial production. Such criticism has frequently been outspoken and forceful, and it may happen that a lagging British minister of defense, for instance, is challenged and criticized by a NATO member who may have previously been a British civil servant in the minister's own department. Against this record, it remains true that member governments have not delegated any final authority to their representatives on NATO concerning the key economic and financial questions on which military integration rests. "The most they have conceded—and this is a good deal—is that national policies in matters affecting NATO should be scrutinized and discussed from the standpoint of common interest and with a free exchange of full information." [13]

[13] Royal Institute of International Affairs, *Atlantic Alliance,* Oxford, New York, 1952, pp. 124–125.

Continuous consultation and continuous adjustment of policies is the key to maintenance of the alliance. So long as ends remain a matter of agreement and disharmony stems primarily in the realm of methods and means, mutually acceptable compromises can almost always be worked out and flexibility preserved. No member has surrendered any of its sovereignty—formally speaking—and this is guaranteed by the unanimity principle. However, each has bound itself to submit all national policies of defense in the North Atlantic area to the NATO process of consultation. Hence even the United States, like all other members, annually submits its defense budget to the scrutiny of its allies in the Council, an action unprecedented in American history. The "NATO method" of making decisions and plans rests not on formal voting but on the continued readiness to consult, discuss, adjust, and only then to take internationally directed and supervised action in the military sphere.

NATO Military Integration. Within the military sphere of NATO, different forms of organization and methods of making decisions arise. Once a top-level economic and financial policy is fixed by the Council and implemented by each member government, and once a fixed military target has been set in the same manner, implementation and planning are taken over by integrated military organs. Strategic plans of forming, equipping, and deploying divisions are made by the Military Committee composed of all members. In practice, however, detailed decisions are worked out by the Standing Group, the general staff of NATO composed of the military representatives of the United States, Britain, and France. It is continuously in session in Washington. Three regional commands function under the Standing Group, of which the largest and most important is the imposing organization known as "Supreme Headquarters Allied Powers Europe" (SHAPE). While national armies continue to function everywhere in NATO, the structure of command has been integrated. Dutch troops take orders from SHAPE in Paris, and SHAPE is commanded by an American general. The Italian army obeys the commands of the Allied Commander for Southern Europe (an American admiral), who, in turn, receives his orders from SHAPE. In peace, standardization of weapons, of production, of tables of organization, and of chains of command remains the task of NATO; and in war centrally directed operations will be the major responsibility. For the first time a truly internationally commanded, organized, and equipped coalition army functions before the outbreak of actual hostilities.

Adapting to Change: Axis Failure. Continuity of consultation and compromise, essential to maintenance of alliances, were striking by their total absence from the Axis system. The vicissitudes of change posed problems no less serious in scope for the Axis than for NATO, although the composition of the elites governing Germany, Italy, and Japan remained constant. Reinterpretations of interest, such as Hitler's swing from anti-Bolshevism to

Nazi-Soviet pact to war with Russia in the course of two years, placed critical strains upon the alliance, yet little effort was made by any of the partners to cope with the impact of change within or without the system. Rome was given twenty-four hours' notice of the Nazi-Soviet pact. At three o'clock on the morning that Nazi panzer units struck across the Soviet border, Mussolini received Hitler's lengthy letter announcing the Führer's latest venture. Mussolini, rankling under repeated slights at the hands of Hitler and Ribbentrop, attacked Greece in the winter of 1940–1941 without co-ordinating policy in Berlin. Not only did this weaken Italy's ability to campaign in North Africa against British units in Egypt, but it required intervention by Nazi units, striking through Yugoslavia and Bulgaria, to save Mussolini from complete disgrace at the hands of victorious Greek armies.

Similarly, consultation between Berlin and Tokyo was more apparent than real. When Hitler endeavored to make Soviet Russia a full-fledged member of the Axis in November, 1940, he first dispatched an outline of his proposed scheme to Tokyo.[14] However, no further liaison was maintained throughout the Nazi-Soviet talks, despite the fact that a major stumbling block proved to be Soviet insistence upon explicit definition of Japan's anticipated "new order of Greater East Asia." Typical of Hitler's basic attitude was his directive of March 5, 1941, "The Japanese must not be given any intimation of the Barbarossa operation"—Barbarossa being the code reference to the anticipated attack on Soviet Russia.[15]

Japanese efforts to consult with their German allies assumed slightly more substance, although never was this consultation institutionalized as in NATO. For instance, Foreign Minister Matsuoka hopped back and forth between Berlin and Moscow in April, 1941, attempting to arrive at an understanding with the Russians which would prove compatible not only with Japan's interests but those of Germany as well. Hitler flatly avoided divulging his plans against Russia. While Ribbentrop deceived Matsuoka, he was paid in kind. No hint was made of war games already under way in the Pacific which were to prepare the Japanese navy for attack upon Pearl Harbor.

In fact, both Berlin and Tokyo played a devious game. After an explicit warning from Matsuoka on behalf of the Japanese cabinet on May 28, 1941, that war between Germany and Russia was inimical to Japanese interests, Ambassador Oshima received the first official German confirmation on June 6 that a Nazi-Soviet war was imminent. Similarly, not until a few days before Pearl Harbor was Hitler informed of Japanese intentions to broaden the war by attacking the United States, despite repeated statements to Japanese officials by Ribbentrop and Hitler that "Germany considers war with the United States undesirable."[16] The Tripartite Pact was characterized not by

---

[14] H. Feis, *The Road to Pearl Harbor*, Princeton University Press, Princeton, N.J., 1950, p. 146.

[15] Hitler Basic Army Order 24 as quoted in Feis, *op. cit.*, p. 183.

[16] F. H. Hinsley, *Hitler's Strategy*, Cambridge, New York, 1951, pp. 17 ff.

multilateral diplomatic intercourse but primarily by "the statesman's monologue." [17]

6. Utilizing the Alliance. The final test of an alliance comes when its partners rely upon it to achieve specified ends of policy. The test may be purely political, frightening opposition into submission or deterring opposition from attack. The mere existence of an agreement among nations may serve to accomplish ends without that agreement being put into the crucible of battle. Should the situation preclude so inexpensive a victory, however, economic coordination among the allies may attempt to increase the pressure upon a target group. Failing this, the only alternative is resort to military action, calling into operation the full force of the system.

The Distribution of Power. Two imponderables reduce the certainty of victory, the distribution of power and the reaction of the target group. The first may be structured in any of four ways: (1) the alliance may be stronger than both its target-group and "neutral" areas; (2) the alliance may be stronger than its target group but weaker than a combination of target and "neutral" areas; (3) the alliance may be weaker than its target group but hold predominance if "neutral" areas come to its assistance; and finally (4) the alliance may be approximately equal in strength with that of its target group, "neutral" areas offering certain preponderance to whichever side they might join. The predictability of success or failure decreases radically as the situation moves from the first to the last possibility. By definition "neutral" areas are uncommitted and therefore incapable of predictable action. Thus the first situation offers certain victory; the second, probable victory; the third, probable defeat; and the fourth offers stalemate, defeat, or victory, depending entirely on the course of unforeseen events.

Statesmen seldom seek an actual "balance" of power; rather it is an *im*balance of power which assures success to an alliance. "Preservation of the balance of power" may cover a multitude of aims ranging from "preserving our present superiority in power" through "preserving an apparent power equality" between the major antagonists, to "avoiding committing all areas with power to either of two strong opponents."

Policy makers must ascertain which of these situations confronts the alliance. However, the calculation of comparable power is seldom capable of accurate measurement. Furthermore, power may breed power in the familiar phenomenon of the arms race. Power predominance within the alliance may stimulate its accumulation outside the alliance. Military power does not increase at a constant rate. Once the leveling-off period arrives, the ratio of superiority over competitors continually lessens as they mobilize their total resources.

[17] J. Huizenga, "Yosuke Matsuoka and the Japanese-German Alliance," in G. Craig and F. Gilbert (eds.), *The Diplomats, 1919–39,* Princeton University Press, Princeton, N.J., 1953, p. 637.

Target-group Reaction. The question of the arms race raises the second imponderable for alliance makers: "How will the target group react?" The intent of the alliance might be misunderstood, bringing the reverse response from that anticipated. Although this is not common, it has been operative at least to a limited degree in tensions between the two major blocs in Europe. An elaborate postwar network of bilateral alliances interlocked Soviet Russia with all countries of Eastern Europe. Explicitly worded as instruments of defense against a revived Germany, the pacts were viewed by many non-Communists as instruments of offense against Western Europe. NATO was, to a large extent, a response to this alliance system. In turn, groups within the Soviet bloc viewed NATO as an instrument for attack against the Communist sphere. Both systems, despite their basic aims of self-preservation, aroused reactions which interpreted them as aiming at self-extension.

Far more common is the alliance which fails because recognition of its aim brings an unanticipated response by the target. Thus a major purpose behind the Tripartite Pact was to frighten the United States out of interfering with Japan or Germany in their destruction of the British Empire. As phrased by Matsuoka, "Germany wants to prevent American entry into the war, and Japan wants to avoid a war with the United States." [18] Actually, the pact proved an impetus for those groups striving to carry out American mobilization and aid to Great Britain. It provided them with an argument against a neutralist position by suggesting a world-wide totalitarian conspiracy aimed at defeating the democracies piecemeal. Similarly, NATO served as a convenient scapegoat for Soviet propaganda, seeking to maintain control over Eastern Europe. Particularly was this true with respect to repeated American efforts to bring a rearmed Western Germany into the alliance, a step which could not but be viewed with alarm by groups within the Soviet bloc. The creation in 1955 of a militarily integrated Soviet-satellite treaty organization was the response.

Undoubtedly the most significant miscalculations in response followed the signing of the Tripartite Pact. The American reaction has already been cited. No less important for Japan as well as Germany was the hoped-for Soviet adhesion to the Axis. By flanking the Soviet Union, Germany, Italy, and Japan would have compelled Russian acceptance of a sphere of influence outside their respective "new orders" and would have won Russian manpower and industry as a reservoir of power. Moscow took no such action, however. Insisting upon interests in East Europe and China, opposed by Germany and Japan, respectively, Molotov refused to accept Hitler's proposals. The Tripartite Pact had failed to cow Soviet Russia, just as it failed to cow the United States.

Such are the obstacles to successful utilization of alliances. Nothing could

[18] Foreign Minister Matsuoka at Imperial Conference approving Tripartite Pact, Sept. 26, 1940, as quoted in Feis, *op. cit.,* p. 111.

be wider of the mark than regarding them as "mere scraps of paper." However, by recognizing their limitations as well as their potentialities, a more realistic appreciation of the role played by alliances in international relations can result.

7. The Impact of the Twentieth Century. Like diplomacy, alliances cannot be in the twentieth century what they were in the era before the Industrial Revolution. At that time, international coalitions of elites, sharing similar values and interests, could agree to act together for the attainment of certain ends. They remained responsible to a limited court hierarchy, the composition of which remained constant in terms of interest if not of personnel. However, the succession of elites in democratic governments lessens the possibility of assuring a constant regard for the obligations of an alliance. Furthermore, the variety of conflicting interests which must be considered by policy makers representing not only a coalition of elites but facing opposition groups in the pluralistic community compels negotiators to tread a careful path in forming and maintaining alliances. Even so explicit and dramatic a guarantee as that given by Great Britain and France to Poland in March of 1939 underwent serious debate in the French cabinet before being honored in September, 1939.

NATO has not been without its inner strains and conflicts. Field Marshal Viscount Montgomery, often critical of American strategy and tactics, made no secret of his feelings in 1953 when he called upon Canada to take "an increasingly important part in the NATO affairs. . . . Do not be influenced unduly by the great nation of 160,000,000 people lying beyond your border. . . . Go right ahead, Canada, and lead the Western world." [19] In view of Canadian criticism over United States policy in Asia, his remarks bespoke underlying tensions. Far more vitriolic critics of NATO on the American side are typified by the anguished comments of a Middle Western Senator, "You remember that glorious picture of the four Marines lifting the American flag over the bloody ground of Iwo Jima? Today the Marines are hauling down the American flag and raising the NATO flag on our soil." [20]

Nor are dictatorships, despite their absence of shifting elites and representative government, more prone to honor long-term commitments. As has been seen, Mussolini failed to support Hitler in September, 1939, although the declarations of war by Great Britain and France clearly came under the *casus foederis* of the Pact of Steel. Similarly, within the councils of the Japanese cabinet, the German attack on Russia brought forth determination to avoid a Soviet conflict "for some time, but we will steadily proceed with military preparations against the Soviets and *decide our final attitudes independently.*" [21] Authoritarian regimes seem inherently hostile to the necessary

[19] Speech of Aug. 28, 1953, *The New York Times,* Aug. 29, 1953.
[20] Hon. William E. Jenner, *Congressional Record,* Aug. 18, 1952, p. A5250.
[21] Imperial Conference of July 2, 1941, in Feis, *op. cit.,* p. 216.

consultations and compromise which make alliances viable. The tendency to "go it alone" epitomizes the behavior of the Axis partners, as well as much of the Soviet actions in the wartime coalition with Great Britain and the United States.

From Alliance to Regional Association. Despite these internal strains, however, the global alliance systems of our era are gaining rather than losing in cohesion. Encompassing ever more nations, the American and Soviet-led coalitions are gaining in geographical scope. More important, however, is the rapidly expanding authority delegated to the central organs of the alliance, perhaps taking away, step by step, from the theoretically still unimpaired sovereignty of the member states. This has clearly happened in the Soviet Eastern European system, which is dominated rather than led by Moscow. The Organization of American States, ANZUS, and SEATO, by contrast, show very little evidence that habits of cooperation and common planning have taken precedence over the separate national policies of the allied nations. NATO, however, furnishes some hints of the gradual process by which the forces of the twentieth century are gradually transforming a calculated alliance of sovereign governments into a regional association of peoples, united by loyalty to common myths and symbols as well as by concrete interests.

NATO began as a simple military pact, without hint of common armies, integrated economic planning, permanent institutions, standardization of weapons, and coordination of foreign policies. It is one of the obvious lessons of the twentieth century, however, that policies of economic welfare and development cannot be pursued simultaneously with policies of rapid rearmament and military training when resources of men and money are scarce, currencies weak, and living standards in peril. Military planning thus presupposes economic planning and coordination. Further, common military policy is meaningless unless the over-all foreign policies of the participating nations aim at the same goal. In short, the military alliance demands the coordination of foreign and economic policies before the purely military aims can be achieved.

Consequently, the unique "NATO method" of decision making—consultation, discussion, compromise, and national implementation of centrally determined policy—took shape first in the realms of foreign and economic policy. Only later did the military command achieve the power and prestige which now makes it the acknowledged center of loyalty for most European, as well as Canadian and United States, officers. Despite lingering resentment and occasional bursts of insubordination—especially by French generals—the system has continued to gain momentum, so that some of the Western European armies have begun to lose a measure of their individuality with the growth of standardized weapons, command structures, and supply systems, and jointly operated airfields, pipelines, and railroads, not to mention such visible symbols as international shoulder patches and insignia.

Lord Ismay, first Secretary General of NATO, thus described the manner in which the NATO members allocated in 1953 the financial burden of rearming: [22]

> They dumped the whole problem in my lap, so I called in three assistant secretary-generals and each of us drew up our own list of what we thought the percentages should be, and then we averaged them out. . . . Then we got into the Council meeting and everyone thought it was a jolly good distribution except for their own [share] which they thought too high. But we got agreement within 1.8 percent, and so we simply divided up that 1.8 among the 14 [nations] and that's all there was to it.

Without attachment to a common overriding goal, such dispositions would hardly be acceptable to sovereign governments. The growth of institutions and techniques such as NATO's, therefore, provide evidence that the easily terminable alliance of the past is giving way to the permanent regional association of nations of the present and future.

Alliances today surpass the scope and power of international organizations in many ways. With the emergence of "total war" and its demands upon economic, political, and military planning, alliances acquire increasing responsibility in all fields of endeavor. From military planning to full regional integration is a long step, but it is an unmistakable trend in both NATO and the Soviet system. Standardization of weapons, elimination of national economic barriers, pooling of resources, and ultimately the meshing of policy—though not always successful—all remain characteristic of the efforts of both major alliance systems. Despite the many obstacles hindering achievement of these aims, they remain as evidence of the profound impact of the twentieth century upon alliances as a traditional means of foreign policy.

ADDITIONAL CASE-STUDY MATERIAL

"Athens, Ankara and Belgrade," *World Today*, vol. 9, July, 1953.

Boutros-Ghali, B. Y.: "The Arab League," *International Conciliation*, no. 498, May, 1954

Boyd, Andrew, and Frances Boyd: *Western Union*, Public Affairs Press, Washington, 1949.

Churchill, Sir Winston: *The Second World War*, Houghton Mifflin, Boston, 1948–1953

Craig, G., and F. Gilbert (eds.): *The Diplomats, 1919–1939*, Princeton University Press, Princeton, N.J., 1953.

Deane, J. R.: *The Strange Alliance*, Viking, New York, 1947.

Fay, S. B.: *The Origins of the World War*, Macmillan, New York, 1928.

Feis, H.: *The Road to Pearl Harbor*, Princeton University Press, Princeton, N.J., 1950.

Ferrell, R.: *Peace in Our Time: The Origins of the Kellogg-Briand Pact*, Yale University Press, New Haven, Conn., 1952.

Haas, E. B.: "The Balance of Power: Concept, Prescription, or Propaganda," *World Politics*, vol. 5, no. 4, July, 1953.

Khadduri, M.: "The Arab League as a Regional Arrangement," *American Journal of International Law*, vol. 40, October, 1946.

[22] *The New York Times*, May 10, 1953, p. E1.

Killen, E. D. L.: "The ANZUS Pact and Pacific Security," *Far Eastern Survey*, vol. 21, Oct. 8, 1952.

Kulski, W. W.: "The Soviet System of Collective Security Compared with the Western System," *American Journal of International Law*, vol. 44, July, 1950.

Mansergh, N.: "Britain, the Commonwealth and Western Union," *International Affairs*, vol. 24, October, 1948.

"NATO and World Peace," *The Annals of the American Academy of Political and Social Science*, vol. 288, July, 1953.

North, R. C.: "The Sino-Soviet Agreement of 1950," *Far Eastern Survey*, vol. 19, July 12, 1950.

Roberts, H.: *Britain and the United States*, Council on Foreign Relations, New York, 1953.

Rossi, A.: *The Russo-German Alliance*, Beacon Press, Boston, 1951.

Royal Institute of International Affairs: *Atlantic Alliance*, Oxford, New York, 1952.

Seabury, P.: "The League of Arab States: Debacle of a Regional Arrangement," *International Organization*, vol. 3, November, 1949.

Voigt, F. A.: "Comintern," *Nineteenth Century*, vol. 142, December, 1947.

Wiskemann, E.: *The Rome-Berlin Axis*, Oxford, New York, 1949.

Chapter 9

PROPAGANDA AND SUBVERSION

1. Defining Propaganda and Subversion. What is international propaganda? Is any attempt to persuade the members of a foreign elite to anything a manifestation of this technique of international relations? To some degree, obviously, the attempt to persuade is implicit in diplomacy, alliances, and most other means. What, then, are the peculiar qualities of propaganda? Observation rather than strict definition might furnish a clue.

Propaganda. Clearly the flaunting of military power, whether through atomic explosions or naval maneuvers in distant waters, has a different effect on groups abroad from the testing of weapons in full secrecy. Similarly the diplomat who speaks at the public banquet fulfills a different function from the one who exchanges views at a confidential tête-à-tête. Cultural exchange programs may be carefully conducted tours, limiting the observation of participants to officially selected items, or they may be completely unstructured, permitting the members to explore whatever facets of a country's culture prove of interest. In each of these cases the distinguishing characteristic is the degree to which "a systematic attempt by an interested individual (or individuals)" is present, seeking "to control the attitudes of groups of individuals through the use of suggestion." [1]

It is primarily the difference in emphasis of intent underlying these activities which makes it possible to set them in a separate category of means. Thus we may define international propaganda as "the transfer of meaning, whether by written, spoken or pictorial symbols, or by various types of action," aimed at bringing about politically relevant attitudes and actions on the part of target groups in different nations. [2] It is important to note what is included—as well as what is excluded—in this definition. It stresses two basic techniques of persuasion: symbol manipulation and demonstration. The definition serves to reveal the basically similar purpose of the official radio broadcast beamed abroad and the use of diplomatic ceremonial or military demonstrations. No reference is made as to the nature of propaganda, whether it is true or false, whether it is hostile or friendly; nor is any value

---

[1] L. Doob, *Propaganda, Its Psychology and Technique,* Holt, New York, 1935, p. 89.
[2] W. P. Davidson and A. L. George, "An Outline for the Study of International Political Communications," *Public Opinion Quarterly,* vol. 16, no. 4, winter, 1952–1953, p. 501.

judgment suggested in terms of its being "bad" or "good." It assumes two groups, a communicator and his audience, bridged by a variety of media but separated by belief in different myths, by belonging to separate national communities.

Subversion. Subversion differs from our definition in one essential: it assumes three groups in the communicating process. It involves a communicator and a target group in different countries, but includes participation by a third group, nationals of the target community, but actually sharing the interests and values of the foreign communicator. Thus instead of Soviet policy makers' relying exclusively on Soviet propagandists, they employ Communists and fellow travelers throughout the world, groups in various countries who profess allegiance to their respective nation but who always identify their interests and values with those of the Soviets and never with the ruling elites of their own country. In terms of groups, subversion then is unique in that it relies on the enlistment of the target country's citizens on behalf of the foreign state's aims. In terms of technique, subversion features sabotage, infiltration, and revolution in addition to the tools of propaganda.

Twentieth-century conflicts of myth and ideology encourage the transferral of loyalties across national boundaries. With the rise of fascism and communism propaganda and subversion received prominent emphasis, usurping positions of importance traditionally held by other means of policy, particularly diplomacy. Today they stand as acknowledged, if disparaged, tools at the disposal of policy makers.

2. The Role of International Propaganda. Propaganda may be used as an instrument of alleviating group tensions within a national community. Some effort has been made, furthermore, to employ propaganda externally as a means of lessening international tensions. However, efforts at lessening tension by international communication and stress upon the interdependence of countries have had little significance so far, failing to have any appreciable effect on the incidence of war. UNESCO's attempts to use propaganda internationally as a means of fashioning unity from disunity, while not outside the present definition, remain outside the focus of this chapter.

Conflicting Aims in Propaganda. Assuming that the propagandist or communicator seeks to fulfill policies of self-extension or self-preservation, representative of the interests of national elites, his activities may fulfill any of three different purposes. Directed at a country defined as hostile, his message may drive a wedge between elite and community, or between elites within that community. Directed at a country defined as friendly, his message may cement bonds of alliance and unify the target behind policy. Directed at a country of uncertain status, communication may persuade groups not to align with hostile nations but to join in support of the propagandist's policy.

International propaganda varies according to the classification of the target as enemy, ally, or neutral. However, words and symbols seldom prove capable of being directed at one group to the exclusion of all others. Hence the triple role fulfilled by external propaganda further complicates the limitations which we noted in its internal use. For example, elites both in the United States and the Soviet Union have interests which demand fragmentation of hostile coalitions, cementing of friendly alliances, and neutralization or winning over of uncommitted countries. Obviously the same message cannot meet all situations simultaneously. Bellicose American propaganda may bring vicarious satisfaction to anti-Soviet groups in Eastern Europe, but the same tone alarms allies in West Europe whose interest demands security without war, and it alienates neutrals who seek to avoid alignment with those they believe responsible for increasing international tension. Tempering American anti-Soviet propaganda may reassure allies and soothe neutrals, but it decreases the intensity of resistance to communism within the Soviet bloc. Soviet propaganda encounters similar problems. Agitation against "Wall Street imperialists" may strengthen revolutionary determination among Communist supporters, but its vehemence only serves to solidify American alliances and to drive off neutrals who seek a more moderate position. Relaxation of tirades against the West loosens the bonds of NATO, but at the same time it threatens the *raison d'être* of Soviet hegemony over the Eurasian continent.

International propaganda, like all means of international relations, requires precise policy formulation to give direction to the complexities inherent in its diversity of roles. It is insufficient to define audiences as hostile, friendly, or neutral. Policy must determine the desired ends, prepare to cope with alternative reactions from the target group, and coordinate propaganda with other means of foreign relations. Without policy providing a goal, the communicator is like "a swimmer treading water just to keep from going under; he is unable to strike out in any direction." [3]

To take the Soviet and American examples again, both sides have frequently waged so-called "psychological warfare" without adequate policy formulation. Immediately after World War II Soviet spokesmen unleashed an ever-increasing campaign of vituperation against the United States, accepted by then still pro-Moscow Yugoslavia. In August, 1946, Yugoslav guns fired upon several American planes flying over the country, killing four American airmen in the process. Instead of the anticipated Russian congratulations for carrying out in deed what Soviet spokesmen advocated in word, V. M. Molotov, Soviet Foreign Minister, scolded the Yugoslav delegation to the Paris Peace Conference. Soviet policy failed to anticipate all possible consequences of Soviet propaganda.

Similarly, United States propaganda in a sense proved too successful, bringing results inimical to American interests through no fault of the

[3] *Ibid.*, p. 507.

propagandist. With the intensification of American-Russian conflict in the postwar period, United States propaganda agencies, especially the radio service Voice of America, directed messages to East European countries comparing American prosperity with Communist poverty. Thousands of refugees risked their lives to flee the Soviet countries in hope of migrating to better conditions in the United States. However, for many such hopes were shattered by American groups which remained adamantly opposed to any large-scale immigration.

Propaganda and Other Means. In addition to planning the "why" as well as the "how," policy must coordinate various means with the factors of power. Otherwise, glaring contradictions may be introduced. Postwar Soviet efforts to portray Russian aims exclusively in peaceful terms continued unabated despite the presence of Soviet armies throughout Eastern Europe, armed insurrection by Communists in Iran, Greece, Malaya, Indochina, and Indonesia, and the North Korean invasion of South Korea. Parallel American peace propaganda encountered fewer but similar obstacles in the network of American air bases throughout Europe, Africa, and the Far East, and in the recurring atomic explosions at Eniwetok and Las Vegas.

Propaganda may present its message in a number of ways, but effectiveness lessens the further it departs from the reality level of the audience. The hard facts behind the façade of fancy may expose it as bluff or hypocrisy. The role of international propaganda is indeed a complex one; its purposes are varied and its targets are remote, both geographically and ideologically. Only policy can determine how its role is to be fulfilled, policy which in turn is conditioned by the total situation in terms of all ends and means.

3. Techniques of International Propaganda. *Radio.* Most highly publicized among contemporary ways of communicating propaganda abroad is that of radio. Powerful transmitters cover almost the entire globe with messages designed to weaken foes, bolster friends, and win new supporters for various policies. Similar transmitters attempt to blot out foreign broadcasts from potential target areas, particularly in the Soviet bloc, by "jamming"— emitting a cacophony of growls, squeals, whistles, and static.

Typical of propaganda beamed at hostile coalitions is that of the Voice of America, designed to increase tensions within the Soviet bloc. The following excerpt illustrates the twofold aim of weakening cohesiveness within a community, Czechoslovakia, and driving a wedge within an alliance, between Czechoslovakia and Soviet Russia: [4]

Czechoslovakia's most important uranium mines . . . operated by the Communist regime, produce uranium ore for the Soviet Union. . . . Prisoners work the Bratrstvi [mine]—about 1,700 political prisoners. The pit is guarded by members of the SNB—the National Security Corps—who wear violet insignia instead of

[4] VOA broadcast, quoted by Anthony Leviero in *The New York Times*, Dec. 12, 1951, p. 14.

the usual SNB red. Most brutal of all the guards is a certain chief sergeant by
the name of Frantisek Zlamal. Frantisek Zlamal, about 50 years old, a chronic
alcoholic. When drunk, very brutal to prisoners. Chief Sgt. Frantisek Zlamal, SNB
guard at the Bratrstvi uranium pit outside the Czechoslovakian village of Jachymov.
His name is known.

Here is the multiple wedge, seeking to set individual against individual,
group against group, ally against ally.

Striking at the Soviet Union directly, VOA broadcasts include themes
urging groups to flee to the West where they can organize an underground
movement within Russia. Here propaganda suggests subversion, although
the message is still communicated over an official United States broadcast to
Soviet listeners, and does not constitute actual subversion. An interview
with a Soviet *émigré* concluded, "I fled, fled so that here, abroad, I can
give all my strength to the fight with ·Communism, for the liberation of the
Russian people." [5] A few days later the theme reappeared, linking World
War II underground movements in "France, Belgium, Holland, Norway,
Denmark, Italy, Yugoslavia, and Greece" with the Korean War. Four million refugees had fled North Korea, and the broadcast described how many
had since returned as "anti-Communist partisans. They work in the rear
of the Communist armies, carrying on the fight for freedom against tyranny.
Thus in North Korea a second front has been created, a front of partisan
war against Communists." [6]

Soviet themes for West European targets similarly try to exploit areas
of tension within countries and to split off members of NATO from the
United States. A favorite stratagem is to search Western periodicals for anti-
American material so as to imply that the words are truly representative
of West European opinion and not merely those of the Soviet propagandist.
Such was the purpose of the following quotation from *Le Monde,* read by
Andrei Vyshinsky at a UN gathering held in Paris, "At present more than
100,000 American soldiers and officers are located in France. This time they
have not come to pay courtesy visits to Lafayette. . . ." [7] Detailed accounts
of misdemeanors by American soldiers stationed in West European countries, coupled with allegations of plots to plunge NATO into an aggressive
war for American and German interests, highlight Soviet propaganda beamed
abroad.

   Demonstration. Actions, no less propagandistic than words, have played
a dramatic role in the efforts of Soviet and American policy makers to
weaken each other's alliance system. One of the most highly publicized epi-
sodes of this nature was the American handout of free food packages to East
Berliners and ultimately to hundreds of thousands of East Germans, during

[5] VOA broadcast, Feb. 24, 1952, translated by A. Whiting.
[6] VOA broadcast, Mar. 3, 1952, translated by A. Whiting.
[7] A. Y. Vyshinsky at Sixth Session of United Nations General Assembly, Nov. 16, 1951.

the summer of 1953. Following a wave of strikes and popular uprisings stemming primarily from economic dislocation, the American move won an overwhelming response from persons in the Soviet zone of Germany, many of whom risked serious consequences by accepting the food packages. As opposed to this humanitarian aspect of propagandistic action, Soviet and American explosions of nuclear weapons posed the possibility of total annihilation before mankind. United States demonstrations in the Pacific and on the Nevada desert were highly publicized, being reported by television, newsreel, and radio and observed by hundreds of American and foreign personnel. Soviet explosions were held in full secrecy and announced dramatically to the world by Soviet spokesmen such as Stalin and Malenkov. The effect was similar in both cases. The reverberations of such means of destruction as atomic and hydrogen bombs were calculated, in part, to weaken the confidence of opposing coalitions in their ability to win a military conflict. Actions, here, indeed spoke more eloquently than words.

Cultural Exchange. Different propaganda techniques are generally employed to maintain friendly relations within an alliance, techniques which frequently are the exact opposite of those used to drive a wedge in a hostile target. One of the more highly publicized efforts has involved cultural exchange programs. Used extensively by both the Soviet Union and the United States, these serve to emphasize the peaceful, productive prosperity of the socialist and capitalist communities. For several years, a United States Information Service maintained libraries abroad, distributed films, and aided foreign scholars and officials. A 1952 report on USIS in London [8] told how it

answers hundreds of questions daily from editors, members of Parliament, clergymen, and other leaders of opinion. It conducts exhibitions depicting the American way of life in various parts of the country, and a daily summary of American news is distributed to the ten wire services and the hundreds of national and provincial newspapers, weeklies and other publications. American labor and industrial news is distributed to trade and technical papers as well, with the emphasis recently on the need for higher productivity and how it is being attained in the United States. The USIS film unit . . . has 1,500 films. . . . Documentaries have been shown in commercial movie theaters and broadcast by the BBC on television. Under the Exchange of Persons Plan, British writers on industrial subjects, labor relations and military subjects, and economists and teachers are given a grant to enable them to visit the United States and investigate their favorite subject.

Although there are different points of emphasis, this program is duplicated in the Soviet bloc with a constant flow of films, literature, and persons prominent in various fields, moving between Peiping and Prague, circulating among the capitals and major cities of Eastern Europe, Russia, and China. Virtually every month a "friendship" celebration is held between representatives from some two countries in the Soviet alliance system,

[8] *The New York Times,* Nov. 24, 1952, p. 8.

accompanied by exchanges of art, entertainment, and pledges of perpetual harmony. During Sino-Soviet Friendship Month, November, 1952, Chinese authorities announced membership of 39,000,000 in the Sino-Soviet Friendship Association. The SSFA

contributed articles to 74 periodicals and 580 smaller publications, supported 200 film-projection teams and 2500 lantern-slide groups in the field . . . and played host to a score of Russian peasant, worker and entertainment teams which toured China. . . . The flood of Soviet publications reaching China was said to include 13,505,000 copies of translations of 3,131 Russian works published in the period 1950–52. Thirty-five Russian newsreels and 53 Russian films were dubbed in Chinese. . . . for an audience reported to total 580,000,000 persons in 1952.[9]

Impressing One's Allies. Actions within an alliance system not only serve to increase the actual strength of the partners but also possess symbolic value of considerable importance. Again, the summer of 1953 proved one of feverish activity in this respect. Catastrophic earthquakes rocked islands off the coast of Greece, killing hundreds and leaving thousands homeless. Within hours American ships and planes struck out to carry medicinal supplies, parachute food packages to stricken villages, and evacuate persons from dangerous areas. Not only did this prompt American response emphasize the ability of the United States to effectuate immediate assistance should Greece be in peril, but its generosity demonstrated American willingness to help allies even when not so obligated by any legal agreement. Similarly, the signing of the Korean armistice found Soviet Russia publicly pledging 1 billion rubles in aid for reconstruction of ravaged North Korea. This move paralleled an earlier announcement on the part of the United States that congressional appropriations had been earmarked to the sum of 200 million dollars for relief and rehabilitation in South Korea.

Similarly, military demonstrations, whether they are American fleet maneuvers in the Mediterranean or Russian jet aircraft flying over Red Square, prove reassuring to weaker members of alliance systems. As a symbol of unity, few actions proved so colorful as the endless march of troops from all corners of the globe which demonstrated Commonwealth cohesiveness at the coronation of Queen Elizabeth in 1953. These examples furnish added evidence of the subjective nature of power. Nothing in the flight of Soviet planes, the sailing of American ships, or the marching of Commonwealth troops gives proof of military superiority in case of conflict. However, each of these actions seeks to impress friend and foe with symbols of strength, frequently with considerable success.

Wooing Neutrals. Finally there is the message aimed at neutrals who may become allies or enemies, depending upon which side is more persuasive in

[9] R. Plunkett, "China Views Her Russian Tutor," *Far Eastern Survey,* vol. 22, no. 8, July, 1953, p. 99.

the war of words. Cultural exchange programs find Indian delegations traveling to Moscow, Peiping, and Washington, returning with varying degrees of praise for their respective hosts. An alternative tactic is to attack the competing country in terms of values and interests held by the neutral target. Thus American propaganda to India stresses Soviet forced labor camps and shortcomings in Soviet consumer production, while Soviet missions in New Delhi declaim the vices and shallowness of American culture, particularly as represented through Hollywood films.

With the spotlight upon meetings of the United Nations Assembly and affiliated organizations, a new type of propaganda becomes of increasing importance. Both Soviet and American representatives seek to demonstrate their sympathy with the aspirations of the Arab-Asian countries by speeches and votes. Positions of prestige within the organizations are championed by delegates of the two major powers as being symbolically enhanced when occupied by an Asian representative. Counterthrusts in the form of resolutions are so worded as to inflame anticolonial prejudices or antimilitarist sympathies. In this wooing of neutrals, accompanied by a relentless Soviet effort to embarrass, if not split off, avowed supporters of the United States, propaganda seems to be in its most suitable environment, since interested governments are appealed to directly.

"Fact" and "Lie." It should be noted that the majority of these examples rely less on fabrication than on selection and emphasis of facts. No greater misconception of propaganda exists than the assumption of its falsity, that it is simply "the big lie." The consequence of this misconception is to assume either that "a bigger lie" will win or that "the fight for truth" automatically promises success. However, the reality level of the target remains all-important; propaganda occasionally is pure fabrication, but in such instances it runs the risk of fatal exposure.

Undoubtedly the most highly touted piece of Communist propaganda since World War II was based on allegations of American use of bacteriological warfare in Korea. For well over a year, a relentless campaign emanated from Communist capitals, particularly from Peiping, seeking to brand American action in Korea as inhumane. In one sense, this propaganda was well suited for international use, since its message needed no alteration for the three different target areas: Soviet allies, neutrals, and Soviet enemies. Exploitation of fear might strengthen the anti-American coalition. Exploitation of disgust might persuade neutrals of United States' callousness with respect to Asian peoples. Exploitation of distrust might raise dissenting voices within the United Nations' coalition from those resentful of American hegemony and tendencies toward unilateralism in the Korean War.

In another sense, however, germ-warfare charges proved to be the weakest type of international propaganda because they referred to actions, not to attitudes, and therefore required a more substantial foundation in reality.

Obviously it is one thing to charge America with intending to conquer the world; it is quite different to claim it is dropping germ-laden bombs among civilian populations. For all the effort put into this campaign Soviet propagandists failed to win striking successes in non-Communist countries because they never exposed the bases of their charges to detailed examination by any observers except those especially invited by Communist authorities. By opposing an investigation of the evidence by the International Red Cross and by a United Nations team of scientists representing nonbelligerents in the Korean conflict, Soviet propaganda suffered a serious setback, evidenced by the quiet abandonment of germ-warfare charges when a Korean armistice was signed in July, 1953.

Multipurpose Messages. Since propaganda seldom can be limited to the target groups, multiple-purpose messages eliminate the hazards of embarrassing contradictions or propaganda working at cross-purposes. Another Soviet effort to hit different targets with one propaganda blast came in the so-called Stockholm Peace Campaign. Preceded by "congresses for peace" in New York, Paris, and Prague in 1949, all directed primarily by communists, a "peace congress" convened in Stockholm in 1950. A petition sponsored by the congress advocated prohibition of atomic warfare. Emanating from the capital of a traditionally neutral country and limiting its stated aim to a cause supported by virtually millions throughout the world, the petition nevertheless implicitly had American policy as its whipping boy. Particularly with United States troops in Korea and Soviet forces represented only by Chinese "volunteers" and North Korean troops, the Stockholm appeal proved eminently suitable to Soviet interests.

Impressive as were the hundreds of millions of signatures gathered on this petition in virtually all countries of the world, it stands as an interesting example of propaganda whose results affect attitudes and actions only remotely connected with policy formulation. Obviously the vaguer or more general an appeal, whether against atomic bombs, against germ warfare, or simply against war, the more persons there will be who will respond to it. However, the effectiveness of their response diminishes in inverse proportion to the general acceptability of the appeal. Thus little responsibility was required to sign a petition banning atomic bombs, nor was any conflict of loyalty involved for the majority of signatories. No politically relevant action ensued. However, had the petition required participants to refuse to pay taxes which might finance production of atomic bombs, its political significance would have been increased but its support would inevitably have radically decreased.

4. Ideological Problems. The basic problem confronting the international propagandist is the ideological gap which separates him from his audience. Propaganda is designed to bring a reaction in groups of one nation which will serve the interests of groups in another nation. Yet by definition, the fundamental factor which distinguishes national communities is the unifying myth, providing an all-inclusive interpretation of interests and values for those within the community but unacceptable to those outside it.

What does this mean for the propagandist? In the first place, he must have adequate information. He must understand the interests and values shared by his audience. Only by comprehending the frame of reference which shapes his target's view of the world can he hope to establish contact, in the ideological sense of the word, with that target. Secondly, the propagandist must have adaptability. He must be able to shape his message to fit each particular frame of reference held by different target groups. This is dependent upon but supplementary to adequate information about his audience. It requires of the propagandist that he divest himself of those symbols and terms which are employed within his own group and among groups within his own community, but which are unacceptable or incomprehensible in a foreign milieu. This translation into the frame of reference of another community must be done, of course, without losing sight of the interests which his propaganda seeks to implement. The form must change but the content remain the same. Finally, he must have independence. He must be free from the pressure of domestic groups so that he may adapt whatever techniques are demanded by his specific target. In using the frame of reference of his target instead of his home community, the propagandist runs the risk of being accused of disloyalty by his compatriots. Yet without the independence to shape his message according to external needs, his efforts to appear "non-American" or "non-Soviet" to his audience will boomerang in his being viewed as "un-American" or "anti-Soviet" by domestic elites.

A Case Study: Propaganda in the Middle East. Illustrative of these problems of information, adaptability, and independence is the contest between Soviet and American propaganda in the Middle East. Throughout this area attitudes of interest groups range from cautious but critical support of the United States to vociferous, militant Communist championing of the Soviet Union. Within this continuum, the bulk of sentiment seems to center in a so-called neutralist sector, although this so-called "neutralism" frequently expresses more vocal criticism of the United States than of the Soviet Union. Much of this anti-American predisposition stems from the association of American policy with colonialism in North Africa and support for Israel. Nevertheless, we must still examine other factors which account for the failure of American propaganda to persuade more groups that support of United States' policy, or at least opposition to communism, is in keeping with their interests.

Viewing this problem exclusively from the situation of the propagandist, several points emerge. First, it is clear that American propaganda is not working unopposed in the Middle East; it is countered by Soviet efforts throughout the entire area. Russia enjoys a distinct advantage so far as information of the audience is concerned. Within its own territory the Soviet government has long experienced the problem of bringing a desired response from illiterate, rural populations. Furthermore, it is familiar with the various faiths dominant in the Middle East, possessing a sizable Moslem population within the Soviet Union. Secondly, American propagandists are far removed culturally from their Middle Eastern targets. To take three important features of rural life—time, religion, and human relations—there is an almost unbridgeable gap between the agrarian East and the industrial West. One marks time in moons, the other in minutes. One finds its Hindu, Moslem, or Buddhist faith an all-embracing way of life; the other relegates religion to a fixed time of worship with a minimum of ceremony. Human relations in the East move by indirection and elevate self-effacement to a virtue; in the West, directness is preferred to politeness and humility is scorned.[10] Even where certain Asian groups, such as the bureaucracy or the intelligentsia, have borrowed from the West through cultural or commercial contacts, they remain rooted in native values and enjoy security only so long as they can defend local interests.

These cultural differences between East and West not only complicate the problem of information for American propagandists, but place a high premium upon adaptability and independence. So far as adaptability is concerned, Soviet and American communicators seems to be evenly matched, sharing similar assets and liabilities, although the American position is handicapped because it is further removed from Middle Eastern groups. Thus despite Soviet efforts to modify or to suppress temporarily the militant atheism which is part of the Bolshevik ideology, constant tensions vis-à-vis Moslem groups within Soviet Russia, and, in turn, the Middle East, are an obstacle to effective propaganda, particularly in such countries as Pakistan. Similarly, American officials who advocate measures of land reform, an ever-present problem in this area, find themselves constantly frustrated by conflicts with American values rooted in the sanctity of contract and the inviolability of private property. Hence United States propagandists can seldom win widespread support from landless groups by advocating radical solutions to agrarian unrest. That both Soviet and American propagandists are aware of the need to adapt to specific audiences is amply illustrated by their efforts in dealing with religion and property respectively in a manner somewhat at variance with policies pursued within their own communities.

It is the sphere of independence which provides the final, perhaps decisive, advantage for Soviet propagandists. Working in the framework of an authoritarian system dominated by a single elite, their actions are responsible to one group, the Presidium of the Russian Communist Party. Within the Central Committee of the Communist Party is the Agitation and Propaganda Section, known as Agitprop. The foreign activities of this agency are directed

[10] B. L. Smith, "Communications Research in Nonindustrial Countries," *Public Opinion Quarterly*, vol. 16, no. 4, winter, 1952–1953, pp. 526–538.

exclusively by party officials, drawing on a vast supply of technicians trained in an elaborate network of special schools for propaganda and agitation established in the Soviet Union and allied countries. Funds for propaganda work abroad are virtually unlimited, as evidenced by the millions of Soviet books, pamphlets, magazines, newspapers, posters, and films which permeate the most inaccessible regions in a multitude of languages and dialects.

Soviet propaganda beamed at the Middle East employs a variety of techniques, but its over-all direction remains monolithic. This is not to say that it is always consistent, for consistency is a virtue almost unknown among propagandists, especially those who must follow the zigzags of dialectics. However, this does mean that Soviet magazines and radio broadcasts will mesh with Soviet cultural missions and local Communist propaganda in spelling out an identical message; until new orders come from Agitprop the line has been established for all Soviet communication.

Limitations on American Propaganda. Far different is the fate of the American propagandist seeking to merge the conflicting interests of several elites in a democratic community into a single, coherent message. The Department of Defense seeks Middle Eastern bases. American capitalists exploit Middle Eastern oil reserves. American congressmen look askance at spending money in foreign countries, particularly if criticism of the United States is rampant abroad. American patriotic groups insist on advancing principles of free enterprise and private property at every opportunity.

Somehow, out of this tangle of interests, policy must determine which are to be given priority in shaping American propaganda. Even when an agency has been established with this responsibility, and such agencies have come and gone with considerable frequency in recent years, it has no monopoly over American statements to Middle Eastern groups. Inherent in the pluralistic-democratic system is the right of each group to speak in defense of its own interests. Only in extreme cases can disciplinary action be effected. Remarks by Secretary of Navy Francis Matthews in 1950, suggesting preventive war against the Soviet Union, brought prompt repudiation by high government officials, although the damage to American efforts abroad had already been done. Similarly, efforts by Senator Joseph McCarthy in 1953 to identify and ban all books and materials used in overseas USIS libraries written by persons associated in any way and at any time with groups later felt to be suspect or unduly critical of the United States led to even more serious repercussions. Amidst a confusing series of directives, many so ambiguous as to defy interpretation, USIS librarians removed books by suspect authors from their shelves, destroying the publications in some cases. This move proved to be highly damaging to American prestige abroad through the subsequent exaggeration and misinterpretation of the so-called "book-burning" episode. Yet such instances are symptomatic of an inherent democratic incapability to make those supposedly in charge of conducting propaganda activities solely responsible for the manner and methods employed.

Many limitations on the propagandist stem from the way in which American elites view international relations. Some groups advocate a campaign of truth, demanding a direct attempt to convince others of the correctness of the American appraisal of events, the superiority in the American system of values, and the inferiority of all things Soviet. Others advocate a more aggressive program, matching Soviet propaganda in form and content by raising tensions through every possible means within the Soviet bloc. For some, propaganda is no more than an extension of American advertising to other countries, "selling American policy abroad." For others, propaganda is an instrument of warfare, differing in means but not in ends from military operations. All this does not preclude success for American propaganda; but it does increase the difficulty of attaining it in many situations.

5. Technological Problems. Just as the target group is ideologically predisposed, if not bound, to its national myth, so its media of communication are controlled by national groups. The communicator attempting to penetrate another country can never enjoy the technological advantage over his opponent. Newspapers may be censored or banned, public gatherings may be watched or forbidden, radio sets may be restricted or foreign wave lengths jammed. Even the ingenious use of gas-filled balloons to carry American propaganda into East Europe met Soviet countermoves which punished unauthorized persons caught taking messages off balloons after landing.

Problems of Control. Not only do material obstacles arise in attempting to hit specific target groups in other countries, but there often is an additional problem following from the need to restrict the message from groups other than the desired target. As Hans Speier noted, [11]

A politically important statement may aim at one particular group, say the enemy government, but will reach at the same time other groups as well, for example the neutrals or the domestic critics of the man who made the statement. The statement may also miss the intended target altogether and reach only others instead. There is no fire in political warfare without the possibility of backfire, no percussion without its repercussion, and duds sometimes blast the wits out of the gunner. All this deprives the laws of political warfare of the imposing simplicity of ballistics.

Further obstacles confront the international propagandist which his domestic counterpart does not face. For instance, he often has no control over the situation in which the audience receives the message. Obviously, timing plays a pivotal role in the effectiveness of propaganda, yet the greater the tension between countries the less opportunity the propagandist has to make his message coincide with the most propitious moment. An interesting example of this problem arose in connection with RIAS, the American-controlled

[11] H. Speier, *Social Order and the Risks of War,* Stewart, New York, 1952, p. 385.

West Berlin radio station which attempted to undermine Soviet control in East Germany after the Russian zone of occupation became a satellite of the Soviet bloc. RIAS, together with its American counterpart the Voice of America, frequently stressed the theme of liberation and revolt among those disaffected with the Soviet regime. However, when economic crisis and political instability led to a wave of workers' strikes in East Germany in mid-June of 1953, RIAS lagged behind the tempo of events, failing to co-ordinate resistance activities or to prolong the spirit of defiance.[12]

Paralleling the problem of timing, the communicator frequently has no way of checking on the effectiveness of his efforts. Without seeing his audience and with no means of conducting a survey within the target group, he is left with none of the techniques of ascertaining failure or success which aid the domestic propagandist. Initial errors become compounded. Unanticipated reactions among the target group may defeat the very policy communication is designed to support. The only mitigation of this factor comes with wider access to the audience, found usually in friendly and occasionally in neutral countries.

Finally, the propagandist does not control the range of response open to his audience. All his efforts to stir systematic unrest may be of no avail should fomenting unrest merely expose groups to extermination by ruling elites. Especially is this true in authoritarian communities where, as Hans Speier has remarked, "the primary condition for the fall of totalitarian regimes is not 'tension' or dissatisfaction among its masses, but organized defection among the armed forces and the police who have access to the modern means of violence." [13] The situation in East Germany well illustrated this point, the 1953 strikes being suppressed in short order by the presence of thirty-seven Soviet divisions, including tanks, armored trucks, and artillery.

These obstacles decrease in direct proportion to the decrease in tension between two countries. However, even communication among allies en-counters difficulties so long as conflicts of interest remain and national myths preclude the coalescing of allies into federated units. Here the problem be-comes one of developing symbols and points of reference ambiguous enough to cover conflicting interests among the elites within the coalition but clear enough to give the coalition as a whole a sense of direction.[14] Should the American propagandist attempt a precise definition of the phrase "free world" in addressing the various allies of the United States, he might arouse hostili-ties instead of bettering relations. We need only cite the regimes of Tito, Franco, and Chiang Kai-shek to demonstrate the ambiguity of "free," whether applied in an economic, religious, or political sense. Yet recourse to a term

[12] J. Wechsberg, "A Report on Germany," *The New Yorker,* Aug. 29, 1953, pp. 33 ff.
[13] H. Speier, "International Political Communication: Elite versus Mass," *World Politics,* vol. 4, no. 3, April, 1952, pp. 305–318.
[14] D. Lerner, "International Coalitions and Communications Content: The Case of Neutralism," *Public Opinion Quarterly,* vol. 16, no. 4, winter, 1952–1953, p. 682.

such as "freer world," albeit more accurate, would give less direction and impetus to the propaganda and the coalition.

Impact of Propaganda. In view of the serious ideological and technological barriers limiting effective communication between groups in different countries, it must be concluded that the situation is quite different from that pictured by those who would eliminate wars or conquer enemies by the manipulation of word and deed. If propaganda is something less than a panacea in domestic politics, it is definitely of subsidiary importance in international politics. This is said, of course, in the qualitative sense; quantitatively, the efforts of international propagandists produce statistics of astronomical proportions with respect to the number of books, magazines, newspapers, and radio-hours aimed at groups in different countries. The very barriers between propagandist and audience hamper scientific research into the achievements of international propaganda.

This, however, does not mean that propaganda will cease to be utilized. Such means tend to have a self-perpetuating quality stemming from the propagandist convincing his superiors, if not himself, of his own effectiveness through fascination with his own message. Furthermore, they are, in part, conditioned by the nature of tension between Soviet and non-Soviet elites. As Harold Lasswell has remarked, "Instead of the incessant realigning of national blocs in maneuvers of encirclement and counter-encirclement, the principal strategy becomes that of penetration, which puts a premium on dividing an elite against itself and from the rank and file." [15] Finally, the high value placed on proselytizing in both Soviet Russia and the United States, the former epitomized in the communist firebrand and the latter in the missionary and the traveling salesman, will leave a continual emphasis upon the use of international propaganda, whatever its effectiveness in achieving ends of policy.

6. Types of Subversion. Penetration, as noted by Lasswell, is indeed a constant aim of competing elites in the twentieth century, and no means of policy is better adapted to this end than subversion. Symbolized in antiquity by the Trojan horse, subversion has a lengthy and colorful history. However, seldom has it won such prominence as a way of attaining ends as in the contemporary period. No longer the monopoly of totalitarian ideologies such as fascism and communism, subversion now serves policy makers in democratic as well as authoritarian states, in their search for more effective means of safeguarding or extending their interests.

Subversion, like propaganda, may appear in any one of several situations. Its hallmark, however, is the utilization of a group allegedly loyal to the interests and values of one community but actually furthering the policy of a rival nation. The subversive group may rationalize its position and

[15] H. Lasswell, "Psychological Policy Research and Total Strategy," *Public Opinion Quarterly,* vol. 16, no. 4, winter, 1952–1953, p. 494.

attempt to conceal even from itself its actual position. Such efforts make no difference so long as the group consistently responds in favor of a foreign elite whenever domestic elites encounter conflict in international relations. Note that unless this element of conflict is present, necessitating a choice of foreign versus domestic interests, it is impossible to classify a group as subversive unless there is material proof—seldom available—of its acting on orders from a foreign agency.

Penetration through Ethnic Ties. The most limited and at the same time the most pervasive use of subversion is for ideological penetration. Ideological penetration may use as its vehicle groups which share primarily ethnic affiliation or ideological ties. Among instances of subversion by groups of ethnic affiliation, the most celebrated contemporary example is that of Nazi Germany. According to Hitler's credo, all Germans living outside the territory of the Third Reich were duty-bound to advance the cause of Nazism and to assist the Fatherland in any way possible. In the United States, German-American bunds organized sports and social activities for the purpose of propagandizing the Nazi myth and for building centers of public opinion favorable to Hitler Germany. In a similar manner, the Soviet Union exploited ethnic affiliations among those of Slavic descent in the United States during and after World War II. Lacking the flags, arm bands, and uniforms which clearly identified the bundists as supporters of a foreign cause, Nazism, these groups appeared to champion non-Communist principles, emphasizing cultural appreciation and mutual understanding. Actually, they were so-called "front" organizations, consistently supporting the Soviet position in controversial affairs and ardently campaigning on behalf of any issue which could lower the prestige of the United States government.

Ideological penetration, while a fascinating phenomenon of the twentieth century, represents a limited use of subversion. It aims at indirect attitude controls, as compared with more direct measures, such as the *coup d'état* and territorial annexation. Because it must compete with the all-pervasive ideology embodied in the national myth, ideological subversion is seldom more than a subsidiary measure used in conjunction with other subversive means to "soften up" a community by pitting group against group. Its limitations are particularly evident when ethnic affiliation is the main tie between the subverted group and the foreign elite, for ethnic groups are readily identified and consequently easily isolated from other groups in the community.

Penetration through Ideological Ties. Considerably greater effectiveness comes from utilizing groups whose main tie with the foreign elite is an ideological affiliation. While they lack the emotional and personal associations with the foreign country which facilitate discipline, they are less readily identified as members of a group apart from others. They can easily mask their subversion in the guise of patriotism. Because they employ many symbols of the community in which they operate, such as the national flag, national holidays, and national heroes, these groups often succeed in concealing their subversive nature and win acceptance of their views as ideas advanced for the best interests of the community. Closer examination, however, reveals these ideas as advanced in order to undermine the community for the interests of a foreign group.

Fascism and communism epitomize this second technique, penetration by groups ideologically affiliated. The end may be immediate and radical, such as reducing French resistance power prior to Nazi conquest, or it may be distant and limited, such as building public opinion in India hostile to the United States and favorable to the Soviet Union. In any case, the vehicle is usually the "front" organization, employing groups sympathetic to a foreign ideology as cancerous cells within the body politic. Because of the difficulty of diagnosing the true nature of these cells, they are able gradually to eat away the tissue of the national community, belief in the national myth.

The Case of France. In France, no more serious problem has confronted governments of the past twenty years than the cancer of ideological subversion. Hitler's lightning-swift victory over French legions in May, 1940, was largely the result of Nazi penetration into antirepublican elites. Today, although German subversion is almost nil, Communist subversion has affected much of the country. According to official American estimates in 1951, the French Communist Party numbered about 500,000 but its activities were better measured by the 2 million trade unionists belonging to the Communist-controlled General Confederation of Labor (CGT), by the 5 million votes— one-fourth of the total cast in 1951—won in parliamentary elections, and by the 15 million signatures claimed for the Stockholm peace petition.[16] Although the degree of ideological penetration varies considerably from case to case, especially as between membership in the Communist Party and signing Communist petitions, these figures remain symptomatic of the underlying malady affecting French politics.

Coup d'Etat. Subversion may fill a more radical role when designed to support a *coup d'état,* placing in positions of authority persons of nominal independence but actually subservient to the government of another country. This strategy uses ideological penetration primarily as a means of preparing public opinion for the new regime, but in addition seeks to plant subversives in key positions so as to facilitate overthrowing the present regime. Chief targets for such subversion are, of course, the instruments of force—the police and the military—and the instruments of service—the trade unions— particularly those in communication and transportation.

Preparation for a *coup d'état* focuses attention on the sensitive areas of the community, control of which makes success almost certain. It is no coincidence that in East European governments after World War II, Communists

[16] *The New York Times,* Dec. 13, 1951.

frequently were content to control the Ministries of Justice (law administration) and Interior (police administration), while letting other positions go to non-Communist parties. Unlike ideological penetration, activity did not center on mass proselytizing but rather on infiltrating groups with trusted supporters. Opposition organizations were steadily weakened by the systematic use of terror, tolerated by Communist-controlled police or actually directed by them. When the time came to suspend the electoral process or to outlaw hostile parties, few pockets of effective resistance remained to be overcome.

Subversion and Democracy. Subversion as an instrument of authoritarian elites has received ample study. Considerably less is known about the role of subversion in the foreign policy of nonauthoritarian regimes, largely because of its more recent adaptation by Western governments in response to the Communist challenge before 1946 to 1948. The United States, in particular, eschewed the use of subversion except during wartime. During the postwar decade, however, American groups turned increasingly to a type of subversion quite dissimilar from those conventionally employed by fascist and Communist elites.

Thus the groups employed for subversion within the Soviet bloc share only one value in common: they oppose the Communist governments now in control of their countries. They do not, however, embrace the principles of the American myth unequivocally, differing widely with respect to their political, economic, and religious beliefs. Nor are they able to agree on a common program for the countries to be liberated, as evidenced by the failure to unify the various anti-Soviet *émigré* groups in the United States.

This role of subversion further differs from others in that it assumes that the agents of subversion will include exiles and refugees living outside the target country. Although obviously less effective than well-organized groups within a community, these "governments-in-exile" maintain contact with loyal elements in the "conquered homeland," provide symbols of prestige around which resistance movements may rally, and possess a knowledge of local conditions seldom enjoyed by American strategists.

Without further information, it is impossible to define more fully the role of subversion in American policy. It is by no means a technique of ideological penetration. It is less clear how much it is designed to effect a *coup d'état*, particularly because its targets lie within the Soviet bloc and the Russian reaction to such a move might bring about open conflict—too great a risk for American strategy, at least in the past. Where American-sponsored subversion has aimed at a *coup d'état* in non-Soviet countries, particularly in Central America, it has enjoyed some success. However, with respect to its role in the postwar situation the most that can be said is that it aims at weakening Soviet power by increasing tensions within the Soviet system.

Annexation. Finally, subversion plays an overt role in the situation of open, complete penetration: annexation. The activities of the Sudeten Germans, as a prelude to Nazi annexation of this sector of Czechoslovakia, have already been reviewed. Utilizing ethnic minorities abroad as provocation for seizing territory is generally known as "irredentism," borrowed from the Italian term of pre–World War I, *Italia Irredenta* ("Italy Unredeemed"). This referred to Italians living in Trentino and in the Tyrol who remained under Austrian rule, but the use of "irredentism" soon spread to all countries possessing "lost" peoples living outside their frontiers. Although population transfers since 1945 have eliminated many possible cases of irredentist subversion, notable instances remain, particularly in the problems of Trieste and the Saar.

7. Czechoslovakia: Subversion in Operation. No more striking instance of the role of subversion in the postwar world can be found than that of Czechoslovakia. The multiple use of ideological penetration, infiltration, and territorial annexation culminated in the Communist *coup d'état* of February, 1948.[17]

Ideological penetration came through various ways. Communist groups were, of course, active in the wake of the Red Army in 1945, assuming command of liberated areas with the sanction of Russian officers and forming "national committees" resembling the famous soviets of the 1917 Russian Revolution. Their prestige soared with Red victories; their power rested on possession of weapons, offices, printing presses, and other paraphernalia of propaganda seized from the Germans and their collaborators. Given America's withdrawal from Europe after World War I, the failure of Western Europe to help Czechoslovakia in 1938 and the anti-Nazi, "liberating" role of Soviet Russia, it is easy to see how suitable was the situation for Soviet subversion.

By fostering Slovak autonomy, Communists won support among disaffected elements in Eastern Czechoslovakia. No less important was activity among "peasant unions, youth clubs, student associations, intellectual groups and purely professional associations."[18] Capturing these nonofficial organizations proved important in agitating against non-Communist parties as well as for effecting a display of public unity behind the newly established Communist government in February, 1948. Such organizations were, in Czechoslovakia as elsewhere, readily susceptible to Communist infiltration. While non-Communists took part in such activities only on a part-time basis, Communists could devote their full-time attention to winning positions of influence because they were paid by the party for such activity. Fellow travelers, whatever their motivation, helped to give prestige and influence to Com-

---

[17] This section is based on two articles by Ivo Duchacek, "The Strategy of Communist Infiltration: 1944–1948," and "The February Coup in Czechoslovakia," *World Politics,* vol. 2, no. 3, April, 1950, pp. 345–372; *ibid.,* no. 4, July, 1950, pp. 511–533.

[18] *Ibid.,* p. 359.

munist ideological penetration, disguising the systematic subversion of Czechoslovak democracy as harmless reformist efforts made in good faith by a bona fide political party.

As professional revolutionaries—the term was repeatedly used by Lenin—Communists infiltrated the police, military, and labor organizations preparatory to the *coup d'état*. In the reorganization of police, necessary after German occupation, the Communist Ministry of the Interior made changes which placed both police and investigative services into the control of the Communist Party. Infiltration into the army was facilitated by the purge of officers after the war and the introduction of "educational officers" to provide political indoctrination to the troops. Although this operation proved less thorough than that within the police, the loyalty of the army was in such question that President Beneš refused to rely on it when confronted with the February coup.

Undoubtedly the most impressive aspect of subversion so far as the external aspects of the coup were concerned was in the labor unions. Communist cells honeycombed the Central Labor Union as well as the Peasant Union. Agitation and slogans among these groups portrayed the parliament as anti-working-class, while distribution of weapons among them on the eve of the coup created an atmosphere pregnant with revolt, augmenting the power of the Communists by cowing their unorganized opponents. The sudden appearance of armed workers patrolling the streets with tommy gun and rifle, apparently with the acquiescence of the police, provided a forcible demonstration of the planning behind the *Putsch*.

It is significant that to bolster their hand, the Communists convened mass meetings of workers' and peasants' groups in Prague just prior to seizing power. This maneuver presented a façade of mass support at sharp variance with other evidence.

Even the Communist-controlled Ministry of Information reported a 10 to 15 per cent drop in Communist support in a poll of December, 1947. Some observers felt the February coup was necessary to prevent a Communist defeat at the elections scheduled for later that spring. In any event, every effort was made to present the coup as a widespread popular movement. The Ministry of Information served as a valuable instrument toward this end, with its nationwide broadcasting system available for calling meetings, whipping up sentiment against oppositional elements, and giving an impression of complete success by monopolizing public information services.

In addition to these many techniques for seizing power, the role of nearby Soviet troops should be mentioned. These were present in neighboring countries, perhaps ready to intervene. President Beneš remained unwilling to risk civil war and possible Soviet intervention, especially with such uncertainty as to the Western reaction. Better to accept defeat with as little destruction as possible; such was his reasoning. Although no direct, visible support for the coup came from Soviet Russia, the presence of V. A. Zorin, Deputy Soviet Foreign Minister, in Prague for the week of the coup, had at least propagandistic effect in lessening the security of the anti-Communists while increasing the prestige of the Communists.

Propaganda, police control, seizure of key governmental agencies, mobilization and arming of workers, immobilizing industrial activity by means of a general strike, undermining army discipline—all proved instrumental in placing Czechoslovakia within the Soviet bloc. Actually the surface change was somewhat deceptive; subversion had placed Communists within reach of power long before February, 1948. In terms of control, they had remained in the ascendancy since liberation in 1945, especially as they had emerged as the single largest party.

8. Impact of Subversion. Revolution is the technique through which most authoritarian regimes gain domestic power. Small wonder, therefore, that these elites attach so much importance to the kindred technique of subversion in their efforts to extend their sway abroad. Indeed, the policies and practices of Hitler Germany, Franco Spain, Peron Argentina, and Soviet Russia suggest that subversion is an integral part of the means of authoritarian elites for the conduct of foreign relations, whether for winning friends or weakening foes.

Subversion has had a twofold impact on nonauthoritarian regimes. On the one hand, its dramatic successes have won it new adherents among democratic elites, although their acceptance of it has been tardy and incomplete. On the other hand, its successes have at times been inflated beyond all reality, leading democratic elites to assume that subversion is the source of most, if not all, domestic disturbances. Especially because the techniques of revolution and of subversion are often similar, the situations are mistakenly identified as one and the same problem.

Revolution and Subversion. Admittedly the distinction is not always clear in practice. Subversion seeks to capture, control, and capitalize upon revolution. The dissent of the few must become the grievance of the many; so runs the credo of the agitator, whether he be a subversive or a revolutionary. In the case of contemporary China, for instance, debate raged among non-Chinese circles for more than twenty years concerning the nature of the Chinese Communist movement. Strong evidence came forth to support both views: (1) that it was essentially a subversive movement controlled from Moscow and hence to be handled by police methods, and (2) that it was essentially a revolutionary movement resting on indigenous unrest and upheaval and hence to be handled by reform measures striking at the source of domestic dislocation. In fact, the Chinese Communist government was directed from Moscow and constantly served the interests of the Soviet elite, while gaining power because of basic economic and political dilemmas unsolved by the Nationalist government. Thus the Communist movement was both subversive, directed from without, and revolutionary, rooted in domestic problems.

The problem is complicated by the fact of world-wide subversion fomented by communist movements at the disposal of decision makers in Soviet Russia. There is no doubt that such subversion exists. It by no means follows, however, that every movement which purports to be communist is equally controlled by Soviet leaders. Much evidence which has come to light in the Tito-Stalin controversy indicates precisely the contrary. Finally, not all Communist claims of success necessarily reflect more than a wishful boast put out in the hope of being identified with all revolutions, regardless of their true character. All these factors serve to emphasize the point that revolution and subversion are different phenomena, springing from essentially different sources although often overlapping in the process of seizing power. The criterion of differentiation lies in the extent to which the participating groups seek to advance the interests of a foreign elite.

No means short of war seem to encounter more opprobrium among nonauthoritarian groups than those of propaganda and subversion. Yet it would be naïve to assume that because of the disfavor with which they are viewed these means are exceptional, utilized only in rare and marginal cases. Their acceptance by authoritarian elites as a preferred means of policy, in peace as well as in war, has compelled nonauthoritarian groups to counter them or to accept them. Fighting fire with fire seems to have been the choice made by responsible groups in the West, for today propaganda and subversion remain among the most important instruments of American strategists in their conflict with Soviet elites.

ADDITIONAL CASE-STUDY MATERIAL

Adamic, L.: *The Eagle and the Roots,* Doubleday, New York, 1952.
Barrett, E.: *Truth Is Our Weapon,* Funk, New York, 1953.
Bellquist, E.: "The Overseas Information and Cultural Relations Program of the Department of State," *World Affairs Interpreter,* vol. 18, spring, 1947.
Burge, M. R. K.: "The British Council," *Political Quarterly,* vol. 16, October–December, 1945.
Cantril, A. H. (ed.): *Tensions That Cause Wars,* University of Illinois Press, Urbana, Ill., 1950.
Carr, E. H.: "Propaganda and Power," *Yale Review,* vol. 42, autumn, 1952.
Carroll, W.: *Persuade or Perish,* Houghton Mifflin, Boston, 1948.
"Confessions of a German Propagandist; Testimony by Dr. Herbert von Strempel," *Public Opinion Quarterly,* vol. 10, summer, 1946.
Davidson, W. P., and A. L. George: "An Outline for the Study of International Political Communications," *Public Opinion Quarterly,* vol. 16, winter, 1952–1953.
Doob, L.: *Propaganda, Its Psychology and Technique,* Holt, New York, 1935.
Duchacek, I.: "The Strategy of Communist Infiltration, 1944–1948," *World Politics,* vol. 2, April, 1950; "The February Coup in Czechoslovakia," *World Politics,* vol. 2, July, 1950.
Harter, D. L., and J. Sullivan: *Propaganda Handbook,* 20th Century Publ., Philadelphia, 1953.

Hovland, C., and W. Weiss: "The Influence of Source Credibility on Communications Effectiveness," *Public Opinion Quarterly,* vol. 16, winter, 1952–1953.

Kris, E., and H. Speier: *German Radio Propaganda,* Oxford, New York, 1944.

Lasswell, H. D.: *Propaganda Technique in the World War,* Peter Smith, New York, 1938.

——: "Psychological Policy Research and Total Strategy," *Public Opinion Quarterly,* vol. 16, winter, 1952–1953.

Lerner, D.: "Inter-coalitions and Communications Content: The Case of Neutralism," *Public Opinion Quarterly,* vol. 16, winter, 1952–1953.

——: *Sykewar, Psychological Warfare against Germany, D Day to V-E Day,* Stewart, New York, 1949.

Padover, S. K.: "France in Defeat: Causes and Consequences," *World Politics,* vol. 2, April, 1950.

——: "Symposium: Propaganda and World Politics," *Columbia Journal of International Affairs,* spring, 1951.

Peterson, H. C.: *Propaganda for War,* University of Oklahoma Press, Norman, Okla., 1939.

Plunkett, R.: "China Views Her Russian Tutor," *Far Eastern Survey,* vol. 22, July, 1953.

Siepmann, C. A.: "Propaganda and Information in International Affairs," *Yale Law Journal,* August, 1946.

Smith, B. L.: "Communications Research in Non-industrial Countries," *Public Opinion Quarterly,* vol. 16, winter, 1952–1953.

——, H. D. Lasswell, and R. D. Casey: *Propaganda, Communication and Public Opinion: A Comprehensive Reference Guide,* Princeton University Press, Princeton, N.J., 1946.

Speier, H.: "The Future of Psychological Warfare," *Public Opinion Quarterly,* vol. 11, spring, 1948.

——: "Inter Political Communication: Elite versus Mass," *World Politics,* vol. 2, April, 1952.

——: *Social Order and the Risks of War,* Stewart, New York, 1952.

Stalin, J. V.: "Economic Problems of Socialism in the USSR," *Current Digest of the Soviet Press,* supplement, Oct. 18, 1952.

Wechsberg, J.: "A Report on Germany," *The New Yorker,* Aug. 29, 1953.

Chapter 10

ECONOMIC MEANS: TRADE AND COMMERCIAL PRACTICES

1. Economic Means and Ends of Policy. Economic measures play a major role in contemporary international relations. They may serve economic ends, such as the maximization of profit or the optimum allocation of resources, or they may serve political ends, such as increasing national security or extending control over other countries. Before examining the techniques of manipulating the flow of goods and money as well as the problems inherent in their use, it is necessary to analyze the various purposes for which these techniques are employed.

Economic Ends. Economic ends served by these means are of three basic types. The first group represents specific interests within the community. Tariffs provide the most common example, restricting foreign imports by assessing a duty at the port of entry. Thus levies against Danish blue cheese or Swiss watches serve specific American manufacturers by restricting foreign competition.

A second type represents general material interests of the community, aimed at decreasing unfavorable repercussions from economic events abroad. The phenomenon of interdependence examined in Chapter 1 compels all countries to enact measures coping with fluctuations in world trade and commerce and to lessen the domestic impact of inflation or depression in other countries.

Finally there are economic ends derived from general tenets of the national myth. Many American elites, who favor in principle the "free market" in the domestic economy, have generally favored "free trade" abroad. Reciprocal tariff reduction and multilateral trade conferences are among the chief means employed toward this end. Authoritarian elites traditionally stress economic self-sufficiency or autarky, espousing policies of controlling the flow of goods and money so as to achieve optimum use of export earnings and to import only militarily and politically essential items. Elites in underdeveloped countries, in pursuit of goals of industrialization and higher standards of living, may adopt rigid controls on foreign investment and trade.

Political Ends. As opposed to policies directed toward financial return for specific groups or for an entire nation, economic means may also be utilized for what have been termed "uneconomic" or political ends. Tariffs may be lowered for allies, raised for enemy countries. Boycotts may shut off trade from a given country in order to weaken it, regardless of the sacrifices involved for those undertaking this measure. Commonly, when political ends underlie economic means, the term "economic warfare" is used. Economic warfare aims at supporting the basic policy of the nation by appropriate techniques, especially such measures as freezing an enemy nation's assets, discriminating against its trade, black-listing its merchants and manufacturers, or even blockading its shipping and keeping it in want through the preemptive buying of raw materials.

The political consequences accompanying economic policy techniques may be far-reaching. When one nation alleviates unemployment and depression by artificial stimuli to its exports and controls over imports, another nation may suffer loss of foreign markets and influx of foreign goods. Its ruling groups may face political difficulties should they prove unable to cope with these economic problems caused by policies of groups abroad. Domestic and international tension may result.

In another sense, economic measures are intertwined with political ends, since any change in economic well-being affects the power available in support of policy. Swiss watches may be excluded by American tariffs to ensure a domestic supply of precision craftsmen as well as to guarantee profits to an interest group. State trading, once the exclusive practice of totalitarian regimes such as Soviet Russia, now enjoys widespread use in selected items considered important in national economies. Foreign-aid programs provide the most comprehensive example of economic measures which support a complex of economic and political ends. Thus although these means are distinguished as economic because they involve manipulation of goods and currencies, their consequences are of political importance.

2. Representative Trade Policies. Certain basic features within each national economy tend to produce major trends in the economic goals pursued by ruling groups. Before elaborating the techniques of manipulation, their end product must be examined according to the different needs of various countries.

Industrialized Economies. The highly industrialized countries of Western Europe as well as Japan have an overwhelming interest in exporting their manufactured goods, to each other, to underdeveloped countries, but especially to the United States. Since these nations are deficient in the raw materials and energy resources needed for manufacturing, they seek to import these goods at the lowest possible prices. Conversely, they seek to obtain high prices for their exports while also having to compete with each other for sales abroad. All industrialized economies, except the American, are compelled to earn foreign currency, especially dollars, because of their dependence on foreign supplies of raw materials and food. Whenever their exports of manufactured goods do not suffice to earn enough of this currency—

and this has frequently been the case—they seek to earn the difference by selling their shipping and insurance services to other countries. When these additional efforts fail to bridge the gap between import demand and export needs, standards of living must be cut through "austerity programs" or foreign aid secured. The Marshall Plan was thus a device to bridge the European dollar gap.

Agricultural Economies. Nonindustrialized countries fall into two groups, those with a highly developed and modern agricultural economy, and those familiarly known as "backward" or underdeveloped agricultural areas. The former, such as Argentina, Australia, or New Zealand, depend upon specialized exports for prosperity. They seek guaranteed markets with the highest possible prices and definite quantities fixed over a period of years for their dairy and meat products. Because their items may be regarded as luxuries abroad, they remain dependent upon such agreements to tide them through depression or recession in consumption areas. One of the most cogent arguments for Commonwealth unity for Australia and New Zealand is the preferential system whereby these countries are assured of a guaranteed British market.

Underdeveloped agricultural countries, found in most of Asia, Africa, and South America, have far less security and enjoy much lower standards of living than countries in the modern agricultural category. They tend to specialize in the production of one exportable crop, such as rice, cotton, or sugar. When the world demand declines, prices drop, and poverty and starvation may set in among the agriculturally backward nations. To assure a semblance of stability, countries producing the same commodity may be compelled to agree on production and export quotas, thus seeking to avoid sudden excesses of supply. Since their universal aim is a more diversified economy and industrialization, these countries often manipulate trade so as to avoid spending the earnings from exports on consumer goods. The importation of machinery and capital is to be achieved instead.

The Soviet Bloc. Although the countries within the Soviet bloc partake of both groups discussed above, industrial and agricultural, an over-all policy tends to alter the general characteristics of policy. Industrialization remains the primary aspiration of the bloc as a whole, requiring almost unlimited supplies of producer goods for Eastern Europe and Communist China. Unable to meet this need in Soviet Russia, these countries must limit domestic consumption so as to offer maximum exports of marketable commodities, such as wheat and rice.

At the same time, periodic resistance on the part of consumers within the Soviet bloc compels the Communist elite to import a limited amount of luxury goods to check discontent. Whether this resistance is active as in Eastern Europe during 1952–1953 or passive as during the last years of Stalin's rule in Russia, its impact upon the hard-pressed Soviet economy demands palliative measures. Thus Soviet foreign trade is generally characterized by importing items directly related to strengthening the industrial base, intermittently broken by purchases of butter or textiles in exchange for gold or raw materials. Another variant in the pattern comes from sudden shifts in support of particular political ends, seeking to increase Soviet prestige and weaken opposition coalitions by offering large orders for British machinery or Finnish ships.

The United States. Finally, the general trade pattern of the United States is characterized by its being both an industrial and an agricultural country. Its manufactured items face constant competition from British, German, and Japanese producers. Its agricultural produce is so abundant as to present a constant problem of surpluses. To complicate the picture further, postwar political developments place the United States among allies sorely dependent upon its market or its help for economic viability, yet at the same time competing with its products. Contradictions between economic and political ends will be discussed at the close of this chapter. Suffice it to say that the United States frequently pursues a policy of advocating free trade abroad while protecting manufacturers and farmers at home, and at the same time giving large-scale economic assistance to both industrialized and underdeveloped allies.

3. The Flow of Goods and Money. Economic controls operate on two interrelated fields of activity: the flow of goods, or international trade, and the flow of money, or international payments and investments. So different are the problems of manipulation in each of these two fields that they must be analyzed separately. However, their inseparability is amply demonstrated in what is known as a country's balance of payments.

Balance of Payments. The balance of payments might be compared with the financial statement of a corporation. It represents an accounting of the total flow of goods, services, and money into and out of a country. A major item is the balance of trade. If exports and imports balance, foreign trade is essentially a type of barter in which no money is exchanged. Seldom does this occur, however. More generally, exports and imports are in imbalance. Imports may then be paid for by other earnings in the balance of payments: shipping services, tourist trade, and income from foreign investments or loans abroad. Great Britain has long financed an import surplus by extensive shipping services and returns from foreign investments and loans. When imports are paid for by exports or by other earnings, so-called "invisible exports," the balance of payments is held to be in equilibrium.

The alternative to these ways of financing imports is to pay for them with money. Since this entails dipping into a nation's reserves, it is a means of last resort, particularly when those reserves reach a dangerously low level. An added complication comes from the fact that since 1933 there has been no single world currency. When all national currencies were expressed in terms of gold and converted freely according to a gold standard, multilateral trade permitted a country to build up its reserves through earnings in one area so that it could purchase from another area. Abandonment of the gold standard forced trade to be accounted for bilaterally, in terms of specific earnings between two countries. In other words, British pounds sterling were of no value for purchases in the United States. Only American dollars or gold, the basis of American currency, could finance British imports from this country.

Thus the interrelation of goods and money is illustrated in the balance of payments. If exports do not cover imports, payment must be made in national currency. The only alternative is grants or loans from the creditor nation. Countries dependent on imports from the United States must finance those imports, and frequently face balance-of-payments problems which entail a constant drain upon their limited holdings of gold and dollars.

Exchange Controls. The balance-of-payments problem will be examined in greater detail in the discussion of controls upon the flow of money. It should be clear at this point, however, that the net effect of controls upon goods and controls upon money is identical. If a country cannot sell abroad, it cannot buy abroad except by dipping into reserves or by borrowing. Similarly if foreign currencies are not made available, importers cannot finance their purchases. If Argentina erects tariff barriers against American goods or exercises exchange controls on American currency, a decrease in Argentine-American trade results. Similarly if Britain devalues the pound, making British goods cheaper in the United States, or the United States drops tariffs on British products, an increase in British-American trade is certain to take place.

Because of the greater attention given to the balance of trade, traditional controls centered more on the tangible flow of goods than on the less obvious, though no less important, flow of money. With the impact of the Great Depression and the consequent repercussions throughout the world, governments not only discouraged imports by tariffs but limited or prohibited them by exchange control. The interrelation of goods and money was demonstrated in the marked decrease in total world trade, combined with a radical altering of trade from multilateral and triangular to bilateral patterns, following the proliferation of exchange controls. Thus not only material interdependence but monetary interdependence characterizes international relations.

4. Import Controls: The Tariff. Controls on the flow of goods may hit imports or exports. Domestic groups often argue that import controls hurt "foreign competitors" while export controls hurt "home business." This fallacy fails to recognize the fundamental fact that for domestic producers to sell abroad, foreign purchasers must have means of payment. Ultimately, then, import controls affect exports. For analytical purposes, however, the two aspects of trade may be examined separately.

Protective Purposes. The most celebrated import control is the tariff, duty levied upon goods brought into a country. Tariffs may serve as a source of revenue or as protection for so-called "infant industries," although these cases prove of minor importance in international relations. A recent study estimated that if present import duties in the United States were abolished, imports would jump by 2.6 billion dollars, but of this amount two-thirds "would not appear to be disastrously competitive with domestic output." [1]

More common and more important is the tariff which serves group interests by reducing foreign competition. American producers of low-priced cars seek to cut imports of foreign makes by maintaining import duties. During the Great Depression, enactment of the Hawley-Smoot Tariff Act protected American industry with one of the highest and most all-inclusive tariff structures in the world.

Swift and far-reaching international repercussions occurred. Typical of the official protests sent by twenty-four countries was that of Greece, warning "that the export of American products, agricultural as well as industrial, holds the first place in Greek imports, and whatever changes occurring in the tariff would necessarily affect the purchasing power of Greece to the detriment of American goods." [2] Within two years some forty countries took retaliatory measures. For instance, Spain increased its duty on American automobiles by 50 per cent and on American safety razors by almost 700 per cent. French export promptly replaced those from the United States in the Spanish market. "In this way we [the United States] ruined a trade relationship which amounted annually to about $79,300,000 in sales as opposed to the $35,800,-000 of purchases from Spain." [3]

Types of Tariffs. Tariffs differ according to form and application. They may be specific, figured in terms of physical units such as a hundredweight or a gross. They may be ad valorem, figured in terms of "value" assessed at point of entry. They may be single-column, with identical duty charged for all items regardless of point of origin. They may be double- or multiple-column, with two or more rates according to specified criteria. Finally tariffs may be conventional, the initial rate determined by law but changes introduced by international agreement.

As an instrument of policy the conventional tariff is highly important. An interesting application of its principles came in the Reciprocal Trade Act of 1934 wherein the United States softened the impact of the Hawley-Smoot Act. This permitted the President to alter tariffs up to 50 per cent of the 1930 schedule provided reciprocity was won by executive agreement with other countries. The impetus for this measure stemmed largely from the hope

[1] H. Piquet, *Aid, Trade and the Tariff,* Crowell, New York, 1953, as quoted in "Free Trade Is Inevitable," *Fortune Magazine,* March, 1953, p. 99.

[2] A. Isaacs, *International Trade,* Irwin, Homewood, Ill., 1948, p. 231.

[3] *Ibid.,* p. 235.

of stimulating the depressed American economy by increasing exports which, in turn, required lower tariff barriers abroad. Implementation of the Reciprocal Trade Act has seen a continuous conflict of interests between protectionist groups and those advocating international free trade. Its basic principle, however, emphasizes the role of economic means in general and of tariffs in particular as instruments of foreign policy.

"Invisible Tariffs." Frequently administrative procedures permit general obstruction of imports or particular discriminatory treatment. This camouflaged control is termed an "invisible tariff." Thus a pre-1914 German tariff reduction was applied to all "large dappled mountain cattle or brown cattle reared at a spot at least 300 metres above sea level and which have at least one month's grazing each year at a spot at least 800 metres above sea level." [4] Despite its "general" phrasing this reduction was actually limited to Swiss and Austrian cattle.

Other restrictions act like a tariff in requiring additional manufacturing or shipping costs. An interwar Argentine law required each imported apple to be wrapped in special paper marked with the name of the grower or shipper, in addition to charging a flat duty of 32 per cent of delivered value.[5] Similarly a postwar United States law required Dutch bricks to be stamped "Made in Holland," thereby raising production costs.

"Invisible tariffs" may operate through administrative application of apparently innocuous laws. In an investigation of obstacles restricting European exports to America conducted in 1949, it was revealed that a Dutch manufacturer of candied figs was unable to gain entry for his products because United States custom authorities ruled the product did not properly come under "figs" and no "candied figs" could be found on the tariff schedule.[6] The same study told of another Dutch exporter, this time of earthen ashtrays, who could not plan his market in advance because he did not know whether his export came under the classification of household articles with a 15 per cent duty, smoking requisites with a 30 per cent duty, or luxury earthenware with a 50 per cent duty.

Another variation on the theme lies in sanitary and health regulations which serve to impede or exclude imports. The Argentine law cited above required that each shipment of apples be thoroughly inspected at the port of entry, even though it had been inspected at the port of shipment. This may have been in retaliation against United States legislation which permitted the Department of Agriculture to ban all livestock and fresh and frozen meat from countries with foot-and-mouth disease. Regardless of the fact that a country as large as Argentina has many areas free of this disease,

---

[4] P. Ellsworth, *The International Economy,* Macmillan, New York, 1950, p. 659.
[5] Isaacs, *op. cit.,* p. 659.
[6] Ellsworth, *op. cit.,* pp. 659–660.

strict interpretation of this law led to the virtual exclusion of Argentine beef from the United States market.[7]

5. Import Quotas and Licenses. Last but not least in the category of import controls come quotas and licenses. The first of these practices specifies the total amount of a given commodity which may be imported during a given period, usually allocating the source of imports by countries according to a percentage of imports from an earlier year. The second method requires importers to receive specific permission from their government before carrying out their transactions. Current practice generally finds a mixture of the two systems, with licenses being allocated in terms of an unannounced quota.

United States quotas restrict imports of cotton, wheat, sugar, butter, cattle and beef, and linseed oil to amounts far below domestic demand in order to ensure a minimum price and steady market for domestic producers. In at least sugar, butter, cattle and beef, and linseed oil it appears that removal of such quotas would lead to significant increases in imports.[8] Similar to import quotas are mixing and milling quotas, fixing the maximum amount of foreign-produced commodity which may be employed in domestic manufacturing. Thus French law has required that flour made in France must contain from 75 to 97 per cent domestic grain, the exact amount fluctuating according to domestic conditions.[9]

Although all import controls affect relations between countries in some way, those of a more clearly discriminatory nature prove most explosive. Thus a general tariff on luxury products may affect a number of countries equally, but import licenses channel purchases along specific lines. Similarly, mark-of-origin requirements or "Buy American" acts serve as general deterrents to imports, but preferential tariffs provide special advantages for one country over another. For ends of persuasion or coercion, then, those import controls which permit maximum discrimination are most suitable. Thus tariffs have come to occupy less attention and import licenses have enjoyed increasing usage.

6. Stockpiling, Preemptive Buying, and Boycott. Two import controls seek to expand, rather than to decrease, the flow of goods. The first, stockpiling, entails official purchase of commodities far beyond contemporary needs, hedging against future contingencies in which the cost or availability of the material will be prohibitive. After World War II, for instance, the United States undertook an extensive stockpiling program of goods such as rubber and manganese which had to be imported across the Pacific and which, in time of war, might prove inaccessible. Stockpiling tends to unbalance the economy of the exporting country, inasmuch as it creates an abnormally high demand for a limited time, after which demand may fall

---

[7] R. Mikesell, *United States Economic Policy and International Relations*, McGraw-Hill, New York, 1952, p. 68.

[8] Piquet, *op. cit.*, p. 98.   [9] Isaacs, *op. cit.*, p. 645.

off altogether. Its effects are less obvious, politically, than another type of control, preemptive buying. Originally designed to buy up supplies in wartime to make them unavailable to the enemy, preemptive buying is now recognized as an instrument of policy in times of "peaceful" tension, such as the cold war. Its operation is simple: if the United States wishes to deprive Soviet Russia of rubber, it buys up all the rubber available, regardless of economic considerations. Under the more acceptable guise of stockpiling, preemptive buying places a premium upon the availability of foreign exchange and foreign trade, a situation which leaves Soviet Russia at a perpetual handicap compared with the United States. During World War II, however, preemptive buying flourished on both sides, with America, Britain, and Germany bidding frantically in such neutral areas as Spain, Turkey, Sweden, and Latin America in an effort to keep materials out of each other's reach.

The reverse of preemptive buying is the boycott, the complete exclusion of products from a given country. Facilitated by marks of origin, the boycott has been of varying effectiveness, depending upon the reliance of the boycotted country on the given national market. China, for instance, officially sponsored crippling boycotts against Japanese exports during the interwar period.

Import controls, then, are diverse in their operation and identical only in the general purpose of controlling the flow of goods. They vary considerably in the degree of control effected, ranging from the tariff, which may merely discourage imports, to the boycott, which prohibits all imports according to point of origin. Because their first repercussion is upon the foreign exporter, import controls enjoy general support within the importing community and can often be used with impunity as a means of securing specific ends.

7. Export Controls: Unilateral, Bilateral, and Multilateral. Essentially, import controls are unilateral although, as has been noted, tariffs are often fixed by negotiation and reciprocity. Export controls, however, may be classified as unilateral, typified by the embargo; bilateral, as written into barter agreements; and multilateral, represented chiefly by international marketing agreements.

Among the unilateral export controls, licensing and embargo parallel their import counterparts. Export licenses may restrict the flow of goods by commodity or by point of destination or both. With increasing tension between the United States and the Soviet bloc, the American government resorted to export licenses in an effort to keep strategic goods from going to Soviet Russia or her allies. A more drastic measure, the embargo, is the reverse aspect of the boycott. Applied against Communist China by the United States, it was used to choke off all exports to China in retaliation for Chinese intervention in the Korean War.

Dumping. Not all export controls limit or stop the flow of goods. Governmental subsidies, for instance, seek to expand the export of goods by reimbursing the producer for loss incurred at the prevailing market price. In a parallel practice known as "dumping," goods are sold on the world market at prices below those charged at home, the difference in price being assumed as a loss by the exporting country in order to maintain exports in the face of competition from other countries.

The extensive use of both measures suggests that objections stem less from principle than from political reasons. The United States, for instance, while consistently opposing "dumping," subsidized wheat and wheat-flour exports in 1938 and cotton exports in 1939. It has continued to "support" prices of agricultural goods by governmental purchases from domestic producers at prices higher than those offered on the world market into which these goods enter. "Dumping" in the precise sense is difficult to detect since those states most frequently charged with practicing it, such as Soviet Russia, lack a foreign exchange rate which permits accurate comparison of external prices with those charged in the domestic economy.

Bilateral Agreements. Bilateral agreements serve to fix exports between two countries—simultaneously, of course, regulating imports. They vary according to the specificity of terms, one type being represented by an agreement concluded between Spain and Switzerland in 1949, fixing quotas for the shipment of Spanish fruits, wines, iron ore, and other items, in exchange for Swiss dairy goods, industrial and agricultural machinery, chemicals, and other products. This agreement fixed ceilings on each item but did not guarantee the actual amounts to be shipped. More rigid and more picturesque was the interwar agreement whereby Hungary exported 29,000 pigs to Czechoslovakia in exchange for 20,000 wagonloads of wood.[10] Another type represents the familiar "tie-in" sale, binding the importing country to take less desirable or less essential items with imports of more important goods. Its use in the postwar period resulted in Denmark's being compelled to import 100 million kroner worth of "unwanted" imports out of total imports valued at 1,400 million kroner.[11] Such bilateral agreements provide an effective instrument of manipulation particularly between countries of unequal economic strength. While obviating the need for foreign exchange, they permitted countries such as Nazi Germany and Soviet Russia to exploit their economic position for winning political hegemony over countries in Eastern Europe.

It is in the area of multilateral export controls that the most ambitious efforts have been made in the interwar and postwar periods. Operating primarily among agricultural and raw-material products such as tea, coffee, wheat, tin, and rubber, these multilateral agreements aim at stabilizing fields

[10] *Ibid.,* p. 632.
[11] *A Survey of the Economic Situation and Prospects of Europe,* United Nations, Geneva, 1948, p. 96.

of activity most susceptible to changes in world demand yet least adaptable in terms of world supply.

International Commodity Agreements. International commodity agreements are of two types. The first includes only producer countries and attempts to restrict production in order to keep prices up and supply down. Typical of this arrangement was the interwar International Rubber Agreement. Combination among producers was facilitated by the fact that 95 per cent of world rubber came from countries of Southeast Asia, most of which were colonies of Great Britain, France, and Holland. By regulating production and export of rubber, the member countries introduced some stability into their economies despite world depression. Furthermore, by prohibiting the export of "any living portion of the rubber plant that may be used to propagate it," they preserved their near-monopoly position. Not until Japanese invasion of this area compelled the United States to sponsor rival rubber plantations in Latin America did this form of export control collapse.

A second type of commodity-control agreement includes both producing and consuming nations. Here the attempt to balance the interests of exporters and importers as well centers on assigning quotas and prices to ensure a minimum price for producers and a maximum price for consumers. One of the major postwar efforts in this direction was the International Wheat Agreement of 1948. Thirty-seven importing countries agreed to purchase a total minimum amount of wheat over a five-year period from specified exporting states at not less than $1.50 a bushel. Four exporting countries, the United States, Canada, Australia, and France, agreed to sell a corresponding amount of wheat during the same period for not more than $2 per bushel. Thus the world price was to settle between the two figures, since both sides were bound to meet their commitments regardless of price fluctuations above or below the specified points.

Soviet Russia and Argentina, the two authoritarian regimes, refused to participate because of the limitations on policy inherent in such an agreement. The refusal of an important exporter to participate nullifies much of the multilateral effort, since escape clauses permit importers to renege if they suffer a shortage of necessary exchange and can purchase wheat below the agreed minimum price outside the system. Nevertheless, implementation of the agreement through a two-chamber international council in which importers and exporters were represented in proportion to their participation in the wheat trade provided a pattern for subsequent ventures of this type.

8. State Trading. Obviously the most effective control over the flow of goods comes with the monopolization of trade in the hands of the state. Long practiced exclusively by totalitarian states, especially by Soviet Russia, state trading is now a widespread phenomenon. Its advantages as an adjunct of policy make it an accepted procedure, even in a private-enterprise-oriented country such as the United States.

To be sure, the scope of state trading varies considerably. At one extreme are countries, such as the United States, which exercise governmental monopoly only in the importation of selected items, like rubber, held to have strategic significance. At the other extreme stand the Communist countries, all of whose imports and exports pass through governmental agencies. In the case of the Soviet Union, a Ministry of Foreign Trade exercises exclusive control by means of import and export licenses over the flow of goods across Soviet borders. These in turn are issued to so-called trading combines representing various branches of industry and agriculture, all state-owned. In the case of trade between Soviet Russia and East European Communist countries, joint-stock companies, in which Soviet control is shared with participation of the respective country, carry out operations as outlined in negotiations between the two governments.

State trading, even in individual commodities, plays an ever-increasing role among non-Communist countries. Almost all wheat enters the world market through state agencies, whether Argentinian, Canadian, or otherwise. Under British "bulk-purchase" agreements, all exportable surpluses of Australian and New Zealand farm products are purchased for given periods at fixed prices. Except for Cuba, practically all Latin-American countries employ state-trading monopolies for a substantial part of their trade. In the case of Ecuador, as much as 20 to 30 per cent of governmental income is thus derived.[12] With the increasing nationalization of key industries in raw-materials-producing countries, the role of state trading may be expected to assume increasing importance.

State trading represents the logical culmination of increasing controls over imports and exports. It eliminates the vagaries of the free market and the idiosyncrasies of the private trader, replacing these with planning and political manipulation. Its effectiveness has been amply demonstrated by Soviet practice. Employed in the monopolistic purchase of such items as Iranian caviar, state trading provides Soviet policy makers with an effective means of persuasion or coercion. Even in the absence of monopolistic conditions, as in Yugoslav-Soviet relations, dependence upon the Soviet bloc permitted the Cominform to effect a partial blockade against Tito, thereby jeopardizing the economic balance of the country. Finally, state trading facilitates swift and coordinated use of trade offers in support of political objectives. Thus in 1946 a Soviet offer of 500,000 tons of grain on favorable terms was made to the French government prior to a national election. Negotiations proceeded through Maurice Thorez, simultaneously head of the French Communist Party and a vice premier in the French government. The political nature of this move was highlighted by the depressed level of Soviet consumption standards at the time.[13]

12 Isaacs, *op. cit.*, p. 652.
13 H. Schwartz, *Russia's Post-war Economy,* Syracuse University Press, Syracuse, N.Y., 1947, p. 86.

Under conditions of state trading, tariff restrictions become unimportant inasmuch as political rather than economic considerations determine the flow of goods. With the extension of this phenomenon, accompanied by the proliferation of bilateral trade agreements freezing trade into rigid patterns, tariffs, subsidies, and similar indirect controls on the flow of goods may be discarded in favor of more overt practices.

9. Exchange Controls. No more serious or lasting blow was dealt to advocates of free trade than the introduction of controls on the flow of money subsequent to the Great Depression. The entire trend away from unhampered trade and toward government manipulation of economic levers parallels an increasing awareness of the significance of material and monetary interdependence, and the consequent need of cushioning national economies against fluctuations abroad.

Exchange rates determine the related value of different national currencies. Long subject to the fluctuating demand of the open market, these exchange rates became arbitrarily determined by the respective governments in an effort to stabilize national economies. By "overvaluing" a currency, i.e., by fixing its exchange rate higher than the normal market would allow, a government may increase its holdings of foreign currencies or foreign exchange with relatively small exports. Similarly by "undervaluing" a currency, a government may stimulate exports through offering better terms than would otherwise be the case. The effectiveness of such measures depends on the absence of black market or uncontrolled exchange.

The Sterling Area. When currencies are not freely convertible, trade becomes restricted along bilateral lines. Chinese exporters amassing credits in pounds sterling are unable to exchange these for dollars in order to purchase American commodities but rather must buy something in Great Britain with their accounts. One escape from this restriction has been to widen the number of countries agreeing to free convertibility of their currencies, all of which are expressed in terms of one common denominator. Since sterling enjoys wide confidence and London had long operated as the central banker for the Commonwealth, the so-called sterling bloc became the prototype of this arrangement. Made up of Great Britain, Ireland, Union of South Africa, Iraq, Pakistan, India, Burma, New Zealand, Australia, and Iceland, the sterling bloc provides the largest multilateral exchange area in the world. The pivotal position of Britain as central clearinghouse for payments within the bloc and between the bloc and nonbloc countries permits considerable manipulation upon the flow of money. Particularly is this true between sterling and dollar accounts.

Exchange controls may serve other purposes than those illustrated by the sterling bloc. By compelling all exporters to change foreign earnings into domestic currency and all importers to purchase foreign exchange through government-controlled sources, administrative discrimination may effectively regulate the flow of goods as completely as if direct import and export controls were utilized. Such discrimination is more readily concealed, however, since the official holdings of exchange at any given time may be a carefully guarded secret. Thus exchange may be denied for the import of luxuries but granted for the import of raw materials if the domestic policy of the government calls for industrialization. Similarly, different exchange rates may tax those exports certain of a steady high level and favor those which are sensitive to competitive prices abroad.

Argentine Practice. Argentina provides a classic example of exchange-rate manipulation designed to serve a number of ends simultaneously. A multiple exchange rate, varying both for exports and imports, serves the threefold purpose of bringing revenue to the government, fostering Argentine processing and manufacturing industries, and encouraging some imports while discouraging others. For example, exporters of beef and staple grains must exchange their foreign earnings at the lowest of three rates, permitting the government to profit from the high sales of these items abroad and from the fact that alternative use of resources used in their production is limited at home. Exporters of wool, meat extracts, canned meats, and similar items received, as of 1950, an exchange rate 50 per cent higher than that for beef, government policy thereby encouraging export of items that otherwise might find alternative use in the domestic market. A third rate of exchange, three times that offered for beef and grain sales, subsidized the export of leather, tungsten, mica, and other products so that Argentine producers could sell competitively on the world market and be reimbursed for their loss by the government.[14]

A parallel pattern of import rates permits Argentina to import essential industrial raw materials such as coal and petroleum, while penalizing imports of "nonessentials" such as perfume and liquors. The high rate of exchange sought for purposes of foreign travel or study abroad intentionally discourages such activity. Additional measures seek to meet the "dollar shortage" by limiting imports from the United States in favor of those from Great Britain and elsewhere.

Import Licenses and Exchange Control. The combination of import licensing and exchange controls best illustrates the interrelation of goods and money in international economics. Import licenses may operate independently as discussed earlier, seeking protection against specified commodities, or they may operate in conjunction with exchange controls. In the latter case, governments may publish lists of approved imports in order of their decreed "essential" nature, issuing licenses on a simple priority system or in conformance with specified percentages of foreign exchange currently available. Alternatively, a straight list of imports requiring licenses may have no direct ex-

[14] S. Enke and V. Salera, *International Economics,* Prentice-Hall, New York, 1951, pp. 297 ff.

change restrictions, but securing of a license is no guarantee of receiving the necessary exchange. British practice assumes that granting of an import license automatically guarantees issuing of the necessary exchange; Latin-American practice is to the contrary.[15]

10. Devaluation and the Drive for Exports. As has been seen, exports provide an important means of payment for imports in addition to providing markets for domestic producers. With the postwar insistence on full employment so characteristic of most governments of Europe and particularly of Great Britain, economic dislocations resulting from a decline in exports can prove politically fatal to the groups in government. This, coupled with balance-of-payments problems, presented British leaders with a dilemma. On the one hand, exchange controls and tight restrictions on sterling convertibility were necessary to assure a means of payment for imports. On the other hand, American pressure continued urging a lifting of such controls, particularly stressing sterling convertibility. As written into the loan agreement whereby the United States advanced 3.75 billion dollars to Great Britain in December, 1945, the British undertook "to relax import and exchange controls, including exchange arrangements affecting the sterling area." [16]

As a result of acquiescing in July, 1947, to free sterling convertibility, Britain suffered a swift drain of gold and dollar reserves. In addition, exports lagged as British industry, already hampered by inefficient methods and labor difficulties, reeled under one of the most crippling winters in modern British history.

After a number of futile measures, British leaders resorted to the one certain means of boosting exports, devaluation. In September, 1949, the pound was pegged at U.S. $2.80 instead of the former $4.03. By permitting the dollar to purchase more pounds, British goods became cheaper for American buyers as did goods throughout the sterling area, since these countries kept their currency linked with the pound sterling.

Devaluation is far-reaching in its consequences, since its use by one country generally compels competitive devaluation by others in order to maintain their share of the world market. As an unstabilizing force in international commerce, its use is particularly risky. Not only does it serve to increase the tension among countries affected, but it may set off a chain of devaluations which nullify the original end for which it was undertaken. In the British case, it did not worsen relations between Britain and the United States, because it had been undertaken with prior consultation between the two countries. It did, however, introduce a discordant note into Anglo-French relations, already strained because of other problems. Its failure

---

[15] H. Chalmers, "Operation of Foreign Import-license and Exchange-control Systems," *Foreign Commerce Weekly*, vol. 36, no. 7, Aug. 15, 1949, p. 3.

[16] Truman-Attlee statement, quoted in N. Palmer and H. Perkins, *International Relations*, Houghton Mifflin, Boston, 1953, pp. 748–749.

to provide a permanent remedy for Britain's economic ills was illustrated by the graphic comment of Sir Winston Churchill shortly after examining the residue of Labor's efforts in 1951, "We were within a few months of national bankruptcy and having to choose between charity, if we could get it, and starvation."[17]

11. Bilateral Clearing Agreements. Bilateral clearing agreements, as their name implies, balance out all trade exchanged between two countries, stipulating that any surplus earnings must be used to purchase from the respective signatory. When coupled with state trade, as in Nazi Germany and Soviet Russia, bilateral clearing agreements strap the weaker country to the stronger one in near-permanent economic servitude. Germany employed bilateral clearing agreements as a means of penetrating Balkan economies, offering initially favorable terms of trade and then exploiting her position to unload products which could find no market elsewhere. Thus during the inter-war period, Yugoslav exports accumulated bank balances in Germany which could not be used for anything except imports from Germany. By 1938, Yugoslavia's credits in Berlin totaled 23 million marks, requiring her to import items at high cost or of less desirability than would have been purchased elsewhere through normal exchange procedures.[18]

Ends of self-preservation, no less than those of self-extension, may dictate the use of bilateral clearing agreements. In postwar British-Swedish relations, such practices guaranteed that Swedish sales to Britain would not be used to purchase dollar-scarce American goods. Sometimes specific export-import quotas are attached, as in the British-Italian clearing agreement of 1936. Italy pledged to spend 46 per cent of her sterling receipts for imports of British coal, and 41 per cent for other specified commodities. Here the concern was to assure a steady market for British coal, already in a depressed condition.

Although it is commonly believed that the debtor is in a subservient position to the creditor, the complexities of international economics and politics sometimes effect just the opposite. During World War II, Great Britain established blocked sterling accounts for many countries, particularly within the Empire, from whom she had to buy goods and services in order to prosecute the war. Egypt, for instance, found herself at the end of the war with a sizable store of sterling balances in London, placing her in the position of creditor on British sterling reserves. By suggesting that, with a less adamant stand on the British positions in Suez and Sudan, Egypt might receive these balances for purchases outside Britain, Labor negotiators presented a persuasive argument in the prolonged Anglo-Egyptian talks Although the stratagem failed, it illustrated the use to which blocked accounts and accumulated balances, actually "debts" owed to an exporting country, may be put to further ends of policy.

[17] *Ibid.*, p. 751.   [18] Ellsworth, *op. cit.*, p. 640.

12. The Clash of Economics and Politics. Having surveyed the general motivations behind economic controls and described the techniques of manipulation, this analysis must now highlight its central problem: the conflict between economic and political ends. This conflict is multidimensional, operating not only between groups within the national community but also between nations in the international arena.

Taking first the domestic conflict, different agencies in the United States government pursue diametrically opposite ends. On the one hand, Department of Agriculture policy, responsive to farm and cattle interests, promotes protection through price supports, quotas, embargoes, and tariffs. On the other hand, Department of State policy advocates loans and gifts to foreign governments which will permit them to tide over balance-of-payments problems until their exports to the United States can pay for their imports. While American delegates to international conferences appeal for fewer restrictions and free trade, new barriers spring up to shield American producers from foreign competition. Nor are imports the only key issue in United States commercial policy, as emphasized by the fact that in 1949 almost 40 per cent of the wheat crop went abroad, as did one-third of the cotton grown and almost one-third of the machine tools produced.[19] Export subsidies and state trading increase in direct antithesis of avowed policies voiced by American representatives in councils abroad.

Since 1947 American foreign policy consistently pursued ends of meeting Soviet expansion by strengthening a cordon of allies, extending around the world from Great Britain to Japan. Yet against the pleas of Presidents Truman and Eisenhower for assisting these countries through facilitating their overseas markets in the United States, powerful interest groups continued to press for serving domestic interests first. Or as a spokesman for the American Sugar Cane League warned, " 'Free trade' would completely disrupt the economy of this nation. Widespread unemployment, lower wage rates, lower profits, and the complete extinction of many industries would inevitably result." [20] Given the alternative between throwing thousands of watchmakers out of work or vetoing a prohibitive tariff on Swiss watches, the close balance of party politics may well dictate the decision of the President, who is simultaneously responsible for foreign policy and party victories.

Where economic and political motivations parallel, economic controls act as a useful adjunct of policy. During the past decade, American efforts to restrict all outside trade with Soviet countries as a means of weakening their economies found enthusiastic support from American producers thereby enabled to increase markets abroad. Particularly in the case of Japan, American political and economic interests coincided, with the result that Japan was compelled to import coal across the Pacific instead of from nearby Communist China.

[19] Mikesell, *op. cit.*, p. 318.   [20] Piquet, *op. cit.*, p. 99.

From the international aspect, the contradictions become even more complex. Perhaps nowhere is the dilemma more acutely presented than in the case of postwar Britain. Domestically, full employment and expanding social services have remained important desiderata, coupled with the need to expand exports so as to lessen the pervasive "dollar gap" in her balance of payments. Externally, American insistence on rearmament and objections over exchange controls threaten to negate all the domestic efforts, particularly since congressional resentment may express itself in less trade, as well as less aid, through raising tariffs on British goods.

Overseas the situation is no better. With China, for instance, British policy followed a moderate course vis-à-vis the Peiping regime, hoping thereby to safeguard and enlarge the financial future of Hong Kong, if not to reopen a market on the mainland. American opposition to this policy remained adamant, however, and the recriminations following Chinese intervention in the Korean War placed a serious burden on Anglo-American relations. Similarly, in the Middle East, British efforts to maintain oil investments in the face of rising nationalist sentiments for expropriation among the Arab countries ran afoul of the American alliance, which eschewed actions that smacked of imperialism. In addition, the necessity of appeasing Arab sentiment so as to safeguard the oil supply clashed with American sympathies in the founding of Israel. To paraphrase Sir Winston Churchill, Britain's economic position remained a problem wrapped inside a dilemma, shrouded in catastrophe.

Nor is the authoritarian elite free of the conflict between economics and politics. Communist China, for instance, spurned British offers of recognition in 1950 and obstructed British trade efforts on the mainland—all this despite the pressing need for machinery and manufactured goods with which to set out on an avowed program of transforming the economy from an agrarian to an industrial one. In part these rigid controls on British trade came from domestic motivations, enhancing the prestige of the Communist elite by showing its ability to twist the tail of the long-hated British lion. In part they were dictated by the Soviet alliance, which found Russian policy furthering Chinese dependence on Moscow. The strains on the Chinese economy reached such proportions by 1952, however, that the Minister of Foreign Trade was compelled to answer domestic critics, "It is quite wrong of some people to think that the expansion of our trade with the Soviet Union and the People's Democracies will adversely affect our trade with Western countries. . . . Only after the American government launched an embargo was this trade restricted and brought to a standstill." [21]

To demonstrate these problems is not to deny the effectiveness of economic means as an adjunct of foreign policy. Indeed, the widespread practice of

[21] Minister of Foreign Trade Yeh Chi-chuang, article of Oct. 2, 1952, translated and quoted in R. L. Plunkett, "China Views Her Russian Tutor," *Far Eastern Survey*, July, 1953, p. 98.

controls on the flow of goods and money suggests that elites prefer the economic and political risks inherent in manipulated trade rather than the alleged advantages of free trade. According to estimates made in 1949, "out of 85 foreign countries and colonies . . . all but 8 now either require an official license to be obtained as a condition of importation of many, if not all products, or control the granting of foreign exchange necessary for paying the supplier, or do both." [22] Economic means, then, promise to be of ever-increasing importance in the dynamics of international relations.

ADDITIONAL CASE-STUDY MATERIAL

Chalmers, H.: "Operation of Foreign Import-license and Exchange Control Systems," *Foreign Commerce Weekly*, vol. 36, Aug. 15, 1949.

Condliffe, J. B.: "International Trade and Economic Nationalism," *International Conciliation*, no. 476, December, 1951.

Diebold, W.: *Trade and Payments in Western Europe*, Harper, New York, 1952.

E.C.A. Special Mission to the United Kingdom: *The Sterling Area: An American Analysis*, London, 1951.

Ellsworth, P.: *The International Economy*, Macmillan, New York, 1950.

Enke, S., and V. Salera: *International Economics*, Prentice-Hall, New York, 1951.

Feis, H.: *The Diplomacy of the Dollar; First Era, 1919–1932*, Johns Hopkins Press, Baltimore, 1950.

"Free Trade Is Inevitable," *Fortune*, March, 1953.

Hilton, H. J.: "Hungary: A Case Study of Soviet Economic Imperialism," *Department of State Bulletin*, vol. 24, Aug. 27, 1951.

Hirschman, A. O.: *National Power and the Structure of Foreign Trade*, University of California Press, Berkeley, Calif., 1945.

Isaacs, A.: *International Trade*, Irwin, Homewood, Ill., 1948.

Jones, J., Jr.: *Tariff Retaliation*, University of Pennsylvania Press, Philadelphia, 1934.

Linder, H.: "The Problems of Economic Pressure on Soviet Bloc Countries: Economic Relations between Eastern and Western Europe," *Department of State Bulletin*, vol. 25, Nov. 12, 1951.

McKitterick, T.: *Russian Economic Policy in Eastern Europe*, Fabian Society, London, 1948.

Marx, D., Jr.: "Economic and Political Factors Affecting Trade between Eastern and Western Europe," *Political Science Quarterly*, vol. 66, June, 1951.

Mason, C. S.: *Controlling World Trade: Cartels and Commodity Agreements*, McGraw-Hill, New York, 1946.

Mikesell, R.: *United States Economic Policy and International Relations*, McGraw-Hill, New York, 1952.

Piquet, H.: *Aid, Trade and the Tariff*, Crowell, New York, 1953.

Plunkett, R.: "China Views Her Russian Tutor," *Far Eastern Survey*, vol. 22, July, 1953.

Schwartz, H.: *Russia's Postwar Economy*, Syracuse University Press, Syracuse, N.Y., 1947.

"Soviet Economic Bloc," *East Europe and Soviet Russia*, London, Jan. 17, 1952.

Stocking, G. W., and Others: *Cartels in Action; Case Studies in International Business Diplomacy*, Twentieth Century Fund, New York, 1946.

United Nations: *A Survey of the Economic Situation and Prospects of Europe*, Geneva, 1948.

Warren, H. (ed.): "Economic Diplomacy with Europe," *Inter-American Economic Affairs*, vol. 4, spring, 1951.

Williams, B.: "Economic Warfare," *Military Review*, October, 1950.

[22] Chalmers, *op. cit.*, p. 3.

Chapter 11

FOREIGN AID AND FOREIGN POLICY

1. Types of Aid Programs. While economic means have long been used for furthering political ends, the most important recent innovation in this field is the utilization of foreign-aid programs as an adjunct of foreign policy. Wholly unprecedented in scope and design, these measures have played an important role in the foreign policies of the United States and Soviet Russia. Their ramifications affect most countries of Europe and Asia, and, to a lesser degree, have proved operative in the Middle East, Africa, and Latin America. Differing radically from economic controls on the flow of goods and money, foreign-assistance programs furnish economic, technical, and military aid in an effort to develop conditions in receiving countries favorable to the interests of the donor. After reviewing the basic types of aid programs, it will be necessary to examine the various ends to which foreign-assistance programs have been adapted, survey the types of controls characteristic of such programs, and review the salient problems connected with the application of this means of policy.

Foreign-assistance programs may be distinguished by their emphasis on (1) economic aid, consisting of grants and loans; (2) technical assistance, making available information and advisers; and (3) military aid. Beneficial as such measures may have been to the recipients, the fact remains that these programs are tools of foreign policy and deserve close attention as alternative ways of building allies, acquiring satellites, and dissuading uncommitted nations from becoming enemies.

Soviet Economic Aid. The most comprehensive aid scheme ever developed was the American Marshall Plan. Because of the complexity of controls built into it, it will be examined in greater detail after surveying other types of foreign-aid programs. Soviet policy makers also have employed economic aid as an adjunct of policy, though by no means on so comprehensive a scale as in the United States. While few over-all figures are published officially, some indication of the scope of the use of loans and grants is given in the Soviet credit to China of 300 million dollars in 1950, and the Soviet grant to North Korea of 1 billion rubles in 1953. The loan to Peiping was to cover five years of purchase at a nominal rate of interest, but nothing is known as to the conditions which may have attended this move. The grant to North Korea, designed for rehabilitation and relief following the Korean War, was paralleled by similar United States action in South Korea. Moreover, the Soviet Union has begun to offer low-interest development loans without attaching political "strings," as to India in 1955.

Another type of Soviet economic assistance provides more obvious measures of control. This consists of joint-stock companies established in the East European and Asian Communist countries, in which the Russian and allied governments shared in the exploitation of raw materials and the manufacture or trade of selected articles. In view of the disparity of economic and political power, these ventures were not of equal partners but instead served to extend the dominance of the Soviet elite. In return for providing equipment and capital funds, the Soviet Union received a tangible return in the form of raw materials or profits. Intangible returns included the prestige accorded the donor government as well as the controls over the local economy afforded the dominant partner. Thus, from 1950 to 1955, Sino-Soviet companies operated oil and mining concessions in Sinkiang and controlled civil airlines throughout China. In Eastern Europe, joint-stock companies supervised pivotal points in local economies, such as Romanian oil, Hungarian bauxite, and Danubian shipping, while maintaining a semblance of national independence. Apparently, Chinese resentment of such overt Soviet control forced the Russian leaders prematurely to abandon these mixed corporations in 1955, although their original term of contract was to last until 1980. Simultaneously, joint-stock companies in Eastern Europe were dissolved. However, repayment of Soviet shares was to be in the form of future deliveries of goods and services, thereby continuing Russian intervention in domestic economic development.

Commonwealth Economic Aid. A third area of assistance programs, the Colombo Plan, focuses attention on the recipient rather than the donor. Initiated among Commonwealth countries of Southeast Asia in 1950, this move has endeavored to improve living standards of economically undeveloped countries such as India, Pakistan, Ceylon, Malaya, and British Borneo by coordinating their approach to foreign assistance. Great Britain and Australia assist in providing technical assistance and money. All the countries face similar problems of population pressures, agrarian improvement, and local unrest. Anxious to avoid Communist uprisings and loath to accept the kind of foreign loans which might mask a return to colonial status so recently thrown off, these countries have voluntarily shared experience, information, and planning in order to provide a sound basis for economic development. Although the independent members retain full national sovereignty and merely consult through a council, their coordinated efforts serve to bolster their collective strength.

That the Colombo Plan is dependent upon foreign loans and investments was recognized from the start. Indeed, it was felt that such funds would be more readily forthcoming under mutually satisfactory terms if local efforts showed initiative and foresight in estimating the needs and resources of the member countries. In the first three years of operation, Colombo Plan countries received about one billion dollars in aid from the United States, the United Kingdom, Australia, New Zealand, and the International Bank for Reconstruction and Development.[1] Most of the money financed irrigation, hydroelectric, and railroad projects.

United States Technical Assistance. Whereas economic aid programs center around the providing of credit whether in grants or loans, technical-assistance programs center around the transmission of information and experience, generally in training programs and overseas missions. Here the emphasis is upon social and economic measures of a long-range nature whose beneficial effects will make the recipient country a stronger and more cooperative supporter of the donor's interests. Typical of such a venture was the celebrated Point Four Program, launched in 1950 as a new means of furthering American interests abroad. United States' expenditures during the first four years of operation totaled less than 400 million dollars, a slight sum in comparison with the 11 billion dollars of the Marshall Plan.[2] However, the effectiveness of technical assistance is not indicated by statistical comparison alone, since its field of operation so far as the United States was concerned lay chiefly in food, health, and education. Thus with a relatively small expenditure a considerable amount could be accomplished by expert advice, improvement of methods, and training specialists from various countries. Point Four will be examined in greater detail later in connection with the problems and prospects of each type of program.

Soviet Technical Assistance. Technical assistance has received special consideration in Soviet foreign policy, although with somewhat different emphasis from that in the United States. Throughout the Soviet bloc, Russian agricultural and industrial experts act as advisers while groups from Czechoslovakia, Hungary, China, and elsewhere travel in the Soviet Union to receive training and experience. In many instances, evidence indicates that Russian experts ordered rather than advised their non-Russian colleagues, thereby extending Soviet control into countries bordering on Russia. In particular, continual interference and exploitation by Soviet advisers fostered Yugoslav resentment, which underlay tensions surrounding the Tito-Stalin controversy in 1948. However, fragmentary reports from Communist China indicate that although technical assistance has been more important than direct economic aid, Soviet officials exercise less control and intervention, remaining discreetly aloof from the actual management of many operations. A relatively inexpensive type of foreign-aid program, technical assistance fits Soviet policy well as a means of extending prestige as well as control throughout East Europe and Asia.

[1] *The New York Times,* Oct. 18, 1953, p. 5.
[2] *The New York Times,* Sept. 26, 1953.

Military Aid. Finally, foreign aid may be of the strictly military type, giving money, equipment, and advisers for the explicit purpose of building up a country's armed forces. Unlike technical-assistance programs, which generally offer help with few obligations in return, military aid may bind the recipient to coordinate policy with the donor. If part of a formal alliance, commitments may be embodied in precise terms. Alternatively, they may be loosely phrased, as in treaties providing American aid where the recipient agrees to "take such action as may be mutually agreed upon to eliminate causes of international tension" and to contribute to "the defensive strength of the free world." Since 1949, more than 12 billion dollars were appropriated for military programs, most of which served to strengthen NATO forces. Soviet statistics are unavailable, but much aid was certainly given. As tensions between the Soviet Union and the United States mounted, military aid became of increasing importance, with a corresponding deemphasis on economic- and technical-assistance programs.

Of course, the three main types of aid program are not rigidly exclusive of one another. They may be used in conjunction or as alternatives; all may support similar objectives. As one American official put it, "United States technical assistance participation is a world-wide approach and military assistance is also a world-wide approach. The two are companions rather than oppositionary approaches." [3] Nevertheless, the programs vary considerably according to the controls employed and to their applicability to specific problems. These points require a closer examination of each type of foreign assistance.

2. Economic Aid: The Marshall Plan (European Recovery Program). As a comprehensive economic assistance program the Marshall Plan—or ERP, as it is called—has no parallel. In terms of expenditure as well as in terms of impact, it proved to be a major event in postwar international relations. Although officially terminated in 1951, ERP remains as a striking example of how economic means may serve political ends.

Main Objectives of ERP. The underlying motivations of ERP may be summarized quite simply. The primary challenge facing America in 1947 was Soviet expansion, particularly through Communist governments in East Europe and Communist movements in West Europe. Continuing economic crisis, rooted in the disequilibrium following world wars and depressions, plagued efforts to introduce stability and prosperity into regimes confronted by large dissident agrarian and industrial groups. If communism were to be checked, economic help would have to be rendered the non-Communist elites. So ran the thinking behind ERP.

Secretary Marshall phrased it with considerable eloquence: [4]

---

[3] Mutual Security Director Harold Stassen, *The New York Times,* Sept. 27, 1953, p. 6.
[4] G. C. Marshall, "Assistance to European Economic Recovery," *State Department Bulletin,* Jan. 18, 1949, pp. 71–72.

So long as hunger, poverty, desperation, and resulting chaos threaten the great concentrations of people in Western Europe . . . there will steadily develop social unease and political confusion on every side. . . . The vacuum which the war created in western Europe will be filled by the forces of which wars are made. Our national security will be seriously threatened. But if we furnish effective aid to support the now visibly reviving hope of Europe, the prospect should speedily change. The foundation of political vitality is economic recovery. Durable peace requires the restoration of western European vitality.

Although Secretary Marshall here avoided naming the antagonist of the United States, other officials showed less caution. Thus the Harriman Committee, appointed by President Truman to examine the over-all problem, concluded,[5]

The interest of the United States in Europe cannot be measured simply in economic terms. It is also strategic and political. We all know that we are faced in the world today with two conflicting ideologies. . . . If these countries by democratic means do not attain an improvement in their affairs, they may be driven to turn in the opposite direction. Therein lies the strength of the Communist tactic: it wins by default when misery and chaos are great enough.

Subsidiary Objectives of ERP. Moving from the general to the specific, implementation of this over-all objective was to follow two main lines. One approach aimed at overhauling damaged and dilapidated economies so as to increase productivity, decrease inefficiency, and generally create conditions of high employment and prosperity. At the same time, efforts were made to increase the multilateral trade of Europe, including trade between Soviet and Western Europe, to break down discriminatory trade barriers between nations, and ultimately to achieve some sort of economic integration which would approximate the single-market conditions of the United States. The first objective, increasing efficiency and productivity, encountered few objections as to ends, although many as to means. The second, fostering West European integration, ran afoul of innumerable problems, not the least of which was the unclear way in which this objective was formulated by American policy makers. As summarized by an official spokesman in 1952, no reference was made to this point in Secretary Marshall's proposal of 1947 or in the initial legislation of 1948.[6]

In 1949, however, the Congress set forth "unification of Europe" as an explicit objective. . . . The Mutual Security Act of 1951 stated that the funds . . . should be used "to further encourage economic unification and political federation of Europe." In the Act of 1952, the Congress "welcomes the recent progress in polit-

[5] *European Recovery and American Aid,* report by the President's Committee on Foreign Aid, November, 1947, p. 4.

[6] D. Stone, "The Impact of United States Assistance Programs on the Political and Economic Integration of Western Europe," *American Political Science Review,* December, 1952, p. 1101.

ical federation, military integration, and economic unification in Europe and affirms its belief in the necessity of further vigorous efforts toward these ends."

Both objectives entailed differences of opinion between donor and recipient, as well as among the recipients themselves. The determination of the most efficient allocation of resources or the best way of increasing productivity, not to mention the far more complex problem of eliminating trade barriers and achieving some sort of integration, was often viewed quite differently by European and American elites. This was particularly evident where disagreement stemmed from the fundamental cleavage between groups embracing some type of socialist ideology as opposed to groups supporting capitalistic principles. The critical factor in ERP was the degree of control open to the United States which might be exercised in pursuit of basic objectives.

Donor Controls in ERP. The most fundamental control, of course, lay in the economic dependence of the recipients upon continued American aid. Although ERP funds during the first year accounted for only 5 per cent of the European national production during that period, it was a crucial 5 per cent, comparable in size and importance to the spark plugs of an automobile. In effect, it provided the wherewithal to purchase food, raw materials, and capital equipment necessary to produce the remaining 95 per cent. Yet American aid could be suspended or terminated at any time if one or more of the many obligations were unsatisfactorily met by the recipient nations. Among these were pledges to obtain the highest possible productivity, to stabilize currency, and to balance the budget, to establish "valid" exchange rates, to reduce tariff barriers, and to make "efficient" use of all domestic and imported resources. Given the desperate state of West European economies, termination of ERP provided a persuasive argument for fulfilling American objectives.

Additional controls shaped the specific direction of economic development. American officials determined which commodities were to be purchased with ERP funds, and allocated these commodities over fixed periods of time. Each recipient government made quarterly schedules of needs, subject to American approval. Since the purpose of the program would be defeated were non-ERP funds to be used for purchases disapproved by ERP officials, in effect the United States won the right of review over the total import program of each recipient.

Furthermore, after commodity requests had been screened and allocated, the United States issued export licenses in order to limit exportation of goods in short domestic supply and to prevent strategic goods from reaching the Soviet bloc. While East-West trade in general was an objective of the program, any trade which would strengthen the military power of the Soviet bloc was anathema to American officials. Hence not only American exports but European exports which were in any way facilitated by ERP funds came under the purview of United States officials.

One more control must be mentioned to illustrate the extent to which foreign assistance provides possibilities for implementing policy. Under a device known as counterpart funds, recipient countries deposited local currency in amounts equal to the dollar value of grants made to each country. These deposits, made to the central bank of each recipient, then came under the veto power of the United States officials whose approval was necessary before these funds could be used. Since these deposits could be spent only in a way commensurate with ERP objectives, a considerable control over the entire economy was possible, especially since the size of these deposits sometimes equaled the entire national debt of the recipient country. Through these measures, investment and monetary policy in some countries could be completely controlled by American officials, should they so desire.[7]

These controls and their attendant obligations were written into identical bilateral treaties concluded between the United States and Greece, Turkey, Italy, Portugal, France, Switzerland, Luxembourg, Belgium, Netherlands, United Kingdom, Ireland, Denmark, Norway, Sweden, Iceland, and the occupied areas of West Germany and Austria. In addition, a multilateral treaty bound the recipients, among themselves, to over-all coordination through the Organization for European Economic Cooperation (OEEC). American supervision of the program came through a specially created agency, the European Cooperation Administration (ECA), with a representative acting as liaison with the OEEC and special missions in each of the participating countries. ECA was expected to consult with the Department of State but was not subordinate to the Secretary of State. Administration of ERP required a large staff to survey its operations abroad and to manipulate the controls written into the program. Thus in every respect it constituted a major endeavor of American foreign policy.

3. Greece: ERP Controls in Action. Although the possibilities of control were indeed far-reaching, the degree of intervention varied considerably from country to country. In some instances, as in Sweden, the amount of aid was so negligible and the implementation so efficient that virtually no exercise of American controls took place. In other cases, as in the United Kingdom and France, some pressures were applied with varying degree of success but outright suspension or termination of aid never took place, despite the refusal of these governments to accept all American suggestions. Particularly adamant stands on the part of the British and French in opposing American preferences as to internal monetary policy and over-all European integration brought no overt interference from United States representatives. In view of the many political as well as economic measures undertaken during the duration of ERP contrary to American policy, it is safe to conclude that neither Paris nor London became wholly subservient to Washington.

[7] ERP legislation as embodied in Public Law 472, 80th Cong. 2d Sess., Apr. 3, 1948. The Economic Cooperation Agreement was signed in Paris on June 28, 1948, and published in *Treaties and Other International Acts Series, 1783.*

The picture changes somewhat in moving to the Mediterranean countries of Italy and Greece. Here the Communist challenge was in many ways more serious, in Greece actually erupting into civil war. Here, too, political and economic problems were more pressing, particularly in view of the extensive wartime destruction and the lack of overseas possessions to serve as sources of revenue. However, while Greece provides an atypical example of ERP in operation, it serves as a revealing case study of the manner in which economic controls elaborated in foreign-assistance programs may be utilized to serve political ends.

The Greek Problem. Two interrelated problems confronted American representatives in Greece. A large armed Communist minority, organized during the resistance movement of World War II, carried on guerrilla warfare against the Greek government with considerable assistance from the Communist regimes of Albania, Yugoslavia, and Bulgaria. At the same time, internal economic and political conditions rooted in wartime destruction, corrupt officials, extremes of wealth and poverty, and undemocratic practices threatened to leave Greece in perpetual instability and crisis. Termination of the civil war required primarily military means. Solution of the internal crisis demanded political and economic remedies. Both problems became the concern of America, because of the strategic location of Greece. Anglo-American strategists viewed supply lines to vital oil supplies in the Middle East as endangered if unsettled conditions were to result in a Communist victory.

Aid to Greece. In March, 1947, President Truman made an emergency appeal to Congress for stopgap aid to Greece. Later this aid was formally incorporated into ECA activities so that although Greece was geographically apart from Western Europe, it represented a vital part of the European Recovery Program.

By the end of ERP on December 31, 1951, more than $614,000,000 had been allocated for economic assistance to Greece. Of this amount two-thirds went for purchases of commodities, $293,500,000 going for food and agricultural products and $169,800,000 for industrial goods. In addition, $4,200,-000 provided technical assistance.[8] This discussion is not concerned with the military assistance as such, particularly in view of the extraordinary conditions prevailing in Greece during the civil war. Suffice to say that as a result of the Tito-Stalin split, Yugoslavia ultimately stopped all aid to the Greek guerrillas. This, coupled with increased assistance and direction from American quarters, enabled the Greek government to end the civil war victoriously in the winter of 1949–1950.

Although the amount of economic aid extended to Greece appears small in comparison with over-all appropriations, it bulked large in proportion to the Greek economy. As a lever for manipulation, foreign assistance offered

[8] *Procurement Authorizations and Allocations,* Mutual Security Agency, Statistics and Reports Division, Jan. 31, 1953, p. 10.

considerable promise for the attainment of American objectives. These objectives were outlined in the special address to Congress by President Truman, March 12, 1947: [9]

> Greece must have assistance if it is to become a self-supporting and self-respecting democracy. . . . It is of the utmost importance that we supervise the use of any funds made available to Greece, in such a manner that each dollar spent will count toward making Greece self-supporting, and will help to build an economy in which a healthy democracy can flourish. . . . We have condemned in the past, and we condemn now, extremist measures of the right or the left. . . . It must be the policy of the United States to support free peoples who are resisting attempted subjugation by armed minorities or by outside pressures. . . . Our help should be primarily through economic and financial aid which is essential to economic stability and orderly political processes.

In short, American policy aimed not only at halting Communists within Greece but at providing a government based on a sound economy and democratic principles. Aid was not to consist of a blank check to be filled out at the discretion of Greek officials. As noted in President Truman's remarks, constant supervision was to accompany all assistance. Under the terms of assistance agreed to by the United States and Greek governments, the chief of the American mission was empowered to determine "the terms and conditions upon which specified assistance shall . . . be furnished" while the Greek government guaranteed complete freedom of observation and information for American representatives. Assistance was to be withdrawn "if the President of the United States determines that such withdrawal is in the interest of the United States" or if the Greek government failed to "take reasonable steps to effectuate those measures proposed in its note of June 15, 1947, or subsequently agreed upon which are essential to reconstruction and recovery in Greece." [10] No wider latitude could have been left to United States representatives, short of assuming direct control of the Greek government. In fact, American advisers were admitted to all important government agencies and took part in overhauling the entire administrative, financial, and military structure in Greece.

ERP Intervention in Greece. The first two years of ERP in Greece provided little more than stopgap remedies. Until the end of civil war in 1949–1950, it was all the American mission and the Greek government could do to prosecute the war and put a brake on inflation, much less attempt any far-reaching reforms. With the return of peace, however, opportunity for improvement appeared. Yet in order to effect the changes in exports, taxes, wages, and social policies implicit in the American program, it was necessary

---

[9] "Aid to Greece and Turkey," *Department of State Bulletin*, supplement, May 4, 1947, pp. 829–832.

[10] *Agreement on Aid to Greece*, in First Report to Congress on Assistance to Greece and Turkey, U.S. Department of State, November, 1947, pp. 35–38.

to cope with the oligarchy of vested interests which had traditionally ruled Greece. In the seventeen cabinet changes between the liberation of Greece in 1944 and the end of the civil war in 1949, politics had resembled a game of musical chairs played among essentially the same figures, with the occasional loss of one or more through natural death. The coalition of landed, business, and royalist elites remained in the ascendancy, despite the deterioration of government and country.

It was this interconnection between politics and economics which ultimately brought overt American intervention in Greek affairs and the utilization of ERP controls. Already in 1948 and 1949, first Ambassador Dwight P. Griswold and then his successor, Ambassador Henry Grady, had vainly attempted to use the pressure of economic assistance as a means of changing the pattern of Greek politics.[11] Although the election of March, 1950, indicated a sharp swing away from the dominance of the two major conservative parties, the new premier, Venizelos, threatened to suspend Parliament for three months. This was designed to perpetuate the rule of the traditional elites. Ambassador Grady thereupon presented the Greek government with a thinly veiled ultimatum which he made public immediately, without waiting for a reply. Its juxtaposition of politics and economics merits quoting. After summarizing measures undertaken to remedy the dislocation caused by world war and civil war, Grady noted that basic improvements had been delayed. "It should be frankly recognized that an important reason for the delay has been a less than satisfactory performance by the Greek Government in its conduct of economic affairs." He interpreted the election as a manifestation of widespread demand for an improvement in the situation. Grady bluntly advised that any Greek government "which hopes to continue to receive the aid which [the United States] have generously offered" must "utilize this assistance to the fullest extent. . . . Only a stable and efficient Government" could do this. "Irresponsible talk of adjourning Parliament or of new elections before the new Parliament has had an opportunity to rise to its responsibility, can only create a climate of political and economic uncertainty which may do grave damage to the country's future."

Grady demanded these unpopular measures: sharply curtailed government spending, a ceiling on the national debt, curtailment of subsidies, and enforcement of a revised tax program. In addition, "the improvement should include the establishment of a Cabinet with a minimum of Governmental ministries, a greater decentralization of responsibility . . . and the enactment of a civil service code. . . . Elections of local officials, which have not taken place for fourteen years, should be considered for the very near future."

On April 15, Venizelos resigned and a new cabinet more amenable to American advice was formed. Through parliamentary maneuvers, Venizelos succeeded in overthrowing the new cabinet within six months and rewinning

11 *The New York Times,* Jan. 20, 1948, and June 28, 1949.

control of the government. American reaction was immediate. On September 13 Venizelos took office. On September 16 ECA officials in Washington announced a cut in appropriations for Greece because "the rate of progress . . . has not been sufficient to allow complete and effective utilization of the amount originally contemplated."[12] The cut in American aid exceeded 67 million dollars. Within two weeks Venizelos promised to undertake the "necessary steps," and tensions eased temporarily.

That Greece continued to pose problems for American policy was indicated only a few months after termination of ERP. Further assistance was held to be necessary to achieve American objectives, and accordingly an additional 175 million dollars was appropriated to be administered by the Mutual Security Agency, the successor to ECA. With elections imminent in March, 1952, Ambassador John E. Peurifoy expressed publicly his opposition to the extant proportional-representation system. Implicitly favoring a majority system which would return candidates believed better suited for carrying out policies favorable to American objectives, Ambassador Peurifoy claimed that proportional representation, "with its inevitable consequences of continuing governmental instability, would have a disastrous effect upon the efficient use of American aid in Greece."[13] Athens responded accordingly; the electoral system was revised, and a new government supposedly more compatible with American policy took office.

The point need be elaborated no further. The case of Greece under ERP is one of halting economic and political reform, spurred on at the repeated instance of United States intervention. But despite the tensions and difficulties, American efforts succeeded in ending the civil war, maintaining a semblance of representative government, and gradually strengthening the position of Greece in NATO. It is no coincidence that Greece consistently supported the United States in United Nations voting, occasionally in isolation from other European countries, and that Greece contributed a military unit in the Korean War. In short, economic assistance proved a valuable adjunct of American foreign policy.

4. Technical Assistance: Point Four. Point Four, officially known as the Technical Cooperation Program (TCP), shared one feature in common with ERP. It employed foreign assistance for furthering political ends. ERP was initiated as a short-run emergency measure to save European economies from complete collapse. TCP began as a long-range venture in assisting underdeveloped areas to raise living standards and to cope with problems of industrialization. ERP appropriations frequently exceeded 1 billion dollars to a single country. TCP never allocated more than 100 million dollars to one recipient. Finally, TCP remained essentially a one-way program involving a minimum of intervention by the United States.

[12] *The New York Times*, Sept. 17, 1950, p. 32.
[13] *The New York Times*, Mar. 15, 1952, p. 1.

Objectives of TCP. That both programs, however, were motivated by political ends is clear from the statements of American officials. President Truman
called on Congress to legislate Point Four aid for underdeveloped countries
lest "they turn to false doctrines which hold that the way of progress lies
through tyranny." [14] More explicit was the analysis given by a TCP official
in 1952: [15]

> The United States cannot afford to let the free countries of Asia and the Middle
> East, to say nothing of Latin America, fall under Communist domination. The
> rest of the free world would then be fatally deficient in raw materials and man-
> power. . . . The people of the underdeveloped areas . . . are going to find it in-
> creasingly difficult to resist the promises of communism in an atmosphere of con-
> tinued stagnation or deterioration. They will move one way or the other. . . .
> Our Point IV program . . . provides a positive answer to the wiles of commu-
> nism. . . . There will be no use building a shield against Communist aggression
> through our defense programs if the area behind the shield is allowed to become
> soft and subject to subversion from within.

Additional motivations voiced by government spokesmen included boosting American exports to countries by raising their economic level and thereby
increasing their purchasing power, as well as appeals based on humanitarian
grounds. However, the absence of specific figures and the general lack of
emphasis on these points indicated the priority of political over economic
and humanitarian objectives.

Implementing TCP. Implementation of TCP was essentially threefold in
nature. Technical advice flowed through special missions of experts in sanitation, education, agriculture, and industry dispatched to participating countries. By 1953, some 1,400 Americans were functioning in this capacity in
thirty-five countries. In addition, training for nationals of the recipient states
was provided in the United States, with more than 1,300 persons participating
in this phase of the program. Finally, funds for specific projects decided upon
and financed jointly with recipient governments served to provide equipment
in conjunction with the overseas missions and training programs. During
the first four years of Point Four, American contributions totaled $399,000,-
000 as compared with $490,200,000 invested by recipient countries.[16]

Unlike ERP, TCP counterpart funds provided by recipient countries were
not necessarily equivalent in value to that furnished by American grants.
Subject to negotiation in each individual case, these voluntary contributions
provided an index to the desire and ability of recipient governments to help
finance TCP. At the start American allocations averaged six times recipient

---

[14] Message to Congress, June 24, 1949.

[15] Acting Administrator, Technical Cooperation Administration, J. B. Bingham, *Mutual
Security Act of 1952*, Hearings before Committee on Foreign Relations, U.S. Senate,
82d Cong., 2d Sess., 1952, pp. 616–619.

[16] *The New York Times,* Sept. 26, 1953, p. 4. See also S. Andrews, "The United States
and Underdeveloped Areas," *Department of State Bulletin,* Feb. 23, 1953, pp. 306–310.

contributions; by 1953 projects were financed on practically a 50-50 basis. In some cases, local contributions exceeded those from the United States.

In bilateral treaties concluded between the United States and each of the thirty-five participating countries, the terms of aid differed considerably from ERP. No specific economic obligations were written into the agreements, although many general pledges were included, calling for "cooperation in mutual exchange of technical knowledge" and promising to "endeavor to make effective use of the results of technical projects carried on . . . in cooperation with" American aid. This general phraseology paralleled that of the Technical Cooperation Act of 1950 wherein Congress defined as its purpose "to exchange technical knowledge and skills and to encourage the flow of private investment capital."

Controls were not wholly absent, however. As indicated earlier, recipient governments established counterpart funds for the joint financing of specific projects. All projects required the approval of an American-appointed TCP Director; hence some control on domestic development as well as on domestic funds was involved. However, the recipient country could refuse the appointment of any Director, and could expel TCP missions upon ninety days' notice without loss of any equipment or materials invested in the projects. No country was obligated to undertake any project, congressional legislation prescribing only the most general type of economic development to be financed. Furthermore, local counterpart funds could be financed by selling commodities provided by TCP, decreasing the burden on national budgets. Finally, the proportionately small amount of the recipient's efforts financed by TCP funds sharply limited the impact of possible intervention.

Although the initial congressional action had included stimulus of private investment as a TCP objective, this phase of the program received little direct supplementation. As one State Department official remarked after three years of TCP, so far as private investments were concerned, "We have a long way to go." [17] Although separate agreements were often concluded between the United States and recipient countries with guarantees against expropriation and against nonconvertibility of earnings, these apparently were not made a prior condition for TCP aid. However, they were probably helpful in persuading Congress to continue TCP appropriations.

5. India: TCP in Action. TCP aid to India was initially negotiated in December, 1950, but not until January of 1952 did the two governments sign supplementary agreements covering the first appropriations. In June, 1952, an official breakdown of TCP allocations indicated the following projects, together with the agreed division of contributions: [18]

---

[17] Andrews, *op. cit.*, p. 307.

[18] Based on breakdown published in *Hindustan Times,* June 15, 1952, as quoted in *Indian Press Digest,* May, 1953, p. 57. Indian contribution calculated from rupee figures at official exchange and then rounded off.

Project	United States	India
Tube wells for irrigation.........	$13,700,000	$ 8,890,000
Fertilizers.....................	10,065,000	880,000
Community development........	8,671,000	68,766,800
Iron and steel................	8,385,000	240,000
River-valley schemes...........	4,784,000	100,000
Marine fisheries..............	2,462,000	1,379,000
Malaria control...............	648,000	7,500
Locust control................	230,000	48,000
Soil-fertilizer research..........	200,000	168,500
Training for village workers......	166,000	1,505,000
Forest research; desert control....	104,000	41,600
Total......................	$50,000,000	$81,026,400

One year later approximately one-fifth of the American appropriation and one-fourth of the Indian contribution had been expended. These figures indicate the relatively slow pace of TCP aid as well as its primary points of emphasis, in contrast with the comprehensive operations of ERP.

Politics and TCP. More important for purposes of this discussion, however, is the political impact of TCP. On the one hand, the hope behind TCP was that improving conditions and demonstrating American efficiency and good will would keep Communist influence in uncommitted countries at a minimum. On the other hand, the Indian government hoped to remain aloof of cold-war conflicts and to maintain good relations with Communist countries. Not only does India have a 2,000-mile border with Communist China, but the Indian Communist Party is the strongest single opposition to the dominant Congress party. From the Indian viewpoint, foreign assistance is limited to economic development, with no commitment to join forces with America in containing communism. To further complicate matters, India's sorely won freedom from foreign domination meant that any controls attending foreign assistance would be certain to encounter serious opposition.

The American Congress, however, was unwilling to support a "do-good" or a "giveaway" program, without a pro-Western realignment in New Delhi. Stress upon anticommunism brought Indian objections. In March, 1952, Secretary of State Acheson warned Congress that

The advice of all our observers on the ground is that unless the newly independent government under Prime Minister Nehru can show substantial progress in economic development over the next five years there is the likelihood that in the next elections democratic forces will be endangered either by extremists or Communists.

These remarks were promptly quoted by influential opposition groups in India as foreshadowing loss of Indian independence in foreign relations, ultimately forcing an official denial from the Nehru government.[19]

[19] S. Ramabhai, "Agreement or Slavery Bond?" in *Harijan*, May 10, 1952, pp. 95–96.

Nehru himself came under constant attack as the chief proponent of foreign aid, not only from virulent Communist opposition but from his own Congress party. When challenged with the avowed anti-Communist motivations behind American aid legislation, he replied, "The point is what we do about it, not what the wishes were of the American Congress when they passed the Act." [20]

Unlike the situation in Greece, Indian objections over TCP did not stem from specific controls or from instances of disagreement between Indian and American officials as to how assistance should be utilized. Indeed, the absence of such controls and intervention was emphasized by an Indian official in a detailed rebuttal to attacks prominent in the Indian press: [21]

No agreement . . . is being entered into . . . except for an object which is essential and fits into the framework of the Five Year Plan. . . . There is no obligation . . . to buy any equipment for projects under the TCP from the United States. India is free to buy equipment through her own agencies wherever the price factor and the delivery situation are favourable. No American experts are employed in India or sent to India unless they are specifically requested for by the Government of India. . . .

Limitations on TCP in India. Yet the criticism continued. The attack varied, sometimes charging that too little money came to India as compared with Europe, sometimes picturing a flood of American advisers and equipment which would disrupt India's village communities. Sometimes the type of aid was questioned on the basis that India needed to employ all her manpower, while American emphasis was on machines and electric power. Whatever the form, the theme of distrust and suspicion indicated widespread opposition to TCP among vocal groups in India. While the peasant in the village may have had few objections, he was far removed from dominant elites in urban Indian politics.

Whatever may have been the long-range hopes of TCP advocates, it was clear that in the short run it had brought few tangible results in the country of greatest TCP effort and with the most immediate importance for American policy. In part, the problems were of a propaganda nature, such as congressional insistence upon adequate publicity and a share in directing expenditures. In one of the major projects, a community-development program designed to encompass some 16,000 villages, American appropriations did not exceed 15 per cent of the total funds. Yet the publicity given TCP participation both in India and in the United States caused Indian groups to protest the distortion of fact and to question the degree of American control.

More fundamental, however, to the success of the program was the basic nature of the situation. Implicit in the granting of American assistance was

---

[20] *The New York Times,* July 5, 1952.
[21] Gulzarilal Nanda, Minister for Planning and River Valley Schemes, in *Harijan,* Aug. 23, 1952, pp. 209–210.

the hope that so-called "benevolent neutrality," if not full-fledged cooperation, would be forthcoming. The unwillingness, if not the inability, of Indian
leaders to support American policy in time of international crisis—especially
in Korea—brought forth congressional reactions distinctly unfavorable to
continuing aid of any sort. These statements in turn only served to convince
Indian circles that regardless of American assurances to the contrary, "strings"
came with aid. The absence of control permitted Indian independence of
policy which, in turn, alienated American legislative support for TCP. These
short-run crises threatened to thwart any long-range utilization of technical
assistance as an adjunct of American policy.

6. Military-assistance Programs. Of the types of foreign-assistance programs utilized in support of foreign policy, military assistance is the oldest
and most widely practiced. Its advantages are several. A guarantee of control
accompanies military aid when the recipient is unable to provide the necessary ammunition, replacement parts, and maintenance equipment vital to
effective use of weapons. The cost to the donor is negligible when the aid is
rendered in the form of obsolete or outdated equipment. What may be of
little use to the advanced military power is generally of considerable value
to the more poorly equipped country. Finally, the granting of military aid
carries fewest overt manifestations of foreign intervention. Indeed, by bolstering a country's armed forces the donor may be said to have increased the
sense of independence and nationalism, contrary to the attitudes on both
sides which often accompany economic and technical assistance.

As might be expected from these advantages, military-assistance programs
have enjoyed widespread support in the postwar period. Soviet aircraft, tanks,
artillery, and ammunition served to keep North Korea and China fighting
against the United Nations for three years. Communist China, in turn, helped
to supply the Viet-Minh forces under Ho Chi Minh, fighting the French in
Indochina. Similarly, on the American side, extensive United States military
aid flowed into Europe through NATO. In turn, Great Britain continued her
traditional equipping of Trans-Jordan legions, while France was able to
supply Viet-Nam forces fighting under Bao Dai. In addition, the armies of
South Korea and Nationalist China were virtually created and maintained
by American military assistance during the last decade.

Soviet Military Aid. Quantitatively, too, military aid has been impressive.
During 1955 and 1956, for instance, American expenditures in support of foreign armed forces totaled $2,595,200,000. The entire air force of the Soviet
bloc, including all Communist countries of Eastern Europe and Asia, had
come from Russian factories. Of course, it is impossible to tell how much
was given outright and how much was offered in exchange for raw materials,
but in view of the reequipping of Polish, Hungarian, Romanian, and Bul-
garian armies, it is doubtful that the major part of Soviet military supplies
was covered by payments in the form of goods or services.

The Soviet approach to military assistance is simple and direct. It aims at the maximum strengthening of allied armies consonant with maintenance of maximum control by the Soviet Union. That this approach has not always been successful, as evidenced by the defection of Yugoslavia in 1948, does not deny its effectiveness throughout most of the Soviet sphere. In East Europe, this included a complete revamping of the chain of command in every country so that organization was everywhere identical with that of the Soviet army. All commanding positions are staffed by Communist Party members, whose prior allegiance is supposedly to the Russian Communist Party rather than to their national governments. At the highest levels, personnel are recruited from nationals formerly resident in the Soviet Union and sometimes, as in the case of Konstantin Rokossovsky, head of the Polish army, former Soviet citizens. Finally, the pervasive Russian secret police serve as an added check upon the attitudes and actions of East European military forces. Periodic purges testify to the use of terror as a means of control.

Similarly, in the past decade the armies of East Europe have been completely reequipped with standardization of weapons along Soviet lines. Although little is known about the existence of munitions factories other than those in Czechoslovakia, it appears that maintenance and supply for critical artillery and armored units rest exclusively in Russian hands. In short, there is little independence left to the armed forces of Russia's allies in East Europe, their separateness being maintained only in the symbols of flag and uniform and in the semblance of national commands.

In Asia, Soviet military assistance has had less sweeping success, primarily because of the greater strength of the Chinese Communist government. Mao Tse-tung won power largely on supplies and weapons captured from the Japanese in World War II and from the Nationalist army between 1946 and 1949. Although Soviet assistance in the form of captured Japanese arms played a minor role in 1945–1946, it was not until after the Red Army victory in 1949 that Soviet military aid became of increasing significance. Of course, throughout the Korean War, Chinese transport and air power depended on Soviet Russia. Furthermore, no invasion of Formosa could be contemplated without critical supplies from Moscow. Nevertheless the fact remains that for further expansion into South Asia, Russian aid was not vital to Mao's regime. Hence the degree of control necessarily diminished as compared with that accompanying Soviet military assistance in East Europe.

It should be noted that, at least in East Europe, Soviet military assistance served as a control over internal as well as external policies of the respective governments. Although not the only means of such intervention, it provided the Soviet elite with a monopoly of organized violence, capable of being turned against any manifestation of internal dissent. This so-called "Russification" of the East European armies served as an effective safeguard against any underground resistance movement on the part of disaffected groups.

American Military Aid. American policy with respect to military assistance differs radically from that of the Soviet elite. In exceptional cases, such as South Korea and Nationalist China on Formosa, military assistance has been utilized as a significant means of control over foreign policy, if not over internal policy. More generally, however, military assistance has been extended to strengthen avowed allies and is merely one of a series of pressures applied in an effort to win continuing support for American objectives. This is true for the majority of NATO countries. Finally, in the exceptional case of Yugoslavia, military assistance was granted in the hope that it might serve as a means of bringing an uncommitted country to greater support of American objectives, but with no known conditions attached to the aid rendered.

In recognition of the interrelationship of all assistance programs with respect to bolstering a recipient's strength and thereby supposedly strengthening the defense of the United States, an over-all scheme emerged in 1951, known as the Mutual Security Program (MSP). While MSP was to combine all three types of foreign assistance, the ascendancy clearly lay with military aid. Behind the general conditions specified by Congress as binding upon recipients of MSP aid stood the avowed purpose of offering military assistance as a means of strengthening anti-Soviet forces. "No military, economic, or technical assistance authorized pursuant to this Act shall be supplied to any nation to further military effort unless the President finds . . . such assistance will strengthen the security of the United States and unless the recipient country has agreed to . . . take such action as may be mutually agreed upon to eliminate causes of international tension. . . ." [22]

General as these conditions might appear, they proved sufficiently detailed to deter neutralist-minded nations in South Asia from adhering to MSA pacts including such obligations. Initialing a pact of this type led to the political downfall of the responsible official in Indonesia in February, 1952. Not until December, 1952, were Indonesian leaders willing to conclude a more limited agreement for technical assistance exclusively. According to a United States governmental spokesman, ten countries refused to accept American military aid because of the attendant obligations. [23]

Implementation of this program has been fourfold. Military items manufactured in the United States, equipment manufactured elsewhere under so-called "offshore purchasing" agreements, military-training programs, and delivery of supplementary commodities vital to defense were all financed with MSP funds. Once the initial equipping of NATO was established, supplementary commodities such as food, clothing, and raw materials received increased emphasis. Instead of economic aid being rendered to improve living

[22] *Mutual Security Act,* 82d Cong., 1st Sess., Oct. 10, 1951. The current name of the United States government agency in charge of all foreign-aid programs is "International Cooperation Administration."

[23] C. R. Dekker, MSA Administrator for the Far East, *The New York Times,* Feb. 26, 1952.

standards, it was more closely linked to rearmament and served as a direct prop for military development.

Control over American Military Aid. The degree of control varied considerably. In South Korea, for instance, a successful attempt was made to keep President Syngman Rhee in line with American policy following the Korean armistice by threatening to cut off vital military supplies should he violate the truce unilaterally. Since South Korea lacks all industry necessary to maintain a modern army, the threat to withdraw military aid had the effect of making any unilateral military campaign impossible.

Another aspect of American military assistance highlighted the limitations in terms of control, namely, the offshore purchasing program. This served to finance production and purchasing outside of the United States in order to simplify logistics problems and to economize wherever possible. Thus jet engines might be manufactured in Great Britain, mortar weapons in France, and signal-corps equipment in West Germany, all financed by congressional appropriations. The net effect was to bolster the armaments industries of NATO members and to lessen the direct control by the United States. In NATO generally, American military assistance served as a prod toward standardization of weapons and over-all integration of command, but it bore little resemblance to the sweeping control effected in East Europe.

The judicious use of military-aid controls is illustrated by Yugoslavia. Marshal Tito's forces were strong and well organized at the time of the break with the Cominform in 1948. However, they were held to be inadequate in the face of a combined assault by Hungary, Bulgaria, and Albania, particularly if that assault should be supported by the Soviet Union. Following serious American reversals in Korea during the winter of 1950–1951, President Truman announced extension of 29 million dollars in "raw materials . . . basic to the needs of the Yugoslav armed forces." [24] After one year of deliveries, largely of light weapons, signal equipment, and supplementary commodities, American policy boosted the reward for Tito's continued anti-Cominform stand. A new Yugoslav air force of Sabre jet fighter-bombers, medium tanks, heavy artillery together with thousands of trucks, maintenance equipment, and gasoline composed the bulk of increased military assistance provided by the United States. In return, it was made clear that Yugoslavia was to integrate her defense with that of Greece and Turkey, thereby serving as a direct prop for NATO defense.

While Yugoslavia moved slowly to implement liaison with NATO forces, American spokesmen emphasized their abstention from interfering with Yugoslav affairs. As Ambassador to Yugoslavia George Allen remarked, "Realistically, our two governments recognize that our economic and political systems are fundamentally different, but this has not prevented us, as sovereign independent nations, from recognizing the responsibility we share

[24] *The New York Times,* Apr. 16, 1951.

in helping to preserve the free world." [25] Prompted by economic and logistical motivations, as well as by a growing confidence in Yugoslav cooperation, United States assistance provided $5,300,000 for an "offshore-purchasing" project to finance a munitions industry in Yugoslavia.

This gradual strengthening of Yugoslavia's military power bore unexpected fruit in the Trieste crisis of late 1953. Refusing at first to accept an American-sponsored plan for dividing Trieste between Italy and Yugoslavia, Marshal Tito publicly threatened to use "armed force" against Italian troops, warning, "We have said many times we are grateful for aid, but we cannot sell our bloodsoaked country for aid. We refuse aid if this is the situation." [26] High Yugoslav officials emphasized their ability to "go it alone" by calling attention to the possibility of supplying and equipping their armed forces on existing facilities financed and built with American assistance. Eventual Yugoslav-Italian agreement on the partition of Trieste was not, apparently, influenced by controls over aid.

Between the two extremes of South Korea and Yugoslavia came the manifold problems attending military aid to Western Europe. Arguments over German rearmament, atomic defense, integration of Spain into NATO, and withdrawal of American forces from the Continent all served to highlight the considerable scope left to NATO members for maneuver, despite their recognized dependence on United States assistance for the bulk of their defense. Since the battle is the proverbial pay-off, the effectiveness of military assistance could not be fully measured in time of peace. In so far as it acted as a deterrent to Soviet expansion, such aid had proved its worth. Its future results remained open to question. By 1953, however, it was clear that American officials had fixed on military assistance as a primary adjunct of foreign policy, with decreasing emphasis on economic and technical assistance as such.

7. Problems of Aid Programs. *Dilemmas of the Donor.* Those employing foreign assistance as a means of policy must maneuver between Scylla and Charybdis, between nonintervention and application of controls. Where foreign assistance is given unconditionally, it provides no assurance that the donor's objectives will be reached. It may be squandered or wasted. It may be used effectively, yet leave the recipient not only stronger but better able to act independently of the donor's interests. Alternatively, where controls are utilized, cries of "imperialism" and "intervention" may increase the tensions between elites and ultimately lessen the support for the donor's policy. Short of all-out controls, partial intervention threatens to act as a weapon for dissident groups in the recipient states, capable of whipping up nationalistic fervor against the "foreign imperialists."

The donor's problems are compounded when the aims of its elites include the desire to dispose of agricultural surpluses or encourage the exportation

[25] *Ibid.*, Mar. 11, 1953.   [26] *Ibid.*, Oct. 11, 1953.

of goods not wanted by the recipients. Both these pitfalls have intermittently plagued American aid programs. Further, ill will rather than friendship may be fostered if the donor insists on the recipient's accepting military aid in lieu of economic assistance, or if aid of all kinds is made conditional on the recipient's shifting the economy to military production, sacrificing butter to guns.

These problems are particularly critical where the future course of the recipient is in doubt. In France and Italy large groups favor a so-called neutralist position, while strong Communist minorities champion outright support of Soviet policy. Finally, there is the great shadow-area of the Middle East and South Asia, where no certainty whatsoever exists that recipients of American assistance will be willing or able to keep their countries in at least "benevolent neutrality" vis-à-vis the United States, if not rendering outright support. The gamble of uncontrolled aid as compared with the onus of intervention leaves the American policy maker with a serious dilemma.

To a far lesser extent, a similar problem confronts the Soviet elite. In Eastern Europe the decision to control at any cost resulted in one fiasco and in recurring minor tensions. In the last analysis, of course, the dominant groups in these countries realize that their survival depends on accepting Soviet controls. Communist China, however, presents a more delicate situation embodied in the problem of how to render assistance so as to ensure a strong yet willing ally. The long-standing bitterness with which the Chinese have regarded interference by "foreign long-noses" was not wholly subsumed under protestations of Communist brotherhood.

Expectations of the Donor. Another problem in foreign assistance is linked with the expectations of the donor. It seems to be almost axiomatic that, whatever may be the benefits derived from foreign assistance, gratitude and good will are seldom among them. As an American participant in a recent international conference in India remarked, the United States seems to have been caught in a "damned if you do and damned if you don't" situation. When little or no assistance is rendered less well endowed countries, accusations of "have nots" against the "haves" abound. When an abundance of economic and technical assistance is forthcoming, charges of imperialism and intervention proliferate.

Yet belief in the fostering of good will and increasing allies abroad continues, particularly among certain American groups. This leads to a publicizing of foreign aid which often serves to undo whatever good will might possibly have resulted from aid efforts. It arouses a negative reaction among the donors when sensitive nationalist temperaments on the receiving end flare up against alleged patronage, charity, or worse, exploitation.

The expectations of the donor include not only intangible returns but also such consequences as increases in productivity, elimination of subversive unrest, and a strengthening of elites consonant with the donor's interest. Here other weaknesses in foreign-assistance programs come to light. With few exceptions, they apply short-run solutions to long-run problems. In Western Europe, the fundamental economic disequilibrium reflected in balance-of-payments problems and productivity stagnation was rooted in almost a half century of development. It was incapable of remedy with four years of Marshall aid, no matter how lavishly or how wisely administered. In agrarian countries such as Greece and Italy, economics could not be dissociated from politics. Only by transformation of the ruling elites could reforms be effected necessary for rising productivity and prosperous stability. In countries like India, the conundrum of population explosions amidst conditions of near starvation defied short-run palliatives.

Expectations of accomplishment turn into frustrated realization of delayed crisis. Recriminations between donor and recipient and substitution of one program for another result. The heart of the dilemma inherent in utilizing foreign assistance as an adjunct of foreign policy is that, in many cases, foreign assistance can accomplish its objectives only as a continuing program. Foreign policy, however, generally moves in a series of short efforts, adjusting to the dynamics of international relations and eschewing long-range commitments. This is especially true for all countries where the alternation of elites brings a new combination of interests to be pursued in foreign relations. Continuity of a single elite with an attendant fixed objective defined by its ideology, as in the Soviet Union, encourages the longer view compatible with foreign-assistance programs. Yet even here hazards arise when a transformation of external conditions permits the recipient new alternatives beyond the control of the donor.

The Impact of Neutralism. One final limitation must be noted. Reference has already been made to the cautious manner in which both India and Indonesia approached the question of accepting assistance without accepting obligations. Foreign-aid programs may appear at first glance as a most attractive way of winning over uncommitted areas such as prevail in the Middle East and South Asia. Actually, insecure elites often propound "neutrality" as a necessary means of surviving internal and external political pressures. A case in point was that of Burma. Between June, 1950, and June, 1953, the Burmese government accepted more than 30 million dollars' worth of economic and technical assistance from the United States. However, despite serious internal disturbances from various Communist and opposition elements, the government took no part in military-assistance programs. Moreover, the activities of pro–Chiang Kai-shek forces on Burmese soil brought forth protests and pressure from Peiping. Choosing the politically acceptable path of "neutrality," the Burmese government in 1953 even terminated acceptance of American economic aid, hoping thereby to make its position more acceptable to internal as well as external critics.

It should come as no surprise, in view of the many risks attending foreign-assistance programs, that this means of policy gained prominence only in the intensified international tensions following World War II. As a corollary, it appears that as crisis lessens, so will reliance upon this type of action, particularly upon economic and technical assistance. As an emergency measure, the means enjoy widespread support. As a long-range policy, they encounter strong opposition. Despite the claims of their proponents, then, foreign-assistance programs remain an important, but by no means omnipotent, means of attaining ends in foreign relations.

ADDITIONAL CASE-STUDY MATERIAL

"Aid to Greece and Turkey," *Department of State Bulletin,* supplement, May 4, 1947.

Andrews, S.: "The United States and Underdeveloped Areas," *Department of State Bulletin,* Feb. 23, 1953.

Barber, J. (ed.): *The Marshall Plan as American Policy,* Council on Foreign Relations, New York, 1948.

Basch, A.: "The Colombo Plan: A Case of Regional Economic Cooperation," *International Organization,* vol. 9, February, 1955.

Blelloch, D.: "Technical Assistance: Programmes and Policies," *International Affairs,* vol. 28, January, 1952.

Bowles, C.: "Point Four Begins an Indian Revolution," *The New York Times Magazine,* Nov. 16, 1952.

Carr-Gregg, J.: "The Colombo Plan," *International Conciliation,* no. 467, January, 1951.

Chand, T.: "The Impact of Western Civilization on Eastern Ideology and Ways of Life," *International Social Science Bulletin,* vol. 3, winter, 1951.

Diebold, W., Jr.: "East-West Trade and the Marshall Plan," *Foreign Affairs,* vol. 26, July, 1948.

————: *Studies in Economic Cooperation, 1947–51,* Harper, New York, 1952.

Ellis, H. S.: *The Economics of Freedom,* Harper, New York, 1950.

Harris, S. E.: Foreign Aid and the Domestic Economy," *Proceedings of the Academy of Political Science,* vol. 23, January, 1950.

————: *The European Recovery Program,* Harvard University Press, Cambridge, Mass., 1948.

Hoffman, P.: *Peace Can Be Won,* Doubleday, New York, 1951.

Hoselitz, B. (ed.): *The Advancement of Underdeveloped Areas,* University of Chicago Press, Chicago, 1952.

Kaplan, J. J.: "The United States Foreign Aid Program: Past Perspectives and Future Needs," *World Politics,* vol. 3, October, 1950.

Kennan, G. F.: "Foreign Aid in the Framework of National Policy," *Proceedings of the Academy of Political Science,* vol. 23, January, 1950.

Lutz, F.: *The Marshall Plan and European Economic Policy,* Princeton University Press, Princeton, N.J., 1948.

Madan, B. K.: "The Economics of the Indian Village and Its Implications in Social Structure," *International Social Science Bulletin,* vol. 3, winter, 1951.

Marvel, W. W.: "Foreign Aid and United States Security," unpublished Ph.D. thesis, Princeton University, Princeton, N.J., 1951.

Motwani, K.: "The Impact of Modern Technology on the Social Structure in South Asia," *International Social Science Bulletin,* vol. 3, winter, 1951.

Neal, M.: "Implementation of Technical Assistance," *International Conciliation,* no. 468, February, 1951.

Rubinstein, A. Z.: "Soviet Policy toward Underdeveloped Areas in the Economic and Social Council," *International Organization,* vol. 9, May, 1955.

Staley, E.: "Technical and Economic Assistance under Point Four," *Proceedings of the Academy of Political Science,* vol. 25, May, 1952.

Stone, D.: "The Impact of United States Assistance Programs on the Political and Economic Integration of Western Europe," *American Political Science Review,* vol. 46, December, 1952.

Wolf, C.: "Political Effects of Economic Development," *Far Eastern Survey,* vol. 20, May 2, 1951.

PART FOUR

FOREIGN POLICY AND POLITICAL INSTITUTIONS

Chapter 12

THE UNITED STATES: IDEOLOGIES AND INSTITUTIONS OF PLURALISTIC DEMOCRACY

The United States "bestrides the world; she is the colossus of our time. Whatever is said and done in the United States may easily change the lives of unnumbered millions thousands of miles away."[1] Thus wrote a friendly British critic of American foreign policy, and he comments that to America's allies, "It is like being locked in a house with a whimsical drunken giant." How gigantic is the United States in terms of its population, resources, and military power, and what are some of the important socioeconomic features which make it so whimsical?

The United States covers over 3 million square miles and is inhabited by over 160 million people. Its armed forces numbered 3.5 million in 1954, 1.1 million of whom were stationed in Europe, Africa, Arabia, Korea, Japan, and the Caribbean. The American people have been spending over 30 billion dollars annually for defense since 1951. While its per capita national income of about $1,500 a year is the highest in the world, over half its government's budget was allocated to assuring victory in the cold war.

Yet so extensive are its resources and industrial apparatus that it proved possible to expand war production and raise living standards simultaneously, assuring both guns and butter. In 1953 America produced 110 million tons of steel, was able to refine over 7 million barrels of oil per day, and generated 80 million kilowatts of electric power. Through constantly rising productivity it was able to increase its armory of tanks and planes while offering ever-growing numbers of automobiles to the consumer at the same time.

[1] J. B. Priestley, as quoted by N. D. Palmer and H. C. Perkins, *International Relations*, Houghton Mifflin, Boston, 1953, pp. 1005–1006.

Less than 20 per cent of the American people gain their livelihood from agriculture and live in farming communities. Still, agricultural production was so great as to result in government holdings of a fifteen months' surplus of wheat, a nine months' surplus of cotton, and a two months' oversupply of butter in 1953. American agriculture is notoriously unstable, and fears of depression are generated by falling farm prices and incomes, resulting from overproduction. During 1953 the United States consumed 62 per cent of the world's rubber production, 56 per cent of world manganese, 53 per cent of global zinc output, and 52 per cent of all tin mined. An American depression would invariably result in a sharp reduction of such purchases— and thereby spread a domestic slump to other countries. Conversely, American industrial and agricultural immensity facilitated military victory in both world wars. No wonder the rest of the non-Communist world is afraid of the impact of the American colossus.[2] The mere economic importance of the United States is such as to make most of the world somehow dependent on domestic industrial and agricultural trends and therefore on policies determined in Washington.

1. The American Myth and the Moods within It. *Middle-class Egalitarianism.* If a superficial and inevitably subjective attempt be made to reduce the welter of American beliefs, hopes, and expectations to a concise formula, the task is slightly facilitated by the striking absence of important belief systems which dissent from the dominant American consensus. No significant revolutionary groups of the right or left are effective in American politics. No coherent "un-American" dogma challenges the basic precepts of the "way of life" of the people of the United States. Indeed, Americans seem to take pride in their conformance to central values. The so-called "average man" is respected by all, from presidents to advertisers. The "average" American thinks of himself as belonging to the middle classes, no matter how much economists and sociologists may challenge such opinions through statistics of income and status. "Americans have a strong aversion to thinking of themselves as markedly different from the average man. . . . The major party politicians . . . have long tended to personify the American people as the average man. . . ."[3]

That the average man accepts a belief in individual freedom and equality is obvious. Special social and economic privileges are repugnant to the American myth. Yet the belief in liberty is frequently qualified to exclude those suspected of falling outside the national consensus. Toleration and freedom of opportunity are watchwords of the American way; but they are

[2] Statistics on military manpower, industrial production, agricultural surpluses, and strategic imports in *The New York Times,* Aug. 2, 1953; Dec. 13, 1953; Jan. 17, 1954.

[3] A. N. Holcombe, *The Middle Classes in American Politics,* Harvard University Press, Cambridge, Mass., 1940, pp. 205–206.

not necessarily applied to deviant groups who challenge the values of the average middle-class man.

Egalitarianism begets a distrust of special claims to leadership and eminence, and therefore it fosters the dominant American belief in the virtues of common sense. While the technological expert is highly respected, the statesman who fails to identify himself with the average man's search for common-sense answers to basic issues skates on dangerously thin ice. Americans prefer the simple and straightforward to the sophisticated and abstract —in art and literature no less than in politics and economics. A boundless faith in human—and especially American—ingenuity and in the certainty of progress persuades the average man that common sense applied to any political or social problem is bound to yield the "right" answer. If the issue fails to be resolved in this fashion, "someone" is likely to be blamed for incompetence, corruption, or even treason. The democratic faith of America, therefore, carries with it a common-sense devotion to progress achieved by individual and private exertion.

Business versus Missionary Values. This devotion to progress and individualism is closely tied to the prevailing business values of American society. The fabled ascent "from rags to riches" typifies admiration for the individual who, through skill and dedication, can rise to positions of power, especially in the business hierarchy, which continues to receive the greatest respect of all American elites. Business assessments of what is good or bad policy, wise or unwise investment of effort and money, correct or wasteful application of talent tend to prevail in politics as well as in agriculture or finance.

In general, therefore, America in the midst of the twentieth century is dedicated to the continued supremacy of individual private initiative in business as well as in social and political relations. Agreement rests partly on a sharing of these values by all major segments of American society and therefore "without design the system as a whole tends to produce conformity to its values. . . ." However, "a powerful discipline makes it difficult for a businessman to call his soul his own, that is, if he wants to stay in business. He must have regard for his customers, his suppliers, his bankers, his stockholders, his brokers, his lawyers and all others with whom he deals." [4] The same is true of the labor leader, the lodge president, the farmer, and the politician.

So strong is this dedication that some Americans have been speaking of our era as "the American century," and others have emphasized the mission of America to carry its values and belief to less fortunate portions of the world. American progress is held to have resulted from the unerring pre-

[4] V. O. Key, Jr., as quoted in J. M. Burns and J. W. Peltason, *Government by the People,* Prentice-Hall, New York, 1952, pp. 331–332.

scription of faith in common sense, hard work, and private initiative. The prescription is considered equally applicable to other regions and nations. Hence United States foreign policy tends to be assessed in terms of this formula. If the "investment" is judged to be a bad one, a change in course is demanded and the rascals must be thrown out. The consistent application of the American myth to foreign policy thus may carry with it the simultaneous extension of American values abroad.

Thus the ethic of the businessman is wedded to the values of the Christian missionary in American beliefs. But while one emphasizes practicality and tangible results in efforts at home and abroad, the other implies dedication to humanitarian principles and to welfare on a less material base. One rests on hard work and often ruthless competition for success and survival; the other insists upon disinterested service. Yet both are very much in evidence in American political attitudes; their simultaneous presence introduces ambivalences, doubts, and frustrations. Whatever the cause of the dualism—on which sociologists and anthropologists continue to disagree—it seems to be responsible for marked oscillations in the American view of political life. Within the basic myth the moods of withdrawal and intervention, optimism and pessimism, superiority and inferiority toward other nations tend to alternate. The ambivalence of the myth, therefore, contributes to the fluctuating manner of American policy at home and abroad. Hence the moods within the myth deserve a closer analysis.[5]

Oscillations in Mood. These oscillations are particularly clear in the attitudes of Americans toward the outside world which have prevailed since 1945. At the end of World War II, a pattern of optimism, tolerance, and idealistic dedication to a new world of harmony dominated.

But as specific conflicts with the Soviet Union broadened into the general impasse of the Cold War, the American foreign policy mood changed again. Optimism about the future of peace gave way to pessimism. Idealist internationalism faded into "security realism." Overtones of impatience and intolerance began to emerge in public reactions to our relations with the Soviet Union, England, China; but the continuance of threat precluded an unequivocal expression of these reactions.[6]

The mood of withdrawal from a "hopeless" situation was linked with pessimism, while the drive for active intervention often met an optimism of obtaining speedy results. Thus General MacArthur in 1944 thought that Europe, being hopeless, was a wasteful investment from which America must withdraw, while more active intervention in the Pacific seemed to offer optimistic possibilities of future American strength.[7] Intervention and with-

---

[5] G. A. Almond, *The American People and Foreign Policy,* Harcourt, Brace, New York, 1950, chap. 3, provided the framework for this analysis.

[6] *Ibid.,* p. 67.

[7] MacArthur's interview with foreign correspondent Bert Andrews, entered in the diary of Defense Secretary James E. Forrestal, Nov. 22, 1944. W. Millis (ed.), *The Forrestal Diaries,* Viking, New York, 1951, pp. 17–18.

drawal, pessimism and optimism are both represented. But in the American oscillation between the two in postwar China policy, the continuing meaning of the dualism is manifest.

Similarly, the tolerance for Soviet communism shown by the Roosevelt Administration gave way to intolerance when the assumptions of peaceful cooperation which had motivated American policy until 1945 crumbled after Yalta. Tolerance implies patience in dealing with others and the willingness to compromise values. Intolerance results when the compromise seems to redound to the antagonist's benefit, and withdrawal or unilateral intervention may develop as the impatient reaction. Thus in 1945, the American Cabinet disapproved of the growing communization of Poland. Secretary of War Stimson and presidential naval adviser Leahy advised patience and "hoped we would go slowly and avoid any open break." Secretary of the Navy Forrestal, Ambassador Harriman, and Secretary of State Stettinius demanded strong action and less tolerance. President Truman decided that "if the Russians did not wish to join us they could go to hell." [8] Disappointment with tolerance led to unilateralism and intolerance, not only on the popular level of the average man but in the highest government ranks.

An ambivalence between cynicism and idealism was equally implicit in this period. In 1945 it seemed that the American people embraced the idea of peace and security through the United Nations. National foreign policies, armaments, and alliances were to be scrapped in favor of the collective measures envisaged in the UN Charter. This unbounded idealism, encouraged by many government officials who wished to avoid the fate suffered by the League of Nations Covenant in the Senate debates of 1919, was by no means shared by all. Severe doubt, the opposite side of the coin, was voiced by John Foster Dulles, who urged that "these questions of a viable machinery for world peace are questions that have been perplexing the minds of statesmen for centuries and . . . it was unwise . . . to assume that they would be settled overnight." He felt that the UN idea was being "oversold." [9] Similarly, the ideal of disarmament was greeted by Forrestal with open cynicism: [10]

I suggested that once discussions in the Security Council appeared to hold out a plan for a disarmed utopia there would perhaps be irresistible public pressure to adopt such a plan forthwith, regardless of world conditions which for some time will require existence of force to accomplish stability.

By 1950 the "irresistible public pressure" which the Secretary had feared as overly idealistic had indeed been transformed into acquiescence toward

[8] Report of a Cabinet meeting, Apr. 23, 1945, *ibid.*, pp. 47–50.
[9] *Ibid.*, pp. 41–42, as paraphrased by Forrestal's diary entry.
[10] *Ibid.*, pp. 241 ff., 290–291. Forrestal's comments to other high officials, Jan. 20 and July 11, 1947.

the contemporary drive for military strength as necessary for national security. Cynicism toward the UN was supreme, at least temporarily.

A final dualism in the American myth is of vital significance to foreign
policy: the ambivalence between apathy to events abroad as opposed to the
desire to take immediate action on the basis of an oversimplification of the
issue. When American policy suffers a reverse, somebody must be guilty of
incompetence or treason; when apathy is rewarded with loss of influence
abroad, the demand will be for immediate and drastic action for "liberation
of oppressed peoples" through unprecedented propaganda or military build-
up. Thus oversimplification was demonstrated in the report of a Senate committee investigating the Far East policy of the United States. "China fell"
because America failed to support the Kuomintang adequately with matériel
and advice, the Senators concluded. Other and more complex reasons for
Chiang's debacle—such as fifteen years of unrest, runaway inflation, and
lack of unity among Kuomintang leaders—received no recognition in this
assessment.[11]

Moods and the Unattached Individual. America's basic tenets of belief,
therefore, are characterized by conflicting moods which tend to offset one
another. Withdrawal alternates with intervention, pessimism competes with
optimistic assessments, intolerance takes the place of patience and understanding, while oversimplification and the cry for action succeed periods of
apathy and indifference. Many groups, to be sure, possess ideologies which
rise beyond such oscillations. The positions of churches and business tend
to show more permanence than these moods would suggest. Yet the unattached individual whose link with organized groups is remote and peripheral
turns from one extreme to the other. In periods of optimism, feeling confident and superior to the complex forces of society around him, he favors
toleration and participation in world affairs; but struck by doubt, frustration, and feelings of inferiority to the impersonal forces which tax his income and conscript his sons, he turns to intolerance and withdrawal at times
of pessimism.

Thus withdrawal and doubt were the earmarks of this assessment of America's world role at the height of the Korean troubles: [12]

"Why doesn't Truman get rid of those Communists in the government?" Mrs.
Hunter demanded. "With our boys dying in Korea, he won't kick out the people
who are fighting us—it makes me sick!" . . . Although the Hunters saw no chance
of agreement with Russia, they were reluctant to say that war is the only alternative. Nor were they content with the present nightmarish twilight of neither war
nor peace. "We ought to do something to show those Russians where they get off,"

[11] *Military Situation in the Far East,* Hearings before U.S. Senate, 82d Cong., 1st Sess.,
Committee on Foreign Relations and Committee on Armed Services, 1951, pt. V, pp.
3593–3595.
[12] S. Lubell, *The Future of American Politics,* Harper, New York, 1951, pp. 156–157.
Based on an interview in Knox County, Ohio.

said Hunter. "When Malik and Vishinsky say those things about us in the United Nations, someone ought to go up to them and slap their faces!" As I got ready to leave, Hunter tried to sum up his feelings, "I guess what I've been trying to say is that it's time we got back to the American way of living."

American values, having been spurned by a foreign world dominated by other views and aims, seek refuge in negation, withdrawal, denunciation of the enemy, and the affirmation of the "old" way of life.

If the optimistic and tolerant extreme of the American dualism be represented by the "magnanimous Goddess of Liberty" extending her arm in New York harbor and asserting the Christian missionary aspect of national thought, the practical and frequently intolerant aspect of the society resting on the ethic of private business enterprise can be symbolized by "horse-trading Uncle Sam." [13] Both are key aspects of the American myth. They alternate in importance as optimism takes the place of pessimism, and vice versa. But in the impact of American power on external friend and foe alike, both are known, feared, and cherished. The role of these and other tenets of America's beliefs in the ideologies of key interest groups now remains to be explored.

2. Interest Groups and Their Ideologies. Of the thousands of American interest groups whose aspirations enter the process of making and implementing foreign policy, seven categories of groups have been selected because they function continuously, possess a large membership, and are led by articulate and powerful elites. The categories comprise business, labor, agriculture, veterans, women's organizations, religious groups, and important ethnic minorities. In each case, the position defended by the largest or most influential interest groups in each category has been used in this analysis.

Business. In the realm of business, the United States Chamber of Commerce is the largest and most representative organization. Conservative in its social and economic beliefs, the chamber is an unflinching supporter of free private enterprise at home and abroad, tending to equate the national interest with the interest of the businessman. Sound business principles are stipulated as the only valid guides for government policy abroad; the welfare state, planning, and the concomitant high taxes and unbalanced budgets are opposed on principle. Continued participation of the United States in multilateral international activities is urged as essential, because "no nation, be it ever so strong and prosperous, can remain unaffected by political and economic developments outside its own borders." [14] Foreign aid was approved, but "The best hope for industrial development in other countries lies in a flow of American private capital for investment in new enterprises." [15] The

---

[13] The symbols are those of G. Gorer; Almond, *op. cit.,* pp. 44–45.

[14] Chamber of Commerce of the United States, Board of Directors, *Annual Report to the Members,* 35th meeting, Washington, 1947, p. 2.

[15] Hearings before Committee on Foreign Affairs on International Technical Cooperation Act of 1949, U.S. House of Representatives, 81st Cong., 1st Sess.

chamber, in its opposition to planning and socialism, adamantly opposes government competition with the private investor in economic activities abroad; yet the chamber also insists that no political conditions be attached to foreign-aid measures.

While the business ethic and its ideological derivatives form the substance of these demands, the missionary aspect of American thought is implicit in the ideology of the affiliated Junior Chamber of Commerce: [16]

> With each grain of wheat and coppery penny [sent in foreign aid] we should send as a companion of equal dignity and importance a dose of the old-fashioned gospel of democracy—pointing out that only under our system of free opportunity and enterprise has a people been able to work and produce enough to relieve the chaos of a troubled world. This is no time for false modesty. The scream of the American Eagle must be heard around the world. . . .

The chamber generally favors free trade, though with reservations against destructive competition. The powerful National Association of Manufacturers, controlled by the sixty largest American industrial firms, is less enthusiastic over free trade and more anxious than the chamber to use foreign aid as a means to fashion American-style business institutions and ideologies abroad.

A small business group of Eastern executives, the Committee on Economic Development, however, is squarely in favor of completely free trade even if this should involve the restructuring of the American economy. Represented by such men as Paul Hoffman, CED has been a major supporter of the internationalist wing of the Republican party, favoring accommodation in foreign affairs and permanent American participation even at the risk of compromise. Because of its close ties with the Republican leadership, CED's political importance is far greater than its limited membership suggests.

The aspirations of the millions of small American businessmen, however, seem to bear little resemblance to these currents of opinion. Merchants, shopkeepers, small manufacturers, and wholesalers regard themselves as the "backbone of American democracy," as the grass roots of traditional American individualism and private initiative. This devotion has led to a condemnation as "Marxist" and "socialist" of American foreign-aid "giveaway" programs. Small business opposes any kind of domestic government planning and is adamantly against a permanent pattern of high taxation. Alliances, permanent external commitments, and compromises with allies or enemies abroad are equally repugnant to this segment of American life. Dedication to traditional values of exclusion or vigorous self-assertion rule instead.[17]

---

[16] Almond, *op. cit.*, p. 165.

[17] This material is systematically developed in the Ph.D. dissertation of John H. Bunzel, instructor in political science at San Francisco State College. The dissertation is in the library of the University of California, Berkeley, Calif.

The total impact of the business ideology on American thinking is symbolized by the attitude which characterizes American foreign-assistance programs. While political, humanitarian, and long-range economic aims are of course implicit in these measures, the language which prevails in foreign-aid debates is reminiscent of the simple, hard-headed business approach. Thus TCA chief Jonathan Bingham told Congress that "dollar for dollar, the United States can make no better investment than in the point IV program." [18] In a national myth geared to business concepts and values, commercial standards and criteria have a tendency to dominate political planning.

Labor. American labor leaders differ only in degree from these aspirations. The labor elite identifies itself with business because "mutual interests in the welfare of America" compel such cooperation, especially since "democracy is possible only in a society of free enterprise and trade unionism can live only in a democracy." [19] The American labor elite considers itself "cocustodian of American prosperity" with the business elite and therefore accepts the free enterprise system *in toto,* provided collective bargaining and large-scale unionism are permitted to prevail. Both the CIO and the AFL accept the institutional and ideological *status quo* of America and claim to represent not merely the interests of labor but the welfare of the national economy on the whole.

Hence the foreign policy demands of labor differ only in degree from those of business. Like the CED and the Chamber of Commerce, the Brotherhood of Railroad Trainmen accepts large-scale foreign aid and involvement and even campaigns for it through its Public Affairs Institute. The CIO upholds the virtues of containing communism but insists that this can best be achieved by favoring the principles of planning and the welfare state among America's allies. The AFL agrees but tends to stress the participation of labor leaders in planning and implementing American policy. It shows little interest in furthering welfare-state principles abroad. Generous demands for foreign aid and moderate pleas for disarmament give labor's elite a slightly different approach to foreign policy, as compared with business; yet despite attachment to the UN, patriotism prevails without major challenge. The CIO "is an institution with a single national allegiance, to our own country, the United States of America," as its own leaders proclaim.[20] In addition to favoring permanent American participation in world affairs on principle, however, the AFL sees in Point Four a major device for assuring the United States of access to strategic raw materials. The CIO's major criticism of the Eisenhower Administration's policy abroad hinged not

[18] Hearings before Committee on Foreign Relations on Mutual Security Act of 1952, U.S. Senate, 82d Cong., 2d Sess., 1952, pp. 616–619.
[19] C. Wright Mills, *The New Men of Power,* Harcourt, Brace, New York, 1948, p. 115.
[20] CIO, 9th annual convention, *Report,* Atlantic City, N.J., 1947, p. 274.

on principle but on the tendency to favor "big business as usual" at the expense of labor participation.[21]

Agriculture. American farm groups range from the conservative National Grange to the radical Farmers' Union, though the largest organization is the middle-of-the-road American Farm Bureau Federation. The Grange represents the intervention-withdrawal dualism at its extreme, since the organization is at once pacifist and favorable to world government while it opposes extensive foreign aid and a relaxation of tariffs. Failing to obtain the millennium of global peace and stability on American terms, it falls back on unflinching exclusivism. Opposed to the Grange on domestic ideological and policy questions, the Farmers' Union still exhibits somewhat similar traits. While this group favors government planning in agriculture and supports welfare-state ideas, it endorses policies of foreign participation through alliances and aid measures only if these are not motivated by power aims. If "power politics" seem to intrude, the union falls back on withdrawal from the sullied world of compromise, since it refuses to compromise its faith in the fellowship of all humanity. Hence it has not always supported recent American foreign policy, especially in its military commitments.

While total planning for welfare and unfettered free enterprise are the opposing symbols of these groups, the Farm Bureau Federation has generally avoided basic statements and favored government policy. It declared that "the best and most effective defense is to maintain this American free choice system," but it holds that deficit spending, cheap money, and federal controls are undesirable. The Federation has been especially critical of large military-aid programs to allies abroad, and it regards the alleged policy of making the European economy dependent on America's as unsound because it wishes to favor the increased exportation of agricultural surpluses instead.[22] Immediate economic interests, therefore, find a more consistent expression in political activity than do the basic value aspirations of the other farm groups.

Veterans and Patriots. American veterans' organizations and the American Coalition of Patriotic Societies exhibit many common ideological traits. While the former are small in number but huge in membership, the Coalition consists of eighty-five separate groups, mostly with a small membership.[23] Patriotism is their watchword, but this implies marked disapproval of both major political parties as being "socialistic" and not sufficiently aware of their responsibility in defending traditional American values of freedom and private enterprise. The American Legion and the Veterans of Foreign Wars, similarly, stress patriotic devotion, which they equate with the maintenance

---

[21] CIO, 12th constitutional convention, *Report,* 1951, p. 185. Also *The New York Times,* Nov. 18, 1953, p. 13.

[22] Hearings before Committee on Foreign Affairs on Amendments to the Mutual Security Act, U.S. House of Representatives, 82d Cong., 2d Sess., 1952.

[23] Almond, *op. cit.,* pp. 204–208.

of free enterprise and procapitalistic values in public policy as well as education and the activities of other interest groups. Hence they stand on "100 per cent Americanism" and single out the military strength and ideological unity of America as vital. Their unilateral devotion to national values makes them leery of extensive participation in international organizations in which the United States can be outvoted, and their opposition to UNESCO has been bitter. Foreign aid is to rest on private initiative and a minimum of government participation; military aid is to be restricted to those who seem ideologically reliable. The Daughters of the American Revolution identify active international cooperation with the one way to "ensure the triumph of socialism" and to "bankrupt" the United States.[24] Unilateral self-assertion and a distaste for compromise are implicit in this ideological complex.

Women's Groups. Politically articulate American women are organized into the conservative National Federation of Business and Professional Women and two liberal groups, the League of Women Voters and the General Federation of Women's Clubs. The National Federation is close to the NAM in ideology and takes the same stand on public policy as that business group. The League and the General Federation, by contrast, agree with the American Association of University Women to [25]

act on our knowledge that the whole world is one, by assuming our full share of responsibility in international problems, by educating ourselves and our communities in these problems and in their relation to community life, and by supporting the United Nations, Unesco, and other related agencies in promoting human welfare, international cooperation and peace.

The UN is a key symbol of attraction to these liberal groups and only the intensification of the cold war has brought about their support for unilateral and multilateral American military and economic commitments. Even so, they stress the nonmilitary aspects of foreign activity and continue to cluster their policy demands around the pole of toleration rather than withdrawal.

Religion. Organized religion provides one of the focal interest groups of American society. Catholics as well as Protestants prefer to recognize "the United Nations as our existing instrument for world order. . . . We should seek by every possible means to uphold its hands in the hope that it may become a more effective world organization, guided by Christian principles." [26] Yet both agree that military preparedness and alliances are necessary for the United States and hence they have minimized their former advocacy of disarmament. The recognition of the cold war, however, has by no means become all-important in Church ideology. Christian principles demand that nonmili-

[24] *Daughters of the American Revolution Magazine,* vol. 82, no. 4, April, 1948, p. 232.
[25] *Journal of the American Association of University Women,* vol. 40, no. 4, summer, 1947, p. 224.
[26] *The United Lutheran Church in America Speaks on World Order,* New York, 1949, p. 3.

tary foreign aid be stressed and rigidly separated from military assistance. UN agencies are to be used for such purposes, and American unilateralism is to be held at a minimum. Private enterprise, access to raw materials, and the containment of communism are explicitly eschewed as exclusive national aims in foreign-aid policy by many such groups; the extension of American values abroad which they generally seek is limited to the advocacy of freedom of religion and respect for Christian ethics.

Ethnic Minorities. General ideology gives way to specific claims based on feelings of ethnic affinity in the demands of the myriad of groups representing the national minorities of the United States. In 1950 there were almost 1,000 foreign-language newspapers in America, published in forty languages and enjoying a readership of over 6 million.[27] No common denominator gives cohesion to the claims of such groups. The Ancient Order of Hibernians restricts its activities to counseling pressure on Britain to effect the unification of Ireland. The American Polish Congress is largely concerned with liberating Poland from communist rule. The Zionist Organization of America seeks to mold a United States policy friendly to Israel and critical of the Arab League, while the National Association for the Advancement of Colored People is concerned with raising living standards in colonial areas and giving political rights to subject peoples.

Conflict and Consensus. Because of the very diversity of aspirations here represented, the process of foreign-policy formulation is rendered ever more complex, especially since these group claims do not necessarily dovetail with the basic demands voiced by business, labor, or the churches. Yet the streaks of general consensus running through this welter of ideologies and claims are impressive. One supreme end of American policy is accepted by all: the protection of national institutions and beliefs against communism. Certainly there is continuing and bitter disagreement over the means and the widest variety over the intensity of the anticommunist feeling. But few businessmen, clergymen, lodge presidents, Legion post commanders, or farm leaders would quarrel with former AFL President William Green's dictum that "with a totalitarian enemy that discredits all that we believe, there can be no compromise. Aggressive, atheistic materialism cannot coexist with Christian civilization."[28] Some evidence of Soviet "good faith," such as domestic reforms, is to be a precondition for negotiation.

Nor would most Americans, despite their heterogeneous ideologies, dispute that the increase in living standards and the spread of freedom represent the "true revolution" of our time and that all free nations should join with the United States to make it triumph over the "Communist conspiracy." Despite partisan strife, therefore, the American myth is sufficiently cohesive to permit mass acceptance of this credo. Yet the dualism remains embedded in the

[27] Almond, *op. cit.,* p. 184.
[28] *American Federationist,* August, 1951, p. 16; *ibid.,* February, 1952, p. 17.

myth. Disappointment with policy expectations will lead to renewed withdrawal; the concurrent claims of horse-trading Uncle Sam and of the magnanimous Goddess of Liberty are not easily reconciled.

3. Political Parties and Factional Ideologies. American political parties lack the ideological cohesion of specific interest groups. Instead, they are merely federations of regional, local, and frequently scattered political interests which find common advantage in formal cooperation in national politics. Neither the Republican nor the Democratic national platform is a clue to the policy of either party; each set of principles is phrased as ambiguously and generally as possible in order to attract to its banner the maximum number of voters in all interest groups. Not coherent ideology, but the affiliation of specific interest groups gives American parties whatever distinction on principle they do possess.

Instead of national party ideology and organization, local and regional pressures tend to determine the stand of individual legislators on the basis of these conflicting forces. The party label means little and national conventions of party leaders usually result in no more than a polite and veiled registration of disagreement. Each party faction must therefore be examined to determine its supporters and constituents, its regional or class basis, the pressures to which it seeks to adjust, and the principles on which it seems to vote and act.

What are these party factions which make political discipline impossible in the American legislative system? Republicans can be divided into a liberal or "internationalist" wing, the "Eisenhower Republicans," opposed by the conservative or "isolationist" faction. Democrats, in turn, are split into a liberal, or "New Deal–Fair Deal" group, which is opposed by a faction of conservatives who find the party label useful for local electioneering purposes but who really side with the conservative Republicans. Finally, the Southern wing of the conservative Democratic faction has given rise to a regional group, the Dixiecrat (or States' Rights Democrats) party, with which a good many conservative Democrats sympathize though the party has been unsuccessful at the polls.

Conservative Republicans. The fundamental rift within the Republican administration, preventing it from presenting a clear legislative program conforming to the ideologies of all its supporters, is attributable to the division between conservative and liberal party members. Conservative Republicans consider themselves the champions of free private enterprise, defending the businessman against greater and greater encroachment of state power. They stand for minimum Federal outlays, reduction of Federal activity, return of Federal powers to the states; in short, "small" government with low, balanced budgets and a low level of taxation. Their adherence to the ideal of pre–New Deal American practices and traditions makes them opponents of extensive presidential powers. Continuing heavy outlays on foreign aid, especially economic and technical assistance, are anathema to this faction, as is the station-ing abroad of large numbers of American troops. The regional and cultural backbone of this group lies in the rural areas of the Middle West, Great Plains, and Far West, but they have scattered supporters in Maine, Pennsylvania, and New Hampshire. The group epitomizes the tendency to seek all-or-nothing answers to foreign policy problems, alternating between the wish to withdraw from "foreign entanglements" and the desire to strike a mortal blow for American democracy and thus end the Communist threat. In terms of strategy, this faction favors Hoover's idea of a "Western Hemisphere Gibral-tar" and MacArthur's desire of dominating the Pacific with sea and air power, because this "line of defense is a natural one and can be maintained with a minimum of military effort and expense." [29]

Attachment to a minimum of government activity, the desire for low taxes and balanced budgets, and the wish to defeat communism without sacrificing "traditional American" principles of government have led these Republicans to a policy of favoring Pacific security over Europe's, of relying on unilateral air and atom supremacy in preference to the compromise-imbued coalition land forces of NATO and the UN. The Pacific promises a clear-cut issue of asserting the American values of Christianity and expansion of free business activity—which have been favored by successive Republican administrations ever since 1898—and obviates the necessity of compromising with other Western nations professing slightly different values and less concerned with the assertion of the American credo.

Conservative Democrats. In principle, the conservative wings of the Demo-cratic party accept most of these Republican positions. Many Southern and Western Democrats share the faith in small government, low taxes, and bal-anced budgets. Southerners consider states' rights preeminent and abhor a New Deal administration in Washington as "socialistic." They agree with the unilateralism implicit in the conservative Republican position. But pro-nounced economic interests in foreign trade make them favor foreign aid and commitments abroad. To be sure, many of them have supported the pre-1952 Democratic foreign policy consistently. But they have done so because the policy stands involved were not crucial to their reelection. When the ideologi-cal issue, however, is clearly joined, they vote with the conservative Republi-cans, possibly against a Democratic President, whose extensive powers they distrust. In terms of geographic and strategic considerations, however, these men lack the Republican attachment to the Far East and show more interest in European defense.

Liberal Republicans. In the complex of contemporary American foreign policy formulation, the liberal Republicans are the faction of chief interest since they control the Presidency, the Cabinet, and certain key congressional

---

[29] MacArthur's address to Congress, Apr. 19, 1951, *Congressional Record,* Apr. 19, 1951, pp. 4233–4235.

committees. Moreover, since 1940 they have succeeded in capturing the GOP Presidential nomination on every occasion. Liberal Republicans come predominantly from the Northeastern seaboard, with scattered supporters in the Middle West and along the Pacific Coast. They enjoy the support of many groups in the big-business elite, just as America's small businessmen tend to back the conservative Republicans. Men like Dulles, Lodge, Flanders, Saltonstall, and Ives are as firmly in favor of private enterprise and opposed to communism as their conservative colleagues; but they differ in their emphasis on these tenets. Long-term foreign commitment is taken for granted. Economic and military assistance, binding alliances, heavy defense outlays, and perhaps even deficit financing are accepted items in the program. Unilateral American self-assertion is less pronounced; the necessity for compromise with allies in NATO and the UN—and even the possibility of negotiating with the Soviets—are all part of the Eisenhower credo. Crusading zeal in this complex takes second place to an "investment" approach to American policy: liberation of oppressed peoples is anathema since it may "invite war with Russia"; a belligerent foreign policy, as advocated by Senators McCarran and Jenner, "would leave the Russians with the feeling that they have no alternative but an eventual war." "All this is not to say we should not stand against evil nor that we should ever reconcile ourselves to it. But this is a dangerous idea—that we have a destiny not merely to struggle against evil but to set the whole world right overnight." [30] Yet in terms of geographical preferences, these Republicans are divided. They favored European defense commitments, to be sure, but their Far Western and Pacific Coast supporters sought to put more emphasis on China, Korea, and Japan than had been advocated in the East. Consequently, the Eisenhower Republicans now follow a policy of firm commitment in Europe as well as in the Orient, with a consequent reduction of material aid to NATO.

Liberal Democrats. The backbone of the Fair Deal Democratic faction is in the large urban centers of the Northeast, the Middle West, and parts of the Pacific Coast. This group is supported by organized labor, some farm groups, and many ethnic minorities. Further, it enjoys the backing of many professional associations. Domestically, it stands for a subsidized agricultural economy, government planning against depressions, civil rights for minorities, and less emphasis on free enterprise than any other party faction. In foreign policy, it initiated the containment policy, the European Recovery Program (in close cooperation with the liberal Republicans), NATO, and the principle of binding external commitments. Geographically, it favors Europe over the Far East and attaches more importance to large land armies than atomic air power, despite the larger financial cost of the former. This crucial difference in attitude as contrasted with the Republican party stems, in part at least, from the interest groups affiliated with the Democrats. Ethnic mi-

---

[30] Editorial from *The Wall Street Journal,* "A Dangerous Crusade," Sept. 2, 1952.

norities of European origin press for a satisfaction of their claims. Business interests with trade and investment in Europe—though normally Republican—nevertheless support Democratic programs of European peace, stability, and prosperity. Professional and fraternal groups alive to the cultural and ideological ties between the United States and the "old countries" across the Atlantic stress the importance of maintaining the common values and aims of Western civilization, thus perforce committing the power of the United States to the defense of Europe.

Conflict and Compromise. In terms of support for extensive Presidential powers, a high rate of taxation, and the doctrine of "negotiating from positions of strength" with the Soviets, liberal Democrats and liberal Republicans therefore vote alike. Yet those Democrats object to the idea of "America's mission," as espoused by Dulles: [31]

> The United States now has the opportunity to bring about peacefully what every Western leader . . . recognizes ought to be done, but what will not be done unless there is friendly but firm outside pressure. The United States can and should take that opportunity and exert that pressure. We have not only the moral right, we have not only the experience, we have not only the worthy motive, but also the responsibility.

Crusading zeal and a conviction of America's right to lead and "pressure" others are accepted by many Republicans. Democrats of the Fair Deal variety, however, stress the material causes of communism and therefore emphasize social reforms. In the words of Justice William O. Douglas: [32]

> We cannot remake the world in our image; but we can help those who are seeking an escape from squalor to find alternatives to communism. We cannot do it by talking democracy and peace. We can do it only by making our foreign policy understandable in terms of the aspirations of these people. We should be behind those who sincerely have as their motto—"the man who works the land should own it."

No single one of these Republican and Democratic factions possesses a majority in Congress or in the nation. Interest groups are not always consistent in their support of any one faction. Many legislators fail to identify themselves clearly with any one party group and waver between factions, especially some Southern and Southwestern Democrats. Hence coalitions of groups rule Congress and shape Presidential recommendations. Liberal Republican opinions must be compromised with conservative Republican aims if the party is to hold together. If such a compromise proves impossible—as it has on numerous occasions—a liberal Republican President must tailor his

---

[31] Dulles, as cited in L. L. Leonard, *Elements of American Foreign Policy,* McGraw-Hill, New York, 1953, pp. 561–562.

[32] W. O. Douglas, *Strange Lands and Friendly People,* Harper, New York, 1951, as quoted by Leonard, *op. cit.,* p. 579.

program to enlist the support of kindred liberal Democrats. Coalitions and compromises thus shape American policy not only on the interest-group level, but in the policy-making hierarchy as well. How policy can be formulated in accordance with consistent precepts at all in such a heterogeneous milieu now remains to be discussed.

4. Political Leadership and Policy Making. The United States Constitution endows the President with the power to conduct the country's foreign relations. In this task, the President is advised by his Cabinet. But the members of this group must be confirmed by the Senate in order to be appointed, thus permitting Congress to participate in choosing policy makers. Furthermore, the Senate has the power to "advise and consent" to the ratification of treaties, a process which demands a two-thirds majority. Finally, all foreign policy measures requiring government financing—and this includes all important aspects of foreign policy—depend for their implementation on appropriations voted by both Houses of Congress. It appears, therefore, that while the President can certainly exercise leadership and initiative in proposing policy, he cannot conduct it without majority support in Congress regardless of the text of the Constitution.

The President's Leadership. Of what does this leadership consist? Does it follow the moods of the public and clamor of groups, or does it seek to shape them? Presidents have acted with scant regard for public support in concluding treaties with foreign states which did not require submission to the Senate, so-called Presidential executive agreements. They have withheld information from the public and from Congress, and they have taken measures abroad committing the country to later action, without specific authorization from Congress. Franklin D. Roosevelt, "when confronted by an apathetic public and a critical foreign menace, felt compelled to deceive the people into an awareness of their peril." [33] Yet other Presidents have declined to assume such responsibilities.

The dilemma of Presidential leadership and dependence upon public and congressional support is well illustrated by the contemporary military strategy of the United States. President Truman's desire to station American troops in Europe without congressional approval, but in conformance with treaty obligations, was challenged by conservative Democrats and Republicans alike, and the President's freedom of action was circumscribed. President Eisenhower's administration sometimes speaks of a strategy of "massive atomic retaliation," depending on American air power rather than on coalition ground forces. Who can order such retaliation? When and where shall it be applied? War is certain to result from it; but the President as commander in chief of the armed forces seems to have the power unilaterally to make the crucial decision. Yet that power is disputed by many and according to one conservative Republican, "The fundamental issue . . . is whether the

[33] Burns and Peltason, *op. cit.*, p. 609.

President shall decide when the United States shall go to war or whether the people of the United States themselves shall make that decision." [34] Liberal Republicans and liberal Democrats do not agree and insist on the President's primacy. Hence a case study of how leadership was actually exercised by a "strong" President should prove instructive.[35]

Leadership and the Cabinet. These ambiguities of Presidential leadership in policy formulation, depending as they do on the Chief Executive's ideology, consistency, strength of conviction, and advisers, are compounded further if the participation of the Cabinet is taken into account. Just as political parties are coalitions of diverse groups and beliefs, most American Cabinets reflect the same heterogeneity. Conflicts on the ends of policy can and do arise in the thinking and recommendations of the President's advisers, reflecting usually the ideological preconceptions of the members. No wonder that Cabinet meetings did not always prove able to resolve conflicts, especially if the President had not made up his own mind or chose to be vague. Thus Secretary of War Stimson confided to his diary that Cabinet meetings in 1945 were "the same old two-and-sixpence, no earthly good." [36]

Disagreement on Ends: Germany. Ideological conflict among Cabinet members prevented the formulation of a clear postwar policy for Germany. Initially, Roosevelt appointed a committee of Hull, Stimson, Hopkins, and Morgenthau to work out a plan. Hull and Stimson favored a Germany strong enough to survive economically, able to trade and manufacture, for "unless this commerce was protected she could not probably feed her population by agriculture." [37] Morgenthau and Hopkins, however, were determined to reduce Germany to a pastoral state, by razing the great Ruhr and Saar industrial centers and making industry impossible. Roosevelt's trusted adviser and the Secretary of the Treasury were far more intent on punishing Nazi Germany for her sins and keeping her weak than was true of the heads of the War and State Departments, who were more interested in achieving a stable postwar world, in which Germany would not remain an economic burden for the Allies. They argued merely for "control or trusteeship or even transfers of ownership [of industrial plants] to other nations," but not the pastoralization of Germany.

Before a final decision was made, Churchill met Roosevelt at Quebec and the two approved the "Morgenthau plan." "Hull was so angry when he got this message that he expressed a desire to resign." [38] A journalistic leak to the public then focused popular attention on the plan, and opposition imme-

---

[34] Robert A. Taft, *A Foreign Policy for Americans,* Doubleday, New York, 1951, pp. 21–23.

[35] See the discussion of the destroyers-for-bases deal, Chap. 13, for illustration.

[36] H. Stimson and McG. Bundy, *On Active Service in Peace and War,* Harper, New York, 1948, p. 561.

[37] *Ibid.,* p. 568.

[38] Millis, *op. cit.,* p. 12.

diately developed. Thereupon, Hull and Stimson counterattacked and demanded that Roosevelt withdraw his approval. The President did retract his endorsement of the impetuous Morgenthau in October, 1944, but the initial occupation directive still enjoined American officials to "take no steps (*a*) looking toward the economic rehabilitation of Germany, or (*b*) designed to maintain or strengthen the German economy."[39] In later years, Stimson's supporters in the occupation continued to berate the Treasury Secretary's as "Morgenthau boys."

Disagreement on Means: The Far East. Policy differences in the Cabinet with respect to the Far East, however, exemplify possible disagreements over factors other than ideology. The objective assessment of the situation may differ from department to department. Means for carrying out universally accepted ends may differ radically in proportion to these varying assessments, and basic disagreements over proper policy may result, even though no ideological cleavage divides the warring secretaries.

Thus the Departments of State and Defense, after 1949, differed sharply in their evaluations of the military and political power of the exiled Kuomintang regime on Formosa, and on the importance to American strategy of Syngman Rhee's South Korean government. Defense wished to withdraw from Korea and support Formosa; State argued for—and obtained—commitment in Korea in 1950 and a momentary reduction of aid to Chiang.[40] These implications of Far Eastern policy will be examined in a later case study.[41]

The National Security Council. Is there no mechanism for overcoming these clashes on ends as well as means in the President's official family? Joint planning by all departments concerned has long been in use. A multitude of interdepartmental committees has sought to achieve liaison and coordination to bring the policies of all concerned into line. The record indicates, however, that joint planning and careful coordination or thinking do not necessarily produce agreement, especially if rival ideological positions are involved. The most far-reaching of such attempts at permanent interdepartmental planning was taken in the creation of the National Security Council.

The Council has had its ups and downs, and it has by no means overcome the difficulties inherent in the political leadership problems of a pluralistic democracy, in which not even leaders of the same party agree on all basic principles. The Council is composed of the President, the Vice President, the Secretaries of State and Defense, while the heads of the Central Intelligence Agency and of the Joint Chiefs of Staff participate when requested. It has its own small secretariat, and its secretary works in close conjunction with the President and Central Intelligence. The task of the Council is simply to dis-

[39] J. L. McCamy, *The Administration of American Foreign Affairs,* Knopf, New York, 1950, pp. 138–139.
[40] *Military Situation in the Far East,* pt. IV, pp. 2577–2645; pt. I, p. 384.
[41] See Chap. 13, Sec. 2.

cuss and plan basic policy decisions or meet specific emergencies, not on the basis of improvised consultations but through permanent association and cooperative judgments.

How has the Council worked? The epitome of smooth functioning is indicated in the 1948 decision to return Trieste to Italy. Early in March of that year, one week before a crucial Italian election in which the Communists were feared to win, Washington learned that Moscow had promised to support the return of the international city of Trieste to Italy, thus supporting the Italian Communist party. State Department experts then recommended that the United States beat Moscow to the punch and promise Italy the same boon first. But what would be the military implications of such a move, since American troops were garrisoning the city? The Secretary of the National Security Council then drafted a research report, in consultation with the professional military and diplomatic advisers of the Council, in which the political and military factors were weighed and assessed. They concluded that return to Italy would be preferable in order to forestall a loss of the entire Italian peninsula to Communist rule. On the lower levels, therefore, agreement between the military, naval, and diplomatic staffs had been secured. The report was then circulated among the members of the Council, who discussed it in secret session a few days later. After some debate between Forrestal and Marshall, the paper was approved and implementation ordered by President Truman. A day later, the United States, Britain, and France informed Italy that she was to be given Trieste. Whether because of this or because of other factors, the Communists were defeated in the election.[42]

Interdepartmental planning thus functioned in the Trieste case. It did not work in the Chinese situation, in the Palestine dispute, or in the Berlin blockade crisis. Decisions in all these situations requiring political leadership were left to the President working with some Cabinet members, but excluding others. We must conclude that not even the National Security Council is a panacea in the search for unified political leadership. Only when the members of the administration are in close agreement on the aims of policy and when their outlooks permit them identical evaluations of foreign crises can the mechanism of permanent joint planning take the place of interdepartmental warfare and diplomacy. This was rarely achieved in the heterogeneous Truman Administration. It appears, however, that with the more unified Eisenhower team the Council has been playing an increasing and consistent planning role. But then it is likely that a Cabinet which represents essentially only one faction of a major party can achieve a unified approach even without the mechanism of formal joint planning.

Congressional Leadership. So far we have limited the discussion of political leadership, or lack thereof, to the President and his Cabinet. Agreement or

[42] J. Alsop and S. Alsop, "How Our Foreign Policy Is Made," *Saturday Evening Post,* Apr. 30, 1949, pp. 30–31, 113–116. Millis, *op. cit.,* pp. 453–454.

disagreement on ends and means has emerged as the chief problem once more. The same conclusion will appear in our examination of the final source of political leadership, the Congress. Congress, as the forum of discussion for leaders of the majority party as well as of the opposition, naturally represents a microcosm of the ideological and policy issues confronting and confounding the various elites. A firm policy stand taken by a highly respected Senator, such as the late Arthur Vandenberg, can give leadership to a divided house in supporting or opposing the administration. Hence the role of Congress is the crucial imponderable for any President anxious to provide leadership, since the aspirations originating from Capitol Hill may well counter those of the White House. As Cordell Hull saw his problem in relation to the lawmakers: [43]

Our policy of international cooperation faced almost overwhelming isolationist opposition during the years 1933–1941. . . . Hence, while advocating international cooperation at all times, we were faced with the extremely delicate task of being careful not to present and urge measures in such numbers as to alarm the people and precipitate isolation as an acute political issue in the nation. Had we done so, the Roosevelt Administration would have been thrown out of power bodily as soon as the American public had a chance to go to the polls, and the nation would have been thrown back still farther to the extreme isolationist period. . . . Our only alternative, therefore, was constantly to urge upon the country a general policy of international cooperation in every way we could, and from time to time present for Congressional approval such proposals as an arms embargo applied against an aggressor . . . and more flexible Neutrality legislation. These on their very face contravened nationalistic policies. . . . Wherever the matter before Congress seemed about to become a serious national isolation issue, we did not press it to the point of a national campaign.

Partisan debate rules Congress, even though it may not be on the basis of strict party divisions. Hence the President's opponents will challenge his leadership almost by definition, while his supporters will rally behind him. Enemies and critics on Capitol Hill, for example, insisted that President Truman had no right to commit American forces in the Korean conflict without a previous congressional declaration of war. "Now I would like to know what the difference, what special category this particular war is in whereby it does not require a declaration of war, but that the President, as you say, can start the war and conduct the war," Senator Byrd said.[44] Other advocates of congressional supremacy chastised the Truman Administration for failing to give Congress sufficient information on foreign affairs to make policy, while Senator Wiley argued that the President lacked the power to dismiss General MacArthur if he failed to present a bill of particulars to

---

[43] Cordell Hull, *Memoirs of Cordell Hull,* Macmillan, New York, 1948, vol. I, pp. 176–177.

[44] *Military Situation in the Far East,* pt. V., p. 3583; pt. III, pp. 2013–2017.

Congress.[45] Naturally, the supporters of the Truman Administration took issue with all these claims for congressional dominance, but the controversy demonstrates the role of partisan conflict and the likelihood that leadership will take the form of two opposing sets of principles competing for public attention. What are the proposed remedies for this manifestation of pluralism?

Bipartisanship. Bipartisanship is the panacea held out in this area. Senator Vandenberg, one of the architects of a bipartisan foreign policy during World War II and after, thought that "regardless of political differences at home, we are serving notice on the world that America is united to protect American rights everywhere and through firmness in the right to seek peace with justice for ourselves and the other peace-loving peoples of the world." [46]

This definition means little unless one examines the situations in which it was applied and the mechanism through which it was to become operative. It rests on the basic assumption that "politics should stop at the water's edge" and that a united nation should respond to policy leadership once a certain external danger point has been reached. How can consensus emerge from heterogeneous groups and parties, or more basically, how can agreement be reached on where the "water's edge" begins? Advocates of bipartisanship explain that this requires some or all of the following procedures: constant collaboration between the President and Congress; participation of *minority-*party members in the planning, drafting, and discussion of legislation; appointment of minority-party members to international conference delegations and to the United Nations; frequent informal briefing of minority-party members by the Executive; bipartisan congressional study and research committees to explore new legislation in cooperation with the Executive.

To what policy decisions has this process been applied and where has it been omitted? One student concludes that [47]

Bipartisanship applies to "new departures" in foreign policy which marked a significant break with past undertakings, or preceded the adoption of novel and costly foreign policy ventures which constituted major milestones on the march against Soviet imperialism. In both categories, interparty consultations operated only where Congress played a part in policy formulation.

Such ventures included the drafting of the UN Charter, of the post-1945 inter-American treaties, the North Atlantic Pact, the peace treaties with the Axis satellites and with Japan, the Truman Doctrine, and the European Recovery Program. Equally significant, however, are the areas in which the process was not used. These include the Yalta and Potsdam conferences, all aspects of policy regarding China and Korea, all aspects of foreign economic

[45] *Ibid.,* pt. I, p. 413; pt. V, p. 3598.

[46] Vandenberg's radio address of Oct. 4, 1948, *Vital Speeches of the Day,* Oct. 15, 1948, pp. 11–14.

[47] R. A. Fuller, "Case Studies in Bipartisanship United States Postwar Foreign Policy," unpublished Ph.D. dissertation, University of Wisconsin, Madison, Wis., 1953, p. 1.

policy, except ERP, the Mutual Defense Program, and the exclusion of foreign policy questions from Presidential election campaigns, though in the contests of 1940, 1944, and 1948 partisan debate centered around the means rather than the ends of policy.[48]

The Touchstone: China. The reasons which persuaded the administration to by-pass the interparty consultation process are most revealing of the true nature of bipartisanship. "This area included policies in which Congress played no significant role . . . in which the prior assumptions of the two leading parties varied so greatly as to preclude inter-party understandings, and areas which were primarily of a negative or 'wait-and-see' nature, like China. . . ." [49] Domestic pressure groups in cooperation with Nationalist Chinese representatives were quick to utilize the divergence among the parties and therefore attached themselves to the conservatives in encouraging sweeping criticism of the administration's vacillations. Democratic overtures to discontinue aid to China were countered with Republican demands for more support to Chiang. Even Vandenberg exclaimed that,[50]

We virtually "sold China down the river" at Yalta and Potsdam and in our subsequent demands for coalition with the armed Chinese Communists. I have always opposed this program. . . . I favor an affirmative policy of vigilance and helpfulness in the Far East. . . . We must not surrender the Far East to the Soviets.

Senator Wiley agrees that the bipartisan mechanism will work only if the parties are previously agreed on the basis of policy: [51]

I believe that the basic reason the Administration failed to consult the Republican minority in the Senate and House on Far Eastern policies was that the Administration knew that it would run into the severest opposition. . . . For bipartisanship to succeed, it is essential that the Administration be willing to accept frank criticism and to act upon it, assuming it is, of course, constructive. The Administration, however, felt "what they don't know won't hurt us. The less they know the better."

Consultations on the controversial mutual-security and technical-assistance programs were initiated only *after* the opposition had begun to emasculate the administration proposals and the "bipartisan" process was then resorted to only to save something of the Truman foreign-aid approach. Neither unity nor leadership was in evidence as the unilateralism of the conservative opposition found its way into the programs.

On balance, it appears that bipartisanship by no means overcomes the diversity of opinion implicit in a pluralistic nation wedded to democratic

[48] *Ibid.*
[49] *Ibid.*, p. 197.
[50] A. Vandenberg, Jr. (ed.), *The Private Papers of Senator Vandenberg,* Houghton Mifflin, Boston, 1952, p. 536.
[51] Fuller, *op. cit.*, p. 276.

group expression. At best, it results in common planning in essentially non-controversial areas, and at worst it is merely an alliance between the administration and certain leaders of the opposition who are predisposed to favor the administration's course.[52] And incidentally, the administration may succeed in stifling opposition comment by branding its critics as "sabotaging" bipartisanship and thereby weakening national policy while "the Kremlin is watching." Consistent and firm political leadership in policy making, whether from the President, Congress, or the Cabinet, therefore, cannot be expected in American society unless firm traditions of either withdrawal or intervention—but not both—become part of the American myth. So far, this has not happened, but the future may decree otherwise.

5. Professional Leadership and Policy Making. If the elected and appointed politician is unable to bridge the ideological chasms of American life, it still remains possible that the permanent official, whether civil servant, Foreign Service officer, or military man, can give direction and firmness to the nation's foreign policy. Military officers or bureaucrats who owe their permanent positions to appointment on the basis of merit and competence, who are independent of the electorate and of interest groups, could, presumably, see the "national interest" in dispassionate terms. But this would presuppose that they somehow "think alike" and bring a uniform code of disinterested service to bear on the policy recommendations they send to their political chiefs. It assumes objectivity, detachment, and freedom from ideological thought patterns.

One preliminary question, however, must be raised with respect to professional leadership. In principle, the civil servant is "neutral," i.e., he carries out policy but he does not make it; nor does he object to or protest decisions made by his political superiors. If this were the case in actuality, there could be no question of professional leadership, since an exclusive activity of implementation would preclude a public or private stand on the basic questions of policy aims. Is the American bureaucrat, civil or military, a neutral administrator in this sense? The evidence suggests that he is not.

Ideology and the Civil Service. The motives which impel many persons to enter government service provide one clue as to the ephemeral nature of bureaucratic neutrality in American life. Frequently, individuals seek government employ precisely because they hope to influence the course of policy. They may be technically trained as economists, conservationists, or lawyers and thus search for a creative outlet for their ideological convictions in public service. Planning or *laissez faire,* public control of forests or private exploitation, may be the very values which these men hope to implement and which private employment or private life would render inaccessible. Hence they enter government to translate values into policy and not to be neutral.

Military officers may display the same urge to express their beliefs through

[52] *Ibid.,* pp. 409, 430, 445. A. Vandenberg, Jr., *op. cit.,* pp. 532–533.

policy. General Omar Bradley could say, "I am neither a Democrat nor a Republican. I think it would be improper if I were, in my position. I have never voted, and if I ever do, which I expect to do after I retire . . . I expect to vote on the issues." [53] General Marshall could argue that an officer while on active duty should never speak up against higher policy but argue his beliefs in private through the proper channels.[54] But these instances of neutrality must be balanced against the equally prevalent view that "the fact that any group in authority, in carrying out its responsibilities makes decisions, that when they make that decision every man accepts it as an infallibly correct one is absurd." [55] The same professional, General Mac-Arthur, went so far as to argue that the political leadership should exercise no control over the handling of troops in war, while Air Force commandant Hoyt Vandenberg maintained that an officer has the duty to disagree publicly with the political leadership when he thinks its policies incorrect.[56] Clearly, there is no consistent and universally practiced neutrality among professional officials. Their efforts to influence policy must be taken for granted.

Hence detached policy planning is extremely difficult even if done by professional civil servants. Awareness of issues, dangers, and the need for planning prevails; but awareness alone does not permit the sorting of factors in the "national interest" and the discarding of "irrelevant" demands. The State Department possesses a professional policy-planning staff, but its advice is often disregarded by the political leadership as unsuited to the needs and aspirations of the elites in power. Further, the duties of the staff are so heavy that little time for planning remains, even assuming that the planners are really able to achieve a separation of personal beliefs from the public good. The values and interests of the professional civil servant and military man therefore remain in the forefront of the policy-making process. However, it does not appear that State Department or military officials *as such* are characterized by any distinct set of beliefs and evaluations. Like the rest of the civil service, their values run the gamut of the aspirations found generally among American interest groups.

Quarrels among Civilian Professionals. State Department personnel is divided into a career Foreign Service and technical personnel in the regular civil service or hired temporarily. Conflict between these segments has at times been severe. Foreign Service people, from the lowest ranks to the career ambassador or minister, have tended to be recruited from the upper classes, especially from the Northeastern seaboard. In 1950, 40 per cent of the Political Affairs officers had attended private preparatory schools and 19 per

[53] *Military Situation in the Far East,* pt. II, pp. 753, 811.
[54] *Ibid.,* pt. I, p. 389.
[55] *Ibid.,* p. 289, p. 102.
[56] *Ibid.,* pt. II, p. 1385.

cent of all Foreign Service men had come from either Harvard, Yale, or Princeton.[57] State Department workers outside the Foreign Service ranks have considered these career men overly conservative, biased in favor of the country to which they were accredited, prejudiced against nonpolitical research and negotiation, and intent on preserving the *status quo* instead of fostering reforms abroad.[58] These accusations are undoubtedly exaggerated, but they indicate the basic policy differences which may exist among professional civil servants.

Technical civil-service personnel and *ad hoc* professionals from the universities have become increasingly important in the conduct of American foreign policy as gigantic policies of foreign aid, technical assistance, supervised investment, military integration, agricultural productivity, and land reform have become part of the United States programs abroad. President Roosevelt favored the use of such personnel because he considered the politically oriented Foreign Service officer too conservative and unimaginative for these functional tasks. Since these technical people frequently enter public service because they are anxious to influence the foreign policy of their government, their ideological convictions have frequently clashed with those of the Foreign Service, giving rise not only to rival policies abroad but to clashing recommendations at the political leadership level at home.

The quarrel between the State Department and the Economic Cooperation Administration is a classic example of such difficulties. State was interested initially in a financially modest program of assistance to Europe, geared to the traditional policy of encouraging a maximum of free trade through the reciprocal relaxation of tariffs, exchange controls, and quantitative restrictions, but opposed to extensive American intervention in the economies of the recipient countries. ECA, however, was led by many liberal Republicans and business executives on temporary government service, who were concerned with exporting the American business philosophy to Europe. Furthermore, they tended to favor the economic integration of Europe and the rapid modernization of European industry, without insisting on the re-creation of global free trade at the same time, thereby necessarily engaging in a species of intervention. Conflict between State and ECA missions abroad was continuous, especially since the two were administratively separated in each foreign country. Ends as well as means were in dispute among servants of the same government and the same national interest. Professional leadership displayed the same diversity of aims as did the political policy makers and the elites with whom they were associated.

Quarrels among Military Professionals. In the area of military policy the same conclusion must be reached. Hence it is fallacious to speak of a "military

---

[57] McCamy, *op. cit.,* pp. 91, 194.

[58] Hoover Commission, *Task Force Report on Foreign Affairs,* GPO, Washington, 1949, pp. 113, 123.

mind" coming dangerously close to dominating American policy making, based on the principle of civilian supremacy. Interservice cooperation has existed for a long time, first through the Joint Board and later through the Joint Chiefs of Staff (JCS); yet administrative coordination has failed to produce a uniform state of mind within each service or among them. Stimson notes: [59]

> Differences between the Army and Navy were frequent. . . . Some of the Army-Navy troubles . . . grew mainly from the peculiar psychology of the Navy Department which frequently seemed to retire from the realm of logic into a dim religious world in which Neptune was God, Mahan his prophet and the United States Navy the only true Church.

Forrestal had continuous difficulties with the JCS because of their refusal to make joint policy instead of merely defending the aims of each service. An interservice conference on Guam, in 1945, was conducted "almost on the level of international diplomacy." [60]

Pivotal Role of Military Leaders. This diversity in aims and outlook, however, does not imply that military personnel is not of key importance in political decisions. In 1941, General Marshall and Admiral Stark took it upon themselves to outline the basic aims of American policy in their endeavor to plan industrial production requirements: [61]

> Those major national objectives of the United States which are related to military policy may broadly be stated as: preservation of the territorial, economic and ideological integrity of the United States and of the remainder of the Western Hemisphere; prevention of the disruption of the British Empire; prevention of the further extension of Japanese territorial dominion; eventual establishment in Europe and Asia of balances of power which will most nearly ensure political stability in those regions and the future security of the United States; and, so far as practicable, the establishment of regimes favorable to economic freedom and individual liberty.

"Military policy" in such a setting came to include almost every aspect of American foreign activity. Apparently on "military" grounds alone the military chiefs approved joint Anglo-American plans in 1940 and 1941 to give first priority to the defense of Europe and the Atlantic and consider Japanese occupation of Thailand the *casus belli.* In the absence of firm political guidance from the President, the naval commanders took it upon themselves to initiate cooperation with British and Dutch forces in Southeast Asia several days before the Japanese struck at Pearl Harbor.[62] More recently, mili-

---

[59] Stimson and Bundy, *op. cit.,* p. 506.

[60] Millis, *op. cit.,* pp. 45, 391 ff.

[61] Memorandum of Sept. 11, 1941. Quoted in K. Thompson, "Collective Security Reexamined," *American Political Science Review,* vol. 47, no. 3, September, 1953, p. 765.

[62] H. Feis, *The Road to Pearl Harbor,* Princeton University Press, Princeton, N.J., 1950, pp. 128–140, 167–168, 302, 322–338.

tary considerations and planning entered continuously into the drafting of the Japanese peace treaty, both in the timing of the pact and in terms of its substance. It was the JCS who recommended in September of 1947 that a free South Korea was not essential for the military security of the United States. The key importance of military evaluations and recommendations thus cannot be denied. Yet it does not follow that such activity either contravenes the preferences of civilian officials or results from a uniform military outlook.

The conduct of the Korean War lucidly illustrates the impact of various patterns of thought among civilian and military professionals in government. Generals MacArthur, Wedemeyer, Van Fleet, and Clark, as well as Admiral Radford, backed by conservative lawmakers in both parties, refused to assess the Korean hostilities as a "police action," in which the United States was subject to allied and United Nations control. They argued for all-out war, or withdrawal—not for the "limited" war endorsed by Generals Marshall, Gruenther, and Collins and liberal politicians. Cooperation with America's allies, common front with NATO and the UN, firm but cautious commitment abroad, these were the guiding concepts of the administration and the Joint Chiefs of Staff. Unilateral action or isolation were the opposing alternatives suggested by the administration's critics. Thus all the ambivalences and conflicts of mood in American society are present in all levels of leadership, political and professional, civilian and military.

Having analyzed the American myth and the group ideologies functioning within it, and having examined the structure of political and professional leadership, its modes of thought and conflicts, it now remains to analyze American foreign policy in action. How does policy emerge from this welter of aspirations, and how are the groups of American society represented in the process?

Chapter 13

THE UNITED STATES: PRINCIPLES OF DEMOCRATIC FOREIGN POLICY MAKING

1. Decision Making in a Pluralistic-democratic Milieu. Suggestions for initiating specific foreign policy measures may originate anywhere in the hierarchy of governmental bureaus, political parties, or private interest groups. Key elites are always ready to urge on Congress and the President their particular demands, whether they be the admission of displaced persons to Israel, the raising of the tariff on watches, or the liberation of Lithuania from Soviet control. Party factions always stand ready to fight for the exportation of agricultural surpluses (if the member of Congress comes from the farm belt) or the relaxation of immigration laws (if the member happens to hail from New York). Yet basic policy matters, such as the conclusion of alliances or the adoption of policies of containment, rarely originate on these levels.

Fundamental policy departures develop as a result of close interaction among all these groups, but they usually originate in the professional ranks of the government hierarchy. Continuous foreign intelligence reports flow into the Central Intelligence Agency, which collects, analyzes, and disseminates whatever information is amassed. State Department missions abroad report daily on the most general and the most minute trends and events in foreign countries. Diplomatic and intelligence data thus find their way in an unbroken stream to the desks of the bureaucrats responsible for policy recommendations. Once a point has been reached at which the information received from abroad seems to call for a definite step by the United States, memoranda analyzing the problem and suggesting remedies will be submitted to the political leaders of the government.

At that level, policy making becomes a function of the President, individual Cabinet members, and the National Security Council. Intensive consultations among these men now set in. But a major decision on foreign policy depends on the acquiescence of a sizable congressional majority. After a decision has been made by the policy makers, the legislators have to be convinced as well, if they differ from the party faction in control of the White House. This, in turn, calls for extensive consultations with the elites who are closely associated with congressional and executive leaders. Consequently, private conversations with leading members of interest groups will be undertaken; radio addresses will be made by Cabinet members, the President, and friendly legislators; attempts will be made to mobilize the press in favor of the new course. On occasion, though this is by no means true generally, foreign policy issues will be fought out in the context of national elections and thus call for continuous submission by the policy makers to the public at large.

Still, it is evident that the process of decision making must vary a good deal with the circumstances. In a crisis situation a sudden and secret decision may have to be made, of which policy toward China in 1944 and 1945 will serve as a case study. Special decisions in which domestic groups have a direct interest may be called for, such as the course of American policy toward Palestine in 1948. Finally, basic new courses are demanded at times, calling for the most extensive kind of consultations and publicity. In this category fall the case studies of the development of the destroyers-for-bases deal in 1940 and the European Recovery Program.

2. Crisis Decision Making: China Policy, 1944 to 1945. In 1944 both China and the United States were seeking to defeat Japan. China, however, was split into two factions: the Kuomintang regime under Chiang Kai-shek ruling the southwest from Chungking, the Communists ruling the northwest from Yenan, with the eastern portion of the country under Japanese control. Which faction was to be supported by American military and political aid? That was the question confronting policy makers in Washington, especially after the Japanese surrendered in August of 1945 and the rival factions began to fight for military control of all China, while the Soviet Union moved into Manchuria and millions of Japanese soldiers had to be repatriated to their homeland.

Conflicting Local Reports. American personnel in China disagreed sharply on this question. During the latter half of 1944 Foreign Service officers felt that the Kuomintang was dictatorial, financially corrupt, militarily unable and unwilling to fight the Japanese. The Yenan Communists,[1]

if shown friendship by us . . . could align their actions to the policies of the West; or if they failed to do so and broke with the United States, they would lose the support of Chinese democratic public opinion. While . . . if we turned our back on them and our arms against them, they would go over to Moscow; and with or without Soviet aid might well come into power in China.

Hence they argued for American military support to Yenan, supplemented with pressure on Chiang to form a coalition government and to cease fighting the Communists.

Ambassador Hurley and General Wedemeyer felt otherwise. They sympathized with Chiang and "found the company and ways of the members

[1] H. Feis, *The China Tangle,* Princeton University Press, Princeton, N.J., 1953, p. 263.

of the government agreeable." [2] They were satisfied with Chinese military performance against Japan; and while they agreed to the desirability of a coalition government, they were unwilling to make American aid to Chungking conditional on domestic reforms and accommodation with Yenan. Ideology and objective evaluations clashed sharply in the American mission. The quarrel was carried to Washington, the Foreign Service officers denouncing the Ambassador for sending "incomplete and nonobjective" reports, and Hurley going home in March of 1945 to accuse his accusers and ask for a clear policy of support to Chiang. All government departments overtly agreed with Hurley; the dissident officers were transferred, but no basic policy decision was made. [3]

Disagreement in Washington. In February of 1945, however, President Roosevelt in cooperation with the JCS and some members of the Cabinet had made the Yalta agreement, under which the Soviet Union promised to enter the war against Japan and was assured of a special economic position in Manchuria. As regards China, the JCS recommended that aid be continued for six months after the end of hostilities, in terms of both matériel and personnel to train a modern Nationalist army. Before a Presidential decision on these recommendations—basically in agreement with the Hurley-Wedemeyer outlook—had been made, however, the final struggle between Yenan and Chungking over the control of north China began. The JCS met with State, Navy, and War Department representatives to hammer out policy. The civilians, and especially the State Department, argued that aid should be continued only if Chiang reformed his regime and admitted members of China's other parties into it. The JCS, however, held out for an aid policy seeking merely to create a "friendly, unified, independent nation [in China] with a stable government resting, insofar as practicable, on the freely expressed support of the Chinese people." [4] A vague compromise was finally decided upon, extending aid to Chiang with the possibility of discontinuance if the Generalissimo failed to make efforts to come to terms with Yenan. Discussion and bickering were confined entirely to the departments concerned; the public had little knowledge of these considerations.

Indecisive Intervention. As the situation in north China deteriorated to Chiang's disadvantage late in the summer of 1945, the Generalissimo requested American assistance to transport his troops to Manchuria. The service secretaries now came out for using American forces in the area for that purpose, while the State Department held out for restricting them to repatriate the remaining Japanese. Another compromise resulted under which American naval forces were to carry troops to Manchuria, Marines were to protect the major ports, but efforts were to be made at the same time to

[2] *Ibid.*, pp. 260 ff.
[3] *Ibid.*, pp. 265–272.
[4] *Ibid.*, p. 375.

arrange a truce and reconstitute the Kuomintang regime. General Marshall was sent to China to carry out the negotiations in December of 1945. Yet the chasm separating the departments seeking to make a rapid and secret decision was by no means overcome. Marshall's instructions, though drafted after consultation with the JCS, the local commanders and the departments concerned, continued the ambiguous compromise policy which had been followed for over a year. Marshall was to use the activities of the American forces to threaten the Communists to come to terms and also hint at the withdrawal of armed support if Chiang proved to be recalcitrant. Yet in case of doubt, Marshall was instructed to use these forces to the exclusive advantage of the Kuomintang.[5]

The Marshall mission of spring, 1946, was a failure, and with the growing success of the Communists, American military opinion in Washington and Tokyo hardened in support of Chiang. Secretary Forrestal took up the cry, holding out for more and more aid, while Secretary of Labor Schwellenbach —in agreement with several other Cabinet members—argued that "he saw no reason why we should continue to interfere in the affairs of China; [if] they wanted to have a civil war they should have it, but that we should not be in the position of trying to impose any form of government on any nation." [6] The State Department thereafter sought to wash its hands of the matter and quietly advocated the withdrawal of American personnel, since it was felt that Chiang's government had progressed too far toward disintegration to make continued shoring-up feasible. But the halfway policy of continuing some aid was carried on nevertheless.

Who participated in the making of the China "policy" beside the State and Defense Departments and the JCS? At first, the quarrel was within and among these groups only. After 1945, however, opposition leaders in Congress, backed by Forrestal and vocal interest groups in the country, urged the continuation of aid; the policy of "some but not enough aid" to Chiang resulted as the compromise between these dissident pressures, while the Kuomintang was being defeated and Chiang's regime collapsed. Finally, China policy fanned out into a major national issue to take its place as one of the crucial items in the partisan debates of 1950 to 1952, mixed with charges of espionage and treason and the search for scapegoats. A secret policy decision which could not be made in 1944 had become a political football by 1950. Even though the problem originated within the ranks of the professional policy makers and concerned only the President and the department heads later in the game, the mere fact that basic disagreement existed among these participants in the policy-formulation process made a final entry of Congress and interested elites a possibility.

[5] *Ibid.*, chap. 37.
[6] W. Millis (ed.), *The Forrestal Diaries,* Viking, New York, 1951, pp. 177–190; quotation on p. 190.

3. Limited Group Participation in Decision Making: Palestine Policy, 1948. Interest groups, however, were vitally concerned with America's policy toward Palestine right from the beginning, and no possibility ever existed of keeping the problem within the ranks of the professional and political leadership. Public interest began to be focused on Palestine when a number of Jewish organizations, supported by such groups as the National Council of Churches, called attention to the plight of the European Jews who, at the end of World War II, had survived Nazi persecution. These were kept in displaced-persons camps on the Continent while the British government refused to give permission for their resettlement in Palestine. The reason for Britain's stand lay in her policy of supporting the Arab countries generally and in her unwillingness to fight Arab riots and insurrections which were certain to break out with large-scale Jewish immigration. Should the United States support Britain, an allied nation, and therefore the Arabs? Or should the principle of a Jewish national home in Israel be the cornerstone of American policy? Powerful forces worked in both directions.

Departmental Bickering. Thus when the UN sought to find a solution to the rival claims over Palestine in the summer of 1947, Undersecretary of State Lovett reasoned in favor of supporting the Arabs: "While much emphasis has been placed on the distress, the commotion among the Jews, there was an equal danger of solidifying sentiment among all of the Arab and Moslem peoples against the United States." [7] State's policy was attacked in a Cabinet luncheon on September 4, 1947, when Democratic National Chairman Hannegan wished President Truman to make a public statement advocating the immediate admission of 150,000 Jewish displaced persons to Palestine. Fund raising for the Democratic party would be facilitated in this fashion, reasoned Hannegan. While Truman opposed this as interfering with the negotiations underway at the UN, Forrestal called for a pro-Arab policy because he wished to initiate the construction of a new oil pipeline in the Middle East to make up for the fuel deficiencies of America's armed forces.[8] "No group in this country should be permitted to influence our policy to the point where it could endanger our national security," he said in opposing Zionist policy demands.[9] The Defense Secretary lectured his Cabinet colleagues long and hard on the military necessity of making friends of the Arabs and even showed his opponents intelligence reports to back up his arguments. He tried, in cooperation with New York banker Winthrop Aldrich, Thomas Dewey, and Lovett, to take Palestine "out of politics" entirely.

Party Politics Are Supreme. The pro-Zionist Cabinet faction, supported by much of the press and the work of religious and ethnic interest groups, coun-

[7] *Ibid.*, p. 306.
[8] *Ibid.*, pp. 309–310, 323–324.
[9] *Ibid.*, p. 344.

tered by saying that "there were two or three pivotal states which could not be carried without the support of people who were deeply interested in the Palestine question," [10] a pointed reference to large blocs of Jewish voters in New York, Illinois, and California. They pointed to the support which Jewish groups had traditionally given the Democratic party and Attorney-General McGrath therefore wanted the United States to back up a pro-Jewish partition plan with troops.

The pressure on the President for not taking the decision "out of politics" was overwhelming in the end and he refused to submit the case to the National Security Council. Judge Rosenman urged Truman to support the Zionists because if he failed to do so in time, the GOP would embrace Zionist aims first.[11] Lovett's and Forrestal's opposition to a more consistent pro-Zionist policy by America's representative at the UN faded after more and more key Democratic leaders supported partition and no formal recommendation at all was made to the President.

Truman, however, made the decision independently of his Cabinet advisers. When the Jews in Palestine declared their independence on May 15, 1948, Truman ordered the new state recognized almost immediately. Further, he ordered the pro-Zionist James G. MacDonald to be appointed as minister to Israel, despite Lovett's protests. "The President had told [Clark Clifford, presidential aide] he did not want any discussion of the matter but to have action followed at once . . . by the State Department," Lovett was informed by the White House.[12] The process of discussion, consultation, and coordination within the Executive was resolved by a Presidential decision taken on the basis of interest-group demands. Forces and elites allied with the Democratic party carried the final choice before the political leadership, while such oil interests as were identified with the Republican party and conservative Democrats were defeated. The unity of domestic with international politics is here clearly demonstrated. Policy makers cannot decide issues on any other basis, since the total process of participation takes in groups on all levels if the question is one which concerns them intimately.

4. Basic New Departures: General Participation in Decision Making. Policy decisions which imply a major new departure, however, cannot be made on the basis of professional and Cabinet discussion alone, nor with the participation of only a few groups which are vitally interested. Congress must be informed and persuaded. If the policy goes against the values and aspirations of significant segments of the public and its elites, an effort must be made to rally them behind the new program and, if necessary, compromise its terms so as to give it a maximum of acceptability.

Intervention in 1940? Thus in the summer of 1940 the Roosevelt Administration faced the task of persuading the nation to the policy of supporting

[10] *Ibid.*, p. 344. [12] *Ibid.*, pp. 440–441.
[11] *Ibid.*, pp. 346–347, 360–361.

the cause of Britain more actively than had been done that far. Repeal of neutrality legislation, speedy reorganization of the economy for war production, economic planning, and the institution of compulsory military service were the major facets of the Administration's program.

The opposition to this major break with decades of isolationism was spearheaded by the America First Committee, an interest group composed of liberals and conservatives alike; their common aim was to prevent American entry into the war. Its members included prominent persons from all groups and elites: General Wood, Sears, Roebuck executive; Senator Burton K. Wheeler; Charles Lindbergh; and President Robert Hutchins of the University of Chicago. The Committee opposed aid to Britain precisely because it might lead to ultimate involvement in war. As Representative Thrill of Wisconsin put it: [13]

If Hitler wins the war, will it promote friendly relations for him to know that we aided his enemies and sought to ruin him and his country with our war equipment? . . . If the Allies win, will they not criticize us for having given too little and for giving only at a price?

Implicit in this evaluation was the age-old distrust of Europe. "We will never again be fools enough to send a single American mother's son to double-crossing Europe," was the succinct summary of one isolationist.[14] The corrupt Old World would not prove amenable to American efforts and would scoff at American values. Why bother with "saving" the Old World, then, instead of concentrating exclusively on America's defense?

The President Arouses Opinion. To this widespread sentiment Roosevelt and his advisers had to reply. As early as December of 1939, the President himself had taken the initiative in suggesting privately to the famous and respected editor of the *Emporia Gazette,* William Allen White, that [15]

Things move with such terrific speed these days that it is really essential to us to think in broader terms and, in effect, to warn the American people that they, too, should think of possible ultimate results in Europe and the Far East. Therefore, my sage old friend, my problem is to get the American people to think of conceivable consequences without scaring the American people into thinking that they are going to be dragged into this war. . . .

In his State of the Union address of January 3, 1940, Roosevelt expressed these same opinions publicly and strongly, thus in effect throwing the gauntlet openly to the isolationist opposition. At Charlottesville, on June 10, 1940, the President used Italy's "act of treachery" against France as his symbol

---

[13] W. L. Langer and J. S. Gleason, *The Challenge to Isolation,* Harper, New York, 1952, p. 504.

[14] *Ibid.,* p. 683, statement of commentator Hugh Johnson, radio address, Aug. 23, 1940.

[15] F. D. Roosevelt to W. A. White, Dec. 14, 1939; *ibid.,* pp. 347, 516.

for calling on the nation to rearm and to give greater and greater material aid to embattled Britain.

Opinion Supporting Intervention. This trend of thinking within the ranks of the political and professional policy makers had its counterpart among many private interest groups who had no need for this kind of persuasion. Some liberal Republicans, such as Presidential candidate Wendell Willkie, agreed with the President. White urged the President to go ahead more speedily. But it was the countergroup to the America Firsters, the Committee to Defend America by Aiding the Allies, which bore the brunt of the interventionist battle. "Government of the people, by the people, for the people— if Hitler wins this will be the discarded ideal of a decayed civilization," was the battle cry of the group in its campaign to "stop Hitler now!" [16] An inner circle within the Committee, known as the Century Group, advocated immediate full-scale help to Britain, including the sending of American warships, and open war if necessary. The group included prominent members of many of America's elites—naval and military men, lawyers, businessmen, men of letters, and journalists.[17] It was the Century Group which took the initiative in proposing the destroyers-for-bases deal and in defending the program before the public. Private elites committed to intervention worked in cooperation with the political leadership, while private elites opposed to the same course worked with the opposition in Congress. The showdown came with the British request of June, 1940, asking for unprecedented American aid including the sale of 100 destroyers and large quantities of additional arms.

The Destroyers-for-bases Deal. Roosevelt felt unable to comply because of continued isolationist opposition to such a blatantly unneutral act and because there was some doubt as to the legality of the sale under legislation then in force. American military leaders and the ambassador in London, Joseph Kennedy, were skeptical of Britain's ability to resist with or without the aid. Yet the Century Group immediately argued for honoring the request, supplied the President with legal memoranda to prove the admissibility of the action without changes in the law, and urged a new survey of Britain's position to prove her capabilities of continuing resistance to the Nazis. Its members propagandized in the press and called upon Cabinet members to aid in changing the President's and the public's reactions. A *quid pro quo* was developed by the Group and submitted to the administration: in exchange for the destroyers, Britain was to give the United States access to bases in British Western Hemisphere possessions. Through this device, the Group hoped to kill two birds with one stone: the argument of the illegality of the

---

[16] Advertisement by Robert Sherwood, June 10, 1940; *ibid.*, p. 506. Privately, Roosevelt agreed with the program, though not with the timetable, of this group. J. L. McCamy, *The Administration of American Foreign Affairs*, Knopf, New York, 1950, p. 143.

[17] *Ibid.*, pp. 710–711.

sale was to be overcome by demonstrating that American security was safe-guarded more directly by the acquisition of new Atlantic bases for defense; and isolationist objections could be met by satisfying the opposition's long-standing demand for the expulsion of European powers from the West Indies.[18]

As new and urgent telegrams poured in from London, Roosevelt's Cabinet took up these proposals on August 2, 1940. They were accepted, with the double proviso that William Allen White be persuaded to obtain Republican Presidential candidate Willkie's approval and that leading Republicans in Congress be sounded out prior to submitting the necessary legislation to Capitol Hill. White agreed, and the process was underway.

Negotiations with the British went forward, and even though the number of vessels was reduced to fifty and the terms of the transfer of bases modified in Britain's favor, no serious difficulties were encountered in this sphere. Willkie, however, balked and refused to support the deal publicly. Undaunted, the Century Group induced the most respected of American military leaders, General Pershing, to make a radio address in favor of the proposal, while the Committee to Aid the Allies, in its 600 local chapters, arranged meetings and had petitions signed by millions sent to Washington. Influential naval leaders publicly supported the plan. Yet opposition continued unabated, and the administration despaired of getting the enabling legislation past Congress. Hence Roosevelt proceeded to by-pass Congress and transfer the destroyers through executive action alone, while presenting the deal to the country in such terms as to make it appear that Britain had given up its West Indian bases unilaterally and without expecting a *quid pro quo*.

The great new departure in American policy was an accomplished fact. Still, the political leadership had failed to explain and explore the issues clearly with all interested elites and groups and had declined to submit the matter to a vote of the lawmakers. Discussion there had been plenty; group participation had been loud and lengthy. But no effort had been made to mesh the aspirations of all concerned with the formal process of policy formulation. The opposite procedure was used in another great new inter-ventionist departure in American policy: the European Recovery Program.

The European Recovery Program, 1947 to 1948. The mechanics, purposes, and effects of ERP have been explored previously. This discussion is con-cerned only with the process whereby the new departure was formulated in the democratic environment in which the American policy maker must work. The initiative for the multi-billion-dollar program for the revitalization of the Western European economic and social structure came from the Execu-tive, confronted at that time with a Republican Congress. Secretary For-restal, in a Cabinet meeting on March 7, 1947, suggested to his colleagues that the American business community be mobilized in a campaign to stop

[18] *Ibid.*, pp. 744–762.

the advance of communism in Europe through timely, far-reaching, and long-term countermeasures. President Truman thereupon deputized Forrestal, Acheson, and Treasury Secretary Snyder, a St. Louis banker, to confer with business leaders, listen to their ideas, and persuade them toward an attitude of partnership with the political leadership in an unprecedented economic reconstruction program abroad.[19]

These informal consultations eventually led to formal studies for such a program. Policy memoranda were prepared by the State, Commerce, and Agriculture Departments, several special commissions were appointed by the President, and two congressional committees began to examine a course of long-term American involvement, even before Secretary Marshall made his historic address at Harvard University. Studies and consultations embraced representatives of business, labor, agriculture, the universities and the professions, both major political parties in and out of Congress, and all government departments concerned. When draft legislation for ERP was given to the Eightieth Congress, it represented not only the results of bipartisan discussion but the extensive participation of the most diverse interest groups.

Why Was ERP Accepted? Hence it is only natural that the supporters of ERP saw in the Program the means for translating their particular values into reality. To the members of the President's Committee on Foreign Aid the Program was to ease European social and economic tensions and thus preserve Western institutions and values in Europe. Some spokesmen for agriculture welcomed it because it provided them with European markets for surplus commodities. Patriotic and veterans' groups argued for it since it would sap Communist strength and preserve Western Europe militarily. The National Association of Manufacturers wished the Program to represent a crusade for private enterprise and have it used to discourage the nationalization of industries and economic planning in Europe, while the Committee for Economic Development saw in ERP a way to demonstrate the superiority of American-style free competition over monopolistic practices and cartels. Labor groups favored the Program as well, since they saw in it the means for saving European trade unions from Communist control and because it seemed to give the labor elite its first large-scale opportunity to participate in executing national policy. Opposition to ERP was negligible on the interest-group level; only groups which deplored the by-passing of the UN structure and opponents of any American activity abroad—if this implied working with alien socialists and internationalists—argued against the plan. In Congress, only the consistent defenders of "little government" and tax reduction voted against it. The passage of the Program seemed to presage a new American mood of extensive foreign commitment.

The major credit for the overwhelming acceptance of this major new de-

[19] Millis, *op. cit.,* pp. 251–252.

parture in American policy must go to the process of extensive consultation and group participation. The Democratic administration conceded in advance to the Republican leadership in Congress that the Program should be run on "sound business principles" and conduce toward deflationary policies of high taxes, balanced budgets, and reduced government spending in the recipient countries. Further, it conceded that members of the American business elite should head the Program and that the State Department should not have exclusive control over its implementation. The extensive process of consultation thus made ERP a catchall for a multitude of different and sometimes self-contradictory aspirations, all of which were satisfied to a degree. The appointment of Studebaker Corporation president Paul Hoffman as Administrator of ERP succeeded in giving the whole gigantic effort the appearance of a business undertaking cast as a "sound investment" and designed to "sell America" abroad.

The contrast between the formulation of the European Recovery Program and post-1944 policy in the Far East is striking. One was characterized by publicity, consultations, discussions, hearings, and participation of all the private and public levels of America's infinitely complex society. The other thrived on executive secrecy, interdepartmental bickering, congressional misgivings, and the exclusion of interest groups from policy planning. The reasons for the dichotomy are plain. A consensus could be obtained for a relief program to Europe provided it was made a compendium of group aims. No such possibility existed for the Far East, where the alternatives ranged from the withdrawal favored by some segments of the political leadership and the public to a full-scale intervention at the other extreme. No general formula could—nor can it now—possibly bring all claims under the roof of one consistent policy. Hence the variety of policy-formulation techniques will subsist and recur. Unity of purpose, on the basis of these case studies, can by no means be expected in the American milieu.

5. Objectives of American Foreign Policy before 1940. Group conflict has characterized American foreign policies ever since the struggle between Jefferson and Hamilton about America's stand toward the French Revolution. The tradition of noninvolvement fought with the mood of intervention on behalf of European liberal republicans in 1848; it lost out to its opponent over continental expansion, when America seized and settled the land now covered by the forty-eight states, at the expense of Mexico and Great Britain; and intervention carried the day in the imperialist crusade of 1898. Neutrality and aloofness did not prevent American conquest of Cuba, Puerto Rico, and the Philippines; but the recurrent mood toward withdrawal facilitated their emancipation. A policy of self-assertion was implicit in Hay's Open Door notes, and a disdain for Europe's quarrels did not keep the United States out of two world wars. Clearly, the "tradition" implicit in Washington's oft-quoted Farewell Address is not a political principle which has en-

joyed the universal and unswerving support of all American groups. Past
and present American aims abroad reflect a good deal more than the aspiration toward aloofness.

Noninvolvement and Europe. Yet it is true that Americans overwhelmingly recognized no important interests to defend in Europe prior to 1917.
Europe was considered decadent and corrupt; its wars were held to be
endemic and irremediable. The only alternative to isolation was the complete
remaking of Europe in the American image. This was accepted even by the
groups identified with the Wilsonian crusade of reforming the world toward
democracy and national self-determination. Involvement on the basis of
existing European institutions and practices was rejected by the United
States. Only with the increasing recognition that politics in Europe bear an
intimate relationship to events in other portions of the world in which American groups did acknowledge a lasting concern—the Far East and the Western
Hemisphere—did the attitude of aloofness suffer gradual disintegration. It
must be stressed, therefore, that the attempt to withdraw was observed in
American policy largely vis-à-vis Europe, and in no other part of the globe.
To many American groups only World War I and its aftermath of unrest,
poverty, and revolution demonstrated that this country did possess permanent interests in the Old World; though to others these very disturbances led
to a reassertion of the old creed.

Intervention in the Americas. In any event, in New World relations almost all American parties and groups accepted the dictum of "hands off"
implicit in the Monroe Doctrine. The basic policy of not permitting the
powers of Europe to assert political control over the states of Latin America
or to expand their colonial possessions in the Western Hemisphere was not
seriously questioned after 1824. However, it is equally true that for lengthy
periods the Monroe Doctrine lay forgotten and that it was unearthed only
when specific group aims had to be defended. Thus when American bankers
wished to safeguard their loans to unruly Central American republics and
the State Department felt anxious about European interventions to recover
similar financial outlays—and incidentally to threaten America's strategic
control over the Caribbean—the Monroe Doctrine reappeared in the guise
of the Roosevelt Corollary: the United States would assume responsibility for
peace and stability in the Caribbean, even if this implied the use of armed
force. The doctrine, therefore, was a multipurpose device which enjoyed the
support of varying groups at different times. It was a unilateral American
policy assertion until its conversion into the mutual nonintervention guarantees accepted by all American states in 1936, and until its *de facto* replacement by the multilateral security arrangements explicit in the modern Organization of American States.

Self-assertion in the Far East. If aloofness was striking in its absence
in America's Western Hemisphere policy, much the same can be said

about the Far East. Decades of flourishing trade with China had created an early American interest. in the Orient, especially in New England and later in California. Demands for "opening" the Far East to American traders led to Perry's visit to Japan and to the establishment of American merchants' settlements in China. It contributed heavily to the aim of wresting the Philippines from Spain, to give America a "window opening on the Chinese coast." Generations of missionaries, furthermore, had preached an American duty to convert the millions of the Celestial Empire. Hence Washington's first major assertion of permanent interests took shape in the efforts of John Hay to extract guarantees from Europe and Japan to respect the territorial integrity and independence of the moribund Chinese empire. While the effort proved unsuccessful it nevertheless gave notice that Americans too were interested in China and wished to reserve a share of Far Eastern trade, investment, and missionary activity to themselves.

In marked contrast to post–World War I policy in Europe, Washington was willing to accept binding commitments in the Far East, in the effort to keep Japan and Russia from encroaching on the fabled Chinese mainland. Naval limitations were bartered for reciprocal guarantees of China's integrity in 1921. Yet when the pact was violated ten years later, the mood of commitment and participation had once again changed to withdrawal in the controlling Republican party. As President Hoover declared with respect to America's policy toward the Japanese attack on Manchuria: [20]

This is primarily a controversy between China and Japan. The United States has never set out to preserve peace among other nations by force and so far as this part is concerned we shall confine ourselves to friendly counsel. . . . These acts do not imperil the freedom of the American people, the economic or moral future of our people. I do not propose ever to sacrifice American life for anything short of this. . . .

The historical aims of American policy, therefore, centered around aloofness toward Europe, United States predominance in North America and the Caribbean, and the commitment toward equal access with other nations to the spoils in the Far East. None of these policies was absolutely free from conflict among contending groups, though the Monroe Doctrine was accepted as a minimum by all. Despite the objectives, policies wavered, changed, and responded to alterations in interests and moods. The drive toward expansion in the Far East was countered by the anti-imperialism of Bryan and Wilson. The willingness toward commitment abroad voiced by Root, Taft, and Hughes was rescinded by the urge toward withdrawal expressed by Hoover and Kellogg. The ambivalences of the American myth were present even in the historical aims of policy.

[20] Cited in L. L. Leonard, *Elements of American Foreign Policy*, McGraw-Hill, New York, 1953, p. 220.

6. Objectives of American Policy since 1940. It is often argued that a new trend toward a willingness to make binding commitments and to engage in a policy of multilateral sharing of aspirations and aims with like-minded nations has emerged since 1940. In that year, both major parties took their stand on the necessity of defending not only the continental United States but the entire Western Hemisphere. But they both added that kindred nations abroad engaged in fighting aggression were to be supported short of war.[21] The embryo of the far-reaching commitments later accepted in the United Nations Charter, the Rio Pact, and the North Atlantic Treaty is apparent in this admitted concern over the status and development of other nations. Certainly, the trend reflected in the pacts and programs entered into by Americans is toward more and more participation in joint planning and action. It remains to be seen, however, whether legal and institutional commitment alone suffices to establish such a tradition. American ideologies must be related to the institutional pattern in order to support the contention that full and permanent international participation is now the chief feature of policy.

The Grand Alliance Disintegrates. With the defeat of the Axis in 1945 almost all American groups and segments of opinion voiced strong approval of the United Nations as the instrument to maintain the peace which had just been won by force of arms. Freedom, democracy, stability, and an expanding world trade on a nondiscriminatory basis were to be realized through the new organization, thus meeting the major aspirations of most American elites. Yet the collapse of the Grand Alliance between the West and the Soviet Union soon shattered this hope. With the growing concern at the expansion of Communist ideology and the power of the Soviet state, voiced first by the conservative elements in American society, the now dominant focus of United States policy emerged: anticommunism on a global scale.

The keynote of the new orientation was sounded by President Truman in the doctrine which bears his name: [22]

> The seeds of totalitarian regimes are nurtured by misery and want. They spread and grow in the evil soil of poverty and strife. They reach their full growth when the hope of a people for a better life has died. We must keep that hope alive. The free peoples of the world look to us for support in maintaining their freedoms. If we falter in our leadership, we may endanger the peace of the world—and we shall surely endanger the welfare of our own Nation.

From the initial program of sending military equipment and training missions to Greece and Turkey in 1947 developed the global program of anti-Communist alliances and regional security pacts which now binds America to forty other nations. "Anticommunism" is a negative way of stating the major

[21] Democratic and Republican party platforms, Langer and Gleason, *op. cit.*, pp. 669–671.

[22] President Truman's message to Congress, Mar. 12, 1947; *Department of State Bulletin,* supplement, May 4, 1947, pp. 829–832.

ends underlying the contemporary focus of policy: put positively, the policy holds out the desirability of maintaining the world's institutional and ideological *status quo*. On this depends the realization of American aspirations, the stability of free political institutions, and the continuity of the free-enterprise system in economic organization. The victory of communism would shatter these aims.

The willingness of liberal Democrats and liberal Republicans to implement this policy is manifest in enforcement measures against Communist sallies, in the seven military alliances now in force, in permanent interallied planning even in time of peace, and in the 40-odd billion dollars which had been spent on foreign aid between 1945 and 1954.

General Support for Anticommunism. Since anticommunism is the basic motive which pervades all these activities, the permanence of this policy appears to be well accepted by Americans. Certainly, military, economic, legal, and institutional involvements surpass any similar experience in America's past. That the faith of many American leaders is pinned to such programs is clear from the assertion by conservative Republicans that if greater aid had been given to Nationalist China the regime of Mao Tse-tung would never have triumphed.[23] Liberals support foreign aid no less, for as Dean Acheson put it,[24]

Weakness invites aggression. The free nations must be strong to deter attack by the enemies of freedom. . . . All our actions abroad, whatever form they may take, have a single purpose. That purpose is to advance the security and welfare of this country. There is no other possible justification for any policy or program. There is no other justification for asking the American taxpayer to finance any policy or program.

Other aims of policy are by no means forgotten in the overwhelming dedication to anticommunism. The support of democracy elsewhere is accepted by many as an end in itself, as is the encouragement of American investment abroad or the relaxation of world trade barriers. But in the over-all context of American aims, these aspirations are subsidiary to the larger focus, and in the programs of successive administrations they have been subordinated to the basic aim of anticommunist world stability.

Yet even this dedication continues to contain within it the dualism of America's complex myth. Hence the acceptance of large-scale commitments does not necessarily imply a developing tradition of permanent involvement, and it certainly does not guarantee the cooperative sharing of aims and values with other nations in the noncommunist camp. The contemporary

[23] *Military Situation in the Far East,* Hearings before Committee on Foreign Relations and Committee on Armed Services, U.S. Senate, 82d Cong., 1st Sess., 1951, pt. V, pp. 3593–3594.

[24] Hearings before Committee on Foreign Affairs on the Mutual Security Program, U.S. House of Representatives, 82d Cong., 2d Sess., 1952, pp. 7–9.

struggle between the proponents of containment as opposed to the advocates of liberation makes this evident. This conflict is doubly significant since the rift is so pervasive as to coincide broadly with the division of groups into liberals and advocates of multilateralism on the one hand, as opposed to conservatives and friends of unilateral intervention and/or withdrawal, on the other. The ideological characteristics of the two camps will provide the clues as to the extent to which the multilateral sharing of aims implicit in aid programs, alliances, and international organizations has gained acceptance in the American myth.

The aim of containing the expansion of Soviet and Communist power, which took shape during the Fair Deal administration in which liberal Democrats were charged with the conduct of American foreign relations, carries with it a number of highly significant ideological and procedural assumptions. First, it rests not on the destruction and annihilation of the Soviet Union and its orbit but on its "containment." Further encroachments on what Americans have come to call the "free world" are to be prevented; but the Communist elites of Russia, China, and Eastern Europe are not to be attacked and eliminated. Containment, further, was conceived to rest on the principle that continued demonstrations of free-world unity based on voluntary cooperative effort would produce "positions of strength" militarily, economically, and politically, from which negotiations with the Soviets looking toward peaceful coexistence could be conducted.

Implicit in containment, therefore, is a definite moderation of American values. Advocates of the policy are no less anticommunist in sentiment than their conservative critics. However, in their efforts not to invite war with a system reprehensible to almost all Americans they put the emphasis on merely *restraining* the Soviet elite. Hence proponents of containment seek to gain American institutional and ideological security by constructing a firm anti-Soviet alliance designed to win World War III if it proves inevitable in their estimate, but designed primarily as a deterrent to the initiation of that war by the Soviet elite. Hence liberal Democrats insist that the enforcement action in Korea derived its primary value from the clear demonstration of firm intent implicit in the Western alliance; but they also insisted that "refusing to enlarge the quarrel to the point where our global capabilities are diminished is certainly not appeasement, but is a militarily sound course. . . ."[25] The Korean and Geneva negotiations of 1954, therefore, are a consistent policy derived by liberal Republicans and Democrats alike from these precepts.

Procedurally, policies of containment put a heavy stress upon the cooperative efforts of alliances and international organizations. They are based on voluntary associations of like-minded national elites, for whose stabilization the unprecedented international military and economic aid programs of the

[25] *Military Situation in the Far East,* pt. II, pp. 729 ff., General Bradley's testimony.

United States were initiated. They presuppose a willingness to share common anticommunist values, implying compromises on policy when rifts appear. They cannot operate without constant give-and-take among allied nations even if this should imply a retreat from exclusive American values and aspirations. A constant willingness to participate in efforts abroad and even to intervene—but never to withdraw—are the earmarks of this segment of American opinion. Multilateralism in diplomacy, in military planning, in economic reconstruction, and in negotiating with the Communist elite stands in the forefront of the values of containment-oriented Americans. Policies of favoring Nationalist China—against the wishes of Britain—or of insisting on German rearmament—flying against the values of Frenchmen—are inconsistent with this approach. Multilateralism implies value sharing, and value sharing calls for compromise of cherished national beliefs.

Anticommunism and Unilateralism: Liberation. At the opposite pole from the containment-oriented focus of present and future American policy stands the extreme of liberation. Thus General Wedemeyer said that [26]

Communism is a political and economic philosophy that visualizes subordinating the individual to the state. It is atheistic and it would regiment the economy, would deprive individuals of their freedom. It abrogates definitely the dignity of man. It does not accept the spiritual side of life. It places a premium on the bestial qualities of human beings.

A truce or negotiations with such an enemy are rejected. Only complete surrender on his part is acceptable, since any other policy is "appeasement." The containment policy, thought General MacArthur,[27]

seems to me to introduce a new concept into military operations—the concept of appeasement, the concept that when you use force, you can limit that force. . . . The concept I have is that when you go into war, you have exhausted all other potentialities of bringing the disagreements to an end.

Negotiations, limited wars, and restraint all fall under the heading of appeasement. A positive approach is urged by the advocates of liberation, an approach which would end the compromising of American values abroad. As Patrick Hurley phrased it: [28]

We should quit supporting ideologies abroad which if successful will destroy the American system of liberty. We should quit the policy of appeasement and present again a positive foreign policy based upon the principles of individual liberty, self government, regulated free enterprise and justice.

Implicit in this dedication to the purity of American values in the relations with other nations is a tacit rejection of alliances, international organization,

---

[26] *Ibid.,* pt. III, p. 2476.
[27] *Ibid.,* pt. I, p. 39; and the Republican Committee view, pt. V, p. 3579.
[28] *Ibid.,* pt. IV, pp. 2827–2828.

and extensive foreign commitments, precisely because these instruments of multilateralism call for compromise. Advocates of liberation stress the necessity of freeing the peoples of Eastern Europe and of China from Communist rule. They argue for a "rollback" of the Iron Curtain, and hence they scoff at those of America's allies who have staked their future on a policy of peaceful coexistence. Proponents of liberation distrust the UN and NATO. They feel that America's allies have not supported the policy of the United States with sufficient vigor, especially the dissident minority in the UN which opposed the Korean enforcement action. Liberation is the positive policy consonant with American values. "My hope would be . . . ," said General MacArthur, "that the United Nations would see the wisdom and utility of that course, but if they did not, I still believe that the interests of the United States would require our action . . . alone, if necessary." [29]

"Alone, if necessary" states the crucial implications for American foreign policy involved in the liberation ideology. When aroused by a sharp external threat the advocates of liberation favor quick, decisive, and uncompromising action and commitment, at the risk of more extensive hostilities than the friends of containment think desirable. But when this type of action fails to materialize, they argue for withdrawal as the rational alternative. The consistent, patient, and long-term commitment implicit in the containment view is lacking in the doctrine of liberation. Unilateralism, whether through vigorous self-assertion abroad or through withdrawal from the alien external world, is the keystone of the liberation ideology.

Groups and Policy Aims. It follows that the groups in American life most insistently concerned with the preservation of the traditional values of free enterprise, class harmony, and "little government" are in favor of the liberation approach. They include patriotic societies, veterans' organizations, small-business groups, many ethnic minorities, and the conservative wings of both major parties. The proponents of containment and multilateralism, by contrast, are to be found in the ranks of groups standing for big business, labor, liberal women's organizations, and the largest farm groups, as well as the liberal factions of the major parties. Yet the lines are by no means firmly drawn. On some issues implying a choice between a unilateral American mission and crusade on the one hand and a multilateral sharing of aims on the other, the breakdown fails to apply. Specific issues blur the total picture, and the future course of American policy can by no means be predicted on the basis of this group distribution.

Significantly, many groups and individuals share the beliefs of both extremes in many respects. They show impatience at the restraint followed by the containment wing but shrink at the possibility of conflict held out by the liberation school. They decry the compromising of values implicit in the

[29] *Ibid.,* pt. I, *passim;* and the endorsement in the Republican viewpoint on the Committee, pt. V, pp. 3584 ff.

multilateral diplomacy of regional and universal security organizations as inconsistent with Americanism, but they admit the need for friends and allies abroad. In the middle group, the ambivalences of the American myth are most pronounced and its wavering allegiance makes the clear victory of either containment or liberation in American thought an unlikely event. Multilateralism and unilateralism, intervention and withdrawal, optimism and pessimism, are likely to remain fixed poles in American society toward and between which group aspirations will keep on fluctuating. Ideological support for both prevails, but the fragmentation of American group beliefs and aims is such as to make possible the decisive advent to power of one or the other only if the anticommunism dominant in the minds of all American elites is provoked by serious external action. Friction and tension between all group beliefs in the United States and those professed by Communist elites abound. Interests clash on every level, and their impact is driven home to the public at large in every newspaper. But the bipolarization of thought in the United States is obscured by the mixture of attitudes which prevails among large segments of the population and the variety of group interests which seek defense in foreign policy. Sometimes these can be satisfied through containment; sometimes liberation seems to hold the answer. But a clear polarization is rendered all but impossible; and a decisive policy of either containment or liberation is unlikely to take the place of improvisation and of the momentary yielding to the varying internal pressures generated in a democracy.

7. Characteristics of American Foreign Relations. The pushing and pulling of groups, the rivalry among ideologies, and the conflict and compromise among competing interests may define American policy in its substantive content from year to year. Clear policy may not be in evidence often. Yet certain recurring features of American behavior are hidden in these manifestations, and they govern the nature of America's diplomacy and warfare. What is more, they are typical in general of all heterogeneous democratic communities whose foreign policies represent perhaps a less ambivalent myth than America's but whose substantive claims abroad must reflect the demands of many groups and parties. The major characteristics of American policy can be summarized as the tendency to stand on principle, the difficulty of defining the ends of policy clearly and unambiguously, and the inconsistency in the choice of means to implement given aims of policy.

The Stand on Principle: Morality. The recurrence of such terms as "crusade," "morality," and "mission" in the basic aims of American policy is no accident. Recourse to these symbols signifies a deeply embedded belief on the part of all American elites that abstract principles of right and wrong, religious in their origin and context, form an important part of public consciousness. This tendency is as evident in domestic politics as it is in certain types of advertising and public relations work. It is supported by the inveterate tendency of Americans traveling abroad to lecture other nations on America's unique values and contributions and to insist that the salvation of the world lies in a global imitation of America's way. Whether the sermon takes the form of denunciations of the British "blood traffic"—i.e., the trade with Communist countries—or exhortations to permit greater leeway to the private investor makes little difference. Moral principles are invoked in either case and departures from the "right way" must necessarily smack of compromise, or, in the American vernacular, a "sellout."

The chief consequence of the American stand on moral principles, therefore, is the difficulty of retreating from a diplomatic position once assumed. A retreat would be precisely the kind of "selling out" which no political party likes to contemplate if it has to justify itself before the electorate. It makes negotiations with enemies and allies alike a most difficult procedure, and it may operate to postpone international settlement until the elite in power considers it safe from the viewpoint of domestic politics.

The Stand on Principle: Legalism. Closely allied to moral preaching is the tendency of American leaders to invoke abstract legal principles to justify their policies, even if such a course cannot possibly help in maintaining a diplomatic position, at least in the short run. At the height of the delicate negotiations with Japan over the future of the Orient—and while the Roosevelt Administration was intent on concentrating all national efforts on the Atlantic while keeping the Pacific peaceful and uninvolved with Hitler's campaigns—Cordell Hull defined America's legal rights in this form: [30]

1. Respect for the territorial integrity and the sovereignty of each and all nations.
2. Support of the principle of non-interference in the internal affairs of other countries.
3. Support of the principle of equality, including equality of commercial opportunity.
4. Non-disturbance of the *status quo* in the Pacific except as the *status quo* may be altered by peaceful means.

No doubt, these principles supported the basic diplomacy of the United States in seeking to keep Japan from absorbing China and Southeast Asia. But they were phrased in such terms as to be unacceptable to a Japanese coalition of elites bent on expansion—whether through violent or peaceful means—and thereby tended to defeat the immediate American aim of reaching a *modus vivendi* with Japan while Germany was being defeated.

Moral principles and legal definitions combine to introduce a series of rigidities into American foreign policy which seriously limit ease in the formulation of policy aims and the choice of means. A given course is not easily

[30] A. Feis, *The Road to Pearl Harbor*, Princeton University Press, Princeton, N.J., 1950, p. 178. From a memorandum of Hull's to Ambassador Nomura, Apr. 14, 1941.

changed, and desirable policies must either be abandoned or so presented as to fit somehow into the accepted moral and legal pattern. In the contemporary political setting the difficulty seemed to be demonstrated by the inability of the Truman Administration to conclude the Korean negotiations which it had haltingly begun in 1951. The Republican charges of "treason" and "espionage" which accompanied these attempts at negotiation, however, prevented the weakened administration from carrying through a policy which might have embarrassed it in the elections of 1952. Conversely, the very same negotiations were successfully concluded by the incoming Eisenhower Administration in 1953—despite the fact that they ended in a compromise—partly because the now victorious Republican party had no wish to disavow its own leader during the first months of his tenure. That the rigidities are still operative, however, is made clear by the reluctance shown by all American negotiators in dealing with the Chinese and Russians, in Panmunjom no less than in Geneva, and the repeated assurances of leading Republicans that the negotiations did not imply a sellout. The principle can be documented, however, from a study of American-Japanese relations during 1941.

A Case Study: Negotiations with Japan, 1941. To reach a temporary agreement with imperial Japan so as to be free to support Britain against Germany, or to stand on principle and restrain any further Japanese advance —those were the alternatives confronting the political leadership in 1940–1941. Counsel was divided, and both policies—incompatible though they were—found application.

Serious negotiations for a *modus vivendi* with Japan were begun in the spring of 1941. Japan's determination to expand either unilaterally or through some agreement with Washington was beyond doubt, but Hull's reactions were less clear. He continued to lecture and to preach, but he made no counterproposals meeting the Japanese even halfway. Indeed, he admitted in August that "nothing will stop them except force. . . . The point is how long we can maneuver the situation until the military matter in Europe is brought to a conclusion. . . ." [31] That such a strategy might be aided by a short-term agreement was accepted but not condoned by Hull. Yet Roosevelt came close to acting on this reasoning, for he discussed with his advisers during November an offer to Japan which would have postponed a final decision for six months. [32] The "compromise on principle" would have given the United States a badly needed respite, after which the situation would have had to be faced once more. Yet domestic groups favoring China, supported by the arguments of Secretaries Knox, Stimson, and Hull, opposed the scheme precisely because it would have weakened the moral and legal position of the United States. Instead, the administration presented Japan

[31] *Ibid.,* p. 248. See pp. 123–140, 154, 240, 276–277 for further documentation.
[32] W. L. Langer and J. S. Gleason, *The Undeclared War*, Harper, New York, 1953, pp. 872 ff.

on November 26, 1941, with a completely unacceptable proposal which was not expected by Washington to result in agreement, but which had the inestimable advantage of remaining true to past American pronouncements and therefore maintained ideological consistency.[33] Furthermore, the government knew that Japan was determined to move; it had information of Japanese troop shipments and therefore felt that a "last offer" would demonstrate American consistency and unveil Japanese bad faith.

Negotiations, consequently, were never conducted on the serious basis of finding a compromise, because such a course was inconceivable in terms of the thought pattern of the leadership. Rigidities are obvious in such a setting and they remain fixed in American foreign relations. Only an extremely secure and firmly established political leadership thinks itself able to dilute these principles and depart from them, and American society and politics are too fragmented to permit the ready development of such an elite.

The Definition of Aims. The fragmentation of American groups and elites highlights the second major principle of American foreign policy, the difficulty of defining policy aims. Each major party is merely a coalition of opposing groups of politicians and reflects an uneasy alliance of interest groups whose aspirations coincide in some but not all respects. Members of the Democratic as well as of the Republican party, despite formal membership in the same organization, favor policies of liberation as opposed to containment. Democrats from New York stand behind heavy foreign aid and liberal immigration quotas; Democrats from Virginia and Nevada oppose both demands. Republicans from Massachusetts stand for the UN and NATO as pillars of American policy; Republicans from Wisconsin and California have grave misgivings about both. The same divisions in ideology and policy prevail within some interest groups and among such organizations, while significant portions of the public are simultaneously attracted to several positions and arguments.

Consistent aims of policy do not emerge easily in this setting. The problem is compounded by the inevitable alternations of elites in the American system. Not only do parties yield power to one another after elections, but each party and each interest group tends to be subjected to a struggle between older and younger leaders, "ins" against "outs," experienced officeholders giving way to challengers with different views and values. Thus the policy aims of each group in America are themselves subject to debate and ultimate change within the organization itself. While this may not obstruct the political leadership in times of dire emergency, it implies friction and difficulty in the definition of policy aims in ordinary times, or in eras when tension is expected for decades. The alternations of elites and the developments of ideological patterns within them therefore introduce a complex of factors which renders the making of policy more difficult still. A national con-

[33] *Ibid.,* pp. 891 ff., 894 ff.

sensus which agrees merely on the desirability of maintaining American institutions, values, and security against communism is not sufficiently precise to act as a cohesive in these rifts and chasms.

Persuasion by Leaders. The political leadership, to be sure, has attempted to simplify the process by conducting its own propaganda in favor of given aims. Press conferences by officials, unending speaking tours throughout the country by State Department personnel, pamphlets and documents distributed free and en masse by the Department, radio addresses, and a painstaking policy of answering private letters of inquiry addressed to these officials are all mobilized to "sell" the government's policy to an apathetic or hostile public. Controversial new treaties and commitments, such as the UN Charter, are praised in extravagant language by the professional and political leadership, thus frequently raising false hopes. Demands for sudden action are couched in "crisis" and "emergency" terms in order to overcome apathy and opposition, as with the Truman Doctrine in 1947. But once the public is aroused, policy makers may have the greatest difficulty in quieting it once more and resisting the demands for drastic and immediate action abroad. Emphasis for orderly policy formulation is therefore focused on the stable elites in American society, a need which the Department of State recognizes in maintaining close relations with over four hundred national groups and in cultivating the opinion leaders among them, especially clergymen, teachers, and journalists.

Yet these techniques have not sufficed in the past and do not suffice now to overcome the varying strains in American thought and values. Manipulation and propaganda, consultation and participation, bipartisanship and stopping politics at the water's edge have not produced a detailed and explicit foreign policy consensus any more than agreement on domestic issues. Thus,

> Franklin Roosevelt repeatedly deceived the American people during the period before Pearl Harbor. . . . He was faced with a terrible dilemma. If he let the people slumber in a fog of isolation, they might well fall prey to Hitler. . . . If he came out unequivocally for intervention, he would be defeated in 1940. . . . If he was going to induce the people to move at all, he would have to trick them into acting for their best interests, or what he conceived to be their best interests. . . .[34]

But the temporary consensus achieved through these means did not outlast the actual war emergency and was effected only because of the timely Japanese attack on Pearl Harbor. The definition of policy aims through executive leadership, but without the acceptance of the bulk of the population, is therefore a possibility in American society. Further, it may be and has been used

---

[34] Thomas A. Bailey, *The Man in the Street,* pp. 11–13, as cited in N. D. Palmer and H. C. Perkins, *International Relations,* Houghton Mifflin, Boston, 1953, p. 965.

on occasion. But the very vituperation with which such manipulation has been greeted after the passage of the emergency is enough to suggest that no American elite anxious for survival is likely to risk this method of achieving unity on ends of policy indefinitely or with great frequency. And the definition of policy aims remains subject to all the currents and crosscurrents of group aspirations.

The Choice of Means. Finally, in our array of principles of American policy, the limitation on the choice of means is clearly implied in the uncertainty over ends. What is moral, right, and acceptable to one set of leaders may well spell a violation of American values to another. Foreign intervention, for instance, is today accepted by many elites who are convinced of the rightness of American methods and techniques. Competition in American business is held applicable to European industry. Principles of crop rotation used by the farmers of Minnesota are urged with equal determination on the peasants of India or Syria. What is good at home must be good abroad, and the exportation of American techniques—with the values implicit in them—through propaganda and subtle pressure is accepted by many. But these means of implementing the containment or liberation policies are rejected by those who argue for the inviolability of other cultures and societies. They protest the imposition embedded in these acts of intervention and therefore challenge the permissibility of given means of policy. Intervention versus the self-determination of other nations constitutes an area of disagreement which has by no means been overcome by the withdrawal of American Marines from Central America. More subtle methods of intervention are in vogue today, and they remain subject to controversy from extreme liberals as well as from conservatives.

War. The inconsistency and difficulty in the choice of means to implement American policy aims—once they have been fixed—are most pronounced in the limitation on the ability to go to war, in the relations with America's allies, and in the possibility of negotiating with the enemy. The United States, it is true, has taken the initiative in declaring war on a number of occasions. In each case, however, the majority of the public was firmly wedded to whatever principles the war was to be fought about: the protection of settlers in Texas in 1845, and the suppression of Spanish barbarism in Cuba in 1898. Even the case of World War I supports the position that the United States cannot easily go to war. Opposition to abandoning neutrality in 1917 gave way only after the Germans had been sufficiently careless to sink American ships and to promise Mexico the reacquisition of Texas, Arizona, and New Mexico if she would join in an attack against America. Only then did President Wilson think it possible to enter the war, though it appears that both he and many other leaders in government and business had favored a more active policy of defeating Germany and her allies before that time.

The limitation on this means of policy, however, is most explicit in the period since 1940. That isolationist opposition induced the Roosevelt Administration to postpone entry into a conflict which the leaders considered imminent has already been shown. That they were unwilling to pay a price in principle and law for a short respite has become clear. War, they feared, had become inevitable nevertheless, but to assure public support war could not be declared by the United States. As Secretary Stimson explained: [35]

In spite of the risk involved . . . in letting the Japanese fire the first shot, we realized that in order to have the full support of the American people it was desirable to make sure that the Japanese be the ones to do this so that there should remain no doubt in anyone's mind as to who were the aggressors.

The same principle applies today. As a nation which is committed to peace first and foremost, with the exception of the extreme advocates of liberation, the United States must permit the enemy to fire the first shot. American good faith and consistency in values cannot be demonstrated in any other fashion. Hence years of border incidents in Korea brought enforcement only with an overt attack and endorsement by the UN. The civil war in Indochina, since it neither was an attack on the United States nor was branded as "aggression" by the UN, was characterized by an absence of an overt American commitment—in manpower, at least. The limitation remains real for the policy maker who believes that war is once more inevitable and should be anticipated by timely counteraction. Preventive war, therefore, is impossible in the American setting unless it can somehow be made to stem from the enemy's initiative.

Alliances. The choice between working with allies or "going it alone" characterizes the second major inconsistency in America's armory of possible means. Since key groups differ on principle as to whether the United States should compromise with its allies to achieve a united free world or whether strong unilateral action is to be preferred, the selection of means is likely to be as unstable as the ends to be attained through them. American stands in firm opposition to the Soviet Union are frequently greeted abroad with efforts at mediation. Naturally, if compromise seems inevitable, the tendency is to forgo the alliance and make a solely national effort at success in war or diplomacy.

Of course, America's allies are likely to greet these shifts in emphasis with cries of dismay. Britons complain that the tendency to "go it alone" is, for a smaller country, like "sleeping in the same bed with a giant." Philippine spokesmen assert that America's refusal to allocate more funds to foreign aid "is indeed disheartening."

It is certainly not pleasant to contemplate food surpluses going to waste and billions being spent on movies, television, entertainment and so on, while millions

[35] Stimson's testimony before the Joint Congressional Committee on the Pearl Harbor Disaster. B. Rauch, *Roosevelt from Munich to Pearl Harbor*, Creative Age, New York, 1950, p. 473.

of people in the less fortunate countries of the world are condemned to a state of poverty.[36]

When these demands coincide with a period of Soviet pressure, the means may shift to a greater allocation of national resources to allies abroad; but with an abatement of Communist challenge, withdrawal reasserts itself. Thus the choice has to be made constantly between a greater and a lesser amount of cooperation with allied nations; but the instability in mood and the varying impact of group aims make possible no simple selection of means.

Negotiating with the Enemy. Negotiating with the enemy poses the supreme problem to American policy makers. If the aims of policy shift between the extremes of containment and liberation and if the means alternate between support of and disregard for allies, how can long-term negotiations ever be carried on? If the power of the Soviet state is feared by American elites, a proportionate growth of allied power should lay the basis for a measure of mutual accommodation, as Kennan and Acheson, for example, have argued. But if Communist ideology is the enemy, no such means can be chosen. As Senator Hickenlooper put it: [37]

I don't want to see a slackening of our diplomatic policies in any way on the basis that those people tell the truth at any time or that they have any moral purpose behind their statements. If we get mousetrapped again, it is going to be bad indeed for us. . . .

Sentiments of this kind imply absolute opposition to any move of the enemy, except surrender. Advocates of liberation therefore oppose any negotiations whatever, and many of the uncommitted segments of the American public regard attempts at reaching a compromise with communism with the gravest misgivings. Public talks therefore almost invariably degenerate into propaganda campaigns, while secret diplomacy is feared to result in more "appeasement" and "sellouts" of the Yalta and Geneva variety. Serious negotiations are all but impossible in such a setting.

Positions of principle render retreat almost impossible. The difficulty of defining the aims of policy subject American foreign relations to shifts and changes and constant reinterpretation. The inconsistency in the choice of means makes the implementation of any one course difficult beyond description. Yet policy is made and carried out. Negotiations do take place, though they result in agreement only in rare and unusual instances. But no violent shifts in American policy have taken place since 1947, though changes in emphasis recur constantly. This suggests that the balance among interest groups and elites is such as to make a decisive departure into new directions

[36] *The New York Times,* Oct. 22, 1953, p. 7.

[37] *NATO,* Hearings before Committee on Foreign Affairs, U.S. Senate, 83d Cong., 1st Sess., 1953, p. 19.

a most difficult procedure. Policy limps from situation to situation, but it cannot advance steadily. Techniques are improvised but cannot be planned over long periods. The result is an unsteady policy and faltering leadership for the anti-Soviet coalition. Yet it is a leadership which continues to be accepted and which has succeeded in introducing more stability into world relations than had been in evidence since the onset of Soviet self-extension. Whether it will keep acting in this role depends, as in the past, on the stability of American moods and the relations among America's elites.

ADDITIONAL CASE-STUDY MATERIAL

American

Almond, G. A.: *The American People and Foreign Policy,* Harcourt, Brace, New York, 1950.
Alsop, J., and S. Alsop: "How Our Foreign Policy Is Made," *Saturday Evening Post,* Apr. 30, 1949.
Bailey, T. A.: *The Man in the Street,* Macmillan, New York, 1948.
Bendix, R.: *Higher Civil Servants in American Society,* University of Colorado Press, Boulder, Colo., 1949.
Brady, R. A.: *Business as a System of Power,* Columbia University Press, New York, 1943.
Burns, J. M., and J. W. Peltason: *Government by the People,* Prentice-Hall, New York, 1952.
Douglas, W. O.: *Strange Lands and Friendly People,* Harper, New York, 1951.
Feis, A.: *The China Tangle,* Princeton University Press, Princeton, N.J., 1953.
————: *The Road to Pearl Harbor,* Princeton University Press, Princeton, N.J., 1950.
Fuller, R. A.: "Case Studies in Bipartisanship United States Postwar Foreign Policy," Ph.D. thesis, University of Wisconsin, Madison, Wis., 1953.
Holcombe, A. N.: *The Middle Class in American Politics,* Harvard University Press, Cambridge, Mass., 1940.
Hoover Commission: *Task Force Report on Foreign Affairs,* GPO, Washington, 1949.
Hull, C.: *Memoirs of Cordell Hull,* Macmillan, New York, 1948.
Klapp, O. E.: "Hero Worship in America," *American Sociological Review,* Feb. 14, 1949.
Langer, W. L., and J. S. Gleason: *The Challenge to Isolation,* Harper, New York, 1952.
————: *The Undeclared War,* Harper, New York, 1953.
Leonard, L. L.: *Elements of American Foreign Policy,* McGraw-Hill, New York, 1953.
Lubell, S.: *The Future of American Politics,* Harper, New York, 1951.
McCamy, J. L.: *The Administration of American Foreign Affairs,* Knopf, New York, 1950.
Mathews, D. R.: *The Social Background of Political Decision Makers,* Doubleday, New York, 1954.
Millis, W. (ed.): *The Forrestal Diaries,* Viking, New York, 1951.
Mills, C. W.: *The New Men of Power,* Harcourt, Brace, New York, 1948.
Rauch, B.: *Roosevelt from Munich to Pearl Harbor,* Creative Age, New York, 1950.
Sapin, B., and R. C. Snyder: *The Role of the Military in American Foreign Policy,* Doubleday, New York, 1954.
Sargeant, H. H.: "The Overt International Information and Education Exchange Programs of the United States," *Department of State Bulletin,* vol. 26, 1952.
Schriftgiesser, K.: *The Lobbyists,* Little, Brown, Boston, 1951.
Stimson, H., and McG. Bundy: *On Active Service in Peace and War,* Harper, New York, 1948.
Taft, R. A.: *A Foreign Policy for Americans,* Doubleday, New York, 1951.
Trotter, R. G., et al.: *Canada in World Affairs,* 4 vols., Oxford, New York, 1953.
Vandenberg, A., Jr.: *The Private Papers of Senator Vandenberg,* Houghton Mifflin, Boston, 1952.

Foreign

Aron, R.: "French Public Opinion and the Atlantic Treaty," *International Affairs,* vol. 28, January, 1952.

Bassett, R.: *Democracy and Foreign Policy: A Case Study,* Longmans, New York, 1952.

Brown, W. N.: *The United States and India and Pakistan,* Harvard University Press, Cambridge, Mass., 1953.

Bulwer-Thomas, I.: *The Party System in Great Britain,* Phoenix House, London, 1953.

Cady, J. F.: "Religion and Politics in Burma," *Far Eastern Quarterly,* February, 1953.

Churchill, Sir Winston: *The Second World War,* 6 vols., Houghton Mifflin, Boston, 1948–1953.

Epstein, L.: "British Labour Left and U.S. Foreign Policy," *American Political Science Review,* vol. 45, December, 1951.

———: "British Labour's Foreign Policy," *World Politics,* vol. 6, October, 1953.

Flournoy, F. R.: *Parliament and War,* King, London, 1927.

Furniss, E. S.: *Weaknesses in French Foreign Policy-making,* Princeton University, Center of International Studies, Princeton, N.J., 1954.

Hatta, M.: "Indonesia's Foreign Policy," *Foreign Affairs,* vol. 31, April, 1953.

Heinberg, J.: "Personnel of French Cabinets," *American Political Science Review,* vol. 33, April, 1939.

Howard, J. E.: *Parliament and Foreign Policy in France,* Cresset, London, 1948.

Kahin, G.: *Nationalism and Revolution in Indonesia,* Cornell University Press, Ithaca, N.Y., 1952.

Levi, W.: "India Debates Foreign Policy," *Far Eastern Survey,* vol. 20, Mar. 7, 1951.

———: *Free India in Asia,* University of Minnesota Press, Minneapolis, 1952.

Mansergh, N.: *Survey of British Commonwealth Affairs: The Problem of External Policy, 1931–1939,* Oxford, New York, 1952.

Miller, J. K.: *Belgian Foreign Policy between Two Wars, 1919–1940,* Bookman Association, New York, 1951.

Pickles, D.: *French Politics,* Royal Institute of International Affairs, New York, 1953.

Schuman, R.: "France and Europe," *Foreign Affairs,* vol. 31, April, 1953.

Soustelle, J.: "France and Europe," *Foreign Affairs,* vol. 30, July, 1952.

Strauss, P.: *Bevin and Company: The Leaders of British Labor,* Putnam, New York, 1941.

Tingsten, H.: *The Debate on the Foreign Policy of France, 1918–1939,* Oxford, New York, 1949.

"The West German Political Parties and Rearmament," *World Today,* vol. 9, February, 1953.

Yone, N., and D. Mandelbaum: "The New Nation of Burma," *Far Eastern Survey,* vol. 19, Oct. 25, 1950.

Chapter 14

SOVIET RUSSIA: THE SINGLE-GROUP AUTHORITARIAN ELITE

I. Principles of Soviet Policy

1. The Problem of Analysis. On no aspect of international relations have opinions differed so sharply or changed so abruptly as on the question of Soviet Russia. Analysis is complicated by the wide cultural gap separating Russia from the Western world. It is impeded by extreme Soviet restrictions on the availability and authenticity of evidence with which to judge Russian motivations. The problem is not merely an academic one. Faced with a rival ideology in communism and a rival power center in Moscow, American policy makers for the past decade have been almost exclusively concerned with evaluation of Soviet ends and means.

From this continual sifting and resifting of statements and actions of Russian leaders, three major theories of Soviet political behavior have emerged. The first, primarily geopolitical in nature, describes Soviet foreign policy as motivated by an urge to the sea, a drive for warm-water ports with which to communicate with the economic centers of the world. Another analysis draws, like the first, upon pre-Bolshevik history for its evidence. It sees Russian policy as one of consistent expansion for its own sake, equating czarist nineteenth-century imperialism with Soviet twentieth-century expansionism. Both theories stress the Russian origins of Soviet actions. Wholly different is a third school which sees the wellsprings of Soviet behavior in the goal of world revolution as posited in the Marxist values of Bolshevik ideology. Although all three theories agree that Soviet foreign policy is basically expansionistic, they differ in stressing either Russian or revolutionary origins of that policy.

In the framework of the analysis given here, the interaction of environment and ideology produces a Soviet foreign policy which is both Russian and revolutionary. Marxism began as the writings of a German, Karl Marx, and his colleague Friedrich Engels. Under the impact of its development in backward unindustrialized Russia it became Marxism-Leninism-Stalinism. Russian values and practices merged with Marxist goals and methods to produce

Bolshevism. Thus while identifying the Russian and revolutionary factors operative in shaping Soviet foreign policy, neither one is assumed to be of primary importance. It is the fusion of these factors which provides the clue to Soviet motivations and permits analysis of Soviet ends and means in international relations.

2. Russian Determinants of Soviet Policy. Without attempting an exhaustive survey of the parallels between czarist and Soviet policies, the more important historical roots of contemporary behavior may be noted. Chief of these are the three dominant values of the *ancien régime:* nationalism, orthodoxy, and autocracy. They illustrate the impact of the Russian environment upon Marxist principles.

Russian Autocracy. Theoretically czarist nationalism was the antithesis of Bolshevik internationalism. Actually the czarist tradition of emphasizing all things Russian to the exclusion of non-Russian values is paralleled in recurring efforts to suppress centrifugal forces among non-Russian peoples in the Soviet Union. The Soviet elite has repeatedly fought "bourgeois chauvinism" in the Ukraine while generally avoiding such campaigns among Great Russians. The last fifteen years of Stalin's rule found symbols of internationalism secondary to symbols of Russian nationalism, not only during World War II, significantly called "the Great Patriotic War," but during the postwar decade as well.

The czarist tradition of orthodoxy gave the Russian Orthodox Church official sanction to the exclusion and often persecution of all other religions. Soviet parallels emerge in the ruthless insistence upon Marxism-Leninism as interpreted by an official hierarchy to the exclusion of all other interpretations and of all non-Marxist ideologies. By manipulation of symbol and ceremony, Stalinism substituted the worship of men, Lenin and Stalin, for the worship of a god. Any imputation of mortal weakness on the part of the elite was regarded as heretical and punished by public humiliation, banishment, and often death.

Autocracy rested on the charisma of the czar and the impotence of the legislature. The dictatorship of the proletariat rested upon the charisma of Stalin and the impotence of the Supreme Soviet. Infallibility of the individual leader was coupled with an abuse of Western political practices to produce a type of rule blessed with the modern name of dictatorship, but known throughout the ages as despotism or autocracy.

Anti-Westernism. Nor is it any wonder that Russian values and interests should produce a form of government so at variance with contemporary Western models. The entire stream of czarist history moved in currents far removed from the traditions of Rome, the stimuli of the Renaissance, and the conflicts of the Reformation. The French Revolution had little impact in St. Petersburg. Russia remained essentially isolated from European thought and social change. Yet the debates between Slavophile and Slavophobe which preoccupied the Russian intelligentsia during the eighteenth and nineteenth centuries exemplify a striking ambivalence toward the West. Long sensitive to a cultural inferiority when contrasted with the court circles of Prussia, France, and Britain, Russian intellectuals wavered between hatred and admiration for all things Western. Similarly, Stalinism sought to borrow technologically from the West while vilifying Western democratic values and concepts.

Accompanying this sense of cultural inferiority was economic and military inferiority, no less a problem in Soviet than in czarist times. Particularly in the nineteenth and twentieth centuries did Russian material weakness bring disaster in military conflict. No better summation of the impact of this past upon the present can be found than Stalin's exhortation of 1931 to speed up the tempo of industrialization: [1]

Those who fall behind get beaten. But we do not want to be beaten. No, we refuse to be beaten! One feature of the history of old Russia was the continual beatings she suffered for falling behind, for her backwardness. She was beaten by the Mongol khans. She was beaten by the Turkish beys. She was beaten by the Polish and Lithuanian gentry. She was beaten by the British and French capitalists. She was beaten by the Japanese barons. All beat her—for her backwardness; for military backwardness, for cultural backwardness, for political backwardness, for industrial backwardness, for agricultural backwardness. She was beaten because to do so was practicable and could be done with impunity. Do you remember the words of the pre-revolutionary poet: "You are poor and abundant, mighty and impotent, Mother Russia!" These words of the old poet were well learned by those gentlemen. They beat her.

It would be fallacious to assume that Russia fulfilled the role of the underdog at all times. Just the opposite is true with respect to weaker countries on the periphery of czardom. Hence the inheritance of czarist imperialism must be included as an important feature of the environment in which Soviet policy was formulated and implemented. Prior to the Bolshevik Revolution the Russian empire included Finland, the Baltic countries (Estonia, Latvia, Lithuania), much of Poland, the Ukraine, as well as preponderant influence in Outer Mongolia and northern Manchuria, the last secured by control of the Chinese Eastern Railroad. Such czarist accessions necessarily played a part in the formulation of Bolshevik policy, particularly because of a final factor conditioning policy: the continuity in conflict of interests with elites of other countries.

Inheritance of Czarist Imperialism. Regardless of the intent of Lenin before assuming power, the interests and values of elites in other countries remained essentially the same as they had been during czarist days. In the Far East, Japanese designs upon the mainland of Asia proved no less opera-

[1] J. Stalin, *Leninism: Selected Writings*, International Publishers, New York, 1942, p. 200.

tive in 1918 than they had been in 1904. Russian weakness or withdrawal brought Japanese penetration, whether in Manchuria, Mongolia, or Siberia itself. Similarly in the Middle East and in the Balkans, British policy had long clashed with czarist policy. According to strict Marxist precepts, Bolshevik policy should have renounced all czarist concessions and allowed the principle of self-determination to give free play to all centrifugal forces accumulated under the pressure of the *ancien régime*. To have done this, however, would have been to ignore the opportunities such action would have afforded the historic competitors of Russia in Europe and Asia. Lenin was too well versed in history to have run such risks for the sake of proletarian principles.

These are but a few of the Russian determinants which shape Soviet policy. Their presence in Russian history helps to account for the difference between Russian and non-Russian reactions to similar situations. A fuller understanding of this difference, however, requires a consideration of the revolutionary factors embodied in the theories of Marx and Lenin.

3. Bolshevik Determinants of Soviet Policy. No element of Marxism-Leninism is more central than its assumption of conflict in all nonsocialist relations. Many non-Marxist philosophies assume a basic unity, harmony, or moral order of the universe. So unalterably opposed to this is Marxism that groups in India no less than in the United States find themselves unable to communicate, much less collaborate, with those of Marxist belief. "Bourgeois reformers" and "utopian socialists" typify the terminology of Marxists reserved for those who would deny that conflict is omnipresent in history, whether between classes within a nation or between nations themselves. Slaves versus slaveholders, serfs versus landlords, workers versus capitalists, capitalist versus capitalist, so reads the Marxist record of history. At the highest and last stage of conflict stands the clash between classes on the international plane, in the world revolution that springs from the inevitable conflict between international socialism [2] and international capitalism.

For purposes of this discussion, only two aspects of this assumption of conflict are important: the "contradictions within the capitalist world," and the clash between capitalist and socialist elites. As expressed by Stalin in 1925,[3]

In the capitalist camp there is no unity of interests, no adequate centripetal force promoting consolidation. Within the capitalist camp there is conflict of interests, a tendency toward disruption, a fight between victors and vanquished, a conflict among victors, a dispute among all the imperialistic countries for . . . the opportunity of making profits. . . . In the capitalist camp dissension and disintegration

---

[2] It is essential to remember that in Soviet Marxist terminology "socialist" means "communist." The term "socialist," as used in this chapter, is not to be confused with the nonrevolutionary European socialist movements.

[3] J. Stalin, *Leninism,* Modern Books, London, 1932, vol. I, p. 370, as quoted by N. Leites, *The Operational Code of the Politburo,* McGraw-Hill, New York, 1951, p. 54.

prevail. . . . In the socialist camp, consolidation is advancing and there is an ever growing unification of interests against the common foe.

Contradictions among Capitalists. Stalin said after the war, "It would be incorrect to think that the Second World War arose accidentally as a result of the mistakes of some statesman or other. The war in fact arose as the inevitable result of the development of world economic and political forces on the basis of contemporary monopolistic capitalism." [4] This formulation found little change in Stalin's last published work, appearing in 1952. "In order to eliminate the inevitability of wars, imperialism must be destroyed." [5] Since such wars are inevitable, Soviet policy seeks to turn them to its own interests by "sharpening the conflict among capitalist powers" wherever possible.

Contradictions between Capitalist and Socialist. This assumption of conflict among capitalist countries is paralleled by the assumption of conflict between capitalist and socialist elites. The most famous formulation of the capitalist-socialist conflict by Lenin came in 1919, while Soviet Russia was besieged by foreign intervention at both ends of the continent. "We live . . . not only in a state but in a system of states, and the existence of the Soviet Republic side by side with the imperialist states for a long time is unthinkable. In the end either one or the other will conquer. And until that end comes, a series of the most terrible collisions between the Soviet Republic and the bourgeois states is inevitable." [6]

After the ousting of foreign imperialism, the inevitability of conflict between capitalism and socialism remained a constant element in Bolshevik ideology. Thus Lenin warned in 1921: "The international bourgeoisie, deprived of the possibility of waging open war against Soviet Russia, is waiting, always on the lookout for the moment when conditions will permit the renewal of this war." [7] Stalin phrased it somewhat differently in 1927: "Two world centers will be formed: the socialist center, attracting to itself all the countries gravitating toward socialism, and the capitalist center, attracting to itself all the countries gravitating toward capitalism. The fight between these two centers for the conquest of the world economy will decide the fate of capitalism and communism throughout the whole world." [8]

Bolshevik assumptions of conflict have been reinforced by attitudes and actions of the non-Bolshevik world. In part this resulted from Bolshevik behavior, the phenomenon of the "self-fulfilling prophecy." In 1917 Lenin's

[4] J. Stalin, speech of Feb. 9, 1946, as quoted in "Historicus," "Stalin on Revolution," *Foreign Affairs,* January, 1949, p. 191.

[5] J. Stalin, "Economic Problems of Socialism in the USSR," in *Current Digests of the Soviet Press,* supplement, Oct. 18, 1952, p. 8.

[6] V. Lenin, *Sochineniia* ("Works"), vol. XXIV, p. 122, quoted in E. H. Carr, *The Bolshevik Revolution, 1917–1923,* St. Martins, New York, 1952, vol. III, p. 115.

[7] Lenin, *op. cit.,* 3d ed., vol. XXVI, p. 428, quoted in Leites, *op. cit.,* p. 58.

[8] J. Stalin, *Leninism,* vol. II, p. 71, quoted by Leites, *op. cit.,* p. 55.

followers proclaimed themselves the leaders of world revolution. Groups otherwise favorably predisposed to those who had overthrown czarist autocracy then reacted with hostility, convincing Soviet leaders that all capitalists were sworn enemies of socialism. Similarly after World War II Soviet statements repeatedly accused the United States of plotting to encircle the Soviet bloc with aggressive powers. The belligerency of Soviet words and deeds convinced groups in Europe and Asia that only by allying with the United States could they survive a possible Russian attack. The resulting network of defensive pacts concluded under the impetus of Soviet behavior appeared to "prove" the validity of Bolshevik predictions about conflict between capitalist and socialist elites.

In addition to this "self-fulfilling-prophecy" phenomenon, however, external events since 1917 have frequently reinforced these assumptions of conflict dominant in Bolshevik ideology. In the first years of the Russian Revolution, German troops invaded European Russia, while Japanese forces subsequently occupied the Soviet Far East. Continued pressure from Japan in subsequent decades and attack from Hitler Germany in 1941 followed the pattern of capitalist hostility predicted in the Soviet myth. The combination of expectation and realization hardened into an experienced conviction that the gap between the socialist and capitalist world was permanently unbridgeable.

4. Decision Making in Soviet Russia. Bolshevik ideology and Soviet institutions exemplify authoritarian rule to a degree unparalleled in modern history. The locus of power lies in the all-powerful Presidium of the Central Committee of the Communist Party, formerly called the Politburo. The overwhelming majority of persons in the Soviet government are party members and hence subordinate to decisions made by the Presidium. In time of crisis, such as World War II, the fiction of separateness between party and state is cast aside and Presidium members personally fill the key government posts. Thus V. M. Molotov officially directed foreign policy, relinquishing his position of Minister of Foreign Affairs to a non-Politburo party member, A. Vyshinsky, in 1949.

Dominance of the Party. Soviet leaders make no effort to conceal the dominant role of the party and, within the party, the directing influence of the Politburo or Presidium. As phrased by Stalin, "Here in the Soviet Union . . . not a single important political or organizational question is decided by our Soviet and other mass organizations without directions from the Party." [9] Lenin commented in 1920 that "the Politburo decided all questions of international and internal policy." [10] Activity of the Politburo in the realm of foreign policy reached the point prior to Lenin's death where he concluded,

[9] J. V. Stalin, *Problems of Leninism*, p. 34.
[10] V. Lenin, speech to 9th Party Congress in 1920, quoted by J. Towster, *Political Power in the USSR*, Oxford, New York, 1949, p. 160.

"Are not petty as well as large-scale questions of 'moves' on our part in answer to 'moves' of foreign powers . . . discussed in the Politburo from the Party standpoint?" [11] In short, this small group of from five to ten persons is "the highest organ, not of the state, but of the Party, and the Party is the highest directing force of the state." [12]

It is here that the critical difference between the Nazi and the Soviet state appears so far as decision making is concerned. In Germany no central party body asserted continuing supervision over all party affairs, nor did any systematic penetration of governmental positions subordinate all official activity to the direction of the party. This was the ultimate goal of Hitler, but he failed to control completely the bureaucracy, the military, and the business groups. They continued to vie for power and intermittently tried to participate in policy formulation as separate and distinct interest groups. In Russia the control of the party is complete and explicit. All decisions of the Politburo or Presidium of the Communist Party are binding upon all party members; these persons in turn exercise a near monopoly on all positions of influence in the bureaucracy, the army, and the secret police.

Individuals as individuals may still have differing concepts of policy implementation and may participate in struggles for control of the governing apparatus. Repeated purges of the instruments of violence, the army and the police, testify to Stalin's suspicions of these groups. Success of the purges, however, also testifies to his unlimited control over potentially rival centers of power. In thirty years of rule, despite serious personal schisms within the highest party echelons, so far as is known no separate action was taken by the bureaucracy, military, or police which conflicted with the policy defined by the major faction in the Politburo.

The Politburo. The Politburo, or Presidium, is the monolithic, semipermanent elite par excellence of the twentieth century. The absence of regular party congresses permits it to be self-perpetuating, evidenced by its secret purging and replacement of members. Recruited exclusively from lower ranks of the party, it has awarded membership on the basis of faithful party work as viewed by the dominant figures in the Politburo.[13] With the ascendancy of Stalin, Politburo membership stabilized, and removal appeared to stem more from natural death than from political circumstance.

Beyond these general statements it is impossible to go. There is virtually no knowledge of the method or manner of decision making within the Politburo. Stalin's purges indicated an insistence upon accepting his word as final in all cases, but there is no way of determining how policy was formulated when he chose to remain silent. In view of the continued strength of the Soviet Union in the last decade of his regime and the absence of collapse immediately upon his death, it is probable that his leadership had little re-

[11] V. Lenin, writing in March, 1923, quoted in Towster, *op. cit.,* p. 162.
[12] J. Stalin in 1925, quoted in Towster, *op. cit.,* p. 160, footnote 7.
[13] G. Schueller, *The Politburo,* Stanford University Press, Stanford, Calif., 1951.

semblance with that of Hitler. His associates in the Politburo probably played a more rational role in decision making than did Goering, Ribbentrop, or Himmler. Lack of specific information on this point in no way invalidates the importance of our study, particularly in so far as the relationship of the Politburo to the party and consequently to the state machinery is concerned. It is truly the purest form of the single-group authoritarian elite.

5. Ideology and Aims of Policy: Self-expansion and Unilateralism. One of the most important characteristics of Soviet foreign policy stemming from Bolshevik ideology is its inherent self-expansionism. Self-expansion is rooted in the positing of world revolution as the fixed goal of Soviet policy. Because this revolution spells the end of capitalism, all capitalist elites are by nature held to be hostile to the Soviet Union. Differences in the intensity of this hostility stem only from weaknesses within the different elites, according to Bolshevik theory, and are not to be taken as signs of genuine acquiescence to Soviet survival. Because these elites are hostile, revolutions abroad must be used to weaken the capitalist system.

Areas of Self-extension. Thus the dictates of Leninism-Stalinism insist on means of self-extension to serve ends of self-preservation because all capitalist elites are viewed as determined to destroy the socialist elite. These means of self-extension, ranging from ideological subversion to planned revolution abroad, spring in part from the necessity to defend socialism against "capitalist encirclement." They operate in three major areas: the periphery of the Soviet Union, especially Eastern Europe; the capitalist-controlled colonies, especially in Asia; and the capitalist countries themselves, especially in Western Europe. The *cordon sanitaire* built by French diplomacy in Eastern Europe after World War I to "contain" Bolshevism becomes the chain of "people's democracies" serving as a "bulwark against American imperialism." The foundations of empire laid by British and French diplomacy in South Asia during the nineteenth century become "the weakest link" of capitalism, to be shattered by "raising the banner of national liberation." Finally, the industrial centers of Western Europe stand as the challenging citadel "to be assaulted by the shock troops of the proletariat, the Communist party." While this strategy is argued in the name of defending socialism, other motivations are present in addition to that of self-preservation.

Russia as the Base of World Socialism. The equation which identifies Russian interest and the interests of world revolution provides one key to Soviet foreign policy. Ostensibly the Communist International (Comintern) and its stepchild, the Communist Information Bureau (Cominform), were collective centers of like-minded world revolutionary groups. Actually they were instruments of Soviet foreign policy. If socialism were to advance in the world it must have a base from which to operate. Any weakening of Soviet strength simultaneously weakened world socialism. Conversely, only by strengthening Russia could revolution triumph elsewhere. So argued Lenin's followers.

Thus the Comintern abandoned its revolutionary slogans during the Great Depression. Instead of fomenting unrest among the millions of unemployed, it compelled Communist parties to support the noncommunist regimes of Chiang Kai-shek, Franklin Roosevelt, and Léon Blum. Outwardly championing the "antifascist coalition," this policy actually served the interests of Soviet Russia, weakened internally by collectivization and threatened externally by the fascist elites of Germany and Japan. Again after World War II, French and Italian Communists relinquished their commanding positions in resistance movements to enter parliamentary coalitions under noncommunists and to restore exiled governments to power. This followed the interests of the Soviet elite which sought to maintain good relations with the Western countries while consolidating its positions of power in Eastern Europe.

According to the precepts of Bolshevism, self-expansion also serves as an end in itself. That self-expansion is desirable as well as necessary is evident in the following statement of Stalin containing a parallel internal quote of Lenin: [14]

The very development of world revolution . . . will be more rapid and more thorough, the more thoroughly Socialism fortifies itself in the first victorious country, the faster this country is transformed into a base for the further unfolding of world revolution, into a lever for the further disintegration of imperialism. . . . The development of world revolution will be the more rapid and thorough, the more effective the aid rendered by the first Socialist country to the workers . . . of all other countries. In what should this aid be expressed? It should be expressed, first, in the victorious country "carrying out the maximum realizable in one country for the developing support, awakening of revolution in all countries." . . . It should be expressed secondly, in that the "victorious proletariat of the first country . . ." after organizing its own Socialist production, should stand up . . . *against* the remaining, capitalist world, attracting to itself the oppressed classes of other countries, raising revolutions in those countries against the capitalists, in the event of necessity coming out even with armed force against the exploiting classes and their governments.

The Role of Revolution. Herein lies the second responsibility of the Comintern and later of the Cominform, the promulgation of revolution as an end in itself. Decreasingly evident during the past three decades of communism in Western Europe and North America, the revolutionary role of communism in Asia took on new significance after World War II. In China, Indochina, Malaya, Indonesia, and the Philippines, armed insurrections sparked by Communist agitation and assistance sought to advance the banner of revolution throughout the Asian world. Revolutions and Red armies— these became the twin weapons for advancing Soviet ends by self-extension: ends of self-preservation dictated by the inevitability of conflict and ends of self-extension dictated by the desirability of world revolution.

[14] J. Stalin, writing in 1924, quoted by "Historicus," *op. cit.,* pp. 198–199.

Against the contention that the Soviet elite has long since abandoned hopes of world revolution and that therefore self-expansion is only a means, not an end, in Soviet policy, it must be noted that renunciation of world revolution cannot yet be explicitly voiced in the Soviet Union. Until it can be so renounced, the Soviet elite remains beholden to all revolutions which partake of causes championed by the Bolshevik ideology, even where these revolutions are in no way controlled or directed from Moscow. Failure to uphold such revolutions, whether in Southeast Asia, Africa, or Latin America, in principle if not in practice, threatens the *raison d'être* of the elite. Not even Stalin—who, as will be seen shortly, had definite reasons for wishing to restrain more enthusiastic comrades in Yugoslavia and China—dared to declare publicly his convictions or to disavow Soviet support for Communist activity abroad. Thus, even with a slackening of external "capitalist hostility" or a lessening of the internal impetus toward world revolution, Soviet policy makers find themselves intimately linked with unrest abroad, carrying Soviet values and interests into non-Soviet territory and underwriting a policy of self-expansion.

Bolshevik Unilateralism. Another aspect of Soviet policy derived from Bolshevik ideology is its unilateral orientation, regarding all agreements with non-Communist elites as certain to be exploited by them for ends detrimental to Soviet interests. Stalin's traditional formulation of this danger warned against being used "to pull chestnuts out of the fire" for capitalist allies. Ambiguous as were his many statements on the possibility of coexistence between socialist and capitalist worlds, they consistently emphasized the temporary nature of such coexistence. In his celebrated interview with an American trade-union delegation in 1927 Stalin said: [15]

The matter concerns, obviously, temporary agreements with capitalist states in the field of industry, in the field of trade, and perhaps in the field of diplomatic relations. I think that the presence of two opposed systems . . . does not exclude the possibility of such agreements. . . . The limits of these agreements? The limits are set by the opposition of the two systems between which rivalry and struggle go on. Within the limits permitted by these two systems, but only within these limits, agreements are fully possible. . . .

That such "temporary agreement" is reluctantly undertaken as a necessity of Soviet weakness is revealed in remarks made by Stalin for domestic consumption the same year as this trade-union interview: [16]

We cannot forget the saying of Lenin to the effect that a great deal in the matter of our construction depends on whether we succeed in delaying war with the capitalist countries, which is inevitable but which may be delayed either until proletarian revolution ripens in Europe, or until the colonial revolutions come fully to

---

[15] J. Stalin as quoted by "Historicus," *op. cit.,* pp. 208–209.
[16] J. Stalin to the 15th Party Congress, quoted by "Historicus," *op. cit.,* p. 207.

a head, or finally, until the capitalists fight among themselves over division of colonies. Therefore the maintenance of peaceful relations with capitalist countries is an obligatory task for us. The basis of our relations with capitalist countries consists in admitting the coexistence of two opposed systems.

Here Stalin was speaking to his party associates; his frankness is indicative of the hostile unilateral nature of Soviet policy toward non-Soviet countries.

While conflict of interest usually exists among allies, Soviet ideology emphasizes the clash of aims to the exclusion of confluence of interests. The Russian approach toward Britain and the United States in the World War II coalition was consequently marked with hostility and distrust. Soviet representatives pounced on any hint of conflict or deceit, and charges of bad faith continually came from Moscow, frequently before investigation or explanation could be made by the Allies. Accuse first, investigate later, apologize never—these seemed the precepts for Bolshevik relations with allies.

Another manifestation of unilateralism is the Soviet refusal to recognize international arbitration or to submit Soviet actions to the scrutiny of international organizations. According to the assumption of conflict between capitalist and socialist elites, there can be no arbitration impartial to both sides. Similarly international organization must remain hostile to socialist interests so long as it is dominated by capitalist countries. The basic economic conflict underlying capitalist-socialist relations is not susceptible to international adjudication or legislation. So runs the Soviet argument. Trusteeship systems merely camouflage colonial control. International arms inspections only seek to discover weaknesses in the socialist economy. Schemes for helping underdeveloped areas are no more than palliatives for surplus capital searching for new markets and raw materials.

These assumptions do not preclude Soviet participation in international organizations, however. Just as temporary coexistence and even limited cooperation with capitalist countries can be dictated by objective circumstances, so membership first in the League and later in the United Nations was expedient for Soviet policy. These forums had no equal for appealing to uncommitted nations and for "unmasking the imperialistic capitalists." Examination of Soviet actions in the United Nations and its affiliated agencies, however, reveals the definite limits to the term "participation" when applied to the Soviet Union.

Relations with Communist elites, as with capitalist elites, frequently demonstrate Soviet unilateralism. The premises differ, but the result is similar. Moscow may view Warsaw or Prague with paternalism rather than hostility, but its alliances with Eastern European countries are marked by dictation rather than by consultation. Since history is regarded as a series of stages marked by progressive economic development, Soviet leaders insist on the prerogative to guide Communists outside Russia toward the socialist state already attained in Russia. Enunciated in principle by Lenin in 1920, this doctrine dominated Stalin's policy with respect to the Comintern as well as toward Communist governments after 1945. The purges which swept Eastern European capitals, accompanied by the expulsion of Titoist Yugoslavia from the Cominform, marked the culmination of this insistence upon obedience to orders from the Soviet elite. In short, Bolshevik ideology permitted satellites but not allies.

Only in the case of Communist China is the question of satellite versus ally a moot one. Yet even here the bulk of evidence indicates Moscow's commanding position in the activity of the Chinese Communist Party from its inception in 1921 to its seizure of power in 1949. No major Chinese Communist policies were enunciated without approval of the Kremlin. In many instances these policies originated with the Russian elite; when they failed leading Chinese Communists fell as scapegoats in sudden purges.[17] Whatever shift in this relationship may have occurred since 1949 is determined by the superior power position of the Chinese Communist elite compared with that of Eastern Europe.

6. Ends and Means of Policy: Flexibility amidst Rigidity. Having given so much attention to the fixed principles of doctrine and policy, it might well be assumed that Soviet policy makers enjoy little choice of ends and means and consequently their task is highly simplified, if somewhat stultifying. Nothing could be further from the truth. Those formulating policy may choose from a variety of means, may abandon one approach for another, and may justify interminable zigzags wholly within the framework of Bolshevik ideology. In the decade 1936 to 1946, Soviet policy espoused antifascism, scrapped it for a Nazi alliance, made a wartime coalition with Britain and America, and junked it in favor of an assault on Western positions by all means short of war. The key to such chameleonlike changeability lies in the dialectical interpretation of history.

Dialectical Thinking. This interpretation presupposes constant conflict of contradictory forces in any situation. Inasmuch as conflict is dynamic and history is assumed to be progressing to ever higher stages of development, the task of the policy maker is to determine the level of development, the degree of conflict, and to adjust his means accordingly. In Marxist parlance he must avoid mistaking "subjective appearance" for "objective reality." Thus policy may be defended against critics as "subjectively" appearing to contradict Bolshevik interests but "objectively" appropriate for the extant historical stage of development. In 1925 Stalin sought a closer relationship with Japan, arguing that Japan was "subjectively" the most imperialistic state in Asia but "objectively" it was a "progressive" country because it had the most highly industrialized economy in Asia.

The dialectic sanctions almost infinite flexibility for Soviet policy makers.

---

[17] See R. C. North, *Moscow and Chinese Communists,* Stanford University Press, Stanford, Calif., 1953.

A tactic which fails once is not relegated to the dust bin. It may merely have been a case of improper "timing," or an "incorrect analysis of the objective material forces." Scapegoats may suffer and officials may be purged for having failed to exercise Marxist-Leninist principles correctly, but the tactic will reappear. Its reemergence will be justified on the basis that the "objective" situation has changed.

Soviet-German relations provide a case in point. Seeking to build an anti-Western power, Soviet leaders secretly rearmed Germany in the 1920s and early 1930s. The rise of Nazism reversed Soviet policy. In 1934 came an alliance with France, entry into the League of Nations, and a world-wide campaign against fascism. In 1937 came the liquidation of the entire top echelon of the Red Army on charges of conspiring with German circles and/or plotting a German alliance. With the vacillation of England and France, Soviet policy suddenly reversed itself again and concluded the Nazi-Soviet pact of 1939. While Russia furnished military and economic aid to Hitler's marching armies Communist groups throughout the world scrapped antifascism for "the fight against participation in the imperialistic war." Every turn in policy was justified in terms of the dialectic and advanced as a striking victory for the scientific basis of Soviet foreign policy.

Stalin explained the necessity for this zigzag policy in terms of Bolshevik ideology when he elaborated his concept of the "ebb and flow" of world revolution: [18]

> The epoch of world revolution . . . is a whole strategic period, embracing a whole series of years and, I dare say, even a number of decades. In the course of this period there can and must be ebbings and flowings. . . . For the time being the international revolutionary movement is in the declining phase; but . . . this decline will yield . . . to an upward surge which may end in the victory of the world proletariat. If, however, it should not end in victory, another decline will set in, to be followed in its turn by yet another revolutionary surge. Our defeatists maintain that the present ebb in the revolutionary tide marks the end of the revolution. They are mistaken now just as heretofore. . . . The revolution does not develop along a straight, continuous and upwardly aspiring line, but along a zigzag path.

Advance and Retreat. Along with the assumption of constant change, and therefore the need for constant shifts in means to attain the given end, is a basic belief in the inevitability of victory. Retreat is only temporary and prerequisite to advance. This formula of two steps forward and one step backward was repeatedly enunciated by Lenin and Stalin, generally in the verbiage of military strategy. As Lenin put it during the early twenties when certain radical measures of "war communism" were abandoned in favor of capitalistic concessions during the "New Economic Policy": "We are retreating because we have won enough to enable us to hold the necessary posi-

[18] J. Stalin, *Voprosy Leninizma,* as quoted in Leites, *op. cit.,* p. 62.

tions, and had we not won these positions in the period of 1917–21, we should not have had any room to retreat geographically, economically and politically." [19] Stalin drew the military parallel more explicitly: [20]

This is often the case in war, when one side wants to save the cadres of its army and lead them out from under the blows of the excellent forces of the enemy. Then it begins a planned retreat and gives up, without fighting, whole cities and areas for the sake of winning time and collecting forces for new decisive battles in the future . . . to gain a breathing space, to create a new army, and thus to secure future strategic gains.

Tactics and Strategy. Flexibility of means contrasts with rigidity of ends. Concessions may be justified in terms of ebb and flow, advance and retreat, but all concessions are to be considered as only temporary. If safety of the center is jeopardized, outward pressure on countries bordering the Soviet bloc may be eased, but it must be reasserted according to concepts of conflict and self-expansion. The alteration of means, or tactics, toward the achievement of given ends, or strategy, is constantly stressed by Soviet theorists. Again to quote Stalin,[21]

Tactics, guiding itself by the directives of strategy and by the experience of the revolutionary movement . . . calculating at every given moment the state of forces inside the proletariat and its allies . . . as well as in the camp of the adversary—marks out those *concrete courses* for winning the wide masses to the proletarian side and leading the battle stations of the socialist front which most surely paves the way for strategic success.

7. Unity on Ends; Disunity on Means. Having placed so much emphasis upon the monolithic nature of the Soviet elite, the challenge naturally arises as to the source of repeated schisms which have fragmented though not shattered that elite. The phenomenon of disunity amidst unity has given rise to Western prognoses of imminent collapse, of revolution against the party, or of conspiratorial cliques plotting to assassinate the Soviet leadership. Whatever may have been the hopes or plans of dissenters along these lines, Stalin never suffered the open challenge to his rule such as Hitler suffered in the bombing of July, 1944. However intense has been the struggle for control at the top, seldom has the structure been shaken to its foundations. Even the Stalin-Trotsky feud, extending for almost two decades and in part responsible for the liquidation of thousands of party stalwarts, failed to cripple the authoritarian controls of the regime.

Agreement on Ends. In part, this impressive unity stems from the forbearance of those contesting for control. Thus Trotsky, despite his wide influence in the party and particularly in the Red Army, which was his per-

---

[19] V. Lenin, *Selected Works,* vol. IX, p. 313.
[20] J. Stalin, *Sochineniia* ("Works"), vol. V, pp. 167–168.
[21] 1921 article by J. Stalin, quoted in "Historicus," *op. cit.,* p. 205.

sonal creation during the civil war, allowed himself to be expelled from the country and driven from country to country without once attempting an uprising against Stalin. Even the instruments of violence, the army and the police, were purged at will by Stalin without a single incident of organized resistance coming to the fore.

Unity stems not only from self-imposed restrictions, or from the excellent manipulation of purge and police, but also from an extremely high consensus on the ends of policy. Such unanimity is a natural corollary of the single-group elite, established by forcible elimination of all organized opposition during the November revolution of 1917, the civil war of 1918 to 1920, and the "Stalinist revolution" of 1925 to 1931. By the time of the purges of the old Bolsheviks in 1937, potential group conflict in trade unions, peasantry, and military had been eliminated by deportation, execution, and penetration of mass organizations by party members. Neither the initial defeats of World War II nor the passing of Stalin found this unity in peril.

Disagreement on Means. How then explain the persistence of disunity within the elite not only long after Lenin's death but down to the death of Stalin? Why should accusations of "Trotskyism" and "imperialist agent" recur against highly placed persons in long-established positions of authority if the consensus is so universal? The answer lies in the disagreement over means of attaining agreed ends. As has already been seen, considerable flexibility is accorded Soviet policy makers seeking to analyze the dialectic process of history. Dissenting analyses of "the objective reality" or arguments over the vital question of "timing" policy fill the early pages of Bolshevik polemics. Disunity is the stepchild of the dialectic.

Disunity springs from other than dialectical diagnosis, however. Two fundamental problems, the internal industrial weakness of the Soviet Union and the external failure of world revolution, have plagued Soviet policy makers since the seizure of power in 1917. No Marxist formula lay at hand for the resolution of dilemmas posed by these situations. Their persistence has occasioned schisms within the Soviet elite throughout its history.

Thus two generations of Soviet leaders have grappled with the problems of inadequate agricultural production and a forced tempo of industrialization which strains resources, human and natural, to the breaking point. Failure to solve these problems within the avowed Bolshevik framework of collectivization and centralized planning has, in turn, driven Soviet foreign policy to compromise with the capitalist world and to curtail assistance to insurrection abroad. Such retreats inevitably arouse disunity within the elite as to the degree to which, and the duration for which, compromise is necessary. The interrelationship of foreign and domestic policy widens this circle of disagreement to include the manifold problems of resource allocation, heavy versus light industry, rearmament levels, and long-delayed consumer needs such as housing.

Disunity and Personal Insecurity. Complicating solution of these problems is the struggle for personal survival, present in all elites but exacerbated by the conspiratorial and violent traditions of Bolshevik politics. From Marx's strictures against his contemporary Lassalle to the execution of Beria as "traitor and imperialist agent" by his former associates Khrushchev and Malenkov, internecine accusations and ruthless purges fill the pages of Communist history.

If the penalty for disagreement is liquidation, the reward for successful polemics is promotion and power. Given the roots of disagreement in the dialectic, it was natural for those seeking favor or power to manufacture or to magnify "errors" of opponents. Indeed, it is not improbable that the individual heading an authoritarian elite might encourage such "safe" disunity, inasmuch as it lessens the possibility of unified opposition to his policies and permits him to build a following by coming out in favor of one or another protagonist.

Disunity amidst unity, then, proves to be highly dramatic in the personal sense although less significant politically. Schisms represent not differences on ends or conflicts among groups but rather disagreement over means among individuals within the elite. These disagreements extend toward the base of the pyramid in so far as these individuals are able to build personal followings by means of promoting friends and demoting foes. Disunity lessens the total power in terms of leadership and human resources and may heighten feelings of insecurity which are omnipresent in the authoritarian regime. Suppression of debate within the ranks of the Central Committee or the Presidium does not eliminate secondary indications of disagreement over tactics with respect to both domestic and foreign policy. Such signs as the gradual elimination of men associated in the past with Andrei Zhdanov following his death in 1948, and their replacement by those thought to be favorites of Georgi Malenkov, suggest the association of individuals along differing concepts of policy. So far, however, such disunity has not brought about revolution or collapse within the Soviet elite.

II. Soviet Policy in Action

8. A Decade of Stalin: 1939 to 1949. No better illustration of ends and means operative in the single-group authoritarian Bolshevik elite can be found than in the last years of Stalin's rule. During the decades after Lenin's death, Stalin eliminated organized opposition and tamed internal dissent. Despite the economic dislocation of collectivization, the elimination of celebrated leaders in both party and army in the purges, and the failure of revolution to succeed outside the Soviet Union prior to 1949, Stalin's elite preserved its monolithic structure and strength. From the replacement of Litvinov by Molotov as Commissar of Foreign Affairs in 1939, the pattern became one of ever-increasing responsibility in the hands of the Politburo members. Stalin, Molotov, Malenkov, Beria, and Voroshilov formed the nexus of direction of all military, political, and economic affairs. Their success was registered in the lack of serious schism in the Soviet community in the face of drastic policy reversals, occasioned first by the Nazi-Soviet pact and later by the Soviet-British-American coalition, and in the face of widespread destruction resulting from the lightninglike victories of Nazi forces in 1941–1942.

In this decade, 1939 to 1949, Soviet policy coped with the problems of war and peace in various ways. During the first period, 1939 to 1941, it won a limited war with Finland and observed a limited alliance with Germany. In the second period, 1941 to 1944, the military crisis resulting from the German attack on Russia found the Soviet elite allied with the capitalist countries of Britain and the United States in a struggle for its very survival. Finally, during the years 1944 to 1949, military success was followed by economic crisis stemming from the ravages of war and the reconversion to peace. Thus the ten-year sample offers divergent backgrounds against which the Stalinist elite played its role.

Obviously not every aspect of policy which was examined in the previous section will be found equally operative in all three periods. Furthermore, the limitations of evidence on Soviet motivations must be kept in mind as we attempt to infer aims from actions. Within this framework, however, a case study of Stalin's policy over a ten-year period illustrates the way in which such principles as self-expansionism, unilateralism, and flexibility manifest themselves.

9. Nazi-Soviet Alliance and Self-expansionism. The full documents concerning the negotiations carried on simultaneously between Soviet Russia and Germany on the one hand, and Soviet Russia and Great Britain on the other, during the fateful summer of 1939, are not yet available. Nevertheless, it is clear from the published records of Nazi-Soviet relations that one impetus to the Berlin-Moscow entente was its promised rewards for Soviet expansionism. In a secret protocol concluded between Ribbentrop and Molotov on August 23, 1939, it was agreed that [22]

In the event of a territorial and political rearrangement of the areas belonging to the Baltic States [Finland, Estonia, Latvia, Lithuania], the northern boundary of Lithuania shall represent the boundary of the spheres of influence of Germany and the USSR. . . . In the event of a . . . rearrangement of the areas belonging to the Polish state the spheres of influence of Germany and the USSR shall be bounded approximately by the line of the rivers Narew, Vistula, and San. . . .

[22] A. Rossi, *The Russo-German Alliance, 1939–1941.* Beacon Press, Boston, 1951, pp. 40–41.

With regard to South-Eastern Europe attention is called by the Soviet side to its interests in Bessarabia.

With one stroke of the pen, Soviet Russia won extension of its frontiers along lines similar to those of czarist Russia. Reincorporation of the Baltic states (with the exception of Lithuania), which had declared their independence after the Bolshevik Revolution of 1917, annexing Poland up to the so-called Curzon line proposed by British representatives as being ethnically fair in 1919, and winning back the Romanian-seized strip called Bessarabia, all served to reward Stalin for promising "nonaggression" vis-à-vis Hitler Germany. By later offering Hitler a large slice of Poland in exchange for Lithuania, Soviet Russia won an exclusive position in the Eastern Baltic.

Only a few days of fighting were necessary to "seal in blood" the Nazi-Soviet partition of Poland. Moscow then sought concessions from Finland, particularly with respect to territorial changes north of Leningrad. When Helsinki balked in late November, the Red Army attacked. Initial failures on the military front were paralleled by the futile effort to set up a rival "Red" Finnish regime on Soviet soil in hopes of winning defections from the opposite side. Finally in March, 1940, the disparity of power compelled Finland to sue for peace. As a result, Soviet frontiers were moved forward along most of the Soviet-Finnish border and a Soviet naval base in the Gulf of Finland provided not only protection for Leningrad but domination over the Finnish capital as well.

Following full annexation of the Baltic states of Estonia, Latvia, and Lithuania in 1940, endorsed by so-called "plebiscites" in these territories already dominated by the Red Army, Stalin moved to satisfy his claims in southeastern Europe. His ambitions prompted the first serious split in the Nazi-Soviet alliance. Although Bessarabia had been promised in the 1939 agreement, Bucovina had not; in June, 1940, Molotov laid claim to both pieces of Romania.[23] A compromise settlement finally ceded northern Bucovina to Russia, but the basic question of Soviet hegemony over the Balkans remained unsettled.

The most complete and official statement of Soviet expansionist aims came in 1940 when Ribbentrop invited Russia to join the Tripartite Pact linking Germany, Japan, and Italy. Soviet counterproposals included the following points: [24]

> The area south of Batum and Baku in the general direction of the Persian Gulf is recognized as the centre of gravity of the aspirations of the Soviet Union. . . . Bulgaria geographically is situated inside the security zone of the Black Sea boundaries of the Soviet Union. . . . A base for land and naval forces of the USSR [should be] within the range of the Bosporus and the Dardanelles by means of a long-term lease.

[23] *Ibid.*, p. 133.
[24] *Nazi-Soviet Relations, 1939–1941*, Didier, New York, pp. 258–259.

Hitler refused to countenance further Russian expansion in the Balkans and made no reply to these proposals; his response was to be the attack of June 22, 1941.

10. The Assumption of Conflict: 1939 to 1941. Basic to an understanding of the Nazi-Soviet aspect of Soviet foreign policy during these years is the deep distrust with which the Soviet elite viewed the capitalist world, a distrust rooted in the assumption of the inevitable, basic conflicts between the two economies. Soviet suspicions of British-French motivations were clearly voiced by Stalin in March of 1939: [25]

> The majority of the non-aggressive countries, particularly England and France . . . have taken up a position of non-intervention, a position of "neutrality." . . . [This] reveals an eagerness, a desire, not to hinder the aggressors in their nefarious work: not to hinder Japan, say, from embroiling herself in a war with China, or better still, with the Soviet Union; not to hinder Germany, say, from enmeshing herself in European affairs, from embroiling herself in a war with the Soviet Union . . . egging the Germans on to march farther east, promising them easy pickings, and prompting them: "Just start war on the Bolsheviks, and everything will be all right."

With this distrust of Allied motivations, the Soviet elite played its hand cautiously. Pursuing simultaneous negotiations separately with Nazi and Allied representatives, Stalin sought for the best safeguards of Russian security in case of general conflict. Beyond this he looked for whatever gains might be picked up at little cost. His suspicions were in no way relieved by the failure of London to speed talks, to send highly placed persons such as had been used in negotiations with the Germans, and to compel Poland to accept Soviet terms of assistance. Although the final impetus to the Nazi-Soviet pact was undoubtedly the promised territorial rewards, the failure of the Russian-British talks stemmed in part from this deep-seated assumption of ulterior motives on the part of the traditional center of the capitalistic, imperialistic world.

So far as Nazi-Soviet relations were concerned, the assumption of conflict played a less obvious role, but it is clear from the acrimonious exchanges between Molotov and Ribbentrop that the Nazi-Soviet pact did not run smoothly. While Nazi ideology made inevitable such friction between Hitler and his allies, Bolshevik assumptions of conflict made the Soviet elite in turn suspicious of German policy. Among the Soviet counterproposals to the Nazi invitation for Russia to join the Tripartite Pact was one insisting "that the German troops are immediately withdrawn from Finland, which, under the compact of 1939, belongs to the Soviet Union's sphere of influence." [26] Similarly, Molotov protested in January, 1941, against the fact "that German

---

[25] J. Stalin to 18th Party Congress, Mar. 10, 1939, quoted by F. Schuman, *International Politics*, 5th ed., McGraw-Hill, New York, 1953, p. 420.

[26] *Nazi-Soviet Relations*, p. 258.

troops in great numbers were concentrated in Rumania and ready to march into Bulgaria." He warned that since "the Soviet Government had repeatedly called the attention of the Government of the Third Reich to the fact that it considered the territory of Bulgaria and the Straits as a security zone of the USSR, . . . it would consider the appearance of any foreign armed forces [there] . . . as a violation of the security interests of the USSR." [27] Such was the distrust with which the Soviet elite viewed its Nazi counterpart.

The Sharpening of Conflict. In both Europe and Asia, Soviet tactics successfully freed the hands of Germany and Japan so as to precipitate war between them and other capitalist powers, simultaneously safeguarding the Soviet center and permitting extension of Russian power. Concise statement of these tactics came in secret telegrams explaining policy to the Soviet ambassador to Japan in 1940.[28] Moscow explained its acceptance of Japanese conciliatory moves along the Manchurian border:

. . . Japan plans intensifying pressure on foreign interests in China and southeast Asia by securing the safety of Manchuria. We considered that this action on part of Japan would collide with foreign nations to advantage of the Soviet Union and China. We may alleviate our pressure upon North Manchurian border if Japan lifts her pressure upon Soviet Russia and China. . . .

A second wire clarified this policy:

. . . An overall agreement with Japan including peace between Japan and China would spoil Soviet-American relations. Considering a probable Soviet-German dispute in the future, we do not desire the cooling of friendly relations with America. Also such overall agreement with Japan might destroy our work proceeding among the suppressed peoples of Asia, and it would, on the one hand, guarantee Japan's free activities in China and in the Pacific, and on the other, it would not instigate the Japanese-American war which we desire. So we are planning not to develop the negotiation into an agreement but merely to alleviate tension between Japan and the Soviet Union. We concluded an "Agreement with Germany" because a war is required in Europe. . . .

In short, the pattern of the Nazi-Soviet pact could not be repeated in Asia because it would alienate revolutionary groups whose aims fit Bolshevik strategy of smashing capitalism by eliminating European imperialism. Also it would eliminate American aid in the event of a Russo-German war. Moscow's policy thus led to the Russo-Japanese Neutrality Pact of 1941, which proved a prerequisite for Japan's advance into South Asia and its attack on America. "Sharpening the conflict among the capitalist powers" here served two ends: self-preservation in terms of safeguarding the Soviet Far East,

---

[27] *Ibid.,* pp. 270–271.

[28] These telegrams were intercepted by the Imperial Japanese Government's consul general in Harbin. Japanese copies were examined by A. S. Whiting and accepted as authentic.

and self-extension in terms of maintaining Soviet penetration of national-revolutionary movements throughout Asia.

11. Flexibility: 1939 to 1941. Perhaps no more dramatic example of Soviet zigzags can be found than in the first part of the decade under examination. In March, 1939, Stalin had summed up Soviet foreign policy in an explicit, succinct program which included the following declarations:

> We stand for peaceful, close and friendly relations with all the neighboring countries which have common frontiers with the USSR . . . as long as they make no attempt to trespass, directly or indirectly, on the integrity and inviolability of the frontiers of the Soviet state. We stand for the support of nations which are the victims of aggression and are fighting for the independence of their country.

Yet within six months the Soviet Union invaded Poland and annexed much of its territory. Within a year, the Soviet army attacked and defeated Finland. Within a period of eighteen months the Baltic countries and part of Romania were absorbed into the Soviet Union. Stalin's declared ends of self-preservation and avowed means of "businesslike relations" coupled with self-defense had shifted. In the case of Finland, means of self-extension, annexing strategic territory, aimed at ends of self-preservation. Elsewhere the establishment of Soviet institutions and the formal incorporation of non-Russian populations into the Soviet Union could be interpreted only as means of self-extension, aimed at ends of self-extension.

No less drastic was the change in Soviet policy vis-à-vis the Axis. Throughout the 1930s Litvinov had led the attacks within the League of Nations against the expansionism of Japan, Germany, and Italy. Communists had joined in "Popular Fronts" with socialists and other non-Communists and had sent men and munitions to assist the Loyalist forces in Spain against the Franco armies, supported by Hitler and Mussolini. Overnight, with the signing of the Nazi-Soviet pact, the "fight against fascism" became "the imperialist war." Stalin explicitly blamed the Allies for World War II. "It was not Germany who attacked Britain and France, but Britain and France who attacked Germany; . . . the British and French Governments had brusquely rejected the German proposal and the USSR's efforts for a settlement." [29] In other words, Great Britain and France were guilty of aggression because they refused to accept Nazi domination over Poland supported by Soviet Russia. As Molotov explained before the Supreme Soviet,[30]

> Germany has clearly become a dangerous rival to Britain and France, the chief imperialist powers in Europe. It was for this reason that, under the pretext of fulfilling their obligations to Poland, these two countries declared war on Germany. . . . They have shown increasing hostility toward the USSR, since the USSR has refused to become the accomplice to Britain and France in carrying out their anti-German policy.

[29] Stalin, interview with *Pravda*, Nov. 30, 1939, quoted in Rossi, *op. cit.*, p. 82.
[30] V. Molotov, speech of Mar. 29, 1940, quoted in Rossi, *op. cit.*, p. 83.

That the credulity of Russian Marxists was sorely strained is suggested by Molotov's frantic efforts to work out an understanding with German leaders which would permit the Soviet invasion of Poland to be explained according to ends of self-preservation. His first hope was to "declare that Poland was falling apart and that it was necessary for the Soviet Union, in consequence, to come to the aid of the Ukrainians and the White Russians 'threatened' by Germany." [31] German objections resulted in a joint communiqué proposed by Berlin but rejected by Stalin on the basis that "it represented the facts all too frankly." [32] Stalin's draft prevailed, explaining Soviet intervention as designed "to restore peace and order . . . and to bring about a new order by the creation of natural frontiers and viable economic organizations." [33]

12. Military Crisis: 1941 to 1943. On June 22, 1941, Hitler's armored units swept across the Soviet frontier in what was formerly Poland. Within six months they hammered their way to the gates of Moscow. Soviet summary of Russian losses in the first weeks of the war notes: [34]

> On the territory that had been occupied by the Germans in November, 1941, lived about 40 percent of the whole Soviet population. About 65 percent of the whole prewar output of coal had come from there, 68 percent of all pig iron, 58 percent of all steel, 60 percent of aluminum . . . 38 percent of the grain . . . 41 percent of all railway lines.

Nor was the picture relieved elsewhere in the world. France lay under the heel of Nazi occupation, Britain stubbornly fought off Nazi air assaults but enjoyed no striking power, and in the winter of 1941–1942 the United States suffered a series of defeats in the Pacific at the hands of Japan. The high tide of Axis victories found the German-Italian-Japanese coalition dominant over all of Europe, most of North Africa, the richest area of Russia, much of China, and all of Southeast Asia, as well as the sea lanes of the world.

Under such conditions it might be supposed that Bolshevik determinants of policy would prove inoperative, that aims of self-expansion and assumptions of conflict would be absent from Soviet foreign policy. Indeed, such was the conclusion of many who saw only the surface aspects of relations among the Allies, a conclusion which received apparent support in the official disbanding of the Comintern in April, 1943. Was this not an explicit abandonment of world revolution as an aspiration of the Soviet elite? Did it not indicate a renunciation of self-extension and intervention in the internal affairs of other countries?

So sanguine an analysis received a rude jolt immediately following the

---

[31] *Nazi-Soviet Relations*, p. 91.
[32] *Ibid.*, p. 99.
[33] *Ibid.*, p. 100.
[34] N. Voznesensky, quoted in I. Deutscher, *Stalin, A Political Biography*, Oxford University Press, New York, 1949, p. 470.

war. Even the fragmentary evidence at our disposal suggests that in the years of adversity as well as in the years of success, the Soviet elite remained motivated by factors salient in the Bolshevik ideology. As early as December, 1941, Anthony Eden flew to Moscow, where Stalin made the following demands, among others, as Soviet objectives in the postwar world: (1) approval of the Soviet borders as of June, 1941, thereby sanctioning the annexations effected under the Nazi-Soviet alliance of 1939 to 1941, including Estonia, Latvia, Lithuania, and part of Romania within the Soviet Union; (2) the Curzon line to demarcate the Russo-Polish boundary, a line roughly corresponding to ethnic divisions but refused by the Polish government as being inadequate; (3) Russian bases in Romania; (4) territory seized from Finland in the Russo-Finnish war of 1939–1940 and Russian bases on Finnish territory.[35] This remained the consistent minimum program of Soviet policy throughout this period.

Other clues to Russia's intentions in East Europe came even during this time of military crisis. Exploitation of Pan-Slav sentiments was calculated to split off Hitler's satellites in East Europe and to lessen the pressure on southernmost Russia. However, the historical precedents of this doctrine, which emphasized the unity of the Slavic peoples under the leadership of Russia, hinted at Soviet expansionist ends and means in Poland, Czechoslovakia, Yugoslavia, and Bulgaria. Similarly, Stalin's sudden reinstatement of the Holy Synod in September, 1943, with the attendant refurbishing of the Russian Orthodox Church, served not only to revive Russian sentiments of loyalty to the regime but also to render Stalinism more acceptable to non-Communist Orthodox groups of Eastern Europe.

Nor was the dissolution of the Comintern as complete a break with Communist groups throughout the world as it appeared. They continued to champion the interests of the Soviet Union regardless of the implications for their domestic elites, as with their incessant demands in England and the United States for a "second front." They also acted as channels of propaganda from Russia and for espionage information to Russia, frequently with the connivance of Soviet embassies. Postwar trials in Canada, Great Britain, and the United States revealed an extensive network for espionage directed by official Soviet agents through members of local Communist parties. Disbanding of the Comintern, then, in no way eliminated the utilization of groups abroad for the extension of Soviet prestige and power.

Traditional Russian-British rivalry in the Balkans and Middle East and Winston Churchill's vigorous anti-Bolshevism of the intervention years, 1918 to 1920, offered historical precedent for Soviet assumptions of conflict with wartime capitalist allies. The prolonged delay of a second front appeared as part of a British plan to bleed both Germany and Russia to mutual annihilation.

[35] C. Hull, *The Memoirs of Cordell Hull,* Macmillan, New York, 1948, p. 1167.

When American shipments of lend-lease aid were forced to delay in Scottish harbors awaiting adequate protection along the Arctic route to Russia, Soviet officials charged Britain with "stealing" supplies. Stalin personally attacked Churchill bitterly in August, 1942, for having failed to launch a second front. His insinuations about British "fear of losses" and his accusations of a "broken promise" epitomized the distrust with which he viewed Allied strategy.[36] Again in May, 1943, Stalin dispatched a note to Churchill flatly accusing the Allies of "bad faith."

Symptoms of unilateralism were evident in the adamant refusal to permit Allied observers on the Russian front, the reluctance to publicize Allied aid, and the paucity of information given to support Russian military and economic requests to the Allies.

The most critical unilateral action came in the spring of 1943 over the question of the so-called Katyn massacre. When Radio Berlin announced discovery of the mass graves of Polish officers allegedly executed by Russians in 1940, the Polish government-in-exile in London immediately requested a neutral investigation. This strategic blunder, giving credence to an enemy broadcast designed to split the Allies, was magnified by Moscow's prompt termination of relations with the London Poles. American efforts to repair the breach failed. This unilateral action proved to be the first in a series of Russian moves extending Soviet power into Poland over the protests of Britain and the United States. The desire to absorb Poland, more than any other issue, demonstrated Soviet determination to disregard Allied advice which countered Russian interests.

Flexibility in the Soviet's foreign policies has already been noted in the disbanding of the Comintern, rehabilitation of the Orthodox Church, and replacement of proletarian internationalism with Pan-Slavism. Similarly the early years of the Allied coalition found Soviet policy able to shelve temporarily its entire anticapitalist program. Gone were the Communist strictures against the "imperialist war"; abandoned was Lenin's classic injunction to convert "the imperialist war into a civil war." Communists throughout the resistance movements of Europe accepted the symbolic leadership of De Gaulle, Beneš, and Queen Wilhelmina. Churchill and Roosevelt were no longer the "reactionary leaders of a decadent capitalist regime" but "the progressive leaders of a fighting antifascist coalition." Stalin, who had presided smilingly over the signing of the Nazi-Soviet pact, now publicly toasted the Anglo-American leaders and called for the extermination of "every single German who has set his invading foot on the territory of our Fatherland."[37]

[36] Sir Winston Churchill, *The Second World War,* Houghton Mifflin, Boston, vol. IV, pp. 480 ff.
[37] Deutscher, *op. cit.,* p. 489.

13. Economic Crisis: 1944 to 1949. By the Teheran Conference in December, 1943, bringing together for the first time Stalin, Churchill, and Roosevelt, the military crisis had been overcome and Red Army attacks were hammering the Nazi line in a grinding drive to the prewar Russian borders. It was clear that even with no Allied landing in Europe, the Soviet Union could liberate itself and perhaps drive on into the territory of the Third Reich. Militarily the advantages lay with Stalin. Not only had he demonstrated the superiority of the Red Army but he knew that his help would be desired in the final offensive against Japan. With decimation of German forces the Red Army would remain the dominant military power on the Eurasian continent.

A wholly different picture confronted the Soviet elite, however, with regard to domestic conditions. As noted in a postwar speech by Georgi Malenkov, 1940 figures for productivity were only reattained "in coal output in 1947, in steel and cement production in 1948, in pig iron output and oil extraction in 1949, in production of footwear in 1950, and in production of cotton textiles in 1951." [38] The following table traces the decline of Russian industry under the destruction of war and its slow recovery in the postwar years:

U.S.S.R. INDUSTRIAL OUTPUT IN PER CENT OF 1940 PRODUCTION

	1940	1944	1945	1946	1947	1948	1949
All industry.......	100	104	92	77	93	118	141
Producers' goods...	100	136	112	82	101	130	163
Consumers' goods..	100	54	59	67	82	99	107

SOURCE: G. Malenkov to 19th Congress of the Russian Communist Party, translated in *Current Digest of the Soviet Press*, vol. IV, no. 38, Nov. 1, 1952, p. 6.

These figures take on added significance when it is recalled that in 1940 the Soviet Union had the lowest ratio of productivity per person as well as per square mile of any of the major countries of Europe or North America, and that after World War II its population was increased by almost one-fourth. To put the picture in still another focus, direct destruction during the war included 84,000 schools, 43,000 libraries, 31,000 factories, 13,000 bridges, 40,000 miles of railway track, 7,000,000 horses, 17,000,000 cattle, and perhaps as many as 10,000,000 men.[39]

If Bolshevik ideology could be written off for naught, it might follow that

[38] G. Malenkov to 19th Congress of the Russian Communist Party, translated in *Current Digest of Soviet Press*, vol. IV, no. 39, Nov. 8, 1952, p. 3.
[39] Schuman, *op. cit.*, p. 429.

so demanding a task as rehabilitating the Soviet Union would compel the elite to abandon concepts of self-expansion, unilateralism, and conflict with capitalism in favor of self-restoration and cooperation with non-Soviet elites. Such is not the case, however. Events from the end of 1943 to the beginning of 1949 demonstrate the primacy of basic motivations stemming from Bolshevik ideology.

14. Self-expansion: 1943 to 1949. Considering only territory annexed outright by Soviet Russia, its size was expanded by some 274 million square miles since 1939. In addition, Poland, Czechoslovakia, Hungary, Albania, Bulgaria, and Romania, totaling 360 million square miles, have been brought under Soviet domination. The status of Eastern Germany remained essentially that of a Soviet satellite throughout the decade following World War II, although its final disposition in a united Germany might remove it from Russian hegemony. Similarly, Yugoslavia lay within the Soviet orbit for several years; its loss resulted from an open split between Stalin and Tito in 1948. Finally there is the Communist apparatus throughout the world, most of which—with the possible exception of groups in Asia—remains subservient to Moscow. Such is the record of Soviet expansion.

This expansion has been, for the most part, calculated and voluntary. No less significant, however, has been the unplanned, "involuntary" expansion. As has already been seen, there is an ideological link between the Soviet elite and all revolutions which champion Bolshevik principles, although these revolutions may be beyond Moscow's direct control. Even when Stalin felt such movements doomed to failure or strategically unwise in terms of his over-all program, he remained ideologically committed to them. In this sense, they represented "involuntary self-expansion."

Remarks of Soviet leaders to Western representatives during and after the war indicated little conviction that the Chinese Communist movement was on the threshold of seizing power.[40] Stalin is alleged to have once told the Yugoslav Foreign Minister: [41]

After the war we invited the Chinese comrades to come to Moscow and we discussed the situation in China. We told them bluntly that we considered the development of the uprising in China had no prospect, and that the Chinese comrades should seek a *modus vivendi* with Chiang Kai-shek, that they should join the Chiang Kai-shek government and dissolve their army. The Chinese comrades agreed here with the views of the Soviet comrades, but went back to China and acted quite otherwise. . . . Now . . . we admit we were wrong.

Similarly, in Greece it appears that a revolution "from below," as opposed to one directed "from above" in Moscow, sought to extend Soviet power and prestige against the will of the Soviet elite. In 1944, British action against

---

[40] J. Byrnes, *Speaking Frankly,* Harper, New York, 1947.
[41] V. Dedijier, *Tito,* Simon and Schuster, New York, 1953, p. 322.

the Greek Communist party passed with no challenge from Stalin. A previous understanding with Churchill divided the Balkans into tentative spheres of influence, Greece remaining wholly in the British camp. Whatever may have been Stalin's role in the initiation of the Greek civil war in 1946–1947, once American reaction was perceived to be hostile, he attempted to terminate all outside assistance to the Greek Communists. Safety of the Soviet center took priority over the success of revolution abroad. Soviet Russia never recognized the rebels' claim of a *de jure* government, although during the Soviet-Finnish campaign of 1939–1940, Moscow had bolstered a Finnish "government" of far less indigenous nature. In the Stalin interview quoted above referring to the restraint attempted with the Chinese Communists, he ordered the Yugoslavs to cease aiding the Greek rebels: "We do not agree with Yugoslav comrades that they should help further the Greek Partisans. . . . That struggle has no prospect whatsoever." [42] Regardless of Stalin's desires in China and Greece, however, the activities of local Communists were properly regarded by the outside world as potential extensions of Soviet power.

Such instances are exceptional. Far more familiar is the triple pattern of Soviet expansion by territorial annexation, political control over allied elites, and subversive activities among hostile elites. Unwilling to risk general war or to jeopardize the center, territorial annexation becomes possible only by means of implicit or explicit sanction on the part of those potentially capable of attacking the Soviet Union. Thus it is operative only in marginal situations such as World War II when both the Nazi-Soviet pact and the Allied coalition compelled Stalin's protagonists to buy his support by acceding to his demands. Nevertheless, territorial expansion differs only in degree from political expansion as evidenced by Russian domination over the governments of Eastern Europe and direction of large Communist minorities in Western Europe.

In this way, the three-pronged policy of postwar expansion becomes intelligible. At Teheran and Yalta, Stalin won British-American approval for annexing part of Poland and the Baltic states, while securing a dominant position in Manchuria and promise of southern Sakhalin and the Kurile Islands in the Far East. Concealed expansion through establishment of satellites came in a sphere-of-influence arrangement with Churchill, which recognized the preponderance of Soviet influence in Romania, Hungary, and Bulgaria, while presuming an equal British-Russian role in Yugoslavia. So far as Poland was concerned, British acceptance of a Russo-Polish frontier totally unacceptable to the London government-in-exile cut the ground out from under that group as a contender with the Soviet-sponsored "Lublin government." Finally, Communist parties abroad provided the third prong of expansion as Moscow ordered those in Western Europe to sabotage the

[42] *Ibid.*, pp. 321–322.

Marshall Plan while pushing Southeast Asian Communists to open insurrection.

The consequence of Soviet expansion is writ large on the maps of the world and the pages of history. It needs no elaboration here. Given the Marxist predilection for communism throughout the world, the conviction that "capitalist encirclement" placed the socialist state in perpetual danger, Russian aspirations for hegemony in Eastern Europe, and the historical heritage of foreign invasion from both ends of the Eurasian continent, it is small wonder that expansionism should be an integral part of Soviet policy. In terms of values and interests it appears to the Soviet elite as both necessary and desirable.

15. Unilateralism and the Assumption of Conflict: 1943 to 1949. Although some Soviet moves came after consultation with London and Washington, the *fait accompli,* particularly in Poland, remained dominant. As Secretary of State Edward Stettinius remarked in defense of the Yalta pact, "It was not a question of what Great Britain and the United States would permit Russia to do in Poland but what the two countries could persuade the Soviet Union to accept. . . . What did the Soviet Union gain in East Europe which she did not already have? . . . If we had made no agreements at Yalta, the Russians would still be in full possession of the territory." [43]

Despite American efforts to mediate between the London Poles and Moscow, Stalin had refused to permit outside intervention. A rival Polish group, formed under Soviet auspices, accompanied the Red Army on its march across the 1939 Polish-Russian border. In July, 1944, it received official Soviet recognition as the *de facto* regime, the so-called "Lublin government."

In August, 1944, the Red Army reached the outskirts of Warsaw and in special broadcasts called upon the populace to revolt against the Germans. Once the revolt began, the Red troops remained in the neighboring suburbs; the Red air force sent no assistance. The following month saw Warsaw leveled and the bulk of the local populace exterminated under the furious Nazi attack. Soviet refusal to cooperate in any way with the uprising, accentuated by dilatory tactics designed to obstruct Allied planes from parachuting supplies to the Poles, stemmed from more than military strategy. As Molotov frankly admitted to American Ambassador Harriman at the time,[44]

Stalin had promised Mikolajczyk [representing the London Poles] . . . to give aid to the Poles resisting the Germans in Warsaw. However, because of statements emanating from the Polish government in London, *it had become evident that the movement in Warsaw was inspired by men antagonistic to the Soviet Union, and therefore the Soviet government could no longer countenance any association with the uprising.* [The Soviet government] could not object to

---

[43] E. Stettinius, *Roosevelt and the Russians,* Doubleday, New York, 1949, pp. 301 ff.
[44] Hull, *op. cit.,* pp. 1446–1447. Italics supplied.

British or American planes dropping arms in the region of Warsaw but they objected to the planes landing in Soviet territory since the Soviet Government did not wish, either directly or indirectly, to associate itself with "the Warsaw adventure."

The Soviet rupture of relations with the London regime in 1943, the calculated abandonment of the Warsaw uprising in 1944, and the repeated delays in postwar elections accompanied by intimidation of all non-Communist opposition formed a consistent pattern of policy. Unilateral interpretation of the Yalta agreements sought to form an interim government dominated by the Lublin Poles. Roosevelt protested to Stalin on April 1, 1945, "I cannot conceal the concern with which I view the lack of progress made in the carrying out . . . of the political decisions which we reached at Yalta, particularly those relating to the Polish question." [45] Roosevelt's efforts were of no avail. His death a few weeks later came as sixteen members of the Polish underground, having been promised safe conduct if they went to Moscow to consult on the new government, were arrested by Soviet authorities on charges of espionage. Despite a special flight by Harry Hopkins at the instance of newly installed President Truman, Stalin refused to release them. He insisted that only "four or five" of the eighteen positions in the Polish cabinet could go "to representatives of groups" other than the Lublin Poles, and he commented that such freedoms as speech and assembly could "only be applied to full in peacetime and even then with certain limitations." [46]

Soviet assumptions of hostility produced endless recriminations between Russian and Allied officials. At one point Vyshinsky told the American officer supervising the Soviet end of military lend-lease aid, "Neither the United States nor the United Kingdom [is] seriously opposing Hitler." [47] One month after Yalta, preliminary contacts between German and Allied military representatives in Italy, although made known to Soviet authorities in advance, brought charges from Molotov that Great Britain and the United States were "carrying on negotiations . . . behind the back of the Soviet Government." [48] Despite clarifying cables from Roosevelt flatly denying that negotiations for surrender of German forces had begun, the Soviet Premier replied bluntly,[49]

My military colleagues . . . do not have any doubts that the negotiations have taken place. . . . I think my colleagues are close to the truth. . . . As a result of this agreement, at the present moment the Germans on the Western Front have in fact ceased the war against England and the United States. At the same

[45] C. Wilmot, *The Struggle for Europe,* Harper, New York, 1952, p. 686.
[46] *Ibid.,* p. 707.
[47] J. Deane, "Negotiating on Military Assistance," in R. Dennett and J. Johnson (eds.), *Negotiating with the Russians,* World Peace Foundation, Boston, 1951, p. 7.
[48] Wilmot, *op. cit.,* p. 688.
[49] *Ibid.,* pp. 688–689.

time, the Germans continue the war with Russia, the ally of England and the United States.

In view of the Allied pledge of "no separate peace" this was tantamount to charging treachery as well as falsehood on the part of Britain and the United States.

Because of the basic hostility with which Bolshevik ideology views capitalist elites, unilateral actions should have been no surprise. Much less anticipated, however, was parallel treatment of Communist elites in Eastern Europe. For instance, Georgi Dimitrov, celebrity of the interwar Comintern and leader of postwar Bulgaria, concluded a treaty of alliance with Tito prior to the Tito-Stalin split, and openly proposed a Balkan federation. Stalin's veto of the entire project and Dimitrov's public reversal of policy revealed the extent of Soviet interference with Communist allies.

Similarly, Soviet policy with respect to Yugoslavia both before and after the ousting of the Germans was undertaken without consultation with the Titoist elite. Tito apparently had no foreknowledge of the Churchill-Stalin agreement whereby British influence was to be permitted, the monarchy reestablished, and radical economic measures indefinitely postponed.[50] Soviet bargaining over Trieste likewise ran counter to Yugoslav policy. At the 1946 Paris Conference, Soviet acceptance of a French proposal unsatisfactory to Belgrade came without prior warning to the Yugoslav delegation.[51] Among the central issues of the Tito-Stalin dispute was Tito's refusal to accept Soviet unilateral direction of the entire military, political, and economic development of Yugoslavia.

16. Flexibility: Advance and Retreat, 1943 to 1949. During the period of economic crisis, Soviet Russia suffered recurring strains and Eastern Europe even more so. War with the West could only be viewed with alarm, particularly while America held atomic superiority. Recourse to the flexibility inherent in the dialectic, to the principle of advance and retreat, provided an alternative to policies of self-expansion and unilateralism which threatened to involve Russia in open hostilities.

A salient example of this came in the Soviet-imposed Berlin blockade which sought to seal off all channels to the British and American sectors of Berlin, thereby forcing the withdrawal of Western units from the symbolic center of Germany. The gigantic Berlin airlift proved that the West was prepared to exert all effort short of war to maintain its position. Despite incidents during the winter of 1948–1949 between Allied and Soviet aircraft, neither side moved to full hostilities. Rather than risk further provocation Soviet policy retreated, representatives negotiated a settlement, and the blockade was lifted.

[50] Dedijier, *op. cit.*, p. 233.
[51] *Ibid.*, p. 265.

Flexibility of a different sort, involving a shift of propaganda or alteration of tactic, is evident throughout the change from wartime to peacetime relations with the West. "The valiant Allies" became "the fascist imperialists." Photographs of the meeting on the Elbe wherein Soviet and American troops embraced victoriously in 1945 disappeared, to be replaced with crude caricatures of American generals with swastikas and bacteriological-warfare apparatus.

It is with respect to Germany that Soviet policy ran the gamut of approaches during this period. The start of the war found "death to the German invaders" as the Red Army's watchword. At Teheran, Stalin expressed himself unequivocally on the need to render Germany impotent and incapable of military aggression for all time to come. Just before Yalta he warned, "It would be naive to think that Germany will not attempt to restore her might and launch new aggression. . . . History shows that a short period— some twenty or thirty years—is enough for Germany to recover from defeat and re-establish her might." [52] With the end of the war, such violent anti-German sentiments might well have propelled this pivotal area into the arms of the Allies. Accordingly in April, 1945, his approach shifted: "Hitlers come and go, but the German nation and the German state remains." [53] By 1949, Stalin's domination of East Europe and particularly his control of Poland allowed him to bid higher for support in Germany. On October 13, 1949, his letter to Wilhelm Pieck, president of the East German regime, declared that the Germans and Russians were "the two peoples possessing the greatest potentialities in Europe to complete great actions of world significance." [54] Thus did Soviet policy with respect to Germany shift in the course of four years.

17. In Summation. Russian environment and Marxist theory have combined to produce the Bolshevik ideology, an ideology which shapes and directs Soviet policy. Expansionism is an inherent part of this policy, designed to serve ends of self-preservation by means of weakening the defined enemy, capitalist elites, and to serve ends of self-expansion by means of revolution which will establish communism, i.e., Soviet power, throughout the world. Unilateralism and an assumption of conflict with non-Soviet elites result in an abuse of alliances, an open disregard for traditional diplomacy, and an inveterate impugning of non-Soviet motivations. As a consequence those elites tend to regard Soviet motivations with hostility, to ally themselves against Soviet expansionism, and in short to behave precisely as predicted by Bolshevik precepts. Such is the self-fulfilling prophecy in Soviet policy.

Throughout the decision-making process authoritarian controls are manifest, offset only by disunity over tactics, by disagreement over the way to

[52] Deutscher, *op. cit.*, p. 538.
[53] *Ibid.*, p. 539.
[54] Y. Gluckstein, *Stalin's Satellites in Europe*, Beacon Press, Boston, 1952, p. 205.

weaken "capitalist encirclement" and to secure the Communist world. Yet despite the monolithism of the elite and the rigidity of the ideology, compromise and amelioration come as tactics sanctioned in the Marxist concept of history, in the mystery of the dialectic.

In the years following this selected case study, certain external factors altered the environment within which Soviet policy was formulated. Soviet inferiority in atomic weapons gradually lessened, and by mid-1955 it appeared that parity with, if not supremacy to, American hydrogen-bomb development had been won by Soviet research. Industrialization reached levels permitting greater attention to the badly neglected consumer sector of the economy. Communist China appeared as an important, if demanding, ally. To offset these gains, the United States threw back the North Korean invasion of South Korea in 1950. In 1953 came the death of Stalin, followed by dissension in Eastern Germany, unrest in Eastern Europe, and political shake-ups in the Soviet Union.

Although these changes were accompanied by shifts in Soviet tactics, there was little indication that any basic changes in Soviet policy and practice had occurred. After almost forty years of development Bolshevik ideology has crystallized, the elite has solidified, and the resulting policy has stabilized. Its every tactic may not be anticipated; its goals in each instance may not be clearly defined even by the Soviet elite. Nevertheless, the over-all motivations remain constant. Such is the pattern of ends and means within the single-group authoritarian elite of a Communist community.

ADDITIONAL CASE-STUDY MATERIAL

Beloff, M.: *The Foreign Policy of Soviet Russia,* 2 vols., Oxford, New York, 1947.

Byrnes, J.: *Speaking Frankly,* Harper, New York, 1947.

Carr, E. H.: *The Bolshevik Revolution, 1917–1923,* St. Martin's, New York, 1952.

Churchill, Sir Winston: *The Second World War,* 6 vols., Houghton Mifflin, Boston, 1948–1953.

Dedijier, V.: *Tito,* Simon and Schuster, New York, 1953.

Dennett, R., and J. Johnson (eds.): *Negotiating with the Russians,* World Peace Foundation, Boston, 1951.

Deutscher, I.: *Stalin, A Political Biography,* Oxford, New York, 1949.

Fischer, L.: *The Soviets in World Affairs,* Princeton University Press, Princeton, N.J., 1951.

Gluckstein, Y.: *Stalin's Satellites in Europe,* Beacon Press, Boston, 1952.

"Historicus": "Stalin on Revolution," *Foreign Affairs,* vol. 27, January, 1949.

Hull, C.: *The Memoirs of Cordell Hull,* Macmillan, New York, 1948.

Inkeles, A.: "Social Stratification and Mobility in the Soviet Union," *American Sociological Review,* vol. 15, August, 1950.

Leites, N.: *The Operational Code of the Politburo,* McGraw-Hill, New York, 1951.

Levi, W.: *Modern China's Foreign Policy,* University of Minnesota Press, Minneapolis, 1953.

Moore, Barrington: *Terror and Progress—USSR,* Harvard University Press, Cambridge, Mass., 1954.

Moore, H. L.: *Soviet Far Eastern Policy, 1931–1935,* Princeton University Press, Princeton, N.J., 1945.

Nazi-Soviet Relations, 1939–1941, Didier, New York.

North, R. C.: *Kuomintang and Chinese Communist Elites,* Hoover Institute Elite Studies, Stanford University Press, Stanford, Calif., 1952.

Rossi, A.: *The Russo-German Alliance, 1939–1941,* Beacon Press, Boston, 1951.

Rostow, W. W.: *Dynamics of Soviet Society,* Norton, New York, 1953.

Royal Institute of International Affairs: *Soviet Documents on Foreign Policy, 1917–1941,* 3 vols., Oxford, New York, 1951–1953.

——: *The Soviet-Yugoslav Dispute,* London, 1948.

Schueller, G.: *The Politburo,* Stanford University Press, Stanford, Calif., 1951.

Stalin, J.: "Economic Problems of Socialism in the USSR," *Current Digest of the Soviet Press,* supplement, Oct. 18, 1952.

——: *Leninism: Selected Writings,* International Publishers, New York, 1942.

Stettinius, E.: *Roosevelt and the Russians,* Doubleday, New York, 1949.

Towster, J.: *Political Power in the USSR,* Oxford, New York, 1949.

Wilmot, C.: *The Struggle for Europe,* Harper, New York, 1952.

X: "The Sources of Soviet Conduct," *Foreign Affairs,* vol. 26, July, 1947.

Chapter 15

EGYPT: AN OLIGARCHICAL ELITE

1. Political Bases of Oligarchy. Oligarchy, the limitation of decision making to a few groups and the exclusion of the bulk of the population from politics, prevails in most of Latin America, the Middle East, and much of Asia. Egypt provides a typical case study with characteristics common to oligarchical regimes elsewhere. Thus its historical traditions have failed to encourage democratic development. Its religious doctrines have provided a suitable atmosphere for rule by a few and passivity of the many. Its constitutional practices have sanctioned abuse of parliamentary methods. Finally its public acceptance of violence as a means of settling group conflict has substituted compulsion for persuasion. Egypt's basically agrarian economy dependent upon single-crop exports parallels that of oligarchical countries in the Middle East and Latin America. The roots which nourish oligarchy in Egypt prevail wherever underdeveloped countries are ruled by a limited elite. Whether Moslem or Catholic, whether influenced by Britain or America, whether dependent upon cotton or coffee, the essential framework shows striking similarities.

Egyptian apathy toward government and politics is in part a consequence of history. As one writer observed, "For over twenty-five centuries, Egypt was never ruled by Egyptians. The seat of government might be in Persepolis, Rome, Constantinople, Damascus, Baghdad, or it might be in Alexandria or Cairo. But the rulers, the army, and the higher ranks of the bureaucracy were almost without exception foreigners." [1] The winning of autonomy in the nineteenth century and of *de jure* independence in the twentieth failed to give rise to pluralistic government. Rule from above remained.

Islamic doctrine, originally proclaiming unity of church and state in the caliph, receded before the challenge of secular government until it focused exclusively on personal relationships and not political ones. "Political and administrative institutions . . . lay outside its range of effective action. . . . The atomism of the Muslim mind, by its rejection of abstract 'law,' hindered Muslim thinkers from evolving a systematic and practical political doctrine. . . . Orthodox thought rarely ventured into political economy or philos-

---

[1] C. Issawi, *Egypt: An Economic and Social Analysis,* Oxford, New York, 1947, pp. 4–5.

ophy." [2] Not only did religion present no obstacle to oligarchy; its conservatism favored the *status quo* and promoted acquiescence in rule by a few in its tendency to keep the impoverished masses content with their lot in life.

Nor was oligarchy replaced by democracy during British hegemony, established in 1882 and continuing in modified form through World War II. In fact, the record suggests British connivance to continue an oligarchy favorable to British interests in Suez and the Sudan. In 1923 Egypt established a constitutional monarchy, but practice soon indicated clear supremacy of the king. Suspended in 1928, modified in 1930, restored in 1936, and abolished in 1953, the constitution did little to further representative government. Rigged elections, British intervention in cabinet appointments, and inevitable dissolution of parliaments receiving valid electoral majorities all combined to make politics a succession of struggles between the Palace and its chief political rival, the Wafd party. Between 1923 and 1942 only four cabinets out of nineteen enjoyed parliamentary majorities; the king dismissed all four. Down to 1950 only one parliament lasted out its appointed term of five years. Small wonder that Western institutions made little headway among Egyptian political circles.

Assumption of Violence. Oligarchy in Egypt draws strength from the contrast between formal institutions such as the constitution and the reality of political struggle. Assassination arouses little horror in a country where the incidence of murder is officially placed at 224 per million inhabitants annually compared with 5 per million in Great Britain.[3] Those who have fallen before the dagger or pistol include a British governor-general of the Sudan, a prime minister, and Hasan al-Banna, founder of the Muslim Brotherhood. The assumption of violence made Hasan one of the most powerful figures in contemporary Egypt as his followers terrorized British and Egyptian opponents alike. In turn government police failed to intervene at Hasan's assassination, nor were his assailants brought to trial. Only strong groups can compete in this struggle; the unorganized mass must remain outside the political arena.

Mob violence enters politics in "the Street." Devoted student agitators, restive unemployed groups, and sheer hooliganism form a volatile mixture for political agitators. The pattern is familiar, from the initial gatherings of slogan-shouting nuclei to the surging throngs of burning, pillaging, and fighting rioters. Used principally against the British, "the Street" proved no less important in the struggle for ascendancy among the Wafd, Muslim Brotherhood, and Palace. Occasionally mob violence passes out of control of those behind it, and the excesses may well boomerang. Thus anti-British riots of 1952 killed over a dozen foreigners, burned one of Cairo's most famous

---

[2] H. A. R. Gibb, *Modern Trends in Islam,* University of Chicago Press, Chicago, 1947, pp. 89, 116.

[3] Issawi, *op. cit.,* p. 156.

hotels, and destroyed much valuable property. King Farouk won a handy pretext for ousting the Wafd leader, Nahas Pasha. Nahas could not win support from his wealthy patrons, who realized the danger of uncontrolled mob action by Egypt's impoverished and oppressed population.

Finally imprisonment followed by secret trial and swift execution may prove a more circumspect though no less coercive means of consolidating power. As an instrument of violence this police action smashes political organization and makes force a prerequisite for winning control of government. It proved particularly effective during the military regime of General Mohammed Naguib in 1952 and that of his successor, Colonel Gamal Abdel Nasser, in 1954.

2. Economic Bases of Oligarchy. Egypt, like similar countries throughout Asia and Latin America, is primarily agricultural and has traditionally been dominated by a small class of wealthy landlords. At the top, a minuscule 5 per cent of the landowners hold more than one-third of the land. Against this, 93 per cent of the landholders own 33 per cent of the land.[4] The fellah, or peasant, averages only ten to fifteen days of work a month at bare subsistence wages. Raising cotton, which accounts for more than 80 per cent of Egypt's exports, the fellah remains wholly at the mercy of a money market where usury rates range from 25 to 50 per cent.

The hard pressure of population upon land determines the oppressed state of peasantry and proletariat. While the population of Egypt has quintupled within a century to reach more than 20 million, the amount of cultivable land has remained constant at slightly more than 6 million acres. The surplus rural population of between 5 and 6 million persons offers an unlimited labor market for industry, effectively blocking organized labor. Neither fellah nor worker is in a position to enter political action except through sporadic mob action.

Egypt's intelligentsia faces parallel problems. For many of the yearly 30,000 graduates from high schools and universities, knowledge is the only reward. Other than government they have little hope of employment, yet only 180,000 jobs are open in the bureaucracy. The absence of a regularized system of examination or promotion permits these jobs to be used as rewards for support of contending groups within the oligarchy. As a result Egypt has two complete teams of officials which alternate in office according to which group holds power. The intelligentsia remains caught in the economic squeeze, unable to be an independent political force and beholden to patronage from above for survival.

The pyramid of Egypt's economic classes rests upon an extensive base of impoverished agricultural workers supplemented by an unimportant industrial nucleus. Above this level in status stands a diminutive middle class of

[4] *The Middle East: A Political and Economic Survey,* Royal Institute of International Affairs, London, 1950, p. 182.

shopkeepers, displaced intelligentsia, and officials. At the pinnacle stands a small group of wealthy, frequently absentee, landlords, industrialists, bankers, and exporters. In their hands rested the process of decision making before 1952.

No system is static. In 1952 a military junta seized power in Egypt from the landowning elite. Throughout the Middle East, as elsewhere, traditional oligarchies face new challenges from discontented popular movements. Basically, however, these populations remain as undifferentiated masses to be exploited by clergy against military, Palace against landholder, or to be periodically marshaled to the polls in a demonstration of loyalty for a dominant group. The focus of analysis must shift from the population as a whole to the few groups which contend for control—the oligarchy.

3. Political Forces: Islam and the Muslim Brotherhood. Articulate group ideologies are absent where political participation is limited, illiteracy is universal, and bullets hold sway over ballots. Competition within the oligarchy centers around the economic *status quo*. Differences arise over the division of spoils, not the elimination of spoils. General tenets and attitudes which distinguish groups and thereby influence policy, while identifiable, operate at a lower level of intensity than in authoritarian or pluralistic political systems.

Islam as a political force has traditionally stood aside from politics in Egypt. Only recently has it emerged as a dynamic factor in the hands of militant Moslem leaders. Al-Azhar University, the thousand-year-old source of muftis and judges who interpret Islamic conduct and law throughout the villages, stands for traditional conservatism. Its graduates voiced little objection to Palace corruption or landowner exploitation. As a reaction to Al-Azhar orthodox interpretation of Islam as a justification for property, privilege, and poverty, the so-called modernists formed two important rival organizations: the Young Man's Muslim Association (YMMA), and the Muslim Brotherhood. These have made Islam a revived political force in Egypt.

Mahdism. The modernist Islamic doctrine weighs heavily in foreign policy since its ideology is typified by mahdism, a belief that the Moslem world must be purified and united by the sword under an all-powerful charismatic leader. Mixing the romanticism of Islamic thought and the charisma of the Mohammed cult, mahdism's essentially negative character is described as "not a rational assertion that one type of political organization is more desirable than another, but a revolution against what is felt to be . . . an intolerable state of affairs. . . . What is to follow is left to the future to decide." [5]

A paramilitary organization somewhat smaller than the Brotherhood, the YMMA has exercised a strong influence among students and young military

[5] Gibb, *op. cit.*, p. 113.

officers since 1927. Each member swears "to be active as a warrior, fighting for the revival of the glory of Islam by restoring its religious law and its supremity." [6] Stressing Moslem unity against divisive nationalism and foreign imperialism, the YMMA pursued a militant anti-Zionist policy and showed a marked sympathy for the Axis during the early part of World War II.

The Muslim Brotherhood. Started in 1929, the Muslim Brotherhood rose rapidly in power under its dynamic founder, Hasan al-Banna. Hasan's charismatic attributes were accompanied by an ability to organize and control disciples. His appeal to the deep-seated superstition and romanticism of both urban and rural Moslems met the qualifications for a mahdist leader who seeks "to convey to others the idea that he is especially chosen by Allah; his is given light and blessing and is, on that account, superior to the rest of mankind. . . . With leaders of the Hasan al-Banna type, much is expected of them. The state of expectation must be satisfied . . . [by] indulging in such violent activities as demonstrating against the enemies of Egypt and Islam, be they supposed or real." [7]

Hasan mobilized "the Street" as an adjunct to a tightly controlled secret movement built on personal loyalty. The chief target of violence was Great Britain. A typical postwar Brotherhood manifesto demanded, "All British employees in Egypt should be dismissed from their posts, no landlord should accept a British tenant, no Egyptian should have any dealings with a Britisher, and all British should be deported." [8] Nationalism is not the basis of this xenophobia, for in all its declarations the Brotherhood raises the ancient banner of Islamic supremacy. Fighting foreign influence which "sneaks into the affairs of all the Eastern nations and poisons their blood," it calls for a Holy War throughout the Middle East and ultimately throughout the world.

A statement of foreign policy reveals the expansionistic character of the Muslim Brotherhood: "The desire of conquest and world domination has its basis in Islam which directs its conquerors toward the best system of colonization and conquest. . . . It requires us to spread the teachings of Islam over the whole earth with all means at our disposal . . . to see the banner of the Muslim world rise over the whole world and the flag of the Holy Writ wave in every place." [9] With more than 500,000 members in Egypt and strong branches in Syria and Iraq, the Muslim Brotherhood remains a dynamic force in oligarchies of the Middle East, even when persecuted by hostile elites in control of the state.

[6] J. Heyworth-Dunne, *Religious and Political Trends in Modern Egypt,* published by the author, Washington, 1950, pp. 55–56.

[7] *Ibid.*

[8] *Ibid.,* p. 44.

[9] *Da'watuna* ("Our Propaganda Aims"), Cairo, 1943–1944; translated in F. Rosenthal, "The 'Muslim Brethren' in Egypt," *The Muslim World,* October, 1947, pp. 289–290.

4. Political Forces: The Wafd: The closest resemblance to Western-type political parties in Egypt centers around the Wafd and its offshoots. From inception of the constitution in 1923 to the seizure of power by military junta in 1952, the Wafd was the self-styled spokesman for Egypt's electorate. Its impetus, like that of the Brotherhood, came largely from its leader, Saad Zaghlul. Saad headed a delegation, in Arabic called *wafd,* to present Egypt's demand for independence in 1918. As the symbol of nationalism the Wafd won overwhelming support for three decades.

Its major competitors at the polls came from internal splits over tactics and from revolts against the personal leadership of Saad's successor, Mustafa Nahas Pasha. In 1938 the Saadist party arose in opposition to Nahas Pasha's espousal of a militant anti-Palace policy. In 1944 a second schism gave birth to the Kutla party. Only the Wafd could hope for electoral majority, however, because only the Wafd had money and organization. An Egyptian scholar has noted, "All parties, whatever their labels, are composed of members of the same social group and are inspired by the same leading ideas." [10] Promotion of landed interests, toleration of corruption, and hostility to Great Britain mark the constants in party politics.

Xenophobia. The Wafd, organized around the exclusive purpose of driving Britain from Egypt, became an amalgam of groups whose use of xenophobia served their own ends. At the top stood entrenched landed interests. The Wafd secretary-general, along with other prominent figures, held large estates dependent on cotton for income. Manipulation of land taxes, raising of tariffs, and regulating legislation to facilitate speculation all served to enrich this group at the expense of the fellah. Demands for economic reform failed as internal tensions were channeled against a safe target, the British.

Displaced intelligentsia provided a second source of strength in the "Wafdist Youth," combining anti-British agitation with promise of future employment in government positions. Strongly nationalistic and economically insecure University of Cairo graduates worked "the Street" when a show of force was called for by Wafd leaders. Their support was contingent upon hope of Wafd success, since ultimately only patronage could keep this group allied to one political party.

Finally the vital factor of nationalism won support among middle and lower classes alike who felt that economic betterment could come only after complete expulsion of British influence from Egypt. So vital was xenophobia as a factor of power that the Wafd infrequently flirted with such extremists as the Muslim Brotherhood and the minuscule Communist movement to retain control of government. Only when the Wafd-directed anti-British riots of 1952 ran out of control and suspicion spread that nationalism was being exploited to cover up widespread corruption in the government of Nahas Pasha

---

[10] Issawi, *op. cit.,* p. 173.

did Egypt's major political party lose popular support. Its fall from power marked the ascendancy of a new military group and a serious transformation of the traditional oligarchy.

Xenophobia combines with opportunism to produce mercurial shifts in policy in oligarchies. As early as 1930 the Wafd sought British intervention against Palace-inspired changes of the constitution inimical to Wafd interests. In 1942 Nahas Pasha accepted power literally on British bayonets when armed units forced King Farouk to dismiss a cabinet suspected of pro-Axis sympathies. Another shift in 1948–1949 found the Wafd standing aside while the militantly anti-British Muslim Brotherhood suffered the loss of its leader and imprisonment of thousands of its members by King Farouk. When the Wafd won at the polls a year later, Nahas Pasha released Brotherhood members in an effort to build up strength against both Britain and the throne.

Nationalism and Corruption. The final burst of nationalism failed to preserve Wafd power. Its last two-year regime, 1950–1952, found cotton speculators filling warehouses with unsold produce purchased by the government to shore up prices and secure high profits to landlords and investors. At the same time investigation revealed widespread corruption and bribery to have been partly responsible for defeat in the Palestine war of 1948. Rather than reform itself, Wafd leadership unilaterally abrogated the 1936 Anglo-Egyptian Treaty and blamed all Egypt's ills on Great Britain. Nahas Pasha charged that economic stagnation which was "stifling . . . every phase of our life" was the work of British economic imperialism. As for Israel, he claimed Whitehall had been "taking only a hostile course [which] has exposed Egypt to the gravest of dangers." Raising high the banner of Egyptian nationalism, he concluded, "The British government still bases its policy on the antiquated principles of colonization and empire that were so unsuccessful in America, in India, and Iran. It still assumes responsibilities that are not its own and restricts national rights with varied excuses and pretexts." [11] Coupled with the mob violence which swept Cairo three months later, Nahas Pasha's regime provided a clear illustration of scapegoating internal tensions against an external target.

In the slogan, "The Wafd is the nation and the nation is the Wafd," Nahas Pasha sought to assert monopoly control over decision making within the government. Thus in 1946 and 1947 he refused to participate in discussions with the British or at the United Nations unless the Wafd had the majority membership and chairmanship of the delegation. Similarly, the Wafd refused to acknowledge supremacy of the military junta after the ouster of King Farouk in mid-1952, balking at General Naguib's land-reform program. Its intransigence resulted in imprisonment and, in some cases,

[11] Nahas Pasha to Parliament, Oct. 8, 1951, in *Vital Speeches*, Dec. 1, 1951, pp. 104–108.

execution of the Wafd hierarchy. Given the inherent instability of any single elite in an oligarchy, it was by no means impossible for the Wafd to rise, phoenixlike, from the ashes. Such rebirth could come, however, only after radical changes in its ideology.

5. Political Forces: The Palace. Although the monarchy was formally abolished in 1953, no analysis of previous Egyptian politics would be complete without analysis of the Palace. Established as a constitutional monarchy in 1923, Egypt had two kings in thirty years. Descendants of Mohammed Ali, viceroy during the early nineteenth century and founder of modern Egypt, neither Fuad (1922–1936) nor Farouk (1936–1952) proved capable of surmounting the many internal and external problems besetting the country. Perched precariously atop shifting forces, their primary concern appeared to be manipulation of individuals and groups in order to preserve power. Little time or energy was accorded policy as such, except in so far as was necessary to assuage the demands of threatening groups, particularly if backed up by British arms.

The monarchy, especially under Farouk, drew support from three quarters. A group of so-called "independents" formed an entourage of strong, capable men with political acumen but lacking popular support. From this group Farouk recruited the bulk of his prime ministers, who ruled in defiance of Wafd-dominated parliaments. Another source of strength lay in Al-Azhar, whose conservative hierarchy could be counted on to side with the Palace against extremist agitation of Wafd or Brotherhood. Finally, if the situation appeared to be seriously threatened, a strong presumption of British backing protected the Palace from direct overthrow. That this presumption proved fallacious in 1952 when the army moved against the throne does not mitigate the importance of its effect during the years when the Wafd repeatedly moved in the direction of insurrection yet never openly challenged Farouk to a contest of power.

An institution as short-lived as the Palace has little in common with the British throne, lacking tradition and resting almost wholly on the ability of the individual monarch. In the case of Farouk, this proved to be catastrophic. Waging a two-front fight, first against the Wafd and secondarily against the British, Farouk displayed little interest in a positive program of reform and progress for his country. His ideology—if his outlook can be dignified with that term—may be summed up in the phrase of an earlier monarch, *"Après moi, le deluge."* His life of self-indulgence and debauchery alienated the population. His reluctant prosecution of those implicated in defeat in Palestine brought the army into open opposition. With no policy for his people and no virtue in his character, King Farouk fled Egypt in 1952, taking with him as much personal wealth as possible and leaving behind no visible evidence of public regret at his departure.

6. Political Forces: The Army. Pivotal in oligarchical politics is the monopoly of organized force held by the military. Mob rule may wreak dramatic but short-lived damage. Extremist groups of left or right may move in a *Putsch* against the capital. In the last analysis, however, no group can maintain power without the benevolent neutrality, if not the actual support, of the military.

To be sure, military regimes are neither permanent nor universal throughout the Middle East and Latin America. Several factors account for this. Military interest in status and a strong army is seldom threatened by the game of musical chairs which represents the periodic change of government among the few competing groups. Conscripting of recruits and awarding of military honors continue uninterrupted. If political intrigue does reach into the army, it seldom penetrates beyond the highest echelon of older officers, or the peripheral positions of newly appointed officers. The elevation of one general accompanying seizure of control by a particular group is certain to be followed by elevation of another, once that group is thrown out of power. The army as an institution, however, is seldom associated *in toto* with one particular contender in an oligarchical regime. Finally, there is the almost universal military tradition which holds the professional position of the soldier independent of and somewhat superior to that of a political leader. When, therefore, army leaders do decide to take over the government directly, they automatically become the sole ruling group—at least as long as unity continues to reign in their ranks. Dissension among military leaders may reopen the door to civilian oligarchs.

Political Independence. In the military in Egypt, except for a small group of older officers beholden to the Palace for positions and status, these factors produced an independent *esprit de corps* which argued against participation in politics. At no time did the Wafd win unequivocal support from the army, although the majority of officers came from middle- and upper-class families whose interests were well represented by the Wafd. Conversely, King Farouk received no open opposition from the army despite his inept rule and abuse of constitutional procedures. Not until his activities affected the immediate interests of the military did Farouk arouse opposition in that quarter. Two weeks before attacking Israel, army leaders had petitioned the government not to begin a campaign in view of the unfitness of the armed forces. Among the signatories was Naguib. The king, acting on other advice, went ahead with the war.[12] Following exposure of this move, in 1950, Farouk dismissed most of his palace generals but found his nominees for the powerful "Officers' Club" rejected in favor of a young group, headed by Naguib. Farouk's attempt to reassert control, culminating in appointment of his brother-in-law as Minister of War, failed to ward off the blow. In July, 1952, Naguib deposed

[12] J. Kimche, *Seven Fallen Pillars*, Praeger, New York, 1953, pp. 369–370.

Farouk and, as head of a twelve-man junta, moved to break the economic power of the wealthiest landlord group, a prerequisite for reforms vital to overhauling the political and economic structure of Egypt.

Sources of Discontent. Discontent among younger officers antedated defeat in Israel. Better educated than their superiors, they had rankled under a system of promotion by seniority instead of by merit. National pride fostered resentment over the continued presence of British troops in a country supposedly leader of the Arab League. As evidence of this discontent, the Muslim Brotherhood exercised an ever-increasing influence in the lower ranks of the army. In March, 1953, it was reported that "two of its [the Brotherhood's] former leaders are now in the Cabinet. At least four members of the Officers Committee which runs Egypt are disciples. Army officers admit that nearly one-third of their ranks participate in the Brotherhood's activities." [13] Nevertheless, not until the connivance of Palace and parliament in corruption, which ruined the prestige of Egypt as well as of the army, did this discontent explode into the coup of 1952.

The Ideology of the Military Junta. The group of young officers, led by Colonel Nasser and using the well-known and popular General Naguib as their temporary figurehead, who staged their successful coup against the King in 1952 took the "harm to Egypt's reputation in the eyes of the peoples of the world" as their initial justification. Yet their program for Egypt represents a sweeping scheme of reform and modernization, which, if successful, will transform the country into either a democracy or a system of mass-based totalitarianism. Thus Nasser claims that the mission of the army is "to check despotism and make the nation itself the source of powers, and to put an end to foreign intervention and the usurpation of Egypt's resources. . . . Now [the army] understood its position and joined the ranks of the people to head the movement for national liberation." [13a] The oligarchy thus claimed and organized the masses as the basis of its revolution, departing from the traditional pattern of ignoring them.

What are the aims of the new oligarchy? "These," answers Nasser, "are the aims of the revolution: to end the exploitation of the people, to realize national aspirations and to develop the mature political consciousness that is an indispensable preliminary for a sound democracy. The revolution seeks to bridge the gulf between social classes and to foster the spirit of altruism which marks a cultivated individual and a cohesive group. Our ultimate aim is to provide Egypt with a truly democratic and representative government." [13b] The army's revolution is to be realized by mass land redistribu-

[13] D. Peters, "The Muslim Brotherhood—Terrorists or Just Zealots?" *The Reporter,* Mar. 17, 1953, pp. 8–10.

[13a] Gamal Abdel Nasser, "The Egyptian Revolution," *Foreign Affairs,* January, 1955, pp. 202–203.

[13b] *Ibid.,* p. 208.

tion, government-planned industrialization, the diversification of foreign trade away from dependence on cotton exports to Britain, the complete ejection of foreign dominating influences, and the assurance of Middle East security by a collective organization of the Arab states, aloof from ties with East or West.

The first two "aims in foreign policy" announced by General Naguib in January, 1953, included "(1) strengthening relationship with the Arab peoples to bring about effective cooperation among them in all fields, (2) fostering the Arab League Charter to turn it into an efficient instrument in the service of its peoples." [14]

In this sense the nationalism of the military, like that of the Muslim Brotherhood, is more anti-British than pro-Egypt. The "national aims" of the Egyptian Liberation Organization reflected this clearly, swearing "to drive foreign troops out of the Nile Valley unconditionally and to liberate it from any kind of political, economic, or social colonization"; but it promised "to enable the Sudan to determine its future status freely and without any outside influence." [15] Most Egyptian groups had long demanded expulsion of the British from Suez. No such universal support came for an independent Sudan, however, even if only suggested in a propaganda statement. Xenophobia was not coupled with chauvinism in this form of nationalism. An agreement subsequently concluded between Cairo and London opened the door for Sudanese independence, a far cry from Wafd championing of Farouk as "King of Egypt and Sudan."

7. Factors in Foreign Policy. Chief among the factors operative in the foreign policy of this oligarchy is the constancy of anti-British sentiment. Target of Muslim Brotherhood extremism, whipping boy of Wafd agitation, and a primary concern of both Naguib and Nasser, British policy has long been the focal point of Egypt's foreign relations.

Britain's role in Egypt has been a complex one. Loath to annex Egypt outright, British rulers pursued a policy of occupation and intervention from 1882 to 1922, describing Egypt as a "protectorate" of Great Britain. Protection of the Suez as a line of communication to overseas empire and joint Anglo-Egyptian control of the Sudan as a barrier to French imperialism motivated British policy down to World War I.

Negotiations. As we have noted, the Wafd originated as a protest movement in 1918 demanding "complete autonomy" for Egypt. British refusal touched off a wave of riots and bloodshed. Ultimately London was forced to recognize Egypt as "an independent and sovereign State" in 1922, subject however to "the following matters [which] are absolutely reserved to the discretion of His Majesty's Government . . . (a) the security of the communications of

---

[14] "Charter and Aims of the Egyptian Liberation Organization," *Middle East Affairs,* March, 1953, p. 104.
[15] *Ibid.*

the British Empire in Egypt; (*b*) the defense of Egypt against all foreign aggression or interference, direct or indirect; (*c*) the protection of foreign interests in Egypt and the protection of minorities; (*d*) the Sudan." [16] The importance of the Sudan as the exclusive source of Egypt's vital water supply, the headwaters of the Nile, was emphasized when, in retaliation for the murder of the British Governor-General of the Sudan in 1924, London forced the evacuation of all Egyptian troops and threatened to extend irrigation in the Sudan "to an unlimited figure as need may arise." [17]

Negotiations stalled over implementation of Britain's imposed terms for independence, and not until 1936, under the pressure of Italian invasion in nearby Ethiopia, did the two countries reach agreement. Although the British occupation of Egypt was formally terminated, bases at Alexandria, Cairo, and in the Suez Canal Zone continued, and joint control over the Sudan remained in effect. As one observer remarked of the 1936 treaty, "In reality the new privileges, disguising old rights which Britain had originally acquired in 1882 by dint of occupation, abridged Egyptian sovereignty and thus furnished the elements of future contention upon which Egyptian nationalists were certain to seize." [18]

Under the circumstances, it is small wonder that Egyptian circles entertained varying degrees of hostility to Great Britain in World War II. Support for a German victory was encouraged by Nazi propaganda promising an end to foreign troops and abolition of external limitations on sovereignty. The Muslim Brotherhood and the YMMA openly sympathized with the Axis prior to British victories. During the critical month of June, 1942, when British evacuation seemed imminent, Hasan al-Banna gave signs of preparing to welcome Rommel, and some of his students demonstrated in the streets, crying, "Advance, O Rommel! Advance on Qasr al-Nil!" [19] Even the Palace appeared ambivalent and only British military force persuaded Farouk to take a firmer stand on the side of the Allies.

Violence. After World War II, the rising tempo of anti-British demonstrations provided dramatic evidence of the degree to which violence was a factor in the policy of all cabinets, be they Palace, Wafd, or army. In 1946, for instance, Farouk described street demonstrations as "a healthy manifestation of the people's ambition to realize their just claims," and his anti-Wafdist prime minister removed a recently imposed ban on such activity.[20] The result was mayhem, with burning of British property and stoning of British police resulting in two deaths and considerable damage. Less volatile but no less intransigent was the next cabinet, similarly appointed by Farouk against

[16] J. Hurewitz, *Middle East Dilemmas,* Harper, New York, 1953, p. 70.

[17] *Ibid.,* p. 72.

[18] *Ibid.,* p. 75.

[19] Heyworth-Dunne, *op. cit.,* p. 41.

[20] Royal Institute of International Affairs, *Great Britain and Egypt, 1914–1951,* Oxford, New York, 1952, p. 86.

Wafdist opposition. Its spokesmen insisted that "immediate and uncondi-tional evacuation" of British troops form the *sine qua non* of Egyptian policy. Finally, it should be noted that, despite the military junta's success in settling the long-standing Sudan question, in February, 1953, it, too, approached the Suez problem with caution. So important was this held to be in terms of his support among important groups, particularly the Muslim Brotherhood, that complete secrecy surrounded the talks in the fall of 1953 and little public comment was permitted in the controlled Egyptian press.

Vacillation. It is impossible to deny the deep-seated hostility of the pop-ulace at large against British troops on Egyptian soil. However, it by no means follows that the intensity of the hostility is a constant factor. Indeed, there is much to indicate that the degree of hostility in Anglo-Egyptian relations is in part a function of the insecurity inherent in oligarchical rule. It fluctuates according to the political tactics of the contending groups, serving as a scapegoat for the "ins" and as a means of attack for the "outs." On the one hand, there is the unbroken record of identical demands put forth by Wafdist and non-Wafdist representatives negotiating with the Brit-ish, insisting on simultaneous settlement of the Sudan and Suez questions with no concessions whatsoever on the part of Egypt. Given the pivotal posi-tion of Suez and the obvious weakness of the Egyptian army, the British refused to acquiesce and could not countenance withdrawal from Suez until absolute guarantees were given concerning its future security. On the other hand, there is the constant compromise with the British position which found the Palace, Wafd, and even the Muslim Brotherhood tacitly acquiescing in the *status quo* when it served their purpose. Thus Nahas Pasha assumed power in 1942, thanks to British armored intervention, declaring, "Each one . . . is conscious of the duty of supporting our friend and ally, Eng-land, in the hour of its need." [21] Out of power in 1946, the Wafd led anti-British riots with support of the Muslim Brotherhood. Back in power in 1951, Nahas Pasha blamed Britain for all Egypt's ills. Similarly, the Muslim Brotherhood attacked Nahas Pasha through his acceptance of power in 1942 and campaigned for unconditional expulsion of the British from Suez. Yet when Colonel Nasser prolonged negotiations over Suez for months on end, the Brotherhood, strongly influential in army circles, made moves to employ violence only at the successful end of the talks.

One is forced to conclude that paralleling the constant anti-British factor in Egyptian foreign policy is a variable degree of intensity of xenophobia. Prior to the regime of Colonel Nasser, it would appear that no Egyptian delegation approached the problems of Suez and Sudan with any intention of negotiating, much less with any hope of achieving avowed ends. Implaca-bility served a twofold purpose. It presented the delegation, regardless of its

[21] Ibid., p. 74.

composition, as the unsullied champions of Egyptian nationalism. At the same time, it assured the continuation of British military protection against external or internal threats to the security of the oligarchy. Both aspects were vital to all groups in the close and constant struggle for power which rested as much on means of coercion as on means of violence. Xenophobia is always a volatile factor to manipulate for internal political ends, as Nahas Pasha himself found out in 1952. Yet its continued presence in a country which has chafed under the indignities of semicolonial status makes it a tempting genie to be uncorked at the bidding of any particular group.

Arab Relations. A second constant in Egyptian foreign policy is pro-Arab sentiment, although it too is subject to fluctuations of intensity. As the leading force in the Arab League, Cairo serves as the headquarters of the Secretariat and an Egyptian has been secretary general since the League's inception in 1945. Embracing Egypt, Syria, Lebanon, Jordan, Iraq, Saudi Arabia, Libya, and Yemen, the League is the flowering of so-called Pan-Islamic aspirations to date. As an Islamic entity, the League reacted with prima-facie unity against Israel, and Islamic ritual as a symbol of unity has marked gatherings of League leaders. As has already been seen, a prominent position was given to cooperation with Arab states in the proclaimed program of the ruling military junta.

Behind the façade of Arab and Islamic brotherhood, however, lies a record of considerable tension among League members, tension in which Egyptian groups have played a prominent part. Farouk joined the war against Israel although his Prime Minister correctly warned that the war would only increase the power of Farouk's chief rival, King Abdullah of Jordan.[22] So deep was the schism between Farouk and Abdullah that Jordanian forces made no move to assist the Egyptian legions in full retreat before advancing troops of Israel.

Continual jockeying for position within the League has threatened to split it apart. When Syria and Iraq were negotiating for a union in 1949, both Farouk and Ibn Saud publicly denounced the move. Similarly, when Abdullah sought to expand Jordan's territory deep into Arab Palestine, Egypt took hostile measures short of actually expelling Jordan from the League. With the assassination of Abdullah in 1951, the military coup in Syria in the same year, and the ousting of Farouk in 1952, internal tensions lessened for the moment. But the conclusion of a pact in 1955, tying Iraq militarily to Turkey and NATO, again brought with it a division of the League into neutralist and pro-Western camps, with Egypt leading the former. There seemed little doubt that friction would continue among the Middle Eastern oligarchies, particularly over the unsettled issue of Israel.

Non-Arab Ties. As a final factor in Egyptian foreign policy, economic dependence upon the non-Arab world moves side by side with aspirations for

[22] Kimche, *op. cit.*, p. 207.

a neutralist position which will leave Egypt outside quarrels among the major countries of the world. Sending only 2.5 per cent of her exports to the Middle East as compared with 67 per cent to Europe, and receiving only 10 per cent of her imports from Arab states as compared with 60 per cent from European ones, it is clear that Egyptian stability rested almost exclusively on the detested "Western imperialist powers." With domestic capital unwilling to venture outside cash crops like cotton, and with nothing but "infant industries," no government in Cairo can hope for prosperity. The nation's welfare is intimately linked with the fluctuating world demand for cotton. The absence of tax measures designed to tap cotton profits through landlords and speculators left the Egyptian government with few resources for improvement of the army and virtually nothing for capital projects vital to economic well-being, such as the extension of dam systems along the Nile. Yet industrialization and military security remain fixed targets in Egypt, as in all underdeveloped countries.

Perhaps no more fundamental restraint upon the Palace, the Wafd, and the Muslim Brotherhood in their fight against the British can be found than this recognition of economic dependence. Azzam Pasha, first secretary-general of the Arab League, warned against attempting to destroy the Jews by force, in part "because from a military point of view we are dependent on the big powers." [23] Azzam might well have added that, from a financial point of view, Egypt remained beholden to Britain through the existence of accumulated sterling balances in London which remained blocked by British policy.

Ample demonstration of this twofold reliance upon outside aid came in 1949, when defeat in Palestine and riots at home threatened to unseat King Farouk. Action by the British government made foreign currencies available for purchasing equipment in Italy, provided modern jet fighters to the Egyptian air force, transferred six modern frigates to Egypt's navy, and made possible formation of an entire armored division. Similarly, General Naguib prevailed upon the United States to equip a strengthened and expanded police force immediately after his coup, and later he made a frank bid for foreign loans and investment: [24]

We need foreign capital in Egypt because our resources cannot easily cover all the great projects we intend to carry out [such as] . . . a second large and higher dam, south of the present dam. With this water we could make two million more acres of desert arable. . . . We need electrification projects to bring electricity to the villages. We need a small ammunition industry for our army. We should develop mining . . . fisheries . . . and achieve a balance of trade. . . . But we haven't the money for it all.

[23] Azzam Pasha to Prime Minister Nokrashy Pasha, Sept. 5, 1945, quoted in Kimche, *op. cit.*, p. 56.
[24] *U.S. News and World Report*, Mar. 27, 1953, pp. 28–38.

Neutralism. Yet against this recognition of dependency comes a demand for breaking the reliance upon cooperation with Great Britain, carried in its more extreme forms to a demand for complete withdrawal from all associations which involve partisanship in larger conflicts of interest between East and West. Typical of the first, more moderate viewpoint was the expression of Palace policy in 1945, rejecting a British effort to conclude a treaty guaranteeing London a dominant position in Egypt's economy: [25]

> The raising of the standard of living in Egypt cannot be accomplished without economic collaboration with the Great Powers in general in order that competition may play its part. . . . The United States, France and Russia are ready to lend us assistance in order to uplift our social and economical system.

Similarly, Sidky Pasha, venerable independent leader who often served as Farouk's governmental leader, advocated aligning with NATO policy. "We ought to think of putting ourselves in touch with the Powers whose interests coincide with ours, and who can help us in the realization of our aspirations." [26]

Against such views may be cited the Kutla party organ: [27]

> If we are courted as allies, we must first be shown wherein Egypt's interest in such an alliance lies—unless it is a question of involving her in a war in which Britain would be a combatant and Egypt would have no concern. We have already experienced that sort of alliance in the last war. We were ruined and starved to feed the Allied armies. We are still suffering many setbacks on account of that ally. Lord preserve us from such alliance.

Even more explicit was the approach of the Wafdist newspaper during the last regime of Nahas Pasha: [28]

> We ought to declare the neutrality of the Suez Canal as well as that of Egypt. . . . If the British finally leave Egypt and the various States guarantee the country's neutrality, we shall be, like Switzerland, sheltered from the spectre of the war which threatens the world with ruin. We need peace and quiet, and wish to be isolated from all these influences, which will spare no one and nothing.

Thus Egyptian policy eschewed participation in a Middle Eastern pact sponsored by Great Britain and the United States, while seeking military and economic assistance from both countries. The dilemma continued to

[25] Ahmed Hassanin, Chief of the Royal Cabinet, to Prime Minister Nokrashy Pasha, Sept. 4, 1945, in Kimche, *op. cit.*, pp. 429–430.

[26] Letter of May, 1949, quoted in Royal Institute of International Affairs, *op. cit.*, p. 118.

[27] Written in January, 1950, quoted in Royal Institute of International Affairs, *op. cit.*, p. 121.

[28] Written in April, 1950, quoted in Royal Institute of International Affairs, *op. cit.*, p. 122.

plague General Naguib, attempting to meet the demands of xenophobia and those of national security at one and the same time. He declared flatly in March, 1953, that although Egypt had need of military advisers, he would not countenance British or American personnel in Egypt. They must be "neutrals . . . Swiss or Swedish technicians." [29]

Yet with the achievement of the basic anti-British aim of the military oligarchy, these declarations of neutralist intent lost something of their cogency. Following Anglo-Egyptian agreement on the future of the Sudan, Colonel Nasser in 1954 negotiated an agreement with London under which British control over the Suez Canal and the adjacent military bases was turned over to Egypt. Significantly, however, Britain was granted the right to reoccupy these facilities in the event of aggression against Turkey, Iran, or other Middle Eastern states. In short, Egypt's largest military installation was made subject to the policy and future of NATO, since an attack on Turkey would bring the Western alliance into operation. Almost at the same time, another Arab country sometimes flirting with neutralism—Iraq—accepted American military aid and advice, while Turkey entered into a pact of military consultation with Pakistan. Yet the Nasser government drew closer to neutralist India and Indonesia at the same time, while vigorously denouncing Iraq's turning toward the West and splitting the Arab League into two camps over the issue. Whether "realistic" or not, Egypt's modernizing military oligarchy still caters to the neutralist attitudes of its nationalist supporters.

8. Oligarchical Elites and Foreign Policy. With due regard for the differences encountered in moving from one country to another, Egypt stands as a representative type of oligarchy found throughout Asia, the Middle East, and Latin America. Basic to an understanding of the foreign policy pursued by elites within these countries is the omnipresence of political insecurity. Regardless of the interest group represented, the decision maker is aware that his political life is short. A palace *Putsch* or a "popular revolution" engineered from above may sweep him from power, just as he swept his predecessor from power. Charges of connivance with foreign interests may well prove fatal in countries long restive under the economic and political hegemony of such nations as France, Great Britain, and the United States. Failure to attend to the economic ills of strong groups may be no less effective a weapon in the hands of determined opponents, even though solution of these ills requires compromising with foreign powers on the one hand and liquidation of domestic vested interests on the other.

Small wonder that, given these conditions, the ideology of contending groups in oligarchical regimes posits a few simple points, avoiding any highly structured exposition of ends and means. Chief among these is an assertion of independence against all outside interference. The corollary is

[29] *U.S. News and World Report*, Mar. 27, 1953, p. 30.

to champion the cause of colonial countries in such organizations as the United Nations. At the same time, no move must endanger the chief sources of military and economic succor unless alternative sources exist. Few dare to move so far as did Iran in 1951, nationalizing the Anglo-Iranian oil fields and truly killing the goose that laid the government's only, albeit not golden, egg. Premier Mossadegh proved unable to survive in the conflict of Iranian elites largely because he ignored this rule of successful oligarchy. He alienated the Western-oriented army by his attack on the Shah, offended religious extremists by seeking to negotiate with the West, and impoverished labor by eliminating oil royalties, the main public revenue until 1951. At the same time his domestic insecurity made it impossible for him to accept aid offered on American terms or consider close ties with the Soviet Union. The coalition of dissatisfied elites—led by the army—forced his downfall.

Exploitation of Xenophobia. More usually regimes, as in Venezuela and Bolivia, seek to assuage nationalist pressures by improving their position vis-à-vis foreign interests while avoiding complete alienation of those interests. Xenophobia may come in waves, paralleling economic and political discontent within the country. Occasionally a determined revolutionary group will ride into power on the crest, as appeared imminent in the position of the Communist-dominated Tudeh party in Iran during 1952–1953. Generally, though, xenophobia subsides as the dominant group achieves control of the situation, if only for a limited time. Its roots are genuine, often reaching back into a century or more of foreign exploitation and domination. Its growth as well as its fruition remain susceptible to careful nurturing by local groups, however, according to their political and economic interests.

Military Elites. In Egypt, as elsewhere, the oligarchy of alternating elites has been challenged by new groups, centered in the army. Where military dictatorships consolidate their position, excluding traditional groups from rule and responding to mass discontent from below, the pattern of politics alters but the characteristics of foreign policy remain the same. Domestically the ascendancy of a reformist oligarch like Paz Estenssoro in Bolivia or a Nasser may result in land reforms designed to break rival economic groups and in elaboration of an ideology aimed at winning the support of intellectual and religious groups. Externally, however, xenophobia remains a means of diverting internal unrest as well as a legitimate reflection of basic attitudes within the population as a whole.

To be sure, the enhanced stability of the new military regimes, so marked in Middle Eastern politics, permits greater flexibility in negotiating with foreign countries. It is no accident that both Naguib and Nasser succeeded in effecting agreements with the British which formerly were unacceptable to powerful extremist groups. Instability remains, however, in the possibility of a coup from within the ranks of the military or among groups supporting the new elite. The new oligarchies provide transitional regimes which may, as in Turkey, evolve into democratic-pluralistic regimes or, as in Argentina, aim at establishing authoritarian elites. In their infancy, however, such military juntas remain characteristic of oligarchical elites, especially in their xenophobia.

Alliances. Another feature of oligarchical foreign policy is its espousal of common interest with similar neighboring governments, marred by incessant rivalries and juggling for status. Economic weakness, coupled with desire to find strength outside highly industrialized areas, compels the decision maker to ally with his Latin-American, Middle Eastern, or Southeast Asian confreres. At the same time, internal insecurities compel him to inflate his government's prestige by asserting its leadership in the regional councils. Thus regional conferences inevitably present an impressive façade of "common interest" and "brotherly cooperation," behind which continue the divisive tendencies of insecurity, jealousy, and ambition. Far greater unity comes within the chambers of the United Nations among the so-called "blocs" of Southeast Asia, Arab countries, and Latin America than in the direct, concrete, and all-important economic, military, and political relations among these countries.

Finally, these elites tend to side against the international *status quo* in time of general crisis, so long as it provides no threat to their internal position. In both world wars, Germany found strong support throughout the Arab countries. So marked was this in World War II that armed intervention was necessary to depose local governments hostile to the Allies. Less overt though no less indicative was German influence in Latin-American countries, some of whom declared war only when the balance had swung irrevocably in favor of the United Nations. Similarly, Japan discovered that "Asia for the Asians" struck a responsive note throughout Southeast Asia.

Communism. Because of Communist hostility to private property and religion, two important factors in most areas supporting oligarchical governments, it is less certain how these elites would react in time of full-scale conflict between Soviet Russia and the West. One thing seems clear, however. Whether in Iran, Egypt, or Chile, ruling groups find little difficulty in a *mésalliance* with Communist-oriented movements if it serves to bring victory over a rival group. The degree to which these are well-integrated, Moscow-controlled movements seems to lessen in direct relation with their distance from Soviet Russia. Thus in Iran the Tudeh party exhibits far more of a coherent Communist ideology than a parallel group in Chile. In Egypt, the facility with which terrorists move between Brotherhood and Communist membership suggests not so much infiltration of the former by the latter as a predilection for xenophobic violence, backed by little positive political conviction.

It would be fallacious, however, to assume that Russian-directed Communist leaders are absent in these countries. On the contrary, abundant evidence indicates the familiar "hard core" leadership at the center of rather loosely organized movements of popular agitation. Toleration of these movements serves a twofold purpose for contending groups within the oligarchy. It provides an additional source of popular demonstration and violence against domestic opponents. In addition, by drawing attention to the presence of Communist support, the government has a persuasive argument for winning economic aid, particularly from the United States. As a Latin-American representative is alleged to have remarked after securing promises of additional financial support from Washington, "If there had been no Communist party, it would have been necessary for us to invent one."

Taking these factors into consideration, together with the widespread neutralist movement throughout Asian regions dominated by oligarchy, there is little certainty that in time of war full support would be rendered the NATO alliance. Despite the willingness of many such governments to grant military bases in exchange for economic aid, the security of these bases remains in doubt so long as genuine xenophobia, exaggerated for internal political purposes, remains operative among the population. Oligarchy, then, is of signal importance in international relations, not only because of the crucial role these countries play as sources of raw materials but also because of their possible pivotal position in terms of communications and military operations in time of war. They will be of increasing significance in the dynamics of international relations as the United States ceases to be the sole supplier of aid and Soviet influence grows with offers of technical assistance and loans and with the ever-present possibility of subversive activity.

ADDITIONAL CASE-STUDY MATERIAL

Beals, R. L.: "Social Stratification in Latin America," *American Journal of Sociology,* vol. 52, January, 1953.

Blanksten, G. F.: *Ecuador,* University of California Press, Berkeley, Calif., 1951.

Gibb, H. A. R.: *Modern Trends in Islam,* University of Chicago Press, Chicago, 1947.

Heyworth-Dunne, J.: *Religious and Political Trends in Modern Egypt,* published by the author, Washington, 1950.

Hurewitz, J.: *The Middle East Dilemma,* Harper, New York, 1953.

————: "Unity and Disunity in the Middle East," *International Conciliation,* no. 481, May, 1952.

Issawi, C.: *Egypt: An Economic and Social Analysis,* Oxford, New York, 1947.

Khadduri, M.: "The Role of the Military in Middle East Politics," *American Political Science Review,* vol. 47, June, 1953.

Kimche, J.: *Seven Fallen Pillars,* Praeger, New York, 1953.

Lenczowski, G.: *The Middle East in World Affairs,* Cornell University Press, Ithaca, N.Y., 1952.

Lewis, W. H., and R. Gordon: "Libya after Two Years Independence," *Middle East Journal,* vol. 8, winter, 1954.

Loewenstein, K.: *Brazil under Vargas,* Macmillan, New York, 1942.

Nasser, G. A.: "The Egyptian Revolution," *Foreign Affairs,* January, 1955.

Peters, D.: "The Muslim Brotherhood—Terrorists or Just Zealots?" *The Reporter,* Mar. 17, 1953.

Pierson, W. W., et al.: "Pathology of Democracy in Latin America," *American Political Science Review,* vol. 44, March, 1950.

Rosenthal, F.: "The 'Muslim Brethren' in Egypt," *The Muslim World*, October, 1947.
Royal Institute of International Affairs: *Great Britain and Egypt, 1914–1951*, Oxford, New York, 1952.
Scalapino, R.: *Democracy and the Party Movement in Prewar Japan*, University of California Press, Berkeley, Calif., 1953.
Stokes, W.: "Parliamentary Government in Latin America," *American Political Science Review*, June, 1945.
———: "Violence as a Power Factor in Latin American Politics," *Western Political Quarterly*, September, 1952.
Thompson, E. M.: "Political Unrest in Latin America," *Editorial Research Reports*, June 20, 1952.
Wynn, C. W.: "The Latest Revival of Islamic Nationalism," *The Muslim World*, January, 1948.

Chapter 16

NAZI GERMANY: MULTIPLE VERSUS SINGLE AUTHORITARIAN ELITE

Some dictatorships, like the Soviet Union or Communist China, derive their uniqueness from the fact that only one elite controls all aspects of public—and frequently private—life. A multigroup dictatorship, such as Franco Spain, is characterized by the sharing of state power by a number of allied elites anxious to exclude other groups in the population from access to rulership. Such dictatorships, however, may be converted into the Soviet type if one of the allied elites succeeds in asserting its dominance over the others and manages to reduce their role. Nazi Germany, because it began its authoritarian career as an example of the multigroup variety of dictatorial pattern and underwent a transformation making it into a state ruled by the Nazi party alone, provides a lucid instance of the impact of the associated ideologies and institutions on the pattern of international life.

In tracing the impact of these institutional patterns on international relations it will first be necessary to determine how the elites joined in the making of policy and what the characteristics of the initial phases of German policy were. With the elimination of the allied elites, however, it will be possible to analyze the impact of the Nazi way of thought and of Nazi governmental practices on subsequent German foreign policy.

1. The Elites of Nazi Germany. The advent of Nazism in Germany resulted from the converging interests of four key elites: the civil service, or bureaucracy, the professional army leadership, the leaders of big business, and the National Socialist party. Of these groups, the bureaucracy was certainly the least important in facilitating the Nazi rise to power. Its role was one of passivity, of going along with whatever policy had been decided by party and army. Yet this passivity and acquiescence enabled the members of the civil service to prosper under Nazi rule and to contribute their share to the Nazi impact on world affairs.

Big Business and the Nazis. The leaders of German big business had a far greater impact in shaping the nature of Nazi rule and policy. Even prior to the advent of Hitler, German heavy industry had been characterized by a very high degree of concentration of ownership and control. Competition among firms was absent. Vertical integration (trusts) as well as horizontal agreements on marketing and production (cartels) typified German business practices. The ideology of German business, moreover, drove it directly into close cooperation with the Nazis. Dedicated to the monopoly version of unrestricted private enterprise, German industrialists feared all political institutions which maximized the power of organized labor. They wanted absolute control over the labor market and therefore supported any movement which promised to curb communists, socialists, and trade unions. Their conservatism made them friends of authoritarian movements of the Right, especially those which they expected to be able to control. Hence industrialists like Schröder and Thyssen financed some of Hitler's early political campaigns and diplomat-politician-businessman Papen's connections with them enabled the Nazis to enter the German cabinet in January of 1933. Subsequently the coalition of the Nazi with the business elite became a permanent one, especially as business was left to reap the fruits of the alliance in German domestic as well as foreign policy.

The Army and the Nazis. The German army, however, had still more direct institutional and ideological affiliations with the Nazis. The professional German officer believed that the unique virtues of German thought and life were implicit in his own status, role, and position. He admired loyalty, discipline, and obedience; he abhorred ideological struggle, social unrest, and party politics. His prestige in Germany rested on his reputation for order, patriotism, and professional skill. His conservatism led him to equate internal order with external glory. He held a strong army to be the spiritual salvation of Germany, and a strong army implied acceptance of a foreign policy of vigorous self-assertion, and even war—if it could be successful.

The Nazis. It was the National Socialist party itself, however, which provided the impetus for the characteristic later features of German foreign policy. Numerically much larger than the other German elites, the mass membership of the party also represented a large segment of the population, as did the vote the party received in the last free German elections before 1933.[1] Sociologists still hotly dispute why the membership was so large and in what lay the particular appeal of the party to German society during the Great Depression and after. It is known, however, that Germany was torn by bitter party and group conflicts. Its economic, political, and social life was marked by mutually incompatible ideologies competing for adherents. Patriotic Germans were outraged that great territorial and economic losses had been suffered as a result of World War I. The Nazi party emerged as the catchall for all these accumulated grievances. It promised employ-

---

[1] Membership was estimated at 9,500,000 in 1943, on the basis of German newspaper reports. The party received 13,779,000 votes in the elections of July 31, 1932. F. Neumann, *Behemoth, The Structure and Practice of National Socialism,* Oxford, New York, 1944, p. 539.

ment and prosperity to the jobless. A new social importance and status was predicted for the middle classes, which had been impoverished by the inflation and felt themselves threatened by socialism and communism alike. Security for the small businessman and "dignity of work" for the laborer were held out by Nazi orators. International glory and the rise of Germany were outlined to those who grieved over the losses of the war and the "humiliations of Versailles." Nazi appeal was as widespread as it was vague, but party membership figures testify to its success among the Germans.

The nature of the appeal in large measure answers the question: "Who were the Nazis?" Apart from the support enjoyed as a result of parallel or identical interests with the army, the civil service, and big business, the party itself was largely made up of those segments of German society who felt their status and security threatened by inflation, depression, thwarted nationalism, and party strife. Overwhelmingly, the administrative positions were occupied by members of the lower middle classes whose status was threatened under the republic; the paramilitary and terror apparatus was controlled by dissatisfied World War I officers and veterans; and the huge propaganda machine was the realm of unemployed intellectuals, scholars, and students for whom life under the republic seemed to offer no scope of activity.[2] Thus all the groups whose separate existence was in doubt after World War I, and who tended to blame their insecurity on those who allegedly had caused Germany to lose that war, congregated in the Nazi party. To these people the creation of 492,000 secure party positions, built on the leadership principle, could not but be a welcome relief from class warfare and ideological strife.[3]

Nazi Ideology. What did the members of this party believe? What was the unifying ideology which they accepted and which was to transcend the doctrines of all other German groups? The doctrinal keys to Nazi performance are race and nationality, the total supremacy of the party to other groups, the leadership principle, and the role and rights of Germany.

Hitler and his followers believed that mankind was by nature divided into "inferior" and "superior" races, of which the "Aryan race" was the highest, and Germans were Aryans. Racial superiority implied the absolute right to rule over the inferior. But since races also struggle for survival, the competition of rival races then implied policies of purifying the Germans internally and asserting their superiority externally, by conquering other "races."

The idea of the nation is central to the concept of racial supremacy. Unlike other German thinkers, the Nazis did not emphasize the unifying role of the state over competing groups. They insisted instead that membership in a common biological group, the "folk," constituted the supreme identify-

[2] Daniel Lerner, *The Nazi Elite,* Stanford University Press, Stanford, Calif., 1952.
[3] Neumann, *op. cit.,* p. 82.

ing bond. Germany was not a state so much as a "folk community," a body
of tens of millions of individuals tied together by the fact that they came
of identical racial stock, regardless of whether they lived in Russia, Romania,
Czechoslovakia, Brazil, the United States, or Germany. All ethnic German
groups living abroad, therefore, were part of the community of Greater
Germany. Membership in the nation, so defined, was the greatest honor
conceivable, and the special mission of each pure Aryan German was to
assert the supremacy of his folk.

Under Nazi doctrines, nation, state, and party were ruled according to
the "leadership principle." Authority, instead of being evolved by election
from below, was asserted and delegated by order from above. Each party
cell, factory, economic association, chamber of commerce, youth group,
cultural association, or professional group was ruled by a delegated leader,
appointed by his superior in the hierarchy. The supreme leader, the "Führer,"
was at once the head of nation, state, and party: Adolf Hitler. He possessed
the charisma, infallible insight into all matters, a quality which could be
grasped by the members of party and nation only by faith and not by
reason. Since the government of Germany under Nazism was built on this
principle, it is as unnecessary as it is misleading to analyze the organs of
the state, after the victory of the party over its allies. They functioned only
as a result of orders given by Hitler—or his deputies—with whom all key
decisions originated.

The German nation, in turn, was declared to be the leading nation of
the world. It incorporated the leadership principle by virtue of its racial
character. Germany had the right to everything; inferior nations had privileges only in so far as they were granted and recognized by Germany. The
first and foremost German need, however, was internal strength and the
reconstruction of the armed forces in defiance of the treaty limitations imposed upon her by the victorious states in 1919. Hence Hitler's first major
deduction from these doctrines was the need to get rid of the "shackles of
Versailles," i.e., rebuild the army, navy, and air force, regain lost territories, and reconstitute Germany as the "leading" nation of continental
Europe.

With all the emphasis on the supreme unifying role of the party, however, the Nazis were not always a united and homogeneous group. It took
the "Blood Purge" of 1934 to eliminate those elements in the party which
sought a radical anticapitalist policy and attempted to take over the army.
Some elements in the party, such as Himmler and his Elite Guards, tended
to stress racial purity, while others, such as Göring, were more interested in
building up a separate industrial empire for the party. With Hitler's death
in 1945, a wave of arrests, liberations, and counterarrests occurred, in which
rival leaders sought to eliminate each other, ended, however, a few days
later by Germany's military collapse. Yet the fact remains that in its strug-

gles with the other three elites of Nazi Germany the party usually maintained a common front, and therefore it effectively supplanted them by 1938, when it succeeded in asserting control over big business, the bureaucracy, and especially the army.

The coalition of elites which ruled Germany, therefore, was not a homogeneous one. It contained competing as well as identical interests and aims. While the party emerged triumphant in almost all contests over control, the nature of this contest is nevertheless a crucial factor in explaining the foreign policy of Nazi Germany during the period from 1933 to 1937.

2. The Aims of Germany's Old Elites and Nazi Foreign Policy. The fact that the advent of authoritarian dictatorship in Germany is attributable to the confluence of interests among the three older elites and the forces associated with the rising Nazi party should not be taken to mean that each plank in Germany's post-1933 foreign policy bears the imprint of aspirations shared by all German groups in power. Exhaustive researches into the secret documents of Nazi Germany, conducted by the United Nations personnel who brought top Nazi and German officials to trial in 1946, point to the overwhelming preponderance of party aims in fashioning foreign policy. The other elites, to be sure, cooperated freely with the party for the most part and seldom showed active opposition to Nazi aims. Yet they were never in a position to share in policy making on a basis of equality. When Nazi policy coincided with their interests they worked with the party; but when Hitler's aims seemed to conflict with theirs, resistance was not necessarily shown. Disagreement made itself felt through individual acts of defection. Thus industrialist Thyssen and Deputy Führer Rudolf Hess left their posts and fled Germany in revolt against Hitler. But only once did opposition find expression in open revolt, in the plot of July 20, 1944. Police Chief Himmler's terror apparatus sufficed to keep even the allied elites in check, as graphically demonstrated by the 5,000-odd executions which followed the abortive 1944 plot against Hitler's life.

The Bureaucracy and Foreign Policy. In what respects did Germany's elites have common or parallel foreign policy aims, and in what areas is there evidence of tension and disagreement? This question is crucial to the analysis of Nazi foreign policy. The case of the bureaucracy once more seems to be the least complex. In general terms the German civil service had no quarrel with the preponderance of Nazi power in Germany in any of its aspects. In the realm of foreign affairs, most career officials of the Foreign Ministry agreed with the party as to the necessity of tearing up the Treaty of Versailles. They seemed to favor expansion on principle. Civil servants like Weizsäcker found no serious difficulty in serving a fanatic Nazi foreign minister, Joachim von Ribbentrop, as far as the ends of policy were concerned. Only in the realm of means can differences in outlook be detected. Thus Weizsäcker confesses his acceptance of the need for expansion, in his memoirs, but insists that this should have been accomplished by peaceful means only. In short, he accepted the ends of imperial expansion but preferred means of blackmail, threats, demonstrations, and propaganda to war. He, like almost all high officials of the government departments, found no difficulty in cooperating with the party as long as success seemed certain, even though the civil servants were never given the power to *initiate* any policy of significance.

All overt opposition to Nazi policy aims in the bureaucracy was finally liquidated as a result of the July, 1944, attempt to assassinate Hitler and to end the war. Diplomats like Schulenburg and Hassell and important administrators like Mayor Goerdeler of Leipzig had joined in the conspiracy to oust the Nazis. These men were conservatives, appalled by Nazi brutality and inability to compromise rather than by the policy aims of the party. Yet they were the exception rather than the rule among civil servants. On the whole, the bureaucracy identified its own survival with that of the party and therefore accepted Nazi foreign policy aims even if it did little to state and formulate them.

The Army and Foreign Policy. Much the same picture obtained in the army. The younger officers, especially the nonaristocrats favored by Hitler, identified themselves fully with the ends professed by the party. The army was their calling, and their claim to status, fame, and security lay in the continued primacy of war in German life. War and a policy of active expansion were natural to them. The same, however, cannot be said of the aims characteristic of the older members of the army elite. While the army was their supreme symbol and its welfare, strength, and size their primary concern, they did not cherish the idea of risking this buttress of their own status in adventures whose outcome was doubtful. Certainly the older officers of the General Staff planned aggressive war and consented to policies of conquest. Aims of expansion were fully acceptable to them as long as the risks of defeat were slight. Disagreement over the ends of German policy, therefore, arose only when the army elite differed with the party over the advisability of a given campaign at a given time, not over the principle of expansion. Of this kind of opposition some interesting examples were uncovered after the demise of Nazi Germany.

While men like Keitel and Jodl in the army and Doenitz in the navy— not to mention Göring's party-controlled air force—always agreed with Hitler's plans, the more cautious generals who did not wish to risk the survival of the army for the sake of the party's aims attempted to thwart Hitler more than once. They opposed the march into the Rhineland in 1936 as too risky and advised against eastward expansion in 1937. Some evidence exists which suggests that the General Staff was prepared in the fall of 1938 to arrest Hitler in order to keep him from risking war over the Sudetenland. Only the negotiated settlement of Munich is said to have prevented the effectuation of this coup. Again, while the generals loyally planned the invasions of Poland, France, Norway, Britain, the Balkans, the Atlantic Islands, and the Soviet Union to the most minute detail, many of them expressed opposition to the implementation of these plans if success seemed doubtful. As the war went from bad to worse after 1943 some of these men hoped to displace Hitler, erect a conservative army–civil service regime instead, and negotiate for peace with the Allies before Germany and her army were completely destroyed. Members of the elite, such as Beck, Canaris, and Stauffenberg, stood therefore at the center of the plot of July 20, 1944. But their failure sealed the demise of the army's opposition. The rise of the party's Elite Guard to military prominence demonstrated that in the struggle of elites Hitler and his colleagues had carried the day.

Even after the entire German military, economic, and political apparatus was deeply mired in the war with Britain, Russia, and the United States, divergences over policy occasionally continued to come to the fore. Thus the party's indifference over the rational utilization and efficient administration of conquered territories clashed sharply with the army's insistence on such measures. To the military leadership, efficient administration in Poland, France, and the Ukraine was essential if stability was to reign in the rear echelons, to safeguard communications and supply. The basic aim of winning the war—shared with the party—could be attained only if the industrial and economic resources of conquered territories were rationally and efficiently integrated into German military needs. The party, however, felt no such compunction. Repression, extermination, and forced mass movements of conquered populations were desirable on principle despite army disagreement. The destruction or inefficient relocation of conquered industries was preferred on grounds of ideology and race, despite the inevitable loss of production and supply engendered thereby. Conflicts such as these recurred throughout the war years without detracting from the advent of the party to exclusive control.

Big Business and Foreign Policy. By and large, however, the army's aims coincided with those of the party, though they differed over means. The same, essentially, is true of the leaders of big business. Further, Nazi economic policy within Germany was not such as to permit a conflict of interests to arise. On the contrary, prior to the war years the aims of business elite coincided perfectly with those of the party, with the complete autonomy of the trusts assured by government policy. In the realm of foreign relations, however, the identity of interests is less marked and opportunity for divergent aims arose.

It has been customary to assert that big business was directly concerned in unleashing the Nazi policy of conquest. Monopoly, the argument runs, had to seek areas for sales and raw materials abroad, since the expansion of operations in Germany was precluded by the prevalent industrial struc-

ture. The trials of leading German industrialists after the war, however, have
failed to reveal any direct complicity in the policy of violent self-extension.
In fact, I. G. Farben, for instance, was reluctant to cooperate with the party
on several occasions; it refused to relinquish patent-sharing agreements with
alien firms and opposed the use of its facilities abroad for propaganda and
subversion purposes. There is no evidence that the business elite was directly
involved in the planning and execution of the policy of expansion.[4]

On the other hand it is equally clear that the business elite was ready
to reap the fruits of the war and therefore did not oppose the policy of
expansion. Krupp, Flick, and I. G. Farben, among many, absorbed the
properties of their foreign competitors and were eager to take over their
patents and markets. German business had no quarrel with the Nazi policy
of concentrating all industrial power in German hands and therefore took
full advantage of political and military expansion to achieve monopoly status
over all of Europe. The identity of interests between industry and party in
this kind of expansion is symbolized by the fact that in all conquered areas
the pattern of economic organization followed the German model, with
German chambers of commerce abroad in the ruling positions in France,
Belgium, Holland, Poland, etc., and foreign enterprises compelled to follow
their lead.[5] The German war machine was thereby strengthened, and the
economic aims of business safeguarded at the same time. Conflicts of interest
were implicit in this partnership, however, whenever the military policy
conflicted with that of sound business, or when the party sought to build
its own industrial empire. When the policy of concentrating all of Europe's
heavy industry in German hands could be conducted without making war
on the whole world, the business elite preferred peaceful means to those of
the Nazis.

Conflict and Harmony among Elites. The impact of these patterns of
converging and conflicting elite interests on the characteristics of German
foreign policy can now be summarized. During the first five years of Nazi
rule, a period in which it did not yet prove possible to control the separate
aims and aspirations of the army and of business, the Nazis were apparently
compelled to moderate their program. While rearmament and preparation
for a possible war of expansion were undertaken, of course, the older elites
resisted the lighthearted use of these implements. Police terror and absolute
totalitarian control of all aspects of German life, similarly, reached their
apex only after the showdown struggle between party and army early in
1938, which resulted in the dismissal of General Blomberg and the advent
of military leaders absolutely loyal to the Führer. The converging of elite

---

[4] *Trials of War Criminals before the Nürnberg Military Tribunals,* Washington, 1951,
vols. VII and VIII. See especially the judgment on counts 1 and 5 of the indictment,
vol. VIII, pp. 1096–1128.
[5] Neumann, *op. cit.,* pp. 356–358, 577–585.

interests thus made possible the assumption of power by the Nazis, the gradual rearmament of Germany, and agreement on the desirability of wiping out the territorial losses imposed in the Treaty of Versailles. The conflicts implicit in these elite aims, however, prevented any drastic and warlike implementation of Germany's aims and therefore produced a certain amount of moderation in Nazi foreign policy prior to 1938.

With the progress of unchecked Nazi power, of course, the picture changed radically, and the Munich crisis was the first obvious consequence. The older elites resigned themselves to reaping the fruits of Nazi victories during World War II, but they took no active part in planning basic policy. Only the few who participated in the plot of 1944 carried their conflicting aims to the stage of active and futile opposition. The bulk of the excluded elites remained loyal to the dominant Nazi group and thus preferred to profit from the continuing convergence of aspirations rather than risk life and property over possible conflicts in aims. The characteristics of later Nazi policy, therefore, showed no restraint and lived up to the full logic of the party's ideology.

The war itself provided the final means for completing the ascendancy of the party. While Hitler succeeded in removing some of the civil servants and generals who were not fully in favor of his policy aims by 1938, the massive predominance of Nazi institutions in all spheres of German life emerged only during the war. It was then that the party's industrial machine acquired in conquered lands an economic empire of its own, competing with the business elite. It was in foreign campaigns that the Elite Guard became an army loyal to the Führer and his police chief Himmler, and not to the General Staff. Finally, it was in conquered territories that the party functionaries took over en masse the administrative tasks which had until then been the preserve of the bureaucracy. The war thus released the forces which enabled the Nazis to sidestep and overrule their allies in German society and thus emerge supreme.

3. The Aims of the Nazi Elite. It is clear that while the aims of the older elites generally coincided with those of the party, it is in the position and ideology of the Nazis themselves that the key to Germany's foreign policy aims after 1937 must be found. Since Hitler then took the initiative in every foreign policy decision, without necessarily consulting the other elites until his mind was already made up, the beliefs of the Nazi party in general and of its Führer in particular must contain the major clues to German policy aims. Hence we must examine in some detail the ideology and interests of the Nazi party.

Three ideological tenets in the creed of National Socialism (and fascism anywhere) stand out in such an analysis: the familiar doctrine of racial supremacy and survival, the closely allied importance attributed to the geopolitical notion of "living space" and agricultural resources, and the belief in violence as such, especially as related to the imperialism of the middle classes.

Blood and Soil. "Only a sufficiently extensive area on this globe guarantees a nation freedom of existence," [6] wrote the Führer. Race and the folk were given the importance of a fundamental point of departure. As Hitler told a class of apprentice leaders in 1937, "Today a new kind of state is being created. Its uniqueness lies in the fact that it is based not on Christianity and not on the importance of the state itself, but on the closed folkish community." [7] The idea of a closed geographical "space" for this community emerges side by side with the racial theme. Germany did not have enough land for its peasants and its food supply, the Nazis argued. A large and efficient population has the right to a large and rich soil. "One crop failure of ten percent makes the feeding of our people uncertain for one month . . . It is not possible to feed our nation on the basis of 470,000 or 570,000 square kilometers." [8] Hence the conquest of lands tilled by inferior races, especially Slavs, was necessary and legitimate. "Soil and territory as the goal of our foreign policy" Hitler regarded as basic.[9] Peasants of Aryan stock were to be settled in the east of Europe, and "the mission of the National Socialist movement . . . is to bring our own nation to such political insight as will make it see its future goal fulfilled . . . by the industrious labor of the German plow which needs only to be given land by the sword." [10] Opposition to such a scheme was illegitimate, since the peoples at whose expense this program would be given effect were racially inferior. Russia was ruled by Jewish Bolsheviks who did not know how to use resources efficiently. France's policy, "methodically led by the Jew . . . is a sin against the existence of white humanity and some day will inspire against that nation all the avenging spirits of a knowledge which will have recognized race pollution as the original sin against mankind." [11]

The Lust for Violence. Implicit in these racial and spacial doctrines, however, is a belief in the value of violence of and by itself. The imperial expansion, not of business or the nobility, but of the common man who made up the bulk of the Nazi party, was glorified by asserting his right to land and space because he was stronger. "Only through domination over alien peoples can one learn how to lead," asserted the Führer, and the elite of the party delighted in following him in reducing the major part of Europe to the status of a colonial empire. The careful use of terror, brutality, and violence was systematically taught to the Elite Guard as the party's leaders

---

[6] A. Hitler, *Mein Kampf,* Reynal & Hitchcock, New York, 1941, p. 953.

[7] Speech by Hitler at Ordensburg "Sonthofen," Nov. 23, 1937; H. Picker (ed.), *Hitler's Tischgespräche,* Athenäum Verlag, Bonn, 1951, p. 446.

[8] *Ibid.,* p. 447.

[9] Hitler, *Mein Kampf,* pp. 943–944.

[10] *Ibid.,* pp. 952–953.

[11] *Ibid.,* p. 908.

in future eras. In foreign policy as well, Hitler preferred the use of violence to gaining his ends by negotiation. In Czechoslovakia in 1938, in Poland in 1939, and in Russia in 1941 the Nazis seemed to want war for its own sake in addition to wanting it as a means for gaining living space and protecting German racial purity. Violence is a key part of ideology when the party could teach that "it is immaterial if people love us. So long as they respect us! It is immaterial if people hate us, so long as they fear us." [12]

Removing the "Shackles of Versailles." In addition to these ideological forces propelling the Nazis toward a foreign policy of belligerence and expansion, the position of the party in German politics probably provided further ends of self-extension. The "shackles of Versailles" were perhaps the single most important propaganda point which was utilized by the party in its ascent to power. The reconstruction of disarmed and territorially reduced Germany to at least its 1914 position was a fixed aim which the Nazis shared with most other nonauthoritarian German groups. It was a position from which Hitler could not have retreated even had he wished to live in peace with his neighbors.

By divesting Germany of the limitations imposed upon her freedom of action by the Treaty of Versailles, the Nazis gained their most important set of common interests with their fellow authoritarian elites. The army wished to be free to rebuild and modernize itself, reintroduce conscription, and once more restore the military calling to its pre-1918 eminence. Big business wished to be free from reparations payments and was anxious to circumvent the financial logic of its monopoly position in Germany by expansion elsewhere. Patriotic civil servants chafed under the territorial losses of Versailles. Versailles was the common symbol, uniting all dissatisfied elites. Thus Hitler declared that "one must be quite clear about the fact that the regaining of the lost regions will not come about through solemn appeals to the dear Lord or through pious hopes in a League of Nations, but only through force of arms." [13] This definition of the issue suited his allied elites and at the same time compelled him to follow through with a policy which most Germans seemed to approve.

Domestic Institutions and Expansion. Similarly, the rapid growth of the party bureaucracy—as distinguished from the regular civil service—imposed limitations upon Hitler's freedom of action. The insecure members of the lower middle classes which flocked to his banners sought status and glory in a role which they had never possessed in the past. In so far as Germany could not meet their aspirations through its domestic institutions, external fields of activity had to be found. A horde of office seekers and hangers-on wished to be rewarded for faithful services rendered. The opportunity could be provided only by the conquest of other nations, which were then trans-

[12] Speech at Ordensburg "Sonthofen," Picker, *op. cit.*, p. 450.
[13] Hitler, *Mein Kampf*, p. 912.

formed into colonies and protectorates. Expansion was therefore essential to maintain unity among the members of the ruling elite. Finally, the policy of expansion and war provided the instrument through which the older elites could be safely deprived of their power and stripped of whatever interests and aims conflicted with those of the party.

Ideology and political position combined, therefore, in making a policy of self-extension the only logical aim of the National Socialist party. To an extent, this aim was shared with the other elites. Thus the definition of policy aims in Germany rested on a limited convergence of interests among the segments of all elites, but not on a lasting identity of aims. For the party, war was of importance even if the outcome was doubtful. Business and army, however, were quite content to engage in self-extension without insisting on war, and they tended to oppose Nazi policy when it seemed that defeat would ensue. Hence Nazi policy aspirations in 1937 derived their peculiarities not only from the sharing of interests among all the elites, but also from the conflicts inherent in this relationship. The absence of permanent identity of aims may lead to a disintegration of the coalition of elites at some stage. War became the device through which the party assured itself of control over its not-too-willing partners. Thus, because of shared as well as unique interests, war was the *sine qua non* of Nazi policy. Without it, the survival of the party as the preeminent German elite would have been imperiled.

4. How Germany Went to War: The Story of Nazi Foreign Policy Making. Yet Hitler waged his campaigns on a highly improvised basis. The decision to attack a neighbor was made usually only a few months before the dive bombers struck. Hitler was willing to wage war in 1938 even if Britain had not handed the Sudetenland to him. Despite warnings by army leaders that Germany was not yet "ready," he was psychologically prepared to take the risks of a two-front war in 1939, even if he had failed to conclude the Nazi-Soviet pact of August 23. The question of why a neighbor should be attacked or where the operations should be undertaken was quite secondary to the major principle of the necessity for armed conflict.

Party Dominance in Planning. Nevertheless, it is of particular interest to trace the process of decision making in such situations. In the case of Nazi Germany it appears that the Führer himself monopolized this process. Army and navy were given assignments to plan given campaigns after Hitler had decided to launch them. Naval policy suggestions and memoranda, for instance, were scarcely read by Hitler, and on only one major occasion did he heed the counsel of Admiral Raeder, in his decision to seize Norway. Most significantly, the regular German Foreign Office was all but excluded from active policy making. The memoranda of its officials were contemptuously disregarded by Hitler. In 1933 Heydrich, a chief of the secret police, described the German foreign service as conducting itself "as if no Nazi revolution had taken place in Germany. Jewish interpreters, black-red-gold flags, reactionary diplomats and senile privy councillors. We Nazis have to undertake a thorough housecleaning." [14] Ribbentrop, a high-ranking Nazi who replaced the civil servant Neurath as Foreign Minister in 1938, trusted his own personnel so little that he set up a small Nazi staff within the Ministry which was entrusted with confidential plans and aims, whereas the regular foreign service personnel was given little contact with such work.

Foreign policy making, therefore, was the exclusive prerogative of the Führer. He usually informed the inner coterie of Nazis: Göring, Himmler, Ribbentrop, Hess, and later Bormann. Thus the Foreign Minister was intimately acquainted with his master's aims even when the professional staff of his Ministry remained in ignorance. The practice was to assign the details of economic negotiation and legal drafting to the foreign service personnel, while policy planning was entirely in the hands of the top Nazis.

The army, however, occupied a consultative position on technical questions in the planning process. While its General Staff was never polled on whether the army elite favored a policy of self-extension and war, and while policy decisions to strike were made by Hitler himself, the army was called upon to explain whether given campaigns were possible under given conditions. The generals learned soon enough that it was not wise to give negative answers to these questions. Hitler preferred to ignore information which did not fit his aims and had no place in his ideology. Hence opposition to the plans of expansion, voiced by some generals on technical military grounds alone, was expressed less and less as the war went on. Intelligence information which did not confirm Hitler's fanatic conviction that Germany would win—as late as 1944—was not usually shown the Führer. Plans and schemes not compatible with his outlook and moods did not find their way to his desk. The mechanics of life under authoritarianism made it entirely unsafe to confront the charismatic leader with information and reasoning he might disapprove.

The Decision to Wage War. The interesting question in tracing the evolution of Nazi foreign policy making, therefore, is: "When and how did Hitler and his staff decide to expand?" There is little evidence, prior to the fall of 1937, that detailed plans for taking over the territories of neighboring states were in existence. Hitler refrained from attacking his neighbors, with the exception of his stillborn attempt to take over Austria by terrorism and internal subversion in 1934, a scheme which was foiled by his Fascist colleague Benito Mussolini.

But on November 5, 1937, the Führer told the party and army leaders

[14] Quoted in P. Schmidt, *Statist auf diplomatischer Bühne*, Athenäum Verlag, Bonn, 1949, p. 263.

what his immediate plans were, plans which he considered as "fundamental principles." [15] Nazi Germany, he explained, possessed a temporary superiority in armaments which had to be utilized while it lasted. Germany had to gain more living space while it could, to strike "where the greatest possible conquests could be made at the lowest cost," to conquer "agriculturally useful space." The Ukraine and Poland were the long-range objectives of this policy, but Central Europe had to be consolidated first. Hence, Austria and Czechoslovakia were earmarked for liquidation and absorption. The conquest of these neighbors might be achieved without war—through threats and bluffs—but Soviet armed intervention was considered likely. This, Hitler thought, was a risk which had to be taken. He was ready for a limited war in 1938, in which the Western powers were not expected to intervene.

Göring as well as the army leaders made feeble efforts to oppose these plans. They pointed out the dangers if Britain, France, and Russia were to intervene. But Hitler brushed aside their doubts by asserting that "the German question can be solved only by way of force and this never without risk. . . . We must place 'force with risk' at the head of our program." This indeed remained Nazi Germany's operational maxim for the remainder of its political life.

Phase One: Central Europe. The following seventeen months witnessed the implementation of this policy by Hitler's characteristic diplomacy: the mixture of threats and bluffs, based on the assumption that Britain and France would be too weak and too indifferent to oppose him and the further alternative assumption that war was inevitable anyway and might as well come. Nazi-fomented civil disorders in Austria forced this nation to consent to *Anschluss* in March of 1938. Britain and France did nothing, while Göring assured the Czech envoy in Berlin that with the annexation of Austria Hitler had completed his foreign policy of reuniting all Germans. Yet by summer of 1938 the second phase of Central European consolidation was well under way. The Sudeten German population of Czechoslovakia was now employed to demand large and unspecified concessions from Prague. Hitler intended these internal Czech disorders to lead to a Sudeten German revolt, which he could assist by invading Czechoslovakia and liquidating it. Britain and France, however, now took a hand in the negotiations and proposed the peaceful transfer of the German areas to the Nazis. Baron Weizsäcker, in the Foreign Office, claims to have warned Mussolini of Hitler's plans and suggested that he be headed off by a peaceful solution. In any event, the Munich settlement was the result: Italy, Britain, and France agreed to give Hitler the Sudetenland in return for a guarantee of independence for the remainder of Czechoslovakia. Hitler, sorely disappointed for not having been

---

[15] J. W. Wheeler-Bennett, *Munich: Prologue to Tragedy,* New York, 1948, pp. 11–14. The document cited is known as the "Hossbach Memorandum," introduced at the Nuremberg Military Tribunal as Doc. 386-PS.

able to use his army, consented. But the speedy annexation of all Czecho-slovakia three months later indicated how seriously he took the Munich settlement.

Phase Two: Poland and the Nazi-Soviet Pact. The stage was now set for the expansion into Germany's Eastern European living space for which the annexation of Central Europe had been the prelude. Danzig provided the pretext, not the reason, for going to war. As late as March, 1939, Germany still offered Poland an alliance for a common attack against the Soviet Union to implement the end of gaining living space. Poland refused, and the German claim for Danzig and the Corridor separating East Germany from East Prussia was Hitler's answer.[16] In April Hitler gave his army orders to plan for a fall campaign against Poland. In May he assured his generals that Poland must be crushed before Germany's armaments advantage disap-peared and before the Western powers were strong enough to intervene.[17]

Yet Hitler was not at all certain that Britain and France would remain neutral again. Hence, in order to avoid a prolonged two-front war, it became necessary to assure the neutrality of Soviet Russia. Since Stalin, as early as March 10, 1939, had indicated that he would not be averse to a deal with his dangerous fellow dictator, prolonged, mutually distrustful, and difficult negotiations between Berlin and Moscow set in to arrange a bargain. Hitler's thought that "Russia may be induced to take no further interest in the destruction of Poland"[18] thus culminated in the Pact of August 23, 1939, in which Germany acquired most of Poland and Russia was given an ambiguously free hand in Latvia, Estonia, eastern Poland, and Bessarabia, in addition to promising neutrality in the event of war with Poland, Britain, and France.

With the proposed pact almost concluded, Hitler made his attitude crystal-clear in a speech to his generals on August 22, 1939, three days before the scheduled invasion of Poland:[19]

Our enemies have no personalities; no masters, no men of action. . . . We have nothing to lose—we can only gain. Our economic situation is such that we cannot hold out more than a few years. . . . We have no other choice; we must act. . . . Therefore conflict is better now. . . . The initiative cannot be allowed to pass to others. . . . We must accept the risk with reckless resolution. . . . We are facing the alternative of striking now or being destroyed with cer-tainty sooner or later. . . . I am only afraid that at the last minute some swine will make a proposal for mediation. . . . [There must be] most iron determina-

---

[16] A. Rossi, *The Russo-German Alliance,* Duell, Sloan & Pearce, New York, 1951, p. 7.
[17] F. H. Hinsley, *Hitler's Strategy,* Cambridge, New York, 1951, pp. 22–23. Account based largely on Nuremberg Docs. 798, 1014-PS.
[18] Rossi, *op. cit.,* p. 13.
[19] Nuremberg Doc. 798-PS, as cited in Hinsley, *op. cit.,* pp. 24–25. A slightly different version of the speech appears in *Nazi Conspiracy and Aggression,* vol. III, Washington, 1946, pp. 581 ff.

tion on our side. Retreat before nothing. Everybody will have to make a point of it that we were determined from the beginning to fight the Western Powers.

But since this was a "defensive" war for the Germans, to protect them from the false Polish claims over Danzig, the Western powers could not be provoked too obviously. They would have to declare war on Germany, not vice versa.[20] Hence Hitler was sorely embarrassed when what he termed "swine" —Britain and France—did offer mediation on August 25. The campaign was postponed for one week in order to ward off this unwelcome peaceful gesture. Ribbentrop brusquely repulsed these Anglo-French attempts; Paris and London assured Berlin that they would intervene; Hitler, ready to take his "risk," launched the attack on Poland on September 1, 1939. World War II had begun, to end six years later with the complete defeat of Germany.

Phase Three: Engulfment in Global War. Ultimately, Germany in pursuit of its policy of self-extension brought an unprecedented coalition into arms against her. The central lesson which emerges from this picture of policy making is the difficulty experienced by the expanding state—given its ideology —to stop the process of expansion, once it has been launched. After the defeat of one enemy, there appeared always another key danger which called for liquidation, if hostilities and bonds are defined as rigidly as the Nazis chose to define them. Short of world conquest or internal transformation there was no easy end to this process, as Germany discovered after 1941. World conquest turned into defeat, and the attempt to bring about internal changes ended in the abortive rising of July, 1944.

Among various factors, it was probably the Nazi predetermination to destroy Russia which provided the final undoing. Only four months after the conclusion of the "alliance" of August 23, 1939, Hitler spoke of the dangers posed by the Soviets and the necessity to destroy them: [21]

Pacts are only held as long as they serve their purpose. . . . Russia has farreaching aims, above all . . . in the Baltic. . . . She is striving to increase her influence in the Balkans and towards the Persian Gulf, which is also the goal of our own foreign policy. Russia will do what she thinks will benefit herself.

But, he added, "we can oppose Russia only when we are at peace in the West." [22]

Russian policy during 1940 only served to strengthen these purposes as the Soviet leaders pressed annexations in the Baltic and Balkans and demanded far-reaching controls over the Turkish Straits. Hitler ordered his generals to plan Operation Barbarossa, the liquidation of Russia, immediately after the fall of France in July of 1940; and he ordered the plan to be im-

[20] Nuremberg Doc. 126-C, as cited in Hinsley, *op. cit.*, pp. 28–29.

[21] Nuremberg Doc. 789-PS, Hitler's speech of Nov. 23, 1939, as cited in Hinsley, *op. cit.*, pp. 44–45. See the slightly different version of the same document in *Nazi Conspiracy and Aggression,* vol. III, pp. 572 ff. This citation is a merger of both versions.

[22] *Ibid.*

plemented by June of 1941 as soon as Molotov, in November of 1940, refused to give up Soviet demands in Europe in exchange for being offered India and the Persian Gulf in the projected Axis division of the world.[23]

But why did Hitler decide to take on his strongest enemy *before* having achieved peace in the West? The curious Nazi attitude toward Britain provides one clue. As late as July of 1941 Hitler thought that "the end of this war will be the beginning of lasting Anglo-German friendship. But the presumption of our living in peace with them is a knock-out blow against them; the Englishman expects such a blow from the man he is to respect; 1918 must be eradicated."[24] Repeatedly Hitler spoke of permitting Britain to keep her empire and home islands, provided Germany would be recognized as ruling the Continent.

Thus the initial timetable called for defeat of Britain and peace in the West. However, three separate campaigns in 1940 failed to bring victory: air attacks on Britain resulted in the defeat of the German air force; Italian land attacks on the Suez Canal were halted; and a projected assault on Gibraltar and North Africa failed to be launched because of disagreements between Hitler and his Spanish colleague, Francisco Franco. Britain seemed unwilling to entertain the basis for peace which the Nazis held out.

Stalled in the West, therefore, Hitler had to turn to the East if Germany was to retain the initiative and wrest agricultural land from the Soviets. If the defeat of Britain could not be brought about first, the Russians had to be eliminated as a threat before a final assault on British power seemed feasible. The failure of the campaigns of 1940 left the insecure dictator no alternative. As he explained to his comrade Benito Mussolini on the day before the fateful June 22, 1941: "For the invasion of England it will be necessary to put our last plane into operation. . . . I would not hesitate one moment to take such a responsibility if, in addition to all other considerations, I could be assured that I would not be suddenly attacked or even menaced in the East. . . ."[25]

Expecting quick victory in the East, Hitler threw caution to the winds. Anticipating the eventual entry of the United States into the conflict, he drew Japan into the Axis fold late in 1940. Japan's mission, however, was to attack Singapore and cripple Britain in the Far East, and later to attack Siberia and thus aid the German assault on Russia. These measures were to *deter* the United States from entering the war, by underlining Axis might and demonstrating Anglo-Russian weakness.[26] In fact, of course, Japan at-

---

[23] Rossi, *op. cit.*, pp. 119–163.

[24] Picker, *op. cit.*, p. 43.

[25] A. François-Poncet (ed.), *Les lettres secrètes échangées par Hitler et Mussolini*, Paris, 1946; Hitler's letter of June 21, 1941, pp. 122–127.

[26] Key material on the German-Japanese-American relationship is in Hinsley, *op. cit.*, pp. 177 ff.; and U.S. Department of State, *Nazi-Soviet Relations, 1939–1941*, 1948. pp. 195–196.

tacked the "wrong" enemy by striking at Pearl Harbor and involving the United States directly, instead of concentrating on Britain and the Soviet Union. Nazi policy, instead of neutralizing the United States through the Japanese alliance, had blundered into open hostilities with America. Hitler had foreseen this as an undesirable possibility but had accepted it as one of the usual "risks" that had to be taken.

Thus, the Nazi decision to strike was predominantly the result of ideological forces and assessments which left no other alternatives. Passionate commitments and fallacious evaluations predetermined war against both Britain and Russia. Failure to win against one enemy automatically brought the other reaction into play, ending in fiasco on both fronts as the United States was carelessly drawn into the conflict.

5. Characteristics of Nazi Foreign Policy. The analysis of Nazi Germany's elite structure, the aims entertained by the elites, and the manner in which they formulated foreign policy can be of relevance to the dynamics of international relations only if the characteristics of conduct implicit in these factors can be specified. Multigroup and single-group authoritarianisms, in their past history, can afford insights into the foreign policies of similar systems at other times. It remains to abstract the characteristics revealed by the story of Nazi Germany.

Clearly, the Nazi party, as the policy-making elite, enjoyed precious little freedom of maneuver. The definition of policy aims inherent in the ideology and position of the party, its tools for interpreting its environment, wellnigh compelled it to follow the ends of violent self-extension. It could see itself in no other light in relation to other nations and other values. Furthermore, the relationship of the Nazi elite to the older German leading groups once more precluded internal adjustments except those which would consolidate Nazi rule. Hence the Nazis once more were compelled to follow the ends they had adopted, because any other course would have strengthened the position of their allied elites. Thus the characteristics of Nazi foreign policy, in their general application, may be summarized as (1) the inability to compromise in international relations; (2) the inability to accept general rules of behavior; (3) the inability to deal with defeated enemies, with the possible exception of Vichy France; and (4) the inability to make use of alliances.

The Inability to Compromise. Probably no area of Nazi conduct is more striking and more disturbing to peace than the inability to compromise. Diplomacy and negotiation in the ordinary sense were impossible to the Nazis. Their ideas on international relations precluded the possibility of this kind of conduct. Doctrines of absolute racial superiority and of historic missions to acquire living space brook no diplomatic formulas and despise pacific means for the settlement of disputes. A preexisting preference for violence and armed contests does not fit the traditional ends and aims of national elites in other societal settings. Said the Führer,[27]

The pacifist-humane idea is perhaps quite good whenever the man of the highest standard has previously conquered and subjected the world to a degree that makes him the only master of this globe. Thus the idea is more and more deprived of harmful effect in the measure in which its practical application becomes rare and finally impossible. Therefore, first fight, and then one may see what can be done. . . .

Compromise, in short, was by definition impossible with a system which defined its aims in such terms. Peaceful coexistence could have no meaning, as the Western powers discovered after Munich, a "compromise" settlement. Short of the conquest of Europe by German Aryans, the coexistence of other nations and other values with Germany's were precluded by the Nazi conception of international relations.

More significant still, Hitler's compromising with others—had he been willing—would have been made impossible by the Nazi inability to understand the motives of other nations save in terms of Nazi ideology. Policy analysis and planning were undertaken, not in terms of generally accepted criteria, but solely in terms of Nazi views on race and racial motives, thus leading to some costly blunders. Hitler thought, for example, that the United States would enter the war only after Britain became exhausted so that America could easily annex the British Empire. He took for granted that Washington was motivated primarily by this desire.[28] Further, he continued to believe—and Hess's famed flight proves that he was not alone in so believing—that Britain and Germany were natural allies who should share the world. He hoped for the continued domestic strength of the British aristocracy, because its members would be bound to be sympathetic to German aims. Britain's refusal to see his point he tended to attribute to the decadent socialists in the government. Nazi ideas on international relations led Germany to conclusions incompatible with peace, negotiation, and compromise. Racially determined eternal needs took the place of these factors.

The Inability to Accept Common Rules. The uniqueness of Nazi beliefs and their drastic inability to share any values are equally implicit in their ideas on international law. Unable, of course, to accept the traditional rules of law, Nazi Germany contributed a set of original prescriptions consonant with Nazi doctrine and aims. Thus of international organizations, the Nazi lawyer Carl Schmitt said that "a universal organization in which there is no place for warlike preservation and destruction of human life would be neither a State nor an Empire; it would lose all political character." [29] The equality

---

[27] Hitler, *Mein Kampf*, p. 395.
[28] Picker, *op. cit.*, p. 46.
[29] Cited in editor's footnote to *Mein Kampf*, p. 393.

of states was transformed into the right of each nation to adequate living space, thus supporting German claims. Traditional international law was further denounced as a Jewish creation and as a cloak for British imperialism, because of its claim to universal applicability. The New Order would be regional, i.e., under the domination of racially strong states. Hence Germany claimed preeminence in Europe, just as the United States allegedly used its Monroe Doctrine for the control of the Western Hemisphere. Finally, the Nazis rejected the state as the subject of international law and substituted the race and the nation. The rules of war were changed accordingly: superior races had certain rights, whereas inferior races had none.[30] In essence, it was only Germany which had any rights whatever.

The Inability to Administer. A further key principle of Nazi foreign policy was the patent inability of the party elite to transcend its own racial views in its treatment of conquered nations. This inability made it impossible for the German government to negotiate a peace with its enemies, even had it been so inclined. But more important still, it precluded stable and orderly administration in the conquered areas, which consequently continued to tie down German troops during the war with guerrilla activities. It has been remarked that an enlightened German administration in the Ukraine, for instance, could have produced a strong anti-Soviet and pro-German political sentiment in that region, thus freeing German troops for combat and weakening Soviet sabotage behind the lines. Such a possibility, however, was out of the question. Nazi racial doctrines doomed to failure any arguments for such an administration. Rosenberg, as ruler of Eastern Europe, refused to consider such suggestions when they were made by army or Foreign Office personnel.

Hitler was determined to use Russia and Poland as colonial areas, to be settled exclusively by Teutons—German, Norwegian, Dutch, and Swedish. The Ukraine was to be the area for "planned racial policy, to prevent the inbreeding which is prevalent among us." He outlined his plans in detail: [31]

In our settlement of the Russian space, the German peasant will live in wonderful villages. German government offices will have beautiful buildings, governors will live in palaces. Around these buildings we will build whatever will be needed to support them. We will construct a circle of beautiful villages around the city . . . connected with the best roads. Beyond that will be the other world in which we will permit the Russians to live as they may wish. So long as we dominate them. In case of a revolution we will merely drop a few bombs on the city concerned and then the affair will be over. Once a year a troop of Kirgiz will be led through the capital in order to impress them with the power and size of our granite memorials. The eastern space will be for us what India was to Britain.

[30] Neumann, *op. cit.,* pp. 152–171.
[31] Picker, *op. cit.,* pp. 44–45, 110–111.

Rigid segregation was to keep the inferior Russian blood from mixing with the Teuton. Rosenberg's government was a colonial regime in the full sense of the word, except that the Russian and Polish population was given none of the social services which characterize imperial rule in Africa today. Russians and Poles were to serve as expendable labor for Germany and no more. A peaceful *modus vivendi* with the conquered population was hardly conceivable on the basis of such a policy.

The notions of "colonial administration," however, were by no means confined to Eastern Europe. Throughout conquered Europe the Nazis constructed their administrations on the basis of racial doctrines and the hierarchy of racial virtues, to the further detriment of stability, with "Nordic" Danes and Norwegians enjoying the most local autonomy and all others considerably less.

Race, as the determinant of Nazi administration, moreover, was supplemented by the rationale of geopolitics. Geopolitical notions of the special status of the people which ruled the "central space" and the industrial organs which controlled the "central economy" imposed further features which made peace in occupied Europe a chimera. Thus, the conquered people were constrained to serve as slave labor in German factories and on German farms, regardless of whether they were equal or inferior racially. Further, the studied policy of industrial spoliation, expropriation, and forced sales tended to concentrate all economic power in the hands of German business firms. Such steps, however, were not designed to make German rule palatable to the French and Belgians, even if they were "equal" racially. These features, therefore, contributed further to make impossible any lasting acceptance of Nazi rule and condemned Nazi administration to indefinite repression, sabotage fighting, and insecurity.

The Inability to Work with Allies. The final characteristic of the foreign policy of multigroup authoritarianism is its inability to make use of allies on a dependable basis. The temptation is always to "go it alone," to keep secret one's plans, and to present the ally with a *fait accompli.* Diplomatic negotiation with an ally is no more possible under such conditions than negotiation with the potential adversary. Even the ally may well become the adversary when the temporary convergence of interests ceases. This, in fact, is precisely what happened to German-Italian relations in 1943 when Mussolini fell from power and Germany proceeded to occupy northern Italy as enemy territory. Hitler initiated his campaigns without warning Rome or Tokyo, the Duce attacked Greece without notifying Berlin, and the Japanese military struck against Pearl Harbor when they were expected by their Axis partners to neutralize Singapore first of all. The Tripartite Axis Pact is a symbol of the inability of authoritarian regimes to conduct alliance diplomacy. Rigid ideological preconceptions preclude the policy maker from sharing his long-range interests with others. Authoritarian rule implies autarky and exclusion; it cannot rest on consultation and cooperation, since these imply the compromising of positions which are not fully acceptable to the ally.[32]

Unilateralism is implicit in all these principles of Nazi foreign policy. Discussion, compromise, and acceptance of a minimum of common symbols and aims with other nations are all excluded by definition. Violence is the only logical conclusion which can follow from such a view of the world, and violence has usually accompanied authoritarianisms of this kind when they considered themselves sufficiently strong militarily to challenge other systems. Italy and Japan prove the point. Spain and Argentina, each representing a coalition of authoritarian elites—though they differ markedly from those of Germany—are inclined toward policies of self-extension. Only their military weakness keeps these desires latent rather than overt. Ideologically and institutionally, both are disposed toward unilateralism and the violent primacy of their values. The delicate balance of elite interests internally and the exclusive definition of aims externally may make any other policy extremely hazardous for the domestic stability of the ruling group. If peace prevails under such conditions, much has been achieved; the international sharing of values, however, remains an impossibility.

Additional Case-study Material

Abel, T.: *Why Hitler Came into Power,* Prentice-Hall, New York, 1938.

Blanksten, G.: *Peron's Argentina,* Chicago University Press, Chicago, 1953.

Causton, E. E. N.: *Militarism and Foreign Policy in Japan,* Allen & Unwin, London, 1936.

Chakotin, S.: *The Rape of the Masses,* Alliance Book Co., New York, 1940.

Ciano, Count Galleazzo: *The Ciano Diaries, 1939–1943,* Doubleday, New York, 1945.

Cortesao, A.: "Democracy and Fascism in Portugal," *Political Quarterly,* vol. 16, October–December, 1945.

Ebenstein, W.: *Fascist Italy,* American Book, New York, 1939.

Elsbree, W. H.: *Japan's Role in Southeast Asian National Movements, 1940 to 1945,* Harvard University Press, Cambridge, Mass., 1953.

Feis, H.: *The Spanish Story,* Knopf, New York, 1948.

François-Poncet, A. (ed.): *Les Lettres secrètes échangées par Hitler et Mussolini,* Editions du Pavois, Paris, 1946.

Gerth, H.: "The Nazi Party: Its Leadership and Composition," *American Journal of Sociology,* vol. 45, 1940.

Gilbert, G. M.: *The Psychology of Leadership: Based on an Examination of the Leaders of Nazi Germany,* Ronald, New York, 1950.

Grew, J. C.: *Ten Years in Japan,* Simon and Schuster, New York, 1944.

Hinsley, F. H.: *Hitler's Strategy,* Cambridge University Press, New York, 1951.

Hitler, A.: *Mein Kampf,* Reynal & Hitchcock, New York, 1941.

Kelley, D. M.: *Twenty Two Cells in Nurnberg,* Greenberg, New York, 1947.

Kleist, P.: *Zwischen Hitler und Stalin,* Athenäum Verlag, Bonn, 1950.

Kordt, E.: *Wahn und Wirklichkeit,* Union Deutsche Verlagsgesellschaft, Stuttgart, 1947.

Lerner, D.: *The Nazi Elite,* Stanford University Press, Stanford, Calif., 1952.

---

[32] For detailed examples of this authoritarian characteristic, see Chap. 8.

Neumann, F.: *Behemoth, The Structure and Practice of National Socialism*, Oxford, New York, 1944.

Oliveira, A. R.: *Politics, Economics and Men of Modern Spain*, Gollancz, London, 1946.

Peers, E. A.: *Spain in Eclipse*, Methuen, London, 1943.

Picker, H. (ed.): *Hitler's Tischgespräche*, Athenäum Verlag, Bonn, 1949.

Rich, S. G., Jr.: "Franco Spain: A Reappraisal," *Political Science Quarterly*, September, 1952.

Rossi, A.: *The Russo-German Alliance*, Duell, Sloan & Pearce, New York, 1951.

Salvemini, G.: *Mussolini Diplomatico*, Editions Contemporaines, Paris, 1932.

————: *Under the Axe of Fascism*, Viking, New York, 1936.

Scalapino, R.: *Democracy and the Party Movement in Prewar Japan*, University of California Press, Berkeley, Calif., 1953.

Schmidt, P.: *Statist auf diplomatischer Bühne*, Athenäum Verlag, Bonn, 1949.

Schneider, H.: *The Fascist Government of Italy*, Van Nostrand, New York, 1939.

Schuman, F.: *The Commonwealth of Man*, Knopf, New York, 1952.

Seabury, P.: *The Wilhelmstrasse*, University of California Press, Berkeley, Calif., 1954.

Trials of War Criminals before the Nurnberg Military Tribunals, Washington, 1951.

U.S. Department of State: *Nazi-Soviet Relations, 1939–1941*, 1948.

Ware, E. E.: *Business and Politics in the Far East*, Yale University Press, New Haven, Conn., 1933.

Weizsäcker, Baron E. von: *Erinnerungen*, List, Munich, 1950.

Wheeler-Bennett, J. W.: *Munich: Prologue to Tragedy*, Duell, Sloan & Pearce, New York, 1948.

————: *The Nemesis of Power: the German Army in Politics, 1918–1945*, St. Martin's, New York, 1954.

PART FIVE

INTERNATIONAL LAW

Chapter 17

INTERNATIONAL LAW AND INTERNATIONAL POLITICS

Shortly after President Franklin D. Roosevelt's 1937 speech calling for a more forceful American attitude in opposing international aggression, his Undersecretary of State, Sumner Welles, was constrained to write that "no one can today affirm that such a thing as international law exists or that there is any common agreement on the part of the so-called civilized nations of the world upon the fundamental standards which should and must govern the relations between nations if world order is to be restored." [1] Thus, in one sentence, the existence of a law binding states is denied while the need for it is asserted equally strongly. Is there an international law? Or is there only the demand for one? In some fields of interdependence there undoubtedly is a law acknowledged by nations as binding them. But in other areas it is equally true that what passes as "law" is really no more than national political demands couched in the rhetorical language of "rights" and "obligations." These peculiarities of international legal bonds now remain to be examined in detail.

1. The Nature of International Law. Any organized community, united by emotional and physical bonds of all kinds, recognizes a multitude of rules which fashion the conduct of its members. These vary from the vague injunction that cheating at cards is immoral and that courtesy demands that ladies enter first to the firm rule that murder is a crime to be punished by the courts. Courtesy and game rules, however, are not law. They are not defined in the statutes, and their infraction is not punishable by the organs of the state. Such sanctions as are attached to their violation are informal and non-

[1] Welles to Roosevelt, Oct. 6, 1937, quoted in W. L. Langer and S. E. Gleason, *The Challenge to Isolation,* Harper, New York, 1952, p. 20.

compulsory. Law in a community, however, is characterized by coercive sanctions: compensation, preventive relief, fines, imprisonment, or death. Individuals or groups accused of violating the rules are hailed before the courts whether they consent or not. The rules, finally, are formally defined and applied by the organs of the state acting on behalf of the groups and individuals making up the community.

How do these coercive rules gain acceptance within the community? Whenever any set of injunctions governing conduct, no matter how trivial or how important, is considered by elites as crucial to the peace, order, and stability of the social grouping, the principle of law through coercive force has been accepted. It is vital to note that it is the *principle* of coercive law which gains acceptance, not necessarily the precise rules laid down. While fairly universal consensus among key elites must be considered essential in making for the acceptance of the principle of law, no such consensus is necessary on specific injunctions in fields which are marked by divergent group values and aims. It follows that universal consensus on details is not necessary and that sanctions are imposed even against the will of the violator.

But international relations are not marked by the symptoms of community development. International law, therefore, cannot be expected to possess the firmness of national law. There is in the relations between nations no consciousness of order and stability, no overwhelming recognition of "belonging" to a common entity, no consistent demand for firm and unambiguously binding rules equipped with coercive sanctions. Certainly, if such a social consciousness did exist, uniting groups across national frontiers in common interests and aspirations toward economic and moral order, international law would develop into the same kind of system which now prevails within national communities. The dynamics of legal development are the same for national and international law; they both serve a common function of stability and order. But while national law has achieved this objective, by and large, international law has not so long as it serves merely an association of states and not a community. The characteristic features of international legal rules, therefore, are those of a voluntary association of entities, and not those of a compulsory community.

This distinction becomes evident when the process of legal development is scrutinized. Most legal systems seem to grow through a combination of three processes: (1) the "habitual adherence of the members of the community to certain" traditional and customary rules; (2) the specific creation of new rules of conduct through legislation, regardless of custom and perhaps in the face of dissent; (3) repetition, generalization, interpretation, and compulsory application of customs and legislation through the executive and judicial organs of the state, giving us precedent or case law.[2] All three of these

[2] O. J. Lissitzyn, *The International Court of Justice*, United Nations Studies, no. 6, Carnegie Endowment, New York, 1951, pp. 4–5, 8.

processes are observable in national communities. However, while there is a customary international law, there are no powerful international authorities repeating, interpreting, and enforcing it. Hence the customary rules are not always buttressed through precedent and cases. More important is the absence of an international legislative process, however. New national law can be made by a majority or even a minority. New international law can only come about through nearly universal consent, and even then it cannot be enforced in the usual sense. While some of the functions of international law are the same as those of national law, the fundamental differences in development account for the difference in power and scope.

Thus international law continues to differ from national legal systems in at least four important respects:

1. It requires the consent of the entities subject to it in order to be applicable to them, which raises the question of how the law is to be determined in any one instance. The *sources* of the law are not free from ambiguity and must be defined clearly.

2. While individuals, groups, and governments are the *subjects* of national legal systems, it is by no means clear whether entities other than states and international organizations are subjects of international law. The subjects of the law must be defined, raising the problems of sovereignty, personality, and recognition.

3. If the subjects of the law are in doubt, so are many of its *objects,* i.e., the areas of interdependence governed by international rules. Statutes, court decisions, and custom define these in national law, but such processes are not always available in determining the rules and scope of international legal norms.

4. The problem of how, if at all, violations of international law can be punished or eliminated against the wishes of the violator remains with us, and the *sanctions* of international law must be examined.

Sources. The sources of the law constitute the "evidence" that an alleged norm in relations among nations is really recognized as such by the members of the international society. Thus over sixty states, by adhering to the Statute of the International Court of Justice (ICJ), have agreed that the sources shall consist of (1) treaties, (2) international custom, (3) "the general principles of law recognized by civilized nations," and (4) previous judicial decisions and the teachings of publicists as "subsidiary means" for determining the law.[3] The use of these subsidiary means is not free from doubt, since it is subject to the further recognized rule that "the decision of the Court has no binding force except between the parties and in respect of that particular case."[4]

Treaties and custom will be analyzed in detail below, as they constitute

[3] ICJ Statute, Art. 38.
[4] *Ibid.,* Art. 59.

the major source of the law despite the recognition of additional possible evidence. "General principles of law," whether overtly recognized in international relations or not, can be used to determine the law. Practice, however, indicates that this has rarely been done, since there is little agreement on what these "principles" are. Nor have the writings of publicists been an important source in recent decades. But while judicial decisions are listed merely as a "subsidiary source" of the law, they have in fact been used extensively in fashioning international jurisprudence, thus building up the core of an international case law. By and large, however, the sources are limited to treaties entered into by states and such custom as appears to enjoy universal acceptance.

Subjects. Historically, it has been states and states alone which were considered to possess rights and obligations under the law, or enjoyed legal personality. This meant that only states could bring suits against each other, prefer claims, or receive reparations for wrongs committed by other states. Persons, firms, or other collective entities could not acquire personality in international legal dealings, since they were not sovereign.

Recent practice indicates, however, that the sovereignty concept has undergone a distinct modification to the extent that international organizations are now recognized as possessing legal personality, but only in so far as is necessary to enable them to carry out their functions, as defined by treaty. Their personality is more restricted than that of states. Furthermore, some commentators maintain that in recent years individuals have become subjects of the law in certain fields, while others argue that the trials of pirates, blockade runners, and saboteurs under a military-occupation regime prove that such individuals have always been subjects of the law. Since they were usually tried under some kind of national rules, however, it is doubtful whether the argument stands up.[5] Certain it is that universal consensus exists only on the proposition that the sole definite subjects of the law are states and international organizations.

But how do states acquire the legal personality which makes them subjects? They are said to become members of the international society as a result of *recognition* by already established states. When a colony revolts successfully or when a nation splits into several new states, other governments may recognize it or they may refuse to do so. Similarly, when a revolution results in the displacement of the old government and the advent to power of a new ruling group, other nations have the option of recognizing the successor regime even though no new state has been created. While definite legal consequences are attached to the granting or withholding of recognition, the act itself is not subject to any rule of law. Latin-American elites have long argued that foreign states have a *duty* to grant recognition to a new govern-

---

[5] P. E. Corbett, *Law and Society in the Relations of States,* Harcourt, Brace, New York, 1951, pp. 56–57.

ment, and in recent years others, including Britain, have expressed concurrence with this position. Yet there is no universal practice in support of the assertion, and the United States denies its validity. Political considerations continue to determine whether a new entity will be recognized as such, and it is far from clear at what point the new group acquires the legal personality necessary to give it rights and obligations. So far the United Nations has not been permitted to act as the body to determine whether a new state or government is to be recognized or not, despite numerous suggestions to that effect. In the absence of such a practice, courts are bound by what the foreign ministries of their states determine.[6]

Objects. International law has as its primary objects such fields as the delimitation of the land, water, and air jurisdiction of states; the determination of title to territory; the protection of aliens, their rights and obligations; the immunities of states, diplomats, and consuls; the interpretation and conclusion of treaties; the rules of war; and the rights and obligations of neutrals. Yet this tells very little, since almost all national systems of law also purport to deal with all or some of these fields. Hence the question arises of how and where the realm of international law can be marked off from that of national rules. Some international lawyers have urged that since all rights and duties of states are determined by international law alone, no conflict can ever arise. The international rule will automatically take precedence. While most modern constitutions do, in fact, verbally recognize the superiority of international law and accept it as binding, national ministries and courts will recognize such superiority in practice only when they have no choice in terms of an unambiguous treaty commitment.[7]

The problem of double nationality is a cogent example of the conflict between national and international law. Under the laws of many states emigrants and their children continue to be citizens of the state of origin even if they are naturalized elsewhere. Frequently they are compelled to render military service if they return to the state of origin. General international law is unclear as to whether such practices are legal, and the effort to clarify the situation through the conclusion of multipartite treaties has failed since only ten states consented to these arrangements. Thus there is an international law of nationality for the parties to these treaties but not for the rest of the world.[8]

Sanctions. The key question concerning the nature of international law, however, is: "How can the law be enforced? Assuming that the subjects, objects, and sources of the law are clear and universally accepted—which they are not—how can the norms be made effective?" Obviously, there is no

---

[6] *Ibid.,* pp. 61–67. P. C. Jessup, *A Modern Law of Nations,* Macmillan, New York, 1948, chap. 3. J. L. Brierly, *The Law of Nations,* 4th ed., Oxford, New York, 1948, chap. 4.

[7] Corbett, *op. cit.,* pp. 42–43.

[8] Corbett, *op. cit.,* pp. 167 ff., on the 1930 attempt to codify nationality law.

international police force analogous to the national law-enforcement officers. Some writers maintain, however, that war may be a legal sanction for enforcing a right. Assuming further that this assertion was correct before the United Nations Charter made war inadmissible, it nevertheless raises the question: "How can the law-enforcing state be checked and supervised?" In short, the practice of war as a sanction merely emphasizes that the law tends to be what national elites make of it; when the plaintiff makes himself policeman, prosecutor, judge, jury, and executioner, the peculiar nature of international law becomes evident.

Under the UN Charter, however, collective enforcement measures taken by the organization have been recognized as sanctions for breaches of the peace and acts of aggression. These extreme measures imply the use of violence identical with old-fashioned war in physical effect, despite the different legal phraseology. Partly because of this they have never been used in the manner prescribed in the Charter, and in any event they are applicable only to the most far-reaching violations of law.

Many international treaties, by contrast, permit sanctions of an economic and technical nature. Violations of international narcotics laws are punishable by depriving the violator of its quota of drugs. Infringements of sugar-marketing agreements may call for concerted policies of price discrimination on sugar against the culprit state. Many such sanctions spelled out in specific —and usually limited—treaties are recognized. Execution, however, depends on the willingness of the subject states to carry out the sanctions and on the degree to which the violator will really be hurt by such measures. Experience indicates that neither prerequisite has been met and such sanctions are very rarely taken. As a result, international law has no effective sanctions. Adherence to it depends almost exclusively on good faith and the aims of the subject nations, as defined and recognized by themselves rather than by an outside authority.

It should come as no surprise that an eminent international jurist, the late Judge Anzilotti of the ICJ, has admitted that [9]

The interests protected by international law are not those which are of major weight in the life of states. It is sufficient to think of the great political and economic rivalries to which no juridical formula applies, in order to realize the truth of this statement. International law develops its true function in a sphere considerably circumscribed and modest, not in that in which there move the great conflicts of interests which induce states to stake their very existence in order to make them prevail.

Basic political conflicts, to be sure, may be explained and justified in legal terms, on the basis of fundamental "rights" and "duties" of states. But when

---

[9] *Corso di Diritto Internazionale,* p. 311, as cited in H. Lauterpacht, *The Function of Law in the International Community,* Oxford, New York, 1933, p. 169.

this occurs legal phraseology is being appealed to for reasons of propaganda or with a preference for unilateral solutions based on some show of force. To this extent, it is also in the nature of international law to serve as a façade for such aims of elites as are not intended to be impartially settled.

2. Acceptance of the Law: Custom, Treaties, and International Legislation. If custom and treaties provide the major evidence of what is law at any one time, they fulfill the equally important role of furnishing the means whereby states assume obligations and acquire rights. The aims and desires of elites are expressed by specific interpretations of customary law as well as by the specific treaties entered into or rejected. International legislation, finally, represents an approximation to the domestic legislative process and provides the means for binding the largest possible number of states to the voluminous new rules imposed by technological, social, and economic interdependence, in so far as this is recognized. Each means must now be analyzed in terms of the ideologies of elites accepting it.

Customary International Law and National Aims. The great bulk of rules governing such fields as territorial jurisdiction, the rights of aliens, the freedom of the seas, and the immunities of diplomats and states are not written down in codes or treaties. They are considered law merely because they have been observed, more or less consistently, for centuries. But how many states must observe them, and in what circumstances, before they will be accepted as law? "The elements necessary" to establish custom as law, notes Judge M. O. Hudson, "are the concordant and recurring action of numerous States in the domain of international relations, the conception in each case that such action was enjoined by law, and the failure of other States to challenge that conception at the time." [10] As if to subject the patent ambiguities of international custom to the relative firmness of written treaty law, writers and courts have held that custom must give way to treaties as a primary source of law.[11] Yet why should states be obligated by treaties, however firm, if they are not bound by a prior customary rule that treaties are binding? In short, the binding nature of treaties assumes first a habit of accepting and obeying them. Hence the customary rule *pacta sunt servanda* ("treaties are binding") is held by many to be the basic rule of all international law, because subsequent commitments of national elites depend on its being accepted first. Granting the existence of such a rule, it becomes essential to analyze how and why it could gain acceptance, thereby demonstrating the nature of custom as binding states.

[1] THE WESTERN HERITAGE OF CUSTOMARY LAW. International law, customary as well as treaty rules, grew in the fairly homogeneous conditions of Western Europe and Western civilization. It was based on the notion that

---

[10] As cited in Herbert W. Briggs, *The Law of Nations,* 2d ed., Appleton-Century-Crofts, New York, 1952, p. 47.

[11] G. Schwarzenberger, *International Law,* Stevens, London, 1945, vol. I, p. 12.

the state was a territorially defined unit with a monopoly of internal power. It assumed a legal equality of all states, however small and weak or large and strong. More important, it presupposed the universal acceptance of a common outlook, a uniformity of ideology among its state-subjects, as derived from Christianity and the traditions of Roman and Anglo-Saxon law. Hence the rights and duties of the law meant approximately the same to all states acknowledging it.[12] Customary law thus could be universal ideologically and morally as well as legally. During the nineteenth century a further universal aspect—from the Western vantage point—was introduced by the incorporation of capitalist business conceptions into the law. The sanctity of contracts, the rights of aliens to do business, the application of Western conceptions of justice and judicial procedures fall under this heading. When the power of the West expanded, either through the creation of new states with a Western outlook or through imperialist expansion, these Western notions of the law were imposed upon such communities as Turkey, Japan, China, and Thailand. They were imposed also on Latin America, though its interests were not always reconciled easily with the Western nature of the law. Thus the law gained territorial universality while it lost its basis in a common economic and moral order.

[2] THE DECLINE OF CUSTOMARY LAW. While the rule that treaties are binding was and is meaningful in the homogeneous setting of Western civilization, its customarily binding nature could by no means be taken for granted when applied to communities which did not share the values underlying the doctrine. It is at the hands of Western lawyers, teachers, and statesmen today that customary international law receives its tribute. Hence it should come as no surprise that the vaunted universality of customary international law, as based on a common outlook, is increasingly being challenged by the countries of Asia, Latin America, and the Communist world.

Western lawyers, for instance, insist on the customary rule that a minimum universal standard of justice should apply to the activities of businessmen residing abroad.[13] Yet Latin-American lawyers adamantly refuse to accept this reasoning and argue instead that the equality of states demands merely that aliens enjoy the same rights and duties as the nationals of the state in which they reside, even though this may be under the unstable and revolutionary conditions prevalent in much of the world. Further, the new states of Asia make similar claims. They insist on the superiority of their own law, as opposed to that of the erstwhile colonial ruler, incidentally rejecting customary Western rules.[14]

---

[12] G. W. Keeton and G. Schwarzenberger, *Making International Law Work*, 2d ed., Stevens, London, 1946, pp. 11–12.

[13] F. S. Dunn, *The Protection of Nationals*, Johns Hopkins Press, Baltimore, 1932, pp. 62–64, 114–121.

[14] Ali Sastroamidjojo, "Some Aspects of International Law in Southeast Asia," *Proceedings of the American Society of International Law*, 1953, pp. 49–52.

[3] SOVIET INTERNATIONAL LAW. The major dissenters from the customary law of the West, however, are the authoritarian systems of our times. Nazi notions of international law made a mockery of the claim to universality, and much the same seems to be true of Soviet teachings on the subject. Doctrine is changed as the aims of Soviet policy undergo modification and law is far more a function of policy than is true in the West. Thus for almost twenty years, the Soviets argued that, since all law is merely a function of the class structure of given communities, "bourgeois" and "capitalist" international law could not apply to a socialist setting. As Korovin, a leading commentator, put it: "An intercourse on the basis of intellectual unity (ideological solidarity) between countries of bourgeois and socialist cultures, cannot exist as a rule, and hence the rules of international law covering this intercourse become pointless." [15] Only such rules of law as referred to the *common interests* of all cultures had continuing validity: postal and telegraphic rules, public health regulations, and the preservation of historical monuments. A limited body of law common to both major systems was still recognized. Since 1945, however, it appears that even this tenuous universality has been discarded. One body of law is applicable to the relations among "socialist" (i.e., Communist) states; another body of law applies to the relations between communism and the bourgeois world. Consent and sovereignty are the keystones of this second law, with the apparent presumption that the Soviet Union is by definition in the right on all issues. Thus a war is just, "non-annexationist," and "liberating" if it "has for its purpose either the defense of a nation against external aggression and the attempt at enslaving her, or the liberation of the people from capitalist slavery, or the emancipation of colonies and dependent territories from the imperialist yoke." [16] All other wars are unjust in the Soviet view.

The doctrine of sovereignty has been expanded to include Soviet protection of weak states and colonies against "exploiters" and "imperialists." Quite naturally, the political demand for national self-determination has now been raised to the status of a rule of law by the Soviet Union. Treaties, they admit, are binding, but "unequal" treaties are not, since they conflict with the doctrine of absolute consent and sovereignty. "Yet, at the same time [the Soviets] admit that there are interests of a humanitarian or of a practical economic and political character which may coincide under the policies of Communist and non-Communist states." [17] It may be that the area of

[15] Mintauts Chakste, "Soviet Concepts of the State, International Law and Sovereignty," *American Journal of International Law,* vol. 43, 1949, pp. 26–27.

[16] Korovin in the 1951 Soviet international law text, as cited by W. W. Kulski, "Present Trends in Soviet International Law," *Proceedings of the American Society of International Law,* 1953, pp. 61 ff. See also recent reemphasis in doctrine in Kulski, "Soviet Comments on International Law and Relations," *American Journal of International Law,* vol. 47, 1953, pp. 133–134.

[17] Kurt Wilk, "International Law and Global Ideological Conflict," *American Journal of International Law,* vol. 45, 1951, p. 665.

agreement can expand if the doctrine of the inevitability of conflict between the two systems is weakened or superseded by different international conditions, and that full reciprocity in rights and obligations will then be conceded by the Soviet lawyers. Pending this eventuality, however, only the call of convenience makes possible the present tenuous interideological agreement on some customary rules. There is no universal consensus on the nature of legal obligation or the content of the law based on the acceptance of common doctrines and values.

The retreat from universalism poses some serious problems for the future of the law. If there is no approved legal usage among the world's cultural systems, how can courts and lawyers be expected to settle legal issues? While there seems to be no abatement in fruitful litigation among Western states, the settlement of disputes on the basis of law between the Communist nations and the new Asian states on the one hand and the West on the other continues to be unimpressive. Determination as well as implementation of the law, on a global scale, thus becomes increasingly difficult.

Implementation depends ordinarily on the aims and attitudes of the elites concerned. But while the state which may have suffered a defeat in a suit before an international tribunal court cannot be compelled to mend its ways, voluntary compliance with decisions almost always takes place because "those whose views do not happen to prevail will nevertheless acquiesce as long as the need for an organized social order as such seems more important to them than its particular shape." [18] The only sanction, therefore, remains the desire of all elites for some order, stability, and predictability of conduct. This desire, however, is at present significant largely in the relations among Western states.

Treaties. A treaty is any formal communication through which a state acknowledges a commitment to another state; whether called convention, declaration, agreement, protocol, or exchange of notes, all such communications are "treaties" and subject to the law of treaties. Such instruments contain the huge bulk of the rights and obligations governing the relations of nations. By becoming a party to a treaty, a state formally binds itself to conduct those portions of its policy covered by the instrument within the limits defined in it. Such instruments, of course, bind only the states which consent to be bound. Yet a great deal of controversy exists as to what is a "valid" treaty. It is uncertain whether an agreement concluded by a branch of the government having no authority under national law is binding under international law. Nor is it certain whether treaties "consented to" under duress are valid. Finally, while some argue that to be valid a treaty must be in accord with customary rules of international law, others dispute that such a limitation on treaty making exists in practice.

[18] G. Niemeyer, *Law without Force,* Princeton University Press, Princeton, N.J., 1941, p. 122.

Treaties enter into force when certain conditions specified by the instrument itself have been met. They may enter into force on a certain date, or upon signature. Usually, however, treaties become operative formally only after an exchange of ratifications, i.e., after the organs of the state have approved the agreement. Generally, the legislature is the crucial organ in this process. A signed but unratified pact has no legal significance. The freedom of action of the state not to be bound is manifest further in the right to attach reservations to the instrument of ratification. Thus a ratifying state may indicate how it interprets certain key clauses of the agreement and thereby give notice that its consent is offered only if the national interpretation is accepted by the other parties. The extensive use of reservations, therefore, can easily weaken the original treaty text so as to make the pact worthless. Furthermore, it frequently happens that various parties to multipartite conventions attach varying reservations so that different rights and obligations, in effect, prevail among the parties to the same agreement. Under certain conditions, a reserving state may not be considered a party to a multipartite treaty if the reservation is incompatible with the purpose of the agreement.[19]

How are rights to be defined when the parties disagree over the interpretation of a treaty? While treaty interpretation is a fine art developed by international tribunals, very few "rules" can be considered as definitely established. Thus interpretations by the courts of one party to a convention are not binding on the others; only decisions of international tribunals are binding on all. While there is a general consensus that interpretation should be "logical" and not lead to "absurd" results or render the agreement void, divergence is equally manifest. Some hold that what alone matters in treaty interpretation is to ascertain the original intentions of the parties, while Judge Hudson maintains that "the process of interpreting the text . . . is not . . . a search for some preexisting meaning. . . . Interpretation involves *giving* meaning to the text." [20] New court-made law could come about as a result of interpretation, though international jurisprudence is rare in such instances.

Ordinarily treaties are concluded for a specified period and lapse when they expire, thus ending all obligations contained in them. In some cases renewal is simple; in others, it requires renegotiation. What is more important, states have the right to denounce treaties either because the instrument itself permits this or because the conditions which prevailed on entry into force are alleged to have changed. Denunciation is permitted also when the other party has been guilty of a prior breach of the agreement. While unilateral denunciation has often been considered illegal, it is practiced by almost all nations when the obligations of a major treaty become incompatible

[19] Advisory Opinion on the Genocide Convention, cited in Briggs, *op. cit.*, p. 857.
[20] *Ibid.*, p. 899.

with a new policy. Further, upon the outbreak of war such treaties with the enemy as conflict with the conduct of hostilities are certainly suspended, and some hold that they actually become void. Thus sufficient ambiguity in the rules remains to permit continued maneuverability to states even after they have formally accepted external obligations.

International Legislation. International legislation is the term bestowed on certain multipartite conventions which aim at the administrative regulation of questions of common concern to many states. Such instruments are subject to precisely the same rules as apply to treaties in general, except that the difficulties and clashing commitments introduced by unilateral reservations are of even greater destructive significance. Frequently, such agreements enter into force only after a specified minimum number of states have ratified. Sometimes the states with the greatest interest in the field to be regulated must accede before the agreement becomes operative. Even though these major conventions can be abrogated, denounced, and terminated, it remains true that they are the most significant vehicle for establishing common rules for large areas and numerous states, especially in such fields as labor standards, health, fisheries, and the control of dangerous drugs.

Thus the control of fisheries in the Bering Sea provides a contemporary example of the growth of international law through sweeping multipartite conventions. The United States has been following a policy of conservation among the salmon fisheries off Alaska, including areas on the high seas. Fearful that Canadian and especially Japanese fishermen would catch so much of the carefully protected fish as to undo the conservation effort, a convention was concluded in May of 1952 establishing common legal rules for the United States, Canada, and Japan. A commission has been created which determines whether specific fish stocks are being harvested in excess of conservation needs. If it finds that salmon, for example, is being overfished, the parties are advised to limit the quotas they allow to their fishermen. The parties are agreed further that special conservation efforts made by one of them will be rewarded by the others' refraining from harvesting the protected fish, until the danger point has been passed. Coast Guard vessels of all three nations are entitled to inspect fishing trawlers regardless of nationality to apprehend fishermen violating the conservation quotas.

Similar treaties for the North Atlantic fisheries, for whaling and halibut, attest to the importance of this legal and administrative technique. International legislation can also have indirect influence on national lawmaking. There are in force today seventy-odd treaties establishing uniform labor conditions for the parties. These treaties are written in the hope that they will "contribute toward shaping national social policy" and "leave their mark on the fabric of national legislation even in the absence of any binding international obligations for the States in question." [21] But the fact re-

[21] International Labor Organization, *Fifth Report to the United Nations.* 1951. p. 183.

mains that this is not legislation as that term is understood in a community. The consent of individual states persists in being required before binding law emerges.

3. Determination of the Law: International Codes and Tribunals.

Codes. Apart from the specific assumption of obligations through new rules worked out in treaties, it is possible to create and determine the law also through the operations of tribunals—judge-made law or case law. However, those who prefer the clarity of a specific code of rights and obligations to the initiative of judges have pinned their hopes to the systematic codification of international law. The attempt to persuade elites to agree formally on one common definition of the questionable rules of law has preoccupied lawyers since the days of the League of Nations. The first attempt ended with the acceptance of three codes dealing with conflict between nationality laws, each of which has been ratified by only ten states.[22] Nevertheless, another attempt at codifying the elusive rules of international law is being made by the International Law Commission of the UN.

From among the attempts of international lawyers, as distinguished from governments, to determine the rules applicable to given fields of international relations a Draft Declaration on Rights and Duties of States has emerged. This declaration affirms that each state has the right to independence, territorial jurisdiction, equality, and self-defense, while its duties call for nonintervention in the internal affairs of other states, respect for human rights and fundamental freedoms, peaceful settlement of disputes, and the faithful implementation of treaties even if they conflict with national law. Similarly, the Commission has prepared a Draft Code of Offences against the Peace and Security of Mankind. The code lists "offences which contain a political element and which endanger or disturb the maintenance of international peace and security" and attempts to make aggressive war and the enslavement of other nations a crime.[23]

Yet the retreat from universalism in international law makes itself felt in codification as well as in the customary rules. Hence most codes, and especially the ones dealing with fundamental matters, remain unratified. At the same time, however, it is also true that even unratified codes occasionally serve as supporting evidence in legal pleading and in the decisions of international tribunals. If there were a general desire to further the development of international law, the codes could undoubtedly play a larger role than they have heretofore.

Arbitration. More successful than codification in determining the law has been the procedure known as arbitration. One of the judicial means for peacefully settling international disputes, arbitration consists of submitting

---

[22] Corbett, *op. cit.*, p. 167.

[23] *Report of the International Law Commission, Covering Its Third Session, May 16-July 27, 1951*, UN Docs. A/1858, A/CN.4/48, 1951, par. 58.

a dispute to a body of individuals called upon to decide on the merits of the case. The parties, before entrusting their fate to the arbitrators, spell out in a special treaty what the issue is and on what alleged rules of law they base their respective cases. The arbitrators, in turn, are bound by this treaty and cannot go beyond its injunctions. Through this method such troublesome tensions as Anglo-American fisheries disputes on both coasts have been settled peacefully, though the same procedure failed to settle the Maine boundary question or the frontier in the Pacific Northwest. Through arbitration "thousands of claims were adjudicated during the interwar period by the mixed arbitral tribunals set up under the treaties of peace; other thousands were submitted to the mixed claims commissions set up under agreements between Mexico and six other states, and between Panama and the United States. . . ." [24]

Yet it has been doubted that arbitration contributes greatly to the development of international law into a true legal system. Arbitrators tend to settle disputes on the basis of political mediation and compromise rather than on the law. They tend to skirt the law rather than to state it. In any event, because they are bound by the special treaty creating their tribunal and its jurisdiction they resign to the contesting states the power to define the limits of the applicable law. The judicial procedures of the former Permanent Court of International Justice and its successor, the ICJ, however, are subject to none of these limitations.

The International Court of Justice. According to the UN Charter, the ICJ is "the principal judicial organ of the United Nations." Since its Statute and procedure are practically identical with those of its predecessor, the Court has in effect functioned continuously since 1920 as the only permanent and universal international tribunal. Yet its powers are so far different from those of a national Supreme Court that it has defined "the judicial settlement of disputes, with a view to which the Court has been established" as "simply an alternative to the direct and friendly settlement of such disputes between the parties." [25] The powers of the Court over the parties are defined in the Court's Statute. All member states of the UN are automatically bound by the Statute, but nonmembers may assume the same obligations and acquire the same rights with the approval of the UN, as Switzerland, for instance, has done. The Court consists of fifteen judges, nominated by national groups of eminent jurists and elected by the UN "regardless of their nationality." [26] Independence of the Court from world politics is assured further by specifying that no more than two judges may be of the same nationality at any one time. If a party to a suit happens not to have a judge of its nationality on the Court, it may appoint a special judge *ad hoc.*

[24] Lissitzyn, *op. cit.,* pp. 41–42.
[25] The PCIJ in the Free Zones Case, 1929; Schwarzenberger, *op. cit.,* p. 347.
[26] ICJ Statute, Art. 2.

It is an unwritten rule of the Court, however, that the major powers shall always have judges of their nationality on the bench.

Two types of decisions can be handed down by the ICJ. Judgments on specific suits are delivered, on the basis of judicial procedures not basically different from those of national legal systems, with oral and written pleadings by counsel, discussion by the Court, and decision by a majority vote, with the minority entitled to deliver dissenting opinions. Such judgments bind the parties to the dispute. In addition, the Court may give advisory opinions on legal issues submitted to it for elucidation by organs of the UN and its specialized agencies. Such opinions bind the organ requesting them, but not necessarily the states which may have made the Advisory Opinion desirable through their conduct. A careful analysis of this procedure disclosed that in the marginal issues usually referred to the Court the judges act and vote quite independently of the positions of their governments. In the one politically significant case which arose, however, the Austro-German *Anschluss* Advisory Opinion of 1931, the judges "voted on lines dangerously near to the alignments or to the detached position of their respective countries." [27]

[1] JURISDICTION OF THE COURT. The power of the ICJ to deliver binding decisions, however, is subject to serious limitations since member states are under no absolute obligation to submit to the Court's jurisdiction. In fact, the Court has no sweeping role; it possesses no "compulsory jurisdiction" in the sense that one state may unconditionally sue another. In descending order of legally binding significance, these are the categories of ICJ jurisdiction:

1. States may, by declaration, accept the unconditional jurisdiction of the Court and thereby consent in advance to be sued without special permission.

2. States frequently give the Court exclusive jurisdiction to interpret specific treaties they conclude with each other, thus waiving their right to refuse appearance in court in specified fields, such as labor, health, and trusteeship agreements.

3. States may, by declaration, accept the jurisdiction of the Court in specific fields and for specific periods, on condition of reciprocity and subject to reservations, under the "optional clause" of the Statute.

4. States may agree to give the Court jurisdiction in specific disputes by concluding a special agreement for the case, much as under arbitration proceedings.

It is now an established principle of law that the Court, in case of disagreement among the parties, possesses the power to determine its jurisdiction.

The "optional clause" is by far the most important of these procedures, since it is under this heading that the Court is actually given most of its

---

[27] Schwarzenberger, *op. cit.*, p. 349. Also see the survey in Lissitzyn, *op. cit.*

cases. Thirty-five states of the sixty-two which are parties to the Statute
have accepted the limited jurisdiction of the optional clause, while only five
cases have been handled on the basis of the specific treaties mentioned in
category 2 above.[28] It must be added immediately that many of these thirty-
five attached far-reaching reservations to their declarations, while only nine
Latin-American, three small European, and three Asian states gave the Court
anything like the full powers envisaged under this procedure.[29]

The optional clause provides that a state can sue another without its
special consent in any "legal" dispute concerning "(*a*) the interpretation of
a treaty; (*b*) any question of international law; (*c*) the existence of any
fact which, if established, would constitute a breach of an international
obligation; (*d*) the nature or extent of the reparation to be made for the
breach of an international obligation." [30] Yet such declarations, in addition
to crippling reservations, may be accompanied by stipulations that they will
apply only for certain periods and be subject to the other party's being
reciprocally obligated. Reservations, similarly, have a reciprocally limiting
effect on the Court's jurisdiction, since their invocation by one party re-
leases the other from perhaps more extensive obligations to submit.

It appears that the optional clause is not invariably relied upon in cases
which could be legally subject to it. Since 1920, only a half-dozen cases
were completed on the basis of unilateral proceedings of one state against
another (and only states can be parties in the Court in cases involving
judgments); most others received at least the informal or *ad hoc* consent
of the "defendant." However, in over two-thirds of the cases which arose
no special arbitral agreement had to be concluded first.[31]

[2] ICJ DECISIONS. Since 1920 the Court has delivered forty-five judgments
and thirty-three advisory opinions. Most of the cases involved nothing more
serious than the violation of alien rights, contract claims, nationality disputes, collisions of ships, or the interpretation of labor conventions and of
minorities treaties. Some, however, were of considerable importance to the
economic aims of governments, such as the Anglo-Norwegian fisheries decision which excluded British fishermen from Norwegian waters. Others bore
directly upon political aims, such as the decision of 1953 giving Britain title
to two tiny islands in the Channel over the claims of France, or the judgment ordering Israel to apologize and pay damages for the assassination of
the UN Mediator, Count Bernadotte. In all these decisions the defendants
complied with the judgments. Furthermore, the Court did not hesitate to
pronounce new and far-reaching legal principles in ruling that international

[28] Ruth Lawson, "Problems of the Compulsory Jurisdiction of the World Court,"
American Journal of International Law, vol. 46, 1952, p. 226.
[29] Lissitzyn, *op. cit.,* p. 66.
[30] ICJ Statute, Art. 36.
[31] Lawson, *op. cit.,* pp. 231–232; Lissitzyn, *op. cit.,* pp. 66–67.

civil servants are entitled to damages from states, in holding that Albania
had no right to mine her territorial waters, and in concluding that Britain
lacked the right to take the law into her own hands by unilaterally removing
the same mines.

Yet it remains true that "most of the disputes handled by the Court in
contentious cases were not such as to threaten the peace at the time they
arose" and that "it is not surprising, therefore, that the judgments of the
Court have been in principle obeyed in all these cases." [32] To complete the
picture, it must also be admitted that Iran refused to comply with the
Court's order to abstain temporarily from nationalizing British oil properties; that Bulgaria, Hungary, and Romania failed to observe their duty
with respect to human rights, despite admonitions by the Court; and that
South Africa chose to ignore the ICJ's ruling that South-West Africa should
be subject to United Nations trusteeship. True, Albania consented to be
sued by Britain when the former's mines damaged some British warships
in the Corfu Channel. The Court furthermore ordered Albania to pay over
£800,000 in reparations, but the defendant has failed to do so. Enforcement
of unacceptable decisions, therefore, is impossible short of war. Theoretically,
the Court can call on the Security Council to compel compliance, but it is
unlikely that "enforcement actions" will be risked over human rights, fisheries, or denials of justice.

Other International Tribunals. The feeble nature of international tribunals
is made evident by current suggestions for the creation of an international
criminal court. As early as 1907 plans had been made to establish an international prize court to try and punish carriers of contraband and blockade
runners. Such offenses were and are still punished by national courts, ostensibly administering international law but really enforcing merely the law
of their governments. Since the establishment of the court would have limited
the freedom of states to conduct hostilities, however indirectly, the plan remains a plan to this day. The draft of a statute establishing an international
criminal court has recently been completed. The court's task will be the
trying of *individuals* accused of having violated the code of offenses against
the peace. Its jurisdiction, however, would be even more circumscribed than
that of the ICJ since "no person shall be tried before the Court unless
jurisdiction has been conferred upon the Court by the state or states of
which he is a national and by the state or states in which the crime is
alleged to have been committed." [33] The doctrine of absolute consent is here
restated without reservation. At any rate, since the crimes over which the
court is to judge have not yet been defined and since no major power seems

---

[32] Lissitzyn, *op. cit.*, p. 76, 77–78.
[33] Draft Statute of an International Criminal Court, Arts. 26, 27. C. A. Pompe,
Aggressive War, An International Crime, Nijhoff, The Hague, 1953, pp. 360–361.

particularly anxious to ratify the statute, the court is not likely to begin functioning soon. In fact, the suggestion for its creation is probably rooted in the political and ideological conflict of nations to a greater degree than in their desire for stability and order.

Thus it appears that treaties, custom, and judicial institutions by themselves are an inadequate index of the actual acceptance of legal rules in shaping conduct. Elites do want order and stability in certain fields; but they want freedom of action in others, and frequently the line between these two areas weaves back and forth. The exigencies of given situations rather than basic principles shape international legal relations. Hence the practice of states, the arguments they use to justify their positions, the rules they accept, and the notions they seem to reject in their diplomatic notes and declarations emerge as being of greater importance than tribunals in assessing the degree of acceptance of law as a restraint on power. Hence it becomes of the utmost importance to analyze the still prevalent formulas used to weaken such international law as seems to survive the ideological cleavages of nations.

4. Political Limitations on International Law. The tendency of nations to strive for a measure of stability and order, while wishing to retain freedom of action at the same time, results in the continued presence of some basic ambiguities in international law. These difficulties go far toward depriving much of the law of normative significance. They are represented by the prevalence of the concepts of domestic jurisdiction, nonjusticiable disputes, the doctrine of *rebus sic stantibus,* and the permissibility of self-defense.

Domestic Jurisdiction. "Domestic jurisdiction" is the cry raised by a state whenever it wishes to exclude a dispute or an issue from the purview of international law. The UN Charter recognizes that matters "essentially within the domestic jurisdiction" of a state shall not be discussed by the organization. What is a matter "essentially" within domestic jurisdiction? International law is silent on the subject, as indicated by the difficulty of distinguishing between international and national law. France claims her colonial tensions are domestic, and Egypt maintains that control over the Suez Canal is a domestic concern only, while for the U.S.S.R. almost every piece of Soviet legislation is domestic.

These difficulties are demonstrated plainly by the severe reserve of both the United States and the Soviet Union toward the ICJ's optional clause. Said Soviet jurist S. B. Krylov: "The U.S.S.R. was guided by the necessity of defending the interests of the socialist state, the United States was apprehensive of opposition in the Senate to the ratification of the Charter and the Statute." [34] "Only an angel could be unbiased in judging Russian affairs,"

---

[34] Lissitzyn, *op. cit.,* p. 63.

Maxim Litvinov had remarked in 1922 in opposing Soviet submission to international judicial jurisdiction. Consequently, the Soviets never complied with the famous Article 36 of the Statute. The United States, however, made the necessary declaration but with the following reservation: "Disputes with regard to matters which are essentially within the domestic jurisdiction of the U.S. of America, as determined by the U.S.," are excluded, as are "disputes arising under a multilateral treaty, unless (1) all parties to the treaty affected by the decision are also parties to the case before the Court, or (2) the United States of America specifically agrees to jurisdiction." [35]

Identical reservations have since been submitted with the acceptance of the optional clause by France, Pakistan, and Mexico. While the Dutch claim of domestic jurisdiction has not prevented the Security Council from aiding Indonesia against Holland, the doctrine has operated to keep disputes affecting the major powers from being dealt with decisively, and it certainly has limited the power of the ICJ. International legal predominance is incompatible with national claims of domestic jurisdiction, unreviewable by the Court. Still domestic jurisdiction carries the day in disputes deeply affecting the aims of national groups and their governments.

Nonjusticiable Disputes. Much the same situation prevails in the field of nonjusticiable disputes. How can specific disputes be settled if there are no rules of law applicable to them? Can the Court create law in such cases? Or can it interpret analogous norms to suit them to the case? If it does it runs the risk of being ignored. Hence international tribunals tend to shy away from creating law or reinterpreting very controversial rules and prefer to hold that they lack jurisdiction over the case, as the ICJ did in the Iranian oil controversy. Yet in the issues peripheral to major tensions in which the Court is active it has on occasion created new rules of law. States for decades, however, specifically excluded "political" disputes from arbitration conventions and restricted them to "legal" disputes, not involving the "honor," "independence," or "vital interests" of the parties. Such limitations no longer occur but the enumeration of "legal" disputes in Article 36 of the ICJ's Statute assumes that there are nonlegal and therefore nonjusticiable disputes as well. In some conventions it has been held that disputes over "rights" are legal and justiciable; but does not every international tension involve the "rights" of some state, according to its own claims? [36] If the insistence on nonjusticiability is read together with the domestic-jurisdiction claim, all matters which elites prefer to settle by a show of force instead of judicial procedures are effectively excluded from the realm of law. No government has seriously suggested that the cold war, the Kashmir or Palestine questions, or the use of slave-labor camps in the Soviet Union are

---

[35] *Department of State Bulletin,* vol. 15, 1946, p. 452.
[36] See the brilliant analysis of Lauterpacht, *op. cit.,* chaps. 2, 3, and 4.

justiciable disputes which can be settled by the majority vote of fifteen judges.

Rebus Sic Stantibus. The doctrine of *rebus sic stantibus* is the counterpart to the rule that treaties are binding, since it maintains that treaties no longer impose duties if the conditions which prevailed at the time of entry into force no longer exist. States make use of this formula when they wish to denounce a treaty which has become bothersome in the attempt to realize a new foreign policy. It may be a relatively minor matter, as the invocation of the doctrine by the United States in denouncing the International Load-line Convention, when this limit on loading ships became bothersome in the prosecution of World War II. But it may involve basic ideological aspirations as well, as in Egypt's denunciation in 1948 of the treaty of 1936 with Britain, by virtue of which Britain controlled the Suez Canal. On that occasion, Nokrashy Pasha branded the agreement as "obsolete," "useless," and no longer binding before the Security Council, while Britain's Sir Alexander Cadogan, appropriately, answered that as a general rule of international law, all treaties are binding.[37] Courts are not asked whether the claim is legal or not; states refuse to honor the agreement despite the condemnations of other states. Hence political aims continue to shape legal patterns so long as states in effect are judges in their own cause.

Self-defense. Finally, the permissibility of self-defense is another area in which prohibition and escape from prohibition create a major ambiguity in legal relations. Under the UN Charter, "All members shall refrain in their international relations from the threat or use of force against the territorial integrity or political independence of any state, or in any other manner inconsistent with the Purposes of the United Nations." [38] Not only is war outlawed but even the threat to use force is no longer permitted. Yet elsewhere in the same Charter we read that "nothing . . . shall impair the inherent right of individual or collective self-defense if an armed attack occurs against a Member of the United Nations, until the Security Council has taken the measures necessary to maintain international peace and security." [39] If the Security Council is prevented by the veto from taking action, of course, self-defense measures cannot be subjected to its scrutiny and national freedom of action is maintained. When is an armed attack "aggression," and when is it "self-defense"? No precise definition has ever received universal agreement, despite the fact that, apparently, the first is illegal whereas the second is permitted. Attacks, after all, may be defensive in nature if, for example, they are designed to forestall an intended attack of the enemy. International law posits the right of existence to each state;

---

[37] H. W. Briggs, "Rebus Sic Stantibus before the Security Council: The Anglo-Egyptian Question," *American Journal of International Law,* vol. 43, 1949, pp. 762 ff.

[38] United Nations Charter, Art. 2, par. 4.

[39] *Ibid.,* Art. 51.

but it also recognizes a right of self-defense so ambiguous as to make possible one state's existence at the expense of another's demise, though the second had the same rights under the law. "It amounts to a negation of society," comments Professor Corbett, "when the entity claiming the right [to existence] also claims the exclusive power to determine when it comes into play." [40] Yet this is the situation in contemporary international law. Elites manage to create rules and maintain the escape formulas from the same norms at the same time.

Thus the desire for stability and order has brought about the development of a set of legal principles and the establishment of some judicial institutions. But the parallel desire to maintain freedom of action in the conflicts of our era has made possible the use of these doctrines and institutions for purposes other than stability and order—indeed, for propaganda and political advantage. The rules of law which have grown within this paradoxical framework now remain to be examined.

ADDITIONAL CASE-STUDY MATERIAL

Brierly, J. L.: *The Law of Nations,* 4th ed., Oxford, New York, 1948.
Briggs, H. W.: *The Law of Nations,* 2d ed., Appleton-Century-Crofts, New York, 1952.
———: "Rebus Sic Stantibus before the Security Council: The Anglo-Egyptian Question," *American Journal of International Law,* vol. 43, 1949.
Chakste, M.: "Soviet Concepts of the State, International Law and Sovereignty," *American Journal of International Law,* vol. 43, 1949.
Corbett, P. E.: *Law and Society in the Relations of States,* Harcourt, Brace, New York, 1951.
Cory, H. M.: *Compulsory Arbitration of International Disputes,* Columbia University Press, New York, 1932.
Duguit, L.: *Traité de droit constitutionnel,* de Boccard, Paris, 1921.
Dunn, F. S.: *Peaceful Change,* Council on Foreign Relations, New York, 1937.
———: *The Protection of Nationals,* Johns Hopkins Press, Baltimore, 1932.
Goodrich, L. M.: "The UN and Domestic Jurisdiction," *International Organization,* vol. 4, February, 1949.
Jessup, P. C.: *A Modern Law of Nations,* Macmillan, New York, 1948.
Keeton, G. W., and G. Schwarzenberger: *Making International Law Work,* Stevens, London, 1946.
Kelsen, H.: *The Law of the United Nations,* Stevens, London, 1950; supplement, 1951.
Kulski, W. W.: "Present Trends in Soviet International Law," *Proceedings of the American Society of International Law,* Washington, 1953.
———: "Soviet Comments on International Law and Relations," *American Journal of International Law,* vol. 47, 1953.
Langer, W., and S. Gleason: *The Challenge to Isolation,* Harper, New York, 1952.
Lauterpacht, H.: *The Function of Law in the International Community,* Oxford, New York, 1933.
Lawson, R.: "Problems of the Compulsory Jurisdiction of the World Court," *American Journal of International Law,* vol. 46, 1952.
Lissitzyn, O. J.: *The International Court of Justice,* United Nations Studies, no. 6, Carnegie Endowment, New York, 1951.
Niemeyer, G.: *Law without Force,* Princeton University Press, Princeton, N.J., 1941.
Nussbaum, A.: *A Concise History of the Law of Nations,* Macmillan, New York, 1947.

[40] Corbett, *op. cit.,* p. 44.

Pompe, C. A.: *Aggressive War, An International Crime,* Nijhoff, The Hague, 1953.
Rosenne, S.: "The International Court and the United Nations: Reflection on the Period 1946–1954," *International Organization,* May, 1955.
Sastroamidjojo, A.: Some Aspects of International Law in Southeast Asia," *Proceedings of the American Society of International Law,* 1953.
Schwarzenberger, G.: *International Law,* Stevens, London, 1945.
Vyshinsky, A.: *Law of the Soviet State,* Macmillan, New York, 1948.
Wilk, K.: "International Law and Global Ideological Conflict," *American Journal of International Law,* vol. 45, 1951.

Chapter 18

THE RULES OF INTERNATIONAL LAW

International relations are characterized by the recognition of inter-dependence among nations as well as by the consistent attempt to minimize intimate ties with other peoples. International law, in so far as it incorporates a body of rules acknowledged even by the strongest nations as desirable and necessary, corresponds to the recognition of interdependence. However, the law exhibits the same duality as the relations among nations. To the extent that it is a façade for unilateral policy aims, it functions merely as a device for asserting the superiority of the national community over international society.

It follows that the detailed rules of the law—in so far as they can be stated with any certainty—correspond to the law's dual function. A maximum of agreement among nations prevails in the area of recognized inter-dependence: there the rules seem relatively clear and, what is more, are fairly consistently obeyed. Less and less agreement is possible, however, as portions of the law become primarily useful for the justification of national aims, in the propaganda function of the law. Hence the major fields of the law must now be surveyed in terms of this duality, thus demonstrating the degree of consensus among nations, elites, and national myths.

1. The Definition of Territorial Jurisdiction. International law contains a certain number of rules regulating the manner in which states can acquire and maintain exclusive jurisdiction over the portions of the globe which they claim as their own. By more or less clearly establishing which nation has title to what areas these rules contribute to stability and order. In line with geographical necessity, the rules define land boundaries, jurisdiction over the ocean, and most recently over the air.

Land. Customary international law recognizes four major principles under which a state can acquire title to land areas: prescription, cession, conquest, and occupation. Prescription and cession are fairly unambiguous, conquest is probably no longer legal under modern treaty obligations, and occupation is the source of continued and bitter controversy among nations. Our analysis will proceed from the most generally accepted to the most controversial of these principles.

Prescription implies that a state exercises jurisdiction over a specific area because it has habitually done so, without serious challenge or counterclaim from other states. It is the only principle on the basis of which old and established nations can justify their territorial sway, especially if there is no treaty confirming their title. Prescription applies, therefore, preeminently to the older nations of Europe and Asia whose existence antedates the development of modern international law. It does not apply generally to colonial acquisitions and to the claim for territorial jurisdiction exercised by younger nations. These rest on occupation and cession, if not conquest.

Title to territory is readily acquired by an act of cession. France ceded Louisiana to the United States; Italy, in 1947, ceded most of Istria to Yugoslavia. Cession may be the result of a victorious war, or it may be accomplished by purchase, or without any compensation. Cession, under international law, does not require the voluntary consent of the ceding party —as demonstrated by territorial transfers brought about by peace treaties —and it need not take into account the wishes of the populations concerned. After World War I, plebiscites were used in some cases in connection with cessions of territory, but since 1945 this practice seems to have fallen into disuse as embarrassing to the state making the acquisition.

Conquest, with or without the benefit of a treaty of cession, was undoubtedly an accepted principle of law until the acceptance of the Stimson Doctrine by most states in 1932. Under this doctrine, states refuse to recognize territorial title if brought about by any means which violate international treaty obligations, and it was held that conquest had become illegal as a result of the Pact of Paris. The same principle is expressed in the UN Charter. Thus, despite the fact that conquest seems to recur in the practice of nations, its legality is now very much in doubt.[1]

Finally, most acquisitions of unexplored and previously unclaimed lands rest on the principle of occupation. While according to some, discovery and exploration gives an "inchoate title" to jurisdiction, others hold that such acts must be followed up by "effective occupation" to vest a firm title. As to what constitutes effective occupation, there seems to be little agreement. Some states maintain that a declaration of occupation suffices, even if no more is actually done than hoist a flag and promulgate a decree. Other states and some tribunals hold that there must be evidence of a continuing exercise of sovereign powers, i.e., police patrols, surveying parties, and the like. Denmark's title to East Greenland has been upheld despite a minimum of such acts. Yet the United States, the Soviet Union, Norway, Canada, Argentina, and others claim wide areas of the Arctic and Antarctic wastes on the basis of simple declarations and the assertion that "sectors" of the lands in question are geographically contiguous to the claimants. Since these claims frequently overlap and since the rivals do not recognize each other's declara-

---

[1] J. L. Brierly, *The Law of Nations,* Oxford University Press, New York, 1948, chap. V, par. 2.

tions, the principle of occupation here invoked seems to throw little light on the rights of the parties.

Water. If the law of occupation is more likely to serve the interests of rhetoric than to establish clear title, much the same seems to be true of the law of maritime jurisdiction. Here it is necessary to distinguish among parts of the ocean considered part of state territory (i.e., territorial waters), the high seas, ambiguous areas between these two, and claims for special national jurisdiction over the high seas.

Customary international law, at least since the end of the seventeenth century, has maintained that territorial waters extend to a distance of 3 nautical miles from shore and that everything beyond this belt is part of the high seas, subject to no one state's exclusive jurisdiction. It is true that states having 79 per cent of merchant shipping tonnage registered under their flags recognize the 3-mile limit.[2] Yet, it is also true that the Scandinavians claim a 4-mile limit and that other states have maintained long historical assertions to 6- and 12-mile limits. Probably the most that can be said is that the *minimum* width of territorial waters recognized in international law is 3 miles. Nor does it follow that all other portions of the ocean are parts of the common realm of the high seas. Controversy exists over the "marginal sea," areas within territorial waters technically but used as major traffic routes and therefore not subject to exclusive national law according to many states and jurists. How are bays and gulfs treated? Some hold that if the entrance of a bay is wider than 10 miles, it is part of the high seas; but the ICJ has declined to accept this as a general rule. Further, certain "historical bays" whose entrance may be wider than 10 miles are nonetheless under exclusive national jurisdiction. If other states fail to challenge such a contention, the presumption of national primacy holds good. There are no firm rules on the extent of the high seas, and limited treaties are often used to regulate rights between specific states and their nationals.

Furthermore, it is plain that states have asserted special national rights over varying areas of contiguous portions of the high seas, none of which are regulated by international consensus. States claim the right to patrol the high seas to prevent smuggling, enforce sanitary laws, and drive off or apprehend alien vessels "hovering" just outside the 3-mile limit in the attempt to violate in some way the law of the nearest state. Frequently the very state claiming such a right for itself will deny another nation the same privilege, as Britain did initially when the United States sought to enforce the Prohibition Act 12 miles off the Atlantic shore.

The most striking claim for national jurisdiction over the high seas occurred when the meeting of all American states at Panama decided to proclaim the "inherent right" to prevent "any hostile act" by a non-American

---

[2] S. W. Boggs, "Delimitation of Seaward Areas under National Jurisdiction," *American Journal of International Law,* vol. 45, 1951, p. 241.

belligerent of World War II in a 1,000-mile belt surrounding the Western Hemisphere. Both Axis and Allied belligerents declined to recognize this claim and carried on warfare in the security zone, but American vessels justified their attacks on German craft on the basis of the Declaration of Panama. The "law," obviously, is far from clear. The status of the key Suez and Panama Canals is equally ambiguous. While they are to be kept open during wars and free from any act of war, Egypt and the United States also have the right to defend the waterways and make certain that their use by others will not interfere with national safety.[3] As a result, the canals were *not* kept open and neutral during the world wars.

The alleged "freedom of the seas" is probably most consistently challenged in the practice of states with respect to fisheries. Many nations claim contiguous-zone jurisdiction for purposes of catching and conserving fish, though the extent of such claims varies. Foreign fishing vessels are driven off, seized, and sometimes condemned in national courts, even if active on the "high seas." The United States, in 1945, established "conservation zones in those areas of the high seas contiguous to the coasts of the United States wherein fishing activities have been or in the future may be developed. . . ."[4] The International Law Commission has recognized the existence of such rights up to 12 miles from shore, with the insistence that conservation alone should be the purpose of such an extension of territorial waters. It was urged further that nondiscrimination against other states should be included; but the North Pacific Fisheries treaty among Canada, Japan, and the United States makes plain that states do in fact assert and practice multilateral and unilateral rights of catching and conserving fish on the high seas, with implied discrimination against nonparties to the treaty.[5]

If fisheries beg the question of the extent of maritime jurisdiction, the now-established doctrine of the mineral-rich "continental shelf" contributes more uncertainty. The United States has asserted that the "natural resources of the subsoil and sea bed of the continental shelf beneath the high seas but contiguous to the coasts of the United States" be regarded as "appertaining to the United States subject to its jurisdiction and control."[6] By 1951, thirty states had made similar declarations, thus in effect—though not in strict terms—extending territorial sovereignty to that part of the ocean bottom and high seas not more than 100 fathoms in depth, to accept the estimate of geologists. Freedom of traffic over the areas claimed is to be

[3] Suez Canal regulations in Constantinople Convention, 1888, and Panama Canal rules in Hay-Pauncefote Treaty, 1901; P. E. Corbett, *Law and Society in the Relations of States,* Harcourt, Brace, New York, 1951, pp. 139, 145–147.

[4] President Truman's Proclamation of Sept. 28, 1945; Corbett, *op. cit.,* p. 135.

[5] H. W. Briggs, "New Dimensions in International Law," *American Political Science Review,* vol. 46, 1952, p. 695.

[6] R. Young, "The Legal Status of Submarine Areas beneath the High Seas," *American Journal of International Law,* vol. 45, 1951, quoting President's Proclamation of Sept. 1945, pp. 227–228. Also Briggs, *op. cit.,* p. 695.

permitted, while the International Law Commission insists that such jurisdiction be confined to the exploration and exploitation of natural resources.
If are added the encroachments upon the common high seas represented
by smuggling, fisheries, natural resources, and continental security legislation, it is clear that in the practice of states the doctrine of the freedom
of the seas is in full retreat.

Air. In contrast to the situation on land and water, the realm of air jurisdiction is fairly clear. The airspace over territory and territorial waters is
subject to the unilateral control of the state beneath. Over the high seas,
planes are part of the territory whose flag they carry, just like ships, but
once they enter a national airspace, they are subject entirely to the law of
that state, in the absence of treaty provisions to the contrary. Furthermore,
unlike ships, planes do not possess a blanket right to enter ports. Attempts
to establish general air-traffic rights between nations have failed. At the
moment forty-one states recognize merely the existence of "the privilege to
fly across its territory without landing" and "the privilege to land for non-
traffic purposes." [7] More extensive rights to deposit and pick up passengers
and cargo are frequently granted, but only through bilateral treaty arrangements, based usually on reciprocity. States continue to assert and guard
their unlimited jurisdiction over airspace, thus minimizing freedom of air
traffic. Security considerations explain this trend only in part. Primarily, it
is an assertion of the right to limit the commercial opportunities of other
nations' air lines and thereby strengthen the position of the nation's own
commercial groups. The reaction to interdependence, once more, takes the
form of the search for self-sufficiency.

2. Immunities. In superficially sharp contrast to the scarcity of international air law, the rules acknowledged by most nations in their intercourse
seem to recognize extensive special rights for foreign diplomats and consuls,
as well as the property of foreign states and the employees of international
organizations. While aliens ordinarily are subject to the law of the state
in which they reside—within some limitations—diplomats and states are
said to enjoy "immunity" under international law. Immunities, like much
of the law, however, seem to be undergoing drastic reduction at the moment,
and their scope is by no means unambiguous.

States and Their Property. In view of recent practice it seems clear that
the once established immunity of states from suit and taxation by other
states is no longer applicable. Heads of state, when abroad, are still exempt
from all the obligations of local law; but public property which was similarly
immune at one time now seems to be subject to both suit and taxation under
certain conditions, especially public vessels and goods purchased by states.

---

[7] International Air Services Transit Agreement, Art. 1, sec. 1. The much more liberal
International Air Transport Agreement had been ratified by sixteen states, of which five,
including the United States, subsequently denounced it. Texts in H. W. Briggs, *The Law
of Nations,* 2d ed., Appleton-Century-Crofts, New York, 1952, pp. 322–323.

With the growth of state trading and the development of state-owned merchant shipping, nations have been less and less willing to accord immunity to these commercial aspects of government activity. It is the practice of the United States and many other nations now to accord immunity only to public warships and to the instrumentalities of foreign states in their diplomatic and political activities.[8] In these matters, national courts are guided exclusively by the policy of the nation's executive.

Diplomatic Officials. Once a state has indicated that it regards the diplomatic representative of another as *persona grata,* the diplomat cannot be taxed; nor can he be sued for either criminal or civil offenses. Upon notification that the individual has become *persona non grata,* he still retains his immunity, but he must be recalled by his government. Furthermore, the premises of embassy or legation he occupies constitute, legally, part of the territory of the state which he represents. They cannot be invaded or inspected by the police of the host state. It must be stressed that these privileges exist even in the absence of treaty obligations, but that they have been increasingly challenged in recent decades, especially under the pressure of ideological conflict.

Thus American diplomats in Eastern Europe have readily been made *personae non gratae* and their recall demanded. Their freedom of movement has been restricted and the embassy premises spied upon. American practice retaliated with kindred measures. The inviolability of embassies and legations has been infringed in case of forced detention, abduction, and murder in Paris, Berlin, and Vienna, and even the once-recognized right to asylum in inviolable embassy premises seems to be vanishing. It was always possible for the diplomat to waive his personal immunities and those of his staff, but such waivers have been construed fairly broadly by French police seeking to remove detained persons from the Soviet embassy in Paris.[9] Thus while diplomatic immunities continue to be recognized, there seems to be a definite trend toward reducing the number and types of persons entitled to them.

International Organizations. If the functions of diplomats require immunity from local law, much the same must be said for the similar duties of staff members of the UN and other international organizations. Thus the UN Charter declares that "the Organization shall enjoy in the territory of each of its Members such privileges and immunities as are necessary for the fulfillment of its purposes," while delegates to the UN and staff members shall "enjoy such privileges and immunities as are necessary for the independent exercise of their functions in connection with the Organization."[10] What are these immunities in law and practice?

---

[8] See recent United States policy in W. W. Bishop, "New United States Policy Limiting Sovereign Immunity," *American Journal of International Law,* vol. 47, 1953, pp. 93 ff.

[9] Briggs, *op. cit.,* pp. 753–754, 789–792. Brierly, *op. cit.,* chap. 6, par. 6.

[10] United Nations Charter, Art. 105, secs. 1, 2.

Persons working at the headquarters of international organizations are either diplomatic representatives of governments, and as such analogous to ordinary diplomats, or permanent employees of the organization not owing special obedience to their home governments during their employment. According to recent treaties, diplomatic representatives enjoy the same privileges and immunities as do ordinary diplomats, and the UN headquarters possesses a status of inviolability similar to that of embassies. Employees of the organizations, however, are immune "from legal process in respect of words spoken or written and all acts performed by them *in their official capacity*" and no more, though they enjoy immunity from immigration laws, taxes, and the like.[11] These arrangements, however, are not recognized by the United States, where the major UN site is located!

As far as the inviolability of the UN headquarters is concerned, the United States has confirmed this in a separate agreement, but the UN cannot afford asylum to persons wanted by American law-enforcement officers. All persons having official business with the UN are guaranteed the right of ingress and egress to the premises, "irrespective of the relations existing between the Governments of the persons . . . and the United States."[12] America has agreed to give the chief diplomatic representatives—if they come from countries recognized by the United States—the standard diplomatic immunities. Others are immune only in their residence, at the headquarters, and en route between these points. Staff members of the UN, however, seem to be immune only in the performance of their official duties, and the United States reserves the right to request the expulsion of unwanted UN employees. Thus one UN staff member has been tried and convicted in American courts and was subsequently expelled. American employees of the UN have been subjected to congressional investigations upon waiver of any possible immunity by the Secretary-General of the UN.

3. Rights of Aliens and the Protection of Nationals. When an alien takes up residence in another nation, does he become wholly subject to the law of that nation, or can he claim special rights and call on his home government to protect them for him? Implicit in this question is one of the major problems of order and stability in international contacts. Western businessmen wishing to reside in Latin America or the Middle East prefer to take their accustomed standards of justice, contract validity, and commercial practices with them. The local governments, not always able to enforce the law and frequently subject to riots, disturbances, and revolutions, wish to deny any special responsibility for the alien's safety. They argue

[11] General Convention on the Privileges and Immunities of the United Nations. In force for thirty-eight member states, as of August, 1951. Neither the United States nor the Soviet Union is a party. Briggs, *op. cit.,* pp. 794–797. Italics supplied.

[12] United Nations–United States, Agreement Regarding the Headquarters of the United Nations; Briggs, *op. cit.,* pp. 798 ff. Also the United States International Organizations Immunities Act, 1945, *ibid.,* p. 811.

that the alien must accept the law as he finds it. Western governments, how-ever, to protect the business activities of their citizens, claim the right to demand an international standard of stability and order, and hold default-ing governments responsible for injury to their nationals abroad What ac-cepted legal rules govern these situations? According to Latin American claims, there should be no special responsibility. Aliens are induced to waive any right to appeal to their home governments in case of injury by having the so-called Calvo Clause inserted into contracts concluded with Latin-American governments. Western courts and foreign ministries usually refuse to recognize the validity of such waivers and insist on international responsi-bility for damages suffered by their nationals even though the individual is not clearly a subject of international law. Such legal "rules" as have arisen in this area, consequently, are not firmly established at all. They represent, by and large, the claims of the West, and while they have been developed and upheld by many arbitration commissions, their applicability continues to be questioned by non-Western groups.

Due Diligence. One of the important principles invoked in the creation of an environment conducive to predictable business relationships is the rule of "due diligence." States are under responsibility, it is urged, to exercise due diligence in the apprehension of criminals guilty of lawless acts against aliens. Failure to apprehend, try, and punish them is considered harmful to smooth commercial relations. Yet it has been impossible to define what kind of governmental acts are required under this reasoning, and at least one commentator has concluded that arbitration commissions use intuitive and nonjudicial standards in determining failure to exercise due diligence.[13]

Denial of Justice. An equally important but even more elusive concept is the "denial of justice" to an alien. States frequently protest and demand action on behalf of their nationals abroad when one of them alleges that the local state has violated civilized standards of justice in dealing with him. Delay between arrest and trial, refusal of access to legal counsel, peremptory proceedings in court, and the like have been included under this heading. Some maintain that a denial occurs whenever it proves impossible to obtain redress against arbitrary action by local officials, while others urge that only a miscarriage of judicial proceedings should be so considered. Western nations insist on a minimum standard of "due process of law," which Latin Ameri-cans deny as an international responsibility. No clear definition has yet been accepted, and mutually incompatible claims continue.

Local Remedies. One rule on which there seems to be substantial agree-ment, however, is the insistence of protesting governments as well as arbitra-tion commissions that, before a claim can be heard, the aggrieved alien must

---

[13] F. S. Dunn, *The Protection of Nationals,* Johns Hopkins Press, Baltimore, 1932, pp. 143–146.

exhaust all local remedies. He must ask the local executive as well as judicial authorities for redress under local law before the international responsibility of the foreign government can be engaged. In some cases, where there may not be any local remedies to exhaust, arbitrators will hear the complaint; but their judgments seem to reflect some consensus that adequate judicial institutions in each country are required by generally accepted international law.

The whole field of protecting nationals abroad, however, is confused further by the lack of agreement as to which government officials must be proved delinquent before an alien's claim can be upheld. If local officials are arbitrarily violating the law is the central government liable? Are federal governments to be held responsible for illegal acts of state officials? Must a distinction be drawn between illegal acts committed in a private or a public capacity? Some arbitrators have worked with such distinctions while others have tended to hold the central government liable regardless of the local power structure. There is no clear practice and certainly no firm law.

Moreover, the practice of protecting nationals abroad begs the question of whether individuals are in effect—though not in doctrine—subjects of international law. Practice tends to escape this question by insisting that the alien as such has no right to sue, that he merely complains to his home government, and that the authorities sue on his behalf to uphold the dignity of the sovereign state. In fact, of course, the home government brings action on behalf of its aggrieved citizen, as is proved by the awarding of monetary damages to the mistreated national, in some ratio to the losses he and his survivors actually suffered. Still, as long as it remains true that the individual can act only through his government, the practice of states continues to deny him the status of a subject of the law of nations.

4. Jurisdiction over Individuals. While the rules governing the protection of nationals abroad merely approach the point at which the individual has independent *rights* in international law, the individual's *liability* for violations of national law are clearly established in international practice. Thus, no state denies that each government has full powers over its own nationals, no matter where they happen to be. An American could be sued for acts committed in France, Panama, or anywhere else, and the same is true of other nations, though Anglo-American practice usually declines to assert jurisdiction beyond the water's edge.

Main Principles of Jurisdiction. Yet the rules defining jurisdiction over aliens in criminal questions are not so readily stated. There are three grounds generally admitted by states to give jurisdiction over aliens accused of violating the criminal law of a nation: the territorial principle, the nationality principle, and the protective principle. Under the first, the place where the offense was committed determines jurisdiction, and an alien is clearly liable wherever he violated local law. Under the nationality principle, the citizenship of the violator is the criterion of jurisdiction, and his home state can claim the power to try him for acts committed against the laws of another country. Since both the first and second principles are recognized by all, concurrent jurisdiction is in effect admitted for many offenses: both the home state and the nation whose law was violated can try the offender. Finally, under the protective principle, many states claim the power to try any alien, no matter where he may be or where the offense was committed, if the act violated the national interest or security of the aggrieved country. Most nations admit this kind of jurisdiction for offenses such as counterfeiting or espionage, but some deny it for lesser offenses.

Extradition. How can individuals be delivered into the hands of the state claiming jurisdiction over criminal offenses? International law recognizes the practice of extradition to accomplish this end. Yet it has never proved possible to secure agreement on whether a duty to extradite exists in the absence of specific treaty provisions. Moreover, extradition is hedged with procedural limitations of various kinds, usually recognized in the treaties concluded among nations. Thus offenders are frequently delivered only for alleged crimes actually enumerated in the treaty of extradition, and the offenses must be in violation of the requesting as well as of the extraditing state's law. Political offenders are almost never extradited, and the extraditing state usually reserves the right to review the evidence against the accused, delivering him only if he could be convicted under the law of the state where he happens to be. Finally, many countries refuse on principle to deliver their own nationals to another state's criminal jurisdiction.[14] The values of nations differ, and the divergences are mirrored in the weak nature of extradition law.

All these situations involve individual liability for violations of national law and no more. It must therefore be asked whether nations recognize individual offenses *against the law of nations,* offenses which can be tried and punished under international rules by international tribunals. If there are such crimes, clearly the individual has become a subject of international law.

Individual liability for offenses against international law has long been recognized in the obsolete field of piracy. And since 1945 some efforts have been made by certain member states of the United Nations to make individuals responsible for the waging of aggressive war, for violating the law of war, and for committing crimes against humanity. These offenses have become known as the "Nuremberg principles" because twenty-two German political and military leaders were tried under them. They were defined and applied by nineteen victor nations in World War II, in these terms: [15]

---

[14] See United States–Great Britain, Extradition Treaty, Dec. 22, 1931, *ibid.,* p. 590, and discussion of various state practices, pp. 595 ff.

[15] Charter of the International Military Tribunal, Art. 6, London, 1945. The same crimes and the same objections apply to the similar trial held in Tokyo for Japanese offenders.

(*a*) Crimes against Peace: namely, planning preparations, initiation or waging of a war of aggression, or a war in violation of international treaties, agreements or assurances, or participating in a common plan or conspiracy for the accomplishment of any of the foregoing.

(*b*) War Crimes [i.e., violations of the law of war, as defined in applicable treaties and customs].

(*c*) Crimes against Humanity: namely, murder, extermination, enslavement, deportation, and other inhumane acts committed against any civilian population, before or during the war, or persecutions on political, racial or religious grounds . . . whether or not in violation of the domestic law of the country where perpetrated. Leaders, organizers, instigators, and accomplices, participating in the formulation or execution of a common plan or conspiracy to commit any of the foregoing crimes are responsible for all acts performed by any persons in execution of such plan.

For the first time in history, individuals were judged and condemned for these offenses against what the victors claimed as international law. Violations of the law of war have long been regarded as making individuals liable to prosecution, though very few persons had actually been tried before 1945; but the other two categories are definite legal innovations. Are they really recognized as international rules today, or were they merely part of the invocation of "law" for the propagandistic purpose of justifying the Allies and castigating the Axis?

Legal opinion is divided on the point, and the practice of states is far from unanimous. Many lawyers urge that a valid precedent has been created, but the objections to this view seem overwhelming. The rules were defined by the victors, not by international society. The trial was conducted by judges representing the victors and not impartial elements in international society. Abstract and nonuniversal criteria of justice supplanted the primacy of generally accepted law, so that the procedures were of an ex post facto nature in the sense that the Nazi leaders were condemned for acts which were not clearly criminal at the time that they were committed.[16] Thus it appears that, as Lord Hankey put it, "Under a cloak of justice these trials were the old, old story—one law for the victors and another for the vanquished. Vae victis." [17] The precedent created in our environment of ideological conflict may merely be one of sanctifying the principle of trying and condemning as war criminals the leaders of any future vanquished nation.

Nor have nations since that time been anxious to codify these new "principles" of individual responsibility. Their detailed restatement and formulation by the UN International Law Commission has not received the assent of the General Assembly, even though that body unanimously "affirmed" them in 1946, an act of disputed legal significance. By 1953 many of the

[16] Corbett, *op. cit.*, pp. 227–229.
[17] C. A. Pompe, *Aggressive War, an International Crime*, Nijhoff, The Hague, 1953, p. 247.

very nations which had argued for the principle of unconditional individual responsibility when it applied to the Axis in 1945 had decided that "no one may be subjected to trial for the international crimes they had recognized before, except by or with the consent of the State of which he is a national." [18] The limited jurisdiction of the proposed criminal court bears ample testimony that individual responsibility has not been recognized.

The problem of the status of the individual under international law acquires most cogency in the attempt to safeguard human rights through treaty arrangements. Under the Genocide Convention, which entered into force in 1951,[19] certain individual acts, even if performed by government officials, are made international crimes. These are killing, injuring mentally or physically, seeking to destroy in any way, or taking away children from members of any "national, ethnical, racial or religious group." The aim of the new international law is to prevent the extermination of minority groups by states. Offenders must be extradited so that they may be tried in the country in which the offense was committed, though the proposed criminal court may also be given jurisdiction. The fact remains that, in the ideologically charged climate of our era, an unwilling state would have to be compelled by armed force to extradite the accused, and it seems doubtful that nations are willing to risk modern war for the sake of minority rights. Thus the impact of the convention is at present restricted to further the ability of antagonistic national communities of charging each other with violations of the law, without incurring the risk of concrete legal action.

The ambiguous status of the Genocide Convention between accepted law and mere assertion of limited national claims may serve as a model to the definition of additional human rights to be guaranteed by the law of nations. Under the auspices of the United Nations two draft covenants of human rights have been prepared, but have not been adopted. Nevertheless, these documents are utilized as propaganda material in global ideological conflicts.

Conflict, indeed, was the main constituent of the drafting process. The Western nations were willing to establish firm rules on personal rights in the realm of political and civil liberties long part of Western constitutional tradition. The Communist nations, however, were far more interested in defining the right to social security, work, minimum pay, and the social and cultural rights of minorities. They, as well as the Arab-Asian and Latin-American delegates, favored national self-determination as an international right and wrote it into the Covenants. As matters stand, the nations least

---

[18] *Ibid.*, pp. 332–333.

[19] The United States has refused to ratify the convention in order not to be compelled to extradite or try offenders against international rules which are not clearly illegal under national law. The Soviet Union's ratification contained such extensive reservations that other parties refused to consider it a ratification, an exclusion upheld by an advisory opinion of the ICJ.

conspicuous in the actual enforcement of such rights are most interested in writing them into law, while the states which habitually recognize most of the demands in question see no pressing need for international definition. The texts of the Covenants, consequently, are full of exceptions, limitations, and escape clauses.

The matter of enforcing these rights, once they are accepted by nations, is perhaps the most puzzling problem. Many of the smaller states, fearing with good reason that the Covenants might develop merely into sources of propaganda charges, demanded that individuals should be empowered to bring complaints against their governments before an international organ. The larger nations unanimously opposed this, and their view won out. Enforcement is limited to governments' lodging complaints of violations by other governments before an international Committee on Human Rights, to be appointed by the ICJ. This Committee could call for hearings and explanations, make recommendations, and brand the violator before the world, but it could take no other action.[20]

The record seems to prove once more that international law cannot grow in an area subject to basically conflicting values and aspirations. When and if legal rules are formulated in such an environment, they are made to serve the national claims and purposes of specific communities, but they will not necessarily contribute to the development of an international community. Western Europe enacted a regional code of human rights in 1953 with a minimum of difficulty, thus suggesting that a certain amount of cultural homogeneity is essential before law can be made to represent values. Such a homogeneity, however, is patently absent in the universal law of nations.

5. The Law of War. Prior to 1919 there can be no doubt that the waging of war for any purpose was completely legal. Consequently there grew up a multitude of customary and treaty rules under which war was regulated by protecting prisoners, the wounded, civilians, and neutrals. Belligerents, however, had equal rights and duties, regardless of who was the "aggressor." Certainly, some rules were violated by the belligerents, but the fact remains that in principle they were accepted and fairly consistently observed. Today, however, war is no longer completely legal, while actual hostilities are more unrestrained and incomparably more destructive; war has become both "illegal" and "total."

Yet, the International Law Commission concluded in 1949 that "war having been outlawed, the regulation of its conduct has ceased to be relevant. The majority of the Commission declared itself opposed to the study of the problem." [21] Granted that the political reality of war is still with us, is it

---

[20] M. Neal, "The United Nations and Human Rights," *International Conciliation*, no. 489, March, 1953, pp. 135–140.

[21] J. L. Kunz, "The Chaotic Status of the Laws of War and the Urgent Necessity for Their Revision," *American Journal of International Law*, vol. 45, 1951, p. 43.

true that such conflicts are illegal and therefore no longer subject to regulation?

Legality of War. The fact seems to be that while war is declared illegal, lawful hostilities are possible in two marginal situations, fully as cogent and destructive as unrestricted war: self-defense and collective enforcement measures. Thus the UN Charter prohibits the use of force, or even the threat to use it. Still, each state under the same Charter retains the right to self-defense; and what nation does not justify each of its armed conflicts as defense against a foreign attack? Moreover, the question of the continued need for rules of war is confused by the possibility that coercive measures may be employed by the United Nations itself. At what point can the world organization resort to such means legally, thus perhaps bringing into play rules for the regulation of hostilities?

Accepted techniques for the pacific settlement of disputes must be examined in order to delimit this marginal situation. Traditional international law recognizes four such methods: (1) good offices and mediation, (2) enquiry and conciliation, (3) arbitration, and (4) adjudication. All four have been carried over into the UN Charter. Arbitration and adjudication are methods in which the dispute is put into legal terms and offered for binding settlement to the impartial persons who serve on the arbitration commission or the international court. This manner of disposing of disputes is subject to all the political and legal difficulties discussed in the preceding chapter and has never been used to settle major international tensions. However, force could legally be used by the UN to carry out the award of an international tribunal.

Mediation and conciliation are political techniques in which the legal rights of the parties need not be taken into account. The mediator is a neutral state making available its "good offices" to bring the parties together, with the aim of persuading them to negotiate and conclude an agreement, without the mediator's entering into the substance of the controversy. Yet mediation is frequently rejected because the two antagonists tend to feel that the mediating state is not really neutral and "interferes" for political reasons of its own. Conciliation is a different and today more universally accepted technique. It involves the submission of the dispute to a neutral group of states, who recommend a settlement on the basis of inquiry into the facts of the controversy. In principle, the Security Council of the UN is a conciliation body, charged with encouraging the parties to negotiate their difficulties, investigating a dispute as to its facts and merits to see whether it threatens international peace, and recommending a settlement to the parties. If the parties refuse the recommendation and go to war anyway, a "breach of the peace or an act of aggression" will have taken place, within the meaning of the Charter. At that time, the UN can institute armed enforcement action against either or both of the parties, provided the Security Council does not consider the war an act of self-defense.

It is at this point that the question arises as to whether the traditional law of war, which made no distinction between aggressor and attacked and gave all belligerents equal rights, is to be operative. For it must be remembered that UN enforcement action is the only "just war" possible under modern law and that it is contrary to the spirit of collective security to give equal belligerent rights to the police powers and the aggressor.

Violence continues to be legal, therefore, in the realms of self-defense and collective measures. It is clearly illegal in the case of *aggressive* applications of armed force, and it is in this area that, in principle, equal belligerent rights should be denied to the lawbreaker and the international organization or its agents. But what constitutes "aggression"? Attacking another nation, encouraging civil strife in it, having armed bands invade its frontiers, flying over its territory, or merely arming against it, perhaps in violation of a disarmament treaty? [22] The UN has so far wrestled in vain with a definition satisfactory to all, and the fact is that few major powers are anxious to circumscribe their freedom of action by agreeing in advance not to "defend themselves" in some specified category of conflict. Only the Soviet bloc favors a simple definition of the term "aggression," limited to overt acts of armed attack.

Thus it is clear that illegal wars still occur and that perfectly legal conflicts can and do arise in the case of self-defense and collective enforcement action. In the practice of states since 1945 it has become plain that the traditional treaties and customs of war continue to be observed regardless of the contrary implications of the Charter. Witness the use of the term "all cases of declared war or of any other *armed conflict*" used by the drafters of the Geneva Convention of 1949 in specifying the scope of application of the most recent treaty on belligerent rights and duties.[23] Witness further the voluntary adoption of the rules of 1949 by both belligerent camps in the Korean conflict, despite the fact that the UN was, in principle, engaged in a collective-enforcement action. As far as practice is concerned, therefore, the legality or illegality of the conflict seems to make no difference. The humanitarian rules protecting prisoners, the wounded, and civilians, at least, are still observed. The military themselves prefer these minimum restraints upon unlimited brutality, despite the apparent violation of the law by local commanders on occasion. As Lauterpacht concludes,[24]

[22] See the enumeration in the Draft Code of Offences against the Peace; Pompe, *op. cit.*, pp. 340–342. UN Doc. A/2211, Oct. 3, 1952.

[23] H. J. Taubenfeld, "International Armed Forces and the Rules of War," *American Journal of International Law,* vol. 45, 1951, pp. 673–674, p. 678. Italics supplied.

[24] "Rules of Warfare in an Unlawful War," in G. Lipsky (ed.), *Law and Politics in the World Community,* University of California Press, Berkeley, Calif., 1953.

It is possible that international society in the future will develop a body of appropriate rules and principles governing the collective use of force. However, unless the force at the disposal of the international community [sic] is so overwhelming as to approach rapid police action permitting of no organized resistance, it is doubtful whether such rules can differ appreciably from those governing the relations of belligerents in an ordinary war.

Forbidden Weapons. What, then, are these rules? Ever since the Hague Conventions of 1899 and 1907—and these are still the basis of the modern law of war—certain weapons have been outlawed. At first, they included merely gas warfare, aerial bombardment, magnetic mines, and some explosives. After World War I these prohibitions were reaffirmed, and submarine warfare was restricted to procedures under which the passengers and crew of the doomed ship had to be removed before sinking the vessel. But these prohibitions meant little because under the "general participation" clause of the conventions a party was bound only if the opposing belligerent had also ratified the treaties. Since not all the nations involved in the world wars had complied, the forbidden weapons except gas were widely used by all belligerents. Additional attempts to outlaw such weapons as heavy artillery, forbid the bombing of unfortified towns, and ban the use of the atom bomb have failed because nations expecting future violence are loath to forgo the use of arms on which their survival is considered to depend, so long as no guarantee exists that prohibitions will be observed. There is no accepted law of war in the realm of weapons and tactics, despite the treaties, and the demand for further prohibitions usually reflects the desire to embarrass an opposing elite and no more.

Civilians, Prisoners, and Wounded. Generally, the most consistently observed portion of the pre-1919 law of war dealt with the rights of civilian populations, the treatment of the sick and wounded, and the status of prisoners of war. The basic purpose of the rules was to exempt these persons, as far as possible, from the suffering normally engendered by large-scale hostilities. Civilian installations were to be left inviolate, enemy aliens were to be permitted to depart, and the shelling or bombing of unfortified towns was banned. The enemy wounded were entitled to the same treatment as casualties of the captor's nationality. Medical installations and personnel were exempt from capture and shelling if they were unarmed and clearly identifiable through Red Cross markings. Prisoners were to be humanely treated, paid according to the captor's pay scale, and not compelled to work on projects related to the war.

Almost all these rules were in fact violated in both world wars, though the Germans and the Western Allies tended to observe most of the law with respect to each other's prisoners. Captured Russian soldiers and all prisoners taken by Japan, however, exercised none of these rights. True, most of the

Hague rules were readopted and even expanded in the Geneva Conventions of 1949. The repatriation of prisoners of war was made mandatory, though they may be given asylum by the captor.[25] But with the intensification of warfare and the ever weaker distinction between civilians and soldiers, the future observance of the Geneva rules remains very much in doubt.

Belligerent Occupation. Once we turn to the law of belligerent occupation, however, the contrast between treaty obligations and actual behavior is again strikingly real. In the Hague and Geneva Conventions it is provided that in the event of a military occupation the private and commercial rights of citizens of the occupied state will be left undisturbed. Reprisals and mass penalties were forbidden, the general assumption being that war was fought between armies, with the victorious side refraining from remolding the legal and political structure of the vanquished. Practice in World War II was otherwise. Germany and Japan observed none of these rules in their occupation regimes. The Allies, moreover, ignored them just as consistently in their policy of reshaping the German and Japanese social and economic order toward democracy. It is plain that the restraint called for by the law cannot be exercised if the fighting deals with the survival and assertion of values and institutions. Defeating Nazism meant more than military victory; it included the destruction of Nazi institutions, but implied incidentally the violation of the traditional law of belligerent occupation. The practice of collective enforcement obscures the picture further. In principle the aggressor should enjoy no belligerent rights, but practice may well decree otherwise, as it has done in other areas of the law of war. The last important—and perhaps most controversial—area of rules governing the hostile relations among states now remains to be examined: the law of neutrality.

6. Neutrality. Before the advent of universal collective-security principles any state could acquire the rights and assume the duties of neutrality by merely declaring its aloofness from a war. As in other portions of the law of war, however, the UN Charter has thrown some doubt on the traditional status of neutrality. Legal war is either self-defense or collective-enforcement action, involving in principle the interests of all against the aggressor. Hence neutrality would become theoretically impossible, since every state would be either part of the collective effort or a supporter of the aggressor. Thus many writers have urged the obsolescence of neutral rights in situations in which the UN is seeking to maintain peace or punish aggression.[26]

[25] Twenty states had ratified the Geneva Conventions of 1949 by 1953. The United States is not among them and therefore continues to be bound by the less sweeping agreement of 1929. However, the UN Korean command has accepted the 1949 rules by declaration and considers itself bound by them. The repatriation of prisoners is discussed by J. L. Kunz, "Treatment of Prisoners of War," *Proceedings of the American Society of International Law,* 1953, pp. 100 ff.

[26] P. C. Jessup, *A Modern Law of Nations,* Macmillan, New York, 1948, chap. 8.

Once again, however, practice has decreed otherwise. Not only have non-members of the UN, such as Switzerland, asserted their continued neutrality, but other states have recognized it. Further, even in the event of collective enforcement neutrality has again been stressed by India, for example, and the UN has intimated that its own members can be considered "neutral" if they have failed to contribute armed forces for the collective action. Despite the advent of collective security, neutrality continues to be a recognized legal status, at least for certain purposes. But its implications are far from clear.

Under the traditional law of the Hague Conventions, a neutral was entitled to complete inviolability by the belligerents if it refrained from aiding either side. Trading with the belligerents was permitted provided both sides were free to purchase supplies. Neutrals could not give unlimited shelter to belligerent warships and were bound to intern belligerent personnel crossing their borders or flying over their territory.

Reciprocally, neutrals were entitled to extensive rights during hostilities. Their ships had to be permitted to trade with the belligerents provided they did not carry "contraband" cargo, i.e., goods useful in waging war. If one belligerent was actually blockading the ports of another, neutral ships were prohibited from entering and could be seized if they tried to run the blockade. But the freedom of the seas was asserted traditionally as a neutral right.

The facts of the law, however, were quite different from its treaty form. With the growth of total war and the participation of civilians and all branches of the economy in the conflicts of nations, the distinctions between "contraband" and "free" goods, between "effective" and "paper" blockades, all went by the board. In both world wars, the belligerents declared every possible kind of cargo to be contraband. Goods destined for neutral countries were confiscated by national prize courts if it was suspected that through "continuous voyage" they would ultimately find their way to the belligerents. Britain systematically stopped and inspected all neutral ships bound for European ports on the "legal" assertion that a blockade of all shores under German control had been declared, even though it could not be enforced through continuous naval operations. Militarily as well as commercially, neutrality was somewhat of a fiction. British units fought with German craft in neutral Norwegian waters, and the Allies planned an invasion of Norway despite its avowed aloofness and adherence to the Hague Conventions. Belgium, in the face of its neutrality, conducted carefully secret military talks with France; the United States, before 1941, supported the Allies while discriminating actively against Axis foreign trade. As a British Prime Minister summarized situations of this kind: [27]

---

[27] Asquith in the House of Commons, Mar. 1, 1915; Corbett, *op. cit.,* p. 253.

In the retaliatory measures we propose to adopt, "blockade," "contraband" and other technical terms do not occur, and advisedly, in dealing with an opponent who has openly repudiated all the restraints of law and humanity, we are not going to allow our efforts to be strangled in a network of juridical meshes.

Belligerent violations of neutral rights, of course, do not imply ready acquiescence by powerful neutral nations in these practices. The United States protested vigorously against British infractions of the freedom of the seas before 1917. In 1939, however, the United States only made a show of protesting against renewed British practices of interfering with neutral commerce but assured London privately that as long as "incidents" were avoided Washington would acquiesce in the measures. America asserted its neutrality in excluding all belligerent warships from the 1,000-mile security zone but privately informed British men-of-war of the presence of Axis vessels and encouraged joint measures against them.[28] Neutrality, then, is a function of national policy. Its rules are asserted, reinterpreted, or violated with impunity in accordance with the aims of governments. Except for small and permanently neutral nations, the law of neutrality is a support for unilateral national preferences and not a restraint against them.

The dual function of the law of nations is thus manifest. With respect to immunities, fisheries, postal communications, and territorial boundaries it serves a universally recognized purpose in ordering relations. Even in the field of alien rights and state jurisdiction over individuals the same tends to apply. In these fields it is true that [29]

Violations of law are rare in all customary systems, and they are so in international law. The explanation of that fact is simple, and so too is the explanation of the common belief to the contrary. For the law is normally observed because . . . the demands that it makes on states are generally not exacting, and on the whole states find it convenient to observe it; but this fact receives little notice because the interest of most people in international law is not in the ordinary routine of international legal business, but in the occasions, rare but generally sensational, on which it is flagrantly broken. Such breaches generally occur either when some great political issue has arisen between states, or in that part of the system which professes to regulate the conduct of war. . . . The laws of peace and the great majority of treaties are on the whole regularly observed in the daily intercourse of states.

That the law orders relations and gives stability to some fields of international intercourse is undeniable; and to that extent it certainly restrains the uni-

---

[28] W. L. Langer and S. E. Gleason, *The Challenge to Isolation,* Harper, New York, 1952, pp. 208, 214–218, 283, 286–287.
[29] Brierly, *op. cit.,* pp. 72–73.

lateral preferences and aims of ruling groups. However, it is evident that the law also serves a rhetorical purpose in clothing the aims of governments in the garb of legal respectability. The mere fact that even the Soviets, who deny the possibility of a truly universal law, have accepted certain rules in common with the West proves "what Western governments have long known, that they can find in the most authoritative literature and records of international law and practice rules and precedents for any policy that pleases them." [30]

In addition to regulating limited fields of contact in which the desirability of order is acknowledged by all, therefore, international law also serves definite functions of maintaining continued freedom of national action. Since the law is not easily determined or changed, it tends to preserve the existing order—or, more likely, disorder. It resists its expansion to cover individuals as well as states and therefore keeps an unreal static content. It makes possible the hiding of true national aims behind a smokescreen of conventional phrases and claims, all equally "legal" in international practice. Consequently it can be utilized in the perpetration of discord, conflict, and disagreement as easily as it can be applied in the peaceful regulation of issues. Basically, international law remains a function of political relations among nations and not a restraining force against them. Though it antedates the invention of modern mass propaganda techniques and is likely to appeal much more to literate elites in allied and neutral countries than to the apathetic or uninformed bulk of the world's population, it is useful in much the same fashion as modern propaganda media. Therefore it ranks as yet another of the means available to elites in the effort to realize ends abroad; but the aim of order and stability emerges rarely as the dominant purpose of those who invoke legal techniques and arguments.

Additional Case-study Material

Bishop, W. W.: "New United States Policy Limiting Sovereign Immunity," *American Journal of International Law*, vol. 47, 1953.

Boggs, S. W.: "Delimitation of Seaward Areas under National Jurisdiction," *American Journal of International Law*, vol. 45, 1951.

Brierly, J. L.: *The Law of Nations*, 4th ed., Oxford, New York, 1948.

Briggs, H. W.: *The Law of Nations*, Appleton-Century-Crofts, New York, 1952.

———: "New Dimensions in International Law," *American Political Science Review*, vol. 46, 1952.

Corbett, P. E.: *Law and Society in the Relations of States*, Harcourt, Brace, New York, 1951.

Dunn, F. S.: *The Protection of Nationals*, Johns Hopkins Press, Baltimore, 1932.

Kelsen, H.: *The Law of the United Nations*, Stevens, London, 1950; supplement, 1951.

Kunz, J. L.: "Treatment of Prisoners of War," *Proceedings of the American Society of International Law*, 1953.

———: "The Chaotic State of Laws of War and the Urgent Necessity of Their Revision," *American Journal of International Law*, vol. 45, 1951.

---

[30] Corbett, *op. cit.*, p. 50.

Langer, W., and S. Gleason, *The Challenge to Isolation,* Harper, New York, 1952.

Lipsky, G. (ed.): *Law and Politics in the World Community,* University of California Press, Berkeley, Calif., 1953.

Neal, M.: "The United Nations and Human Rights," *International Conciliation,* no. 489, March, 1953.

Oppenheim,L.: *International Law,* 6th ed., Longmans, New York, 1947.

Pompe, C. A.: *Aggressive War an International Crime,* Nijhoff, The Hague, 1953.

Preuss, L.: "Consular Immunities: The Kasenkina Case," *American Journal of International Law,* vol. 43, 1949.

Taubenfeld, H. J.: "International Armed Forces and the Laws of War," *American Journal of International Law,* vol. 45, 1951.

Young, R.: "The Legal Status of Submarine Areas beneath the High Seas," *American Journal of International Law,* vol. 45, 1951.

PART SIX

WORLD COMMUNITY OR WORLD SOCIETY:
THE RISE OF INTERNATIONAL ORGANIZATION

Chapter 19

VARIETIES AND ROLES OF INTERNATIONAL ORGANIZATION

A casual glance at the morning newspaper should suffice to convince the modern citizen that the age of exclusive relations among single national states is past and gone. Cryptic initials such as UN, NATO, UNICEF, FAO, or ECOSOC are ample evidence of this. These letters refer to attempts to organize international relations on a permanent basis at a level higher than mere day-to-day contacts between individual states and their governments. They refer to institutions created to bring all national communities "under one roof" in the sense of formal association rather than informal contact. They symbolize the recognition by elites that the world has grown too small to permit them to make policy as if no other national communities existed.

The recognition of interdependence, however, by no means guarantees the absence of strife or the unanimous acceptance of this aspect of international life. Permanent international organizations, though restricted in scope, confined in power, limited to budgets smaller than those of most American metropolitan municipalities, and staffed by less personnel than New York's police force, arouse a great deal of controversy. Ardent advocates of the international sharing of values see in them steppingstones in the process of fashioning a world community. They see peace, freedom, and global welfare largely as the result of the ever-expanding scope and power of such agencies as the UN, and they propose the creation of new agencies on a large scale. However, defenders of the purity of exclusive national values fear international organizations as saboteurs of national institutions and loyalties. They suspect them of unwarranted interference with traditional ways and of promoting of alien ideologies. How justified are these hopes and fears?

To answer this question it is necessary to inquire into the functions, powers, successes, and failures of international organizations. This inquiry must determine their significance as agents of integration in a world split into opposing nations and seek to spell out the conditions under which they might be expected to bring about a world community. Finally, it must examine the arguments of critics of world organization and assess some of the proposals for reform and redirection of efforts which continue to be made.

While the essence of empire is coercion, the basis of international organization is consent. In the words of one contemporary student, "International organization refers to nations united for the achievement of a purpose, and to the institutions and methods they have created to assure the necessary collaboration." [1] That "they" rather than merely one of them have created such institutions proves the element of consent implicit in these developments. The discussion which follows of the role of international organization in international relations will rest on the assumption that consent is the basis of association.

1. Why Organize beyond the State Level? The Needs for Larger Organization. If the primary impulse of national communities is the preservation of their uniqueness, why do these same communities consent to the creation of organizations and procedures having some measure of authority over them? The answer must vary with the intensity of national feeling prevalent in each community. At the level of greatest intensity and therefore greatest exclusiveness, participation in any nonnational organization may be impossible. Thus, until very recent years, for example, the tribal kingdom of Saudi Arabia has felt no need or desire to be permanently associated with any other state. Such intensity is rare, however. Most commonly, contemporary states consent to participation in larger organizations because they recognize that certain of their policy aspirations are so dependent upon similar aims in other countries as to make common action essential if the aspirations of any single group are to be realized. Common action then represents a recognition of permanent interdependence of group aims. A survey of the variety and tasks of contemporary international organizations will illustrate the areas in which such recognition has found acceptance.

Communications, Drugs, and Rivers. The demands of ease and convenience in transport and communication provide the most elementary level of need to be met by formal organization. Thus in 1874 some twenty-two states agreed to ignore national boundaries for purposes of carrying the mails. They were concerned exclusively with overcoming certain annoying obstacles to the rapid and efficient international traffic in letters, parcels, and post

---

[1] Levi, W., *Fundamentals of World Organization,* University of Minnesota Press, Minneapolis, 1950, p. 3.

cards. Here the Universal Postal Union (UPU) was established to abolish exorbitant and inequitable rates charged by governments for sending mail to other countries. Today the rate for a piece of mail in international traffic has been standardized for the whole globe, no matter how distant the country, how many other countries have to be traversed in transit, or what route the letter takes. The maintenance and extension of efficient international mail service remains the sole task of UPU today.

Convenience and ease have provided the need for a number of additional organizations. The task of the International Telecommunications Union (ITU) is the standardization of international telephone, telegraph, and radio links: to assure that a message sent from one country may be received in another. This requires complementary electrical equipment and the absence of interference in the allocation of wave lengths.

Similarly, the safety of international air traffic is a prime minimum need of modern life. Unless the air-safety rules of various countries are identical, passenger flights might collide or crash when cruising in foreign air lanes or landing in overseas airports. Hence the International Civil Aviation Organization (ICAO) regulates air-safety rules. Similar arrangements are in force for ocean shipping, as well as road and rail transport.

The example of international control over the drug traffic is another instance of the recognition by groups everywhere that common aims can be met only by common action, if the nature of the problem is international. Drug addiction is recognized as undesirable everywhere. Dangerous drugs, however, also have a beneficial use if employed as anesthetics. The problem was how to make certain that the drug-producing countries would sell enough to meet medical needs but not permit the remainder of the production to enter the illicit drug traffic which is international in its contacts. This need was met by the creation of the Permanent Central Opium Board and its Supervisory Body, which assign production and consumption quotas to member states and propose common rules for the suppression of the illicit traffic.

Geographic propinquity makes even higher demands on the need of convenience. Nations bordering on the same waterway are interested in seeing that no single one of them has the ability to block or obstruct the traffic and trade of the others. They experience a common need in keeping the river free from physical and legal barriers. Hence Holland, Belgium, Germany, France, and Switzerland created the Rhine Commission to make common trade and navigation rules for them all. The Balkan countries, similarly, united in creating a Danube Commission for the same purpose. It should be noted, however, that in both instances the regulation of navigation proved possible only when the member nations were not deeply divided by rival political aims. The operations of the Danube Commission were long disrupted, for instance, when the Soviet Union assumed *de facto* control over the member countries, while only Yugoslavia remained outside the bloc.

Finance, Tariffs, and Agriculture. Common economic aspirations the world over have resulted in the creation of an impressive number of international organizations, many of which are equipped with powers and possess a scope of activity surpassing that of river commissions and the UPU. The practice of competitive currency devaluation and its underlying cause, the instability of balances of payments, was responsible for the creation of the International Monetary Fund (IMF). In principle the IMF has the power to approve or disapprove national requests for currency revaluation; it is also designed to afford short-term loans to nations whose balances of payments are temporarily dislocated. A sister institution, the International Bank for Reconstruction and Development (IBRD), is given capital, the right to borrow from private and government banks, and the power to lend funds to nations anxious to develop their economies. National economic planning for the member countries of these institutions, therefore, is to some extent subject to common rules and common decisions.

Post–World War II efforts to lay down common minimum rules among nations for the conduct of international trade have largely been a failure. Agreement on exchange-rate manipulation, import and export quotas, cartels, and dumping could not be obtained, since interested groups within nations clearly did not profess common aims internationally. Limited consensus, however, emerged in a common desire to reduce gradually the level of tariffs and to achieve some certainty that given national tariff rates would not be altered hastily and discriminatorily. To this end there was established the General Agreement on Tariffs and Trade (GATT), through which thirty-odd nations can negotiate reciprocal tariff reductions and exchange guarantees of tariff stability. More than this GATT is not empowered to do, thus demonstrating the ephemeral nature of recognized mutual needs in the area of trade and finance.

The demand for a measure of international economic planning, however, came closer to recognition in the realm of food and agriculture. Famine, malnutrition, and the inequitable distribution of food are the conditions the Food and Agriculture Organization (FAO) was called upon to remedy on a global scale. FAO "collects, analyzes, interprets and disseminates information relating to nutrition, agriculture, forestry and fisheries. It promotes and, where appropriate, recommends national and international action [in these fields]. . . . The Organization furnishes to its member governments such technical assistance . . . as they request."[2] In scope, then, FAO is concerned with such highly controversial activities as the processing, marketing, and distribution of food, conservation of resources, agricultural credit, rural development, and international commodity price setting.

The membership, however, reflects the most diverse economic aims and

[2] *Handbook of the United Nations and the Specialized Agencies,* United Nations, Department of Public Information, New York, 1949, pp. 84–85.

interests. American and Western European governments are concerned with low commodity prices and free enterprise. Asian governments are committed to obtaining ever-higher levels of food production and high prices for commodities which they export; they frequently favor regulation and planning. The Soviet bloc seeks aloofness from possible obligations and hence refuses to associate itself with FAO. Can a common global policy emerge from this diversity?

The first Director-General of FAO, Lord Orr, failed to overcome these clashing aims, and the Organization, therefore, has almost no planning functions. The Western nations in 1947 refused to adopt a plan whereby FAO would have become a world food board, buying commodities when the price was low and selling them when it rose beyond the purchasing power of needy nations. As a result, FAO now is restricted to surveying world food needs and making recommendations for relief measures to member governments. Its most important task, however, has been found in the field of technical assistance.

Technical-assistance activities are designed to improve standards of living in underdeveloped countries by means of advice, instruction, exchange of information, the demonstration of new techniques, and some limited gifts of modern seeds, fertilizer, hoes, plows, and tractors. Thus in 1952 FAO announced "that 174 experts from 38 countries were working in 51 countries principally in the fields of land and water development, crop improvement, animal disease and control, nutrition, agricultural economics, the conservation and management of forests and the development of fisheries." [3] Eighty-one students were studying abroad under FAO-financed fellowships, while 200 more were being sought. When early in 1952 an invasion of locusts threatened all crops in the Middle East, FAO-supplied chemicals and crop dusters brought the invasion to a halt and stopped a potential famine. However, the 5 million dollars annually available, and grudgingly appropriated by the developed member states, have not gone far toward increasing the scope of work.

Welfare Standards. A desire to provide for uniformly high standards of working conditions and wages for all workers was the reason which led to the creation of the International Labor Organization (ILO). The ILO concerns itself not only with wages, hours, and working conditions in industry, but also with labor migration, the rights of agricultural workers, the status of women in industry and agriculture, freedom of association for collective bargaining, and the prevention of exploitation of native labor in colonies. It represents, in short, the aspirations of most national labor groups to assure fellow workers everywhere the highest possible living and working standards, and indeed to protect everyone's jobs by means of international antidepression policies. ILO seeks to achieve these purposes by drafting and submitting treaties embodying new labor legislation to member states, by making studies

[3] *International Organization,* vol. 6, no. 3, August, 1952, p. 432.

and disseminating the findings, by rendering advice and technical assistance, and by investigating and debating complaints.

Raising global standards of health is the task of the World Health Organization (WHO). Like ILO and FAO, it undertakes studies of specific international problems: in this case, the manner in which epidemics spread and the means for their control. Like the other agencies, it renders advice and assistance to national governments on how to improve welfare services, such as clinics, dietary programs, and nursing and medical education. As in the ILO, rules for the control of diseases which spread with utter disregard for national frontiers are worked out and offered to states by means of draft treaties.

Yet the welfare activities of both ILO and WHO are by no means free from controversy. An American business delegate to ILO argues that "the ILO is a threat to the way of life which has fostered the religious, political and economic freedom of our country and which has brought us the highest standard of living in the world. . . . ILO . . . can only be an obstacle in the way of other countries choosing to follow our example." [4] The socialist beliefs of many of the delegates to ILO, of course, find their way into the Organization's activities. Hence capitalist spokesmen seek to prevent an expansion of its work and object to its very existence. In WHO, Western nations have succeeded in preventing the Organization from undertaking any projects suggesting "socialized medicine." The Soviet bloc has left the WHO because it refused to tackle the social problems which, the Communists argue, are responsible for bad health. Clearly, the acknowledgment of a need by no means excludes controversy on the basic purpose of international organizations when they approach such areas as economic and social planning.

Culture Sharing. Joining together in organizations designed to assure common access to the sea or stable wheat prices implies only the most rudimentary sharing of values and ideals. Spiritual aims, however, form an essential part of the demands which lead to the establishment of international agencies in the cultural realm. Governments call conferences, appoint committees, and draft treaties to be able to exchange students and teachers with other countries, obtain access to art collections, and standardize the statistical devices used by their scientists. The aim which is advanced through such measures redounds to a general sharing of taste, knowledge, and the enjoyment of life. In the long run this may also result in the sharing of values and ideologies across national boundaries—the basic aim of many such activities.

This aim is most consistently expressed by organizations dedicated to the task of building the ideological supports for a community transcending several nations. Since 1949 the Council of Europe has been meeting twice a year for the express purpose of creating the myths and symbols of a united

---

[4] George V. Moser, "The International Labor Organization," *Harvard Business Review,* vol. 30, no. 4, July–August 1952, p. 109.

Europe, a new community to be created by cultural appeals, but not yet in existence institutionally. And if the exponents of Atlantic union or world federation had their way, governments would soon be calling similar meetings for NATO or the entire globe.

On a global level this same task has been entrusted to the United Nations Educational, Scientific and Cultural Organization (UNESCO). "Peace based exclusively upon the political and economic arrangements of governments," declares the preamble to UNESCO's Constitution, "would not be a peace which would secure the unanimous, lasting and sincere support of the peoples of the world . . . peace must therefore be founded, if it is not to fail, upon the intellectual and moral solidarity of mankind." Peace thus is made dependent upon a general consensus as a result of which the world would be a single community in terms of its myths, symbols, and aspirations. More specifically, UNESCO's function is defined thus: [5]

> The purpose of the Organization is to contribute to peace and security by promoting collaboration among the nations through education, science and culture in order to further universal respect for justice, for the rule of law and for the human rights and fundamental freedoms which are affirmed for the peoples of the world, without distinction of race, sex, language or religion, by the Charter of the United Nations.

How is this ambitious task to be carried out? The Constitution states that the organization is to "collaborate in the work of advancing the mutual knowledge and understanding of peoples through all means of mass communication . . . to give fresh impulse to popular education and to the spread of culture, . . . to maintain, increase and diffuse knowledge . . ." *without intervening* in the domestic affairs of the member states.

Literally all spheres of cultural, educational, scientific, and philosophical contacts fall into the Organization's scope. At first, the attempt was made to use UNESCO as the developer and disseminator of a distinct and coherent ideology to which all nations and cultures could subscribe. While the member states of course never agreed on the content of such an ideology, even the attempt is enough to disturb elites whose rule is based on myths of exclusiveness. International culture sharing, however, is practiced on a large scale despite this inability to agree formally on an ideology. Pamphlets combating racial hatred and religious intolerance are distributed by UNESCO; the books of one culture are translated into the language of another; constant conferences are called in order to persuade the scientists, artists, and writers of various cultures to work on the same projects and for the same purpose; peace is sought through internationally shared values. UNESCO encourages the exchange of works of art among states and takes a most active role in furthering basic education in underdeveloped countries by means of technical

[5] UNESCO Constitution, Art. I, par. 1.

assistance in the realm of teaching and research methods. Clearly, through these activities minds could be changed and loyalties might well be transferred to a world community—if the Organization were permitted to develop its projects freely in such a direction.

Program demands differ, of course, with the policy aspirations of member governments. Thus the French government has been interested primarily in activities promoting cultural contact among artists, philosophers, and scientists, while the Western European nations on the whole demand assistance in their scientific undertakings, such as internationally provided computers and cyclotrons. The underdeveloped countries of Asia, the Middle East, and Latin America, however, ask that assistance to their programs of eradicating illiteracy and raising the levels of primary and technical education should take first place. The United States, by contrast, has been primarily interested in the UNESCO-sponsored development and application of mass communication techniques and the world-wide broadcasting, televising, and teaching of democratic values. These conflicts have not been resolved at all, since the program reflects compromises by meeting almost all demands made regardless of their relevance to UNESCO's primary task of changing men's minds toward peace. For the most part, however, the technical-assistance demands receive the greatest attention, though far less than their recipients claim they should. In terms of working out a world ideology, the Organization has apparently ceased to be interested in philosophical and moral questions. Since no agreement could be reached on what ideology was to take the place of existing nationalisms, UNESCO has quietly forgotten about this aspect of its functions and concentrated on technical assistance instead, though educational advancement in underdeveloped countries by no means necessarily implies the strengthening of peace.

Peace and Security. UNESCO's task is directly related to the preservation of peace even though the accomplishment of changing men's minds is obviously a very long-range project. Indirectly, FAO, ILO, and WHO are held to advance the cause of peace by bringing about conditions under which groups would be less likely to go to war against one another. Again, however, no immediate and drastic changes can be expected. Hence maintaining peace, stability, and orderly change *now* is the special function of collective-security organizations, regional or universal. The United Nations, in its political and military aspects, is charged with this task. NATO, SEATO, and the Organization of American States fulfill kindred functions on the regional level. While these collective-security or collective-self-defense organizations also exercise considerable influence in the realms of social, economic, colonial, and communications policy, the fact remains that their primary task is the preservation of peace in the immediate future, before the long-range effects optimistically expected from the specialized agencies can bear fruit. Each security organization, in a sense, is a parent body for a multitude of activities not directly connected with security; yet the basic purpose remains that of preserving peace.

2. How to Organize beyond the State Level: Forms, Aims, and Symbols. Modern international organization exhibits the widest variety and the greatest scope. Yet diversity of function and role does not confer power. How important are the decisions and debates of ILO and UN? Can UNESCO and WHO influence or direct national policies? Do these organizations administer, tax, and legislate like governments? Are their activities so vital as to approximate those of governments? Answers to these questions call for an examination of the structure, powers, symbols, and expectations associated with international organization.

Legislation. One of the pillars of governmental activity in any nation is the power to make binding law. If international organizations could exercise a legislative power they would become supranational governments, at least in their particular sphere of competence. Such a power, however, does not exist. The only approximation to legislation is the ability to prepare draft treaties, which may become part of the domestic law of the member states—if they choose to ratify. In essence, therefore, international organizations can only *propose* laws to their members but not *make* them.

In addition to the power of legislation, modern governments also exercise a decree-making power, i.e., the formulation of specific legal rules by the executive branch of the government within the framework of a basic law passed by the legislature. It is in this realm that some international organizations approach the national model. Thus ICAO has the power to define new air safety standards which are presumed to become binding for the member countries, unless they give notice to the contrary within a specified time limit. WHO has the power to work out new regulations to prevent the spread of epidemics which become binding under rules similar to ICAO's. Finally, UPU can determine new postal regulations which are accepted as binding by the member states as a matter of custom and convenience rather than on the basis of legal obligation. Obviously, the legislative power is severely restricted. It extends only to noncontroversial issues in which there is not likely to be a dissident minority in any event.

A further approximation to legislative activity is represented by the practice of convening conferences, discussions, and study groups on topics ranging from atomic disarmament to the protection of whales or the improvement of seeds. Common policy again is debated and considered, data are exchanged, and expectations are set forth, but binding law emerges from these conferences only if each participating nation chooses to ratify the decisions, if any.

Representation and Voting. Democratic legislative bodies consist of representatives elected by their home districts. They debate and vote as their conscience and interests dictate; they receive no binding instructions from their constituents. It is otherwise in international agencies. In almost all organizations, supreme power to make policy rests in an assembly composed of *instructed delegates* from member states. Each state usually has one vote, regardless of size, power, or importance. Naturally, the delegates merely carry out the orders of their home governments and seek to shape the policy of the organization in terms of national aims.

In addition to assemblies, however, most international organizations have another policy-making organ, usually called "council" or "executive board," or "executive directors" in the case of the IMF. Whenever the sphere of activity of the organization impinges directly on important national policy aims, it is this organ which exercises the bulk of the agency's power. Usually representation in the council is on a *qualitative* basis: states are given membership if they are considered particularly vital to the achievement of the organization's task. Thus the leading industrial states are automatically members of ILO's Governing Body; the countries most active in international air traffic automatically sit on ICAO's Council; and the nations most prominent in international finance—the United States and Britain—dominate the Executive Directors of the IMF and the IBRD. The principle of qualitative representation, of course, is clearly illustrated by the composition of the UN Security Council. As in assemblies, representatives on councils are usually instructed delegates of national governments.

How do these organizations make decisions? The traditional voting rule of international organizations used to be that of unanimity, regardless of the size or importance of the state. This is no longer the case. Almost all assemblies can pass resolutions by simple majority or two-thirds majority votes. However, it must be stressed again that, with the exception of UPU and some WHO resolutions, the results of these votes are *never* binding on the members. Majority voting is the basic rule in the councils as well. A new factor is frequently introduced here through the principle of *quantitative* voting: Some states are given more than one vote—or even a veto power as in the UN—by virtue of their special position and power. This is most clearly shown in the IMF, in which the United States as the largest financial contributor wields 50 per cent of the vote. However, the significance of majority decision making is far less striking in international organizations than in national legislatures because of the restricted scope of binding supranational power and because of the inability to enforce decisions once made.

Administration. National governments enforce the laws they make through the process of executive action, or administration. This requires a permanent civil service, a veritable army of officials who can regulate, tax, and conscript the individual citizen. Is there a parallel relationship between international organizations and the national communities which created them? The answer is "No."

International organizations do possess permanent civil services, their secretariats. Individuals agree not to accept orders from their home governments while they are in the employ of UN, ILO, or FAO and to give their loyalty exclusively to the top permanent officials of their organization, the Secretary-General or Director-General. Yet the function of the secretariat is extremely circumscribed. It cannot direct, coerce, threaten, or arrest anyone. It does not "administer" or "implement" in the same sense as a national bureaucracy. Its functions are confined to making studies and undertaking research in areas of international interest defined by the assembly or council, and to giving advice to national governments when requested to do so. Secretariats, also, fulfill an important function in preparing for and aiding in international conferences. Thus, today, the rendering of technical assistance is the major function of the international civil service. As such, its contributions to higher living standards and increased national bureaucratic efficiency have been considerable, without, however, having brought about a redirection of loyalties to a supranational symbol.

One of the most vital powers of national governments is the ability to tax. Here again, international organizations occupy a quite different position. With the exception of the European Coal and Steel Community and some river commissions, no agency possesses a taxing power. International organizations are financed through annual contributions assessed against the members, but not necessarily paid by them. No state can be coerced to pay up; many remain in arrears on their membership dues.

Investigations and Sanctions. Thus most international organizations neither legislate nor administer. But to the extent that member states voluntarily bind themselves by accepting the treaties and rules drafted by these agencies, what can be done to enforce the obligations? True, the violator of a sanitary or postal convention can be sued before the International Court of Justice. But that tribunal, in turn, is powerless to enforce its decisions. Is there a parallel to the policeman of the national community who can bring about compliance?

With the exception of the ILO, the IMF, and the UN itself, no international organization possesses such a power, the power of "sanction." The UN can investigate and discuss the violation of international rules in any realm, and if a breach of the peace has occurred, it can undertake collective-enforcement action, as in Korea. IMF has the power to fix the value of a nation's currency. If the nation decides to change this value without the approval of the Fund, sanctions can be taken by preventing the violator from borrowing scarce currency from the Fund when its currency becomes endangered. Used only once, this form of sanction soon demonstrated its complete ineffectiveness.

In ILO, however, the power of sanction is linked with the power of investigation. The alleged violator of an international labor convention can be accused by a government, employer, or trade union before the ILO Governing Body. Hearings may be held, missions sent to the accused state—if it permits this—and recommendations condemning the violator passed. ILO hopes that the mere act of investigation and possible verbal condemnation will prove sufficient to bring about a change in the violator's policies, through "moral" pressure. If this proves inadequate, the organization may call on the membership to undertake an economic boycott of the violator, a sanction which has never been invoked in the thirty-five-year history of ILO, despite the occurrence of violations.

Research, Advice, and Recommendations. Clearly, the efficacy of international organization does not derive from any powers analogous to those of national governments. It rests instead on the need felt by national groups and elites for the services commonly performed by assemblies and secretariats. If the research is judged impartial and useful, its findings may see application. If the advice rendered by technical assistance missions is such as to meet the interests and values of local groups, it will usually be accepted. The long-run, unspectacular impact of international organizations, therefore, is to be found in the research and advice function of the agencies.

How significant are the sweeping recommendations of international organizations as restraints on the unilateral capacity to make national policy? In the short run, the "moral" impact of recommendations is minimal. Still, the essence of international organization is its permanence and continuity. Decisions are made in accordance with procedures which do not vary from year to year, but follow an institutionalized pattern representing a minimum consensus of the member states. A forum for meeting common needs by common debate and common action is provided. Decision making grows easier. Obligations can be enacted more readily. A permanent staff is made available, even when it is not used for important tasks. Such organizations provide a framework for social action and a means for integrating and changing established behavior patterns among nations, even when the framework and the means are not always applied. Whether national states will avail themselves of the opportunities afforded by these creatures of their own making, however, still depends on the degree of incompatibility between clashing aims. Some may be adjusted by means of these processes; others—and usually those most related to intense conflict—may never even be submitted to the organization because the primary impulse for discussion may be lacking.

Symbols and Expectations. The impact of international organization on modern life, of course, depends in large measure on the amount of loyalty which individuals and groups—rather than governments—show toward these agencies. Further, it depends very largely on the extent to which common aspirations and expectations can be gratified by these institutions rather than by national governments. But most international agencies are concerned with matters which form no essential part of national beliefs and hopes. Sanitary standards, postal rates, and even the eradication of malaria or the growth of mass literacy are not symbols to which men will flock and for which they will forswear loyalty to national myths.

Even the preservation of peace—an aim with which, in the abstract, all can usually identify themselves—is an inadequate symbol. The UN or FAO, unlike national government, does not deal directly with individuals and is therefore not "experienced" by them. Individuals read of these agencies in the newspaper; but most of them have never seen a UN official, document, or building, while the corresponding manifestations of national government are familiar to all. As long as this continues, international organization will remain a field of intergovernmental activity and contact, but not an area with which groups and individuals will have any direct relationship.

Further, the abortive attempt of UNESCO to fashion a global ideology illustrates a definite hostility on the part of national elites to endowing international organizations with a life of their own. Loyalty to symbols larger than those approved by elites in power would of course endanger the sociopolitical status of those groups. They would be undermining their own justification to rule by erecting rival centers of loyalty and identification. Culture sharing and international myth building must stop short of providing substitutes for national myths, unless elites are willing to abdicate. So long as they are not, the symbols associated with international organizations cannot possibly take the place of national loyalties—and animosities.

ILO's record in its task of creating a uniform world labor code suggests the symbolic weakness of the program and task of contemporary international organizations. Between 1919 and 1952 the Organization wrote and adopted 100 labor conventions. However, of seventy-one past and present member states, ten had never ratified a single treaty, and half the members had ratified only seventeen or less. In fact, only thirteen countries ever ratified more than one-third of the total conventions adopted by the Organization. In terms of sacrificing national beliefs as well as adjusting national policies, therefore, the impact of international organization on world relations is far from overwhelming.

An international agency which does possess a set of symbols accepted by key groups in its member states, which has the rudiments of a central myth acknowledged by individuals within its territories, may facilitate the transition to a more integrated type of international life. This is true of confederations and federations. Confederations are usually established for purposes of mutual defense—they imply cooperative military, financial, and foreign policies. Though the central organs of the confederation may lack the power to bind member states to definite decisions, the ideological ties among the confederated groups are usually strong enough to permit the voluntary execution of central dispositions. The doctrinal support enjoyed by such entities is usually the incipient nationalism of an emerging nation-state, as was the weak national cohesion of the Thirteen Colonies under the Articles of Confederation, or the inklings of a larger German loyalty under the nineteenth-century German Confederation. With the fruition of this new myth, spurred and encouraged by the common institutions of the confederate structure, a new state—frequently a federal state—will ultimately develop. A basic common need—defense—will have led to the evolution of a new community with its own values, beliefs, and government.

The forms of organization, therefore, fall into a hierarchy in terms of the degree of identification the participating communities exhibit toward their creatures. Federation represents the birth of a new community, or of a very high degree of identification, of loyalty on the part of groups and individuals. International organization shows little evidence of such traits, while confederations occupy a middle position. To trace the process of political integration and assess the role of international organization in it, four constituent factors of the process appear vital: (1) communication, or the degree of understanding which exists among the participating groups; (2) standardization, or the degree of uniformity which characterizes the institutions of the participating groups; (3) cooperation, which refers to the amount of continuing common effort made by all member groups; and (4) organization, which represents the permanent institutions created to carry out the common aims of the cooperating groups.[6]

These four factors, of course, are interdependent. An increase in communication usually begets greater standardization and organization. An increase in organizational endeavor may also result in greater cooperation and standardization in the long run. It remains true at the same time, however, that organization is the last factor to be effected by a chain of stimuli which results first in an increase in communication, and then spreads along the whole ladder of factors. Organization thus occupies the position of the single most revealing index, since it facilitates the assessment of the three other constituent factors.

3. International Organization and Global Integration. What properties of international organization can be isolated as measures of group integration? What aspects of organization should be examined in order to determine the degree of communication, standardization, and cooperation in it? Four aspects of organizational life emerge as significant measures of development:

1. Scope of the Organization's Activity. If an international organization performs functions immediately related to key aims of interest groups, it may be assumed that the organization is connected with the pulse of international life. If, on the other hand, the stated task is peripheral and unimportant, the organization concerned can hardly be considered as one ap-

[6] Q. Wright, in W. F. Ogburn (ed.), *Technology and International Relations*, University of Chicago Press, Chicago, 1948, pp. 174–175.

proximating a larger community, even if it makes its decisions by majority vote and executes its own program.

2. Representation. Diplomatic representation, appointed and instructed by the home government, is indicative of a minimum of integration. Participation of private groups and the election of delegates are procedures promising a more rapid pace of intergroup cooperation in international organizations.

3. Decision Making. Majority voting by uninstructed delegates, again, is an indication of great integration of aims and aspirations. Veto powers, extremes in quantitative voting, and similar institutions are typical of the opposite condition. The question of whether the organization's decisions are binding on the membership is a related index of integration.

4. Access to Individuals. A wide scope of power touching the essentials of international life, coupled with majority voting by uninstructed delegates, able to bind governments, are not enough. In order to qualify as approaching a true community, a given organization must possess access to individuals and groups. Short of such access, the organization continues to be no more than a forum of intergovernmental consultation and cooperation. Direct contact between government and governed is an essential condition for the development of supranational loyalties and symbols.

Expanding the Scope of Activity: ECOSOC. The organs of government of a true community must exhibit a high degree of integration in *each* of the four measures stated. Still, the single most important one of these is undoubtedly the scope of action—the task—allotted to the organization. Unless the task meets the interest and support of many groups and individuals it will hardly cause a ripple in the flow of international life. Within the framework of the peace-preservation machinery of the UN, there has been established an Economic and Social Council (ECOSOC), whose task meets the core of human aspirations: to promote higher living standards and full employment, to solve economic and social problems which might create warlike tensions if permitted to fester, to encourage respect for human rights and freedoms.

Communication is provided for by having ECOSOC meet twice a year to discuss issues arising under these headings. Eighteen nations, elected periodically by the General Assembly, compose ECOSOC; however, national delegates are diplomats who receive instructions on how to vote. The possibilities of free communication, therefore, are impaired. Standardization of institutions might result from its activities as well. Resolutions aiming at the coordination of national policies and treaties designed to bring about new universal rules are the techniques for achieving standardization. Yet ECOSOC's resolutions are only recommendations; they have no binding significance. Cooperation might result nevertheless among those who choose to implement the resolutions and carry out, voluntarily, the recommendations of ECOSOC's commissions and experts. Further organization would be the net result of all these activities, and especially of the efforts of uninstructed technical experts, who, through disinterested advice, might influence the competing policies of member nations. Finally, integration could be furthered in ECOSOC's wide tasks and responsibilities through the efforts of private international groups, or nongovernmental organizations (NGO's), permitted to participate in the policy-making process. How significant have these innovations been in contributing to global integration through international organization?

The discussion of basic economic and social issues is the basic task of ECOSOC. Delegates examine and debate the world employment picture, the flow of international trade, and the conditions which make for rapid economic development. Does consensus emerge from the discussion? As a rule, each representative merely expounds the policy of his own government and hopes to persuade other nations to the same view. Since a simple majority vote suffices to pass resolutions, conclusions favoring one set of policies over another sometimes emerge. But they have no effect on international life, since no state is obligated to implement them. Discussion remains discussion; an increase in communication is hardly noticeable.

Only when the fear of alienating the sympathies of neutralist and under-developed countries motivates elites in the Western and Soviet spheres is an increase in cooperation and organization discernible. For years the West refused to contribute to the UN International Finance Corporation (IFC), designed to make low-interest loans to underdeveloped nations. The Soviet denounced the IFC as an imperialist trap. But when both camps realized that they were losing support because of their stand, they changed their positions in ECOSOC and rallied to support IFC, which began to function in 1955. The logic of the cold war had compelled cooperation which had been rejected initially.

In certain fields of contact, however, discussion is accompanied by expert study and consultation, designed to promote common international action by standardizing procedures and rules. Thus certain types of international discussion and study are designed primarily to change conditions *within* countries. No attempt is necessarily made to increase international obligations or augment the powers of international agencies. For instance, ECOSOC has studied conditions and drawn up treaties in the fields of drug addiction and control, statistical method, treatment of the blind, various aspects of economic development, and the status of women. Many of the recommendations and even treaty commitments have been accepted and the lot of individuals improved. Yet since few new international rules of a controversial nature are involved, the measure of standardization has been small, and neither cooperation nor organization has been facilitated on a supranational basis.

Other types of ECOSOC studies and draft treaties, however, deal directly with new international standards and rules and aim at the creation of new forms of international cooperation and organization. The Genocide and Human Rights Conventions are important examples.[7] Studies undertaken for the protection of minorities, the suppression of forced labor and slavery, and the assuring of freedom of information and the press are other instances of attempted standardization and cooperation through treaty drafting by ECOSOC. Studies by technical experts supplemented the assertions of government delegates. National policy statements compete with earnest and insistent presentations by numerous NGO's interested in these fields. The results in some cases have been draft treaties, laden with compromises, ratified by some states, but not usually the crucial ones. In other instances, however, the process of discussion and investigation was merely a lengthy exchange of charges and recriminations, in which not only government delegates but spokesmen of rival NGO's sought to blame and embarrass one another. The net consequence of the effort at expanding the scope of vital tasks of international organization, in such cases, is neither the achievement of cooperation nor the furthering of global integration. Instead, it merely reproduces the global ideological tensions of the cold war in the UN mirror.

To date, the processes of discussion, study, and convention drafting have brought international agreement in noncontroversial and peripheral matters. They have failed to standardize conduct and rules in the vital arenas of economic development, investment, antidepression planning, and human rights. A final field of activity of ECOSOC remains to be assessed, however: the coordination of economic and social activities undertaken by other global international organizations—e.g., ILO, FAO, IMF, and WHO—called "specialized agencies" of the United Nations. It is one of ECOSOC's functions to assure cooperation between these agencies, to avoid duplication and overlapping of effort, and to take the initiative in the creation of new specialized agencies. Coordination of activity is complicated by the fact that each of the specialized agencies is autonomous, with its own assembly, budget, and civil service. Coordination has proved to be a process of joint discussion and planning, not an act of direction by ECOSOC over the others. Joint planning, for the most part, is restricted to the exchange of information and the mutual right to attend meetings and to criticize budget and programs—without the right to dictate alternative courses. Only in the area of technical assistance to underdeveloped countries has the coordination process been carried beyond this "diplomatic" level of cooperation. Technical-assistance funds contributed by UN member nations are divided up by a Technical Assistance Board, composed of the heads of all participating agencies. Further, interagency assistance programs are here planned so that joint ILO-WHO-FAO teams of experts, for instance, may operate together in an aid-requesting

[7] See Chap. 18 for detailed discussion.

nation. Beyond this point, however, contemporary international organizations are "sovereign": they do not admit the central directing role of UN's ECOSOC.

Expanding the Scope of Activity: Colonialism. Economic and social aspirations provide one example of the attempt at expanding the scope of international organization. Another crucial area in which modern international agencies are increasingly active is the field of colonialism. The spectacle of colonial unrest and emancipation since 1945 has, of course, been striking. A dozen new nations have sprung up since the end of World War II, together accounting for almost one-third of the earth's population. At the same time, almost 200 million people remained under colonial rule—mostly in Africa and the Pacific. Many of them are now engaged in a struggle with their colonial masters for self-government and independence. More important still, the nations with newly won independence are desperately trying to bring national independence to the nonwhite populations of the Belgian, Dutch, British, French, Portuguese, Spanish, American, Australian, and New Zealand colonies.

While the policies of the colonial powers differ appreciably one from the other, it is generally true nevertheless that the West is anxious to avoid the immediate abolition or forcible transformation of the colonial system. Britain is eager to provide increasing self-government and link the advancing colonies to the Commonwealth in a confederationlike arrangement. France, by contrast, seeks to raise her colonies to a position of equality with the mother country but retain close, federationlike ties with her possessions, through the French Union. Portugal, Australia, and Belgium are making few changes in their empires, while Holland, New Zealand, and the United States are in the process of introducing full local self-government into theirs, without promising independence.

Opposition to empire among some Western groups, Asian and African impatience with imperialism, but especially the Western desire to make some concessions to colonial emancipation without giving up the colonial system, resulted in the allocation to the United Nations of important tasks dealing with non-self-governing peoples. The colonial powers were enabled to place some or all of their holdings under the supervisory authority of the United Nations, under the trusteeship system. Trust territories are to be prepared for "self-government or independence"—the West stressing the former and the East the latter—and colonial administration is to be carried on in such a fashion that the interests of the native peoples receive paramount attention. The administering power is obligated to report annually on the record of its rule and to pay heed to UN "recommendations."

Within the UN, there was set up a Trusteeship Council, composed in equal numbers of colonial and noncolonial powers. Members of the Council are governmental delegates who act, debate, and vote in accordance with instructions. The Council receives the annual report from the administering states, may send visiting missions to trust territories to inspect conditions on the spot, and may receive written and oral petitions from the native population, complaining against the administering power's policies. To date, however, only eleven of seventy-odd colonial territories have been placed under the trusteeship system.

The UN Charter also makes provision for these remaining areas. Colonial powers are pledged to ensure the "political, economic, social and educational advancement" of non-self-governing peoples, to respect their customs and institutions, and cooperate for their advancement. The Charter says nothing about missions, petitions, or international supervisory bodies; it merely arranges for an annual report to be submitted on *nonpolitical* matters to the General Assembly. Still, since 1946 a special committee of the Assembly has in fact become the informal "trusteeship council" for these territories, examining the reports and the reasons given for their nonsubmission, seeking to advance self-government and independence in colonies, and hearing oral petitioners protesting against colonial policies. Clearly, institutional development in the colonial realm has been striking since the end of World War II.

But has integration come about also in the realms of communication, standardization, and cooperation? A glance at the activities in the UN may suggest an answer. The anticolonial nations—Latin-American, Asian, Arab, and Soviet—have sought to press on the West a definite timetable for granting independence to trust territories. They have charged violations of the trust obligation and demanded an ever faster pace of development. Further, in the General Assembly the attempt is made to treat the nontrust colonies as if they too were under the trusteeship system. Exploitation of colonial peoples is denounced and held up for public condemnation whenever and wherever it is alleged by these powers. In short, the colonial sphere of UN activity is used to expedite the West's withdrawal from its former great empires.

The West, naturally, has used the colonial competence of the UN to defend its basic aims. Through the device of "strategic trusteeship" the United States has found it possible to reconcile its opposition to colonialism with the acquisition of the former Japanese islands in the Pacific. The trusteeship system was expected to facilitate the neutralization of international tension areas and to justify the continuation of Western rule over undeveloped peoples. In UN debates, the West points to its record of setting free colonies and advancing others to self-government and thus supports its claims of acting within the letter of UN Charter commands. It accuses the anticolonial nations of violating the Charter by setting up new organs and asserting powers not defined when the organization was created.

Certainly, the annual debate has not produced an international consensus. When the United States gave Puerto Rico a new constitution under which the island enjoys full local self-government, Washington ceased to submit an annual report on its administration to the UN. The anticolonial nations charged that no state could unilaterally cease transmitting information—thus in effect demanding that the UN pass on the status of Puerto Rico. When South Africa refused to place its dependency, South-West Africa, under the trusteeship system and all but annexed it in 1954, the same charges were made and action demanded. In neither instance did the accused nations change their policies as a result of the dispute. In 1952, the British evicted Africans from their land in the Tanganyika trust territory and linked the Togoland trust to a contiguous self-governing colony, the Gold Coast. Petitions and complaints from Africa arrived at the UN. Visiting missions were dispatched to the scene as the anticolonial bloc took up the cause of the petitioners. None of these efforts availed, and British policy remained unchanged. Nevertheless, it is undoubtedly true that because of continuing UN supervision and criticism, definite restraints are imposed upon the colonial powers. New Zealand granted Western Samoa a new constitution in 1947, partly as a result of UN intervention. The United States, in 1954, promised her Pacific Islanders relief from damage wrought by nuclear tests in the trust territory, partly because the Islanders complained in the Trusteeship Council. Yet no fundamental facet of colonial policy seems to have been changed because of pressure in the UN.

It must be concluded, therefore, that the mere expansion of tasks and scope under the UN—whether in economic, social, or colonial questions—has not brought with it any significant degree of international integration. Task expansion there has been. But it was not accompanied by similar changes in the pattern of representation, the process of decision making, or increasing access to groups and individuals by international authorities. Representation in ECOSOC, the Trusteeship Council, and the General Assembly is confined to instructed delegates. Voting, even though based on simple majorities, cannot result in binding decisions. Access to individuals is confined to visiting missions, petitions, and technical-assistance teams without governmental power. Task expansion, unaccompanied by these additional steps, has resulted merely in institutional and organizational development. It has failed to bring with it, thus far, any substantial increase in the amount of communication, standardization, or cooperation among contending nations.

Changing the Pattern of Representation. It is clear, therefore, that global or regional integration can take place only if representation in international organization is permitted to develop along new lines. The basic pattern of the moment is the principle of instructed, diplomatic representation. Delegates repeat and reiterate the positions of their governments and cannot depart from them. The participation of private groups is tolerated; the assistance of uninstructed experts is sometimes sought. But these departures from the diplomatic principle have so far failed to be significant whenever basic issues of national policy entered the international arena. Alternative patterns of representation, however, are suggested by the procedures followed by ILO and UNESCO.

Delegates to all ILO policy-making bodies are chosen on a tripartite basis. Each country is represented by four delegates, one each from labor and industry, and two from the government. These delegates tend to vote in accordance with their interest-group affiliation, not on the basis of nationality. Industry delegates join to vote against a united international labor opposition. Government delegates vote in accordance with instructions, but varying with the nature of the regime at home. Thus the delegates of a socialist government, for instance, will vote with labor in ILO. Interest groups are thus brought into direct and powerful relation with the organization.

In UNESCO, policy making is partly a function of national UNESCO commissions, composed of domestic interest groups concerned with international cultural and scientific issues. These groups help pick the delegations and assist in implementing the program. Nongovernmental organizations, furthermore, are active at UNESCO meetings, and many of the delegates are uninstructed. Has consensus emerged as a result of these novel forms of representation? Certainly, UNESCO has been unable to carry out its basic task of achieving ideological unity despite the minimization of governmental influence. Conflict rages in ILO despite tripartite representation. Further, since neither organization possesses any legislative power, the effect of the representational patterns cannot be tested in terms of impact on policy. Among the labor, religious, and educational elites the symbols of ILO and UNESCO certainly enjoy more support than is true of FAO or UPU. But among veterans' groups and industrial leaders opposition to ILO and UNESCO is lively. Negative symbols raised by the opposition encounter the positive identification of ILO and UNESCO supporters, but a net gain in the attraction exercised by international organization can hardly be established. Interest-group representation, therefore, hardly seems to be a panacea when taken by itself.

Changing the Pattern of Decision Making. Majority voting and an increased role for uninstructed experts have been held out as developmental steps through which international organization might make a greater contribution to global integration. As far as the pattern of voting is concerned, the agencies in which unanimity is required are extremely few in number. The trend is in the direction of more and more decision making by simple majorities. Unless this is accompanied, however, by an increase in the scope of authority and legislative capacity, the power of voting alone will do little toward integration.

Those who object to the instructed government delegate as the key actor in international agencies point out that communication, standardization, and cooperation will never come about unless aims and aspirations other than official government policy find expression in international organizations. They point to some of ECOSOC's commissions for confirmation of their thesis that the best and most acceptable international decisions are made by uninstructed experts. The narcotic-drug-control machinery of the UN, for example, is controlled by such personnel; drug allocation and quotas are determined in isolation from the pressures and tensions of international conflicts. Hence the demand is heard that human-rights commissions, economic bodies, and colonial organs be similarly staffed.

In reply it must be stressed that expert decision making thus far has been adopted only in thoroughly noncontroversial fields of activity. Areas of contact tied to contending myths and values remain subject to the established decision-making pattern. Because nations and elites feel strongly on the remaining controversial issues they are unwilling to delegate power to experts over whom they lack control. While integration might well result from a change in the pattern, the decision to make the change would require first an abatement in ideological conflict. Moreover, in such agencies in which the ideological fissures of our era are related to the organization's task—as in UNESCO—uninstructed experts have tended to reflect precisely the same arguments and disagreements which characterize their instructed governmental colleagues.

Access to Groups and Individuals. Communication, and especially cooperation, cannot be expected to develop on a large scale until individuals and groups everywhere are brought into such direct contact with international organizations that symbols of integration can gain acceptance. NGO's, it is true, have such contact; but it makes itself felt only during the policy-planning stage, not in the act of implementation. By and large, international organizations address their recommendations—and occasional orders—to governments only. Departures from this rule are developing, however. What are they, and what significance do they have?

Ever since ECOSOC undertook the preparation of two draft covenants of human rights, one of its commissions has been receiving complaints and petitions on the wholesale violation of freedoms by national governments. By 1952 no less than 25,297 such petitions had been received from all over the world, most of them dealing with acts of political persecution. Clearly, individuals *do* expect action from the UN, even though ECOSOC not only lacks the power to deal with complaints but is not even officially empowered to receive them. Yet discussions of the complaints almost invariably degenerate into ideological and propaganda charges between the rival camps in the organization. A similar fate befell UN efforts to inquire into charges of slave labor in the Soviet Union, though theoretically contact with individuals could be established in the process of investigation.

ILO's efforts to protect the freedom of trade unions to organize have met similar problems. Charges and countercharges by Communist and anti-Communist trade unions resulted in ILO investigations. The hearings involved direct contact with groups and individuals. Yet the organization was never permitted by a Communist state to check the charges. Access to individuals was denied it within the territory of the alleged violator. The right of access, though only for purposes of investigation, continues to be rudimentary. No regular contact has yet been established between global agencies and the individuals who ultimately are to be affected by their recommendations.

The major exception to this rule lies in the field of technical assistance. FAO, WHO, and UN teams of experts, of course, have continuous contact with individuals and groups in aid-requesting nations. It is conceivable that in the long run such relations, as well as the continued efforts of ECOSOC and ILO, will drive the existence of international organizations and their services into the consciousness of individuals everywhere. To result in integration, however, this would call for *equal* access everywhere, including the Communist bloc. The rapid development of symbols of loyalty can hardly be expected on the basis of present trends.

It must be concluded that changes in the pattern of representation, decision making, access to individuals, and even the drastic expansion of the fields of activity of international organizations, taken by themselves, cannot lead to rapid integration of the globe. The ideological drives which condition public policy must first be changed so as to make possible the development of *all* these factors *together*. In short, symbolic cohesion and agreement on aims must *precede* the institutional alterations required for integration. Further, even the drastic alteration of institutional patterns can hardly be expected to result in habits of common action unless the legislative and executive powers of the organizations are enlarged at the same time. Without the power to make vital binding decisions, mere majority voting by uninstructed, elected representatives will not result in new larger loyalties. But the delegation of such powers to international organizations by the national communities which created and use them first calls for sufficient ideological unity among these nations to make the delegation seem desirable.

4. Integration, Federalism, and Functionalism. The discussion of the relationship between group myths and the forms of common action has led to the conclusion that the institutions of cooperation and organization must represent a significant amount of consensus among the myths and symbols of participating groups before the community level can be attained. It is equally true, however, that once institutions are established these forms themselves can become the agents of ever-increasing community sentiments and of ever more closely knit myths and symbols. The pattern of development seems to be circular: a consensus on ends, values, and myths among participating groups in all member nations is necessary for the establishment of a lasting organization aiming at the eventual formation of a community; once these institutions are established, however, they may themselves become the instruments of further integration among the participants and thereby result in the evolution of an even greater consensus on ends and values. As a student of American federalism has said, "The integration of a society like ours, then, depends upon the existence both of common values and of institutions. The former generate the latter, but the latter react to give outward substance to the former." [8]

Critics of modern international organization abound. Nationalists suspect all forms of international cooperation which tend toward the creation of institutions above the state level. But people shaken by the insecurities and tensions of the nuclear era also attack international organization as being an inadequate instrument for the realization of peace and plenty. Ideologically and institutionally they propose alternative approaches to global integration, some of which are gaining in doctrinal importance. Federalism and functionalism—universal and regional—are among these approaches.

Federalism in Principle. Federation differs from all the forms of common action so far examined. It is the one form of unified conduct which results in the creation of a larger entity which has all the characteristics of a new national community and which is, in effect, a new state. It takes over the most important functions of the former states which merge in it; its scope of action can encompass all the areas of governmental activity delegated to it by the constituent members. These in time may become so large as to extinguish for all practical purposes the identity of the member states, who may be left with nothing but the power to license peddlers and dispose of garbage. The usual development of a federation's scope of power begins with foreign policy, defense, and communications. In these areas the member states abdicate all power to make independent policy. Other fields usually slide into the federation's scope soon thereafter. Once a federal government has assumed jurisdiction over a field of action previously subject to member-state regulation, the federal regulations generally command precedence over possibly conflicting state measures.

Clearly, the emergence of a new community, implying the voluntary submersion of the constituent communities in a larger whole, presupposes the existence of an overriding sense of common destiny, of belonging together, of having not only common needs, but a common stake in the future. It presupposes, in short, the existence of a myth transcending the belief systems of the contracting states. Symbols commanding the support of key interest groups in *each* of the federating units are already in existence, such as slogans of "general welfare" or the "common defense." Unanimous acceptance of these symbols by all the people in the federating states is not necessary; but unless important elites are favorably disposed federation is unthinkable. However, once a federation is securely established, once the symbols of cohesion are directed toward the federation and not the member

---

[8] Robert C. Angell, *The Integration of American Society*, McGraw-Hill, New York, 1941, p. 28.

states, the new organization acquires a life of its own. Its preservation then comes to be an end in itself in the minds and beliefs of its constituent groups.

Federations have governments at their head, and not conferences or committees of ministers. Their law is not international law, but law in the usual sense of the word. Legislation is made by representatives chosen by groups and individuals and not by governments, and these representatives cannot be instructed by the state from which they may happen to come. Representation, in short, is based on affiliation with political parties—not states.

Finally, in most federations member states are not free to terminate their association with the union when they choose. Federal constitutions are binding in perpetuity. By joining a federation a state consents to relinquish its identity as an independent political unit and not to recover it, and thereby gives the federal state direct access to groups and individuals. No wonder that advocates of world peace have long held out world federation as the only means for achieving their aim. Federal government, because it rests on the consent of its members to join together in a new community, in effect removes these members from the realm of international relations and transforms their association into a congeries of direct contacts between individuals and groups. Ultimately, these groups join with each other and thus form federationwide interest groups, competing with each other for control over the federal government. Thus a community takes the place of what had been a society before the act of federation.

World Federalism. World federalists are concerned with applying these principles to the integration of the globe *now*. They aim at the creation of a federal community of states—on a global scale—to take the place of the present society of states and their international organizations. Its main ends and values are simply the preservation of peace by depriving the still sovereign members of the world society of the independent power to wage war. As their largest group, the United World Federalists, put it: [9]

We believe that peace is not merely the absence of war, but the presence of justice, of law, of order—in short, of government, and the institutions of government; that world peace can be created and maintained only under a world federal government, universal and strong enough to prevent armed conflict between nations, and having direct jurisdiction over the individual in those matters within its authority.

The overriding assumption of federalists is the proposition that the desire to avoid war is a sufficiently universal value to persuade groups and individuals everywhere to unite. They equate peace with order, with the possibility of initiating change in the relations of interdependent groups by orderly means. The application of peaceful means—majority voting and the

[9] United World Federalist manifesto quoted in F. L. Schuman, *The Commonwealth of Man,* Knopf, New York, 1952, p. 439.

willingness of the defeated minority to abide by the will of the majority—demands the immediate establishment of one government for all potential adversaries. World federalists thus place their faith in the *institution* of common government without reference to the union of national myths which must precede the creation of forms of integration.

Not only do communities depend on unified myths for their creation and development, but significant elites must be swayed by these myths in order to agree to the establishment of common institutions. These elites must be persuaded that their aims and values can be best met by the forms proposed. As long as the values of world federation are not embraced in the ideologies of such elites it seems hardly possible that the institutional changes advocated will find acceptance on the part of the ruling groups. Available information confirms the fact that world federalism is not a myth which finds ready acceptance among significant contemporary elites.

The movement for the integration of Western Europe, however, seems to prove that *regional* federation is possible. The goals and values of this movement explain its greater measure of success. It aims not so much at universal peace as at the military and political strengthening of the Western European democratic community. Its myth is the preservation of the democratic way of life of the member communities against totalitarian dangers from within and without. It seeks prosperity through the merger of Western European industrial and economic life. It works for the strengthening of democratic institutions by making the protection of civil rights and liberties the business of the whole Western European cultural entity. Its beliefs thus rest on the cultural and ideological features which are common to key elites throughout the Western European countries. Its ideology is based on a far larger and more profoundly experienced number of needs than is true of world federalism. In short, it has a reality in terms of important motivations of significant groups.

Functionalism. Advocates of global or regional integration who despair of the speedy realization of the federal principle advance the principle of "functional" integration as a more realistic alternative. They argue that "we are not likely to get peace by trying to argue nations into giving up what divides them, but only by striving practically to strengthen what unites them." [10] Hence they favor the maximization of international communication, standardization, cooperation, and especially organization in the fields of agriculture, labor, transport, and finance. In the long run, they argue, cohesion in these "noncontroversial" areas of international contact will produce an abatement of international antagonisms and thus facilitate integrated political organization as a last culminating step.

Clearly, the functional argument assumes a rather sharp difference between

[10] David Mitrany and Maxwell Garnett, *World Unity and the Nations,* National Peace Council, London, ca. 1950. Quoted in Schuman, *op. cit.,* pp. 296–297.

technical and political questions. Technical matters are held to be uncontroversial. Hence they could be used as a basis for stronger international organizations, since nations would not object to delegating power in an area of little importance. But even though a given question might be technical at one time, it follows by no means that it will continue to be in the future. A change in the nature of the groups constituting the government may invest any issue with a new significance which pushes it into the realm of political controversy. A noncontroversial function, "technical" for the duration of its removal from political conflict, may cease being so as a result of new group demands and aspirations in one or several member states.

Indeed, the record of functional activity in the specialized agencies of the UN seems to prove that the expansion of powers and scope is possible only as a result of a *political* agreement, which is in itself dependent upon the absence of clashing aims among elites in member nations. Task expansion has proved possible—in ILO, FAO, UNESCO, and WHO—only in fields far removed from the tasks vital to global integration. The institutions of these organizations are not such as to make possible the dominance of the majority's will. Disagreement prevails over what is "technical." Hence, in FAO, ILO, and UNESCO, functions and powers related to integration have actually been *reduced,* as studies and advice have gained prominence as the major organizational activities. The distinction between functional and political activities in international organization is meaningless, if we except such purely peripheral activities as postal communications.

The influence of the East-West conflict on functional international organization demonstrates the continued victory of political considerations. Though theoretically outside the realm of political rivalry, almost all the specialized agencies of the United Nations have recently been drawn into the cold-war arena. One after another, they have adopted resolutions pledging cooperation with the political objectives of the United Nations. One after another, they have decided, under the influence of the Western bloc, to reorganize their activities in such a fashion as to be able to play their role in the *political* task of preventing Communist expansion. In short, instead of remaining outside the basic conflict of myths which prevails today, they have become an integral part of it. The intensity of the world conflict has greatly blurred any possible distinction between functional and political activity.

As a result, functionalism remains relevant to integration only in the regional realm, as in Western Europe. In the absence of basic rivalry, functionalist arguments retain some validity. In global terms, however, only such questions as postal rates and weather information can today be considered "noncontroversial."

5. Contemporary International Organization. World federation not being more than an incipient political movement and regional federation being confined to one or two culturally integrated corners of the globe, the bulk of the eighty-odd national communities possess no integrated bonds with each other. In our era, international organization and intergovernmental agreements are the dominant forms of cooperation among states. They show little evidence of anything more than the most rudimentary kind of association and cooperation formalized by entities like the United Nations. International organization with a limited scope of powers and activities, functioning without binding majority voting, dependent upon instructed diplomats, and lacking direct access to groups and individuals is the prevalent approach to common needs and problems. Membership in these organizations, invariably, can be terminated almost at will by a nation which considers that its interests are no longer served by participation.

The fact remains that there exist today a dozen international organizations associated with the general structure of the United Nations, a score or more regional units, and a great many more organizations with modest aims and budgets, associated neither with the United Nations nor with regional groupings. The mere number of these efforts at common action is impressive. Into what over-all categories do these efforts fit, in terms of their contribution to cohesion and integration?

Technical versus Political Organization. Whenever an international activity is recognized as desirable and necessary by elites, appropriate organizations will be created to meet the need. The vital question, however, is: "Under what conditions will the organization be given the power to make decisions binding the constituent governments? When will legislative and executive action be permitted instead of research and discussion?" The record of international organization indicates that in "technical" areas of contact, the powers of the organization are usually greater than in the "political" field.

But how can the two be distinguished, since the discussion of functionalism has demonstrated the absence of a hard-and-fast difference? Modern history seems to support the conclusion that certain types of action are considered so necessary or desirable to nations—regardless of whether they are enemies or friends—that efficient and governmentlike international efforts are possible. This is strikingly true, for instance, in the collection of health and epidemiological statistics, the combating of disease, the setting of postal rates and rules, the standardization of telecommunications equipment, the setting of air safety standards, and the dissemination of weather reports. Binding majority voting, expert decision making, interest-group representation, and the prompt execution of decisions by governments all obtain in these fields.

To stress the "technical" quality of this work, however, is really to point to its lack of relevance to basic world problems as well. In the minds of elites and policy makers, these issues have nothing to do with the fundamental conflicts of world politics and economics. International action has developed strikingly precisely because these activities are so technical as to be far removed from the mainsprings of political motives and aims. Because this is so, moreover, the advance of technical consultation and action bears no relation to the integration of nations into larger units.

Consequently, it is hardly surprising that "political" international agencies lack the governmentlike attributes of the technical organizations. The preservation of security is an obvious instance of competing political aims within the framework of the United Nations. But the same is true of commodity prices, labor standards, medical education, economic development, financial lending, cartel control, and education for world citizenship. All these activities, though necessitating the employment of technical personnel, are political in that they spring from major policy aims and aspirations. Ideology and myth, which hardly enter the areas of postal rates or malaria statistics, are vital in defining policies toward international finance, health, and agricultural development, not to mention security. Thus the bulk of organized cooperation among nations today remains in the political realm and is characterized by mutually antagonistic motives and approaches. Since defeat for a national aim in the voting of the organization would have direct effects on subsequent national policy, elites continue to withhold legislative and executive power from political international organizations. Most importantly, they reserve their right to withdraw from these agencies.

Universal versus Regional Organization. A second major distinction between types of international organization is connected with the geographic scope assigned to them. Some organizations are by design regional rather than universal in their membership. The nature of their task and the need which leads to their creation may be of a geographically restricted variety. Thus the Rhine River Commission, by necessity, had to include primarily the states which had shipping on the Rhine River. Such organizations are usually technical in nature.

A quite different form of regionalism is created when a group of states have made a deliberate decision to unite in common action among themselves, thereby implicitly excluding states outside the area concerned. Since such regional organizations are usually charged with collective security— though this is not uniformly true—they imply the security of their region as opposed to some outside region or regions which might endanger them. Moreover, under the stress of actual or potential world conflict, regional organizations in the Atlantic, the Western Hemisphere, and the Middle East areas have acquired economic, social, and cultural functions which make them rivals of the agencies associated with the UN. Local defense, and not global integration, however, is the aim underlying the effort. Hence regional organizations will be strong and viable in exact proportion to the weakness of universal organization. The record of universal organization in the security realm will be examined in Chapter 20, while the advent of regionalism is the subject of Chapter 21.

ADDITIONAL CASE-STUDY MATERIAL

Alexandrowicz, H.: *International Economic Organizations,* Praeger, New York, 1953.

Allen, C. E.: "World Health and World Politics," *International Organization,* vol. 4, November, 1950.

Angell, R. C.: *The Integration of American Society,* McGraw-Hill, New York, 1941.

Armstrong, J. A.: "The Soviet Attitude toward UNESCO," *International Organization,* May, 1954.

Basch, A.: "The International Bank for Reconstruction and Development," *International Conciliation,* no. 455, 1949.

Bates, M. L.: "Tanganyika: The Development of a Trust Territory," *International Organization,* February, 1955.

Behrman, J.: "Political Factors in U.S. International Financial Cooperation," *American Political Science Review,* vol. 47, June, 1953.

Bidwell, P. C., and W. Diebold: "The United States and the ITO," *International Conciliation,* no. 449, March, 1949.

Corbett, P. E.: *The Individual and World Society,* Publication 2, Princeton University, Center for Research on World Political Institutions, Princeton, N.J., 1953.

De Rusett, Alan: *Strengthening the Framework of Peace,* Royal Institute of International Affairs, London, 1950.

Deutsch, K.: *Political Community at the International Level,* Doubleday, New York, 1954.

Gorter, Wytze: "GATT after Six Years: An Appraisal," *International Organization,* February, 1954.

Hambidge, G.: "The Food and Agriculture Organization at Work," *International Conciliation,* no. 432, June, 1947.

Hexner, E.: "The Soviet Union and the International Monetary Fund," *American Journal of International Law,* vol. 37, 1946.

Hutchins, R. M., et al.: "Symposium on Proposals for Now Revising the United Nations into a World Federal Government," *Congressional Digest,* August–September, 1948.

Huth, A.: "Cooperative Radio Agreements," *International Organization,* vol. 6, August, 1952.

International Labor Organization, *Lasting Peace the ILO Way,* 1951.

"The International Labor Organization since the War," *International Labour Review,* February, 1953.

Laves, W.: "UNESCO and Peace," *Political Quarterly,* April, 1951.

Levi, W.: *Fundamentals of World Organization,* University of Minnesota Press, Minneapolis, 1950.

Maclaurin, J.: *The United Nations and Power Politics,* Harper, New York, 1951.

Mason, A.: "The Nature of Our Federal Union Reconsidered," *Political Science Quarterly,* vol. 65, December, 1950.

May, H. L.: "Narcotic Drug Control," *International Conciliation,* no. 485, November, 1952.

McIntyre, E.: "Weighted Voting in International Organizations," *International Organization,* November, 1954.

Mitrany, D.: *A Working Peace System: An Argument for the Functional Development of International Organization.*

—— and M. Garnett: *World Unity and the Nations,* National Peace Council, London, 1950.

Moser, G.: "The International Labor Organization," *Harvard Business Review,* vol. 30, July–August, 1952.

Niebuhr, R.: "The Theory and Practice of UNESCO," *International Organization,* vol. 4, February, 1950.

Ogburn, W. F. (ed.): *Technology and International Relations,* University of Chicago Press, Chicago, 1948.

Ording, A.: *The Non-governmental Organizations: Some Proposals for Immediate and Long Term Considerations,* Carnegie Endowment, New York, May 31, 1949.

Rees, E.: "The Refugee and the UN," *International Conciliation,* no. 492, June, 1953.

Ristelhueber, R.: "The International Refugee Organization," *International Conciliation,* no. 470, April, 1951.

Robinson, K.: "World Opinion and Colonial Status," *International Organization,* November, 1954.

Schaaf, C. H.: "The United Nations Economic Commission for Asia and the Far East," *International Organization,* vol. 7, November, 1953.

Schuman, F. L.: *The Commonwealth of Man,* Knopf, New York, 1952.

Sharp, W.: *International Technical Assistance,* Public Administration Service, Chicago, 1952.

United Nations: *Handbook of the United Nations and the Specialized Agencies,* Department of Public Information, 1948.

Van Wagenen, R.: *Research in the International Organization Field, Some Notes on a Possible Focus,* Publication 1, Princeton University, Center for Research on World Political Institutions, Princeton, N.J., 1952.

Van Zandt, J. P.: "The Chicago Civil Aviation Conference," *Foreign Policy Reports,* vol. 20, no. 23, 1945.

Woodbridge, G.: *United Nations Relief and Rehabilitation Administration,* 3 vols., Columbia University Press, New York, 1950.

Wright, Q.: *Problems of Stability and Progress in International Relations,* University of California Press, Berkeley, Calif., 1954.

―――― (ed.): *The World Community,* Chicago University Press, Chicago, 1948.

Chapter 20

THE UNITED NATIONS AND COLLECTIVE SECURITY

FAO and WHO aim at raising global living standards; ILO seeks to standardize the welfare of labor; ICAO is designed to assure safety on international air lanes. All these functions and assignments are explicit. They can be implemented with a variety of techniques which generate a minimum of controversy once the basic aims of the organizations have been accepted. The maintenance of "collective security," however, is a far more general task and consequently immeasurably more difficult to define so as to satisfy all nations, not to mention the difficulties implied in carrying it out. Security is a concept including within its confines questions of economic stability and expansion, ideological satisfaction and demand, military fear and safety. By contrast, the regulation of air lanes and the prevention of epidemics are noncontroversial and easily isolated aspects of national policy. To appreciate the altogether different problems involved in the prevention of war through collective security, the properties of this device must be carefully defined.

1. What Is Collective Security? Nations and their elites seek, first of all, their own survival and safety in a competitive international society. Armaments, alliances, propaganda, and foreign aid are age-old techniques for assuring the safety of ruling groups, or cementing the *status quo*. By making the search for national security a "collective" task, emphasis is thrown on universal rights, duties, and procedures as well as institutions, instead of the purely unilateral and bilateral arrangements traditional in the international society. Collective security is a device through which elites hope to bolster the *status quo* by guaranteeing each other's safety on a global basis.

Aims of self-preservation, however, compete with aims of self-extension and imperialism. Preserving the *status quo* assumes that all nations shun expansion at each other's expense. If one member of the international society should seek aggrandizement, the principle of collective security decrees that the other members will unite in defense of the existing order, thus deterring the imperialist state. Collective security also implies, however, the possibility of meeting expansive aims by means short of force. Peaceful change within the framework of a universal international organization is held out as the means whereby the international society can judge the claims for extension put forward by the dissatisfied elite, and perhaps meet it by negotiated adjustments rather than force. Preserving the *status quo* and providing for peaceful change among nations is the dual task of organizations for collective security. It calls for nothing short of banning—or at least limiting—war by reconciling aims of self-preservation with those of self-extension.

Law, Opinion, and Force. This task of collective-security organizations rests on three main pillars: defining rights, duties, and procedures through international law; mobilizing world opinion; and arranging for the international application of armed force. Ideology and institutions would thus combine in these constituents to assure both stability and peaceful change.

International law, on paper, seems to provide the ideological and institutional props required by collective security. It establishes the right of nations to exist and the duty not to resort to force in seeking change. Procedurally, it makes available courts and arbitration tribunals, arguments, and opportunities for meeting claims peacefully. No elite has to use violence to attain its aims—provided it is able to persuade others that its case is a good one.

World opinion is an equally important ideological pillar of the process of pacific settlement in collective security. Thus Woodrow Wilson argued that punitive measures are unimportant as a means to preserve security. He counted on the force of world opinion as being hostile to violations of legal rights. Since each nation has a right to its independent existence, world ideological support for this principle was held sufficient to deter a potential lawbreaker. So long as opinion in all nations accepted the rule that no international dispute was so important as to warrant recourse to violence, sufficient ideological support for collective security would be provided by world opinion. As institutionalized through assemblies and conferences, world opinion would thus buttress the abstract injunctions of international law.

Finally, the use of armed force is a major support for the principle of collective security. The expanding state violating the *status quo* without recourse to pacific-settlement methods would be defeated and punished by the combined might of the law-respecting nations in the organization. But the mere certainty of such force being mustered would be sufficient to deter aggressive elites and induce them to seek change by peaceful means, within the framework of the organization.

Contradictions in Collective Security. Yet collective security is commonly considered a contradiction in terms, a fallacy, and an illusion. Thus Walter Lippmann wrote that [1]

The trouble with collective security is . . . that when the issue is less than the survival of the great nations, the method of collective security will not be used because it is just as terrifying to the policeman as it is to the lawbreakers. It punishes the law-enforcing states, at least until they have paid the awful price of victory, as much as the law-breaking states. . . . There would be little en-

[1] *New York Herald Tribune*, Jan. 15, 1951.

forcement of law in our cities if in order to arrest burglars, murderers and viola-
tors of the traffic ordinances the police had to start a fight in which the court-
house, the jail and their own homes were likely to be demolished. . . . The
method of collective security is, I repeat, too crude, too expensive, and too un-
reliable for general and regular use. . . .

Obviously, the carrying out of a security function by a universal organization implies the existence of some rule or body of rules, such as the principle
of conduct urged by President Wilson. But, as Lippmann's sweeping criticism
indicates, a good deal more is required for universal action against infractions
of the rules. The security of all members of the organization must be equally
important to all these members. Each infraction of the peace, even though
it may be directed by Paraguay against Bolivia and be of no concern to
Europe or Asia, must be considered vital by all member states. The interests
of each must include the security of each, no matter how small, remote, or
unimportant the other's security may seem. In the words of Maxim Litvinov,
first Soviet delegate to the League of Nations, "Peace must be indivisible."
The indivisibility of peace, then, assumes the lasting willingness of all member
states to act and suffer in defense of collective security, however defined in
specific issues.

Collective-security organization, to be successful, assumes further that a
generally acceptable code of law be so framed as to accommodate the aspirations of all the members. Specifically, this presupposes that such national aims
as seek merely to retain unchanged existing international conditions, i.e., the
forces of the *status quo,* be protected in the rules of conduct. It presupposes
further, however, that the aims of those seeking change be satisfied as well.
If either of these sets of aspirations be excluded, the states concerned would
not join the organization, and therefore would not agree to any common
rules of conduct at all.

All these assumptions, of course, can be reduced to one basic proposition:
if the establishment of a collective-security organization rests on a momentary consensus among the aims of ruling groups in the participating countries,
the further success of the organization depends on the continuation of that
consensus or on the evolution of a genuine community from the organization's framework. Motivations of ruling groups are the determinants of policy.
The policies of member states—whether they accord with the assumptions we
stated or not—determine the success or failure of collective security. Success
thus depends on whether the original balance between *status quo* motivations and the desire for change can be reconciled in practical policies assuring peaceful change. Such policies, in turn, depend on the constancy of aims
among key interest groups in the nations on whose cooperation collective
security rests.

Two features in the dynamics of international relations thus would seem
to make the practice of collective security most difficult: the tendency of

aims to undergo change, and the fact that the firm pillars of conduct which must underlie a security organization are of doubtful strength in international society. The examination of national foreign policies has indicated that motivations change as new interest groups come to power within the state and that even the policy aims of given groups are subject to change under the impact of a variety of factors. Furthermore, it is clear that international law is both ideologically and institutionally too weak to buttress firm collective security. World opinion exhibits none of the features of consensus on which Wilson pinned his hopes, and the application of force remains subject to the vagaries Lippmann stated. Consequently the dual task of collective security has been given a number of institutional expressions, each representing a compromise with the basic principle.

Four such compromise patterns have been evolved so far in the history of universal collective-security attempts, each standing for somewhat different concepts of international life and conduct. Briefly, these are (1) the principle of universal security through the "united will of states," the concept incorporated into the League of Nations Covenant; (2) the "concert" principle, expressed in the UN Charter; (3) the "permissive enforcement" principle, practiced and advocated in the United Nations after the advent of the cold war; and (4) the "balancing" principle of security, which made its appearance in the UN in 1951. Each of these is subject to the features and determinants that have been stated. Each must now be examined in turn.

2. The United Will of States: Collective Security under the League of Nations. If the language of the League Covenant is to be taken at its face value, a high degree of consensus as to the universal need to prevent all aggression would seem to have prevailed after 1919. Thus, the members of the organization declared that they "undertake to respect and preserve as against external aggression the territorial integrity and existing political independence of all members of the League." [2] Further, they asserted that "any war or threat of war, whether immediately affecting any of the Members of the League or not, is hereby declared a matter of concern to the whole League, and the League shall take any action that may be deemed wise and effectual to safeguard the peace of nations." [3] Every member state, in short, was responsible for the peace of every other member. Security was a universal concern for all. The united will of all was to be mustered against the designs of the would-be aggressor.

Against this striking concept of collective security, however, must be placed the procedures actually established to implement it. While the League could mediate and conciliate disputes and while members were obligated to avail themselves of such services, no League decision was binding. Even then resolutions, whether to preserve the *status quo* or to change it peacefully, re-

[2] League of Nations Covenant, Art. 10.
[3] *Ibid.,* Art. 11.

quired a unanimous vote for adoption. Each power, large or small, could thus block action. Enforcement measures could be recommended by the organization to the member states—i.e., the alter ego of any member at Geneva could recommend to its home authorities that the guarantees of the Covenant be backed with force. Yet member states, of course, were not obligated to carry out the recommendation. Established treaties—i.e., international conditions favoring the *status quo*—could be changed by the Assembly, but this required the consent of the member at whose expense the change was to be made. Collective security through the "united will of all," then, merely implied joint action if and when the issue was one on which all the members could experience equal need, urgency, and concern. Put more bluntly, in terms of these procedural limitations the principle merely called for joint consultations in the event of a threat to the peace.

Policies of Member States. That the acceptance of the League Covenant did not imply the firm establishment of a balance between those committed to the *status quo* and others dedicated to revision of it is made plain by the history of collective security between 1919 and 1939. That whatever convergence of group motives had prevailed at the founding of the organization was soon to evaporate thereafter is equally implicit in that record. As new motives dictated new policies, the established concepts and procedures of the Covenant ceased to serve any purpose.

As might be expected from the nature of international relations, the rules of the Covenant were interpreted by each of the member states in accordance with national policy aspirations. Thus France and Italy considered these rules primarily as protection for the new lands and rights and powers they acquired as a result of their having been on the winning side in World War I. If a future dispute arose in which Germany should once more claim any of her former rights, the collective-security machinery would work to France's benefit, since a French veto could stop a pro-German decision; but as long as Germany was not a member of the League, France could get support for her anti-German policies through the League. Hence the French even argued for an international army in 1919 and binding decision-making power for the international organization because they were certain that such instruments would redound to French security.

The British interpretation, in many respects, was exactly the opposite. British leaders opposed an international army and binding decision-making power. Collective security for Britain did not imply French security against Germany, or Italian security against a revisionist Austria. Britain was not at all certain in 1919 that she wanted to participate in international action against any and every future attempt to revise the peace treaties, and consequently collective security meant only that the British government would insist on being consulted in future breaches of the peace. The British were quite sure that they would ignore recommendations to use force if the violator of the Covenant was a small state in which Britain was not interested.

In principle, of course, all the victor states believed that collective security meant their security against Germany, Austria, Turkey, and the Soviet Union. These states, in turn, either considered the League as a conspiracy against their security or hoped to join the organization in order to avail themselves of the peaceful-change possibilities inherent in the Covenant. When Germany and Russia were allied with the Western powers they welcomed membership in the League. When, however, their aims of self-extension forced them into a position of opposing the Franco–British–League of Nations policy of stability and peaceful change, Berlin and Moscow denounced and sabotaged the organization.

Before the advent of militantly expansionist Nazism in Germany the League's peacemaking record had been far from impressive. Between 1920 and 1937, thirty-seven major international disputes and crises occurred. Of these only fourteen were referred to the League, while mediation and conciliation managed to settle peacefully only six. The remainder either were settled outside the League framework or else resulted in war.

The Death of the League. With the rise of Nazism in Germany and the initiation of an imperialist policy by Fascist Italy, the entire constellation of forces on which the League had been founded underwent drastic change. In the realm of disarmament, the Western powers had hoped to achieve security for the *status quo* and also to accommodate the German demands for change in the form of permitting democratic Germany a measure of rearmament. The rise of Hitler made this impossible, since the Nazis demanded equality in armaments with their Western neighbors. The disarmament conference therefore ended in complete failure as the dictators sought revision *outside* the consensual framework of the League.

This, in turn, raised a crucial dilemma for France and Britain: should they insist on the pro–*status quo* provisions of the Covenant and invoke collective security to restrain Italo-German self-extension? Or should they meet the revisionist claims through "appeasement"? Paris and London sought to do both and in the process demonstrated the impossibility of collective security through the united will of nations.

When, in 1934, Mussolini gave evidence of wishing to attack independent Ethiopia the test case arose. Hoping to enlist Italy on their side in the effort to restrain German claims, Britain and France indicated to Rome that they would not seriously oppose an Italian move against Ethiopia—despite the assurances of the Covenant—if Mussolini joined an anti-German coalition. When Ethiopia appealed to the League of Nations, indifference and delay greeted her complaints. As Italian troops attacked, the League found that aggression had occurred and voted an economic boycott against Italy—after further delay. However, France and Britain included neither the closing of the vital Suez Canal nor the withholding of oil in the sanctions, which therefore proved completely ineffective.

Absolute collective security had been sacrificed to the hope of obtaining security against one revisionist nation at the expense of appeasing the other. In 1936, Germany took advantage of preoccupation with Ethiopia to reoccupy the Rhineland, while Mussolini left his Western associates in the lurch and concluded a pact with Hitler. Indifference over distant Ethiopia had proved the "united will of states" a fiction. The attempt to reconcile the *status quo* with demands for change by making some concessions had proved to be a failure.

Clearly, the language of the Covenant had not made any serious inroads on the aims and techniques of foreign policy. When safety seemed obtainable through the device of collective security, as in 1919 and 1920, elites supported the League. When, however, an unforeseen situation and changed motives among leading groups imposed the need for a new policy in the thirties, collective security was discarded as inapplicable and undesirable. Motives and situations had changed, and with them the urge to live up to the Covenant. True, national policy preferences defeated an international principle. But the international principle had gained recognition in 1918 only because it seemed to satisfy national policy aspirations—temporarily.

3. The Concert Principle: Collective Security in the United Nations Charter. What seemed to be a temporary agreement among the world's major nations at the end of World War II made possible the writing of the United Nations Charter and launched the second major attempt at universal collective-security organization. As in 1919, each of the participating governments saw in collective security an apparent method for realizing national security. While the earlier efforts were largely directed at keeping the postwar *status quo* against Germany, in 1945 the harmony among the victor states consisted in their common desire to prevent a renewal of the kind of German and Japanese totalitarianism which had challenged their existence and institutions.

Policy Aims in 1945. The common determination to prevent the recurrence of fascist imperialism enabled the three major powers of 1945—the United States, the Soviet Union, and Britain—to approach the problem of collective security with basic agreement. Stalin and Churchill insisted, while Roosevelt agreed more reluctantly, that the wartime concert of the Big Three would in fact dominate the international decision-making process for an indefinite period after the war, both within and outside the United Nations. As a fundamental precondition of collective security, it was held that "there would be agreement among the permanent members of the Security Council upon major issues." [4] Action by the international organization was to be contingent

---

[4] Trygve Lie, UN Doc. A/65, June 30, 1946, Introduction, p. v.

on this agreement; absence of consensus would signify United Nations inaction.

Implicit in this position is a concept of collective security quite different from the "united will of all" which prevailed in the Covenant. It implied that the stability of frontiers and the claims of nations would be judged by the major allies of World War II. They rather than the total membership of the UN would administer change and pass on the aspirations of dissatisfied elites. Each of the great powers expected benefits from the sharing of power. But how can we account for the apparent amity in 1945, which gave way to the cold war so soon?

Hopes for the continuation of the wartime concert of the Big Three were based on the nature of the policies followed by each in 1945. Thus the Soviet Union seemed, above all, anxious to repair the damage done to her industry, agriculture, and manpower by the German invasion. Further, the Communist leaders demanded—and the West granted at Yalta—that a belt of friendly states be erected on the periphery of Russia. It soon developed, of course, that "friendly" meant "Communist" to the Soviet leadership. In any event, Stalin and his colleagues apparently felt that the Yalta agreement had given Russia everything she wished to absorb at that time and they expected the collective-security structure to protect the new *status quo*. Finally, participation in a United Nations based on Big Three unity meant to the Soviet leaders that they would have a permanent and equal voice in all questions of world political importance, whether the issue was raised in Poland, Portugal, Yemen, or Guatemala.

British policy had welcomed the principle of a Big Three concert to the extent of proposing that the postwar collective-security system be based exclusively on a continuing alliance of the large powers, without giving the seventy-odd smaller states a direct voice at all. American statesmen rejected this scheme. Yet London readily accepted the American-sponsored alternative which became the UN Charter because the arrangement seemed to protect what remained of British global interests and influence. Thus British leaders saw in the United Nations the guarantee for stability and common action among the big powers, designed to protect the sorely weakened Empire and Commonwealth.

American aims were less clear-cut than those of Russia and Britain. Liberal internationalists such as Cordell Hull wished the new security organization to be universal in membership and dedicated to the preservation of peace through military action as well as through international economic and legal development. Colonial emancipation was to be another responsibility of the organization, which seemed designed to ushering in a "brave new world" without fundamental international friction, or free from "power politics." Big Three dominance and the veto seemed inappropriate to these groups, since the preservation of a new *status quo* was not their major preoccupation.

While President Roosevelt and Dean Acheson, for example, did not challenge this approach outright, they based their thinking on the proposition
that the war had resulted in the survival of only three large centers of power.
Living in peace with Russia and seeking to maintain world stability through
big-power agreement was their major concern. Hence they accepted the veto
and the inability of the UN to regulate the conduct of the "policemen" as
inevitable.

Finally, there were voices in 1945 which insisted on the veto in order not
to surrender too much American freedom of action—voices of which the
Democratic administration stood in some fear—and a group which foretold
the coming struggle with communism and consequently advised against admitting the Soviet Union to the inner circle of the concert. John Foster Dulles,
for instance, wished the UN to be veto-free so that it could be mobilized
against one of the big powers as well as against minor lawbreakers.

By and large, however, the Rooseveltian viewpoint proved victorious in
American policy—until the first rumblings of the cold war became apparent
in 1945, in the Soviet-American controversy over the postwar governments
of Poland and the Balkan countries. Thus the doctrine of full international
commitment, linked to the admission of the Soviet Union to the inner sanctum of the world's council's, explains the American acceptance of the concert
principle in 1945. Even so, American leaders took the initiative in urging that
France and China be admitted to the charmed circle of big powers, thus in
fact bolstering the anti-Communist camp.

The Big Three—and later the Big Five—thus agreed that collective security could mean only the security of the world against a threat posed by a
minor power. The concert principle, based on the veto, however, precluded
the mobilization of the structure *against one of the policemen*. Indeed, the
UN would never have been created if such a thought had prevailed, since it
would have implied the absence of that basic consensus which is essential to
the establishment of any international organization. Still, the immunity of the
Big Five from the authority of the organization was sharply challenged by
many smaller states. Australia and Canada especially sought to strengthen the
power of the General Assembly and eliminate the veto, all to no avail.

Many of the other founding nations had quite different aspirations as well.
While the Western European countries, weak and war-devastated, did not
challenge the Big Three concern over Germany and Japan and welcomed a
concert of power to prevent the renaissance of militarism, France agreed to
the concert only on the condition that she be admitted to the inner sanctum.
Thus she obtained not only security against Germany but guarantees for the
integrity of her large overseas empire as well.

The opposite aspiration was typical of Egypt, Syria, Lebanon, Iraq, Iran,
and India. These Arab and Asian nations had just obtained their independence
—if not formally, then in essence—as a result of the weakened state of their

erstwhile European overlords. They were desirous, above all, of safeguarding their newly acquired independence. They feared the possible return of the foreign ruler. Collective security to the Arab and Asian countries—including China—meant protection against former imperialist control, whether French, British, or Japanese. To the extent that independence had already been achieved by 1945, these nations were supporting a new *status quo* through collective security. But to the extent that they sought further liberalization of ties with Europe, whether for themselves or other areas still in a colonial position, e.g., Indonesia, they saw in collective security a mechanism for rapid change in the international order. Thus their aims were in essence opposed to those of Britain and France, but collective security was a vague enough concept in 1945 to promise the simultaneous protection of these clashing aspirations.

The twenty Latin-American states, largest bloc in the conference which drafted the United Nations Charter, agreed substantially with the erstwhile colonial nations. But being more secure than the Arab nations, they tended to emphasize the solidarity of the Western Hemisphere in their desire to exclude the influence of European powers from their shores. Hence Latin-American insistence, further, was instrumental in writing the provisions dealing with regionalism into the Charter, thus giving expression to the concern for geographic unity of purpose and agreement on policy.

Different policy aspirations inevitably lead to compromises in the actual drafting of international agreements, and the United Nations rules of conduct are no exception to this generalization. First and foremost, however, these rules represent those points of international policy on which the Big Five were in concert. Four of these Big Five had come to an agreement previous to the San Francisco Conference of 1945 which drafted the Charter, and this prior agreement was changed in only one essential aspect: the rules concerning self-defense and regional security. But the principle of big-power unanimity and domination over the organization, even though attacked by the smaller states, remained in the Charter. The compromise, therefore, was a one-sided affair, since the big powers conceded little and the smaller states left San Francisco far from satisfied.

The Concert and the Charter. If the language of international documents can be used as an index of world solidarity-consciousness, the Charter represents a marked advance toward world community in comparison to the Covenant. The Preamble asserts the determination of the member states to save the world from future wars and to "reaffirm faith in fundamental human rights, in the dignity and worth of the human person . . . and of nations large and small. . . ." Further, it declares a willingness to respect law and justice and to promote social progress, to "live together in peace with one another as good neighbors," and to ban the use of armed forces except for the common good. It remains to be seen to what extent the detailed rules of conduct and United Nations institutions were fashioned to meet these stated aims.

The maintenance of peace and security is affirmed as the major purpose of the United Nations. Hence the organization is declared to possess a monopoly of power for the "prevention and removal of threats to the peace, and for the suppression of acts of aggression or other breaches of the peace" and to bring about the peaceful settlement of all future disputes (Chapter I, Article 1). Further, the use of unauthorized force is definitely outlawed. All members agree to cooperate with the United Nations in measures to carry out these rules against a potential violator and not to aid the aggressor. These rules seem to have taken a great step toward world community. Yet the ability of the organization to act up to these standards is made ambiguous by the recognition of "individual and collective self-defense" in Article 51 and by the exclusion of matters "which are essentially within the domestic jurisdiction of any state" from clear UN jurisdiction.[5]

Since the use or threat of force is no longer permitted in principle, members of the United Nations "shall . . . seek a solution by negotiation, enquiry, mediation, conciliation, arbitration, judicial settlement, resort to regional agencies or arrangements, or other peaceful means of their own choice" in any dispute "the continuance of which is likely to endanger the maintenance of international peace and security" (Article 33, paragraph 1). The rules thus seem clear-cut. No dispute of a nature to provoke war is to be permitted to develop without the organization's taking a hand in solving it through one or more of the methods enumerated. The United Nations is entitled to investigate such a dispute, call for statements from the parties, admonish them, and recommend detailed settlements. But all such measures do not bind the parties. They remain free to reject all recommendations so long as they observe the basic rule not to resort to any "threat to the peace, breach of the peace or act of aggression" (Article 39). Aggression remains undefined, and the self-defense loophole looms ever larger as the Security Council is deadlocked by the cold war.

But what happens if in the course of a dispute one of the parties does commit a breach of the peace, as Italy did in Ethiopia, for instance? In such an event, the United Nations is entitled to "decide what measures not involving the use of armed force are to be employed to give effect to its decisions and it may call upon the Members . . . to apply such measures. These may include complete or partial interruption of economic relations and of rail, sea, air, postal, telegraphic, radio, and other means of communication, and the severance of diplomatic relations" (Article 41). What if these measures prove inadequate, as they did in 1936? Then the United Nations "may take such action by air, sea, or land forces as may be necessary to maintain or restore international peace and security" (Article 42). Unlike the League of

---

[5] For detailed treatment, see Chaps. 17 and 18.

Nations rules, such decisions on the part of the United Nations are *binding upon all members*. They agreed in advance to carry out the organization's decisions to enforce peace and security. As if to give special weight to this point, the Charter calls for the creation of a permanent Military Staff Committee, to be composed of the chiefs of staff of the big powers only, to plan and execute enforcement measures when necessary. The big powers, furthermore, agreed in the Charter to set aside specific units in their armed forces to be in readiness for enforcement action at all times (Articles 43–49). The overwhelming power of the concert thus seemed a fact. Again, however, the consensus proved to be less complete in terms of further details of collective security than these obligations indicate.

Finally, the Arab demand for a recognition of regional collective-security machinery—and the inter-American attachment to hemisphere solidarity—resulted in the admission by the big powers that regional agreements would be integrated in the United Nations system by permitting regional pacific-settlement organs to handle disputes under their jurisdiction, prior to submitting them to the United Nations itself. Thus the Western Hemisphere regional-security pact which had been concluded just prior to the founding of the United Nations was formally recognized. Regional organizations, furthermore, were entitled to take enforcement action of their own, *provided* "no enforcement shall be taken without the authorization of the Security Council" (Article 53, paragraph 1). Thus the big powers on the Council sought to control the use of force even in regional entities for collective security.

In what has since 1945 emerged as the key provision of the Charter, however, even this affirmation of big-power unanimity and domination has evaporated. Since disagreement has become the rule and consensus the exception, the *right of self-defense* has become the legal rationalization under which hostile systems of alliances have developed outside and despite the United Nations collective-security structure. The crucial importance of the right of self-defense can be understood completely only after analyzing how the United Nations makes its decisions.

The Concert and Decision Making. It was clear in the nature of the Anglo-American-Soviet consensus in 1945 that these states would dominate universal collective security. Pacific settlement of disputes and enforcement measures would take place only through their unanimous consent, which implied that such collective measures would not and could not apply to quarrels among themselves. These were to be settled privately and not in the United Nations. In the UN, however, big-power hegemony was permanently consecrated by giving the Security Council the exclusive power to make binding decisions for the whole organization. It was to have charge of disputes and threats to the peace and acts of aggression. It is composed of five permanent members—the Big Five—and six other states periodically elected by the General Assembly. Each of these eleven has one vote—cast, of course, in accordance with instructions received from the home government. Procedural decisions require seven affirmative votes, or a simple majority plus one. Substantive decisions, however, require the unanimous vote of the permanent members plus two additional votes. This is the famous veto; or more significantly, it represents the recognition that peace cannot be enforced against one of the superpowers without large-scale war, the very contingency that the United Nations was to avert.

Within this enormous limitation, then, the Security Council is the supreme political agency of the world, designed to keep the peace by recommendations, threats, or force on the basis of the concert of power among the United States, the Soviet Union, Britain, and to a lesser extent, France and China. For those who had hoped that the veto could be limited by expanding the scope of procedural matters, disappointment came fast. The permanent members soon declared that all matters even remotely related to the maintenance of security, with the significant exception of placing a complaint on the Council's agenda, were substantive in nature. It requires the unanimous consent of all permanent members to change these classifications, a limitation known as the "double veto."

If the Security Council implies the domination of the Big Five, the General Assembly represents the equal representation of all the sixty current member states. Each has one vote, and a two-thirds majority—unqualified by the size or importance of the states—suffices to pass resolutions dealing with security and political matters. However, while the General Assembly may *discuss* any political problem, issue, dispute, or act of aggression, it may merely "make *recommendations* with regard to such principles to the Members or to the Security Council or to both" (Article 11, paragraph 1). Thus, the General Assembly can air disputes and discuss policy, but no member government is bound to anything as a result of such discussion unless it has previously indicated its willingness to be bound. With this most significant difference, the Assembly can perform the same functions as the Security Council in the security field, and since 1950 it has tended to supplant the Council completely.

Such is the formal structure of the United Nations in its security aspects; such are the rules which were to guide international policy in the future, and such the procedures for dealing with breaches of the peace. It is painfully obvious that neither the structure nor the rules nor the procedures have been successful in eliminating the use of violence in the means chosen by ruling groups to satisfy their aspirations. Why has the concert principle of collective security been found wanting, like its predecessor under the League?

Since 1946, of course, it has become all too evident that the original assumption of big-power harmony no longer applies. The United Nations was supposed to prevent wars by easing tensions. Since the United States and the Soviet Union, however, provide the major arena of the vital tensions of our era, the United Nations has merely become one corner of the universal stage of conflict. Instead of dictating peace to others through agreement on the Security Council, the debates on that body are deadlocked because of tension between the policemen. The policemen, indeed, have become the chief protagonists in the key conflict of our times.

It is equally clear, however, that if and when a concert does prevail the United Nations is able to achieve its dual task: preserve the *status quo* and provide for peaceful change. Indonesia was given independence; Israel was protected; war over Kashmir was stopped; the Italian colonies were advanced toward self-rule. Hence, before dismissing the concert principle as superseded because of the disappearance of harmony among the Big Five, it is necessary to explore the possibilities of collective security under the veto rule even *after* the advent of the cold war.

Nevertheless, since 1950 the original assumptions of the UN have changed radically. This is made particularly clear by the role of the General Assembly in the discussion of tensions and security. Since the Korean War the West has consistently attempted to enlist the United Nations on behalf of its efforts to contain the Communist bloc, by seeking General Assembly approval of its program. While no veto can block resolutions in that body, votes supporting the Western position also are no more than recommendations. Hence "moral" approval is sought by the West, leading to a type of collective security in which the UN becomes an instrument of the cold war, in that it sanctions "permissive enforcement" measures by some member states against others, perhaps even states originally protected by the veto.

Not even the veto-free General Assembly, however, can legislate peaceful change. Elites who oppose its votes fail to implement its decisions. Unacceptable resolutions are ignored by those to whom they are addressed. Peaceful change against the will of a major power is impossible without war; but change recommended to a minor power is equally unthinkable unless the Assembly is put in a position to enforce its resolutions. As long as national policies are merely reflected in the international organization but not changed by it, the riddle of reconciling the *status quo* with change remains as deep as ever.

Yet the future role of the General Assembly may be larger than ever despite these problems. If a significant segment of the world opposes both American and Soviet policy aims—i.e., remains neutral in the cold war— while the superpowers seek the friendship and support of the uncommitted nations, bargaining and adjustment may be facilitated through the United Nations. Collective security then takes on the form of "balancing" among hostile blocs within the universal framework, a process to be explored after an examination of the concert in action and of the permissive-enforcement principle.

4. The Concert in Action. In a period when even questions of health, illiteracy, and radio communications are inevitably drawn into the theater of operations of the hostile power blocs, it is hardly surprising that a similar fate should befall collective security. In the absence of a neutral police force applying the law of the United Nations, the law itself becomes one of the bones of contention among the antagonists. Hence the practice of collective security in the solution of major political disputes is not and never has been one of the strict application to the disputants of the rules of the Charter. On the contrary, the application of the rules has been dependent upon the degree of relevance of a specific dispute to the East-West conflict; the policies of the Big Five in that conflict have determined whatever collective-security measures were adopted. When disputes bear no relation to the cold war, they may be expected to be handled more or less as the concert principle dictates. Other disputes take place between states which are not directly allied to one of the Big Five but which nevertheless have direct implications, usually in terms of propaganda, in the cold war. These also remain amenable to solution under the concert principle. Finally the most dangerous disputes have occurred between states directly allied with one of the major powers and therefore directly implicated in the struggle between communism and the West, or between the superpowers themselves. In these situations, the concert principle has given way to permissive enforcement, as symbolized by the Korean War.

The Indonesian Case. The case of Indonesia shows the concert principle in successful operation in ending a war and enforcing a settlement. During World War II Japan conquered and occupied the then Dutch East Indies, and when the Dutch colonial authorities returned in the fall of 1945 they found that their former subjects were organized and armed to resist the reestablishment of the colonial regime. For almost two years Dutch policy wavered between conciliating the Indonesians by offering them some form of autonomy within the Dutch empire and open repression of the independence movement. Distrust grew as armaments increased until the Dutch ceased negotiations and attacked the Indonesians in full force in the summer of 1947. Holland was embarking on a policy of reconquering the islands while the Indonesians were determined to establish their full independence. War was the only possible outcome.

The Soviet Union, true to its policy of encouraging colonial independence movements and breaking up European colonial empires, supported the Indonesian struggle through propaganda statements. Most of the Arab, Asian, and Latin-American countries agreed. Britain, the United States, and especially Australia wished to avoid revolutions, suffering, and instability in underdeveloped regions and therefore supported Indonesian independence within a framework of cooperation with Holland. The fear of the Communist propaganda appeal, always linked with nationalism in colonial areas, dictated a policy of lukewarm support to Indonesia while a good many sympathies existed for Holland as well. France, however, was completely on the side of Holland and wished her to crush the independence movement in order to weaken kindred ideas in the nearby French colonies in Indochina. How was the Security Council going to reconcile collective security with varying concepts of national security?

That the members of the Security Council did not see eye to eye on the issue is evident from the records of the case. When Australia and India called on the Council to take enforcement action immediately to stop the Dutch attack, the United States countered by offering its services as a mediator to the disputant parties without reference to the United Nations, thus hoping apparently to keep the dangerous dispute safely outside the propaganda-charged Security Council arena. Indonesia rejected the offer, and Holland claimed that the dispute was one under Dutch domestic jurisdiction and hence not subject to United Nations action. Since Britain and France supported the Dutch claim, the Security Council at first could only pass a resolution urging the parties to stop fighting and submit their quarrel to arbitration. This appeal went unheeded by the Dutch. As fighting continued, the anticolonial nations on the Council called for the creation of a United Nations conciliation commission to go to Indonesia and report violations of the cease-fire resolution to Lake Success, but since France vetoed this suggestion, the Council merely created a consular commission to supervise the unimplemented cease-fire. A Committee of Good Offices was also appointed by the Council to help the parties negotiate a settlement by themselves. As a result of these measures, fighting eased and a truce was successfully negotiated, though never actually implemented. On the surface it appeared as if the Council's firmness had dissuaded the Dutch from completing their reconquest.

In December of 1948, however, the Dutch suddenly attacked once more, conquered most of Indonesia and jailed all the important leaders of the Indonesian independence movement. Now a significant switch occurred on the Security Council, since the United States openly came to the support of Indonesia and requested firm action by the Council against Holland. The threat of Britain and France to veto such a resolution, however, made it possible only to impose a new cease-fire order without compelling the Dutch to withdraw to the original truce lines. Only open Dutch defiance of the new cease-fire request convinced all the major powers that the situation was too explosive to permit the frank return to imperialism, and on January 28, 1949, the Security Council adopted its strongest resolution, calling on Holland to withdraw to the 1948 truce lines, release Indonesian leaders, and try to reach a peaceful settlement with them, under penalty of enforcement measures. As if to give weight to this declaration, the United States unilaterally cut off economic assistance to Dutch East Indies authorities, pending Dutch compliance. The Dutch did comply: troops were withdrawn, the Indonesians released, and negotiations begun which terminated in the establishment of the independent Republic of Indonesia in November of 1949.

Palestine and Kashmir. In the fall of 1947 the General Assembly was asked by Britain to make recommendations for the disposition of Palestine. Populated in part by Arabs and in part by Jews, Palestine was torn by bitter civil strife as each side wished to exclude the other from a role of influence, while Britain declared her unwillingness to rule any longer. The outcome was a recommendation to partition Palestine into separate Jewish and Arab states. The British withdrew as Jewish and Arab groups fought bitter guerrilla battles for control over crucial towns. On May 15, 1948, the Jewish community declared its full independence and established the State of Israel, while the countries of the Arab League joined the Palestinian Arabs in formally attacking the new state. As both Washington and Moscow recognized Israel, seven Arab League countries made war on the creation of the General Assembly.

The Security Council managed to restore peace, by issuing repeated cease-fire orders and finally establishing a truce patrolled by Mixed Armistice Commissions under the Council's control. Violations by both Israel and the Arab armies continued. At the crucial point in the Security Council's efforts to make peace, threats to use enforcement measures against Israel had to be made, and even then Israeli troops ceased fighting only *after* they had occupied key territory beyond the line fixed by the General Assembly. Security Council efforts to arrange a permanent peace rather than an armistice have failed. UN directives and orders are implemented only with the greatest of pressure on the parties, while certain key decisions—such as the opening of the Suez Canal and the internationalization of Jerusalem—have been ignored by Egypt, Israel, and Jordan. Yet the fact remains that for six years no vetoes obstructed the peacemaking efforts: the concert functioned until 1954, when a Soviet veto finally was cast—in favor of Syria.

The Kashmir dispute, too, has been free from big-power obstruction. When the armies of India and Pakistan moved into the state of Kashmir— each in support of indigenous movements clamoring for annexation to India and Pakistan respectively—war seemed imminent, and the dispute has continued unresolved since 1948. Yet prompt Security Council cease-fire orders, the demarcation of truce lines by officers dispatched by the Council, and the supervision of these "boundaries" since have kept hostilities at a minimum and avoided open war. At the same time, however, UN efforts to settle the issue through an internationally supervised plebiscite and recommendations to the parties to withdraw their troops have met with rejections. The concert functioned in that no veto blocked the orders to cease fighting and the decisions to patrol the truce and make long-range recommendations. But the unity of the superpowers did not go so far as to make possible the enforcement of the recommendations.

All these disputes occurred after the onset of the cold war. Soviet, British, French, and American interests certainly were not identical in these situations. Why, then, was it possible to effect concerted action? Why did the concert function in these situations and fail in every other international crisis which has arisen since 1947?

First and foremost, the interests of the major powers were not directly involved. Further, a glance at the positions of the big powers in the UN may furnish clues. Thus on Indonesia, Britain and France at first backed the Dutch, while China and Russia sided with Indonesia and the United States sat on the fence. At the end, however, all major powers were in favor of halting Dutch attacks, thus implicitly and explicitly backing the Indonesians. Afraid that Communist claims of the "alliance" between colonialism and American "imperialism" would fall on receptive ears in South Asia, the Western powers—like the Soviets, though for the opposite reason—favored the insurgents.

In Palestine, once more, all the major powers—with the initial exception of Britain—favored the Jews. Each for its own reasons, the Soviet and American governments supported Jewish claims and wished to stabilize the Jewish state. Further, when after 1952, both Washington and Moscow began to vie for the loyalty of the neutralist Arab countries, they lessened their support for Israel in the UN, with the Soviet Union going so far as to favor the Arabs exclusively, in her efforts to make friends and influence people in the Middle East. In Kashmir as well, the neutralist position of the belligerents furnishes the clue to the effectiveness of the concert. Both India and Pakistan were and are being courted by the superpowers. Hence the safe course for the Security Council members is a policy of perfect neutrality. Truly, *because* of the exigencies of the cold war, the concert can still function whenever disputes involve neutral countries to which both Washington and Moscow must appeal.

5. Peaceful Change and the Cold War. *Disarmament.* The over-all disintegration of the concert of 1945 and the rise of the cold war have seriously affected ways of peaceful change. This is obvious from the record of disarmament negotiations, for example. The stake in the *status quo* and the demand for revision of it have proved irreconcilable, precisely as they did under the League of Nations. Of these earlier attempts at disarmament, Salvador de Madariaga had this to say:

The animals had met to disarm. The lion looking sidewise at the bull declared: "Horns must be abolished." The eagle, looking at the tiger, said: "Paws and especially claws must be abolished." The bear, in his turn, said: "All arms must be abolished; all that is necessary is a universal embrace."

In an era of global tensions each power wants its opponent to limit the armaments in which it is thought most proficient. In this respect, the disarmament efforts conducted under the auspices of the United Nations do not differ in the least from previous attempts. The position of the United States with respect to the international control of atomic energy is a case in point, as is the Soviet counterproposal.

Mass insecurity and fears engendered by the explosion of the atom bomb at Hiroshima soon affected the security deliberations of the brand-new Security Council. It was recognized by all that the security procedures planned in the Charter were inadequate to stop a surprise atomic raid or secretly planned project of sabotage. Mediation, conciliation, and enforcement measures might come too late to aid a nation already pulverized by a mass atomic attack. Hence the United States, as the then sole possessor of a stock of bombs, took the initiative in proposing a radical way of dealing with the new menace: the internationalization of all production and distribution facilities for fissionable materials. An international control authority was to be planned by the Security Council's Atomic Energy Committee. All major states were to be members of the authority, but a simple majority vote was to suffice in making binding decisions. The authority would purchase all fissionable materials as they were mined, after first making an exhaustive survey of world uranium and thorium deposits and ascertaining that no nation would be able to mine the destructive matter clandestinely. The manufacture of all quantities of these minerals large enough to cause destruction would be the monopoly of the authority, for peaceful industrial purposes as well as arms. Production facilities would be so placed that no one state could seize a sufficiently significant installation without leaving overwhelming numbers of similar installations in the hands of its potential enemies. Security was tied to decentralization.

But the United States—whose atom bomb was its most significant weapon in the cold war—would join its stockpile of bombs and its production facilities to the international organization's only as the last step. The monopoly of the bomb and the strength implied by it would thus be retained until the production facilities and mineral deposits of America's potential enemies were safely internationalized. In the long run unilateral use of atomic weapons would, of course, have become impossible under the Baruch plan, but in the short run the United States retained its major guarantee of security and was in a position to discover something of the Soviet Union's progress in this field through the geological and industrial surveys to be conducted by the United Nations.

Consequently the Soviet Union rejected the American proposal to control the atom. It proposed instead the absolute renunciation of the use of atomic weapons and opposed the internationalization of facilities and the inspection of mining deposits. It took adamant exception to the American insistence on continuous inspection of noninternationalized minor production plants by United Nations personnel and branded such inspection as "spying." Later, the Soviet Union did concede inspection provided it were carried out with prior warning and under control of the Security Council itself, in which Russia would retain her veto. While discussion went on from 1947 until the present, Soviet scientists developed their own atomic bomb, and both super-powers added the dread hydrogen bomb to their armories; but the American monopoly ended.

Clearly, neither the United States—which had the support of almost the entire United Nations membership behind its scheme—nor the Soviet Union wanted to permit the development of control machinery which would in the least detract from its national security. Both plans were so designed as to maximize national security, and since the two concepts of security were apparently mutually exclusive, no possible base for agreement could be reached. Temporarily, at least, a Soviet veto of the American plan ended all major efforts to remove the threat of atomic annihilation from the cold-war climate. American offers to internationalize the peaceful application of nuclear energy have so far failed to change the security stalemate.

In the field of conventional armaments the story was the same. The Soviet Union, possessing the largest land army with modern armor and artillery, offered a flat one-third reduction in the numerical strength of all armed services. The West, lagging in manpower, saw further inferiority but not security in this idea and therefore rejected it. Suggestions for a reporting of national strength before efforts at reduction were made received a cool reception from the Soviet Union. Efforts to ascertain the size and equipment of national armies, navies, and air forces and to inspect them in order to check the honesty of the reporting have met with Western approval and Soviet scorn. Discussions continue, but in the tension-laden environment in which they are being conducted it is hard to resist the conclusion that suggestions are made merely for propaganda purposes and to demonstrate pacific intentions. It seems a foregone conclusion that, as long as distrust dominates, no elite can expect its competitor to disarm or even to consider disarmament except for purposes of propaganda.

Under these conditions, disarmament negotiations can proceed only when the major antagonists have achieved approximate weapons parity and the elites in question consider the financial burden of arms to be prohibitive and incompatible with the achievement of such other policy aims as economic development. It may well be that such a point was reached in 1955, as the opposing powers inched toward a mutually acceptable compromise in secret disarmament negotiations. Thus the West ceased to emphasize continuous and fool-proof inspection while Russia granted the principle of control of weapons by stages and dropped its insistence on the immediate outlawry of atomic bombs. Further, Moscow agreed to the Western formula for controlling conventional armaments by having maximum quotas for men under arms, giving parity to the United States, China, and the Soviet Union. However, in terms of the dominant aims of the elites concerned, a temporary weapons advantage by one of them might well undo the progress toward an agreement, since it would destroy parity, the major assumption for agreement.

Peaceful Change and the General Assembly. The General Assembly, no less than the Security Council, has also been unable to achieve peaceful change, despite its universal membership and two-thirds voting rule. Disagreement among the big powers must of course preclude the possibility of concerted action. But why must the same be true of the General Assembly? Granted the inability of the General Assembly to do more than to recommend specific measures, would not endorsement of a given policy by two-thirds of the world's governments be a powerful force for a general consensus and thereby compel obedience?

Preeminently it is the function of the General Assembly to work out the terms for a peaceful adjustment of established conditions which have come to be intolerable for one or more national communities. This is exemplified by the ever-recurring efforts of the Asian and African nations to use the UN as an instrument for the removal of racial inequality and colonial rule. India, since 1946, has been complaining against South Africa's policy of racial discrimination against Asians; but Assembly efforts to change these conditions peacefully have foundered on South Africa's unwillingness to negotiate. Morocco and Tunisia have demanded independence from France, and their Arab League friends have sought to force the issue into open debate in the UN. Yet French opposition, bolstered by France's NATO allies, has kept the problem off the Assembly floor and no peaceful change has been possible. The complaints of the Wameru people of Tanganyika against British land seizures were aired and debated in New York. But General Assembly censure of Britain has failed to bring about a change in London's policy.

Only the case of the former Italian colonies constitutes an exception to this rule. Interallied inability to agree, after World War II, to a disposition of Eritrea, Libya, and Somaliland resulted in the referral of the issue to the Assembly. After much compromising, the UN voted to make Libya independent immediately (1950), establish a state of Somalia after a ten-year period of tutelage, and federate Eritrea with Ethiopia. Peaceful change, however, was possible only because the major powers had agreed *ahead of time* to accept the Assembly's recommendation.

Colonial and racial issues are obviously crucial to the future stability of the world, especially since the anticolonial nations are also the neutrals in the cold war. Hence attention must be paid to their aspirations, though the West has been slow to respond to the challenge. Issues growing directly out of East-West tensions, however, are taken less seriously. American policy called on the UN to provide for the unification of Korea by peaceful means. The West, similarly, asked the Assembly to aid in the unification of Germany by investigating whether free elections could be held. Soviet delegates demanded an inquiry of alleged American bacteriological warfare in Korea, and the United States called for a probe of Soviet slave labor camps. In almost every case the claimant expected the other side to refuse cooperation. The solution demanded by one was by definition unacceptable to the other— e.g., the unification of Korea or Germany along UN-sponsored lines would have conduced solely to the advantage of the West. Since the accusers know this in advance, their complaint is motivated by the desire to propagandize on behalf of a national policy, and no more. Specific projects aiming at the solution of East-West tensions are at a minimum in these situations; but schemes designed to embarrass the opposition abound. The Assembly thus frequently becomes a propaganda forum in the cold war and ceases to be a deliberative agency to bring about peaceful change.

Voting Blocs. This is inevitable because the smaller states are involved in the cold war precisely as the superpowers are, whether they are pro-Western, pro-Soviet, or neutral. Their own national aspirations can usually be gratified only if they somehow bear a relationship to the major world tensions. Their efforts to influence the large nations and the desire of those states to line up support for their schemes and charges result in the formation of voting "blocs" in the Assembly. States must band together in voting blocs to be able to achieve the same objective. Thus voting in the General Assembly is characterized by the telescoping of national policy aims into bloc demands for a specific world policy. There are five more or less consistent and homogeneous blocs of powers: the Latin Americans (twenty members), Arab-Asian nations (fifteen members), the North Atlantic Treaty powers and their British Commonwealth allies (seventeen members), and the Soviet bloc (five members). Some states do not identify themselves with any bloc, e.g., Israel and Yugoslavia, and these blocs by no means form solid voting fronts on all issues. Through them common national aspirations, which obviously bear a great deal of relation to regional identities of interest, are voiced in the universal collective-security organization.

Decision making on the basis of bloc voting in the Assembly would result in a strengthening of the concert principle of collective security only if the almost unanimous will of the smaller states could bring with it a change of attitude on the part of the major powers. Such, however, is not the case.

The prevailing voting blocs reflect the cold-war alignments; they do not transcend them. On most security issues, the NATO-Commonwealth and Latin-American blocs coalesce to form a majority for the United States, though they frequently fail to muster two-thirds of the total membership.

The General Assembly, therefore, has not been an institution facilitating the continued application of the concert principle either in the maintenance of peace or in the introduction of peaceful change.

Instead, the practice of bloc voting has made possible the introduction of two new principles of collective security: permissive enforcement and balancing. Both depend on support by small states, and both derive their significance from the fact that there are uncommitted regions in the cold war. They imply also that the recent practice of collective security has been a matter for the General Assembly, dooming the Security Council to oblivion. These new concepts now remain to be examined.

6. Permissive Enforcement and the General Assembly. The advent of permissive enforcement implies the submergence of the UN in the cold war. Concerted action had presumed the harmony of interests among the superpowers. Permissive enforcement recognized their basic conflict. In essence, as first proposed by American spokesmen in 1947 in the "Little Assembly" Plan, it enables the General Assembly to take the place of the veto-bound Security Council. It permits the Assembly to investigate and deal with a breach of the peace or act of aggression and designate specific member states to take enforcement action against the guilty nation.

"Uniting for Peace." Such a sweeping plan failed of adoption in 1947 because a majority of the smaller powers feared that it would contribute to the cold war rather than overcome tensions. It was enacted officially, however, in the resolution "Uniting for Peace" in 1950, after the onset of the Korean War. It established a Peace Observation Commission to investigate areas of tension, thus taking the place of the Security Council's powers of investigation, and a Collective Measures Committee to take over the role of the stillborn Military Staff Committee; finally, member states were asked to earmark contingents of their national forces for collective action. It must be stressed, however, that the General Assembly still has only the power of recommendation. In no sense can it order enforcement action if it discovers a threat to the peace or an act of aggression. It may merely, by a two-thirds vote, encourage individual member states to come to the defense of some member who has become the victim of aggression, as determined by the Assembly.

What are the implications of these changes with respect to collective security? Essentially, enforcement action is no longer obligatory but voluntary. It rests on a simple two-thirds majority of the membership and can operate irrespective of the wishes of the major powers. But it has lost its mandatory character and its sense of absolute application, dependent though these features had been on Big Five unanimity. In principle, at least, an attack by the Soviet Union on Yugoslavia or Turkey, a foray of China into Burma, could be met by the collective resistance of the anti-Communist member states. In practice, if the Korean precedent is a valid example, this contingency is an unlikely one. Not all violations of peace will be of equal interest to all members at all times. Furthermore the fear of unleashing a general war—even though this war might be dignified by the term "enforcement action"—is an overwhelming one in many regions of the world. Hence abstentions from any collective effort must be anticipated even if a two-thirds vote could come about. In terms of a general principle of international conduct, the new collective-security principle is likely to be less powerful and less persuasive than the old formula of big-power agreement.

However, from the vantage point of American national policy this conclusion is irrelevant. Under the "Uniting for Peace" resolution, the United States may well count on receiving an approving nod from two-thirds of the membership for any future hostile measures necessitated by the containment policy. It will then appear to the world as the executor of United Nations policy even though its actions may be prompted largely by motives of national policy and even though actual military support from other member states may be insignificant. The political and propaganda advantage of acting not in the name of national policy alone but as the policeman of the United Nations is a tremendous one. Collective security may no longer be what it implied in 1945, but the security of the West has been enhanced by the new developments.

But what if the United States fails to obtain a two-thirds majority when it requests permission to engage in an enforcement action? In short, permissive enforcement depends on American ability to round up support for anti-Communist policies among the neutralist countries of the world, i.e., the Arab-Asian bloc in large measure. The combined votes of this and the Soviet bloc frequently suffice to defeat Western resolutions. Hence, it is incumbent on America to temper its world policy so as to appeal to India, Egypt, and Iran if full advantage is to be taken of the "Uniting for Peace" innovation.

The Balkan Dispute. The Korean conflict is merely the most obvious example of permissive enforcement in action. Much the same was implicit already in the treatment of the Balkan dispute by the UN long before the principle was officially recognized. The quarrel between Greece and her northern neighbors indicates not only that collective action under the concert principle is impossible when the allies of the superpowers are directly involved but also that the permissive-enforcement principle makes its appearance when anti-Communist action, sanctioned by international approval, is desired by the West.

The Balkan dispute had its roots in the civil war which raged in Greece in 1945 and after, in which the liberal and conservative government parties —supported by Britain—fought against the Communist party, supported by Yugoslavia, Albania, and Bulgaria, then all closely allied with the Soviet Union. The issue before the United Nations was the Greek complaint that the civil war was being fanned by the three Communist neighbors of the British-occupied kingdom and the Soviet Union's claim that the presence of British troops in Greece "meant interference in the internal affairs of Greece and caused extraordinary tension fraught with grave consequences both for the Greek people and for the maintenance of peace and security." [6] The real issue was clear to all: the Soviet Union wished to remove potentially hostile Western forces from her satellites' borders, and the West, speaking through Greece, wanted to end the Greek civil war and thus prevent the Soviet Union from obtaining a foothold on the Mediterranean.

The Security Council responded by appointing an investigating commission to look into the truth of the charges, even though the Soviet Union opposed this step. When the commission submitted a report finding Albania, Yugoslavia, and Bulgaria guilty as charged, its Soviet-bloc members submitted a minority report coming to the opposite conclusion. A resolution moving the adoption of the majority report in the Security Council was promptly vetoed, as was a United States suggestion calling for enforcement action against the three satellites.

In September of 1947 the Assembly took up the dispute and during a series of violent debates, in which East and West accused each other of unrestrained imperialism, passed a set of resolutions calling on the parties to negotiate a settlement for themselves after reestablishing diplomatic relations and to refrain from intervening in each other's domestic affairs. Further resolutions urged the disputants to conclude a new border convention which would make further military incidents impossible. A Commission for the Balkans was appointed in order to see whether new violations of the border occurred and to assist the parties in their negotiations. Both Soviet and American representatives served on the Commission, but the Soviet-bloc countries refused to recognize its jurisdiction and restricted its "watchdog" activities to Greek soil. The crisis ended only after Yugoslavia broke with Soviet Russia and the Greek government forces, assisted by American weapons and personnel, defeated the last of the insurgents. United Nations action contributed nothing to the end of the tension. Concerted action being ruled out by the nature of the conflict, the appeal to universal collective security by each bloc was no more than an appeal to world opinion for support. UN endorsement of the West's claims thus in effect sanctioned unilateral American intervention on behalf of Greece.

Korea, Phase One: 1950–1951. The permissive-enforcement principle in United Nations life reached its apex and began its decline in the Korean crisis. The initiation and conduct of military operations reflected the significance of the practice outlined in the "Uniting for Peace" plan; their termination and the prolonged truce negotiations illustrate the advent of the balancing concept of collective security. What were the deep-seated conflicts

---

[6] L. Leonard, *International Organization*, McGraw-Hill, New York, 1951, pp. 185 ff.

in American and Communist Far Eastern policy which led to the first UN enforcement action?

Ever since the end of World War II the 38th parallel, dividing Communist-ruled North Korea from American-supported South Korea, had been the very real boundary between the American and Soviet spheres of influence in the Far East. Both sides spoke repeatedly of unifying all of Korea under one government. But the American plan—endorsed by the General Assembly—would have eliminated Soviet influence from North Korea and was therefore turned down by Moscow. The Soviet suggestions might have resulted in a Communist victory over the entire peninsula, and Washington refused to consider them. To both antagonists, two separate Koreas were preferable to a united Korea whose future affiliation might be in doubt— and the same situation continued to prevail in 1954, after the three-year war.

Tension and distrust, therefore, pervaded life in Korea from 1945 until 1950. Recrimination and border violence flourished. Soviet advice and matériel built a strong North Korean army. Some American aid was given to Syngman Rhee's Republic of Korea, but American leaders were divided about the necessity of defending South Korea. Many considered it unimportant; but to others—inside the armed forces as well as out—a North Korean crossing of the parallel, presumably sanctioned by Moscow or Peiping, would constitute the first decisive challenge to the American policy of containment.

The relevance of this conviction to the practice of collective security became apparent on June 25, 1950, when North Korean forces attacked the Republic of Korea and invaded her territory. On America's demand, the Security Council met in emergency session to consider the situation; the Soviet representative was absent, since the Soviet Union was then boycotting all meetings of the United Nations in order to compel United Nations recognition of the Communist government of China. The United States proposed a resolution stating that an act of aggression had taken place, calling on the aggressor forces to withdraw, and asking "all members to render every assistance to the United Nations" in ending the hostilities. The resolution passed the Council by a unanimous vote, Yugoslavia abstaining. One day later the United States assigned air and naval units to cooperate with the Republic of Korea. Washington had come to the assistance of South Korea *before* such action had been formally authorized by the Security Council.

Since the East-West tension had kept the United Nations Military Staff Committee from making proper plans to repel aggression and since no armed forces had ever been set aside for collective action, direct international sanctions were impossible. Instead, the Security Council adopted on June 27, 1950, an American-sponsored resolution which *"recommends* that the Members of the United Nations furnish such assistance to the Republic of Korea as may be necessary to repel the armed attack and to restore international peace and security in the area."[7] A few days later a unified command under American leadership was established for all United Nations forces made available under this decision, and the United States was authorized to designate the supreme commander for the UN effort. The subsequent struggle in Korea, which ended with a stalemated war at the 38th parallel, proceeded under these broad authorizations.

Several factors in this chain of events deserve closer analysis with respect to the practice of collective security under the concept of permissive enforcement. In the first place, American participation antedated the formal decision of the Council, thus making it a unilateral—though by no means illegal—effort. Secondly, the Council merely gave permission to members to engage in hostilities against North Korea; it did not *order* enforcement action. Thirdly, the "unified command" was in effect the United States Far East Command. Fourthly, the General Assembly never gave the unified command unequivocal permission to cross the 38th parallel in order to unify Korea by force, after the UN victory in the fall of 1950. It appears that invasion of North Korea was begun before the ambiguous Assembly resolution of October 7 was passed, a resolution which merely authorized the Supreme Commander to establish conditions of stability "throughout Korea," adopted with some reluctance by the General Assembly.[8] Lastly, it must be stressed that the UN effort was in reality restricted to the sixteen member states which actually contributed forces. In so far as UN military policy was not exclusively the policy of the United States, it represented only the Committee of Sixteen, and by no means the entire membership. Permissive enforcement thus enabled the United States, eleven of its NATO-ANZUS allies, and three of its Asian-African allies to carry out the containment policy under the banner of the United Nations but not subject to its full control. The same principle, however, failed to make possible a political settlement on American terms. It is in the area of UN political control over the conduct of enforcement action that the concept of balancing in collective security practices made its debut.

7. Balancing and Collective Security. Permissive enforcement implies the delegation of authority by the UN to one nation or a group of nations acting on behalf of the organization. The balancing concept, however, implies restraint, negotiation, and *absence* of military action rather than enforcement. Like the principle of the balance of power, to which the concept bears some relation, balancing operations in the work of universal collective-security organizations call for the efforts of a group of neutral states in mediating and conciliating the clashing aims of the disputants. In the United

---

[7] *Department of State Bulletin,* July 3, 1950, p. 7.

[8] L. M. Goodrich, "Korea: Collective Measures against Aggression," *International Conciliation,* no. 494, October, 1953, p. 173.

THE UNITED NATIONS AND COLLECTIVE SECURITY

Nations General Assembly this role has, since 1951, been assumed by the neutralist Arab-Asian bloc, supported by several of America's NATO partners—including Britain—who disagree with any intensification of the containment policy. With the development of this concept, collective security has undergone one more change in that police actions of the Korean variety are to be avoided under it, rather than encouraged.

The possibility of such practices rests, of course, on the existence of an uncommitted bloc—at the moment led by India—and on the need felt by both the United States and the Soviet Union to cater to it. Should the superpowers prefer to "go it alone" and dispense with the general approval they now demand for permissive enforcement practices, the efficacy of balancing within the UN would lose all meaning. Paradoxically, therefore, future American expectations for receiving the approval of the General Assembly for possible new Koreas also make possible the application of the balancing concept. Future Soviet expectations of keeping the Arab-Asian bloc in the neutralist camp, similarly, compel the Soviet Union to bow to balancing instead of defying the UN overtly and consistently.

American leaders acknowledged the potency of this reasoning when they made peace in Korea without having succeeded in defeating the Chinese. They bowed to balancing once more when, in June of 1954, they agreed to a compromise in Indochina which favored the Communists; any other course might have resulted in the disaffection of Britain and France from NATO and closer ties between India and China. The Soviets, for their part, chose the path of moderation in withdrawing their troops from Iran in 1946, after having been publicly challenged in the Security Council and implicitly accused of imperialism against an independent Asian nation. They, like the West, submitted to compromise in Korea as well as in Indochina, thus keeping the neutral bloc wedded to aloofness and sparking differences between the United States and its allies.

Korea, Phase Two: 1951 to 1953. China entered the Korean War in November of 1950, as UN troops approached the Yalu River, the border of Manchuria. America responded by calling on the General Assembly to brand China an aggressor and authorize military and economic measures against her. Balancing had its origin in this situation. The Arab-Asian bloc, never fully in favor even of the enforcement action against North Korea, opposed such a step and asked for negotiations with China through a group of "neutral" UN members. Balancing became possible because the UN was not fully behind the enforcement action: sixteen states were fighting aggression, while over a dozen others were "neutral" despite membership in the same collective-security organization and despite subjection to the same general legal rules.

While the initial Indian effort to secure peace in Korea through negotiation failed, New Delhi's appeal in the Assembly was sufficient to weaken the condemnation of Red China which was ultimately voted. Intermittent efforts to negotiate on behalf of the UN were continued by these member states while the same UN was also continuing to fight the Chinese aggressors, through the spring of 1951. The anomalous situation was little changed by the Soviet offer to conclude a truce in June of that year, since then the UN Command began negotiations on a basis of equality with the very forces which were to be punished for aggression.

The talks, punctuated by Communist obstruction and American unwillingness to compromise, dragged on for two years. The final deadlock revolved around the question of prisoner repatriation. The Communists held out for the unconditional return of all captured personnel; UN negotiators, with 70,000 prisoners who did not wish to return, demanded *voluntary* repatriation. The moral and ideological appeal of both sides was clearly linked with these claims, and the Communists sought to explain away the defection of their former soldiers by charging brutality and violence in UN prison camps, which erupted periodically in large-scale riots and repression.

Balancing in the UN was instrumental in overcoming this deadlock. In the fall of 1952, India proposed in the General Assembly that repatriation be voluntary, but conducted in an atmosphere free from violence and intimidation, through the efforts of a commission composed of neutrals. This suggestion, first rejected by both superpowers, was finally accepted by them precisely because neither felt it could alienate the Arab-Asian bloc and its own allies. Had the Indian scheme been rejected, Moscow and Washington would have appeared as "warmongers" in Asia; America, furthermore, would have had to combat further strains within NATO, as Britain and others supported India.

Subsequently, teams of Communist and UN explainers worked under the supervision of a commission composed of Czech, Polish, Swiss, Swedish, and Indian officers while Indian troops guarded the prisoners in question. Two nationalities were expected to favor the Communist, and two the Western, point of view, with the neutral Indian the "balancer."

While it is, of course, too early to judge the permanence of balancing practices in the United Nations, the concept is capable of greater application so long as the same international distribution of ideology and power continues, while a full and final bipolarization of world power is avoided. Since the concept assumes a readiness to negotiate and a willingness to compromise, it is obviously at the mercy of extreme ideological strands of opinion among the interested elites. Thus, while the balancing concept now governs the formerly supreme permissive enforcement principle, nations may well dispense with collective-security practices altogether if they are unable to attain their aims through them.

Regionalism and Balancing. Frequent references to NATO, ANZUS, and Arab-Asian "blocs" in General Assembly discussions of Korea and other tension areas make it plain that the practice of collective security is intimately tied to the regional alignments and alliances of modern international relations. Neither the principle of the "united will of nations" nor the concept of the concert of power accommodated this development. However, neither the permissive enforcement nor the balancing approaches to universal collective security could operate without regional ties and commitments. Permissive enforcement derives its value to Western policy from the fact that it enables the extensive regional-alliance systems linking the countries of Western Europe and the Americas to each other to function as enforcement arms of the UN. Korea came close to being exclusively a NATO and Commonwealth effort. Enforcement authority delegated by the General Assembly in future situations, similarly, would owe its power to regional blocs and military systems.

Balancing, of course, rests on the jockeying for position and influence among three major regional aggregates: the West (composed of the NATO-ANZUS and Latin-American blocs) opposing the Soviet bloc, with the Arab-Asians acting as balancers, occasionally assisted by dissident NATO members. Collective security within the universal framework of the Charter and the General Assembly, therefore, has also become a reflection of the world's division into mutually antagonistic regional systems. Universal collective security, instead of transcending and uniting regions—as Wilson's "united will of all" had hoped—has become a function of the delicate interplay among contending regional systems.

That the states of the world do not place any great reliance on any concept of collective security through the UN is made all too plain by the general decadence of universal international organization and the ever-increasing trend toward regionalism. In 1955 the United States belonged to four multipartite regional collective self-defense organizations. After giving lip service to the United Nations, regional arrangements and rights under the self-defense clause are extolled as proper policies to achieve "collective" security. The same trend appears in Europe, the Middle East, Latin America, and most of all among the Soviet Union and its dependent satellite units. Regional structures, preparations, and commitments everywhere are today far more highly developed than the universal security system. The appeal to the Charter as the sanctioning principle of regionalism invariably rests on the weakest link in that document: the right to collective self-defense. Today, public leaders have less and less to say about universal security, while elites in most countries see in mutually antagonistic regional groupings the key to a collective security which is no longer easily obtainable under a split and ambiguous United Nations system.

ADDITIONAL CASE-STUDY MATERIAL

Ball, M. M.: "Bloc Voting in the General Assembly," *International Organization*, vol. 5, February, 1951.

Bernard, S.: "Choice in the West," *World Politics*, vol. 5, January, 1953.

Bonn, M. J.: "How Sanctions Failed," *Foreign Affairs*, vol. 15, April, 1937.

Bryson, L., et al.: *Foundations of World Organization: A Political and Cultural Approach, A Symposium*, Harper, New York, 1952.

Carter, G. M.: "The Commonwealth and the UN," *International Organization*, vol. 4, May, 1950.

Chaumont, C.: "A French View of Security through International Organization," *International Organization*, vol. 4, May, 1950.

Cohen, B. J.: "The Impact of the UN on U.S. Foreign Policy," *International Organization*, vol. 5, May, 1951.

Collins, J. F.: "The United Nations and Indonesia," *International Conciliation*, no. 459, 1950.

Emerson, R., and I. Claude: "Soviet Union and the United Nations," *International Organization*, vol. 6, March, 1952.

Fox, W. T. R.: *The Super Powers*, Harcourt, Brace, New York, 1944.

———: "The U.N. in the Era of Total Diplomacy," *International Organization*, vol. 5, May, 1951.

Goodrich, L. M.: "Korea: Collective Measures against Aggression," *International Conciliation*, no. 494, October, 1953.

Haas, E. B.: "Types of Collective Security," *American Political Science Review*, March, 1955.

Howard, H. N.: "The Arab-Asian Bloc in the UN," *Middle East Journal*, vol. 7, summer, 1953.

Hurewitz, J. C.: "The Israeli-Syrian Crisis in the Light of the Arab-Israel Armistice System," *International Organization*, vol. 6, August, 1951.

———: "UN Conciliation Commission for Palestine," *International Organization*, vol. 7, November, 1953.

Kelsen, H.: *Recent Trends in the Law of the United Nations*, Oxford, New York, 1950.

Kondapi, C.: "Indian Opinion of the UN," *International Organization*, vol. 5, November, 1951.

Korbel, J.: "Kashmir Dispute after Six Years," *International Organization*, vol. 7, November, 1953.

Lourié, S.: "The United Nations Military Observer Group in India and Pakistan," *International Organization*, February, 1955.

Martin, A.: *Collective Security, A Progress Report*, UNESCO, Paris, 1952.

Miller, D. H.: *The Drafting of the Covenant*, 2 vols., Putnam, New York, 1928.

Mohn, P.: "Problems of Truce Supervision," *International Conciliation*, no. 478, February, 1952.

Niemeyer, G.: "Balance Sheet of the League Experiment," *International Organization*, vol. 6, November, 1952.

Rudzinski, A. W.: "The Influence of the UN on Soviet Policy," *International Organization*, vol. 6, May, 1951.

———: "Soviet Peace Offensives," *International Conciliation*, no. 490, April, 1953.

Walters, F. P.: *History of the League of Nations*, Oxford, New York, 1952.

Wheeler-Bennett, J. W.: *The Pipe Dream of Peace: A Study of the Collapse of Disarmament*, Morrow, New York, 1935.

Chapter 21

REGIONAL INTEGRATION

1. The Nature of Regional Integration. Coexisting with and rivaling the universalism of the United Nations and its specialized agencies is the dominant contemporary phenomenon of regionalism. Multipartite understandings, agreements, treaties, and covenants punctuate the conduct of international life at every level. British elites are concerned about the impact of European unity on the Commonwealth. French statesmen worry about the relationship between the Coal and Steel Community and the French Union. Indian leaders are torn between adhesion to the Commonwealth and the building of a neutralist system. American diplomats must strive to fit the overlapping and conflicting commitments of NATO, ANZUS, and the Organization of American States into a framework of consistent policy. Regional considerations and ties dominate in the life of the international society.

Quantitatively, the impact of regional organization is manifest in the fact that of eighty-odd sovereign states, only ten are at present unaffiliated with a regional system: two African, seven Asian, and one European. The bulk of Europe, the Middle East, all of Australasia, and the Americas are regionally committed. The Commonwealth, NATO, the Organization of American States, ANZUS and SEATO, the Balkan Pact, the French Union, the Arab League, the Soviet East European system, the Organization for European Economic Cooperation, the Council of Europe, and the Schuman Plan are the international links which condition the policies and expectations of groups everywhere.

Qualitatively as well as quantitatively, the growth of regional activity is striking. Regional armies with unified command, equipment, and procedures garrison Europe. Regional financial and economic planning organs work and continuously condition policy in Western and Eastern Europe. Regional loyalties and symbols are growing in the Middle East, while neutralists in South Asia band together under the leadership of India. Economic development and investment is sponsored by regional agencies in Asia and the Americas. At the same time, United Nations agencies have no armies, are hampered by scarce financial means, and employ civil servants without administrative power. Regional action and planning is contrasted with United Nations debates and recommendations. Regional loyalties and symbols are

growing while universal ties and values disintegrate. Clearly, regional dynamics are in the center of current international relations, while universal
bonds merely reflect the initiative shown by regional forces in the demands
and charges which thrive in United Nations discussions.

These conclusions, however, still fail to tell us what regional pacts, systems, and understandings really are. Must regional ties be political, military,
economic, or social? Can the membership of a regional arrangement be
geographically defined? Must a "region" be culturally or institutionally
homogeneous? Do regional systems have to possess written constitutions
and regular procedures? Must these be in harmony with the UN Charter?

Regional arrangements may feature pacific-settlement procedures or they
may not. They may include twenty states or two. They may be directed
against a specific enemy or at the collective security of an area in general.
For purposes of this discussion a regional system is any long-term agreement
between two or more states providing for common political, military, or
economic action in specific circumstances, *provided* the commitment extends
to a defined area and specific states. Such a system must possess permanent
organs and fixed procedures. Its membership may vary in constancy and
homogeneity. The "region" may be culturally unified, like the Arab League.
Or it may be as diverse as the "region" comprised by NATO, with its democracies and dictatorships; Protestant, Catholic, Mohammedan, Greek
Orthodox, and agnostic members; capitalist and socialist economies; and
a geographic scope which takes in Florida, Greenland, Norway, Algeria, and
the Caucasus. Consonance with the UN Charter is a useless criterion, since
the elasticity of that document is such as to permit any *defensive* arrangement among member states. Since, moreover, no universal distinction between offensive and defensive intent is accepted by elites, this legal limitation is of no relevance. Finally, regional systems possess the potentiality of
developing into supranational communities, either in terms of their institutions or because of their ideology and motivating spirit. Yet they need no
written constitution: a traditionally accepted "understanding" sometimes
suffices to create real ties and firm symbols of loyalty. Regional systems,
then, may be regarded as possible steppingstones for the integration of national communities into larger entities of some kind, short of the global unity
toward which the UN was to have worked.

Regionalism is thus an elastic concept, defying in its diversity any hard
and fast definition. Yet the common thread running through these contemporary developments is the determination to strengthen supranational
ties for long periods, thus implying the abdication of national freedom of
action in certain spheres to a far larger extent than is true in universal
international organizations. What policy aims can be singled out as vital
in accounting for this decision by governing groups?

One motive underlying regional integration is the desire to realize collective security for a given geographical area, such as the Western Hemisphere. Here the cooperating nations agree to defend one another against aggressors *within* the region. More commonly, however, the basic motive is collective self-defense, i.e., the building of a permanent alliance against the threat of *external* attack. Alliances can thus become regional systems, and today they usually do so develop. Further, the desire to achieve cooperative economic development and maximize physical welfare is an important motive for integration, whether among the industrial countries of Western Europe or the underdeveloped nations of Asia and South America. Regional ties can result also from the desire of a strong nation to control and direct the policies of smaller affiliates, whether through persuasion or coercion or both. And finally, a common desire for the building of regional systems is the will to unify national communities into a larger entity. While such integration may result unintentionally from any of these motives, deliberate intent to integrate may function as an important aim in itself.

2. Neutralist Regionalism: The Idea of a "Third Force." The most significant contemporary regional systems are the result of the fear of external attack. They are alliances directed against some outside threat. While the Soviet-dominated system of Eastern Europe and the American-led systems of Western Europe and the Pacific are the most conspicuous of contemporary regional entities, there is a significant trend in many portions of the world away from either bloc and in favor of a neutral, or "third," position.

European Neutralism. The sentiment known as neutralism therefore shuns alliance and close association with both the Soviet and the American scale of the world balance. Neutralism assumes that peaceful coexistence between the superpowers is possible, and if it should prove impossible the neutralist wants no part of the ensuing conflict. Neutralism opposes the intensification of regional rivalries and emphasizes disarmament. Neutralist states seek to act as mediators between the chief protagonists. As a "third force" in world politics they seek to moderate the intensity of Soviet-American rivalry.

In so far as the desire to stay away from either major power bloc gives rise to the desire for regional unity, neutralism in itself is a motive making for the creation of regional systems of its own. Only one such system has actually been created: the Arab League. Nevertheless, sentiment for the creation of similar neutral systems of strength exists in Western Europe as well as in South Asia. The European federalist movement, for instance, includes some groups and individuals who oppose both the United States and the Soviet Union. They deplore NATO as they fear the Soviet system. Consequently they argue for the creation of a united and federated Western Europe free from any ties with either bloc. They see in regional unity a way of remaining uncommitted in a future war and possibly a deterrent on the desire to go to war as far as the superpowers are concerned. European neutralism is not confined to any one political party or group. It is a general sentiment of some significance in all moderate parties, and receives the encouragement of Western European Communist parties for obvious reasons. While its significance in the general European regional movement is great, it has not emerged as the victorious point of view.

South Asian Neutralism. A somewhat similar sentiment, unexpressed in terms of organizations and treaties, exists in South Asia, particularly in India. Many Indian leaders see in an Asian regional organization a source of strength against both superpowers. They hope to stay out of war and secure the defense of their area against either of the chief antagonists by pooling their resources and their political forces. They hope that neither superpower will start a war if it is uncertain as to where South Asian loyalties will lie in a future holocaust.

These sentiments have so far failed to result in a formal organization. But in the United Nations as well as in direct relations with the Western and Soviet blocs, the governments of India, Burma, Pakistan, Ceylon, and Indonesia have frequently spoken and acted in concert: in pledging solidarity against a return of Western rule to South Asia, and in seeking to avert Communist expansion into the area. India especially has been anxious to foster a sense of Asian consciousness and solidarity, though the other neutralist nations do not seem eager to accept Indian leadership in all situations. Pakistan in particular is less committed to aloofness from the cold war and leans far more heavily on the West than is considered desirable by India and Indonesia. Pakistan's participation in the military and diplomatic efforts of the West may contribute to undermine an incipient regional system of Asian neutrals. But then influential conservative groups even in India oppose Nehru's orientation and tend to favor the West, while South Asia's Communists, of course, counsel the opposite course.

The Arab League. Neutralism as a regional protective philosophy has found expression, however, in the oldest of contemporary regional organizations, the Arab League. Based on strong sentiments of religious and cultural homogeneity among all Arabs—whether in North Africa or in Arabia—the League was supposed to represent the yearning of all Arabs for political unity under one great confederation. Its members are Syria, Lebanon, Iraq, Egypt, Libya, Jordan, Yemen, and Saudi Arabia. While unity of language and customs does bind these nations together, the League merely represents their common *external* aims. As stated in the Pact of the Arab League of 1945: [1]

The object of the League shall be to strengthen the ties between the participating states, to coordinate their political programs, in such a way as to effect real collaboration between them to preserve their independence and sovereignty, and to consider in general the affairs and interest of the Arab countries.

[1] Art. II.

External defense is the watchword, and not any overriding desire to federate the member countries into one entity. In fact, distrust between the single most powerful member, Egypt, and the lesser members has prevailed from the start. Iraq refused to pay its dues for years, and Jordan has on occasion flaunted its disregard for League decisions. Saudi Arabia remains aloof, and Lebanon, with its large Christian population, is not at all at ease in the League. Hence the enthusiasts for Arab unity have condemned the League as inadequate because of the past unwillingness of the member governments to use it as an instrument of internal integration.

In fact, the creation of the League was due to two factors: the desire of the but recently emancipated Arab nations to make impossible the return of their erstwhile British or French overlords, and the determination to prevent the development of a Jewish state in Palestine. At the same time it must be stressed that the creation of the League was supported and encouraged by the British government in the hope of uniting the now independent Arab states behind a generally pro-British policy in the vital Middle East.

The same limited desire to cooperate is shown in the institutions of the League. Decisions are made by a Council on which each member is represented by one instructed delegate with one vote. Only a unanimous decision can bind all members to take collective action, and on the crucial question of collective measures against Israel unanimity could not be obtained. A majority vote binds merely the states which supported the given resolution. On minor matters, the Council possesses more power. It can impose pacific settlement awards in disputes between League members, who are pledged not to resort to force against each other and to settle all their intra-League quarrels peacefully. However, such compulsory pacific settlement is permitted only in disputes not involving the "independence, sovereignty or territorial integrity" of a member. Yet many Arabs continue to aim at making the League the sole executor of member-state foreign policy.

With such a limited consensus in the past it is not surprising that the League's record of common determination and action is poor. A common front by all members did prevent a return of the French to Lebanon and Syria in 1945, and the united bloc the League presents in the United Nations gives it a voice out of proportion to its military power. However, in the acid test of the Israeli-Arab war the tenuous bond of union was openly shown. Not only were the Arab armies defeated in the field but they proved unwilling to bury their political disagreements sufficiently to make a continued united effort possible. Jordan acted contrary to League decisions, and Saudi Arabia showed only token interest. The League thus is not much of a source of strength to its badly divided members and so far even less of an effective neutralist force, though Egypt would like to make it one.

3. Hemisphere Solidarity: The Organization of American States. Of all the regional arrangements, undoubtedly the effort known as "Pan-Americanism," the "Inter-American System," or the "Union of American States" is the best known. Organized efforts at formal and institutional cooperation among twenty-one states of the Western Hemisphere go back at least to 1889, and since that time a plethora of commissions, unions, committees, and boards has been created for meeting what appeared to be common needs. "Up to the time of the formal establishment of the Organization of American States [OAS] in 1948," says one commentator, "eight international conferences of American States had been held, resulting in some forty treaties, together with several hundred recommendations, resolutions and declarations. Special conferences, as well as 200 technical gatherings, resulted in 67 additional inter-American treaties." [2] In terms of regional community building, however, the record is less impressive.

Pre-1947 Inter-American Agreements. Prior to the Rio de Janeiro and Bogota Conferences in 1947 and 1948, agreements among the American states were limited to these: (1) all disputes between American states were to be settled by special Pan-American pacific settlement procedures for which a multitude of conflicting treaties existed; (2) after 1936 intervention in the domestic affairs of any American state was held to be illegal; (3) and after the outbreak of World War II in Europe, it was agreed that the American states would support each other if any one of them were attacked by one of the European belligerents. Thus the principle of "hemisphere solidarity" owed its origin to the twin desire to protect all American states against extrahemisphere pressure and to keep the impact of Europe's war away from the hemisphere. These decisions, however, did not result in any united front once Pearl Harbor shattered America's neutrality. Argentina not only remained neutral but maintained the closest contacts with the Axis powers throughout the war, and not all Latin-American states entered the war immediately. Prior to 1947, therefore, "hemisphere solidarity" by no means implied concerted action and alliances against dangers confronting any one state in the System.

Policy Aims in OAS. Since that time, however, a rigid and well-structured regional organization with all the features of an alliance *and* a collective security system has developed. The bonds which unite the twenty-one member states, it must be stressed, vary with the interested elites. To Latin America, hemisphere solidarity implies the legal and political sanctification of the principle of nonintervention and the equality of states—large or small. Its recognition in a legal system of which the United States is the most powerful member facilitates its observation by that member; denunciation in the Council of the OAS would be the result in the event of violation. Further, for the chronically unstable revolutionary governments of Latin America membership in a noninterventionist regional system is a slight guarantee for the stability of whatever regime was in power at the debut of

[2] L. Leonard, *International Organization*, McGraw-Hill, New York, 1951, p. 304.

the OAS. Finally, for Latin America, the OAS is an excellent device for countering the physical superiority of the "Colossus of the North." The United States can be outvoted on any issue and the united counsel of the Latin Americans can prevail in the limited area of the OAS while it would fail to make its point in the much larger framework of the United Nations. Thus economic aid made available by the United States under the UN must be shared with all other UN members. Economic aid expected under OAS auspices, however, would go to Latin America exclusively. The anticipation of this kind of benefit from a purely American regional system was a powerful factor in persuading Latin America to urge the establishment and recognition of the OAS at the time of the San Francisco Conference of 1945.

United States motives in supporting and joining the OAS were of a somewhat different order. The earlier desire to promote Pan-Americanism as a device for spurring American exports had given way by 1947 to the desire of implementing the Monroe Doctrine with the voluntary cooperation of the rest of the hemisphere. Hemisphere solidarity would imply the automatic concerted action of all American states to meet an outside danger, if it arose. The weak principle of mutual support which obtained during World War II would be replaced by a collective-security system which would (1) make possible the peaceful solution of all inter-American disputes without reference to outside and possibly hostile nations, and (2) give the OAS the character of a firm regional alliance against extrahemisphere threats. In short, to the United States the OAS provides security against the Soviet Union and its designs—if any—against the states in the System. These varying motivations, of course, cannot be reconciled in all situations, and on the question of economic aid especially a good deal of bad feeling has come to the fore between the United States and its OAS partners.

Obligations under OAS. In the formal structure of the OAS, however, both the North and the South American aspirations have found institutional expression. Collective-security arrangements are defined in the Inter-American Treaty of Reciprocal Assistance, known as the Rio Pact of 1947. War is outlawed in this treaty, and recourse to pacific-settlement methods is declared obligatory. Further: [3]

> The High Contracting Parties agree that an armed attack by any State against an American State shall be considered as an attack against all the American States, and, consequently, each one of the . . . parties undertakes to assist in meeting the attack in exercise of . . . Article 51 of the Charter. . . .

Pending a decision by the OAS, following an armed attack, each state is free to help the victim or not to help it. Armed attacks which occur anywhere within the Western Hemisphere, including a 1,000-mile wide maritime belt, and extending to the North and South Poles are to be treated by the OAS

[3] Art. 3.

as follows: (1) a call to the parties to suspend hostilities and restore the situation which existed prior to the attack; (2) recourse to the conciliation of the OAS; (3) imposition of enforcement measures of a financial, communications, economic, and diplomatic variety if step 2 should be rejected; and (4) the use of armed force to restore peace if step 3 should fail. Decisions to impose enforcement measures short of the use of armed forces are binding upon all members if agreed to by a two-thirds vote, but no state can be compelled to contribute its armed forces without its own consent. If an armed attack occurs in Europe or the Far East, the hemispheric-security system takes on the features of an alliance. Then the members are merely obligated to consult and try to make common policy toward the aggressor who threatens one of their number, i.e., the United States as the only member state having interests, personnel, and installations outside the hemisphere. The same loose procedure is to be used if the "inviolability or the integrity of the territory or the sovereignty or political independence of any American State should be affected by an aggression which is not an armed attack." The pact is broadly enough drawn to permit consultations if domestic unrest or subversion should seem to threaten one of the American states.

The System in Action. Within the hemisphere, then, the OAS is a collective-security system, while it represents the principle of hemispheric solidarity with respect to threats originating from outside—in the form of a traditional alliance. The OAS possesses a complete system of arbitration, mediation, and conciliation whose procedures, rules, and obligations differ in no essential respects from the provisions of the UN Charter. This was demonstrated when a series of disputes arose in 1950 to disturb the peace of the Caribbean area. Costa Rica accused Nicaragua of trying to bring about a revolution, and the Dominican Republic accused Haiti, Cuba, and Guatemala of the same intention. The OAS promptly called upon the parties to refrain from any hostile measures, and withdraw their troops to their own frontiers if they had already crossed them. Then investigation commissions with their own guards and agents were flown to the trouble spots to check the claims and counterclaims. After these commissions reported back to the OAS, resolutions were adopted which were diplomatic enough to apportion the blame for the disturbances equally and to admonish all states concerned to refrain from similar interventionist acts in the future. The unanimous will of the OAS members not parties to the disputes sufficed to end the hostile acts, especially since the overwhelming might of the United States was apparent under the formal guise of unanimous resolutions.

Decision Making in OAS. Structurally, the OAS is more ambitious than the United Nations itself. Top decisions are to be made by full-fledged plenipotentiary conferences. Decisions affecting defense and security matters are the business of irregular conferences of Foreign Ministers, while emergencies such as the Caribbean disputes are the business of the Council of the OAS, which is composed of all the Latin-American ambassadors in Washington joined by an Assistant Secretary of State of the United States. The Council not only handles emergency situations but also is responsible for the administrative planning of the OAS, and it is its duty to coordinate the work of the Inter-American Economic and Social Council, the Cultural Council, and a host of lesser OAS bodies which parallel the specialized agencies of the United Nations.

All decisions of these OAS bodies are mere recommendations, with the exception of the measures taken to meet an armed attack. High-flown statements abound, praising unity and solidarity and a common stake in freedom and democracy as hemispheric traditions, but concrete measures are rare. Thus while the OAS Charter provides for an Advisory Defense Committee and an Inter-American Defense Board, their respective functions are far from clear. Common defense planning has been initiated, but it can hardly be compared in intensity with parallel efforts in NATO. There are no common procedures, weapons, command echelons, or army units. Only liaison between staffs has resulted so far, and some reluctance has been betrayed by Latin Americans about these faltering steps. Agreement has been reached, however, on the desirability of pooling knowledge and techniques for the control of subversion, and the United States has urged its OAS partners to exclude Communists from their sensitive services under these resolutions.

Hence neither the structure nor the record of the OAS indicates that this regional system has so far achieved much integration. As an American official recognized, "The Charter does not set up any supernational authority that can exercise its own sovereign powers. Nor do the political bodies established . . . relieve the individual member governments of their responsibility for determining policies and actions of the inter-American organization." [4]

Fissures in OAS. This conclusion must stand even if it be granted that outwardly the OAS has taken a firm and united stand in supporting the United States in the East-West conflict. While the Council of the OAS has endorsed the Korean enforcement action and welcomed the "Uniting for Peace" resolution, basic differences in aspiration abound in the OAS and keep concerted measures down to a minimum common denominator. The issue of whether the OAS should encourage democracy in the Western Hemisphere —as urged by Uruguay—is balanced by the concern for nonintervention. The organization cannot be dedicated to both aims simultaneously; thus intervention by Honduras and the United States against the left-wing regime of Guatemala in 1954 taxed the nonintervention doctrine severely.

[4] John C. Dreier, U.S. Representative on the OAS Council, "OAS Charter Comes into Effect," *Department of State Bulletin,* Jan. 7, 1952, p. 10.

Similarly, dissatisfaction is aroused by the likelihood that the common campaign against Communist domestic subversion also takes the form of persecutions of opponents of Peronismo and similar authoritarian governments in the OAS. Finally, the American insistence that economic aid and development policies under the OAS be geared to the demands of hemispheric defense against the Soviet Union does not always meet with approval south of the Rio Grande, where the world conflict is not as directly experienced. Thus American views that "regional isolation is no more possible for Latin America than it is for the United States" and that "inter-Americanism must . . . be understood in the light of the world situation of which it is a part"[5] would tie the OAS tightly to the anti-Soviet alliance system. Americans view the OAS as a source of strategic materials, manpower, and diplomatic support in the United Nations. Latin Americans, on the other hand, contend that military and economic defense needs are overstressed and that the main contribution of the OAS should be the sharing of technological know-how so as to raise living standards.[6]

Thus, at the moment, the OAS serves as an institutional and diplomatic device for making the leadership of the United States in the anti-Soviet campaign palatable to small and weak states, historically fearful and jealous of American aims and actions. Agreement is reached only on generalities, and the victory of the American viewpoint must be purchased by concessions elsewhere, usually in the realm of trade and economics.

4. Empire to Confederation: The Commonwealth. While there is a fair amount of agreement that the international grouping known as the "Commonwealth" or the "British Commonwealth" is some form of international organization, agreement on a more precise classification is almost impossible. As the *Economist* put it, the Commonwealth is no more than "a sprawling collection of nations with no common obligations, with no coordinated line of action in world affairs and at odds with each other [which] makes up an international system which is a travesty of the word 'Commonwealth.' "[7] The collectivity which at the moment includes Canada, New Zealand, Australia, the Union of South Africa, India, Pakistan, and Ceylon as well as the United Kingdom of Great Britain and Northern Ireland is not an international organization like the United Nations. It has no charter, it rests upon no basic treaty, and membership entails no specific obligations of any kind—nor does it confer any rights. It possesses no standing central institutions of any significance. Nor is it even an alliance, since there is no

---

[5] John C. Dreier, "Taking Stock of Inter-American Relations," *ibid.*, Apr. 30, 1951, pp. 688 ff.

[6] Alberto Lleras, Secretary-General of OAS, "The Inter-American System Today," *The Annals of the American Academy of Political and Social Science*, July, 1952, pp. 97 ff.

[7] Oct. 9, 1948. Quoted in H. J. Harvey, "The British Commonwealth," *International Conciliation*, no. 487, January, 1953, p. 3.

treaty of assistance, no common army, and no obligation to go to war in the event of one member's being attacked or threatened.

Minimum Common Aims. Yet the Commonwealth is more than a mere international organization and more than an alliance in its full scope and significance:

> It is nothing more than a series of governments linked in a common purpose by the symbolic tie of the common Crown and prepared to use methods of regular consultation for promoting that purpose. The efficacy of the Commonwealth depends on the ability of its several governments freely to carry out the policies they undertake.[8]

But what is that common purpose, which after all is the key to any form of supranational association? A minimum conception of the joint aims of the Commonwealth, on which all members are ready to agree, is twofold: common defense against external threats, and common measures for economic well-being. India and New Zealand, the United Kingdom and South Africa, all are willing to combine their efforts and consult more or less regularly to meet threats from countries feared by all. But the mere fact that Communist China is considered a threat by Australia but not by India indicates that a more precise agreement on the nature of a specific threat is no easier in the Commonwealth than in the United Nations. Common welfare is equally difficult to define, since to some it means common investment policies while to others it merely implies preferential trade agreements. Defense and welfare, then, are the common purposes acknowledged as a tenuous minimum, uniting all members of the Commonwealth.

The "Old Commonwealth." For Britain, Australia, Canada, New Zealand, and the South Africans of British origin, however, the Commonwealth means a good deal more. For all the countries whose inhabitants predominantly originated in the British Isles, the Commonwealth is a symbol and an instrument of common policy making for the preservation and protection of British institutions. For them parliamentary government, the rights affirmed by the common law, and the "British way of life" are symbols of identification and of loyalty common to individuals of British descent. Commonwealth ties in the case of the "old" members imply continuing connections with relatives and friends and not merely agreement on certain temporarily shared aspirations, such as defense. Thus the common purpose of the Commonwealth is objective and minimal as far as the "new" Asian members and the South Africans of Dutch descent are concerned. They are subjective and committed to the perpetuation of ideological and spiritual aspirations in the case of the overseas Britons who people Australia, Canada, and New Zealand.

Institutions and Decision Making. While there is agreement on minimum common ends, there is a complete absence of any central coercive machinery.

[8] Royal Institute of International Affairs, *Atlantic Alliance,* London, 1952, p. 105.

The Commonwealth is based squarely on the principles of voluntary association, formal equality of the members, decision making by unanimity, and the voluntary character of the implementation of decisions. This implies a minimum of formal obligations and maximum freedom of action for each member state. Through the development of the Commonwealth an empire which was formerly ruled by imposition from London has transformed itself into a voluntary association of independent nations.

The formal institutions which have been erected on these principles are far less impressive than, for instance, the structure of the United Nations. Thus the only real formal bond of the Commonwealth is the fact that the ruling monarch of the United Kingdom is also the formal ruler of each of the dominions—with the exception of India and Pakistan, which are republics. But Her Majesty's Government in Canada may act quite differently from Her Majesty's Government in Ceylon and in opposition to Her Majesty's Government in South Africa, though the same person is the head of each state. Obviously, the common crown is purely of symbolic significance. Similarly, the recognition of a common body of law is symbolic rather than real, since the Judicial Committee of the (United Kingdom) Privy Council has ceased to act as a final court of appeal for the whole Commonwealth. Common citizenship for all subjects of the Commonwealth countries is recognized by some members but not by others. Thus little institutional significance can be derived from these formal bonds of unity.

More important are the organs of consultation through which the common purposes of the Commonwealth are actually approached. But these are largely *ad hoc* and do not meet regularly. Top common policy decisions in the realm of foreign and defense policies are made by irregular meetings of Commonwealth Prime Ministers. Similarly, conferences of Finance Ministers, Foreign Ministers, and lesser officials discuss matters of common concern in their respective spheres, irregularly. Standing committees in the realm of functional relations do exist, as in agriculture, shipping, and telecommunications, but these do not in any sense make law for the member states. No permanent secretariat has ever been created for any of these organs. Defense liaison is maintained merely by exchanging information and by assigning officers to the staffs of other member states. There is at present no Commonwealth general staff, though such a body has functioned on occasion in the past. The only real continuous evidence of common action is the voluminous and incessant interchange of intelligence of common interest which is conducted through the United Kingdom Office of Inter-Commonwealth Relations. The special position still occupied by Britain herself is also apparent in the fact that the Dominion High Commissioners (Ambassadors) in London meet fortnightly and discuss policy issues, rather than the Dominion High Commissioners stationed in Ottawa or Karachi.

Consultation. These organs make decisions only on the basis of unanimity, and implementation of a decision is dependent upon the interest and concern of each member government. Some decisions are carried out by only two or three or five of the members; others are universally implemented. Some are observed for a while and rescinded when an election in some member state results in a new government opposed to the original decision. One observer notes: [9]

Questions upon which there is not unanimity are put back for later consideration, and circumstances or opinion, or both, may have changed in the interval. . . . Complete agreement has been found to be worth waiting for, because it brings vigorous and friendly common action when it comes.

Yet no conference ever "makes policy" in the full sense of the word. Prime Ministers' conferences are merely exchanges of views to discover whether common interests and aspirations do in fact exist. If they do not, no attempt is made to persuade or coerce a dissenting minority. An exchange of views on whether common action can be taken is the sole aim of the meetings.

Yet even this extremely loose form of consultation and possible common action frequently fails to resolve all conflicts of motivations among the members. Ireland left the Commonwealth rather than "discuss" her policies with the others, and Burma never even consented to join the group. India joined only on condition that she need not recognize the tie of the common crown, and her membership has not prevented a lengthy and extremely bitter series of disputes with three other Commonwealth members: with Ceylon and South Africa over the rights of the local Indian populations, and with Pakistan over Kashmir. The last dispute, of course, resulted in hostilities and the intercession of the United Nations rather than the agency of the Commonwealth. But even though the new Asian dominions and South Africa fail to share the concern for the preservation of British traditions, they still find it useful to remain in the Commonwealth—at least temporarily—because of the obvious economic advantages afforded by inter-Commonwealth preferential trade agreements and common policies of economic development.

Economic Benefits. Thus it is in the realm of economic aspirations that the Commonwealth today offers maximum inducements to all its members. Exporters are assured of a market at predetermined prices and importers of reliable sources of supply in countries not demanding scarce currencies for payment. Preferential trade agreements legalize these benefits and membership in the sterling bloc, which usually goes with membership in the Commonwealth, assures all members of access to a desirable currency in their financial relations. This is as true of the new Asian dominions as it is of the United Kingdom and the British-settled Commonwealth members. The Com-

[9] Harvey, *op. cit.*, p. 15.

monwealth economic development scheme, known as the "Colombo Plan," is visible proof of this community of interests and harmony of aspirations in the economic realm. All the Commonwealth countries with interests in South Asia have joined together in making technical personnel available to India, Pakistan, and Ceylon. All join in formulating development plans for their individual economies by indicating in advance the funds which the industrialized countries can lend to the underdeveloped Commonwealth members. Since all have a common interest in the peace and stability of South Asia and all share a concern over high living standards in this particular region of the Commonwealth, cooperation is so vital to their separate foreign policies that a permanent information and consultation agency for the Colombo Plan has been fashioned.

The Commonwealth as a whole is thus united largely by common economic aims. A political harmony of aims, however, tends to be restricted to the "old" Commonwealth—Canada, Australia, New Zealand, and the United Kingdom—South Africa having embarked on a separate path as a result of the particular racial policy aims of the dominant Afrikaaner Nationalist party. These nations share values as well as economic interests, and consequently they see their fate united in terms of harmonious foreign policies generally and defense policies in particular. To Britain the additional strength afforded by the old Commonwealth connections is sufficiently important to make Britons leery of entering a strictly European union or federation.

From Empire to Free Association. To Great Britain as a colonial power the Commonwealth principle of regional association is particularly vital. It is the stated long-range colonial policy of Britain to develop self-government in her colonies to the point at which a given dependency can become autonomous and choose whether to remain in association with Britain as a free and equal member of the Commonwealth or as an unattached independent state. Burma has chosen the latter course, but with the inauguration of complete self-government in the Gold Coast another colony not settled by Britons will probably decide to remain freely associated with her erstwhile master. Through the Commonwealth principle, the formation of larger communities by consent is possible, even though success is much more likely in the case of permanently shared values than in temporary agreement on common material benefits.

The French colonial system has taken a somewhat different path, reflecting the unwillingness of France's conservative and military elites to associate on a basis of equality with dependent territories. The French Empire is now the French Union, a quasi-federal entity in which the mother country constitutionally shares governing power with the colonies, protectorates, and trust territories, but in which France is the dominant partner in reality. Unlike practice in the Commonwealth, France has sought to compel the protectorates of Morocco and Tunisia as well as the states of Indochina to become "associated states" of the French Union, under an arrangement which leaves with France special powers in the conduct of foreign and defense policies for these states. Unlike the Commonwealth, the colonies are given representation in the French parliament and in the parliament of the French Union, though the latter possesses only advisory authority. Unlike British practice, there is neither formal nor actual equality between the members of the Union, a fact which has found expression in North African riots and Indochinese subversion. With different aims prevailing in Paris, however, it would be possible to adapt the French Union to the needs of voluntary association.

5. Alliances and Integration. Military cooperation without the creation of common economic, colonial, and even social policies among the participating nations is rapidly becoming impossible. Total war and total diplomacy have made obsolete the isolation of military factors from other considerations. Hence it is hardly surprising to see in purely military institutions and obligations the nucleus of permanent regional association, as best exemplified by the development of NATO since 1949.

Pacific Alliances and Integration. Not all regional alliances, however, result in marked integration. Value sharing between the United States and its Japanese, Philippine, and South Korean allies is minimal. Common institutions have failed to emerge; foreign policies are far from unified. Anti-Japanese aims in Australia, New Zealand, and the Philippines counter the anti-Communist aims of the United States, thus giving a quality of dissension to ANZUS as well as the bilateral Pacific pacts.

The difficulties experienced by the United States in building a South East Asian Treaty Organization (SEATO) provide further evidence that not all alliances easily produce integration. The Asian neutrals oppose this organization, and some see in it "not a Pacific security system but an organization of Imperialist Powers for the protection of their interests." [10] Thailand, Australia, the Philippines, and the United States want a Pacific NATO; Pakistan, Britain, and France are lukewarm about firm diplomatic and military commitments. Even with the signature of a formal pact, it is most doubtful that this division in expectations and aims can produce integration.

NATO and Integration. The obligations, institutions, practices, and fissures of NATO were discussed in Chapter 8. However, the impact of NATO on Atlantic integration requires additional attention at this point. Lester Pearson, widely respected Foreign Minister of Canada, holds that in NATO "the sense of community, the experience and the habits of cooperation which the development of collective defense has engendered form the essential basis for the growth of collaboration in fields other than defense." Dean Acheson emphasizes the "unity of belief, of spirit, of interest of the community of nations represented here." [11] Thus some statesmen see in NATO an organi-

[10] *Hindustan Times,* as quoted in *Far East Survey,* Oct. 8, 1952, p. 141.
[11] Royal Institute of International Affairs, *op. cit.,* pp. 100, 131.

zation of ideologically and institutionally similar nations, perhaps emerging toward some form of confederation.

The decision-making procedures of NATO resemble those of the Commonwealth and therefore bear out the impression of evolution toward confederation. Yet it would be erroneous to assume that NATO represents the spontaneous and coordinated expression of all the elites in the member states for Atlantic unity. American insistence on the integration of the European NATO partners has been a powerful stimulus. Successive American administrations have held that Europe was to unify its armed forces, pool its communications and resources, and thus present a common defensive front rather than separate country-by-country programs. Economically, integration was thought to produce a common market, higher production incentives, and therefore general prosperity. Militarily, integration would result in a large unified army, able to deter Soviet expansion, instead of competing and ineffective national contingents.

American influence has been exercised through the economic and military-assistance programs. The Marshall Plan was the initial mechanism, giving way by 1951 to the Mutual Security Program.[12] The receipt of economic as well as of military aid by Europe was made conditional upon the "integrated" utilization of the aid. The relation between bilateral American programs and prodding and the collective effort is most clearly revealed in the fact that the chief of the European MSP establishment was also the American representative on the Council of NATO. "The power he can exercise comes . . . not so much from his position in NATO as from his key position in the planning of his government's economic aid," comments a British observer.[13] The United States, as the main supplier of NATO strength through economic and military aid, is and remains the moving spirit in the organization. By virtue of its ascendant industrial position it can practice either persuasive leadership or plain dominance.

The former has been the practice—without invariable success. Repeated efforts to threaten and cajole the French into joining their armed forces with those of Italy, the Benelux countries, and a rearmed Germany failed with the rejection of the European Defense Community treaty by the French parliament in 1954. Washington's insistence that Britain join the Continent in close and even federal ties has been successfully resisted by London. The entire timetable for European federation has been much slower than American policy makers had hoped and demanded.

Yet patient American efforts to link Yugoslavia with NATO by fostering a close NATO-like alliance among Tito, Turkey, and Greece bore fruit in 1954 with the conclusion of the firm Balkan Pact. Indeed, the failure of immediate European federation has contributed to the development of NATO's

---

[12] See Chap. 11 for details.
[13] Royal Institute of International Affairs, *op. cit.*, p. 82.

institutional significance. American policy makers, unable to achieve economic unity and military integration through the European Defense Community, were persuaded by their British and West German allies to turn to the NATO structure. West Germany's admission to the treaty organization made possible German rearmament under the control and supervision of SHAPE. A Western European Union along military lines, subject to NATO control, emerged in place of the defeated federal plan.

Thus NATO remains the single most important institution of interallied cooperation in the West. In it, American policy makers are able to influence and condition the military and economic efforts of Europe. Through it, however, the United States is also constantly compelled to make concessions to her European allies in order to maintain a united and coordinated structure. The pattern of influence, resistance, consultation, and compromise merges the ascendant position of the United States with the aspirations of the more reluctant Europeans and thereby makes NATO a permanent international association of ever-growing significance.

6. European Integration: An Emerging Regional Community? If American policy since 1948 has been designed to assure the integration of Europe through military and economic aid, and if the multilateral policy of NATO was aimed at achieving integration without formal federation, what have been the trends among European groups and parties with respect to a closer union on the democratic portion of the Continent?

Demands that sovereign national communities of Europe unite into a federation or confederation can be found throughout the post-Renaissance political and philosophical literature. But at no time prior to our own era was the movement for European integration anything like a popular political concern. At no time did it possess a mass membership, and never was it taken seriously by anyone save its few scattered proponents. Since 1945 all this has changed. There are numerically strong groups in all the Continental countries who stand for the immediate federation of Europe. These groups have the support of several key political parties and meet the aspirations of important individuals and interest groups. They do acknowledge a permanent common interest, whether this be expressed in economic, spiritual-religious, or mere political terms. What, then, are the common aims which persuade European industrialists, labor leaders, politicians, and intellectuals to abandon their separate national communities and join in a larger one?

Forces for Federation. The neutralist rationale for federation has already been examined. The possibility of constructing a "third force" appeals to a good many Europeans who object to NATO as well as to the Soviet empire. The aim of such groups, then, is the neutralizing of Europe from the two major power blocs; it is the contemporary example of political isolationism in Europe. Opposed to the neutralist advocates of union, however, is a strong group of statesmen and politicians, such as Winston Churchill, who see in integration—

whether functional, federal, confederate, or intergovernmental—a means for uniting the political power of the divided and competing European systems against the threat of Soviet political and ideological expansion. Politico-military might, thus, is one motive of union.

Closely allied to this conception is the French fear of a resurgent and aggressive Germany, especially after German rearmament. Hence political and military integration, by joining the German forces inextricably with those of other European states, would prevent a future independent German policy and thereby assure the security of France in the minds of such men as Schuman and Monnet. Still other Europeans see in federation the means for realizing an economic motivation. They fear the impoverishment of Europe through economic barriers of all kinds and hold that overlapping and competing national industrial systems result in low productivity and waste of resources. They advocate economic—if not political—integration as a device for maximizing production, consumption, and standards of living and thereby expect to weaken the appeal of communism and socialism. Economic means become the handmaiden to an ideological end: the preservation of a largely laissez-faire economy, an outlook strongly supported by America's policy in Europe.

Spiritual considerations make up the demands of still another group of federalists. They see in Europe the citadel of Western cultural institutions, emphasizing freedom of the individual and democratic government, based on essentially Christian teachings. Integration is regarded once more as a device for pooling the separate institutions of the culturally related European communities and thereby preserving them against the totalitarian danger—internal as well as external. This outlook is typical of Europe's Christian Democratic groups, while the economic rationale more nearly characterizes federalists among professional and industrial leaders. Trade unionists—largely socialist—by contrast, tend to be lukewarm toward these arguments, and if they favor integration at all they do so in order to protect themselves against Communist totalitarianism or to spread socialism uniformly through a democratic federation.

It must be stressed that these trends of opinion and action would in all likelihood have remained paper demands had it not been for the confluence of three forces: American pressure for integration, Soviet threats to European institutions, and the native federalist movement. The Soviet challenge convinced many groups which otherwise would have preferred national exclusiveness to integration. The fact that American economic aid was conditioned upon European moves toward unity was a strong argument in favor of gradual compliance, especially since opposition might have resulted in a renewed American policy of isolation and abandonment of impoverished Europe. In view of these external forces, then, European developments in favor of a new regional community are far less spontaneous than the work of the native federal movements would seem to indicate. A survey of clashing European aspirations will demonstrate the complexity of actual trends.

Forces against Federation. Differences in policy aims characterize not only the various parties and interest groups in Europe but the policies of the European governments themselves. Thus Britain and the Scandinavian countries have been distinctly cool toward the whole idea of formal and permanent association leading to a larger community. Conservatives as well as socialists in Britain favor the closest intergovernmental cooperation, consultation, and coordination—but they want no part of federation or confederation. They applaud NATO and approved of the OEEC—with reservations—but refused to join a political federation or even become a member of functional organs possessing the power to make mandatory policy for national governments. British and Scandinavian stability, mutual economic relations, association with the Commonwealth, and a greater sense of security all have combined in dictating this overwhelmingly powerful attitude of aloofness from intimate association on a community basis. Nevertheless, British as well as Scandinavian policy favors the federation of the Continental states on political as well as on functional lines, and British leaders are willing to cooperate with such groupings on an intergovernmental basis, even to the extent of permanently stationing troops on the Continent.

On the Continent the opposite opinion tends to prevail. Christian Democrats favor unity for spiritual reasons, while some socialists favor integration in order to make continentwide economic planning a reality. Business groups favor economic integration if their production and sales will expand, but oppose it if they fear competition and free market conditions. At the same time, extreme nationalists of the conservative parties as well as the numerous Communists are opposed to integration of all kinds, though for opposite reasons. For those who favor integration on principle, however, the means of unity lie in political federation and not in functionalism, as Belgium's Paul-Henri Spaak (socialist) and France's Paul Reynaud (conservative), for instance, never tire of stressing.

Yet political federation has been opposed by nationalists like De Gaulle and considered premature by socialists who would prefer to win electoral control in the several countries before federating them. While political federation on the Continent has been discussed and a constitution drafted, it has not been implemented. Instead, interest groups have consented merely to create supranational organs of power in those spheres in which common interests are now accepted as dominant—the coal-iron-steel complex.

Institutions for Integration: OEEC. The Continental decision to seek unity through functionalism, however, has not precluded the creation and continued functioning of intergovernmental agencies and advisory political bodies such as the Council of Europe. Thus in the realm of economic planning there exists the OEEC, whose original purpose was to pool the economic aid requests of the recipients of American ERP contributions. On the OEEC all NATO members plus Sweden, Ireland, and Switzerland are equally represented, and a unanimous vote is needed to make a generally binding decision, though a majority is bound to carry out measures for which it

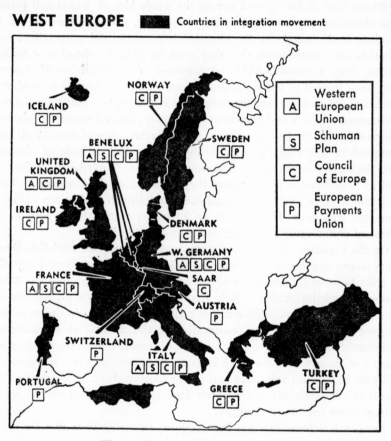

WEST EUROPE ▓▓ Countries in integration movement

A Western European Union
S Schuman Plan
C Council of Europe
P European Payments Union

Western European regional institutions

voted. Through the investigations, studies, and inquiries of the OEEC Secretariat, the economic integration of Europe and its joint policies of recovery were promoted. Studies of the Secretariat were presented to the Council, whose decision would then be translated into proper national policies of investment, employment, relaxation of economic restrictions, etc. Since the demise of ERP and the rise of NATO, the OEEC has become the auxiliary economic planning agency for the NATO Council. Its studies form the basis of the economic decisions reached by NATO. Its prestige in Europe is considerable, and member states have been conscientious in carrying out OEEC recommendations, thus in fact forgoing many of the past practices of uni-lateral economic policy making. Yet Britain opposes the organization and prefers to do its own economic planning. The continued existence of such centrifugal forces makes OEEC merely an approximation to a community and by no means an expression of it.

The Council of Europe. In the city of Strasbourg there meets twice a year a parliamentary body known as the Council of Europe. It consists of members of the parliaments of all non-Communist European countries and contains representatives of all political parties except Western European Communists. In addition, an upper house consists of the foreign ministers of the member countries, and it can make decisions only by unanimity. Resolutions of the Council are binding only if they pass both houses, thus enabling Britain, the least enthusiastic member, to veto proposals of the Continental federalists. The function of the Council is not to legislate but to discuss and to arouse public sentiment in favor of unity. In fact it has merely been the scene of the continuing acrimonious discussion between the Continental federalists and the British-Scandinavian advocates of intergovernmental collaboration. Reso-lutions urging the creation of an integrated army and immediate continent-wide elections to a European parliament have always been stymied by the negative attitude of the Committee of Ministers at the top. Thus, in effect, the Council has reconciled itself to the search for unity through functional rather than political federation.

The European Coal and Steel Community. Advocates of ever closer Euro-pean integration have now pinned their hopes to the prototype of federation in one key area of interdependence: the Coal and Steel Community (CSC). The Community in 1952 established federal governmental features for France, Germany, Italy, Belgium, Holland, and Luxembourg for the regulation of trade, production, investment, and manufacture of coal and steel. Member governments are bound to carry out the decisions of CSC organs, the Com-munity can levy taxes and can control investment and trade as well as borrow and lend money. It is directed not only by an intergovernmental committee of ministers, but primarily by an uninstructed High Authority of experts, a Common Assembly composed of parliamentarians from the member country, a Court, and supranational committees of trade unionists, industrialists, and consumers' representatives.

Under CSC, most economic restrictions on movement of coal, coke, iron, and steel have been abolished among member nations. There has been created a common Western European market in these items, so that competitive price conditions determine whether a Belgian steel firm will purchase French or German coke, for example. It is the hope of many French political leaders that through CSC the economies of France and West Germany will be so intermingled and intertwined that an independent German rearmament and expansionist policy will be impossible. French industrialists expect to be able to purchase high-quality German coke and sell more steel products; German industrialists hope to acquire most of the CSC market for their coal. All participants expect an increase in production, sales, and standards of living, and some hope that the success of CSC will strengthen the general cause of further European integration.

Standardization of economic institutions is expected to result from CSC's power over national mining, production, investment, and marketing policies. Expansion of the scope of power can be anticipated, as illustrated by the initiation of a CSC policy of social security and cheap housing for steel and coal workers in all member countries. Cooperation and even integration among participating groups can be expected from CSC institutions. In the Common Assembly, socialists, whether French, German, or Dutch, vote and act together, as do Catholics and liberals. In the Consultative Committees, industrialists and trade unionists join forces regardless of nationality, in defense of their economic interests. Since these developments take place in an agency with legislative, judicial, and some administrative powers, the net effect of cooperation and standardization is likely to be far more significant for integration than in universal functional organizations.

Governments retain their autonomy to some extent, however, in the Council of Ministers, whose consent is required for certain decisions of the supranational High Authority, which—like the Common Assembly—makes decisions by majority vote. Since the pattern of the future is not clear, it may be that the intergovernmental Committee of Ministers will gain mastery over the federal High Authority. Policy and powers of the Court remain to be tested, and the Common Assembly is still restricted to approving or criticizing the policies adopted by the High Authority, though the Assembly can compel the Authority to resign in the event of lack of confidence. The pattern of CSC, finally, is being held out as the model for additional functional-federal bodies, as in agriculture and transport—so far, without success.

Clearly it cannot yet be asserted that a European regional community exists. Yet there is certainly ample evidence of forces working for such a community, of which the success of the CSC Assembly in drafting a Continental European constitution is a prime example. The institutions and organs for community action do exist in vital areas of contact. The potentialities for their utilization remain great so long as the combined American-Soviet inducement to common action prevails. But the evolution of a community must still depend upon the growth of a mass myth of identification with *Europe* rather than with Holland, Germany, or France before the structure can perform its allotted tasks. Convincing evidence of the existence of such a myth is still lacking.

7. Eastern European Regionalism: Ideological Solidarity or Soviet Domination? At first glance, East Europe presents a more promising picture for regional development than does West Europe. If acceptance of a common myth is the hallmark of a genuine regional community, much of East Europe shares the cultural, linguistic, and philosophic heritage of Pan-Slavism. While consciousness of Slavic ties has centered in the intelligentsia, it has been this group which has dominated much of the symbol manipulation in the political life of Poland, Czechoslovakia, Yugoslavia, and Bulgaria. To be sure, Pan-Slavism has been ambivalent with respect to the role of Russia, at times frankly supporting Russian hegemony over the smaller "Slavic brothers" and at times opposing "Great Russian chauvinism." During World War II, however, Soviet leaders turned to this traditional appeal for instilling support amongst the East European peoples, and in the immediate postwar expansion of Soviet power in the area, Pan-Slavism played a brief but prominent role.

Forces against Integration. A closer examination alters the picture somewhat, and while the centripetal factors are not to be denied, centrifugal forces until recently have been in the ascendancy in East Europe. In the relatively brief interwar period, nationalism fed on bitter border controversies and minority problems. Map making in East Europe has invariably been the result of decisions arrived at among powers which lay outside the immediate area but whose interests have lain with one or another of the small powers. Boundary lines have cut across ethnic as well as economic lines. For almost a century, pieces of Bulgaria, Romania, and Hungary have been moved from one rule to another, according to the pleasures of Germany, France, Britain, and more recently Russia. Such rivalries may be submerged today, as a common ideology is supreme, but nationalist sentiment is certain to smolder among the non-Communist masses.

Offsetting the impact of Pan-Slavism are the non-Slavic areas of Hungary, Romania, and Albania, as well as the Western-oriented Czechs. Rome and Byzantium cast their ageless shadows in the cleavage between Catholic and Greek Orthodox. The fiction of Yugoslavia's alleged national unity was rudely shattered during World War II when Catholic Croats slaughtered Orthodox Serbs in the presence of the common enemy, Nazi Germany. If such cultural and religious barriers to regional unity are no less extant in West Europe, their solution has been on a decidedly more sophisticated level.

Finally, East Europe's past economic development has not fostered economic cooperation. Chiefly an agrarian area, formerly an exporter of foodstuffs and raw materials to West Europe, it is characterized by competitive rather than complementary economies. Smarting under the memory of economic and political inferiority as a result of the interwar depression and its attendant blow to raw-materials-producing areas, East Europeans determined to industrialize after World War II. All countries suffered from a shortage of capital as well as insufficient resources to support an adequate industrial base.

Viewed in the over-all perspective, then, East Europe's problems for regional development appeared no less serious in 1950 than those of West

Europe. That it had thus far maintained a semblance of independent units and avoided formal plans for federation does not tell the full story, however. Behind the façade of sovereign independent states an ever-increasing degree of cooperation if not coordination can be perceived in terms of the impact of Soviet thought and power.

Soviet-Satellite Alliances. But even without Soviet control or Communist appeal the inability or unwillingness of West European governments to save East European allies from Nazi domination in the period from 1938 to 1944 had led many East Europeans to look to new means of protection. Chief among these were treaties of alliance and mutual security, both among the East European states and between them and Soviet Russia. During World War II, the lead was taken by the Czech government-in-exile, concluding a pact with Soviet Russia; the advance of Red troops into the area in 1945 precipitated a veritable rash of interlocking agreements aimed at the common objective of defense against "armed conflict with Germany [in some instances merely specified as 'a third power'] attempting to renew her policy of aggression, or with any other State allying itself with Germany, directly or in any other way, in her aggressive policy." Although the treaties were in every case bilateral, the interlinking came through the parallel treaties between each signatory and the Soviet Union. In 1955 they were capped by a NATO-type collective self-defense pact, setting up the Warsaw Treaty Organization.

Ideological Integration: The Cominform. Although the fear of German recovery was shared by most of the leading political parties in East Europe after World War II, the seizure of power by Communist elites in the 1947–1948 period altered the context of these treaties. Security against Germany became equated with, and then subsidiary to, security against the West, particularly against the United States. Coordination of political activity as an adjunct of the cold war gave rise to the Communist Information Bureau, or the Cominform, in September, 1947. The Cominform sought to rally Poland, Czechoslovakia, Hungary, Romania, Bulgaria, and Yugoslavia to Soviet objectives through uniform propaganda policies. Yugoslavia proved recalcitrant in the face of growing Soviet demands upon her political and economic independence and was expelled in June, 1948. Although Marshal Tito continued to rule an avowedly Communist regime in Belgrade, the treaties binding Cominform members to Yugoslavia were denounced, and Titoism became as rank a crime in East Europe as had Trotskyism in the Soviet Union. The economic implications of the Tito break will be discussed later. At this point, it is necessary to evaluate the problem of nationalism as it affects political regionalism in East Europe.

Communist assaults upon the divisive influence of nationalism have wisely refrained from attacking its symbol referents. National flags, customs, languages, and governments have been tolerated. The form has remained, but the content has been altered. "Bourgeois-nationalist chauvinism" is scourged by Communist propaganda as the great alienator of class-consciousness and socialist unity. Patriotism per se is not anathema, however. Indeed, it is marshaled to counter irredentist strivings which plague East Europe's politics at every turn. In Teschen, for example, a Communist party leader was purged in late 1951 for allegedly displaying less fervor for Prague than Warsaw. While appealing for patriotism at this level, however, Communist elites have fostered substitute symbols at a "higher" level. "Socialist patriotism" places Soviet Russia in a new light for East Europeans.

That local or divisive patriotism is stressed at least as much as Soviet patriotism in Communist mythology is clear from the emphasis in the statement of a leading Hungarian Communist official, "We Hungarian Communists are all Hungarian patriots *as well as* patriots of the Soviet Union." [14] On the one hand, then, local nationalism is used to combat minority tensions within the countries of East Europe. On the other hand, nationalism itself is channeled away from the local capitals and toward Moscow. It was partly Tito's refusal to follow the latter principle to Moscow's satisfaction which precipitated the 1948 break. Whether other East European leaders have balked at this point or not is difficult to say, since "Titoism" has become a catchall charge to condemn all who oppose the Communist elites. However, the constant Communist complaint against "chauvinism" and "bourgeois nationalism" suggests that a high degree of incipient nationalism still runs strong in East Europe.

Economic Ties. Following the pattern of the Cominform, formation of the Council for Economic Mutual Assistance was announced on January 25, 1949. Known in Soviet shorthand as Komekon, this organization for economic coordination includes Poland, Czechoslovakia, Hungary, Romania, Bulgaria, and the Soviet Union as members. There is little doubt of the leading role played by Moscow; its initial chairman was the Soviet Minister of Foreign Trade, Anastas Mikoyan. Although its structure includes a general assembly, direction rests with an executive committee whose meetings are secret. Officially, Komekon's aims include the replacement of bilateral with multilateral trade, the establishment of mutual credit agreements, and the utilization of the pooled raw materials of the region. Whether Komekon also serves as an exploitive instrument for the advantage of the Soviet Union is debatable, inasmuch as the terms of trade with Moscow remain uncertain. Set up partially as a counterpoint to West Europe's Marshall Plan, however, Komekon represents a step toward regional activity when compared with the strictly bilateral trade pattern between Moscow and the East European capitals which preceded its formation.

Concrete instances of intraregional coordination are few thus far. One of them involves the complementary needs of Czechoslovakia and Poland.

[14] Josef Revai, Hungarian Minister of People's Culture, quoted in *Szabad Nap,* Mar. 9, 1952. Italics supplied.

Czech imports of coal were returned in the form of finished steel. In 1948 the two countries concluded a long-term agreement establishing a permanent Czech-Polish Economic Commission, complete with secretariat and numerous committees for establishing reciprocal freight concessions and similar admin-

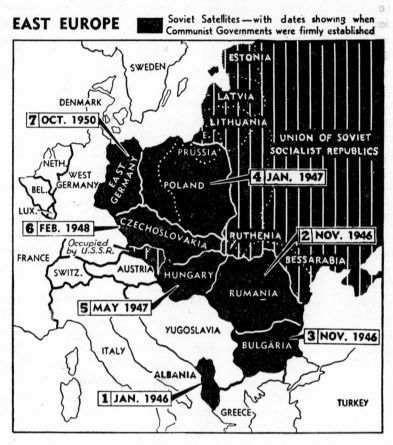

The Eastern European region

istrative procedures. Production agreements for specified industries plan investment and output to the mutual benefit of both economies. Thus Czechoslovakia concentrates on coke manufacturing from low-cost Polish coal, while Poland emphasizes cement and heavy chemical output. Joint construction of a major power station to serve both countries illustrates the degree to which economic coordination has progressed between the two countries whose pre-Communist political relations were seldom harmonious.

That such coordination is the exception rather than the rule in the East European region is testified to by the duplication and overlapping in the various Five Year Plans to be completed by 1955. Both industrialized Czecho-slovakia and agrarian Bulgaria posit production targets for steel, ball bear-ings, and drilling machinery, despite the differences in the raw materials of the two countries. Economic nationalism, with its attendant mania for indus-trial output, limits the degree to which economic coordination can utilize most efficiently the varying resources of Poland and Romania. Yugoslavia's refusal to mesh its plans with those of its neighbors has served as a brake upon Soviet desires to make each East European economy part of a larger unit. Despite this mitigating factor, however, it appears that such integration is the ultimate aim of Moscow, and toward this aim it has additional economic means at hand.

As a consequence of Red Army occupation after World War II, so-called "mixed corporations" were set up by Soviet Russia in the ex-enemy states of Hungary, Romania, and Bulgaria. Industrial enterprises, allegedly German or Italian assets, were transferred to Soviet control under the peace treaties. But in 1955, probably due to resentment and friction in the satellite nations, the Soviet Union sold its portion of stock to the national governments, as Moscow ceased to berate Titoism and "normalized" its relations with Bel-grade. These companies were jointly owned by the Soviet Union and the participating country, but production was extraterritorial and deliveries were listed as "imports from the U.S.S.R." Hungarian bauxite, aluminum oxide, aluminum, and oil thus came under direct Soviet control, as did aviation and navigation. Similar "mixed companies" in Bulgaria and Romania gave Soviet planners a convenient lever for coordination and control of these economies.

Standardization of accounting, equipment, and administrative procedures along the lines of the Soviet system has introduced thousands of Soviet ad-visers and technicians into East Europe. In the Yugoslav-Soviet correspond-ence published after the break in 1948, some hint was given of the dominant role played by these advisers in the planning and production of the various national economies. The growing dependence of East Europe upon Soviet equipment, loans, and raw materials provides these advisers with consider-able power with which to persuade or coerce coordination within the region. Simultaneous with the Marshall Plan and the embargo on trade in strategic goods between Eastern and Western Europe appeared the Soviet-directed ac-celerations of industrialization, absorbing many of the East European prod-ucts previously exported to Western markets. Trade within the Eastern Eu-ropean region has increased precipitously, as has trade between it and the Soviet Union. Deliveries of heavy industrial equipment, machine tools, ores, agricultural machinery, and oil products now tie the East European econo-mies to that of the Soviet Union. It remains to be seen whether the East European economy will develop along lines of mutual benefits or be patterned after the traditional colonial systems of previous great empires.

Military Integration. In the realm of military integration there is again a surface contrast with West Europe, where attention has centered on building an integrated army with new uniforms, flags, and central command. East European armies remain national in form, but integration exceeds anything so far attempted in West Europe. Completely reequipped with Soviet arms, trained by Soviet cadres, and in some cases directed by ex-Soviet citizens, the East European forces are in effect a unified and Soviet-controlled army.

Perhaps more penetrating in its control aspect is the police system of the region, which displays the highest degree of coordination and direction from Moscow. If Jews in Czechoslovakia are suspected of Zionist sympathies—which, by Communist definition, is tantamount to treason—Jews throughout the East European region may be rounded up within hours under identically worded charges. Purges of official as well as nonofficial elites sweep through the region in a series of nearly simultaneous arrests, accusations, trials, and executions. Although the motivations vary, they are consistently parallel, if not identical, with those of Moscow.

Integration and the Communist Party. Paramount in these various cultural, political, economic, and military techniques for integrating the East European bloc is the role of the Communist organization, with its complete domination by the Soviet Communist Party. From 1945 until 1952, Communist elites in the area gradually usurped the power of their fellow partners in coalition governments, until the so-called "people's democracies"—supposedly distinguished from the orthodox Soviet state by a multiparty system —were thin façades for Communist rule. The overlapping of Communist elite and governmental elite assures a monolithic political "line," both internal and external, since this elite holds its position only with the toleration of its Soviet superiors. It is impossible to assess the degree of spontaneity or cooperation operative at high levels of policy making. However, it may be assumed that given the rigidity of the Marxist ideology within which these elites operate, they may tacitly welcome Soviet direction and agree in identifying their interests with those of the Soviet elite—the center of the socialist world. Value sharing on the basis of an overriding ideology is thus facilitated.

As long as this factor of Soviet direction remains operative in East Europe —and the 1953 revolts resulted in no significant relaxation of control—it is impossible to apply the test of cooperative decision making, which might reveal how different the system is from a traditional empire. In so far as the Marxist-Leninist-Stalinist analysis of world history is accepted in East Europe, it may be called a regional community whose interests are identified with a dominant but like-minded neighbor. In so far as the divisive factors made obvious in riots and strikes resist Soviet direction and bring forth coercion from Moscow to achieve its ends, it may be called a colonial system. Only time and a relaxation of Soviet controls may prove how deep are the consensual roots of Communist regionalism.

Thus regional systems vary in the degree of internal integration possessed and achieved. Despite the variation, however, it is quite plain that regional ties today are more diverse, more penetrating, and more appreciated by ruling groups than at any other time. Further regional integration, therefore, may be anticipated as a global organizational development, reducing the number of sovereign units through the consent of their rulers, acting under the stimulus of global tension and fear. But this by no means assures peace among the supranational systems which are growing up.

ADDITIONAL CASE-STUDY MATERIAL

Catroux, General G.: "The French Union," *International Conciliation*, no. 495, November, 1953.

Coudenhove-Kalergi, R. N.: *Pan-Europa*, Pan Europa, Vienna, 1923.

Dreier, J. C.: "OAS Charter Comes into Effect," *Department of State Bulletin*, vol. 26, Jan. 7, 1952.

————: "Taking Stock of Inter-American Relations," *Department of State Bulletin*, vol. 25, Apr. 30, 1951.

Fenwick, C. G.: *The Inter-American Regional System*, McMullen, New York, 1949.

Furniss, E. S.: "French Attitudes toward European Unity," *International Organization*, vol. 7, May, 1953.

Goormaghtigh, J.: "European Integration," *International Conciliation*, no. 469, October, 1953.

Haas, E.: "The United States of Europe," *Political Science Quarterly*, vol. 63, December, 1948.

Harvey, H. J.: "The British Commonwealth," *International Conciliation*, no. 487, January, 1953.

Hudson, G. F.: "Do Regional Pacts Violate the Spirit of the UN," *Foreign Affairs*, vol. 31, July, 1953.

"The Inter-Asian Relations Conference," *Round Table*, vol. 37, June, 1947.

Karp, B.: "The Draft Constitution for a European Political Community," *International Organization*, May, 1954.

Khadduri, M.: "The Arab League as a Regional Arrangement," *American Journal of International Law*, vol. 40, October, 1946.

Levi, W.: "The British Dominions and Regionalism," *Review of Politics*, vol. 9, January, 1947.

Lleras, A.: "Inter-American Relations," *The Annals of the American Academy of Political and Social Science*, July, 1952.

Lord Ismay: *NATO: The First Five Years, 1949–1954*, Paris, North Atlantic Treaty Organization, 1955.

Loveday, A.: "The European Movement," *International Organization*, vol. 3, November, 1949.

McKesson, J. A.: "The Schuman Plan," *Political Science Quarterly*, vol. 67, March, 1952.

Mansergh, N.: *The Commonwealth and the Nations*, Royal Institute of International Affairs, London, 1948.

————: *Survey of British Commonwealth Affairs: The Problem of External Policy, 1931–1939*, Oxford, New York, 1952.

"NATO and World Peace," *The Annals of the American Academy of Political and Social Sciences*, July, 1953.

Poole, B.: *The Caribbean Commission*, University of South Carolina Press, Columbia, S.C., 1951.

Schuman, F. L.: "The Council of Europe," *American Political Science Review*, vol. 45, September, 1951.

Seabury, P.: "The League of Arab States: Debacle of a Regional Arrangement," *International Organization*, vol. 3, November, 1949.

Seton-Watson, H.: *The East European Revolution,* Praeger, New York, 1951.
Vernon, R.: "The Schuman Plan," *American Journal of International Law,* vol. 52, April, 1953.
Warne, J. D.: *NATO and Its Prospects,* Praeger, New York, 1954.
Warriner, D.: *Revolution in East Europe,* Turnstile Press, London, 1950.
Whitaker, A. P.: "Development of American Regionalism," *International Conciliation,* no. 469, March, 1951.

Chapter 22

REGIONAL SYSTEMS IN CONFLICT

The logic of overlapping and conflicting regional systems spells the bankruptcy of the idea of universal collective security through universal organization built on global consensus. It is the Soviet claim that the institutional solidarity of the people's democracies is consistent with the purposes of the United Nations Charter, since it is directed against a resumption of fascist aggression; yet the true implications of the Eastern Empire are far otherwise. Similarly, the pious assertions in NATO and the Mutual Assistance Pacts of the United States that the purpose of Western defense is the strengthening of the United Nations really imply a shift in motivation and a new determination to seek strength through narrow but more cohesive regional association. Thus the dominant principle of large-scale international organization today is the principle of regionalism; it is a direct expression of elite aspirations in the East as well as the West if we posit the survival of ruling groups as the first operational maxim of political life.

Thus the Soviet regional system, or empire, is faced with no less than three Western countersystems: NATO, OAS, and the Pacific pacts. The Arab nations have their own system, whose future position with respect to the two main blocs is not yet certain, and South Asia continues to straddle the fence, thereby preventing the Commonwealth regional system from being a firm member of the anti-Soviet coalition. Yet the symmetry of alliances and counteralliances is a deceiving one. Treaties of mutual help and self-help, manifestoes of ideological solidarity, and affirmations of respect for common traditions are only as strong as the convictions of the groups who make and conclude them. Manifestoes may be repudiated by Titoist heresy; respect for common traditions has come to mean less as brown and black peoples join organizations heretofore monopolized by the white man; and treaties, notoriously, are scraps of paper which seldom survive a radical change in attitude or shift in motive. Hence the solidarity of each regional system cannot be judged from its legal texts and the decisions of its supreme organs at any given instant. Even though most of the earth is now divided into mutually antagonistic regional systems, the internal cohesion of each system must be examined before the full implications of regionalism can be stated.

Cohesion in the Soviet System. On the surface, at any rate, the Soviet empire appears as an integrated and united whole. Yet even it is probably less monolithic than the surface would indicate, though mass manipulation and mass coercion inherent in the system has produced a more unified power bloc than is true of any other regional system. The example of Tito's schismatic Communist regime in Yugoslavia is living proof of the possibility of divergent group aspirations' existing even in the Soviet orbit. Repeated purges and trials in Eastern Europe must mean that nationalist preferences and "Zionist deviations" are symbols of some significance and as such compete with the allegedly supreme symbol of identification: the fatherland of socialism, the Soviet Union. As long as these competing symbols survive, Soviet control is not what it seems on the surface. While orthodox Communists are being accused of spying for the West—a most unlikely charge—and as long as the totalitarian logic compels the ruling elite to seek scapegoats in Eastern Europe's Jewry to detract attention from its own administrative and political blunders, conflicts, strains, and disharmony continue to be latent in the Eastern empire.

But it is likely that the undoubted ascendancy of Soviet power in Eastern Europe will ultimately succeed in eliminating all organized centers of opposition. The efficiency of the police state may be relied upon to eradicate rival symbols of identification, if given time enough to accomplish this task. With the elimination of possible competing elites, ultimate control by the Soviet-sponsored and Soviet-approved ruling circle seems assured.

Whether this development will also occur in Communist China, the eastern flank of the Soviet system, is quite another question. True, ideological solidarity still prevails, and the economic and military dependence of Communist China upon the Soviet Union would argue for the latter's ultimate ability to manipulate Peiping as it manipulates Warsaw and Bucharest. Yet China's population is over twice Russia's, and the loyalty of that population to the symbols of communism is at least open to considerable doubt. Conflicts of interests have characterized Russo-Chinese relations for a century, and it is arguable that such conflicts might arise once more in the future if Peiping should feel less dependent upon Moscow's support. Then, if the Soviet elite insists on treating China as it treats Poland and Bulgaria, the rift in the seemingly cohesive empire might develop in the form of a Chinese heresy, no longer loyal to Moscow's orthodoxy. Symbols of Slavic solidarity, of anti-German feelings, of geographic unity through the Danube, or of a long period of similar cultural patterns are meaningless in Sino-Soviet relations. It requires a great deal of faith in the constancy of the Communist ideology as the sole conditioner of policy to assert that the permanent amalgamation of China into the Soviet empire is a foregone conclusion.

Nevertheless, it remains true that the Sino-Soviet complex—whatever its long-range cohesion or disharmonies may be—functions as one major system in the conflicts of our day, including in its orbit most of the Eurasian land mass and over 750 million people living in eleven nations. One of the keys to future war or peace must lie, therefore, in the nature of the elite ruling the system. Assuming a homogeneous outlook among Communist leaders in China and Russia, can it be concluded that they expect the inevitable decay of the opposing regional systems? Are they irrevocably committed to conflict to hasten the dissolution of their opponents' defenses?

The nature of the Soviet elite provides one clue in this connection. The Communist leadership claims to be omniscient and endowed with a historically justified role in exercising a monopoly of power in the regions under its sway. Soviet ideology does not tolerate the existence of any other leading group and therefore is committed in practice no less than in principle to the eradication of any rival centers of power and allegiance. Its survival, indeed, would be put in doubt if such a course were not followed, major peaceful change within the totalitarian system being extremely difficult. This gives the Soviet elite a homogeneity, a unity of purpose, which is considerably greater than that of the coalition of elites which rule in the countries of the opposing regional systems. Soviet policy is therefore enabled to be more adaptive to outside stimuli than is true of its world rival, though even the freedom of action of a totalitarian system is severely restricted by the shortcomings of manipulation and coercion, but especially by the patterns of expectation built up in the past among its own following.

This very unity of purpose, however, may well be a factor for peace. Once convinced of the risks inherent in war, persuaded that the might of the opposing coalition is such as to make the victory in war of the Soviet elite most questionable, it is possible that a long-range policy of peaceful coexistence may be acceptable merely because it offers the more attractive alternative. Granted that Soviet professions of the possibility of coexistence among the "socialist" and "capitalist" nations is usually only a short-term tactical position, it still remains possible that it may develop into long-range expectations—implying a permanent truce rather than normal peace—if the opposite alternative is sufficiently ugly. A homogeneous elite, then, is more easily adapted to a convincing set of external conditions precisely because it rests on rigid leadership and unswerving allegiance to a "revealed" truth. If, on the other hand, such an elite interprets a given set of external conditions in such a way as to conclude that its survival depends on more drastic measures, the same homogeneity may equally well lead to an acceptance of armed conflict as inevitable.

Cohesion of the Western Bloc. Whatever the latent disharmonies in the Soviet bloc may be, they are dwarfed by the obvious and striking difficulties inherent in the three anti-Soviet systems. Leaving aside the still ambivalent British Commonwealth, whose non-Asian members alone can be considered partners of the anti-Soviet coalition, this analysis must be focused on the

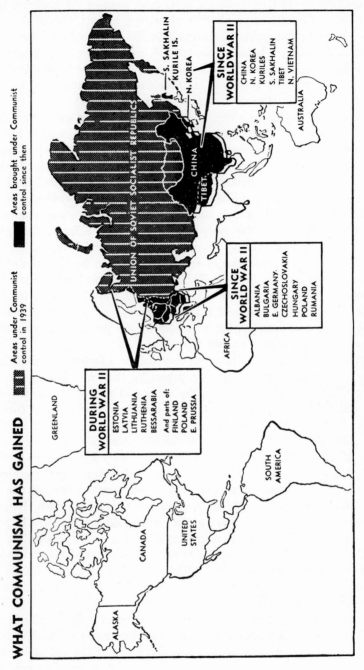

WHAT COMMUNISM HAS GAINED ▨ Areas under Communist
control in 1939

■ Areas brought under Communist
control since then

DURING WORLD WAR II

ESTONIA
LATVIA
LITHUANIA
RUTHENIA
BESSARABIA

And parts of:
FINLAND
POLAND
E. PRUSSIA

SINCE WORLD WAR II

ALBANIA
BULGARIA
E. GERMANY.
CZECHOSLOVAKIA
HUNGARY
POLAND
RUMANIA

SINCE WORLD WAR II

CHINA
N. KOREA
KURILES
S. SAKHALIN
TIBET
N. VIETNAM

GREENLAND

ALASKA

CANADA

UNITED STATES

SOUTH AMERICA

UNION OF SOVIET SOCIALIST REPUBLICS

S. SAKHALIN
KURILE IS.
N. KOREA

CHINA
TIBET

AFRICA

AUSTRALIA

The Communist nations

WHAT THE WEST HAS DONE

Areas covered by treaties and other Western defense arrangements

JAPANESE PACT
JAPAN
UNITED STATES

FORMOSAN PACT
NATIONALIST CHINA
UNITED STATES

S. KOREAN PACT
SOUTH KOREA
UNITED STATES

SOUTHEAST ASIAN PACT
AUSTRALIA
FRANCE
THAILAND
PAKISTAN
NEW ZEALAND
UNITED KINGDOM
PHILIPPINES
UNITED STATES

ATLANTIC PACT
BELGIUM
CANADA
DENMARK
FRANCE
ICELAND
ITALY
LUXEMBOURG
NETHERLANDS
NORWAY
PORTUGAL
UNITED KINGDOM
UNITED STATES
GREECE
TURKEY
WEST GERMANY

RIO PACT
ARGENTINA
BOLIVIA
BRAZIL
CENTRAL AMER.
CHILE
COLOMBIA
CUBA
DOMINICAN REP.
ECUADOR
HAITI
MEXICO
PARAGUAY
PERU
UNITED STATES
URUGUAY
VENEZUELA

UNION OF SOVIET SOCIALIST REPUBLICS

GREENLAND

AFRICA

AUSTRALIA

NEW ZEALAND

JAPAN

S. KOREA

W. GERMANY

AUSTRIA

YUGOSLAVIA

ALASKA

CANADA

UNITED STATES

CENTRAL AMERICA

SOUTH AMERICA

Major contemporary Western alliances

stresses and strains within NATO, OAS, and the Pacific pacts and even more strongly on the fissures between these systems.

Through the pivotal position of the United States all three of these regional groupings are brought into contact with one another, even though they lack all legal and structural ties. An attack on one regional system is almost certain to imply the ultimate involvement of all anti-Soviet systems, including the white members of the Commonwealth. Since American resources and leadership are the key factors in giving strength to each regional system, a large degree of unity seems inherent in their mutual relations. If used to intimidate a potential aggressor, this may be a force for continued uneasy truce between East and West. If the intimidation should fail, however, the interlocking regional system of the West is certain to bring with it another war on a global scale.

True enough, the American-led coalition accounts for over forty nations, including Spain and Yugoslavia. It controls the Pacific, the islands off East Asia, the Western Hemisphere, the Atlantic, and the western rim of the Eurasian continent, and it still rules Africa south of the Sahara. The major share of world industrial might and technological knowledge are still within its confines, and its people number over 680 million. Its colonial subjects account for almost 200 million more, though their attachment to the values of the West may well be doubted.

However, not even the pivotal position occupied by the United States assures the homogeneous functioning of the three systems. Witness the diversity of the participating elites and the heterogeneity of the American leadership: [1]

The Elite in the American world-State is, in global terms, a strange congeries of anomalies: Latin-American dictators, British Socialists, Japanese industrialists, Arab chieftains, French Radicals, German carteleers, Italian clericalists, Yugoslav Communists, Spanish Falangists, and so on. But these are all allies, auxiliaries or mercenaries. What manner of native leadership has America evolved for the accomplishment of its appointed task? It may be asserted, not unreasonably, that the rulership of America and of America's world has become the business, primarily of businessmen, bankers and bureaucrats (recruited partly from the ranks of industrialists and partly from the middle-class intelligentsia), supplemented in ever-increasing measure by career men in the arts of war. The agency of influence abroad is not, as with the enemy, a Party, a brotherhood of converts, or an amorphous mass of "fellow travelers," but the diplomatic, military and economic "mission."

In NATO, American demands are frequently opposed by less demonstrative European ruling groups, and American insistence on military preparation tends to be countered by requests for higher living standards and economic assistance. The same is true in the OAS. American insistence on military and ideological planning tends to be met by Latin-American requests for economic

[1] F. L. Schuman, *The Commonwealth of Man*, Knopf, New York, 1952, p. 225.

aid and technical assistance. Japanese and Philippine reactions tend to follow the same pattern. Furthermore, even though linked through the American position, the aspirations of each regional system are by no means in accord with those of every other system. NATO insists that Europe have first priority in defensive planning and that the United States relegate the Far East and Pacific to a secondary role. ANZUS, quite naturally, tends to take the opposite view, while the OAS puts first emphasis on the defense of the Western Hemisphere and is therefore even less interested in either NATO or ANZUS, with their respective stress on Europe and Asia. Economics imposes a further division of aims. NATO, consisting as it does of the chief industrial nations in the West, is interested in cheap raw materials to permit economies in the manufacture of armaments. The OAS countries, however, export many of these materials and therefore insist on high prices for them, thus making rearmament more expensive but facilitating a rise in standards of living and encouraging economic development in Latin America. How to reconcile these clashing aspirations is the first task of the United States in maintaining a modicum of harmony among the interlocking regional systems. It is a task which cannot be accomplished in all situations, since the opposition of aims may be absolute in nature. Thus the cohesion of the three anti-Soviet systems is and remains dependent upon the ability to harmonize divergent policy aspirations.

This ability, however, is put in jeopardy further by the fact that the motives of leading groups in the United States are by no means constant. Lingering isolationist thought emphasizes the necessity for defending the United States itself and therefore stresses the key role of the OAS. Interest groups identified with European minority groups, with the preservation of free enterprise in Europe, and intellectuals concerned with the preservation of Western institutions all stress the primacy of Europe and of NATO. Yet those more concerned with historical Christian missionary activity in the Far East, with investments and trade in the Pacific, and with undoing the Communist victory in China all insist on the importance of SEATO.

The change from the New Deal–Fair Deal administration to that of the Republican party illustrates the change in dominant motivation which occurred in 1952 and 1953. NATO lost its place of primacy in American planning with the intensification of the defensive effort in the Far East. Respect for European cultural institutions was diminished in proportion to the new stress on immediate defensive steps of integration, coupled with threats of American withdrawal from Europe if the NATO partners failed to respond. Consequently the Pacific pact system gained in importance as far as American motives are concerned. All this is an expression of the fact that with the election of 1952 a new set of interest groups, representing a different set of values and expectations, came into power—values and expectations less concerned with the unity of the West as a cultural entity and emphasizing instead the more limited military position of the United States as a national community. Far from having increased cohesion in the three anti-Soviet regional systems, then, the change in American policy aims has merely demonstrated the latent rifts and antagonisms in these blocs.

There is no unified American elite, then, and no ideological "brotherhood" can be relied upon to give homogeneity to the American camp. The only overriding common purpose is the gratification of certain short-term common interests: physical security against a common enemy, and economic aid to raise living standards. In the minds of most American elites the second aim is merely a means to furthering the first, but in the minds of the recipients it is an end in itself, to be gained from association with the American bloc. Furthermore, the ruling coalition in America is a combination of industrial leaders, professional military men, bankers, and conservative politicians. It is opposed by the leaders of labor, by some national minorities, and by many educational and cultural spokesmen. Agreement on policy is merely the basic common denominator between divergent aspirations, and homogeneity is conspicuous by its absence.

Hence a deliberate and consistent policy in this camp toward the Soviet bloc cannot be expected. Policies of containment must compete with policies of liberation. Group values have to be reconciled to make consistent long-range policy, and group values do not lend themselves to simple long-range reconciliation, either within a national community or among allied nations. Consequently, it is difficult to conceive of a deliberately planned policy of initiating conflict on the part of the United States and its associates and clients. Even if one or two of the elites in the coalition are inclined in this direction, the adoption of a policy of conflict would necessitate the concurrence of allied elites. It may be assumed, then, that the very difficulty of decision making in a democracy and a coalition of democracies, oligarchies, and authoritarianisms is in itself a factor for peace.

This is not to say, however, that the nature of the American and American-led elites precludes the possibility of the West's initiating armed conflict. It is not too difficult to take military and diplomatic steps which will be regarded by the antagonist as final proof of bellicose intentions, so that he may unleash active conflict. Preventive war is a military and diplomatic means of our day which cannot be ignored. It has been advocated even in the pluralist United States in recent years in order to enable American strategy to benefit from a temporary superiority in atomic armaments. Convinced that the adversary is about to unleash war—or armed rebellion in an allied nation— preventive countermeasures may well be undertaken in order to beat the enemy to the punch, especially if a superiority in certain weapons is assumed. To be sure, preventive war is obnoxious to a democratic leadership and may not be accepted by all groups in a democratic society. However, once war has broken out the strength of national cohesion is usually adequate to assure the support of all major groups in the community. Preventive war implies a gamble for a democratic system and its coalition of elites, but it is a gamble which fits the apparent needs of our times as seen by some, and corresponds to the values of some groups. The very nature of a coalition of elites may persuade the spokesmen of one constituent portion to attempt to draw the others along by means of an accomplished and irrevocable fact, such as preventive war.

The West maintains that its military preparations are purely defensive and that they will not be used to attack any nation. This, comments a British group,[2]

. . . sincere though it is, is unlikely to mean much to men like Mr. Molotov and Mr. Vyshinsky. When they read in the declarations of . . . Allied statesmen that the purpose of Western policy is to "create situations of strength" and to "negotiate from strength" they can hardly feel much reassured. For they must understand this kind of negotiation to mean that the western price for what Stalin calls "peaceful coexistence" is likely to be high—the loss of the Soviet Union's preponderant power in Europe and a restriction of expansionist possibilities in other areas across its frontiers.

Assurances of defensive intentions may still provoke a preventive war effort by the Communists if the logical consequences of such intentions are interpreted as being finally and completely irreconcilable with dominant Soviet or Chinese motivations. Immediate survival of the elite would then dictate war while there seems to be a chance of victory rather than long-range peaceful coexistence, which may in fact undermine the security of the elite.

Nor is deliberately planned preventive war the only way through which the two regional systems, though each intent only on defense, may slide into hostilities. What appeared to the West as Chinese "aggression" in Korea was interpreted as warding off "imperialist provocation" by the Communists. The defensive measures of one antagonist always seem as offensive and expansionist designs to the other in a setting of tension and distrust. Hence careless orders to advance naval and air patrols may suffice to create warlike incidents which will appear as evidence of aggressive intentions to one of the antagonists—and, accidentally perhaps, result in global war.

The Imponderable Role of Neutralism. It appears, therefore, that the nature of the opposing elites and their varied aims permit of no clear conclusion. Soviet monolithism and Western heterogeneity continue to be ambivalent with respect to war and peace. Neither condition is absolutely implicit in the conflicting systems. Imponderable factors enter the minds of policy makers and lessen the impact of ideology's dictates.

Among these imponderables the uncommitted portion of the globe looms as the key consideration. Over a dozen nations in the Middle East and South

---

[2] Royal Institute of International Affairs, *Atlantic Alliance,* London, 1952, p. 9.

Asia are resisting the trend toward the polarization of world power into the two antagonistic camps. They have succeeded in remaining aloof so far; the settlement of Korean hostilities in United Nations discussion indicates that their influence is far out of proportion to their military strength. Though they account for 624 million people—not counting their sympathizers in Western Europe and the colonial world—their industrial, technological, and military power is diminutive. Yet their appeal is impressive because it is based on the proposition of peace through compromise among the contending regional blocs. The Soviet elite, which hopes to attract Indians, Indonesians, Egyptians, and Iranians through persuasion rather than coercion, cannot afford to alienate them by acting diametrically in opposition to them. The West, similarly, would weaken its appeal for freedom and peace if it were to reject the overtures of Prime Minister Nehru consistently and indefinitely, especially since those who oppose aspects of American leadership in NATO will give support to the neutral bloc's efforts at conciliation. Thus Britain, when India proposed its compromise formula in the Korean truce negotiations, came to the support of her Commonwealth partner, in effect warning the United States that the West's position was by no means unified. America, ultimately, accepted the Indian formula, as did the Soviet Union.

It is the continued striving for greater strength in each regional bloc rather than acceptance of the neutral ideology which induces Washington and Moscow to bow to conciliation. Neither elite can afford to alienate the crucial uncommitted third of the world's population, and occasional compromise between the antagonistic regional systems comes about as an indirect result of the neutral position. In terms of universal collective security, the balancing efforts of the Arab-Asian bloc imply a softening in the relations among regional-security systems, initially constructed and maintained outside the UN framework. The net impact of the bloc's international position has been a reversal of the trend toward bipolarization of power and ideology. The imponderable factor of denunciation and abandonment by a third of the world's population may well induce the Soviet and the American-led elites to hesitate before closing the door on possibilities of interregional compromise. Granting the ambivalence of beliefs and cohesion in both sets of contenders, the addition of a further factor of uncertainty may result in a moderation of policies of absolute mutual hostility.

In the meantime, peaceful coexistence is not yet an accepted pattern of life for either camp. Each still attempts to strengthen its side; each continues to jockey for a favorable military, economic, and diplomatic position. But each carries on in wooing the members of the neutral bloc. No consistent evidence of a desire of the two rival sets of elites to settle down in the *status quo* is apparent, and so long as such an attitude is not forthcoming, local wars, little wars, and revolutionary situations may well continue and be exploited by both sides. So long as the now dominant motivations undergo no modification, some conflict—though not total war—is inevitable. Only a growing awareness of the futility of attempting the defeat of the other side will bring with it a relaxation of Malayas, Indochinas, Koreas, and Berlin blockades. But before such a change in expectations does in fact come about, it is equally possible that a little war may set the spark for a global holocaust or that one of the two sets of elites will come to prefer the finality of immediate preventive war to the vagaries of a prolonged truce. Paradoxically, it is the very totality of modern hydrogen war which may be the chief deterrent to full hostilities, without, however, ruling out localized conflicts fought with conventional weapons.

INDEX